An International Antitrust Primer

An International Antitrust Primer

A Guide to the Operation of United States, European Union and Other Key Competition Laws in the Global Economy

Fourth Edition

Mark R. Joelson

Published by:
Kluwer Law International B.V.
PO Box 316
2400 AH Alphen aan den Rijn
The Netherlands
Website: www.wolterskluwerlr.com

Sold and distributed in North, Central and South America by:
Wolters Kluwer Legal & Regulatory U.S.
7201 McKinney Circle
Frederick, MD 21704
United States of America
Email: customer.service@wolterskluwer.com

Sold and distributed in all other countries by:
Quadrant
Rockwood House
Haywards Heath
West Sussex
RH16 3DH
United Kingdom
Email: international-customerservice@wolterskluwer.com

MIX
FSC® C103993

Printed on acid-free paper.

ISBN 978-90-411-9095-6

e-Book: ISBN 978-90-411-9108-3
web-PDF: ISBN 978-90-411-9109-0

© 2017 Mark R. Joelson

All rights reserved. No part of this publication may be reproduced, stored in a retrieval system, or transmitted in any form or by any means, electronic, mechanical, photocopying, recording, or otherwise, without written permission from the publisher.

Permission to use this content must be obtained from the copyright owner. Please apply to: Permissions Department, Wolters Kluwer Legal & Regulatory U.S., 76 Ninth Avenue, 7th Floor, New York, NY 10011-5201, USA. Website: www.wolterskluwerlr.com

Printed in the United Kingdom.

Love for the next generation: Valentina, Milena and Breezy

Table of Contents

Preface		xv
Acknowledgements		xix

CHAPTER 1
An Overview of Competition Law Development Around the World		1
§1.01	Background	1
§1.02	The Current Situation	5
	[A] Competition Law Players	5
	[B] The ICN and Convergence	6
	[C] Other International Cooperation	8

PART I
United States Antitrust Law		11

CHAPTER 2
Summary of the United States Antitrust Laws		13
§2.01	The Sherman Act	13
	[A] The Rule of Reason under Section 1	15
	[B] Contracts, Combinations, and Conspiracies	17
	[C] Monopolization under Section 2	19
	[D] The Commerce Requirement	22
§2.02	The Wilson Tariff Act	24
§2.03	The Clayton Act	24
§2.04	The Federal Trade Commission Act	26
§2.05	Remedial Laws Affecting Imports	27
§2.06	Antitrust Exemptions	28
	[A] Exempt Activities Generally	28
	[B] The Webb-Pomerene Act	29
	[C] The Export Trading Company Act	31

Table of Contents

	[D]	The National Cooperative Research and Production Act	32
	[E]	The Foreign Trade Antitrust Improvements Act	32
§2.07	Enforcement Modes		33
	[A]	Department of Justice Antitrust Division	33
	[B]	The Federal Trade Commission	36
	[C]	Private Enforcement	38
	[D]	State and Other Enforcement	39
	[E]	Guidelines	40
	[F]	The Courts	41
	[G]	Modernization	42

CHAPTER 3
The Application of United States Antitrust Law to International Transactions and Foreign Parties   43

§3.01	Foreign Commerce to Which the Sherman Act Applies		43
	[A]	The Historical Development of the Standard	45
	[B]	Enactment of the Foreign Trade Antitrust Improvements Act	48
	[C]	Hartford Fire and the Comity Issue	48
	[D]	Empagran and Application of the FTAIA	52
	[E]	International Guidelines Interpretations	55
§3.02	International Law and Foreign Government Views		57
§3.03	Foreign Government Involvement		60
	[A]	Act of State Doctrine	61
	[B]	Foreign Sovereign Compulsion	63
	[C]	Petitioning Foreign Sovereigns	64
	[D]	Sovereign Immunity	64

CHAPTER 4
US Law Enforcement Procedure   67

§4.01	Procedural Requirements		67
§4.02	Subject Matter Jurisdiction of the Federal Courts		68
§4.03	Personal Jurisdiction		69
	[A]	Due Process of Law and Minimum Contacts	69
	[B]	Corporate Affiliation and Agency Relationships	74
	[C]	Service of Process	76
		[1] The Federal Rules	76
		[2] The Hague Service Convention	80
§4.04	Investigation and Discovery		82
	[A]	Action by the Justice Department	82
		[1] Criminal Prosecutions	83
		[2] Civil Cases	85
	[B]	Discovery Procedures in Federal Courts	85
	[C]	The Hague Evidence Convention	90
	[D]	Foreign "Blocking" Legislation and US Discovery	94
	[E]	Federal Trade Commission Procedures	97

§4.05		Enforcement of US Antitrust Judgments	98
§4.06		International Arbitration	100

CHAPTER 5
Conspiracies, Joint Ventures and Monopolization in US Commerce — 107

§5.01		The Sherman Act § 1	107
	[A]	Contracts, Combinations, and Conspiracies	107
	[B]	Cartels: Price Fixing, Production Limitation, and Market Allocation	109
	[C]	Antitrust Scrutiny of the Tech Industry	115
	[D]	Collective Boycotts and Refusals to Deal	116
	[E]	Standardization Efforts	119
	[F]	Joint Ventures	122
	[G]	Cooperative Purchasing Arrangements	130
§5.02		The Sherman Act § 2	131
	[A]	What Constitutes Monopolization	131
	[B]	Market Definition	133
	[C]	Remedial Action for Monopolization	133
	[D]	Types of Monopolistic Practices	134
		[1] Predatory Pricing and Predatory Bidding	134
		[2] Refusals to Deal	136
		[3] Tying and Other Exclusionary Conduct	137
		[4] International and Other Settings	141

CHAPTER 6
Relationships with Customers or Licensees in US Commerce — 145

§6.01		Vertical Agreements	145
§6.02		US Antitrust Law on Vertical Restraints	146
	[A]	Exclusive Dealing	147
	[B]	Tying Agreements	152
	[C]	Restraints on Resale	156
		[1] Resale Price Maintenance	156
		[2] Territorial and Customer Restraints	157
§6.03		Licensing of IP Rights	159
	[A]	Subject Matter of IP Rights	159
	[B]	Relationship with Antitrust Law	161
	[C]	Territorial Restrictions in International Licenses	166
	[D]	Field-of-Use Restrictions	169
	[E]	Tying Agreements	170
	[F]	Improper Royalty Formulas	172
	[G]	Multiple Licenses, Cross-Licenses and Pooling	174
§6.04		Franchising	176

Table of Contents

CHAPTER 7
The Federal Trade Commission and Robinson-Patman Acts — 179
§7.01 The FTC and R-P Statutes — 179
§7.02 The Federal Trade Commission Act — 180
    [A] Jurisdictional Reach — 180
    [B] Acts and Practices in Violation — 182
    [C] Activity in International Cases — 185
§7.03 The Robinson-Patman Act — 187
    [A] The Scope of the Statute — 187
    [B] Other Provisions of the Robinson-Patman Act — 190
    [C] Competitive Injury — 190
    [D] The Robinson-Patman Act in Foreign Commerce — 193

CHAPTER 8
US Antitrust Aspects of Mergers and Acquisitions — 195
§8.01 Antitrust Treatment of Mergers and Acquisitions — 195
§8.02 Relevant US Laws — 196
§8.03 Premerger Notification — 199
§8.04 Antitrust Analysis of Mergers — 201
§8.05 Joint Venture Policy — 205
§8.06 Merger Case Law — 206
    [A] The Earlier Precedents — 206
    [B] Some More Recent Cases — 208
§8.07 International Aspects — 213

PART II
European Union Competition Law — 221

CHAPTER 9
Overview of the Competition Law of the European Union — 223
§9.01 The EU — 223
§9.02 The EU Institutions — 225
    [A] The Council of Ministers — 225
    [B] The Commission — 226
    [C] The Parliament — 227
    [D] The EU Courts — 228
    [E] The Application of EU Law — 229
§9.03 Overview of the Competition Law Rules and Their Enforcement — 230
    [A] The Competition Law Rules — 230
    [B] Council Regulation 1/2003 — 233
    [C] Overview of Commission Enforcement — 239
        [1] Fines and Penalties — 239
        [2] Leniency for Cooperation by Undertakings — 240
        [3] Complaints — 241
        [4] Investigation — 242

		[5]	Statement of Objections, Hearing, and Decision	244
	[D]		Judicial Review	246
	[E]		Private Enforcement of EU Competition Law	247

CHAPTER 10
Article 101 TFEU: Agreements, Decisions, and Concerted Practices –
Activity Involving Competitors 251
§10.01 Introduction 251
§10.02 Article 101(1): Prohibited Activity 252
        [A] Undertakings 252
        [B] Prohibited Agreements, Decisions, and Concerted Practices ... 253
        [C] May Affect Trade Between Member States 255
        [D] Object or Effect of Restricting Competition Within the Internal Market 259
        [E] Relevant Markets 261
§10.03 Article 10(2) Nullity 261
§10.04 The Application of Article 101(3) 261
        [A] The Past Regime: Notification 262
        [B] The Present Regime: Decentralization 264
        [C] Comparison with US Law 267
§10.05 Article 101(1) in the Horizontal Context 267
        [A] Price Fixing and Market Allocation 268
        [B] Concerted Refusals to Deal (Boycotts) 273
        [C] Limitation or Control of Production 274
§10.06 Permissible Cooperation among Competitors 276
        [A] The Guidelines on Horizontal Cooperation Agreements 276
                [1] Joint Purchasing 277
                [2] Standardization Agreements 278
                [3] Commercialization Agreements: Joint Marketing 280
                [4] Joint Production 280
                [5] Information Exchange 281
        [B] The Block Exemptions 281
                [1] Research and Development Agreements 282
                [2] Specialization Agreements 283
                [3] Insurance 284
                [4] Banking 285
                [5] Agriculture 285
        [C] Cooperation on Exports 285
        [D] Case Law Involving Joint Ventures 286

CHAPTER 11
Article 101 TFEU: Agreements, Decisions and Concerted Practices
– Suppliers, Customers and Licensees 289
§11.01 Article 101 TFEU: Vertical Restraints Generally 289

Table of Contents

§11.02	The BE Regulation	291
§11.03	The Guidelines on Vertical Restraints	292
§11.04	Policies in the Vertical Context	294
	[A] Export Restraints	294
	[B] Resale Price Maintenance	295
	[C] Single Branding	296
	[D] Restriction on Resale Territory or Customer	297
	[E] Noncompete Obligations	299
	[F] Exclusive and Selective Distribution	300
	[G] Franchising	303
	[H] Tying	305
	[I] Hard Core Restrictions	305
	[J] Discrimination in Pricing and Other Terms	306
	[K] Current Rules for Car Distribution and the Aftermarket	307
§11.05	Assignments and Licenses of IP Rights	308
	[A] Introduction	308
	[B] Trademarks	309
	[C] Copyright	310
§11.06	The Digital Market	311
§11.07	The Free Movement of Goods: The Exhaustion Doctrine	312
§11.08	The Technology Transfer Block Exemption Regulation	317

CHAPTER 12
Article 102 TFEU: Abuse of a Dominant Position   323

§12.01	Introduction	323
§12.02	Principal Elements of Article 102	325
	[A] Dominant Position	325
	[B] Abuse	327
	[C] Affect Trade Between Member States	328
	[D] Remedies	328
§12.03	Abusive Practices by Dominant Firms: The Precedents	329
	[A] Excessive, Predatory or Discriminatory Terms	329
	[B] Limiting Production, Markets or Technical Development	331
	[C] Applying Dissimilar Conditions to Equivalent Transactions	334
	[D] Tying	335
	[E] Exclusive Dealing and Loyalty Discounts	336
	[F] Abuses of IP Rights	339
	[G] Joint Dominance	342
§12.04	The Technology Cases	344
	[A] Microsoft	345
	[B] Intel	348
	[C] Google	349
	[D] Amazon	351
	[E] Apple	352
	[F] Qualcomm	352

Chapter 13
Merger Control in the European Union — 355
- §13.01 Introduction to Merger Control — 355
- §13.02 Before the Merger Regulation — 356
- §13.03 Merger Regulation 139/2004 — 358
  - [A] Concentrations Having a Union Dimension — 360
  - [B] Case Referral and Consultation — 362
  - [C] Notification and Review Procedure — 365
  - [D] Remedies — 367
  - [E] Judicial Review — 369
- §13.04 Merger Analysis — 369
  - [A] Market Shares and Concentration Levels — 370
  - [B] Possible Anticompetitive Effects — 371
  - [C] Entry Barriers — 372
  - [D] Efficiencies — 372
  - [E] Failing Firms — 373
  - [F] Vertical and Conglomerate Mergers — 373
- §13.05 Collective Dominance — 375
- §13.06 Full-Function Joint Ventures — 377
- §13.07 Ancillary Restraints — 378
- §13.08 Some Merger Case Highlights — 379

Part III
Other Selected Competition Laws — 391

Chapter 14
The United Kingdom — 393
- §14.01 Background — 393
- §14.02 Later Legislation — 394
- §14.03 Private Enforcement — 395
- §14.04 The Prohibitions — 397
- §14.05 The Cartel Offense — 398
- §14.06 Vertical Agreements — 399
- §14.07 Mergers — 399
- §14.08 Antitrust in the UK After Brexit — 402

Chapter 15
Japan — 405
- §15.01 Historical Background — 405
- §15.02 Overview of the Legislation — 408
  - [A] The Japan Fair Trade Commission — 408
  - [B] Available Remedies and Leniency — 410
  - [C] Private Enforcement — 411
  - [D] Key Terms of the AMA — 412
  - [E] Exemptions — 413

Table of Contents

§15.03	Monopolization		413
§15.04	Unreasonable Restraint of Trade		417
§15.05	Unfair Trade Practices		420
§15.06	Licensing of Intellectual Property		423
§15.07	Mergers and Acquisitions		424
	[A]	Prohibitions	424
	[B]	Premerger Review	425
	[C]	Merger Analysis	426
	[D]	Some Case Law	427

CHAPTER 16
India 431

§16.01	The Background		431
§16.02	Competition Act 2002		432
	[A]	The Competition Commission	433
	[B]	Section 3: Prohibition of Anticompetitive Agreements	433
	[C]	Section 4: Abuse of Dominance	434
	[D]	Enforcement of Sections 3 and 4	434
	[E]	Mergers	436
§16.03	Some Case Law		437

CHAPTER 17
South Korea 441

§17.01	Historical Background	441
§17.02	KFTC Enforcement Powers	442
§17.03	Cartel Activity Prohibition	443
§17.04	Abuse of a Dominant Position	443
§17.05	Prohibition of Unfair Trade Practices	445
§17.06	Mergers and Acquisitions	447
§17.07	Some Case Law	449

Appendices 453

Appendix I
Selected Bibliography 455

Appendix II
Council Regulation (EC) No 1/2003 of 16 December 2002 on
the Implementation of the Rules on Competition Laid Down in Articles 81
and 82 of the Treaty 473

Appendix III
Antitrust Guidelines for International Enforcement and
Cooperation 507

Index 547

Preface

This effort labeled "An International Antitrust Primer" began in 1974 with the First Edition, which I co-wrote with my then law partner and mentor, Earl W. Kintner, who had been Chairman of the US Federal Trade Commission. I produced the Second Edition in 2001, with a foreword by Judge (now Chief Judge) Diane P. Wood. As I observed in the preface to that edition, the twenty-seven-year period which had elapsed marked enormous progress for antitrust jurisprudence. It had passed from a point in time when only a few national and regional authorities, the United States (US) and the European Union (EU) chief among them, took seriously the need for enforcement of competition law, to reaching a point at which more than ninety nations maintained or were in the process of drafting antitrust legislation.

The globalization of commerce worked a transformation in the way in which competition law was perceived around the world. It meant that the few regimes that had championed antitrust enforcement had no longer to legitimize their positions on antitrust by explaining to others' satisfaction the need for enforcing competition laws. It also meant that a common desire had at last been formed to create internationally acceptable and effective means of enforcing antitrust law everywhere. Friction between governments over unilateral antitrust enforcement had been succeeded in many instances by effective cooperation between national competition authorities. Charges of extraterritoriality and affronts to national sovereignty were replaced by intergovernment cooperation over what everyone acknowledged was international commerce.

The fast developing nature of this field prompted a Third Edition of this Primer in 2006, containing substantial revision and additions, only five years after the previous version was laid to bed. Important developments in international cooperation on antitrust, in national competition rules, and in the competition legislation of that vital supra-national regime, the EU, had outdated the 2001 edition.

Merger policy, for example, adjusted to the needs of a globalized economy as it was realized that enhanced size might be necessary for firms to succeed, although as the EU reminds us, abusive practices by "dominant" firms are not to be tolerated.

The ten-year period since 2006 has outdated our Third Edition because of significant new case and legislative developments. In 2017, as this is written, over 130 jurisdictions have enacted antitrust laws. Moreover, much of the terrain upon which competition law operates has been altered as the technological era has descended upon us. Let us pause to consider this phenomenon for a moment.

One of the fascinating aspects of antitrust law is that it permits and indeed requires a study and understanding of markets. There are posed a number of questions. What constitutes a "market" for antitrust purposes and how do you determine its contours? To what extent do two non-identical products in fact compete with each other in the view of the buyer? What is a producer's "ease of entry" in moving from supplying one market to serving another? At the turn of the century, the rules seemed relatively clear. The concept of consumer preference, and hence market definition, appeared to be fully developed, and our antitrust dilemmas concerning the defining of product markets were generally limited to issues like the one that came up in the US *Cellophane* case: was cellophane a distinctive and defining product for antitrust purposes or was it just another interchangeable flexible packaging material?

But then the *Microsoft* cases arrived on the antitrust scene to raise new questions about how "browsers" and "operating systems," "clouds," the Internet itself and other innovative technology affected our concepts of relevant markets and of competition itself. That new era is now fully upon us. Substantial businesses evidenced by brick and mortar are losing ground to "online" sales which have little or no brick and mortar behind them.

Physical barriers to trade have become less important than technological ones. In 2015, Amazon, with only minimal physical presence, overtook Walmart to become the highest valued retailer in the US. Amazon, Alphabet (the parent company of Google), Microsoft, Apple and Facebook, whose power is digital, are currently listed among the ten largest companies in the world by market capitalization. Observers also point out that Uber, the world's largest supplier of car service, owns no automobiles, while Airbnb, the largest provider of housing, owns no real estate. Both rely on electronic commerce.

These companies today have an enormous grip on our collective personal and economic lives. This dramatic rise of the technology companies has been called a "game changer" for antitrust law enforcement, but there is not yet a consensus concerning how or when the "game" will change. As the following pages demonstrate, to date the traditional remedies for monopolization, abuse of dominance, merger control and restraint of trade have been employed in the efforts to curb the market power of these firms.

The EU has just developed a comprehensive plan for the digital marketplace so as to enhance the ability of citizens of the EU to make interstate online purchases. Ever racing to remain fully versed about the competitive process, antitrust law also is attempting to cope with these changing market contours, as we shall see in the pages ahead.

One more precautionary point: as this is written, we are in a period of high political uncertainty. It is too early to tell how and where the Trump Administration will lead US law enforcement policy, including antitrust. It appears also that "Brexit" and other European developments will help shape the economic and political situations in the United Kingdom, in other nations and in the EU itself. We must await the developments and see where they take us. Of course, as Yogi Berra, the great New York Yankee catcher, is reputed to have said, "you can observe a lot just by watching." I hope that this volume is a contribution to the watching process.

Once again, this book is not meant to be a contribution to the extensive literature, some of it multi-volume, which covers all of the jurisprudence that has developed under the US, European, and other competition laws. This volume is not sufficiently detailed to be included in that genre. It is a "primer" designed to provide an explanation and understanding of competition law, as a regime of both domestic and international law, for use by the businessperson, journalist, student, lawyer, or just plain reader, who does not seek to specialize in this fascinating field, but desires to be familiar with it in outline. Hence the principal focus of this book is on describing the main provisions and case law of some key national and regional competition regimes, including their application to international business transactions.

As in the previous editions, in order to make the book's content as informative as possible and its size manageable, I have limited the detailed coverage of the subject to a very few of the competition law regimes extant. For purposes of this Primer, it seems more instructive and interesting (for both writer and readers) to offer a relatively detailed explanation of developments in a few important jurisdictions, rather than covering many jurisdictions by offering summary descriptions of a great number of national antitrust laws. Indeed there is a similarity about these national laws, like multiple drinks of water drawn from the same well, that discourages a repetitive narrative covering a large number of jurisdictions.

The EU and the US continue to be the major economies which are in the forefront in the enforcement and refinement of comprehensive competition laws, although it must be acknowledged that vast strides are being made elsewhere. The EU, which has now expanded to a membership of twenty-eight countries (twenty-seven, if you subtract the UK) conducts a continuous process of modernization of its regime, including a new recognition of the digital marketplace. US and EU antitrust law thus continue to be the main foundations of our presentation.

South Korea, Japan, and India are among the nations which have made great progress in developing their competition law regimes. The United Kingdom, another important economy whose competition law foundation regime has largely relied on the framework of the EU, will soon stand alone after the Brexit has been negotiated. I have selected these four nations for our study here. I hope that you will find their efforts to be as interesting as I do.

July 2017

Acknowledgements

I have received valuable input and advice from many sources for which I am grateful. I am particularly appreciative of the encouragement and help that I have received from Niki DeBruin of Wolters Kluwer publishing. Mrs. Pradhiba and her team have been very expert in assembling the final product.

I deeply thank my wife, Tato, and the "kids," Helen, Daniel and Marisa, for their continuing love and support.

CHAPTER 1
An Overview of Competition Law Development Around the World

§1.01 BACKGROUND

No one claimed credit for having organized the world's first cartel. Conversely, no one is certain as to the earliest antecedents of the concept that governmental vigilance is needed to protect the free market from private anticompetitive restraints. Aristotle is quoted as saying: "It is best to have property private. In this manner industry will be increased as each person will labor to improve his own property." By 50 B.C. Roman legislation prohibited profiteering and joint action to influence the corn trade. Two hundred and fifty years later Diocletian issued an edict, backed up by the death penalty, which forbade concealment of foodstuffs, and hence the artificial creation of scarcity. The Roman Constitution of Zeno, promulgated in 483 A.D., protected consumers against artificial increases in the prices of all foodstuffs and other articles in everyday use. After the decline of Rome, there came a long period of economic and political instability, war, and reduced trade, which was not conducive to either flourishing economies or anticompetitive business activity. It was not until the tenth century that merchants, who were the principal targets of the early Roman competition laws, began to show enthusiasm for the re-establishment of business combinations and monopolies. In response to this re-emergence of anticompetitive conduct, England, France, and several of the Italian city-states, by the end of the thirteenth century, enacted statutes prohibiting specified restrictive practices, such as price fixing by ore traders and the combination of fishmongers for the joint purchase and sale of their products.

From the time of the Magna Carta, English common law judges began to develop principles concerning the "restraint of trade." These doctrines proscribed monopolies and covenants not to compete as unlawful restrictions on the freedom of the individual. In 1349, a statute was enacted providing that merchants who overcharged for victuals must pay to the injured party double the sum charged. These statutes and common law principles were incorporated into the jurisprudence of England's American colonies and, later, into the laws of the newly independent United States (US). Moreover, the American colonists' hostility to the practices of the trade monopolies chartered by the English crown was so great that several of the newly formed states wrote prohibitions against monopolies into their constitutions. These constitutional provisions and laws were designed to put an end to unjustified privilege and to insure a liberal, diversified, and decentralized way of life.

The industrial revolution flourished under these principles favoring the free play of market forces, unrestricted freedom of contract, the freedom to enter into any line of business, and economic individualism generally. The economic, political, and social climate of laissez faire that prevailed in America from revolutionary times until the late nineteenth century (becoming known in the post-Civil War era as Social Darwinism) encouraged individuals to seek the rewards of technological progress through unrestrained competition and the survival of the economically fittest. As the pace of the technological improvements in banking, communications, manufacturing, and transportation quickened, emphasis was increasingly placed upon efficiencies and economies of scale. Mass production required heavy fixed investments, which in turn meant that only well-financed, large enterprises could readily enter a variety of industries. In addition, the economic advantages stemming from control over the sources of supply, the means of production, and the channels of distribution encouraged integration on the part of the firms large enough to have gained entry into the market.

The competitive struggle in this prevailing atmosphere of freedom of contract and laissez faire economics became more and more fierce, as the firms fought for capital, customers, and raw materials. This cutthroat competition and accompanying predatory practices often resulted in the destruction of the weakest members of the industry. The surviving competitors then formed combinations to consolidate their positions or a monopolist emerged. Individual entrepreneurs and small partnerships were steadily replaced by corporations, trusts, and cartels as the customary forms of business organization. The corporate form offered perpetual succession, limited liability and anonymity. But state laws limited the activities of the corporations, and the Standard Oil Company pioneered the use of the common law trust in the US in order to create a still more effective form of business organization. Under this device, the stockholders of a particular corporation would deposit their certificates with a board of trustees that had full management control and power. The trust could then control any number of corporations located throughout the country.

As big business began to affect negatively the lives of individual Americans, protests against its abusive power mounted. The traditional doctrines and remedies fashioned by the common law for dealing with restraints of trade were obviously incapable of countervailing the dominance and abuses of the "robber barons." Small businessmen complained of being driven out of business or of being denied an opportunity to enter a trade. Farmers agitated against the railroad rebate system and the price discrimination imposed on them as between long and short hauls. Labor organizations began to demand government control of large business as a way to obtain better wages and working conditions, as well as of preventing anti-union activities. Consumers and the public rebelled against rising prices, deteriorating product quality, unfair and deceptive practices, and politically threatening

Chapter 1: An Overview of Competition Law Development §1.01

concentrations of power. Outrageous abuses in the petroleum and railroad industries led to the formation of the Grange movement and of other organizations which entered politics in order to militate for government regulation of business.

In 1887, the reform movement in America had gained enough power to obtain enactment of the first federal statute for the regulation of business—the Interstate Commerce Act, which was directed against the abuses practiced by the railroads. In 1888, both major American political parties promised business reforms in their election platforms, and Benjamin Harrison, the newly elected President, lost no time in requesting legislation to curb "dangerous conspiracies" and monopolies. The author of the first antitrust bill to be introduced, Senator John Sherman, described the great concentrations of business power as:

> reach[ing] out their Briarean arms to every part of our country. They are imported from abroad. Congress alone can deal with them, and if we are unwilling or unable there will soon be a trust for every production and a master to fix the price for every necessity of life.

The final version of Senator Sherman's bill passed both houses of the US Congress with only one dissenting vote and was signed by President Harrison on July 2, 1890. However, by 1912 all the major political parties were calling for remedial legislation to strengthen still further the government's ability to deal with abusive business activity. Consequently, within the following six years, three new antitrust laws were enacted, the Clayton and Federal Trade Commission Acts of 1914 and the Webb-Pomerene Act of 1918. In the Depression era, the Congress became concerned with the market power wielded by large buying groups, particularly the chain grocery stores. This led to enactment of the Robinson-Patman Act in 1936, legislation designed to assist small independent competitors by compelling suppliers to treat all buyers on a nondiscriminatory basis. These US antitrust laws will all be discussed in the succeeding chapters.

Such events were not confined to the US. Canada had experienced a very similar trend toward concentration and monopoly, and it had reacted in a similar manner. Indeed, fourteen months before the Sherman Act was enacted in the US, Canada adopted the Act for the Prevention and Suppression of Combinations Formed in Restraint of Trade, which imposed criminal penalties for various anticompetitive conspiracies, combinations, and agreements. Moreover, just as in the US, the first legislation did not quell the demand for government involvement. Therefore, in 1910, Canada enacted the Combines Investigation Act, making monopolies and mergers likely to operate to the detriment of consumers and producers criminal offenses. In 1935, predatory pricing and price discrimination, and, in 1952, resale price maintenance (RPM) were also made criminal offenses. For many years subsequently, the reliance of the Canadian scheme on criminal enforcement, requiring the prosecution to prove its case beyond a reasonable doubt, severely hampered its effectiveness. Amendments enacted in 1976 and the passage of the Competition Act of 1986 resulted in a greatly improved enforcement regime. In 2009, sweeping changes were instituted, including the repeal of some of the offenses, such as predatory pricing and price discrimination, and price maintenance was de-criminalized.

Outside of North America, the years prior to the conclusion of World War I passed without any comparable initiation of legislation designed to regulate anticompetitive business practices. In the developed nations, because of historical national rivalries and the ever-present danger of war, there was a tendency for each national government and business community to believe that the two shared a common overriding interest in their own nation's economic strength and stability. A powerful industrial complex was considered to be a prerequisite for victory in war. Therefore, governments encouraged the development of strong business forces even if that entailed the creation of cartels or monopolies, and they also protected local business from foreign competition by means of high tariffs and other restrictive border devices. It was not uncommon for the leaders of business and government within a nation to consult and collaborate so closely that their aims became interchangeable.

Following the conclusion of World War I, a few countries did become concerned about the financial damage and unemployment being inflicted by the predatory practices of the cartels and monopolies that had arisen. Between 1920 and the onset of the Great Depression, a number of European countries enacted legislation directed against restrictive practices, as did some non-European nations. However, most of this legislation was little enforced or was abandoned as, first, the Great Depression dominated the 1920s and 1930s, and then World War II spread around the globe.

After the war, the US forcefully advocated the adoption of strong antitrust laws in its areas of influence. The military occupation authorities in Germany and Japan quickly imposed American-style antitrust laws in order to prevent the re-emergence of the large, politically powerful cartels that had prospered before the war. US pressure against the conduct of restrictive business practices abroad was also exerted through reconstruction aid programs and treaty negotiations. In addition, as a result of postwar investigations conducted by several governments into the wartime activities of cartels, many countries gained a new awareness of the power of cartels and of the willingness of the latter to place corporate self-interest above the national interest. For a variety of reasons, nations began to enact antitrust legislation in the hope that fair competition would increase their productivity, help to control postwar inflation, and reduce barriers to international trade.

In a development of great importance, the treaties which were drawn up to establish the Common Market in Europe placed significant reliance on the effective enforcement of strong competition law rules. The adoption of such rules served the dual purpose of deterring restrictive business practices and helping to assure the free movement of goods within the Community which was necessary to the economic integration of the European market. Thus, Articles 85 and 86 (now Articles 101 and 102 of the current EU Treaty) of the 1957 Treaty Establishing the European Economic Community (EEC) (also known as the Treaty of Rome) imparted strong proscriptions against restraints of trade and abuses of dominant positions affecting trade between the Member States. In the following years, the Community increased from its original six members to fifteen, and then twenty-eight nations, and the Member States were each urged to take the necessary steps to enact or enhance their national competition laws and to make them consistent with the Community rules.

The importance of dealing effectively with the competitive aspects of multinational mergers led the European Community (EC) to adopt a merger control regime in 1989 and then to upgrade it in 2004. In addition, the difficulties involved in scrutinizing business transactions and practices in an effective and timely manner in a regime that was soon to encompass twenty-eight nations led the EC to partially decentralize its enforcement regime and to place additional responsibilities on national competition authorities. This led to another round of revisions of the Member State competition laws to make them conform to the "modernized" Community model. Under the prodding of the European Commission, private remedies to redress injury inflicted by competition law infractions began to take hold in a number of member nations.

In the final decade of the twentieth century, the collapse of the Soviet Union was followed by a transition on the part of the emerging nations (including Russia itself) from socialist to market economies, a shift which led those nations to adopt competition laws. International lending agencies insisted that debtor nations include competition law in transforming their systems to open market principles, and experts from the US and Europe fanned out around the world to assist the newly emergent nations in designing their new laws.

§1.02 THE CURRENT SITUATION

[A] Competition Law Players

As the impetus to adopt competition laws gained momentum, important new participants appeared on the scene. Russia adopted an antimonopoly law which was ratified by the Supreme Soviet of the USSR in 1991. Subsequently, Federal Law No. 135-FZ, "On the Protection of Competition" was developed by the Federal Antimonopoly Service of Russia and entered into force in 2006. Poland (1990), the Czech Republic (1991), the Slovak Republic (1994), and Hungary (1996) were among the other former socialist states which introduced competition laws. In 1994, Turkey enacted its Law on the Protection of Competition. Switzerland revised its 1995 anti-cartel law several times to pattern it closely after the EC model.

Important development of antitrust laws also took place in Asia as a number of countries of the Pacific asserted their commitments to free markets and pursued their roles in the globalization of trade. Asia-Pacific Economic Cooperation ("APEC"), an intergovernmental organization composed of Pacific Rim nations, has pressed an agenda for the liberalization of trade and investment in the region. Japan has maintained antitrust laws since the postwar period, and it has repeatedly amended that law in an effort to make it more effective to deal with its ongoing competitive concerns, including a tradition in industry of rigging public procurement bids. India adopted its Monopolies and Trade Practices Act in 1969 and enacted a new piece of legislation, the Competition Act 2002, to replace the original scheme.

Since its adoption of the Trade Practices Act 1974, Australia has built a strong tradition in antitrust enforcement. South Korea, after initially ignoring competition policy in an effort to boost exports through large scale enterprises, passed the

Monopoly Regulation and Fair Trade Act ("MRFTA") in 1980 (later amended) to bring free and fair competition to the marketplace. Taiwan has carried out an active competition promotion effort since the Taiwan Fair Trade Commission was established in 1992. Indonesia's Law No. 5 of 1999, for the Prohibition of Monopolistic Practices and Unfair Business Competition, became effective in September 2000. Singapore and Vietnam have enacted competition laws. After more than ten years of drafting and consideration, China adopted a new Anti-Monopoly Law which took effect on August 1, 2008.

In Latin America, among the countries that have taken steps to institute or strengthen competition laws are Argentina, Brazil, Chile, Colombia, Mexico, Peru, and Venezuela. South Africa has enhanced its competition regulation through the Competition Act 1998, which came into effect in September 1999, and other African nations have also adopted antitrust laws.

There is no single model for these pieces of legislation, although a number of voluntary international organizations have offered model competition laws for consideration by governments. Indeed, the existence in each nation of varying points of economic concern and the idiosyncratic uses of language give many of the national competition laws a distinctive look, which the vagaries of translation only accentuate. Nonetheless, a number of commonly held principles regularly appear, evidencing a phenomenon called "convergence." This process of developing universal principles through a sharing of experience and the development of "best practices" has been facilitated by the establishment in October 2001 of a regular forum for the world's competition agency officials called the International Competition Network (ICN).

[B]   The ICN and Convergence

The ICN is a voluntary network of national and multinational competition agencies with the common aim of addressing practical competition law enforcement and policy issues. It was established by antitrust officials from sixteen competition agencies around the world. In addition to the antitrust officials, nongovernmental advisers representing business, academia, economists, and other groups are invited to participate. The ICN now comprises 135 member agencies from 122 jurisdictions. Its work is project oriented focusing on such issues as international best practices in competition matters.

The ICN holds an annual conference at a member nation's venue. At its 2017 conference, for example, the ICN approved new guidance relating to merger remedies, evaluating exclusionary conduct, cartel fines and leniency, and competition agency training programs. There is a Unilateral Conduct Working Group exploring the establishment of a framework for single-firm conduct enforcement. The ICN has adopted a Merger Remedies Guide developed by its Mergers Working Group. The Cartel Working Group has developed a catalog of agency investigative powers and a framework for sharing nonconfidential information. One working group has announced the launch of a new project to analyze the effects of vertical restraints in online markets.

The members of the ICN, by definition, have common interests and even viewpoints. There is essentially universal proscription of "cartels," meaning arrangements among competitors to fix prices, limit output, or allocate markets. Other practices that frequently are viewed as the subject of prohibition are RPM, "predatory" pricing, collective refusals to deal (boycotts), and anticompetitive tying arrangements. On the other hand, except where they are engaged in by dominant firms, some business practices, such as exclusive dealing, are not readily placed into either a bad or a good category for competition law purposes and thus require careful appraisal in terms of the particular situation presented. What the Americans call a "rule of reason," or its functional equivalent, is often applied in national competition laws. Mexico's Federal Law of Economic Competition, for example, approaches this analytical distinction by labeling blatantly anticompetitive agreements as "absolute" monopolistic practices and calling restrictive arrangements that must be assessed in terms of their economic and factual contexts "relative" monopolistic practices.

There appears to be a consensus that hard core cartel activity cannot be permitted and also that the use of market power by dominant firms must be curbed, either by imposing regulatory regimes on the industry or through effective competition law deterrents and remedies. The US has developed the concept of monopolization to address this issue, while the European Union ("EU") has done so in the context of abuse of a dominant position. These concepts are not identical but a significant degree of convergence in approach, based on principles of economic analysis, is emerging with single firm misconduct, as well as with oligopoly. Certain exemptions from otherwise strong competition law enforcement also appear on a regular basis in the different national laws. For example, export cartels that do not cause injury in the exporters' domestic markets are often exempted from the strictures of the law. There is little justification offered for this "beggar your neighbor" policy beyond a narrow nationalism and these cartels seem to be on their way out,

In recent years, the waves of merger activity around the globe have caused the competition law authorities to devote much of their attention, as well as a significant portion of their resources, to the task of assessing the competitive impact of these merger and acquisition transactions. Modern antitrust legislation therefore is carefully crafted to provide appropriate criteria and procedures for review by competition authorities of the mergers and acquisitions subject to their jurisdiction. Bitter experience in a number of jurisdictions, including the US, has taught that, when the merger control law fails to require pre-merger notification, the authorities are badly disadvantaged in trying to restore competition once an anticompetitive transaction has been consummated. Most of the updated laws, therefore, do require pre-merger notification, at the peril of substantial fines for noncompliance.

Since the procedures for submitting a merger for antitrust review have not been harmonized among the different nations—not to mention the forms that must be filled out by the reporting parties—and since a single merger may have to be reported to a dozen or more jurisdictions, the lack of an internationalized approach in this area has been extremely costly and time consuming for the business organizations in question. This is, however, an area in which cooperation by the enforcement agencies under the umbrella of the ICN has brought about a welcome measure of progress.

Significant differences also exist among nations as to the remedies deemed appropriate for antitrust enforcement. The issuance of cease and desist orders, accompanied by the imposition of fines, with the amount of the fine increasing according to the gravity of the offense, is a generally accepted form of remedy. The application of criminal sanctions, including imprisonment for individuals, is not yet a generally accepted remedy, although a number of nations have recently added criminal sanctions for both individuals and enterprises for involvement in hard core cartel activity. Leniency programs, providing incentives for individuals and enterprises to disclose cartel activity to the authorities on an early basis, have gained significant acceptance as a useful anti-cartel enforcement instrument.

Private enforcement of antitrust laws, long a feature of the US system, can play a valuable role in providing an additional deterrent to anticompetitive conduct, as well as in providing compensation to persons and firms injured by that conduct. This view has been gaining adherents in recent years and is now accepted by the European Commission. However, in the EU as elsewhere, these private claims can be pursued only to the extent that this remedy is provided and facilitated by national law. The development of private remedies for antitrust violations is developing slowly in many countries. Several elements of the private enforcement remedy which are important in the US scheme—treble damage awards, contingency fees for the attorneys, and class action procedures—have little support elsewhere.

Moreover, despite the apparent convergence of much competition law from country to country, it can be hazardous to draw the facile conclusion that a universal commitment to antitrust enforcement is being quickly achieved. The fact that Nation A has adopted an antitrust law containing familiar competition policy principles may conceal the fact that Nation A has no serious intention of enforcing its antitrust law because it lacks political appetite for the endeavor and has not devoted sufficient funding to making its enforcement agency successful. Perhaps Nation A grudgingly adopted the law only under duress applied by its international creditors and will largely ignore it. Or, alternatively, it may be that Nation B has every intention of enforcing its new law but will do so selectively for the purpose of disadvantaging foreign investors.

Indeed, the concerns sought to be addressed by enforcement of antitrust legislation often are hostages to larger issues of foreign or domestic policy. National problems created by balance of payments deficits, the need to export, trade barriers, consumer protection issues, treaty obligations, and commitments made to international organizations may shape the scope and content imparted to the enforcement or nonenforcement of an antitrust law at any given time. In sum, the extent of a nation's commitment to competition policy is best assessed not solely by measuring the breadth of its statutory prohibitions, but also by appraising the level and type of enforcement activity that is actually carried on from day to day.

[C] Other International Cooperation

In addition to the ICN, several other international fora serve for discussion of competition law enforcement matters, including the Competition Committee of the

Organisation for Economic Co-operation and Development ("OECD"), the United Nations Conference on Trade and Development ("UNCTAD"), and the Asia-Pacific Economic Cooperation ("APEC") forum.

Bilateral agreements are playing an important role in strengthening the relationships between competition agencies. Close and continuous cooperation in the development of "best practices" with regard to merger and other investigations is taking place on a bilateral basis, as well as in the ICN. For example, the US authorities have entered into bilateral cooperation agreements with many jurisdictions or competition agencies: Germany (1976); Australia (1982); the EU (1981); Canada (1995); Brazil, Israel and Japan (1999); Mexico (2000); Chile (2011); Colombia (2014); and Peru (2016). The US Agencies have also entered into a Memorandum of Understanding with the Russian Federal Antimonopoly Service (2009), the three Chinese antimonopoly enforcement agencies (2011), the Indian competition authorities (2012), and the Korea Fair Trade Commission ("KFTC").

Part I   United States Antitrust Law

CHAPTER 2
Summary of the United States Antitrust Laws

§2.01   THE SHERMAN ACT

The US legal system has sometimes been called the wise restraint that enables freedom. This characterization is certainly apt with respect to the US antitrust laws designed to regulate competition. The US antitrust laws are essentially conservative in nature. Their purpose and design is to protect the vitality of the marketplace by imposing rules that assure that the competitive contest will be fairly waged. These rules seek to prevent coercive practices and the development of giant aggregations of power through unfair means. In *United States v. Topco Associates, Inc.*, the US Supreme Court described the antitrust laws as the Magna Carta of free enterprise, laws which guarantee each business, no matter how small, "the freedom to compete—to assert with vigor, imagination, devotion and ingenuity whatever economic muscle it can muster."

The central US antitrust law relating to agreements in restraint of trade continues to be the Sherman Act. The legislative history of that 1890 enactment speaks eloquently of the popular concern aroused by the condition of the US economy at that time: a relatively small number of corporations and individuals had accumulated vast amounts of wealth; corporate organizations unresponsive to the interests of the general public were being spawned in large numbers; damaging business combinations known as "trusts" were multiplying and were suppressing efforts to compete with them. There was a widespread public view that the weight of these accumulations of corporate wealth and power had been and would be applied to harm the general interest and to oppress individuals, unless protective action in the public interest was taken. The US Congress acted forcefully, in an effort aimed at curbing the business excesses and abuses, while not harming the legitimate competitive process itself.

The wording of the Sherman Act's two substantive sections reflects the statute's intended remedial policies in general terms. Section 1 declares: "Every contract, combination in the form of trust or otherwise, or conspiracy, in restraint of trade or commerce among the several States, or with foreign nations, is declared to be illegal." Section 2 is equally general: "Every person who shall monopolize, or attempt to monopolize, or combine or conspire with any other person or persons, to monopolize any part of the trade or commerce among the several States, or with foreign nations, shall be deemed guilty of a felony."

While these principles have remained constant over the 125 plus years of the Sherman Act, the penalties for violation have been revised upward sharply over the period. A Sherman Act violation, initially a misdemeanor punishable by a fine not exceeding USD 5,000 and/or imprisonment not exceeding one year, is now, by virtue of changes made by the Congress in 2004, a felony punishable by a fine not exceeding USD 100,000,000 for a corporation or USD 1,000,000 for an individual and/or by imprisonment not exceeding ten years. Even these high fine limits are not the outward boundary of the violator's potential liability. Under the Criminal Fines Improvements Act of 1987 (re-enacted), alternative fines may be imposed which equal twice the financial gain to the violator or twice the loss to the victim resulting from the crime.

The Sherman Act can be enforced both civilly and criminally. Civil suits may be brought by the US Department of Justice and by private aggrieved parties. Only the Department of Justice is authorized to seek criminal penalties by initiating court proceedings. The Department has regularly brought criminal prosecutions in the case of the most serious Sherman Act violations, principally price fixing or market division among competitors. With respect to such "hard core" violations, the Department has not hesitated to pursue in the courts the imposition of very heavy fines, even where all or some of the perpetrators were foreign companies and their executives. As we discuss in Chapter 5, in 1999, the Department of Justice announced that Swiss and German pharmaceutical companies had pleaded guilty and agreed to pay over USD 700 million in fines for participating in a worldwide conspiracy to raise and fix prices and allocate market shares on certain vitamin products. The Attorney General noted that these were not only record fines at that time for an antitrust case, but also represented the largest fines obtained by the Department of Justice in any type of criminal case. In addition, a Swiss citizen involved in the wrongdoing agreed with the government to serve a four-month prison sentence in the US. Moreover, private class actions filed on behalf of purchasers victimized by these violations resulted in settlements exceeding more than one billion dollars. Fines in the hundreds of millions of dollars involving violations in disparate industries have followed in later years. For example, in 2015, Citicorp pleaded guilty to joining in the international conspiracy to manipulate currency prices in the foreign currency exchange (FX) spot market, and it agreed to pay a criminal fine of USD 925 million.

A private action Sherman Act claim must be brought within four years after the cause of action accrued unless there is "fraudulent concealment" which "tolls" the statute of limitations.

As the Sherman Act is now in its third century, that basic law designed to protect competition has well served its purpose. Formulated to address competitive threats in basic product markets, we shall see the extent to which the law has proven adept to cope with our new era of breathtaking technological change and innovation.

[A] The Rule of Reason under Section 1

Section 1 of the Sherman Act is, by its terms, directed at joint conduct, but the nature of the joint conduct which is prohibited is described only by the very general phrase "restraint of trade." Under the US common law system, it has been therefore left to the federal courts to impart content to the phrase as they decide specific cases. Initially, the US Supreme Court had some difficulty in determining the appropriate interpretation of the statutory prohibitions. The language of Section 1 is sweeping in the extreme. It declares every contract, combination, or conspiracy in restraint of trade to be illegal. If read literally, this language would outlaw many useful and harmless business arrangements, such as sales contracts extending over a period of time or covenants not to compete incident to the sale of a business. Indeed, when first faced with the task of interpreting the language, the Supreme Court, by a 5-4 vote, adopted just such a literal interpretation of the prohibition. Every restraint of trade was declared to be illegal. Because contracts commonly contain provisions limiting the activities of one or both of the parties in some regard, restraining the exercise of their full rights in trading, this early approach carried grave implications for subsequent enforcement of Section 1.

Almost immediately, however, the federal courts began to withdraw from this literal interpretation. In 1898, a circuit Court of Appeals considered, in *United States v. Addyston Pipe and Steel Company*, the legality of an agreement among manufacturers of cast iron pipe to fix prices and divide markets in areas where they competed in order to avoid the rigors of competition. Circuit Judge William Howard Taft, who later became President and subsequently Chief Justice of the US, wrote the opinion for the court. While recognizing that the anticompetitive arrangements in question could be disposed of by applying Section 1 literally, he nevertheless tested the legality of the agreements by reference both to common law rules and to what subsequently developed into the "rule of reason." At common law, Judge Taft stated, "no conventional restraint of trade can be enforced unless the covenant embodying it is merely ancillary to the main purpose of a lawful contract, and necessary to protect the covenantee in the enjoyment of the legitimate fruits of the contract, or to protect him from the dangers of an unjust use of those fruits by the other party."

The classic example of the sort of valid ancillary restraint to which Judge Taft was referring is the seller's limited covenant not to compete contained in the contract of sale of a going business. In such a case the valid main purpose of the contract is the sale of the business. An ancillary commitment by the seller not to compete with the buyer for a certain period of time would be for the legitimate purpose of maintaining the value of the business and hence should not be illegal. However, to be truly ancillary, the restraint must be no broader than is necessary to protect the main value of the contract. Thus, for example, a commitment by the seller of a local business not to compete with the buyer anywhere in the nation would be clearly in excess of the obligation needed to protect the value of the business being sold.

This principle, Judge Taft stated, was the common law rule with respect to restraints of trade. The English common law courts had declared that only those restraints that were "unreasonable" were illegal. As one English court put it:

> We do not see how a better test can be applied to the question whether this is ... a reasonable restraint of trade than by considering whether the restraint is such only to afford a fair protection to the interests of the party in favor of whom it is given, and not so large as to interfere with the interests of the public. Whatever restraint is larger than the necessary protection of the party requires can be of no benefit to either. It can only be oppressive. It is, in the eye of the law, unreasonable. Whatever is injurious to the interest of the public is void on the ground of public policy.

This approach, which the US federal courts in effect superimposed on the Sherman Act has had a definitive effect on the development of US antitrust law. Only those restraints of trade which are unreasonable have been held to violate the law. In judging reasonableness, courts have often looked at the relationship between the legitimate interest being protected and the breadth of the restraint. Only those restraints designed for and limited to protecting justifiable objectives have been upheld. Not surprisingly, in the *Addyston Pipe and Steel* case itself, the court held that the agreements to fix prices and divide markets were plainly illegal. Far from being ancillary to a valid main contract, the restraints constituted the main purpose of the contracts. The only purpose of the agreements being to suppress competition, a finding of illegality under the Sherman Act necessarily followed.

In 1911, the Supreme Court itself adopted the rule of reason in the famous *Standard Oil* case. Henceforth only those restraints of trade that were unreasonable would be considered violations of the Sherman Act. At the same time, the Court expressed its views as to the interrelationship of Sections 1 and 2. Under both Sections 1 and 2 only those acts or practices that are found to be unreasonable are deemed illegal. Further, the two sections are to be viewed as complementary methods of accomplishing the same goal, that goal being the prevention of monopoly. Section 2 is primarily concerned with a situation that Section 1 cannot reach, that in which a single firm achieves or seeks to achieve a market position of such size and power that it is capable of restraining trade by its own unaided efforts. However, because Section 2 also encompasses combinations and conspiracies to monopolize, joint action which severely threatens competition in an industry may violate both Sections 1 and 2.

Since Section 1 of the Sherman Act has thus been construed to prohibit only unreasonable restraints of trade, every defendant is theoretically entitled to the opportunity to show that its challenged activity was reasonable in view of its business conditions, and that its conduct did not, in fact, substantially and adversely impair existing competitive conditions. However, the courts soon foresaw that allowing such a defense in every antitrust case was not justified and would unnecessarily bog many lawsuits into a mass of unneeded detail. To avoid this undesirable situation, the courts have in the course of time designated certain conduct as being so damaging to competition that it must be condemned as unreasonable regardless of what justification might be proffered in a particular case. To engage in one of the types of conduct that has been so labeled is to commit a *"per se"* violation of the antitrust laws. As the Supreme Court stated in *Broadcast Music v. Columbia Broadcasting System* in 1979:

[T]he court has held that certain agreements or practices are so "plainly anticompetitive" ... and so often "lack ... any redeeming virtue" that they are conclusively presumed illegal without further examination ... .

Among the types of conduct that have been held to violate the statute *per se* are "horizontal" agreements among competitors to fix prices or divide markets and concerted refusals to deal with a particular party (known as "group boycotts").

"Vertical" restraints agreed upon between a seller and a buyer are usually evaluated under the rule of reason. Nonetheless, vertical price fixing, also known as RPM, was first declared a *per se* violation of Section 1 of the Sherman Act in the Supreme Court's 1911 decision in *Dr. Miles Medical Co. v. John D. Park & Sons Co.* However, in 1997, in *State Oil Co. v. Khan*, the Court unanimously determined that agreements fixing the highest price at which a reseller could resell (i.e., the maximum resale price) were not necessarily pernicious and hence should be evaluated under the rule of reason. Subsequently, in 2007, the Court held in *Leegin Creative Products, Inc. v. PSKS, Inc.* that, in the vertical context, both maximum RPM and minimum RPM are to be afforded rule of reason treatment.

In *California Dental Association v. Federal Trade Commission*, a case which involved a code of ethics maintained by a dentists association which restricted advertising, the Court of Appeals for the Ninth Circuit sustained the decision of the Commission holding the restrictions unlawful under an abbreviated rule of reason analysis. The Ninth Circuit applied a "quick look" analysis, employing a truncated rule of reason approach which the Supreme Court had used in some cases. While the Supreme Court's subsequent ruling in the case concluded that the abbreviated assessment made by the Court of Appeals was, under the circumstances, insufficient, the Court recognized that an abbreviated form of analysis was appropriate in situations in which the arrangement in question would clearly have an anticompetitive effect. In 2013, in deciding *Federal Trade Commission v. Actavis, Inc., et al.*, a majority of the Court reiterated that abandonment of the rule of reason in favor of presumptive rules or a "quick look" approach is appropriate only where "an observer with even a rudimentary understanding of economics could conclude that the arrangements in question would have an anticompetitive effect on customers and markets."

[B] Contracts, Combinations, and Conspiracies

The terms of Section 1 of the Sherman Act referring to "contracts," "combinations" or "conspiracies" can be differentiated, although they have often been used interchangeably by the US courts in antitrust cases to characterize the concert of action with is a prerequisite to the statute's application. "Contract" normally means a formal agreement entered into between parties setting forth each party's rights and obligations. "Combination" more generally refers to a union of activity on the part of two or more persons. (The word "person," in the eyes of the law, may include a corporation.) "Conspiracy" is usually defined in law as a combination designed to accomplish an illegal purpose or to carry out a legal purpose by illegal means.

It is critical to understand that the existence of a contract, combination, or conspiracy for purposes of applying the Sherman Act is not dependent upon there being found a written agreement or even an informally styled "gentlemen's agreement" to have been entered into by the parties. For example, the requisite agreement can be inferred from the substance of an informal chat by the executives of competing companies while they are together on a golf course or at dinner. In some circumstances, the agreement can even be inferred by a judge or jury from a course of conduct followed by the parties. In *Eastern States Retail Lumber Dealers' Ass'n v. United States*, a violation of the Sherman Act was found where various associations of retail lumber dealers periodically circulated among their members a list containing names of wholesale lumber firms who were reportedly selling directly to consumers. Although there was no explicit agreement on the part of the retailers to refrain from dealing with the wholesalers whose names appeared on the list, the Supreme Court found the existence of an unlawful combination and conspiracy to boycott these wholesalers because this was the evident purpose of the blacklists and because many of the retail dealers had in fact stopped purchasing from the listed wholesalers.

This doctrine of participation in a scheme evidenced by conscious adherence was subsequently reiterated by the Supreme Court in *Federal Trade Commission v. Cement Institute*, in which the Court stated: "It is enough to warrant the finding of a 'combination' within the meaning of the Sherman Act if there is evidence that persons, with knowledge that concerted action was contemplated and invited, give adherence to and then participate in a scheme."

The development of this rationale led to the question of whether proof of consciously parallel action can be alone sufficient to establish the requisite combination or conspiracy. In the 1954 Supreme Court decision in *Theatre Enterprises, Inc. v. Paramount Film Distributing Corporation*, the Court rejected this notion. It held that, although uniform conduct such as identical pricing may be some evidence of a violation of Section 1 of the Sherman Act, it is not alone sufficient to obviate the necessity of showing that a conspiracy exists. Something more, an evidentiary "plus" factor, over and above the parallel action, must be shown to establish that the conduct of the parties stemmed from an agreement, tacit or express, as distinct from independent decision making. Nonetheless, in a given case, whether the parties solely engaged in consciously parallel conduct or acted identically in compliance with a tacit agreement is often an elusive question left to the wisdom of the fact interpreter—judge, jury, or prosecutor—to discern.

The conclusion that the officers, directors, or employees of a single corporation cannot combine or conspire among themselves or with the corporation to place the corporation in violation of Section 1 has followed from the requirement that there be a showing of concerted action involving two or more parties. Since a corporation can act only through individuals, the contrary rule would be an illogical holding that a corporation can conspire with itself. Moreover, the Supreme Court ruled in 1984 in the case of *Copperweld Corp. v. Independence Tube Corp.* that a parent company and its wholly owned subsidiary cannot conspire in violation of Section 1 of the Sherman Act.

[C] Monopolization under Section 2

"Monopoly" or "monopoly power" has been defined as the holding of such dominance within an industry as to command the power to fix or control prices in or to exclude competition from the industry. It is important to note that Section 2 of the Sherman Act does not forbid the mere status of being a monopoly, but only the act or attempted act of monopolization. Therefore, it is not illegal in and of itself for a company to have achieved great dominance in its industry or for effective competition to be lacking in the industry and marketplace. Indeed, in some instances, monopolies or exclusive privileges may be granted by federal, state, or local governments because of the peculiar nature of an industry or the needs of an area. A business may be in the position of a "natural monopoly." In such cases, however, the government will usually also impose regulation to prevent the abuse of the monopoly status. Lawful monopoly may therefore conceivably be "thrust" upon a firm by historical accident or by the marketplace, because of the firm's unequaled efficiency or product or because, as a practical matter, the market can only support one supplier.

Unlawful monopolization under Section 2 of the Sherman Act, on the other hand, involves the attainment of monopoly power by unfair means or by the use of that power unfairly to maintain the monopoly and exclude effective competition. The Supreme Court reiterated in 2004 in *Verizon Communications, Inc. v. Law Offices of Curtis V. Trinko, LLP* that the offense of illegal monopolization "requires, in addition to the possession of monopoly power in the relevant market, 'the willful acquisition or maintenance of that power … .'"

The degree of market power that must be evidenced to establish the existence of monopoly power has not been definitively fixed by the case law. Where power to control prices or to exclude competitors from the market cannot specifically be shown, the government or other complainant must seek to have the existence of monopoly power presumed by showing that the firm in question controls a massive percentage of its relevant market. Percentages of less than 50 have been held clearly insufficient to indicate a monopoly position and percentages of less than 70 have been characterized as doubtful. While some courts have found a market share of over 75% to be sufficient, it has been generally held that a 90% share of the market is clearly sufficient to allow the necessary inference of market power.

What constitutes unfair monopolizing behavior is often subject to argument. The exercise of superior skill, business acumen, and industry by a dominant firm is not supposed to be actionable under Section 2. Yet, in the famous 1945 *Alcoa* case, the court determined that the defendant, which held a dominant position in the production of aluminum ingot, had violated Section 2 because it had been greatly increasing its production capacity in anticipation of market demand. There is much to be said for the counter-argument that this type of aggressive, diligent, and customer-oriented conduct is precisely what the law should not seek to punish. More typical of the conduct challenged in monopolization cases are acquisitions of direct competitors by dominant firms, use of tie-in sales or refusals to do business except on terms that will maintain or extend the company's dominant position.

The extended antitrust litigation against Microsoft Corporation in the US provides a usefully illuminating exploration of monopolization law in the context of emerging technology. In 1994, the Department of Justice filed suit against Microsoft, alleging that the company was unlawfully maintaining a monopoly in the market for personal computer operating systems by imposing anticompetitive terms in its licensing and software developer agreements. This case was settled by the entry of a consent decree, which was followed by a civil contempt action against Microsoft for violating the decree. In 1998, the Department and nineteen US states brought a new case challenging Microsoft under both sections of the Sherman Act. The plaintiffs alleged that Microsoft had engaged in a broad pattern of unlawful conduct with the purpose and effect of thwarting emerging threats to its powerful and entrenched computer operating system monopoly. This included the taking of alleged predatory exclusionary action against potential competitors, including suppliers of Internet browsing products, to prevent these companies from developing successful "middleware" platforms that could erode Microsoft's operating system monopoly.

After trial, the district court found that Microsoft enjoyed monopoly power, to the extent of a more than 90% market share, in the market for Intel-compatible personal computer operating systems. It held that Microsoft had violated Section 2 of the Sherman Act by maintaining its monopoly power through anticompetitive means and by attempting to monopolize the Internet browser market. It also held that Microsoft had violated Section 1 by "tying" its browser to its operating system. As the remedy, the district court entered an order requiring that Microsoft be split into two companies, one selling the Windows operating system and the other selling Microsoft's suite of word-processing and other software applications programs, with one of the two businesses to be "spun off" to shareholders.

On review, the Court of Appeals agreed that Microsoft commanded monopoly power with respect to the relevant operating systems market and that the company had taken anticompetitive actions to protect that monopoly. However, the appellate court remanded the case for consideration by a different trial judge of the issues of tying and the appropriate remedy. The case was then assigned to a new trial judge who approved the entry of a settlement judgment prohibiting Microsoft from carrying out certain practices. This settlement was supported by the Department of Justice but opposed by a number of nonsettling states on the ground that a more stringent remedy was needed to deter Microsoft from monopolistic activity. On June 30, 2004, the D.C. Circuit Court of appeals rejected *en banc* the two appeals filed against the final judgments entered by the district court in the Justice Department and remaining state cases. The consent decree, which was extended twice, finally expired in 2011.

Antitrust lawsuits based on "predatory pricing" by a dominant firm—generally, selling at a price below some measure of cost—have often proven difficult for the complainants to win. Low pricing is, on its face, the essence of competition and appears customer friendly. While, theoretically, a dominant firm's use of below-cost pricing to destroy or deter competitors is one classic example of monopolistic behavior, proving all of the elements of such a case is often an uphill task. Predatory pricing cases have involved extensive litigation over the key issues of how to measure cost, whether any losses sustained by the seller will foreseeably be recouped by it over time and, in the

Chapter 2: Summary of the United States Antitrust Laws § 2.01[C]

approach used by some of the federal courts, whether a specific predatory intent to damage competitors existed on the part of the dominant firm.

Companies which enjoy a dominant position in their industry may be held liable under Section 2 of the Sherman Act for conduct that a nondominant firm could indisputably engage in. For example, it is well settled that normally a nondominant company may unilaterally refuse to deal with any other party with whom it does not desire a business relationship. On the other hand, a dominant company's refusal to deal with a supplier or purchaser, where designed to injure competition and lacking a legitimate business justification, can be held to constitute unlawful monopolization under Section 2.

In addition to prohibiting monopolization, Section 2 also prohibits attempts and combinations or conspiracies to monopolize. With respects to attempts and conspiracies to monopolize, there is no requirement that the firm or firms involved actually occupy a dominant position in the relevant market. A firm may fail in its efforts to achieve dominance, and yet be guilty of an illegal attempt or conspiracy to monopolize, so long as its market position is sufficiently strong that it poses a palpable threat of achieving monopoly status. To establish an unlawful attempt to monopolize, there must also be evidence that the firm has a specific intent to monopolize. This may be inferred from the firm having committed acts or practices which, if successfully carried out, would result in monopoly.

As is necessary in other antitrust contexts, an appraisal of whether monopolization exists requires preliminary determinations of the relevant product market and the relevant geographic market. Geographic market definition can often be made with respect to the ease and cost of transporting the product. A relevant geographic market may comprise a small portion of the US, where a product—such as cement—cannot be competitively shipped for long distances. Or the relevant geographic market may be the US as a whole or even include areas outside of the US which are part of the nation's foreign commerce. The geographic bounds of the marketer are usually determined by an examination of the sources and locations to which the various customers of the firm under scrutiny may readily turn for supply of the relevant product.

Determining the relevant product or service market may be more difficult than determining the geographic market, because it will often depend upon such factors as product interchangeability and customer tastes. Physical characteristics, uses, the nature and costs of production, distinctiveness of customers, pricing and sensitivity to price changes are all factors that go into determining the interchangeability of two products for relevant product market purposes. Defining distinct product markets in the ever-evolving high tech sectors, as presented in the Microsoft context and others that we will be discussing, can be particularly challenging.

In a use of the term "submarkets" that has evoked some criticism from the commentators as confusing, the Supreme Court noted in *Brown Shoe Co. v. United States* that:

> The outer boundaries of a product market are determined by the reasonable interchangeability of use or the cross-elasticity of demand between the product itself and substitutes for it. However, within this broad market, well-defined

submarkets may exist which, in themselves, constitute product markets for antitrust purposes.

In any event, the ultimate test is interchangeability, the extent to which one group of products competes directly with another.

The problems involved in determining what constitutes the relevant product market were illustrated in another oft-criticized decision, the 1956 Supreme Court decision in the *Cellophane* case. The government had charged du Pont with violating Section 2 by monopolizing the commerce in cellophane. Du Pont produced almost 75% of the cellophane sold in the US, but cellophane constituted less than 20% of all sales of flexible packaging materials. The Supreme Court did not question that du Pont had monopoly power over cellophane itself and also acknowledged that cellophane had advantages over other types of flexible packaging. But the Court found further that cellophane had to meet competition from other materials in everyone of its uses, that a very high degree of "functional interchangeability" therefore existed between the various products, and that high cross-elasticity of demand among the materials existed in that customers would switch from one to another in response to slight price or quality changes. Hence, the Court concluded, cellophane was just a part of the flexible packaging materials market and du Pont could not be found to be monopolizing a partial market. Today, we must add the warning that, the *Cellophane* case notwithstanding, the government often succeeds in its efforts to keep the relevant produce narrow by pointing out elements of distinctiveness in the product allegedly being monopolized. This issue of defining the relevant product and geographic markets also comes up in the antitrust review of mergers, as we shall see.

When should the competitive role of foreign firms selling into the US market in competition with US firms be taken into account in determining whether a particular US firm is dominant in the US market? The significance of foreign competition in the market is certainly considered in restraint of trade, monopoly and merger antitrust review, but the actual impact of foreign competition will vary greatly from case to case. Where foreign firms are able freely to sell into the US, they may still be somewhat handicapped by the transportation costs and by possible customer preferences for domestic products. Where one of these factors is of considerable competitive significance, or where other factors pose a barrier for foreign firms, such as high tariffs or quotas, the status of the foreign supplier as a full-fledged competitor must be discounted in antitrust analysis. For example, it may be relevant that foreign suppliers are potentially subject to attack under the import relief laws, including the US antidumping and countervailing duty statutes, when their pricing injures or threatens to injure domestic competitors.

[D] The Commerce Requirement

As we have noted, the Sherman Act prohibitions are directed against conduct restraining the trade or commerce among the US states or with foreign commerce. This Act, like the other US federal antitrust laws, was enacted under the power given by the Constitution to Congress "to regulate Commerce with foreign Nations, and among the several States ... ". Purely local commerce is left to the individual states to regulate. Accordingly, an initial underlying issue in a federal antitrust case, which may be difficult or simple, is whether certain business activity is in the local, interstate and/or foreign commerce of the US. US courts have held that, in enacting the Sherman Act, Congress exercised the full scope of its powers under the Constitution. In the next chapter, we will focus on a key concern of this volume, the question of what activities in foreign commerce are within the reach of the Sherman Act and the other US antitrust laws. Here, we will explain the analytical approach used by the courts in making the commerce determination by taking a brief look at the concept of US "interstate commerce" as it has been developed for purposes of applying the Sherman Act.

In the late nineteenth century, *a very* narrow definition of "interstate commerce" was first employed. At that time the phrase was deemed to consist only of the actual movement of goods as they crossed the line separating one US state from another. Under this formulation, neither the production of goods by a manufacturer prior to shipment, nor the retail sale of goods by a dealer after he received them, was conceived to be a part of interstate commerce. The first change in this approach came in the 1905 antitrust case against the meat-packing industry, known as *Swift & Co. v. United States*. The meat packers contended that their price fixing conspiracy with respect to purchases of livestock at a stockyard was not in interstate commerce and hence fell beyond the reach of the Sherman Act. The Supreme Court disagreed, describing the movement of cattle from state to state until they reached a stockyard as "a current of commerce among the states," with the purchase of the cattle being "a part and incident of such commerce."

The *Swift* case thus gave birth to what has come to be called the flow-of-commerce doctrine. Briefly, the doctrine provides that any activity which takes place in the flow of interstate commerce, though that activity itself may take place in one state, is within interstate commerce. Over time, the number of activities found by the courts to be in the flow of interstate commerce steadily expanded. Thus, the intrastate sale of goods at retail has often been found to exist within the flow of interstate commerce, as against the contention that the goods have come to rest on the retailers' shelves and have thereby ceased to be a part of interstate commerce. Today there is no longer any doubt that the manufacture of goods which will be shipped across US state lines is in the flow of interstate commerce for regulatory purposes, including the antitrust laws. Similarly, acts relating to the interstate procurement of supplies necessary for manufacturing have been held to be within the flow of commerce. At the retail end of the shipment, even long storage in one state prior to sale in that same state has not been sufficient to withdraw the commodities from the flow of interstate commerce.

Along with the principle that the flow-of-commerce doctrine suffices to bring local activity within the reach of the Sherman Act, it is also established that activities which *affect* interstate commerce are covered by the Sherman Act. For example, in *Burke v. Ford & Kune*, liquor dealers in Oklahoma sued wholesalers under Section 1 of the Sherman Act, alleging that the wholesalers had unlawfully divided up the wholesale market within the state by territories and brands. There were no distilleries in Oklahoma, so the wholesalers had to purchase liquor from outside the state. The district court ruled that the out of state liquor "came to rest" in the wholesalers' warehouses and that the Sherman Act's interstate commerce requirement was thus not satisfied. The Court of Appeals affirmed. The Supreme Court reversed, holding that the "state wide wholesalers' market division inevitably affected interstate commerce" because the market division almost surely resulted in fewer purchases from out of state distillers than would have occurred had the wholesalers been in free competition with each other.

Thus, in the formulation of the Sherman Act, the Congress is deemed to have invoked the full measure of its Constitutional powers over the commerce of the US, which encompasses activities that affect interstate commerce. Of course, the same logic can be applied to extend the reach of the Sherman Act to activities which are within or affect the foreign commerce of the US, but there exist also special rules in that international context which we will be discussing shortly.

§2.02 THE WILSON TARIFF ACT

Sections 73-76 of the Wilson Tariff Act of 1894, although enacted as part of a tariff statute, are antitrust provisions. The purpose of these provisions was to punish efforts to abuse the import laws of the US through agreements or conspiracies between importers and other persons. The Act prohibits "every combination, conspiracy, trust, agreement or contract" made by or between two or more persons or corporations, either of whom is engaged in importing any article from a foreign country into the US, where the agreement is intended to restrain trade or increase the market price in any part of the US of the imported articles, or of "any manufacture into which such imported article enters or is intended to enter." The Act provides for seizure of the imported articles, a feature which has been employed to induce foreign corporations to consent to US jurisdiction. In most cases, the consent has been granted, and there has been no need to use the forfeiture provisions. Moreover, in nearly every case which has involved allegations of violation of the Wilson Tariff Act, there have been coupled allegations of violation of the Sherman Act, treating the former as an application of the latter to importers. Accordingly, the Wilson Tariff Act has little independent significance.

§2.03 THE CLAYTON ACT

The Clayton Act was enacted by Congress in 1914 because of the sentiment that certain shortcomings and omissions in the Sherman Act had to be remedied if the competitive system was to retain its resilience. Notwithstanding the sweeping and seemingly all-inclusive prohibitions of the Sherman Act, new legislation was deemed necessary both because of the judicial refusal to find certain objectionable conduct to be violative of that law and because of the recognition of additional anticompetitive conduct that had not been considered detrimental before. In short, the Clayton Act patched up what were felt to be specific gaps in the Sherman Act by proscribing certain conduct that had proved to be anticompetitive in practice. Since its inception, the Clayton Act has been extended over the years to include additional provisions deemed necessary to bolster the US antitrust regime. The major substantive sections of the Clayton Act, dealing with price discrimination, exclusive dealing, and mergers were all designed to reach in their incipiency acts or practices that might lead to adverse competitive effects. Generally speaking, except in the area of *per se* violations, the Sherman Act is not deemed violated unless a condition of actual and substantial adverse competitive effects is already considered to exist. With the Clayton Act, on the other hand, illegality can be found in conduct that has the probable result of substantially reducing competition. This distinction between actual and potential competitive effects is of the utmost importance in understanding each of the laws in question.

Section 2 of the Clayton Act, which was amended by the Robinson-Patman Act in 1936, is a prohibition directed at discrimination in price, discrimination in the granting of promotional allowances, services and facilities and at certain brokerage payments. While this statute has been widely criticized over its life as a deterrent to aggressive competition, it has survived, largely as a shield for small business. The Robinson-Patman provisions are further discussed in Chapter 7.

Section 3 of the Clayton Act governs product distribution arrangements and makes it unlawful to lease, sell, or contract for the sale of products, whether patented or unpatented "on the condition, agreement, or understanding that the lessee or purchaser thereof shall not use or deal in the goods, wares, merchandise, machinery, supplies or other commodities of a competitor or competitors of the lessor or seller" where the effect of such arrangement "may be to substantially lessen competition or tend to create a monopoly in any line of commerce." This is a prohibition against certain "tying arrangements," practices which may also violate the Sherman Act prohibitions in certain circumstances.

Section 4 of the Act is the provision which authorizes private civil suits by persons injured in their business or property by antitrust violations to recover treble damages and the cost of suit, including reasonable attorneys' fees. Section 4A gives similar rights to the US Government where it has been injured by an antitrust violation. Under Section 4C, state attorneys general are similarly authorized to bring civil damage suits against antitrust violators in the name of the state, as *parens patria* acting on behalf of natural persons residing in the state.

Section 7 of the Clayton Act is a very important statute applying to corporate mergers and acquisitions. It is designed to arrest in its incipiency concentration in the economy that is likely to lead to monopoly or to other restraints of the competitive process. The original provision was strengthened by the Celler-Kefauver amendments of 1950, so as to cover asset as well as stock acquisitions. The prohibition is directed against any acquisition "where in any line of commerce or in any activity affecting commerce in any section of the country, the effect of such acquisition may be substantially to lessen competition, or to tend to create a monopoly."

Notwithstanding the enactment of Section 7, for years much merger law enforcement was thwarted by so-called midnight mergers. This phrase described acquisition or merger transactions which were consummated very quickly after being announced or, indeed, were not announced in advance, thus affording the federal authorities inadequate time to conduct prior examination of the likely competitive impact of the transaction. The government's sole recourse in these cases was to challenge the merger in court after it had been consummated and to attempt, if the challenge proved successful, to obtain a divestiture of assets by "unscrambling" the corporate eggs, often years after the companies had merged their assets and activities. This unsatisfactory situation led to the enactment in 1976 of the Hart-Scott-Rodino legislation (Section 7A of the Clayton Act). This statute requires that parties planning acquisitions of stock or of assets which meet certain thresholds of financial significance give notice thereof to the Department of Justice and the Federal Trade Commission in advance of merger and then observe specified waiting periods to enable the authorities to review the competitive implications of the proposed transaction.

Section 8 of the Clayton Act prohibits, with certain exceptions, a person from serving as a director or officer of two competing corporations if the corporation meets certain size and competition thresholds. The Federal Trade Commission is required to revise those thresholds annually, based on the change in the gross national product. The enactment of Section 8 was prompted by concern over the possibility that a few individuals or groups could effectively control and eliminate vigorous competition between corporations through the use of common directorates and thus circumvent other sections of the antitrust laws.

Section 12 of the Clayton Act provides that any suit under the antitrust laws against a corporation may be brought in the judicial district where it is an inhabitant and also in any US judicial district "wherein it may be found or transacts business." This provision reflects a Congressional intention to make corporations—domestic or foreign—readily subject to suit for antitrust transgressions.

§2.04 THE FEDERAL TRADE COMMISSION ACT

The Federal Trade Commission Act ("FTC ACT"), enacted in 1914, created the Federal Trade Commission ("FTC"), an administrative agency independent of the executive branch. The FTC is composed of five Commissioners, who are appointed by the President with the advice and consent of the Senate for staggered seven year terms. One Commissioner is chosen by the President as the Chair. Not more than three members of the Commission may be from the same political party. The FTC acts by majority vote. The Congress created the Commission in the desire to establish an administrative agency specially competent to deal with the problems of unfair and competitively dangerous practices "by reason of information, experience and careful study of the business and economic conditions of the industry affected." By an amendment to the FTC Act in 1938, the Commission's purposes were broadened to include protection of the public from deceptive business acts.

The FTC has a Bureau of Competition, a Bureau of Consumer Protection, and a Bureau of Economics. It is staffed by lawyers, economists, and statisticians. In addition to its Washington, D.C. headquarters, the FTC has seven regional offices. The FTC's several functions include: (1) the preparation of studies and reports to inform the Congress and the public on competitive developments in the marketplace; (2) the investigation and adjudication of business conduct to determine whether it is in conformity with the laws enforced by the Commission; and (3) the promulgation of rules and guides applicable to conduct in particular industries.

The heart of the Commission's areas of responsibility is found in Section 5 of the FTC Act, which declares unlawful, first, "(u)nfair methods of competition in or affecting commerce" and second, "unfair or deceptive acts or practices in or affecting commerce." The first mandate arose from a congressional desire to empower an agency to halt anticompetitive practices in their incipiency, before they were able to mature into full blown antitrust violations with their attendant deleterious effects. The Supreme Court has held that "unfair methods of competition" includes both conduct that violates the Sherman and Clayton Acts and other conduct that, while not quite violating the standards of those statutes, violates their spirit or policy. The Commission is, in effect, authorized to designate the conduct which falls into the latter category. In addition, the Commission's authority over deceptive acts and practices enables it to perform a consumer protection function, particularly against misleading advertising and other deception aimed at consumers by business.

§2.05   REMEDIAL LAWS AFFECTING IMPORTS

The reader should keep in mind the importance of the trade relief laws to the safeguarding of the competitive process in US international commerce—particularly those addressing unfair competitive practices—even though elaboration of these trade laws is beyond the scope of this book because they are not considered antitrust laws.

The Antidumping Act of 1916 created a private right of action for persons injured by the importation and sale in the US at prices substantially below the prices charged for the same goods in their home market. One of the elements of that cause of action was proving that the importer had the specific intent to injure or destroy an industry in the US or to prevent the establishment of an industry. This law was found in two World Trade Organization ("WTO") panel decisions to be inconsistent with the WTO-GATT rules for national antidumping regimes. The WTO Appellate Body affirmed the panel's findings in both cases. This statute was finally repealed at the end of 2004.

The statute enacted as the 1921 Antidumping Act is still in effect and creates an administrative remedy. This statute enables US manufacturers, wholesalers, unions, and trade associations to petition for the imposition of antidumping duties on foreign merchandise that is being, or likely to be, sold in the US at "less than fair value," if the US industry is materially injured or threatened with material injury by the imports in question. The Department of Commerce determines whether the challenged imports are being sold at less than fair value, and the International Trade Commission ("ITC") (like the FTC an independent US agency) makes the injury determination. The antidumping regime is subject to the international rules adopted under the WTO Agreement on Implementation of Article VII of the General Agreement on Tariffs and Trade 1994. There have been a number of disputes over whether the US laws comply with those rules which have been brought by US trading partners before WTO panels pursuant to the WTO Dispute Settlement Understanding.

The US countervailing duty law provides a similar administrative remedy for US persons where a foreign government is subsidizing imports which injure or threaten injury to the competing industry. This law is subject to the WTO Agreement on Subsidies and Countervailing Measures and the WTO dispute settlement mechanisms. These import relief laws are also relevant, where applicable, under the rules of the North American Free Trade Agreement ("NAFTA").

Section 337 of the Tariff Act of 1930 prohibits "unfair methods of competition and unfair acts in the importation of articles into the United States," or in the sale of such articles after importation, the threat or effect of which is to destroy or substantially injure a US industry, prevent the establishment of such an industry, or to monopolize trade and commerce in the US. Moreover, under this statute, the importation or sale within the US of imported articles which infringe US patents, copyrights, trademarks, registered mask works, or protected designs is unlawful if an industry in the US relating to the protected articles exists or is being established. This law is also administered by the US ITC. While most complaints arising under Section 337 allege infringements of intellectual property rights ("IPR", also "IP rights"), the statute is broadly phrased. Indeed, in 2016, the US Steel Corporation filed a complaint under this law with the ITC alleging a conspiracy by Chinese steel exporters to the US to fix prices, control exports and export volumes, allegations which "sound" in antitrust law principles.

§2.06 ANTITRUST EXEMPTIONS

[A] Exempt Activities Generally

Certain types of potentially anticompetitive activity are expressly or impliedly exempted from the full or partial application of the federal antitrust laws. Under the labor exemption, workers are protected from charges that their formation of labor organizations, engaging in collective bargaining, striking and other enumerated concerted actions constitute unlawful conspiracy or combination. Pursuant to the McCarran Ferguson Act, the regulation of the business of insurance is subject to the laws of the several states, and the federal antitrust laws are inapplicable to the business to the extent that it is regulated by the states. There is, however, an exception to the McCarran Ferguson Act immunity with respect to participation in boycotts.

The "state action" doctrine, which was enunciated by the Supreme Court in *Parker v. Brown*, holds that Congress did not intend the Sherman Act to displace state legislative powers. Thus, the states may decide to displace competition by the regulation of business through their agents. However, state action is only recognized as excluding the application of federal antitrust law where the state has clearly articulated a policy which authorizes the state or its localities to displace the competitive process. The state action doctrine has proven to be both important and controversial in application because the state or local regulatory schemes often tend to involve elements of collaboration by the members of the regulated industry. For this reason, the Supreme Court has made abundantly clear that the states cannot simply authorize private parties to carry on anticompetitive activities and must actively supervise the regulatory scheme imposed.

The National Cooperative Research and Production Act ("NCRPA") of 1993 provides that joint research and development or production ventures will not be deemed *per se* illegal and should be evaluated under a rule of reason standard. This statute also establishes voluntary procedures for notifying the Attorney General and the FTC of joint research and production ventures, and it limits the monetary recovery that may be obtained in private civil suits against the participants in a notified venture to actual rather than treble damages.

The federal courts have developed the *Noerr-Pennington* doctrine, which provides that private collective efforts to influence action by governmental authorities in the US are immune from the application of the Sherman Act, even if the purpose or effect of those activities is to restrain competition. This doctrine is designed to protect genuine communication with governmental officials. It does not apply to confer antitrust immunity on "sham" activities, where the petitioning of governmental authorities is a mere cover for attempts to interfere directly with the competitive process, such as harassing a competitor with onerous, but frivolous, administrative proceedings. The Department of Justice and FTC *Antitrust Guidelines for International Enforcement and Cooperation*, which we will be discussing in greater detail shortly, state that (at p. 36) "[i]t is the view of the Agencies that the principles undergirding [*Noerr-Pennington*] apply to the petitioning of foreign governments. The Agencies, therefore, will not challenge under the antitrust laws genuine efforts to obtain or influence action by foreign government entities."

The Shipping Act of 1984, as amended by the Ocean Shipping Reform Act of 1998 ("OSRA"), confers limited immunity from the antitrust laws for agreements by or among ocean carriers, but the grant of immunity is subject to the participants' compliance with regulation by the Federal Maritime Commission and to other conditions. The OSRA reforms maintained limited antitrust immunity for ocean carriers but limited the scope of permissible concerted activities.

A number of statutes conferring antitrust immunity or inapplicability relate to activities undertaken in the export commerce of the US, a subject which we take up in greater detail below. For years, US companies maintained that they were being unfairly disadvantaged by the stringency of the US antitrust laws inasmuch as those laws allegedly were preventing US exporters from cooperating on sales into foreign markets where the US exporters faced competition from unchallenged foreign cartels The Webb-Pomerene Act was passed in 1918 to address this issue. The Export Trading Company Act ("ETCA") and the Foreign Trade Antitrust Improvements Act ("FTAIA") were both enacted in 1982, after extensive congressional hearings, in further efforts to assuage these concerns of US exporters.

[B]   The Webb-Pomerene Act

The Webb-Pomerene Act declares that an association entered into for the "sole purpose of engaging in export trade and actually engaged solely in such export trade, or an agreement made or act done in the course of export trade by such association" is not illegal under the Sherman Act, provided that it does not have an anticompetitive effect in the US and also is not in restraint of the export trade of any domestic competitor of such export association. Moreover, mergers or acquisitions of corporations "organized solely for the purpose of engaging in export trade, and actually engaged solely in such export trade" are not subject to challenge under the merger provisions of the Clayton Act. Another provision makes unlawful under the Federal Trade Commission Act unfair methods of competition in US export trade, even though occurring outside the territorial jurisdiction of the US.

The Webb-Pomerene exemption applies to the export of goods, wares, or merchandise only. The statute draws a necessary distinction between "export trade" and "trade within the United States." The term "export trade" refers solely to trade or commerce in goods, wares, or merchandise exported from the US or its territories to a foreign country. The term expressly excludes the production, manufacture, or sale for consumption or resale of such items within the US or its territories.

To obtain the exemption, export associations must file their articles of agreement and annual reports with the FTC promptly after their creation and to file periodic reports. Failure to comply with these requirements may result in liability for civil penalties and the loss of the antitrust exemption. There were eight proceedings conducted by the FTC in the 1940s that were taken in conjunction with litigation initiated by the Department of Justice against certain Webb associations. Among the practices determined by the FTC in these proceedings to be improper were the following: obtaining an agreement from nonmembers committing them to export according to Webb association rules; a Webb association entering into an agreement with foreign buyers authorizing them to deduct from the association's assigned quotas the exports of domestic nonmember competitors; an agreement to fix nonmembers' prices; and an association endeavoring to buy out foreign competitors.

In a 1945 case, *United States Alkali Export Association Inc. v. United States*, the Supreme Court held that the Department of Justice could proceed against export associations for alleged antitrust violations without first waiting for the FTC to investigate and make a recommendation to the Attorney General. Those associations were involved in a plot to control the worldwide market for alkalis with other competitors by allocating exclusive territories, assigning sales quotas and selling through joint agents. In the case of *United States v. Concentrated Phosphate Export Association* in 1968, the Supreme Court considered whether export sales to Korea by an export association through the US Agency for International Development ("AID") was exempted from the antitrust laws by the Webb-Pomerene Act. AID had selected the commodities, determined the amounts to be procured, controlled the contract procedure, and paid the contract prices. The Court concluded that the phosphates were purchased, in essence, by US taxpayers though AID, rather than by the Korean Government. Therefore the sales were made in domestic, not export trade, and the antitrust exemption provided by the Webb-Pomerene Act was inapplicable. Thus, where the effect of anticompetitive conduct falls primarily on US taxpayers, federal antitrust jurisdiction may apply.

Ever since the enactment of the Webb-Pomerene Act, proposals to amend it or repeal it have been considered on the ground that it is ineffective to boost exports and may cause more harm than good. On the other hand, the statute has been defended by those who utilize it as necessary to keep US industry competitive with foreign cartels. When last reported, there were only three Webb associations registered with the FTC, these relating to the export of soda ash, specialty crops, and cotton.

As was made manifest by the European Commission's attack on the export activities of members of a Webb-Pomerene Association and others in the *Woodpulp* case brought by the Commission under EC competition law, registration under Webb-Pomerene does not confer any immunity from prosecution under foreign antitrust laws.

[C] The Export Trading Company Act

When the congressional desire to assist US exporters peaked again in the early 1980s, given the consensus that the Webb regime was ineffective, Congress enacted Public Law 97-290, the Export Trading Company Act ("ETCA") as a further legislative effort in that direction. Title III of the ETCA attempts to reduce the uncertainty about the reach of the US antitrust laws in the context of export transactions by providing for exporters to apply for and receive "export trade certificates of review." Such certificates are issued by the Secretary of Commerce with the concurrence of the Attorney General. To obtain the certificate, the applicant must establish, among other things, that the proposed export conduct will not bring about: (1) a substantial lessening of competition or restraint of trade within the US; or (2) a substantial restraint of the export trade of a competitor of the applicant, or (3) the use of unfair methods of competition against such competitors. The ETCA, unlike the Webb-Pomerene Act, covers exports of services, as well as of goods.

The persons named in the certificate are given limited immunity from suit under federal and state antitrust laws with respect to engaging in the activities that are specified in the certificate and that comply with the terms of the certificate. The degree of immunity conferred consists of limiting to actual rather than treble damages the certificate beneficiary's potential liability to persons who have been injured by the specified conduct. In addition, certified conduct is given a presumption of legality in such suits, and the prevailing party is entitled to recover from the other party its costs and attorneys' fees.

The Department of Commerce, in consultation with the Department of Justice, has issued Guidelines which provide interpretations of the ETCA and of the standards applied by the two agencies in reviewing applications. These Guidelines include examples of hypothetical export trade activities, including the use of vertical and horizontal restraints and technology licensing. Many applicants have obtained export trade certificates of review under the statutory scheme, and there is a perception that the ETCA has proven to be a more successful export vehicle than the Webb-Pomerene Act. US business has nonetheless exhibited a degree of wariness over the complexity of the statutory standards, the significant administrative process entailed, the lack of assurances regarding the confidentiality of information, and the narrowness of the antitrust protections afforded. To this list, there must be added the uncertainty —as we have seen in the Webb-Pomerene Act context—over the possibility that a US export trading company will encounter challenges by foreign authorities under their antitrust laws.

[D] The National Cooperative Research and Production Act

The National Cooperative Research and Production Act ("NCRPA"), as amended by the Standards Development Organization Advancement Act of 2004, clarifies the application of the state and federal antitrust laws to joint ventures and to standards development organizations ("SDOs") while the latter are engaged in standards development activity. It requires the US courts to judge the competitive effects of a challenged joint venture or of an SDO covered by the Act under a rule of reason standard. This is consistent with the antitrust law applicable to bona fide joint ventures. Under this legislation, the terms "joint venture" and "standards development activity" are narrowly defined so as to exclude agreements and information exchanges usually deemed to be of an anticompetitive nature. The NCRPA also provides for the possible recovery of attorney's fees by joint ventures and SDOs that are prevailing parties in damage actions brought against them under the antitrust laws. These two benefits, the rule of reason application and the attorneys' fees provision, automatically apply to all joint ventures and SDOs covered by the statute.

A third benefit, avoidance of treble damage liability, is available to joint venture parties and SDOs which meet certain criteria and notify the FTC and the Attorney General of their planned activity and its objective. These parties may be held liable only for actual, rather than treble, antitrust damages. However, this damage limitation provision does not apply to joint production unless "(1) the principal facilities for such production are located in the United States or its territories, and (2) each person who controls any party to such venture (including such party itself) is a United States person, or a foreign person from a country whose law accords antitrust treatment no less favorable to United States persons than to such country's domestic persons with respect to participation in joint ventures for production."

[E] The Foreign Trade Antitrust Improvements Act

Title IV of Public Law 97-290 is known as the Foreign Trade Antitrust Improvements Act ("FTAIA"). The FTAIA does not confer immunity and is a statute that approaches the matter of export support in a different manner, i.e., by restricting the jurisdictional reach of the Sherman and FTC Acts in enumerated situations. The FTAIA provides that, with respect to foreign commerce other than imports, the Sherman Act and Section 5 of the FTC Act apply only to conduct that has a direct, substantial, and reasonably foreseeable effect on US commerce. The statute can be confusing. Its interpretation has been described as follows by the *Antitrust Guidelines for International Enforcement and Cooperation* (at p. 21):

> The FTAIA initially places conduct involving non-import foreign commerce, which means U.S. export commerce and wholly foreign commerce, outside the reach of

the Sherman Act and the FTC Act. What is commonly referred to as the FTAIA's "effects exception" brings such conduct back within the reach of the Acts if the conduct has a direct, substantial, and reasonably foreseeable effect on commerce within the United States, U.S. import commerce, or the export commerce of a U.S. exporter, and that effect gives rise to a claim. (footnotes omitted)

The FTAIA's effects exception thus requires that, to be actionable under the US antitrust laws, the effect of the violation must be on commerce within the US, or on US import commerce, or on the export commerce of a US exporter and be an effect which is direct, substantial and reasonably foreseeable.

Accordingly, as we shall see, in 2004, in the case of *F. Hoffman-La Roche Ltd. v. Empagran S.A.*, the Supreme Court interpreted the FTAIA as designed to exclude from the application of the US antitrust laws anticompetitive conduct causing foreign harm unrelated to any harm inflicted in US markets. In these situations, the aggrieved parties injured by anticompetitive actions must look to foreign, not US law, for relief. We will discuss the case law under this legislation further in the next chapter.

The Supreme Court has declined to consider whether the FTAIA, which added Section 6a to the Sherman Act and Section 5(a)(3) to the FTC Act, amended existing law or merely codified it. The federal courts of appeals have expressed differing views as to whether the FTAIA goes to a claim's merits or to the court's subject matter jurisdiction. This issue will not affect the Agencies' enforcement decisions.

§2.07 ENFORCEMENT MODES

The federal antitrust laws are enforced in a variety of ways. The overlapping enforcement scheme, while perhaps confusing at first impression, has contributed to the high degree of respect, wariness and even fear, with which those laws are regarded by business persons. A business which is charged with having committed a hard core antitrust violation, such as price fixing, will find itself burdened by the sudden notoriety, distraction, huge expense and uncertainty occasioned by the need to fight defensive battles on a variety of legal fronts. At worst, the financial toll on the company can be ruinous and the personal lives of some of its executives may be devastated. The cumulative onslaught may come from federal criminal prosecutors, from civil class actions fueled by private lawyers seeking contingent fee awards, from aggrieved parties demanding individual settlements, and from parallel claims asserted under state antitrust laws.

[A] Department of Justice Antitrust Division

The Antitrust Division of the Department of Justice has several litigating components: six civil sections in Washington, D.C. and offices that primarily handle criminal matters which are located in Chicago, New York City, San Francisco and Washington, D.C. The Antitrust Division is charged principally with the enforcement of the Sherman and Clayton Acts. It is headed by an Assistant Attorney General who is nominated by the President and confirmed by the Senate. The Antitrust Division employs hundreds of professionals, including lawyers and economists. The Antitrust Division's units include a Foreign Commerce Section, which is charged with coordinating the activities of the Division relating to foreign commerce, foreign nationals, and foreign governments. Under the International Antitrust Enforcement Assistance Act of 1994, the Antitrust Division is authorized to enter into mutual assistance agreements with foreign antitrust authorities. Investigations into possible antitrust violations are initiated by the Antitrust Division on the basis of information it receives from a variety of sources, including complaints from the public, news stories, and materials garnered by other federal agencies. Priority areas of activity include criminal cartel prosecution and merger law enforcement.

As we observed earlier, liability under the Sherman Act may be either criminal or civil. Criminal prosecutions are normally brought only with respect to *per se* violations of the Act. Government suits under the Clayton Act are civil in nature. The remedy sought in a civil suit brought by the Antitrust Division may be a declaration by the court that a particular practice is unlawful, the issuance of an injunction forbidding the taking or continuation of certain conduct, or, in a case where a merger has been consummated, the issuance of an order of dissolution or divestiture. The Department of Justice may also bring civil treble damage suits under the antitrust laws on behalf of the US as the directly aggrieved party, for example, where it has discovered a government contract bid rigging conspiracy.

Civil investigations brought by the Antitrust Division are often resolved by the entry of a "consent decree" agreed to by the Division and the party involved. The party thereby agrees to take specified remedial steps without admitting wrongdoing. Pursuant to the Antitrust Procedures and Penalties Act, known as the Tunney Act, the proposed consent judgment must be published and made open for public comment. Subsequently, the consent judgment must be approved by a federal court as being in the public interest.

The Antitrust Division also has "Business Review Procedures" whereby, in certain circumstances, it will review proposed business conduct and state the Division's enforcement intentions. The Division's statement of its present enforcement actions does not bind its actions in the future.

As a matter of prosecutorial discretion, criminal prosecutions are brought by the Antitrust Division only in the case of flagrant violations of the Sherman Act involving agreements among competitors, such as price fixing, divisions of territories, or "bid rigging" with respect to government procurement. These are situations in which the law is clear and the manifest intent of the defendant(s) was unreasonably to restrain trade. Such prosecutions are filed by the Department of Justice in the federal district courts and may result in the imposition of large fines on corporations and individuals, as well as imprisonment of individuals. A corporate officer is a "person" who may be prosecuted under Section 1 of the Sherman Act if he knowingly participates in effecting a contract, combination, or conspiracy which is illegal under the statute. Often the nature of the plea and the terms of the penalties for companies or individuals are negotiated between the government and the defendants' counsel, and are entered as judgments by order of court, thereby eliminating the need for a trial on the merits and likely subsequent appeals. Criminal prosecutions are limited by a five-year statute of limitations.

The *United States Federal Sentencing Guidelines*, which were first issued in 1987, and subsequently amended, include a section on antitrust offenses. These *Guidelines* initially established an appropriate range for fines imposed on organizations, as well as levels of fines and prison sentences for convicted individuals, including mandatory jail sentences of specified lengths based on offense levels. However, in 2005, the Supreme Court held in *United States v. Booker* that the Sixth Amendment to the Constitution, guaranteeing accused persons the right to a jury trial, applies to these *Guidelines*. Moreover, the Court construed the Sixth Amendment as directing that, other than the fact of a prior conviction, any fact that increases the penalty for a crime beyond the statutory maximum must be submitted to a jury and proved beyond a reasonable doubt. Accordingly, the statutory provisions making the *Guidelines* mandatory were declared "severed and excised" by the Court, leaving the *Guidelines* "effectively advisory."

As earlier indicated, in 2004 President Bush signed the Antitrust Criminal Penalty Enhancement and Reform Act increasing maximum Sherman Act fines and prison terms. This new legislation also detrebled the civil liability for amnesty recipients who cooperate with civil case plaintiffs. Now, under the Sherman Act, the fine for a corporate defendant may be as much as USD 100 million, and for an individual USD 1 million and/or imprisonment for up to ten years. The US Sentencing Commission has issued a revised Antitrust Guideline providing for the imposition of sentences with respect to bid rigging, price fixing or market allocation agreements among competitors. The revised guidelines went into effect on November 1, 2015.

Under the Fifth Amendment to the US Constitution, a person charged with a crime that is punishable by death or imprisonment is entitled to have the charges against him first brought before a grand jury. A federal grand jury consists of not less than sixteen nor more than twenty-three persons. An indictment, determining that there is enough evidence to bring the charges to trial, may be returned upon the vote of twelve or more grand jurors. Grand jury proceedings are, with certain exceptions, secret. The government attorney is present, along with the testifying witness, but the lawyer for the latter cannot accompany his or her client into the grand jury room, although the lawyer may remain outside the room for a possible consultation. If an indictment is returned by the grand jury, the individual or, in the case of a corporation, the corporation's counsel, must appear at an arraignment session and answer the charges. The defendant may plead guilty, not guilty, or with the permission of the court, *nolo contendere*. If the case goes to trial, the accused has the right under the Sixth Amendment to a hearing in open court before a jury. Guilt in a criminal case must be established beyond a reasonable doubt.

The Antitrust Division maintains a Corporate Leniency Policy and a Leniency Policy for individuals, both of which are designed to encourage persons who are engaged in activity which is illegal under the antitrust laws to report the activity at an early stage to the Division. "Leniency" under these policies means not charging the firm or the individual criminally for participation in the activity being reported. Among the conditions for the granting of full leniency is that the Division has not already received information about the activity from another source, that complete candor and cooperation be accorded to the Division in the matter, and that the reporting corporation or individual clearly not have been the leader in, or originator of, the unlawful activity. If a corporation qualifies for leniency, all directors, officers, and employees of the corporation who admit their involvement as part of the corporate confession will receive leniency, if they offer complete candor and cooperation. If all of the conditions are not strictly met, for example, if the Division already possesses some pertinent evidence when a party seeking leniency reports the illegal activity, the Division may still grant leniency to the reporting corporation or individual in certain cases.

The Antitrust Division also offers "amnesty plus" to amnesty applicants who self report as to one conspiracy and also offer to disclose the existence of a second, unrelated, conspiracy. In that case, for its cooperation on the second matter, the company will receive amnesty, pay zero dollars in fines for that second conspiracy, and none of its officers, directors, and employees who cooperate will be prosecuted criminally in connection with that second offense.

Prior to the passage of the 2004 legislation, a major disincentive from the viewpoint of potential amnesty seekers was that making a confession of their activities to the government, with resulting public enforcement action, increased the amnesty seekers' risk of exposure to treble damage suits brought by private plaintiffs. As noted, under the 2004 legislation, corporate and executive amnesty applicants who cooperate with the government have their exposure to private civil suits "detrebled," i.e., limited to single damages without joint and several liability—if they also cooperate with the private plaintiffs in their damage actions against the cartel members.

In one case, the Department of Justice attempted to revoke an amnesty agreement that it had entered into with Stolt-Nielsen, S.A. on the ground that the company had not complied fully with the leniency policy requirements by failing to disclose accurately the duration of its involvement in a price fixing cartel. A federal district court held that the Department could not unilaterally void such an agreement and that the amnesty recipient was entitled to judicial review of the matter. This lower court decision was reversed by the Third Circuit on the ground that the court lacked the authority to enjoin the Government's indictments.

[B] The Federal Trade Commission

The FTC is the only agency entitled to enforce the provisions of the FTC Act. In addition, the Commission has the power to enforce the Clayton Act, including the Robinson-Patman Act provisions. All of this legislation is civil in nature. The Commission also enforces several other statutes relating to issues entrusted to it by the Congress. In the areas in which they share responsibility, such as merger review, the Antitrust Division and the FTC engage in regular consultation under the "clearance" agreement between the two agencies, to prevent conflict or duplication. The usual outcome of these consultations is for the agency having the greater expertise or experience with the particular industry or practice to take over the investigative responsibility.

The FTC has a Bureau of Competition, a Bureau of Consumer Affairs, and a Bureau of Economics. It also has an Office of International Affairs. The agency is alerted to alleged violations of the statutes under its enforcement jurisdiction in a variety of ways. Often, letters of complaint, which may be quite informal, are sent to the Commission by aggrieved parties or other members of the public. The Commission has very broad investigatory powers under the FTC Act. It may demand production of documentary evidence, require firms to supply annual and special reports, and issue subpoenas. If the Commission decides to initiate a proceeding regarding an unfair method of competition or unfair or deceptive act or practice in or affecting commerce, it issues a complaint to that effect. An oral hearing is then normally held before an Administrative Law Judge ("ALJ") appointed by the Commission. At the hearing, evidence and arguments are presented by the Commission staff lawyers acting as "complaint counsel" and by counsel for the party charged, the "respondent." The ALJ will then issue a decision.

Either the respondent or complaint counsel can appeal this decision as a matter of right to the Commission itself, and such appeal normally occurs. The Commission will issue an opinion and, if its conclusion is that the respondent has engaged in the prohibited conduct, will also issue a cease and desist order directed at the party and the practice. Following the Commission's ruling, the respondent (but not the complaint counsel) may appeal to the US Court of Appeals presiding over the judicial district in which the alleged violation occurred or where the respondent does business or resides. Under the applicable statute, 15 U.S.C. § 45(c), on appeal, "[t]he findings of the Commission as to the facts, if supported by evidence, shall be conclusive." ("Evidence," as here used, means "substantial evidence.") In addition, the case law establishes that, while the appellate court is to review *de novo* the Commission's legal conclusions and the application of the facts to the law, it must afford the FTC some deference as to its informed judgment that a particular commercial practice violates the Federal Trade Commission Act.

The obligation of the courts to give deference to the expertise of the Commission, as well as the relative finality of the Commission's findings of fact, provide significant support for the agency's position in the course of the judicial review proceedings. After the Commission's order has become final, the Commission may assess any person violating the order in the amount of a civil penalty of not more than USD 40,000 as of August 1, 2016. (This amount is adjusted periodically.) Large penalties may accrue in this fashion because, under the penalty provisions of Section 5 of the FTC Act, "in the case of a violation through continuing failure to obey or neglect a final order of the Commission, each day of continuance of such failure or neglect shall be deemed a separate offense." In the case of violations of FTC orders, in addition to enforcing the payment of the penalties due, the US district courts are empowered to grant mandatory injunctions and any other equitable relief that may be appropriate to enforce the Commission's order. Many cases are, however, resolved by the respondent's entry into a consent order with the FTC. The Tunney Act procedures are not applicable to FTC consent orders. The FTC consent orders are placed on the public record for the receipt of comments from interested persons. Final approval of the order is then a matter within the Commission's discretion, unless someone finds grounds for challenge in the federal courts.

[C] Private Enforcement

Section 4 of the Clayton Act provides that "Any person injured in his business or property by reason of anything forbidden in the antitrust laws may sue ... and shall recover threefold the damages ... sustained and ... a reasonable attorney's fee." Section 16 of the Clayton Act enables antitrust plaintiffs to obtain injunctive relief under the principles normally applicable for such equitable relief. The antitrust laws to which this reference applies include Sections 1 and 2 of the Sherman Act and Sections 2, 3, 7 and 8 of the Clayton Act. Private actions based on asserted violations of the Federal Trade Commission Act may not be maintained. Only the Commission can enforce that legislation.

A "person" for purposes of Section 4 includes natural persons, corporations, unincorporated associations, states, and municipalities. Foreign governments may also be plaintiffs, but they are generally limited by the statute to recovering only actual, not treble, damages. Any action must be brought within four years after the cause of action accrued. The running of the statute of limitations will be "tolled" (deferred) if the defendant has been guilty of "fraudulent concealment" of the violation or by the filing of proceedings instituted by the US.

Pursuant to Section 16(a) of the Clayton Act, if the defendant's antitrust violations have already been established through a civil or criminal proceeding brought by or on behalf of the US after trial or by a guilty plea, a plaintiff seeking treble damages in a civil suit by reason of the same conduct can rely on the government's action as prima facie evidence that the unlawful conduct occurred. This benefit for the private civil case does not pertain where the government obtained only a negotiated consent judgment or decree before any testimony was taken.

As a result of the Supreme Court's 1977 decision in *Illinois Brick Co. v. Illinois*, only direct purchasers may maintain damage actions based on overcharges resulting from cartels or monopolization. In addition, in its decisions in *Brunswick Corp. v. Pueblo Bowl-O-Mat, Inc.* and *J. Truett Payne Co. v. Chrysler Motors Corp.*, the Supreme Court articulated a doctrine of antitrust "standing" as a prerequisite element for private plaintiff damage actions. Under that doctrine, as enunciated in the *Brunswick* opinion, the plaintiff must show that he has sustained "*antitrust* injury, which is to say injury of the type the antitrust laws were intended to prevent and that flows from that which makes defendants' acts unlawful." Such a claimed injury must therefore "reflect the anticompetitive effect ... of the violation ... ."

As is well known, such treble damage suits are very common. They may be brought, for example, by competitors who have been injured by monopolistic or predatory conduct, by distributors who have been boycotted, or by dealers who have been discriminated against in price. Moreover, many private civil antitrust cases are brought as "class actions," i.e., by a few named plaintiffs who assert that they are acting as representatives of a larger group of similarly situated persons or businesses who have allegedly been similarly injured by the claimed antitrust violation. For example, competing manufacturers who are suspected of having conspired to fix their selling prices in violation of the Sherman Act are typically sued for treble damages by one or more classes of purchasers who made their purchases of the affected product directly from the manufacturers. A number of US law firms have staked out positions in the marketplace as plaintiffs' lawyers specializing in antitrust class actions, and they are quick to bring cases when government suits or other signs of conduct in violation of the antitrust laws become public. Few of these cases go to trial but the settlements are often in very large sums.

Rule 23 of the Federal Rules of Civil Procedure lays out the rules by which the trial court may "certify" the class at an early stage of the litigation upon making the requisite findings, principally that: (1) the class is so numerous that joinder of all members as individual plaintiffs is impracticable; (2) the representative parties will fairly and adequately protect the interests of the class; and (3) the questions of law or fact common to the members of the class predominate over any questions affecting only individual members. If the case is successfully brought to a money judgment or settlement on behalf of the plaintiffs, the members of the class are notified by publication and mailing and given an opportunity to share in the recovery or else to "opt out" of the case. The plaintiffs' lawyers, who have generally taken the case on a contingency fee basis, are awarded a fee by the court from the settlement or judgment, with the amount of the fee based on such factors as amount of hours worked and the degree of skill that was necessary to achieve the successful result.

The legislative provisions designed to foster private suits make the institution of private damage actions an almost automatic accompaniment or aftermath to any successful government action. In sum, it is no accident that the history and lore of the US antitrust laws often refer to the private antitrust plaintiff as a "private Attorney General." Much of the governing antitrust law has been developed as a result of private actions. The importance of private enforcement was succinctly described by the Supreme Court's declaration in 1968 in *Perma Life Mufflers, Inc. v. International Parts Corp.* that "the purposes of the antitrust laws are best served by assuring that the private action will be an ever-present threat to deter anyone contemplating business behavior in violation of the antitrust laws."

[D] State and Other Enforcement

Each of the fifty US states may bring treble damage suits under the federal legislation on its own behalf for damages suffered by the state. The state authorities may also sue as *parens patriae* on behalf of natural persons residing in the state to secure relief for injury sustained by such persons to their property by reason of violations of the Sherman Act. This remedy is for the benefit of consumers within the state, who can claim their allocable portions of the recovery received by the state, with the latter receiving the costs and attorneys' fees awarded. In addition, the US states typically have their own statutes (which are known informally as "baby Sherman Acts") which authorize official and private actions against anticompetitive conduct causing injury within the state. The states' attorney generals generally bring the actions which enforce state antitrust law.

As mentioned above, as a result of the Supreme Court decision in the *Illinois Brick* case in 1977, absent special circumstances, only a party who has purchased *directly* from a monopolist or a seller who has participated in a price fixing conspiracy has standing to bring a private action based on the Sherman Act violations. The Court reasoned that permitting suits by indirect purchasers of the product, as well as by direct purchasers, would inflict possible multiple liability on the defendants and would, at the least, greatly increase the complexity of antitrust litigation by allowing arguments over whether the price fix was "passed on" by one level of distribution to the next one. In the case of *California v. ARC America Corp.*, however, in 1989, the court ruled that the principle of *Illinois Brick* does not bar antitrust suits brought by indirect purchasers under state law, where the applicable state law permits such suits. The Court's rationale was that Congress did not intend the federal antitrust scheme to displace state antitrust law and that, indeed, there was a long tradition of state common law and statutory law applicable to restraints of trade and monopolies, with which the federal laws were fully compatible. Nonetheless, a number of state courts have interpreted their statutes to be in harmony with the *Illinois Brick* rule and as thus precluding suits by indirect purchasers.

By virtue of 15 U.S.C. § 15a, the US Government may bring an action for treble damages when it has been injured by an antitrust violation. The Supreme Court held in 1978 in *Pfizer, Inc. v. Government of India* that a foreign nation, like a US state, is a "person" within the meaning of Section 4 of the Clayton Act and hence could bring a treble damage suit when it was injured in its business or property by antitrust violations. However, four years later, Congress enacted the Foreign Sovereign Antitrust Recoveries Act. That statute amends Section 4 of the Clayton Act by limiting the recovery by foreign governments to actual, rather than treble damages, unless the plaintiff is a state entity that carries on primarily commercial activities, and it agrees to waive any arguments of sovereign immunity based on its being a part of a foreign state.

Finally, as we will discuss in Chapter 4, the Supreme Court has ruled that, where an agreement between private parties to arbitrate disputes between them is broad enough to cover claims arising under the US antitrust laws, those claims are to be heard and adjudicated under the law by the arbitrators.

[E] Guidelines

The Antitrust Division of the Department of Justice and the FTC (here together referred to as "the Agencies") from time to time, jointly or individually, issue "Guidelines" and other policy statements which provide advice to the public with respect to the government's current enforcement policies on particular subjects of antitrust concern. The Guidelines, which may be very detailed and include analyses of hypothetical situations, are susceptible to being altered, withdrawn or superseded over time as prompted by changes in enforcement philosophy, case law, or new antitrust legislation. It must be remembered as well that Presidential appointments to head the

Agencies often are "political" in nature. For example, it is generally recognized that the years of the Reagan Administration brought a significant softening of the Department of Justice's antitrust law enforcement philosophy in the area of mergers, the licensing of technology, and with respects to vertical restraints generally. A major reason for this relaxation in policy was that the government enforcement officials were beginning increasingly to view US firms as competitors in a highly competitive international arena, rather than solely as domestic competitors.

In 1995, the two Agencies issued joint *Antitrust Enforcement Guidelines for International Operations*, and the Department of Justice withdrew its 1988 Guidelines in this area. On January 12, 2017, this publication was revised and reissued under the name "*Antitrust Guidelines for International Enforcement and Cooperation*" (hereafter the "*International Guidelines*"). These 2017 International Guidelines are reproduced in this book as Appendix III. We will be discussing these Guidelines further in the pages ahead.

The Federal Trade Commission and the Department of Justice issued revised *Horizontal Merger Guidelines* on August 19, 2010. Guidelines on this subject were first adopted in 1968 and then revised in 1992. These Guidelines outline how the Agencies evaluate the competitive impact of horizontal mergers and whether those mergers comply with US antitrust law. For example, the guidelines explain that the effect of the proposed merger on innovation is an issue that will be considered in evaluating the transaction. Guidelines for vertical mergers were issued in 1968 and revised in 1984. However, the latter *Non-Horizontal Merger Guidelines* have not been revised since and have been criticized as being out of date.

Also pertinent to our interest are the *Antitrust Guidelines for the Licensing of Intellectual Property* which were issued by the Agencies on January 12, 2017, replacing the 1995 original version. On April 7, 2000, the Agencies issued a set of guidelines entitled the *Antitrust Guidelines for Collaboration Among Competitors*. These guidelines are intended to enable businesses to evaluate proposed cooperative transactions with competitors with a better understanding of the antitrust implications, thus encouraging procompetitive collaborations and deterring harmful ones. In 2016, the FTC and the Antitrust Division of the Department of Justice issued *Antitrust Guidance for Human Resource Professionals* concerning business hiring practices. This development was prompted by disclosures that competing employers were entering into agreements to limit or fix the terms of employment for potential hires.

[F] The Courts

Federal antitrust suits by the Department of Justice or by private parties are filed in the federal district courts around the country, which are trial courts. An appeal from the district court's decision may be taken to the US Court of Appeals for the judicial "circuit" embracing the district. There are thirteen judicial circuits. Appeal from the decision of a Court of Appeals may lie to the US Supreme Court, which is the court of last resort. In very rare situations, the Supreme Court may review a district court decision, by-passing review by the Court of Appeals.

Except in a few specified types of cases, review is discretionary with the Supreme Court, dependent on the Court's granting of a writ of certiorari. Under the Court's Rules, a petition for a writ of *certiorari* will be granted "only for compelling reasons." Accordingly, only a minuscule percentage of the federal cases are, in fact, heard by the Supreme Court. It is quite common, therefore, for two or more Circuit Courts of Appeals to reach differing conclusions on important issues of federal law. Until the Supreme Court decides to resolve such a conflict between the Circuits, each Circuit's precedents on an issue control the law on that particular issue within that Circuit, including within the district courts assigned to that Circuit.

[G]   Modernization

The Antitrust Modernization Commission Act of 2002 created the Antitrust Modernization Commission ("AMC"), comprised of twelve members appointed by the President and the leadership of the two Houses of the Congress. The Commission was charged with examining whether there was a need to modernize the US antitrust laws, to identify and study the related issues, and to submit a report thereon to the Congress and the President. The persons appointed to the Commission included former top officials of the Antitrust Division and of the Federal Trade Commission, as well as other experienced antitrust lawyers and economists.

The AMC submitted its report on April 2, 2007. It included eighty recommendations. Among the most important of these were the proposed abolition of the Robinson-Patman Act relating to price discrimination, enactment of legislation which would allow recovery by indirect purchasers, allowing contribution by joint tortfeasors, and limitations of antitrust law immunities and exemptions. The AMC terminated its activity on May 31, 2007 as provided. The recommendations have not prompted significant follow-up.

CHAPTER 3

The Application of United States Antitrust Law to International Transactions and Foreign Parties

§3.01 FOREIGN COMMERCE TO WHICH THE SHERMAN ACT APPLIES

In this chapter, we will consider the extent to which the US antitrust laws extend to activities in international trade and investment, as well as to foreign persons. These questions did not receive extended study when the laws were originally enacted. In those earlier times the Congressional and public concern was focused on the threat posed by domestic "trusts" and on protecting US businesses and consumers from abuses by US businesses. As the focus has necessarily shifted, broadening to the implications of the international economy, the application of the US antitrust laws has adapted to this international setting. Some of the adaptation has taken place by focused judicial interpretation regarding the new situations posed, while other settings have required fresh legislation to address the issues raised. The courts have sought once again to interpret the presumed intent of Congress even where the intent was difficult to glean, if indeed it existed with respect to the novel economic setting. The sovereign interests of foreign nations in matters of international law and comity have had to be understood and weighed. The views of these nations on matters affecting their interests in US litigation have had to be directly considered, no longer through diplomatic notes passed to the courts by the US State Department, but via the filing of *amicus curiae* briefs filed directly by US counsel acting for the foreign governments.

The application and enforcement of national law in any field, including that of international transactions, involves an imposition of jurisdiction in at least two important respects. First, there is a jurisdictional assertion over the specific activities or conduct sought to be regulated, known in US jurisprudence as legislative or *subject matter jurisdiction*. Second, there is a jurisdictional assertion over those persons (including corporations) who will be required to comply by enforcement proceedings brought in the courts of the regulating nation, a concept known in the US as *personal jurisdiction*. US constitutional law has been interpreted as requiring that both subject matter and personal jurisdiction must be established before the antitrust laws can be applied to the conduct of an individual or business. We will consider in this chapter the concept of subject matter jurisdiction and in the next chapter that of personal jurisdiction.

The Congress of the US has the authority under Article 1, Section 8, Clause 3 of the Constitution "to regulate 'Commerce with foreign Nations.'" Congress has used this mandate over the nation's foreign commerce in shaping much legislation, including the federal antitrust laws. The most important of these laws, the Sherman, Clayton, and Federal Trade Commission Acts, each have possible applications to some of the international transactions in or affecting US commerce. The Sherman Act in particular has language permitting a broad jurisdictional sweep, and it is in the context of this law that the question of what has been called the "extraterritorial" reach of US antitrust law has principally been addressed in the judicial decisions.

As we have noted, Section 1 of the Sherman Act declares it illegal for a "person" to engage in any "contract, combination in the form of trust or otherwise, or conspiracy, in restraint of trade or commerce ... with foreign nations ... ". Section 2 makes it unlawful for any "person" to "monopolize any part of the trade or commerce ... with foreign nations ... ." Section 7 of the Sherman Act defines "person" or "persons" for purposes of the Act "to include corporations and associations existing under or authorized by the laws of either the United States, the laws of any of the Territories, the laws of any State, or the laws any foreign country." So it is clear that foreign, as well as US, persons, can be deemed to violate the Sherman Act. The open question has been *when* can a foreign person be deemed to be actionably restraining the commerce of the US? This is a legal, as well as a diplomatic and political question, because US foreign commerce is, by definition, also the foreign commerce of another nation.

In general terms, *trade or commerce with foreign nations* consists of the export from the US or the import into the US of goods or services, and of transportation to or from the US. The notion of "commerce" is a broad one in US law because, in the words of Chief Justice Marshall, the US Constitution authorizes the Congress to enact laws regulating "every species of commercial intercourse between the United States and foreign nations." In particular, US foreign commerce may include commercial activity that commences in the US and is completed abroad, as well as commercial activity that commences abroad and culminates in the US.

As we shall see, it is now settled law that the Sherman Act was intended to apply even to acts of foreign persons in their own countries in certain circumstances. But the case law also now makes clear that the Act applies to none of the "persons" in question, no matter where their activities in foreign commerce take place, unless those activities have a *direct, substantial, and reasonably foreseeable effect* on US trade or commerce. US court decisions sought over the years to interpret this concept definitively and, in 1982, Congress made an effort to clarify its intentions on the jurisdictional issue by enacting the Foreign Trade Antitrust Improvements Act ("FTAIA"). This legislation generated some new confusion over the application of the antitrust laws to international transactions, confusion which the courts have sought to allay.

Definitive Supreme Court pronouncements on the subject did not arrive until 1993 in the *Hartford Fire* case and then again in 2004 with the *Empagran* case. Before we turn to this recent governing case law, it will be helpful to have an understanding of how the principles governing the application of the Sherman Act to international transactions evolved.

[A] The Historical Development of the Standard

The first Supreme Court case involving the extraterritorial reach of the US antitrust laws was the *American Banana* case in 1909. In that case the American Banana Company sued the United Fruit Company alleging that the latter was monopolizing and restraining the banana trade in violation of the Sherman Act. Both parties were US corporations, but the acts complained of took place outside the US, in territory over which Costa Rica claimed sovereignty. The plaintiff's main allegation was that defendant had induced the Costa Rican government to confiscate plaintiff's plantation from which the latter intended to export bananas. The Supreme Court upheld dismissal of the complaint for lack of jurisdiction under the Sherman Act. While the Court seemingly could have based this conclusion on the grounds that no substantial anticompetitive effect on US commerce had been established and that, moreover, a foreign government could not be challenged for acts it undertook within its own territory, the opinion of Justice Holmes for the Court went well beyond these rationales. The opinion spoke of the "general and almost universal rule ... that the character of an act as unlawful or unlawful must be determined wholly by the law of the country where the act is done." Stating that "[a]ll legislation is *prima facie* territorial," the opinion declared that it would be "an interference ... with the authority of another sovereign, contrary to the comity of nations" for another jurisdiction to apply its own laws outside of that nation's jurisdiction. This was a strict expression of the territorial principle of jurisdiction.

However, later decisions in the federal courts limited the holding of *American Banana* in terms of the facts of that case. Only two years later, the Supreme Court reviewed the *American Tobacco* case which involved agreements between American and British corporations to divide world markets in the tobacco trade. The American company had agreed to limit it business to the US, its dependencies and Cuba, and the British company agreed to limit its business to the United Kingdom, except for leaf purchases. Another British company, jointly owned by the two, was to take over the export business of both. The lower court ruled that the British companies were not liable because their contracts had been entered into in England where they were lawful. The Supreme Court reversed this dismissal, reasoning that, notwithstanding the locale of the contracts, "the history of the combination [was] so replete with the doings of acts which it was the obvious purpose of the [Sherman Act] to forbid ... " that the defendants were liable "including the foreign corporations insofar as by the contracts made by them, they became cooperators in the combination ... " Consequently, in the

1927 *Sisal Sales Corp.* case, the Supreme Court, distinguishing *American Banana*, upheld the sufficiency of the complaint under the Sherman and Wilson Tariff Acts because it was alleged that the conspirators "by their own deliberate acts, here and elsewhere ... brought about forbidden results within the United States."

The classic articulation of the potential application of the Sherman Act to persons and conduct abroad was made in the landmark *Alcoa* case in 1945 by one of the nation's greatest jurists, Judge Learned Hand of the US Court of Appeals for the Second Circuit. It is "settled law," his opinion stated that "any [nation] may impose liabilities, even upon persons not within its allegiance, for conduct outside its borders that has consequences within its borders which the [nation] reprehends; and these liabilities other [nations] will ordinarily recognize." This statement reflects the "objective territorial" principle of jurisdiction, as distinguished from the "limited territorial" principle applied in the *American Banana* decision. Under the objective territorial principle, national jurisdiction exists with respect to conduct which has an intentional or at least foreseeable effect on the nation's commerce, and the effect is not insubstantial. The nationality of the wrongdoers is not important, nor is the locale of the damaging activity, so long as the intent and the effect are demonstrable.

The application of this rule to conduct carried on abroad by foreign persons, often in full compliance with the laws of their own sovereigns, prompted much outcry from foreign nations at what they considered the "extraterritorial" imposition of US antitrust law. It was, several friendly nations argued, contrary to international comity and even in violation of international law. The resulting controversy and a thoughtful appraisal of the effects test led the US Court of Appeals for the Ninth Circuit to reach the conclusion in the *Timberlane* litigation that "the effects test by itself is incomplete because it fails to consider other nations' interests. Nor does it expressly take into account the full relationship between the actors and this country."

The *Timberlane* litigation involved a private antitrust suit alleging that the defendant had conspired in Honduras to prevent an Oregon lumber company from buying a plant in Honduras which would export lumber to the US. In the first round of the litigation, known as *Timberlane 1,* the district court dismissed the suit for lack of a showing of a direct or substantial effect on US commerce. The Ninth Circuit reversed. Rejecting the effects test as "incomplete," the Ninth Circuit articulated in this case, in 1976, a new three-pronged jurisdictional rule of reason test for determining whether, in a particular case involving foreign commerce, the Sherman Act *should* be applied to activities which occurred abroad. The first prong was the effects test, and the second prong was that "a greater showing of burden or restraint may be necessary to demonstrate that the effect is sufficiently large to present a cognizable injury to the plaintiffs and, therefore, civil violation of the antitrust laws." The third prong of the test was " ... the additional question which is unique to the international setting of whether the interests of, and links to, the United States including the magnitude of the effect on American foreign commerce are sufficiently strong, vis-a-vis those of other nations, to justify an assertion of extraterritorial authority." The elements to be weighed, said the court, include:

the degree of conflict with foreign law or policy, the nationality or allegiance of the parties and the location or principal places of business of corporations, the extent to which enforcement by either state can be expected to achieve compliance, the relative significance of effects on the United States as compared with those elsewhere, the extent to which there is explicit purpose to harm or affect American commerce, the foreseeability of such effect, and the relative importance to the violations charged of conduct within the United States as compared with conduct abroad.

On remand of the case to the district court, the latter again dismissed the case for lack of subject matter jurisdiction. The Ninth Circuit reviewed the dismissal and, in an opinion known as *Timberlane 2*, affirmed the dismissal on the basis of the application of the three part jurisdictional rule of reason test that it had articulated earlier.

A number of other federal circuit courts essentially joined in taking this approach in ensuing decisions. The Court of Appeals for the Third Circuit approved the *Timberlane* factors balancing analysis in *Mannington Mills Inc. v. Congoleum Corp.* in 1979, somewhat altering the list of factors to be weighed. In the *Montreal Trading* case in 1981, the Tenth Circuit Court of Appeals agreed, stating:

> When the contacts with the United States are few, the effects upon American commerce minimal, and the foreign elements overwhelming, however, we do not accept jurisdiction.

The concept of a jurisdictional "rule of reason" gained significant momentum with the issuance in 1986 of the Third Edition of the *Restatement of the Foreign Relations Law of the United States* (*"Restatement"*). Under the formulation adopted in Sections 402 and 403 of the *Restatement:* (a) a state has jurisdiction to prescribe law with respect to conduct outside its territory, but (b) even when such a base for concurrent jurisdiction exists, a state may not exercise jurisdiction if doing so would be unreasonable in light of the person's or the activity's connection with another state, and (c) where it would be unreasonable for each of two states to exercise jurisdiction over a person or activity, one state should defer to the other, if the latter's interest in the matter is clearly greater. Reasonableness, under this approach, is determined by a "balancing" of various factors relevant to the context of the dispute, as under the *Timberlane* test.

The new approach also had its critics. *Timberlane* received some tactful criticism from the Second Circuit Court of Appeals in 1961 in the *National Bank of Canada* case. Then, in the *Laker Airways* litigation in 1984, the District of Columbia Circuit Court of Appeals was more openly critical of the *Timberlane* doctrine and of the revised *Restatement*. That court declared that there was no basis in international law for determining that one permissible ground for jurisdiction was more "reasonable" than another. The court also declared that, in any event, the US judiciary was not a suitable body for weighing the national interests of various nations and was duty bound to enforce the laws that the US political branches had enacted. The court's opinion, rendered by Judge Malcolm Wilkey, a jurist well versed in international law, concluded that "jurisdiction exists whenever conduct is intended to, and results in, substantial effects within the United States." In addition, some commentators labeled the *Timberlane* decision and its ilk to be flawed for being "uncounselable law." i.e., they questioned how a lawyer striving to counsel a business person on legal compliance under the jurisdictional rule of reason could fairly predict what conclusion a court would subsequently reach in applying the complicated, many-factored jurisdictional test in a given case.

[B] Enactment of the Foreign Trade Antitrust Improvements Act

Efforts to enact a version of the *Timberlane* jurisdictional doctrine into legislation foundered during the 1980s. In 1982, Congress did attempt to make its intentions known with respect to the jurisdictional issue, but managed to generate new confusion while addressing the application of the antitrust laws to export transactions. The primary aim of the 1982 Foreign Trade Antitrust Improvements Act ("FTAIA") was to exempt collective export activities from the provisions of the Sherman Act and the Federal Trade Commission Act. Accordingly, the House Judiciary Committee Report on the legislation indicated that the intent of the FTAIA was to establish that restraints on trade will not violate either of the antitrust statutes unless the restraint has a direct, substantial, and reasonably foreseeable effect on US domestic commerce, on import commerce, or on a domestic firm competing for foreign trade.

Accordingly, as we have previously discussed, the FTAIA, codified at 15 U.S.C. Sections 6(a) and 45(a)(3) makes the Sherman and FTC Act prohibitions inapplicable to conduct involving trade or commerce (other than import trade or import commerce) with foreign nations unless: (1) such conduct has a direct, substantial and reasonably foreseeable effect—(A) on trade or commerce which is not trade or commerce with foreign nations, or on import trade or import commerce with foreign nations; or (B) on export trade or commerce with foreign nations, of a person engaged in such trade or commerce in the US; and (B) such effect gives rise to a claim and, if such claim arises only because of the effect on export commerce, the prohibitions apply to such conduct only for injury to export business in the US. Import trade or commerce is not covered by the FTAIA exclusion and thus remains subject to the basic effects test of the case law.

As we shall see, notwithstanding the insights provided by the legislative history, this untidy language of the FTAIA gave rise to issues requiring considerable attention by the Supreme Court and the circuit courts of appeal in the subsequent years as new situations implicating international commerce arose.

[C] Hartford Fire and the Comity Issue

International comity can be defined as the principle that states will mutually recognize each other's legislative, judicial, and executive acts out of deference, mutuality, and respect. The early Supreme Court decision in *Hilton v. Guyot* described the doctrine of international comity thus:

Comity, in the legal sense, is neither a matter of absolute obligation, on the one hand, nor of mere courtesy and good will, upon the other. But it is the recognition which one nation allows within its territory to the legislative, executive or judicial acts of another nation, having due regard both to international duty and convenience and to the rights of its citizens or of other persons who are under the protection of its laws.

While the drafters of the FTAIA enacted as their basic jurisdictional standard the "direct, substantial and reasonably foreseeable effect" on US commerce test, being aware of the *Timberlane* line of cases, they included language in the House Committee Report to the effect that courts would still be left free to "employ notions of comity ... or otherwise ... take account of the international character of the transaction." It was presumably left to the Supreme Court to shape the unreconciled decisional law and the new statute into a coherent jurisprudence, and there were high hopes that the Court would do so when it agreed to review the *Hartford Fire* case in the early 1990s.

Hartford Fire Insurance Co. v. California was a litigation brought by a number of US states against US and British insurers and reinsurers alleging a conspiracy to limit insurance coverage in the US in violation of the Sherman Act. In part, the complaints alleged that the London reinsurers had agreed to restrict the terms on which reinsurance would be written and to refuse to reinsure certain North American property risks, such as pollution. The US District Court for the Northern District of California dismissed these claims against the British defendants for lack of subject matter jurisdiction, finding that the challenged conduct had been "openly conducted in conformity with British law." Applying the three-part test of subject matter jurisdiction laid down by the Ninth Circuit in *Timberlane*, the district court concluded that the plaintiffs' allegations did not satisfy the international comity requirement of the test because:

> [E]nforcement of the antitrust laws against activities in the London reinsurance market would lead to significant conflict with English law and policy. This conflict, unless outweighed by the factors in the comity analysis, is itself a sufficient reason to decline exercise of jurisdiction.

On the appeal to the US Court of Appeals, and subsequently before the Supreme Court, the British Government filed an *amicus curiae* brief, stating that the conduct of the British reinsurers was subject to regulation under British law and should not be a matter for the exercise of US antitrust jurisdiction. (The author discloses that he was counsel of record for the British Government in this case) However, the Ninth Circuit reversed the district court on this and other issues. It reasoned that the FTAIA mandated application of the direct, substantial, and reasonably foreseeable effect test, and that, by reason of the legislation, it would be only in an unusual case that comity would require abstention from the exercise of jurisdiction. After evaluating the case under the factors of the *Timberlane* test, the Ninth Circuit concluded that the only consideration pointing toward abstention was the conflict with British policy and that this was insufficient to overcome "the weight of the findings already made under the Foreign Trade Antitrust Improvements Act." The Supreme Court agreed to review the case which, in addition to the international issue, involved questions pertaining to the insurance exemption to the antitrust laws contained in the McCarran-Ferguson Act.

In 1993, the Supreme Court, by a five to four vote, agreed with the Ninth Circuit's ruling that the alleged conduct of the London defendants came within the jurisdictional reach of the Sherman Act. The majority opinion, written by Justice Souter, relied on the FTAIA and on the *Alcoa* principle, in holding that "... it is well established by now that the Sherman Act applies to foreign conduct that was meant to produce and did in fact produce some substantial effect in the United States." Justice Souter's opinion did not directly comment on the viability of the *Timberlane* factor balancing test, including the role of international comity, although his opinion did refer to the House Committee Report on the FTAIA which seemingly preserved those principles in appropriate cases. What was controlling in the present case, according to the opinion, was that "even assuming that in a proper case a court may decline to exercise Sherman Act jurisdiction over foreign conduct" any concepts of international comity would only come into play if there was a "true conflict" between domestic and foreign law. There was no true conflict here, said the opinion, because it had not been shown that the London defendants were unable to comply with both the British and the US regulatory schemes.

The majority thus adopted the effects test, cast the future of the *Timberlane* type of analysis into doubt and, as to comity, left open only the possibility that it might play some role where a true clash of legal systems occurred. Justice Scalia wrote the minority's dissenting opinion arguing that, although the US court had jurisdiction, Congress did not intend for the Sherman Act to have extraterritorial application in this type of case, in light of international law and "the limitations customarily observed by nations upon the exercise of their powers." Justice Scalia's opinion relied on the *Restatement* factors in reaching the conclusion that there should here be a dismissal for failure to state a cause of action because it would be "unreasonable" to apply the US antitrust laws in the setting of this case. In applying the *Restatement* factors, Justice Scalia reasoned that:

> The activity relevant to the counts at issue here took place primarily in the United Kingdom, and the defendants in these counts are British corporations and British subjects having their principal place of business or residence outside the United States. Great Britain has established a comprehensive scheme governing the London reinsurance market, and clearly has a heavy "interest in regulating the activity" ... I think it unimaginable that an assertion of legislative jurisdiction by the United States would be considered reasonable, and therefore it is inappropriate to assume, in the absence of statutory indication to the contrary, that Congress has made such an assertion.

The *Hartford Fire* decision squarely settled that the effects doctrine was the law of the land but it left open to debate how much, if anything, was left of the balancing test spawned by *Timberlane* and its kin. In 1996, the Ninth Circuit Court of Appeals, which had given birth to the *Timberlane* doctrine, had occasion to consider what remained of it. In the case of *Metro Industries Inc. v. Sammi Corp.* it observed that "[w]hile *Hartford Fire* overruled our holding in *Timberlane 2* that a foreign government's encouragement of conduct which the US prohibits would amount to a conflict of law, it did not question the propriety of the jurisdictional rule of reason or the seven comity factors set forth in *Timberlane 1.*" Other circuit courts chipped in to the contrary, the First Circuit Court of Appeals commenting in 1997, in the *Nippon Paper* case, that the application of comity analysis in the antitrust sphere was an approach which had been "stunted by *Hartford Fire.*"

Curiously, until the 1997 First Circuit court decision in *United States v. Nippon Industries Co.* all of the leading cases applying the Sherman Act to conduct by foreign persons outside the US involved civil litigation. *Nippon Paper,* on the other hand, involved a Sherman Act criminal indictment brought by the government which alleged that Japanese manufacturers had conspired in Japan to fix prices on the sale of fax paper in the US. One of the defendants, supported by an *amicus curiae* brief filed by the Government of Japan, argued that the effects test did not apply to criminal cases, and the district court dismissed the indictment on the ground that the Sherman Act could not be applied to criminalize conduct occurring solely in Japan. The US Court of Appeals for the First Circuit reversed, concluding that there was no basis for applying a different rule in criminal cases. Common sense, said the court, dictated that the same words of a statute should be given the same reading for civil and for criminal cases. As for taking into account considerations of international comity, the court said that this was more "a matter of grace than a matter of obligation" and that, in the antitrust sphere, *Hartford Fire* left little room for the doctrine.

Notwithstanding *Hartford Fire, t*he Department of Justice and the Federal Trade Commission have elected to give comity analysis broader scope in the formulation of their antitrust enforcement policy. The *Antitrust Guidelines for International Enforcement and Cooperation* (hereinafter also referred to as *"International Guidelines"*) declare that the Agencies take full account of comity factors beyond whether there is a conflict with foreign law. Thus, in determining whether to assert jurisdiction to investigate or bring a proceeding, or to seek particular remedies in a given case, the Agencies consider whether significant interests of any foreign sovereign would be affected. In their view, however, the importance of antitrust enforcement may outweigh any foreign policy concerns.

Accordingly, the impact of a comity assessment on US government antitrust enforcement policy should not be overestimated. It is noteworthy, for example, that one important ground for yielding or deferring US enforcement action in favor of foreign authorities is to give those authorities the prior opportunity to bring enforcement action against the miscreants under foreign law. It is not the purpose of the comity assessment to give the offenders a substantial opportunity to escape enforcement proceedings. In only one well-known case was it acknowledged that foreign policy concerns had caused termination of a case and nonprosecution. This involved termination of the US grand jury investigation into alleged restraints of trade affecting passenger air travel between the US and the United Kingdom. It is said that President Reagan and Prime Minister Thatcher were personally involved in the consideration of that matter.

[D] Empagran and Application of the FTAIA

The FTAIA leaves subject to the Sherman Act strictures anticompetitive conduct which has the requisite effect on a US domestic market, or on a US import market, or on a market for exporting goods from the US, but only if the injury occurs to an exporter within the US.

However, the FTAIA's language created considerable confusion over whether, where a defendant has engaged in international anticompetitive activity affecting both US commerce and non-US commerce, the provisions of the Sherman Act might be invoked by a plaintiff who has suffered injury from these activities outside of US commerce. In *Den Norske Stats Oljeskelskap AS v. Heere MacVOF et al*, a decision rendered in 2001 by a divided panel of the Court of Appeals for the Fifth Circuit, the majority held that, although the plaintiff had alleged a conspiracy affecting US commerce, the district court lacked jurisdiction under the FTAIA because the plaintiff's claimed injury—inflated prices that it paid for services in the North Sea—did not arise from the anticompetitive effects which the conspiracy had inflicted on US commerce. The Supreme Court did not review that decision. Then, in *Kruman v. Christie's Int'l plc*, decided by the Second Circuit in 2002, that court reversed the district court's decision and held that the plaintiffs who paid conspiracy-inflated prices at foreign auctions were not excluded from jurisdiction by the FTAIA where the challenged conspiracy as a whole had the proscribed effect on US commerce, even though that domestic effect was not the basis for the plaintiffs' claimed injury. The Court of Appeals for the Third Circuit subsequently considered the FTAIA issues in a suit brought by foreign travel agents located outside the US. The court affirmed the district's dismissal of the suit and the appellate court affirmed because the plaintiffs had failed to satisfy the requirement of identifying a direct, substantial, and reasonably foreseeable anticompetitive effect on US commerce. Noting the split between the Fifth and Second Circuits in their interpretations of the FTAIA, the Third Circuit observed that the case before it—*Turicentro, S.A. v. American Airlines, Inc. et al.*—did not necessitate that it "take sides in this dispute."

In *Metallgesellschaft AG v. Sumitomo Corporation of America*, the Court of Appeals for the Seventh Circuit's 2003 decision, similarly, noted the disagreement among the circuits regarding the correct interpretation of the FTAIA but found it unnecessary to take sides on the matter presented in the case at bar. That was a suit under the Sherman Act in which the plaintiffs asserted that the defendants had conspired to corner the market for physical copper available to satisfy futures contracts on the London Metal Exchange (LME). The Seventh Circuit determined that the plaintiffs had satisfied the FTAIA's jurisdictional standard on either reading of the statute since they had alleged and demonstrated that they were injured in the US market and that "the alleged foreign activities had a direct, substantial and reasonably foreseeable effect on US non-import commerce."

The application of the FTAIA in the export context had been considered by the Fifth Circuit Court of Appeals in a private antitrust case in 1999, *Access Telecom Inc. v. MCI Telecommunications Corp. et al.* The plaintiff was a Texas business which, using toll free numbers leased from MCI, operated a service allowing Mexican long distance customers to call the US more cheaply than if they used the phone links provided by "Telmex," Mexico's privatized telecommunications provider. When Telmex severed the plaintiff's connections, ending its operation, the latter sued Telmex and MCI in the US courts alleging tort and antitrust law violations. The Fifth Circuit, after determining that the plaintiff's activity was legal in Mexico at the relevant time, held that the plaintiff had properly alleged an antitrust claim of wrongful conduct having a direct, substantial, and reasonably foreseeable effect on the US market for switching services. In reversing the district court's decision, the appellate court also held that, based on the plaintiff's allegations, the US court would have personal jurisdiction over Telmex. The court reasoned that a showing that Telmex, in order to injure the Texas business, shut down phone lines serving Texas residents with Mexican phone service, was sufficient to confer on the US courts specific personal jurisdiction over Telmex for injuries inflicted in Texas.

The Supreme Court finally considered the FTAIA's interpretation in *F. Hoffman-La Roche, Ltd. v. Empagran S.A.* (hereinafter "*Empagran*"). This was a Sherman Act Section 1 suit brought by foreign and domestic purchasers of vitamins alleging a price fixing conspiracy involving vitamin manufacturers and distributors. On the basis that the transactions of the foreign purchasers occurred entirely outside US commerce, the district court dismissed their claims as not covered by any of the exceptions to the FTAIA. A divided panel of the District of Columbia Circuit reversed. Stating that its reading of the statute fell "somewhere between the views of the Fifth and Second Circuits," the court upheld jurisdiction in favor of the foreign purchasers because where the "anticompetitive conduct has the requisite harm on United States commerce, [the] FTAIA permits suits by foreign plaintiffs who are injured solely by that conduct's effect on foreign commerce."

Following a grant of *certiorari* to resolve the split among the Courts of Appeals, the Supreme Court's decision in 2004 articulated an authoritative interpretation of the FTAIA. It reversed the ruling of the District of Columbia Circuit and held that the FTAIA did not intend to apply US antitrust law to conduct having an adverse foreign effect which is independent of any adverse domestic effect. The Court reasoned that Congress, mindful of principles of customary international law implicating the legitimate sovereign interests of other nations, sought to release from antitrust constraints anticompetitive conduct causing foreign effects unrelated to US domestic effects. Noting that several foreign nations had filed briefs in the case, urging that their own antitrust programs and remedies should not be by-passed and undermined by litigants seeking to pursue the more generous US private treble damage remedies, the Court concluded that "principles of prescriptive comity counsel against the Court of Appeals' interpretation of the FTAIA. Where foreign competitive conduct plays a significant role and where foreign injury is independent of domestic effects ... Congress, we must assume, would not have tried to impose the [US antitrust laws on other nations] in an act of legal imperialism, through judicial fiat."

The foreign plaintiffs in *Empagran* had argued, in the alternative, that the injury to them and the anticompetitive conduct's domestic effects were linked to each other, in that, without maintaining higher prices in the US, the sellers could not have maintained fixed prices internationally. The Court left that issue for the Court of

Appeals to consider on remand, if it had been properly preserved for argument. On remand, the Court of Appeals determined that the plaintiffs' asserted link between the higher domestic prices and the prices plaintiffs paid abroad was too indirect to sustain their claims under the Supreme Court's interpretation of the FTAIA. A direct causal relationship was required, which was lacking here.

It should be noted that the Court's opinion in *Empagran* was couched in terms of the law's intended scope rather than in terms of the limitations of the Court's subject matter jurisdiction. As the *International Guidelines* point out, the federal courts have expressed differing views as to whether the FTAIA goes to a claim's merits or a court's subject matter jurisdiction (at p. 18, fn. 82).

For example, the position that the FTAIA's requirements are substantive and nonjurisdictional in nature was taken by the Second Circuit Court of Appeals in 2014 in its decision in *Lotes Co. Ltd v. Hon Hai Precision Industry Co.* In that case, the court also held that the Taiwanese plaintiff's claim that the foreign defendants anticompetitively refused to license their patents to the plaintiff did not "give rise" to a direct, substantial, and reasonably foreseeable effect in the US.

Other recent cases have also considered issues involving the scope of the FTAIA. In *Animal Sci. Prods. Inc. v. China Minmetals Corp.*, the plaintiffs, US purchasers of magnesite, alleged a conspiracy by the defendants, Chinese producers and exporters of the product, to fix the prices of their exports to the US. The district court dismissed the case on the ground that the FTAIA imposed a jurisdictional limitation and that it lacked jurisdiction under the FTAIA. The Ninth Circuit Court of Appeals decision in 2011 reversed on the ground that the FTAIA constitutes a substantive merits limitation rather than a jurisdictional limitation. The court added that a relevant inquiry on remand would be whether the defendants' alleged anticompetitive behavior was directed at a US import market. A Sixth Circuit case decided in 2012, the case of *Carrier Corp. v. Outokumpu Oyj*, confirmed that conduct directly affecting US import commerce is subject to the Sherman Act.

It was established that between 2001 and 2006 there was an international conspiracy between Taiwanese and Korean electronics manufacturers to fix prices for important technology, namely liquid clear display panels known as TFT-LCDs (hereinafter "LCD panels"). The conspiracy ended when the FBI raided the offices of AU Optronics Corporation of America in Houston, Texas. AU Optronics of Taiwan, that firm's US subsidiary and two executives from the parent company were convicted in the district court of violating the Sherman Act. The parent company was ordered by the district court to pay a USD 500 million criminal fine, and the two executives were sentenced to serve prison time and pay criminal fines. The defendants appealed, arguing that because the bulk of the panels were sold to third parties worldwide rather than for direct import into the US, the nexus to US commerce was insufficient under the Sherman Act as amended by the FTAIA.

The Ninth Circuit Court of Appeals affirmed in 2015 in a case titled *United States v. Hsiung*, citing the Supreme Court's "seminal" ruling in the *Hartford Fire* case that "the Sherman Act applies to foreign conduct that was meant to produce and did in fact produce some substantial effect in the United States." Indeed, the FTAIA had displaced the intentionality requirement where the FTAIA applies. In any event, said the Ninth

Circuit Court of Appeals, "[t]he defendants' conduct, as alleged and proven, constitutes 'import trade' and thus falls outside the scope of the FTAIA." While the government had proceeded on a domestic effects theory, rather than on the import trade theory, the court was content to uphold the indictments on the basis of the clear impact of the conspiracy on US import trade, a situation excluded from application of the FTAIA.

However, a different result occurred in a private antitrust case brought against AU Optronics and others by one of the customers of the conspirators. This case, *Motorola Mobility LLC v. AU Optronics Corp.* was decided in 2014 by the Court of Appeals for the Seventh Circuit. Motorola, a US company, and its ten foreign subsidiaries purchased LCD panels from the foreign suppliers which were incorporated into cellphones manufactured by Motorola or the subsidiaries. Motorola accused the foreign manufacturers of the panels of violating Section 1 of the Sherman Act by agreeing on prices with each other. About 1% of the panels were delivered to Motorola in the US for assembly into cellphones—a feature which the court characterized as giving Motorola a solid Sherman Act claim as to those purchases. However, the other 99% of the cartelized components were purchased by, paid for and delivered to Motorola's foreign subsidiaries. Fifty seven percent of these panels were incorporated into cellphones abroad and sold abroad. The other 42% of the panels were purchased by the subsidiaries and incorporated into cellphones that the subsidiaries then sold and shipped to Motorola for resale in the US. The key issue was whether Motorola had a Sherman Act claim beyond the 1% and, if so, to what extent.

First, the court held that the claim for the 57% was clearly frivolous because it was barred from challenge under the Sherman Act by the FTAIA inasmuch as those products never entered the US and thus never became domestic commerce. Second, the court held that the price fixing on the 42% of the panels that were sold abroad and became cellphones bought by Motorola in the US did not have the requisite "direct" effect on US commerce. The effect on US domestic commerce was merely "indirect." Any antitrust injury was to the foreign customers, i.e., the subsidiaries who purchased the price fixed panels. Quoting its own decision in *Minn-Chem, Inc. v. Agrium, Inc.*, the court emphasized: "US antitrust laws are not to be used for injury to foreign customers." The Seventh Circuit also quoted the Supreme Court's warning against rampant extraterritorial application of US law.

In both the Ninth and Seventh Circuit cases, the LCD panels were purchased and integrated outside of the US and the finished product was exported to the US. Were there here two different interpretations of the FTAIA or were the factual predicates different? In any event, the Supreme Court denied review in both cases.

[E] International Guidelines Interpretations

The recently revised and reissued *International Guidelines* of the Department of Justice and the Federal Trade Commission provide an excellent description of the enforcement policies of the two US antitrust enforcement agencies on international matters, as well as a useful discussion of the applicable laws and their interpretations by the US courts.

As we have mentioned, these revised *Guidelines* were issued in January 2017, replacing the 1995 version. They point out that the federal antitrust laws have applied to "commerce with foreign nations" since their inception. The original *Guidelines* did not include in their title the reference to "cooperation," and this concept has now been brought to the fore by the Agencies' greatly increased engagement with foreign competition authorities in recent years, as we have described in Chapter 1. The new *International Guidelines* are reproduced in full in Appendix III hereto.

The *International Guidelines* provide: (1) a brief summary of the antitrust and related laws that are likely to have the greatest significance for businesses engaged in international activities, (2) a description of the connections to the US which are sufficient for the Agencies to investigate or bring enforcement actions challenging conduct occurring abroad or involving or affecting foreign commerce, (3) a description of the Agencies' consideration of international comity concerns and the role of foreign government involvement in determining whether to open an investigation or bring and enforcement action, and (4) guidance on the Agencies' pertinent investigatory tools and their enforcement cooperation with foreign authorities. The *International Guidelines* also include a number of illustrative examples. In short, they contain a valuable amount of information about US antitrust enforcement policies, procedures and applicable laws.

Importantly, the *International Guidelines* declare that the "Agencies do not discriminate in the enforcement of the antitrust laws based upon the nationality of the parties." "When the Agencies determine that a sufficient nexus to the United States exists to apply the antitrust laws and that nether international comity nor the involvement of a foreign jurisdiction precludes investigation or enforcement, the Agencies apply the same substantive rules to all cases."

In considering these valuable guidelines, it is important to recognize, nonetheless, that *statements of enforcement policy*, including such guidelines crafted by agency officials, and *the law* represent distinct regimes and are not necessarily identical. For example, in the antitrust field, law enforcers may choose to act aggressively against business practices which have not yet been evaluated by the courts, in the anticipation the enforcers will succeed in having the practices held unlawful. On the other hand, enforcers may choose to exercise their discretion by *not* filing a case even though applicable law would authorize the bringing of the case, where special factors urge nonprosecution, such as the comity doctrine which we have discussed.

The Agencies thus will pursue under the US antitrust laws: conduct abroad involving US import commerce which has a direct, substantial and reasonably foreseeable effect on such commerce; conduct abroad involving non-import commerce if the conduct has a direct, substantial, and reasonably foreseeable effect on commerce within the US, on US import commerce, or on the export commerce of a US exporter, and that effect gives rise to a claim.

The *International Guidelines* also discern substantial scope for the application of US antitrust law where US Government financial interests—or, put otherwise—"taxpayer interests"—are adversely affected, even abroad. As the *International Guidelines* state at paragraph 3.3 entitled "Conduct Involving U.S. Government Financing or Purchasing":

The Agencies may, in appropriate cases, take enforcement action when the U.S. Government is a purchaser, or substantially funds the purchase, of goods or services for consumption or use abroad. Cases in which the effect of anti-competitive conduct with respect to these goods or services falls primarily on U.S. taxpayers may qualify for redress under the federal antitrust laws. The requisite U.S. government involvement could include an actual purchase of goods by the U.S. government for shipment abroad, a U.S. Government grant to a foreign government that is specifically earmarked for the transaction, or a U.S. Government loan specifically earmarked for the transaction that is made on such generous terms that it amounts to a grant.

There is case law support for this assertion. For example, in 2001, a federal grand jury indicted Bill Harbert International Construction Inc. and others for conspiring to rig bids on US funded construction projects in Egypt in violation of the Sherman Act. One of the individuals involved argued that the court lacked jurisdiction to entertain the Sherman Act charges against him because the activity in question took place in foreign countries and the government had failed to prove that there had been a substantial effect on US commerce. The Court of Appeals for the Eleventh Circuit affirmed the district court's rejection of this argument. It held, first, that the FTAIA did not apply because the matter did not involve commerce with foreign nations, but a US government program paying US companies to perform construction projects abroad. Second, even if the statute were to apply, the defendant's activities had a substantial effect on US commerce, since the bid rigging scheme took money from the federal treasury, decisions and transactions took place within the US, and the contracts required the equipment and materials for the project to be purchased in the US.

The *International Guidelines* cite several other instances in which parties accepted consent decrees with respect to price fixing or bid rigging activities with regard to transactions made abroad but involving US foreign aid programs.

§3.02   INTERNATIONAL LAW AND FOREIGN GOVERNMENT VIEWS

Assertions by the US of prescriptive jurisdiction over conduct carried on outside the US by foreign nationals on the basis of the "effects" doctrine were, for many years, challenged on grounds of foreign relations, international law or comity, even by the US's closest allies. The dispute was sharpened and the debate made more robust by the fact that no international agreement or consensus had ever been reached as to how mutually acceptable rules could be established in this situation. Early on, the displeasure on the part of the foreign governments was manifested primarily by the service of diplomatic notes on the State Department, with the latter dutifully passing on the missives to the Department of Justice or the relevant US court. The US courts presumably considered the diplomatic notes in reaching their decisions.

Occasionally, retaliatory action would be taken by the foreign authorities. For example, the 1952 US court decree, resolving a Sherman Act cartel case against the giant British chemical company, Imperial Chemical Industries ("ICI") and its co-conspirators directed ICI to accord immunity under its British patents to parties who would otherwise be infringers. Another British company, British Nylon Spinners Ltd.

("BNS"), subsequently sued ICI in England to obtain an injunction restraining ICI from complying with the US judgment which would damage the exclusive license rights which BNS had obtained under the British patents. The British courts granted the relief to BNS, reasoning that comity did not require acceptance of a foreign decree which impaired British contract rights.

Foreign policy considerations led to the modification in 1965 of the final judgment in the *Swiss Watchmakers* case, which was aimed by the US at a "collective convention" executed in Switzerland by manufacturers and sellers of Swiss watches and parts. An effect of the agreement was to restrain the manufacture, importation, and export of watches and watch parts in US trade. Since the entry of the US court judgment, the Swiss Confederation had issued official regulations on watch part export permits, so the US court altered its judgment to assure that it did not compel the defendants to engage in conduct contrary to Swiss law.

The battle between the US and some of its closest allies over "extraterritorial" antitrust enforcement escalated in the mid-1970s when the uranium litigation erupted, with a US uranium buyer, the Westinghouse Corporation, at its center. Westinghouse claimed that a foreign cartel, composed of the leading uranium suppliers in the world, had collectively raised prices to the point where Westinghouse was forced to renege on its contracts to supply uranium to public utilities. Westinghouse was unable to prevail in its contract litigation, and it then brought treble damage suits in Illinois under the Sherman Act against the both the US members and the foreign members of the alleged uranium cartel.

The Canadian Government duly advised the court that, acting in cooperation with other foreign governments, it had initiated an international uranium marketing arrangement. The foreign governments maintained that they had been spurred to encourage their uranium producers to market cooperatively by US energy law which barred the use of foreign uranium in US domestic reactors. "The purpose of the international marketing arrangement was to allocate the meager non-U.S. demand among the non-U.S. producers, and to stabilize prices for a transitional period," stated the Canadian Government. As the US litigation proceeded, the primary foreign defendants defaulted, most likely on the advice of counsel to preserve jurisdictional defenses abroad. The US district court then entered default judgments against them.

At about this time, the practice changed concerning the State Department's transmission to the US courts of diplomatic notes submitted by foreign governments wishing to express an interest in pending US litigation. In 1978, at the suggestion of the Clerk of the Supreme Court, the State Department began to encourage foreign governments to present their views directly to the US courts through the medium of amicus curiae briefs. Such a brief, often prepared by private US counsel engaged by the foreign government for that purpose, would describe the sovereign interest of the latter in the pending litigation and make arguments in the context of US law urging the result desired by the foreign government. In the uranium antitrust litigation, the Australian, British, Canadian and South African governments followed the new practice and filed *amicus curiae* briefs with the Seventh Circuit Court of Appeals urging that the damage hearing against the defaulting foreign uranium suppliers be deferred until the district court had conducted a comity analysis with regard to applying US subject matter jurisdiction in this case.

The Seventh Circuit upheld the entry of the default judgments against the foreign companies. Moreover, the Court of Appeals described the foreign governments in its opinion as "surrogates" for the nonappearing defendants, and it stated that "[S]hockingly to us, the governments of the defaulters have subserviently presented for them their case against the exercise of jurisdiction."

The Legal Advisor of the State Department subsequently requested the Justice Department to inform the Court of Appeals that the court's "language has caused serious embarrassment to the United States in its relations with some of our closest allies." For the foreign governments concerned, the US court's chastisement probably added insult to injury. It gave them no confidence that the *amicus curiae* route that the US Government had urged them to employ might be productive. The *Westinghouse* case was eventually settled out of court.

Foreign "blocking" statutes also became a component of this dispute. A package of statutes emerged in several countries which typically included authority for a government minister to direct noncompliance by persons in the country who received discovery requests emanating from foreign proceedings; a declaration that certain types of foreign judgments were to be deemed unenforceable; and statutory authority enabling a party who had made payment under a US antitrust treble damage award to sue to recover the portion of the damages which exceeded single damages (so-called clawback legislation). In this spirit, the British Parliament enacted the Protection of Trading Interests Act (1980), described in a press notice as "primarily a reaction to the accumulation of attempts by the United States since the 1950s to impose its own economic and other domestic policies on individuals and companies outside its territorial jurisdiction, without regard for the trading interests of other countries."

Later, in the *Hartford Fire* and *Empagran* disputes which we have discussed, foreign governments expressed strong opposition, usually through the filing of *amicus curiae* briefs, to the US assertions of jurisdiction over the business activities of their nationals.

Under US law, the theoretical supremacy of international law over so-called municipal law is not always given effect. It is true that there is a presumption that the Congress intends its legislation to be consistent with the requirements of international law, and federal statutes are to be construed so as not to conflict with international law whenever possible. But it is equally well settled that, where the congressional intent and design are inconsistent with the preexisting rule of international law, the US courts are bound to give effect to the congressional will as a matter of US domestic law. In this sense, it does not matter whether the extraterritorial application of the Sherman Act is consistent with international law. Moreover, given the globalized nature of commerce, the traditional international lynchpins of territoriality and nationality are no longer sufficient to govern world commercial events. Indeed, jurisdictional concepts dependent on fixing the territorial base of multinational activity appear increasingly obsolete in the world of the Internet in which electronic impulses can seemingly cause business dealings to be physically taking place everywhere—and nowhere—at the same time.

Historically, the soundness in international law of the "objective" territorial principle of jurisdiction, recognizing the logic of the effects doctrine, was recognized by the Permanent Court of International Justice as early as in 1927 in the *S.S. Lotus* case. That dispute resulted from a claim by the Turkish Government that it had jurisdiction over an accident in which a French ship had run into a Turkish ship, causing the deaths of Turkish subjects. The court ruled that the Turkish ship constituted Turkish territory which had felt the effects of the alleged negligence of the French commander and that hence Turkey was entitled to assert jurisdiction in the matter.

This so-called objective territorial principle is now widely recognized in international law. But this principle alone does not fully resolve the dilemma of which nation's laws should prevail in a dispute in which two or more states have concurrent jurisdiction. As Judge Choy observed in his opinion in *Timberlane 1*, in those cases "the effects test itself is incomplete because it fails to consider other nations' interests." This reasoning quite logically led to the formulation of the jurisdictional rule of reason in the *Timberlane* cases, but, as we have seen, the complexity of the balancing test formulated in those cases frustrated its widespread adoption as a jurisdictional test.

As a practical matter, as other enforcers of competition law, notably the Europeans, themselves began to assert the authority to apply their laws on principles comparable to the effects doctrine, the dispute over what was formerly called "extraterritoriality" waned. The focus these days is more on finding ways for enforcement authorities to avoid conflict and to achieve cooperation in situations of concurrent jurisdiction, for example, with respect to international cartels and transnational mergers.

The argument that the US courts lack jurisdiction to require production of documents located abroad has been repeatedly rejected in cases in which the US court has personal jurisdiction over the party concerned. The procedural issues raised by international discovery are discussed further in Chapter 4.

§3.03 FOREIGN GOVERNMENT INVOLVEMENT

We discussed above some situations in which foreign governments sought to assist their nationals who were embroiled in US antitrust proceedings. Where a foreign government's actions are themselves a focus of a US antitrust case, other legal issues may present themselves. Sometimes a foreign state may have been directly implicated in the allegedly unlawful conduct (as the Canadian Government unsuccessfully asserted in the uranium cases) or else have compelled private parties to act, as distinct from merely giving tacit approval to the conduct in question. Such situations do raise special questions as to whether the conduct should be deemed exempt from the US antitrust laws. These concerns may involve the application of the doctrines of act of state, foreign sovereign compulsion, or sovereign immunity, which we consider below.

[A] Act of State Doctrine

The act of state doctrine was derived from English law and enunciated in the 1897 US Supreme Court decision in *Underhill v. Hernandez*. In that case, the Supreme Court affirmed dismissal of a case brought by a US engineer in the US seeking damages from a Venezuelan revolutionary commander for wrongful imprisonment in Venezuela. Because "[e]very sovereign State is bound to respect the independence of every other sovereign State" said the Court "the courts of one country will not sit in judgment on the acts of another, done within its own territory." In later decisions, the doctrine was described as resting primarily on the separation of powers concepts of the US system, which counsel abstention by the judiciary in the field of international relations. As we shall see, the 1990 Supreme Court decision in *W.S. Kirkpatrick & Co. v. Environmental Tectonics Corp.* described the doctrine simply as a "principle of decision" and emphasized its narrow scope, in effect overruling a number of lower court decisions which had applied it expansively.

The doctrine's application in antitrust law is described in the *International Guidelines* as follows (at 4.2.3.):

> The act of state doctrine prevents courts from "declar[ing] invalid the official act of a foreign sovereign performed within its own territory" [quoting from the Supreme Court's 1990 decision in *W.S. Kirkpatrick & Co. v. Envt'l Tectonics Corp. Int'l*]. Applying this doctrine, courts decline to adjudicate claims or issues that would require the court to judge the validity of the sovereign act of a foreign state in its own territory. This doctrine is rooted in considerations of international comity and the separation of powers. (footnotes omitted)

Accordingly, under this statement, to invoke the protection of the doctrine, the acts under scrutiny must constitute the *public act* of a foreign sovereign, performed within the sovereign's *own territory* (i.e., not within the US) and judicial scrutiny of those acts must be unavoidable for resolution of the case. The restriction of the doctrine to "public" acts is meant to limit its application to the sovereign acts of the foreign state, as distinct from its commercial acts. This distinction is not clearly established in the case law, as a majority of the Supreme Court could not be mustered in 1976 in *Alfred Dunhill of London, Inc. v. Republic of Cuba* for the proposition that there exists a commercial exception to the act of state doctrine (as there is in the sovereign immunity context).

In the 1971 case of *Occidental Petroleum Corp. v. Buttes Gas and Oil Co.* the district court refused to look behind the sovereign acts of the Persian Gulf sheikdoms which had allegedly been induced by the defendants to deprive plaintiff of its oil rights in those countries. The court pointed out that "inquiries by this court into the authenticity and motivation of the acts of foreign sovereigns would be the very source of diplomatic friction and complication that the act of state doctrine aims to avert." This decision was affirmed by the Ninth Circuit Court of Appeals, and the Supreme Court denied further review.

In *Hunt v. Mobil Oil Co.*, another oil industry antitrust case, the plaintiff alleged that the major oil companies had combined unlawfully to prevent plaintiff from reaching a satisfactory oil supply agreement with Libya, which eventually nationalized plaintiff's properties. The Second Circuit held that Hunt's claim should be dismissed under the act of state doctrine, although Libya was not a party to the suit, because adjudication would require inquiry into Libya's motive for the nationalization, raising a "subtle and delicate issue of the policy of a foreign sovereign."

A novel case was presented by a private lawsuit brought in a California federal court against the Organization of Petroleum Exporting Countries ("OPEC") oil consortium and its member nations, alleging that this price fixing group of nations was acting in violation of the Sherman Act. The district court dismissed the suit on grounds of sovereign immunity. On the appeal, resolved in 1981 by the Ninth Circuit in *International Association of Machinists & Aerospace Workers v. Organization of Petroleum Exporting Countries*, the reviewing court agreed that the suit should be dismissed but declared that this should be done on act of state grounds. The court emphasized that the private action might interfere with sensitive diplomatic relationships and pointed out that there existed no international rule condemning the maintenance of cartels or of production quotas by sovereign nations. Indeed, it stated, "The United States and other nations have supported the principle of supreme state sovereignty over natural resources." The court did not explore the issues of whether the conduct of the OPEC nations could be considered "commercial," rather than sovereign, or whether the challenged activity took place wholly within the territorial boundaries of the nations involved, and whether these considerations could make for a different result.

In its 1984 decision in *Clayco Petroleum Corp. v. Occidental Petroleum Corp.*, the Ninth Circuit held that, even where the legal validity of an act of a foreign sovereign was not in question, the act of state defense would not apply since the plaintiff sought to establish that "the motivation for the sovereign act was bribery," and therefore "embarrassment would result from adjudication." It was becoming ever more unclear whether the doctrine extended only so far as needed to avoid US judicial scrutiny of the *validity* of the acts of foreign governments, or if it applied also to avoid review of the *motivation* underlying the acts, or perhaps even to avoiding review of any issue that might cause *embarrassment* to foreign states.

The Supreme Court firmly shut the door against such expansive application in 1990 in the above-mentioned case of *W.S. Kirkpatrick & Co. v. Environmental Tectonics Corp.* That case was brought under anti-racketeering and other statutes by an American company, which had unsuccessfully bid for a Nigerian defense contract, against another American company who was the winning bidder. A central issue was whether there had been bribery of Nigerian officials, bribes being prohibited under Nigerian law in connection with the award of government contracts. The district court concluded that the act of state doctrine applied, citing the *Clayco* case. The Third Circuit reversed, relying on a letter filed with the court by the Legal Advisor to the State Department which stated that embarrassment and interference with the conduct of foreign affairs would not arise from judicial inquiry into the *purpose* behind the act of a foreign government as distinct from inquiry into the *validity* of foreign sovereign conduct.

In an opinion written by Justice Scalia, the Supreme Court held unanimously that the doctrine did not apply here. The Court rejected the reasoning of *Clayco* that the act of state doctrine should apply where a dispute would cause a US court to inquire into the motivation behind the act of a foreign state. It made clear that the doctrine applies only where the relief sought or the defense raised would require "a court in the United States to declare invalid the official act of a foreign sovereign performed within its own territory." It is possible to argue with Justice Scalia's conclusion that the issue of the validity or legality of Nigerian government action was not before the Court. In any event, as defined in the *Kirkpatrick* decision, the act of state doctrine was significantly scaled back.

The OPEC cartel's price fixing activities came up again in the 2011 case of *Spectrum Stores, Inc. v. Citgo Petroleum Corp*. US gasoline retailers brought antitrust claims against oil production companies for allegedly participating in a conspiracy to fix oil prices in the US. Characterizing the suit as alleging "a conspiracy that is orchestrated by the sovereign member nations of OPEC," the Fifth Circuit Court of Appeals affirmed dismissal of the suit as presenting "nonjusticiable political questions" and also as precluded by the act of state doctrine.

The act of state doctrine does not apply to protect the actions of individual government officials acting outside of their official capacity. Nor does it protect the actions of private parties, even when those actions are approved or condoned by a foreign government.

As one can see, the antitrust cases in which the act of state defense has been recognized have involved private complainants. Courts have generally concluded that the defense is not applicable where the suit is brought by the US Government since, in that context, there is no risk that court adjudication will be interfering with Executive Branch functions.

[B] Foreign Sovereign Compulsion

Where private action otherwise violative of the US antitrust laws occurred because it was *compelled* by a foreign state acting within its own territory (as distinct from private conduct which was merely approved or acquiesced in by the foreign state) the defense of foreign sovereign compulsion may be available to the defendant. While the Supreme Court has not directly considered this issue, it is noteworthy that such a defense was not foreclosed by *Hartford Fire*, which recognized that special considerations might apply where there is a direct conflict between US antitrust law and foreign law. However, the case law also indicates that, if the defendant had discretion and the challenged action was merely approved by the foreign government, the defense of foreign sovereign compulsion is not available. The Supreme Court held in *Continental Ore Co. v. Union Carbide & Carbon Corp.* that conduct merely authorized by a foreign government within its territory, and not mandated, is not shielded from the US antitrust laws.

The *International Guidelines* state that courts have recognized the defense when the facts demonstrate that the foreign sovereign has compelled the very conduct that the US antitrust law would prohibit. The Agencies stipulate that they will only recognize the defense when certain criteria are satisfied, namely if (a) the foreign government has compelled the anticompetitive conduct under circumstances in which a refusal to comply would give rise to the imposition of penal or other sanctions, (b) the compelled conduct did not occur within the US and, normally, is conduct that can be accomplished entirely within the compelling state's territory, and (c) the order comes from the foreign government acting in its governmental capacity, i.e., not in a commercial capacity.

The availability of the defense, however styled, in proper circumstances seems to be established. For example, in the 1983 *Japanese Electronics Products Antitrust Litigation*, the Third Circuit Court of Appeals noted that "[w]e may assume, without deciding, that a foreign government mandated export cartel arrangement fixing minimum export prices would be outside the ambit of Section 1 of the Sherman Act." Very recently, in its decision in the *Vitamin C Antitrust Litigation* rendered in 2016, the Second Circuit Court of Appeals considered a case in which the Chinese Government had filed a formal statement asserting that its laws required the defendant Chinese vitamin C producers to fix prices and reduce quantities of vitamin C sold abroad. Applying a *Timberlane* and *Mannington Mills* factor balancing approach, the Second Circuit held that the Sherman Act claims filed by the complaining US purchasers of Chinese vitamins were barred because "the principles of international comity required the district court to abstain from exercising jurisdiction in this case." This decision is a controversial one, and the Supreme Court has asked the Justice Department to state the US Government's view on it.

[C] Petitioning Foreign Sovereigns

As we discussed in Chapter 2, under the *Noerr-Pennington* principle established by US law in the domestic sphere, a good faith effort to influence US federal or state governmental action is immune from the antitrust laws, even if that effort is anticompetitive in its intent and/or effect. Since this rule is grounded on First Amendment concerns, it does not necessarily follow that the immunity concept extends to protecting from antitrust challenge petitioning efforts directed at foreign governments. Moreover, there is a question of whether the principle is appropriate as related to petitioning nondemocratic governments. Accordingly, there is to be found case law supporting different approaches in these situations. However, as we have noted, the *International Guidelines* do not hesitate on the subject. They state that "[i]t is the view of the Agencies that the principles undergirding this doctrine apply to the petitioning of foreign governments. The Agencies, therefore, will not challenge under the antitrust laws genuine efforts to obtain or influence action by foreign government entities."

[D] Sovereign Immunity

Sometimes a US antitrust action will be brought directly against a foreign state or, more frequently, against one of the state's components or entities, such as a state-owned organization. Whether jurisdiction exists in such a case may turn on the special rules relating to sovereign immunity. These rules have been codified in US law since 1976 in the Foreign Sovereign Immunities Act ("FSIA"). The FSIA declares foreign states to be immune as a general principle, but then carves out a number of important exceptions to that principle. When the suits are allowed, some special rules apply, as for service of process.

The enactment of the FSIA adopted into federal legislation the so-called restrictive theory of immunity which has long been embraced by the State Department and enjoys growing international acceptance. Under this principle, states retain immunity to suit for their sovereign or public acts, but not for their private or commercial activities. The principle of absolute immunity, reflected in the phrase "the King can do no wrong," is no longer tenable, particularly given the deep involvement of governments and their owned companies in commerce, including such key industries as airlines, steel-making, and banking.

The FSIA exceptions to immunity include cases in which the foreign government has waived its immunity, or has committed certain torts within the US or has engaged in commercial activity having a substantial nexus with the US. The exception for suits based on the foreign government's commercial activity at 28 U.S.C. 1605(a)(2) is of primary significance in the context of antitrust litigation. The principal question is whether the government is acting as a regulator of the market or as a private player within it. Accordingly, under the FSIA, whether certain activity is sovereign or commercial is determined according to the *nature* of the activity rather than its *purpose*. For example, a government owned steel company could not successfully argue that its participation in an international sales cartel was immune because the company was seeking to maximize the use of public funds. The price fixing would be commercial in nature and hence subject to challenge in a proper case.

The FSIA defines a "foreign state" to include a political subdivision of a foreign state or an agency or instrumentality of a foreign state. This definition includes state-owned corporations so long as the foreign state itself owns a majority of the corporation's shares. We have noted the recurring antitrust litigation in the US against the OPEC nations based on their agreeing with each other to control oil production quotas. Is this sovereign or commercial activity, the management of natural resources or simply a price boosting mechanism? The Ninth Circuit did not decide this issue and was content to dismiss the case under the act of state doctrine.

A suit against a foreign state or one of its entities which relies on the FSIA's commercial activity exception to immunity must satisfy one of the criteria set out in Section 1605(a)(2) ensuring that the commercial activity in question has a sufficient nexus with the US. Under that provision, the action may be brought if it is based on (a) a commercial activity carried on in the US by the foreign state, or (b) an act performed in the US in connection with a commercial activity of the foreign state elsewhere, or (c) an act outside the territory of the US in connection with a commercial activity of the foreign state elsewhere and that act causes a "direct effect" in the US. The Supreme Court has described a direct effect as one which follows as an immediate consequence of the defendant's activity.

In a 2015 case, *OBB Personenverkehr AG v. Sachs*, a California resident who had purchased a Eurail pass on the Internet from a US travel agent fell onto the tracks while in a train station in Austria. She sued OBB, the Austrian state-owned railway, in the US on various theories of fault. The Ninth Circuit ruled that the commercial activity exception to the FSIA applied because the plaintiff's purchase of the rail pass in Massachusetts satisfied the requirement that the commercial activity sued on take place in the US. The Supreme Court disagreed, reasoning that the alleged wrongful conduct and dangerous conditions sued upon took place in Austria, thereby making the foundation of the suit based in Austria.

There have been many antitrust cases brought in the US against companies which are owned by foreign governments. Since Sherman Act application requires a direct effect on US commerce and the cases have been brought against conduct which is commercial in nature, the FSIA's test in this regard has not created significant additional issues.

CHAPTER 4
US Law Enforcement Procedure

§4.01 PROCEDURAL REQUIREMENTS

In the previous Chapter we considered the applicability of the US antitrust laws to activities carried on outside of the US. Our focus was subject matter jurisdiction, in the sense of jurisdiction to prescribe the law to govern particular activity or conduct. We did not address the rules setting forth the circumstances and the manner in which individuals and corporations may be brought before the US courts to respond to US government or private claims that they have infringed antitrust or other federal laws. These are equally critical concerns. Under US law, before the court in which a case has been filed can properly adjudicate the case and enter judgment, it must be established either that the court has personal jurisdiction over the parties before it or else that they have "waived" this defense. The Supreme Court has often declared that the doctrine of personal jurisdiction is one of constitutional dimension in US law. The constitutional notions of fair play and "due process" contemplate that there exist a sufficient nexus between the court and the "person" of the individual or corporate defendant who has been haled into that court by the plaintiff.

In addition to considering the subject of personal jurisdiction, this Chapter discusses the rules for bringing the parties before the appropriate court, including service of process and venue. As we proceed, we shall look into the extent to which investigation and discovery in furtherance of a US antitrust case may be successfully directed against persons and documents located abroad. We will also examine the extent to which US antitrust judgments against foreign parties can, once obtained, be enforced against the person and property of foreign defendants.

A discussion of how cases and parties are brought before the US courts must begin, however, with a discussion of yet another aspect of that potentially confusing subject, subject matter jurisdiction. Here we are not referring, as we were earlier, to the territorial scope of the activities to which Congress intended the antitrust laws to apply. In this Chapter on procedure, when discussing subject matter jurisdiction, we are concerned with the allocation of responsibility among the various courts in the US to entertain particular types of disputes.

§4.02 SUBJECT MATTER JURISDICTION OF THE FEDERAL COURTS

Article III of the US Constitution is the source of the nation's federal judicial power. It establishes the Supreme Court, provides for such "inferior" courts as Congress may ordain, and further provides that the judicial power of the US:

> shall extend to all Cases, in Law and Equity, arising under this Constitution, the Laws of the United States, and Treaties made, or which shall be made, under their Authority, — to all Cases affecting Ambassadors, other public Ministers and Consuls; — to all Cases of admiralty and maritime Jurisdiction; — to Controversies to which the United States shall be a Party; and- to Controversies between two or more States; — between a State and Citizens of another State; — between Citizens of different States; — between Citizens of the same State claiming Lands under Grants of different States, and between a State, or the Citizens thereof, and foreign States, Citizens, or Subjects. [Art. III, Sec. 2]

Among the "inferior" courts established by Congress are the US district courts, which are located in the judicial districts designated within each of the states and non-state territories of the US including the District of Columbia and Puerto Rico. Some of the larger states have more than one district and federal district court. The statutes enacted by Congress to assign subject matter jurisdiction are primarily compiled in Title 28 of the United States Code ("U.S.C."), known as the Judicial Code. With regard to civil litigation, the district courts are given original jurisdiction over, among other things, federal question cases (28 U.S.C. § 1331), diversity of citizenship cases (28 U.S.C. § 1332), actions against foreign states (28 U.S.C. § 1330) and cases "arising under any Act of Congress regulating commerce or protecting trade and commerce against restraints and monopolies." (28 U.S.C. § 1337). On the criminal litigation side, Title 18 of the U.S.C., entitled "Crimes and Criminal Procedure," vests the district courts with original jurisdiction of all offenses against the laws of the US. (18 U.S.C. § 3231).

The federal district courts are, accordingly, the trial courts for actions brought by the Department of Justice or private parties to enforce the federal antitrust laws. These courts are empowered to enjoin violations of the law. They may also award damages, attorneys' fees and other costs in private treble damage suits filed by persons who have been injured "by reason of anything forbidden in the antitrust laws," in the words of Section 4 of the Clayton Act. In criminal cases, the courts may impose fines and prison sentences.

Federal subject matter jurisdiction is thus fixed by the Congress and must be proper under the applicable statute whatever the desire of the parties. By contrast, the requirements that the court must have personal jurisdiction over the parties and that the venue must be proper are personal privileges and can be waived by the parties, either expressly or else simply by a failure to raise them in a timely way as defenses.

§4.03 PERSONAL JURISDICTION

Under US law, the court in which a case has been filed is only authorized to hear the suit and to move it ahead to a possible judgment against the defendant's person or the defendant's assets if the court has jurisdiction over the "person" of the defendant(s) under an accepted legal theory. This means, for example, that, in the antitrust context, personal jurisdiction is not obtained simply because the defendant's conduct has allegedly violated the US antitrust laws. Before the court can proceed to the merits of the case, it must be shown by the plaintiff that there exists an adequate "nexus" between the territory in which the court sits and the defendant's person (or that the defendant has waived the defense). This is not a universal concept internationally, but a requirement of US law that has its underpinnings in the US Constitution.

[A] Due Process of Law and Minimum Contacts

In the US, the jurisprudence relating to personal jurisdiction has been shaped by mandates derived by the Supreme Court from the 5th and 14th Amendments to the federal Constitution. The 5th Amendment, one component of the Constitution's Bill of Rights which protects individual rights from infringement by the federal government, provides that no "person" shall be "deprived of life, liberty, or property, without due process of law." The 14th Amendment, aimed at curbing arbitrary action by state governments, provides that no US state shall "deprive any person of life, liberty, or property, without due process of law ... ." The phrase "due process of law," while inherently vague, has been given significant content over the years by the federal courts, so as to confer on "persons" a broad array of both substantive and procedural rights against arbitrary and unjustified action by government. Corporations, as well as individuals, have been held to be "persons" entitled to due process of law so far as judicial jurisdiction is concerned. Foreign defendants also have generally been considered entitled to constitutional due process protection with respect to the assertion by the US courts of personal jurisdiction over them.

The original US concept of judicial jurisdiction had strong roots in international law notions linking the state's power to territoriality. Joseph Story's influential *Commentaries on the Conflict of Laws* emphasized the principle that, "... no sovereignty can extend its process beyond its own territorial limits, to subject either persons or property to its judicial decisions." Indeed, for many years beginning in 1877, the seminal decision by the Supreme Court in *Pennoyer v. Neff* tied the concept of judicial jurisdiction to strict territorial presence. The realities presented by the nation's rapidly growing interstate and international commerce and the rise to business dominance of the corporation—a legal fiction whose activities were far-reaching and diffuse—inevitably caused the territorial standard for assertion of jurisdiction to weaken and require adjustment. The US states tried to find ways, through judicial proceedings and otherwise, to control the activities of corporations who were headquartered outside the state but affecting the lives of the state's citizens. These regulatory attempts, in turn, raised a variety of constitutional questions. One important issue involved the interplay between the state's assertion of judicial jurisdiction, i.e., personal jurisdiction, over the person and the person's entitlement to due process of law.

Pennoyer's territorial approach to judicial jurisdiction was definitively altered by the Supreme Court in 1945 in the case of *International Shoe Co. v. Washington*. The International Shoe Co. had no offices in the State of Washington and it entered into no contracts there, but it did maintain a dozen commissioned salesmen in the state to solicit orders for its products. The Supreme Court held that this level of business activity within the state was sufficient to satisfy the constitutional "minimum contacts" test, allowing the State of Washington to subject International Shoe to the jurisdiction of its courts. The Court held that "... due process requires only that in order to subject a defendant to a judgment *in personam*, if he be not within the territory of the forum, he have certain minimum contacts with it such that the maintenance of the suit does not offend 'traditional notions of fair play and substantial justice.'"

The "minimum contacts" test left almost as much for *ad hoc* decision making as had the need to define "due process" itself. In a subsequent opinion in *Hanson v. Denckla* in 1958, the Supreme Court explained that a necessary part of the test was that it be shown that the defendant had deliberately engaged in activities that brought about contacts with the forum. The contacts could not be happenstance. The Constitution requires, the Court said, "some act by which the defendant purposefully avails itself of the privilege of conducting activities within the forum state, thus invoking the benefits and protection of its laws."

In 1980, in *World-Wide Volkswagen Corp. v. Woodson*, the Court held that a defendant's foreseeability of forum contacts was not the equivalent of its purposeful availment of the forum. In that case the plaintiffs had purchased a new car in New York State and, while on a trip in the western states, were involved in an accident in Oklahoma. They sued the New York distributor and retail dealer of their car in the Oklahoma state courts, claiming that their injury had been caused by the defective design of the car's gas tank. The US Supreme Court reversed the Oklahoma courts' sustaining of state court jurisdiction, finding a total absence of purposeful contacts in Oklahoma on the part of the defendants. The Court articulated a two pronged due process test: (1) there must be purposefully created minimum contacts between the defendants and the forum, and (2) jurisdiction cannot be exercised unless it is "reasonable."

In 1985, the Court again applied the two prong test in a major decision, *Burger King v. Rudzewicz*. The reasonableness test thus became part of the standard. For some of the justices of the Supreme Court, this prong represented the more important part of the test, with the question of "purposeful availment" of little concern. To this mix of factors was added a proposed "stream of commerce" test, and the entire concoction came up for consideration in the *Asahi Metal Industries Co. v. Superior Court* case in 1987, involving an international setting.

Asahi began with a product liability suit filed in the California state courts by an injured motorcyclist against the Taiwanese manufacturer of the tube for the rear tire. The latter filed a cross-complaint against Asahi, the Japanese manufacturer of the tube's valve assembly. The plaintiff settled his case, leaving only the Taiwanese company's suit against Asahi for disposition. Asahi's tire valve assemblies had originally been shipped from Japan to Taiwan before being incorporated into the tire tubes, and the question was whether the California courts had personal jurisdiction over Asahi in this factual context. The Supreme Court's membership expressed a number of differing viewpoints on the issue. Eight of the nine justices determined that California's assertion of jurisdiction over the Japanese defendant would be unreasonable, in light of both the burden which Asahi would have to assume in defending itself in a foreign legal system and California's diminished interest in the dispute.

In addition, four justices joined in an opinion holding that Asahi's likely awareness that the stream of commerce might carry its product into California did not constitute the requisite "purposeful availment" of the privilege of conducting activity in California. Four other justices reasoned that Asahi's placing its products into the international stream of commerce knowing that they were regularly sold in the forum was sufficient purposeful conduct.

A number of lower court decisions have manifested confusion, or at least disharmony, over the extent to which "purposeful availment," and hence minimum contacts, can be established by reliance on the stream of commerce theory. For example, in a 2012 case, *Carrier Corp. v. Outokumpu Oyj*, the Court of Appeals for the Sixth Circuit held that personal jurisdiction could be established by the allegation that the defendants' unlawful conduct was "expressly aimed" at the plaintiff in the US.

In any given case, it is necessary to distinguish between two types of personal jurisdiction for purposes of the due process analysis, "general" jurisdiction and "specific" jurisdiction. Where the defendant has continuous and systematic activities within the forum, then the court is deemed constitutionally entitled to assert a general personal jurisdiction extending to the adjudication of all claims against the defendant. On the other hand, where the defendant has limited contacts with the forum, those contacts may be sufficient to permit the forum court to assert jurisdiction over the defendant from a due process viewpoint, but it will be only a specific or limited jurisdiction allowing adjudication of claims related to the activities conducted within the forum.

Recent Supreme Court decisions have limited the circumstances in which general personal jurisdiction can be invoked to haul foreign corporations into US courts for acts committed abroad. In *Goodyear Dunlop Tires Operations, S.A. v. Brown*, a 2011 decision, the Court stated that sales of a limited number of goods by foreign tire manufacturers in a US state did not subject those firms to general personal jurisdiction in that state with respect to the deaths of state residents that occurred abroad. The Court has taken the same approach in cases in which a foreign plaintiff sued a foreign defendant based on conduct that occurred in a foreign country. *Daimler AG v. Bauman et al.*, a 2014 case, involved a suit by Argentinean residents against a German multinational for acts done doing Argentina's "Dirty War." The Supreme Court held that the district court lacked personal jurisdiction because Daimler's US subsidiary's contacts with California were not significant enough to justify the exercise of general jurisdiction. The Court reasoned that merely having substantial sales in a forum is not sufficient to justify the exercise of general jurisdiction, which requires that a company's contacts with the state are so "continuous and systematic as to render it essentially at home in" that state. This poses a high standard to meet for general jurisdiction in most cases.

Antitrust law, in any event, has its own rules which differ in some respects and on which we must focus here. To understand the issues raised, it is necessary, first, to introduce the concepts of "venue" and of service of process. Whereas the issue of personal jurisdiction concerns the court's inherent power to hear a case against a defendant, the concept of venue has reference to the particular geographic location in which the case may be brought and determined pursuant to the statutes. The venue provisions enacted by Congress identify the judicial district (i.e., the particular US federal district court) in which a type of case may be heard. An important purpose of these venue provisions is to protect the defendant from being compelled arbitrarily to defend a suit in an inconvenient forum chosen by the plaintiff. The subject of how process is to be served on defendants is also addressed in the statutes.

The general venue and service of process provisions are found in 28 U.S.C. § 1391, which was last amended in 2011. These provisions specify where civil actions may be brought, and they can apply to antitrust as well as other civil cases. In addition, however, there are special rules specifically applicable to federal antitrust cases. Section 12 of the Clayton Act provides: "Any suit, action or proceeding under the antitrust laws against a corporation may be brought not only in the judicial district whereof it is an inhabitant, but also in any district wherein it may be found or transacts business; and all process in such cases may be served in the district of which it is an inhabitant, or wherever it may be found." Also, Section 4 of the Clayton Act provides for treble damage suits in any district court of the US "in the district in which the defendant resides or is found or has an agent ... ." These Clayton Act provisions can be read as alluding to personal jurisdiction, venue and service of process in antitrust cases against corporations. Of course, the personal jurisdiction aspects must be read and applied so as to be consistent with due process, constitutional principles.

A corporation is an "inhabitant" of the jurisdiction under whose laws it is incorporated. A corporation is "found" where it has "presence" and continuous local activities in the district. Being "found" in a district is generally equated with "doing business" there, which requires greater contacts than does "transacting business." In the 1927 *Eastman Kodak* case, the Supreme Court differentiated between the terms "found" and "transacts business" on the ground that the latter was a lesser test of presence within the district than "found." In any event, the carrying on of some substantial business in the district is needed for a corporation to be "found" there.

Unfortunately, the fact that the language of Section 12, in effect, alludes to three separate prerequisites for an antitrust lawsuit—venue, service of process, and personal jurisdiction—has caused confusion in some cases. In particular, the appellate courts have not agreed on whether the express venue provision of Section 12 must be satisfied for the broad service of process and personal jurisdiction principles of the provision to be applicable. It is not useful in this primer to trace in any detail the tortuous flow of the case law on this issue, so we will limit ourselves to discussing a 2013 Seventh Circuit Court of Appeals decision which sought to provide the correct answer to this puzzle.

In *KM Enterp. Inc. v. Global Traffic Tech, Inc.*, the plaintiff sued in the Southern District of Illinois, under the Sherman and Clayton Acts, two Delaware corporate entities which were headquartered in Minnesota. The district court dismissed the suit for improper venue, reasoning that the defendants did not reside in the district and that none of the events at issue in the suit took place in the district. Therefore, according to the district court, the defendants' contacts with the Illinois district were insufficient to support venue under the general venue statute, Section 1391 of Title 28. On appeal, the plaintiff argued that venue was proper under Section 1391 and, moreover, was also proper under Section 12 of the Clayton Act which, as we have noted, provides special rules for venue and service of process in antitrust actions against corporations.

The Seventh Circuit put the key issue this way: "... if a plaintiff chooses to take advantage of Section 12's nationwide service-of-process provision (and thus in effect rely on nationwide personal jurisdiction) must she then establish venue under Section 12 as well, or may she mix and match, relying on the Clayton Act for personal jurisdiction and Section 1391 for venue?" i.e., it must be decided "whether Section 12 is a package deal or an a la carte menu ... " and the answer matters because "if a plaintiff could combine Section 12 service of process with Section 1391 venue, it could drag an alien into court anywhere in the United States .... " The court (per Judge Wood) notes that the federal appellate circuits and scholarly opinion are both split over whether Section 12's clauses are an integrated whole or may be "decoupled."

After a lengthy analysis, the Seventh Circuit's opinion followed the view taken by the Second and District of Columbia Circuits in holding that Section 12's clauses are linked together and must be read as a "package deal." "To avail oneself of the privilege of nationwide service of process, a plaintiff must satisfy the venue provision of Section 12's first clause," said the appellate court. The court therefore affirmed the district court's dismissal of the case for improper venue.

As a practical matter, antitrust lawsuits filed in the US against foreign corporations who are carrying on any substantial business in the US seldom fail to meet the due process test of personal jurisdiction. Even if the foreign company maintains no office, warehouse, bank account or staff in the US market on a regular basis, it will often send salesmen or other representatives to meet with its US customers, and there tends to be a regular flow of product from the company to those customers. The company will usually know precisely what markets it is serving and will seldom, if ever, simply be releasing its product into an undifferentiated stream of commerce.

The arrival of the electronic era has created a new context for application of the concept of personal jurisdiction. The US courts have often held, as did the D.C. Circuit's decision in 2000 in *GTE New Media Services Inc. v. Bellsouth Corp. et al.*, that a firm's maintenance of a website on the Internet, which can be accessed from the forum, is not by itself sufficient conduct directed at the forum to give the latter's courts personal jurisdiction over the firm. If the website is significantly "interactive," to the extent that customers regularly make on-line purchases on it, the result may well be different. One federal court decision has held that the defendant's sending of sixty emails criticizing the plaintiff to individuals with Massachusetts addresses constituted sufficient contact designed to purposefully avail defendant of the benefits—and hence the jurisdiction—of that forum.

The prime point to be taken away from all these procedural conundrums is that the Department of Justice and the Federal Trade Commission have stated that they will bring suit against a party only if they conclude that personal jurisdiction exists under the due process clause of the US Constitution. As we have noted, the Constitution requires that the defendant have affiliating or minimum contacts with the US, such that the proceeding comport with "fair play and substantial justice."

[B] Corporate Affiliation and Agency Relationships

As we mentioned earlier, the Supreme Court held in the *Copperweld* case that a corporation cannot be guilty of conspiring illegally with its wholly owned subsidiaries. This ruling, which is based on understandable policy reasons, represents one of the few exceptions to the general legal principle that the separate identity of corporations will be given effect, even if those corporations are linked in a close corporate family of common ownership and control. In keeping with that general principle, a parent corporation and even those of its subsidiaries that the parent owns 100% will normally be treated as separate entities for purposes of assessing whether a US court has personal jurisdiction over one or the other of the two corporations. That is, one corporation's contacts with the forum will not normally be attributed to the other related corporation. This general rule also has an exception, however, for the situation where the corporate separateness is so disregarded within the corporate group itself that one corporate family member can be viewed as the *alter ego* of the other. Most often, this finding of an *alter ego* relationship occurs when a corporate parent has exercised control over the operations of a subsidiary corporation to such a great degree that the legal distinctions between the two entities are no longer being observed.

The Supreme Court's decision in *United States v. Scophony Corp. of America* in 1948 was a landmark case in the antitrust field on the issue of jurisdiction over corporations. The Court held that continued supervision maintained in New York by a British corporation over a US company that it had formed and wholly owned was a basis for asserting US personal jurisdiction over the parent. Scophony Ltd. ("British Scophony") engaged in a series of patent licensing arrangements with three American corporations, including one which it controlled, Scophony of America. The patent licensing arrangements had territorial and other restrictions that caused the US Government to charge that British Scophony, American Scophony, and others were violating the Sherman Act. The Court concluded that British Scophony was "found" in the Southern District of New York, within the meaning of Section 12 of the Clayton Act, inasmuch as, through key officials in New York, it exercised a continuing supervision over and intervention in the affairs of the American company.

The *alter ego* test is normally one of assessing the degree of control exerted by the parent company over the business operations of the subsidiary. For example, if a foreign parent owns all of the stock of its US subsidiary, places its own personnel as a majority of the subsidiary's officers and directors, controls the subsidiary's pricing and preapproves the latter's customers, it is very likely that the subsidiary's US contacts will be attributable to the parent corporation for purposes of finding that the US courts may assert personal jurisdiction over the parent for antitrust or other US law violations.

Chapter 4: US Law Enforcement Procedure §4.03[B]

It was held in the 1955 *Swiss Watchmakers* case that "where the substance of corporate independence is not preserved and the subsidiary acts as an agent of the parent, this corporate separation has been found without significance." In that case, the Switzerland Information Center, located in New York was a jointly owned subsidiary of two of the alien defendants, FH and Ebauches. Having found that the Information Center was a "mere adjunct of its parent," the court regarded the subsidiary's acts in the New York district as those of the parents. The court seemed particularly impressed by the fact that the subsidiary, the Information Center, had "no independent business of its own." On the basis of this reasoning, the court ruled that the parents were "found" in the New York district, and that personal jurisdiction over them had been obtained by service upon their subsidiary under Section 12 of the Clayton Act.

Conversely, it is possible to attain US jurisdiction and service of process over the foreign-based subsidiaries of US firms, although the subsidiaries may have no property or activities in the US. In *Swiss Watchmakers*, wholly owned foreign subsidiaries were thus reached through their American parents. The parents had permitted the subsidiaries to become parties to a Collective Convention in Switzerland under which anticompetitive practices were engaged in, and the parents had acquiesced in this program. The parents were considered in this way to have voluntarily subjected themselves to the "dominance" of their subsidiaries as to those anticompetitive practices. The court held on that basis that it had personal jurisdiction over the foreign subsidiaries by the effecting of service upon the American parents.

Scophony and *Swiss Watchmakers* can be compared to the factual situation in *O.S.C. Corp. & O.S.C. Corp. of California v. Toshiba America Inc. & Tokyo Shibaura Electric Co.Ltd.*, where the Court of Appeals for the Ninth Circuit affirmed a lower court's holding that a Japanese company lacked sufficient minimum contacts with the district in which it was sued. The court rejected the contention that Tokyo Shibaura, the corporate parent, "transacted business" in Los Angeles through its subsidiary because there was no contention that the corporate separateness between parent and subsidiary should be pierced and because Tokyo Shibaura itself had no personnel, property, bank account or other business links in California.

In *Hoffman Motors Corp. v. Alfa Romeo, S.p.A., et al.*, the court made findings on the propriety of venue and service of process that are also an instructive application of the "minimum contacts" test that must be made for purposes of determining whether personal jurisdiction exists over a non-US corporation, in this case Alfa Romeo, S.p.A.:

> The activities of S.p.A. employees with regard to sales, promotion and warranties alone seem sufficient to meet the relatively minimal contacts necessary to constitute transacting of business ... .But in addition to its direct activities S.p.A. has transacted business through Alfa Inc., its New York subsidiary. Alfa Inc. was an instrumentality used by its foreign parent to perform essential local operations. The parent completely controlled the subsidiary, setting its policies in Italy, appointing its own officers and employees as directors, officers and employees of the subsidiary and paying their salaries. Under such circumstances, the foreign corporate parent will not be permitted to hide behind its local instrumentality.

The above discussion addresses the situation in which a control relationship between corporations has been exercised in such a manner as to ignore the corporate separateness of the entities. The court reasons that the actions of one corporate family member can be attributed to another family member for purposes of claiming personal jurisdiction over the latter. It should be noted that the same result can be reached by a court on "agency" principles, even in situations where there is no corporate relationship involved. Under agency law, where one party—the agent—does not act independently but acts on behalf of and subject to the full control of another party—the principal—the principal is liable for the agent's actions. A foreign-based corporation or individual can, therefore, be held subject to US court personal jurisdiction by reason of its control over persons acting as its business agents in the US.

[C] Service of Process

[1] The Federal Rules

We discussed above the possibility of worldwide service of process in antitrust cases against corporations under Section 12 of the Clayton Act. Service of process in any federal case must be done in conformity with the applicable rules. The Supreme Court held in *Omni Capital International v. Rudolf Wolff & Co.* that, before "a federal court may exercise personal jurisdiction over a defendant, the procedural requirement of service of summons must be satisfied ... ." Accordingly, service of the requisite notice upon a party informing it that it is a defendant in civil or criminal litigation in the US courts is an element of constitutional due process. The notice or "process" normally consists of a complaint and a summons emanating from the court. The procedures relating to service of process in the federal courts are governed by the Federal Rules of Criminal Procedure ("F.R.Crim.P.") and the Federal Rules of Civil Procedure ("F.R.C.P.").

F.R.Crim.P. 3 describes the complaint as a written statement of the essential facts constituting the offense charged. Under F.R.Crim.R. 4, the attorney for the government determines whether a warrant should issue for the arrest of the defendant or whether a summons directing the defendant to appear in court at a stated time and place is sufficient. The warrant may be executed or the summons served at any place within the jurisdiction of the US or anywhere else a federal statute authorizes an arrest.

F.R.C.P. 4 governs service of process in civil cases. It makes the plaintiff responsible for the service of the summons and complaint on the defendant. The plaintiff may ask the defendant to waive the service of a summons. If "a defendant located within the United States fails, without good cause, to sign and return a waiver requested by a plaintiff located within the United States to comply with a request for waiver made by a plaintiff located within the United States, the court must impose on the defendant (A) the expenses later incurred in making service; and (B) the reasonable expenses, including attorney's fees, of any motion required to collect those service expenses." (at Rule 4(d)(2))

Chapter 4: US Law Enforcement Procedure §4.03[C]

As we have seen, in antitrust cases, reference must also be made to Section 12 of the Clayton Act, which provides that process may be served on a corporation in the district of which the corporation is an inhabitant or wherever it may be found.

Accordingly, F.R.C.P. 4 provides the mechanics for achieving proper service in a federal civil case, subject to the minimum contacts test for personal jurisdiction over the defendant being met. Under Rule 4(e), an individual may be served within a judicial district of the US pursuant to state law, or by personal delivery, by delivery to an agent, or else by leaving copies of the documents at the individual's usual place of abode with a person of suitable age and discretion. Under Rule 4(f), unless federal law provides otherwise, an individual may be served at a place not within any judicial district of the US:

> (1) by any internationally agreed means that is reasonably calculated to give notice, such as those authorized by the Hague Convention on the Service Abroad of Judicial and Extrajudicial Documents; (2) if there is no internationally agreed means, or if an international agreement allows but does not specify other means, by a method that is reasonably calculated to give notice: (A) as prescribed by the foreign country's law for service in that country in an action in its courts of general jurisdiction; (B) as the foreign authority directs in response to a letter rogatory or letter of request; or (C) unless prohibited by the foreign country's law by (i) delivering a copy of the summons and of the complaint to the individual personally; or (ii) using any form of mail that the clerk addresses and sends to the individual and that requires a signed receipt; or (3) by other means not prohibited by international agreement, as the court orders.

F.R.C.P. 4(h) provides for service of process upon foreign or domestic corporations, partnerships and other unincorporated associations to be made as follows:

> (h) ... Unless federal law provides otherwise or the defendant's waiver has been filed, a domestic or foreign corporation, or a partnership or other unincorporated association that is subject to suit under a common name must be served: (1) in a judicial district of the United States (A) in the manner prescribed for individuals by Rule 4 (e) (1) for serving an individual; or (B) by delivering a copy of the summons and of the complaint to an officer, a managing or general agent, or any other agent authorized by appointment or by law to receive service of process and—if the agent is one authorized by statute and the statute so requires—by also mailing a copy of each to the defendant; or (2) at a place not within any judicial district of the United States in any manner prescribed for by Rule 4 (f) for serving an individual, except personal delivery under (f) (2)(C)(i).

The Federal Rules of Civil Procedure thus provide a number of modes for making service of US judicial process overseas. It should be noted that such overseas service will normally be successful only if the means utilized are pursuant to an international agreement of the US or are prescribed by foreign law or are undertaken with the assistance of a foreign authority or, at least, are not prohibited by foreign law. Indeed, the 1993 amendments to the Federal Rules dealing with service of process, which are reflected in the above-quoted language, specifically sought to provide greater deference generally to foreign law. Thus, the pertinent provisions of the F.R.C.P. are designed to comply with notions of international comity and to avoid serving US process abroad within sovereign nations in ways that might offend that sovereignty. For the lawyer arranging service abroad, there are also some important practical reasons for punctilious adherence to the provisions of Rule 4. If the service abroad is flawed, then personal jurisdiction over the foreign defendant will likely be found lacking in the US case. Moreover, even if the US court accepts the flawed service of process, any ensuing judgment may be deemed unenforceable on the basis of the improper service if and when the judgment is presented to a foreign court for enforcement.

The cases demonstrate the often complicated nature of assuring proper service abroad. In the private damage case under the Sherman Act of *Dee-K Enterprises Inc. v. Heveafil Sdn. Bhd.*, the clerk of the federal district court had caused service of process to be made on the Indonesian and Malaysian corporate defendants in their respective countries by using a courier service. Plaintiffs argued that this was proper service under F.R.C.P. 4(f)(2)(C)(ii), which authorized service by any form of mail requiring a signed receipt unless prohibited by the law of the foreign country. The defendants, in urging that the provision was not satisfied, submitted the opinions of Indonesian and Malaysian counsel stating that service by courier was not effective service under the laws of those countries. The district court upheld the service as valid, however, on the ground that the opinions did not demonstrate that service by courier was "prohibited" by the national laws. On the other hand, some other courts have reasoned that delivery by a courier service is not "mail" for purposes of the Rule.

In a case decided by the Ninth Circuit in 2002, *Rio Properties, Inc. v. Rio Int'l Interlink*, the Court of Appeals held that the district court had not abused its discretion by ordering service by email upon a corporation based in Costa Rica. The court did not discuss Costa Rican law, and the decision to authorize such service was based on the determination that the defendant had a viable presence and business in the US and had evaded attempts to make physical personal service upon it.

Efforts to serve OPEC, the oil cartel, with a US lawsuit have been mounted from time to time. A decision of the Court of Appeals for the Tenth Circuit in 2003 upheld, on service of process grounds, the dismissal of yet another suit brought against the group of nations. *Prewitt Enterprises, Inc. v. Organization of Petroleum Exporting Countries* was brought as a class action on behalf of purchasers of refined petroleum products in the US, complaining that OPEC's price fixing on production and export of crude oil violated § 1 of the Sherman Act. The district court clerk in that case mailed the plaintiff's summons and complaint to OPEC at its headquarters in Vienna, Austria. The pleadings were signed for and stamped "received" by OPEC's personnel in Vienna. When OPEC failed to respond, the district court certified a class of purchasers, found the existence of a price fixing conspiracy involving OPEC, entered a default judgment against the latter, and determined that OPEC should be enjoined from entering into or enforcing any further oil price fixing agreements for a period of twelve months. At this point, OPEC appeared in the case and filed a motion to dismiss the complaint on various grounds, including insufficient service of process. The district court then dismissed the case on the basis that plaintiff had failed to make proper service under the Federal Rules.

The Court of Appeals affirmed this ruling. The court's analysis first noted that OPEC should be viewed as an unincorporated association, because, "[w]hile its members are sovereign nation states rather than private individuals, OPEC is not a governmental unit or subdivision ... ." Thus, the special rules pertaining to service of process under the Foreign Sovereign Immunities Act and under the International Organizations Immunities Act were inapplicable in this case. The court next pointed out that, under F.R.C.P. 4(h), an unincorporated association headquartered outside of the US may be served in any manner authorized under F.R.C.P. 4(f) for individuals except for personal delivery. As to F.R.C.P. 4(f)(1), the parties agreed that there was no international agreement that stipulated the appropriate means of service, since Austria was not a party to the Hague Service Convention (discussed below). That left the analysis to be done under F.R.C.P. 4(f)(2).

Observing that Prewitt had originally chosen to attempt service of process on OPEC under F.R.C.P. 4(f)(C)(ii), the Court of Appeals held that, "[b]ased on the evidence presented, the district court correctly found that service on OPEC was prohibited by the law of Austria." The court pointed out, in this connection, that the Austrian/OPEC Headquarters Agreement, which had been enacted into law by the Austrian Parliament, specifically forbade service of legal process in the headquarters seat except with the express consent of OPEC's Secretary General. Moreover, even though OPEC had received actual notice of the filing of the suit, the service of process was ineffective because it was not in an authorized mode and hence was not sufficient to permit personal jurisdiction under the US Constitution. Finally, the Court of Appeals found no abuse of discretion in the district court's refusal to order service of process pursuant to F.R.C.P. 4(f)(3), which provides that service may be effected "by other means not prohibited by international agreement as may be directed by the court." Indeed, said the court, it would have been an abuse of discretion for the court to have permitted under 4(f)(3) a form of service of process specifically barred under 4(f)(2) where prohibited by the foreign country.

Undaunted by this history, a group called Freedom Watch, Inc. attempted to launch yet another suit against OPEC in 2012, alleging violations of the Sherman and Clayton Acts. The district court dismissed the complaint for insufficient service of process. It held that Freedom Watch had failed to effectuate valid service of process on OPEC, and it declined to authorize service through alternative means pursuant to F.R.C.P. 4(f)(3). That provision gives the court authority to allow service by any other means not prohibited by international agreement. Freedom Watch had attempted valid service by making hand delivery on OPEC's headquarters in Austria where an individual ostensibly accepted it, and also by sending a copy of the documents to OPEC's headquarters via Austrian mail. OPEC successfully argued in the district court that these efforts did not amount to sufficient process.

On appeal, the US Court of Appeals for the District of Columbia Circuit in 2014 remanded the case, *Freedom Watch, Inc. v. OPEC*, to the district court for further proceedings. Citing the *Prewitt* case as persuasive, the appellate court agreed that the attempted service was invalid. Since OPEC is an intergovernmental organization whose members are foreign governments, the provisions of Rule 4(f) controlled to determine the sufficiency of the plaintiff's efforts to serve process. The court stated that there is no "internationally agreed means of service" here. Although Austria is a party to the Hague Convention on Civil Procedure, the US is not and, although the US is a party to the Hague Convention on the Service Abroad of Judicial and Extrajudicial

Documents, Austria is not. Moreover, in Austria, service of a complaint is a judicial act that may be exercised only by a court unless there is an international convention to the contrary and, indeed, Austrian law prohibits service of process on an international organization holding privileges and immunities under international law (which OPEC does) without the involvement of the Austrian Federal Ministry. In short, neither Rule 4(f)(1) or (2) authorized the service attempt made by the plaintiff.

F.R.C.P. 4(f)(3) allows service "by other means not prohibited by international agreement, as the court orders," but Freedom Watch had neither sought nor secured the district court's authorization to serve OPEC through personal delivery or Austrian mail. Accordingly, plaintiff had failed to make valid process here, which, said the appellate court, quoting *Omni Capital International*, is "[a]n elementary and fundamental requirement of due process." Moreover, the district court did not abuse its discretion in rejecting plaintiff's request for service on OPEC via email and fax since that would constitute a substantial affront to Austrian law.

However, the appellate court concluded, the district court had not adequately considered the possible applicability of F.R.C.P. 4(f)(3), an approach by which a number of courts have sanctioned service on the defendant's US counsel as an alternative means of service. This approach is possibly available even if the alternative means of service would violate foreign law. Accordingly, the appellate court remanded for the district court to exercise its discretion under F.R.C.P. 4(f)(3). One circuit judge dissented in part on the ground that he would simply affirm. Subsequently, in 2015, the district court put an end to the service effort by declining to authorize service through OPEC's US counsel. It reasoned that Freedom Watch had failed to rebut OPEC's argument that serving its US based counsel would be inappropriate because OPEC's headquarters agreement, considered an international agreement under US law, specifically prohibits service on the association without its consent. Under Rule 4, service may not occur by means that are prohibited by an international agreement.

[2] The Hague Service Convention

F.R.C.P. 4(f)(1) expressly authorizes the effecting of service abroad pursuant to an internationally agreed means, "such as those authorized by the Hague Convention on the Service Abroad of Judicial and Extrajudicial documents." ("the Hague Service Convention.") The Hague Service Convention was drafted under the auspices of the Hague Conference on Private International Law, for the purpose of establishing a liberal international regime for the transnational service of process. The US ratified the Convention in 1969, and some seventy nations are parties to the treaty. The Convention does not provide internationally harmonized grounds for transnational service. Rather, it creates a mechanism by which a plaintiff authorized to serve process under the laws of the country of suit can effectuate that service on a defendant abroad in an internationally acceptable manner.

The Hague Service Convention applies in all civil and commercial cases where there is occasion to transmit a judicial or extrajudicial document for service abroad. It thus can generally be utilized to serve complaints, summonses and other documents in

US civil antitrust cases. However, some foreign courts have determined, from time to time, that suits for treble damages are penal and hence outside of the scope of the Convention.

The Convention requires each contracting state to designate a "Central Authority" within its government administration. This Central Authority is charged with receiving service requests from other contracting states, arranging for service to be made by appropriate means, and arranging for return of proof of service to the requesting state. The Central Authority has no discretion to refuse to effect service, unless the request fails to comply with the Convention's formal requirements or if the request is an infringement of the receiving state's sovereignty or security.

The Convention also provides for alternative means of effecting service, without recourse to the Central Authority. As long as the receiving state has not stated its objection to service in this fashion, the service may be made through the requesting state's diplomatic or consular agents, or by sending the document by postal channels, or through "judicial officers or other competent persons," or pursuant to the internal law of the receiving state. Many of the contracting states have, in fact, objected to one or more of these alternative modes for effecting service by lodging reservations to the Convention. In addition, some of the contracting states require that any letter of request be accompanied by translations of the documents to be served.

A significant number of foreign states have objected to use of Article 10(a) of the Convention, which permits the "sending" of judicial documents by postal service directly to the defendant. There has been litigation on the issue of whether a state's nonobjection to the "sending" of documents by mail is the equivalent of its nonobjection to the documents being "served" by mail. Indeed, in 1989 the Japanese delegation to the Hague Conference on Private International Law declared that, while it had no objection to the use of postal channels for sending documents to persons in Japan, this nonobjection did not necessarily imply that the sending by such method would be considered valid service in Japan. Although use of postal channels may appear attractive because it is usually swift as compared to utilization of a Central Authority under the Hague Service Convention, the use of the mails may well create enforcement problems in some instances.

As we have discussed, under US law, service of judicial process may be effected on a foreign parent company by making service on a US corporate subsidiary where the latter is so closely controlled that it acts as an *alter ego* or agent of the parent. In *Volkswagenwerk AG v. Schlunk* the question was posed as to whether this form of service, made in the Illinois state courts on a German corporation, through its US subsidiary, was compatible with the Hague Service Convention. The Supreme Court recognized, in its 1988 decision in this case, that the Convention is intended to be exclusive, in the sense that it "pre-empts inconsistent methods of service prescribed by state law in all cases to which it applies." However, the Court reasoned, it is the law of the forum state that determines whether there is occasion for service abroad, stating that:

> In this case, the Illinois long-arm statute authorized Schlunk to serve [the German parent] by substituted service on [its US subsidiary], without sending documents

to Germany ... we conclude that this case does not present an occasion to transmit a judicial document for service abroad within the meaning of [the Convention.] Therefore the Hague Service Convention does not apply in this case.

As recently as May 22, 2017, the US Supreme Court confirmed in *Water Splash, Inc. v. Menon* that the Hague Service Convention does not prohibit service of process by mail even if there is no use of a Central Authority. The Court observed that service of process by mail is permissible if two conditions are met: first, that the receiving state has not objected to service by mail; and, second, that service by mail is authorized under otherwise applicable law.

§4.04 INVESTIGATION AND DISCOVERY

A US government or private litigant who is investigating or litigating an antitrust case involving transnational activity and/or foreign persons will generally desire access to documents located outside the US. The purpose of this inquiry is, initially, to determine whether a US antitrust violation has occurred and, subsequently, if there has been a violation, to use the information as evidence. For the same reasons, the testimony of foreign persons is often sought. This effort to obtain information, for pretrial or trial use, is broadly referred to in the US as "discovery."

If the foreign custodian of relevant documents or the potential foreign witness does not wish to cooperate, a number of potential problems are posed for the information seeker. As we shall see, US compulsory process does not extend abroad except in certain limited cases. Foreign legal process may be successfully engaged in some instances to obtain the needed information, but, in other instances, the foreign legal system may instead be mobilized by the potential defendant or its government to obstruct the transnational discovery, as in the case of blocking legislation. Indeed, citing grounds of sovereignty, some countries have prohibitions against the use of foreign legal process on their soil even if the parties targeted are willing to participate voluntarily. Admittedly, there is an important multilateral treaty affecting transnational discovery to which the US is a party, the Hague Evidence Convention. However, it too has its inherent limitations, particularly with respect to pretrial discovery. We shall review the procedures available for investigation and discovery in antitrust cases, with a particular focus on the special problems that may arise in the transnational setting.

[A] Action by the Justice Department

As we have previously discussed, liability under the Sherman Act may be either criminal or civil. Under the Clayton Act, (with the exception of a few relatively obscure sections) only civil suits may be brought. As noted, the Department of Justice, through its Antitrust Division, often enforces the antitrust laws through civil, as well as criminal suits

Once preliminary information about possible ongoing unlawful activity has been gathered, a decision is made by the Antitrust Division as to whether a more far reaching scrutiny is appropriate. If so, the additional data needed may be sought either on a voluntary basis or through use of compulsory process. Often the companies and individuals involved decide to cooperate voluntarily with the government investigators, who may include officials from the Federal Bureau of Investigation, as well as from the Antitrust Division. If voluntary cooperation has not fulfilled its purpose or is otherwise inappropriate in a particular situation, the government will utilize its instruments of compulsory process. These include use of civil investigative demands ("CIDs") or subpoenas. As the *International Guidelines* state (at p. 39):

> U.S. law provides authority for such compulsory measures directed to persons over whom the courts have personal jurisdiction. The Agencies may compel the production of documents or information, including documents or information located outside the United States, when the documents or information sought are within the "possession, custody, or control" of an individual or entity subject to the jurisdiction of the United States and are not protected by the attorney-client privilege or the work product doctrine. (footnotes omitted)

Where the suspected violation is serious enough to support criminal prosecution, grand jury proceedings involving the use of compulsory process may be instituted.

[1] *Criminal Prosecutions*

In antitrust criminal prosecutions, as in US criminal prosecutions generally, US district courts have original subject matter jurisdiction. F.R.Crim.P. 18 provides that, except as otherwise provided, the prosecution of a criminal offense shall be in a district in which the offense was committed, and the court is to fix the place of trial within the district "with due regard for the convenience of the defendant, any victim, and the witnesses, and the prompt administration of justice." Of particular importance in antitrust conspiracy cases, where there may be no single locus of commission, Section 3237 of the Criminal Code specifies that any offense begun in one district and completed in another, or committed in more than one district, may be prosecuted in any district where such offense was begun, continued or committed.

Grand juries are convened by the court, from time to time, to consider evidence presented by government attorneys and to decide whether to issue indictments accusing parties of criminal offenses. A criminal investigation is normally begun by the issuance of grand jury subpoenas requiring the recipient of the subpoena to produce documents and/or give oral testimony before the grand jury. Often the witnesses are given "immunity" by the government with respect to their appearing, assuring them that the evidence they provide and evidence derived from it will not be used to prosecute them. Under F.R.Crim.P. 6, the proceedings before the grand jury must be maintained in secrecy by the grand jurors, the government attorneys, and the court staff personnel, unless an authorized exception to the secrecy requirement, such as the showing of a "particularized need" for disclosure, pertains.

The government can also obtain documents in the possession of an individual or a business by obtaining a search warrant authorized by the applicable federal court. The judge or magistrate approving the warrant must make a determination that there exists a reasonable basis for authorizing the search of the premises.

Grand jury subpoenas may not be issued in the US and then served on foreign parties abroad. They may be served on foreign individuals when they are present in the US, or, in the case of corporations, by service on their US agents. There is a statute, 28 U.S.C. § 1783, which authorizes the US courts to direct the service of subpoenas abroad on nationals or residents of the US who are in a foreign country, requiring their testimony in the US and/or the production of documents or other things. To issue such a subpoena in connection with criminal proceedings, the US court must first make a finding that the particular testimony or the production of the document or other thing is necessary in the interest of justice. If a proceeding other than a criminal case is involved, the court must make the additional finding that it is not possible to obtain the testimony in admissible form without the person's appearance or to obtain the production of the documents or other thing in any other manner.

It must be kept in mind that, under US law, once jurisdiction has been established over the "person" of an individual or a corporation by proper service of a subpoena or other demand for documents or other things, the party receiving the discovery demand is bound to produce documents or other evidence in its custody, control or possession wherever that evidence is physically located. The lawyer for the foreign recipient of a US discovery demand is entitled to argue to the court that the demand seeks irrelevant information, or is unduly burdensome, or covers documents that are actually in the control of a third party, not the lawyer's client. In the case of a corporate client, the lawyer may argue that, although another, related corporation has possession and control of the requested documents, his or her client corporation lacks the degree of control over the related corporation necessary to give the latter control over the documents in question. Any of these arguments may succeed or fail, depending on the circumstances of the particular case. Often, a party's lawyer will succeed in narrowing the scope of his adversary's discovery demand without having to take the matter to the judge, by persuading the opposing counsel, whether a government or private lawyer, that the document request is over-broad. But the mere fact that the documents sought are located in a foreign country is no defense, so long as personal jurisdiction exists, except possibly in the case of a foreign blocking statute.

It must also be emphasized that the willful destruction or concealment of documentation, whether by the client or the lawyer, to avoid having to produce materials in response to discovery emanating from an antitrust litigation or investigation invites the most severe sanctions from the court.

The amount of the monetary fines and the length of prison terms that can be imposed for criminal violations of the Sherman Act have increased dramatically over the years and the increase will probably continue in the future. In the majority of cases, the companies and individuals who are being charged with a criminal violation of the antitrust laws do not choose to go to trial and face the risk of the maximum sanctions. It is usually more advantageous for the defendant, with the assistance of its lawyers, to agree to plead guilty and "proffer" to the Antitrust Division all of the information that the defendant possesses regarding the illegal activity. The Division is then likely to agree that it will recommend to the court a specific amount of fine and, sometimes, a prison sentence of a specified duration. The court, after a hearing on the plea, is likely to approve the Division's recommendations. This process obviates the need for a trial on the merits.

[2] Civil Cases

The Antitrust Division generally commences civil investigations by issuing CIDs and/or subpoenas requiring the recipients to produce business records and/or give testimony. CIDs, which are authorized by the Antitrust Civil Process Act, constitute an important investigative tool for the Justice Department for obtaining information relevant to civil antitrust investigations. Through the issuance of a CID, the Antitrust Division is able, prior to the filing of a suit, to obtain from any person having relevant information the production of documents, responses to interrogatories, and the giving of oral testimony. Before the use of the CID device was authorized, the government was compelled to rely on the voluntary cooperation of possible defendants or on any readily available information to determine whether there was a sufficient basis to warrant the filing of a civil suit.

The Antitrust Civil Process Act was enacted in 1962 and substantially expanded in 1976. The 1976 amendments were significant in authorizing the service of CID's beyond the territorial jurisdiction of the US. 15 U.S.C. § 1312(d)(2) provides that service of a CID may be made abroad "in such manner as the Federal Rules of Civil Procedure prescribe for service in a foreign country." We have discussed above the alternative modes for effectuating service of process abroad in civil cases pursuant to F.R.C.P. 4., including the limitations thereon.

The provision authorizing service of a CID abroad also states that, to the extent that the courts of the US can assert jurisdiction over the recipient of the CID consistent with due process, "the United States District Court for the District of Columbia shall have the same jurisdiction to take any action respecting compliance ... that such court would have if such person were personally within the jurisdiction of such court." The Department of Justice has thus been entrusted with a potentially far reaching transnational investigatory power. The Department utilizes that power with care, since it is well aware of the issues of comity that may come into play.

The FTC Act Amendments of 1994, 15 U.S.C. § 57b-1(c), likewise authorize the Federal Trade Commission to use CIDs (in addition to subpoenas) in the investigation of possible antitrust law violations. In merger investigations, the Agencies utilize the mechanisms of the Hart-Scott-Rodino Act to obtain information from parties.

[B] Discovery Procedures in Federal Courts

The Federal Rules of Civil Procedure govern the litigation of civil cases in the federal courts. They provide a variety of discovery devices, available to both private litigants and government agencies after a suit has been commenced. The discovery regime is a liberal one, certainly as compared to the regimes generally prevailing in the legal systems of other nations. It reflects the view of the US legal system that truth and justice will best emerge from an open adversarial process which brings all of the relevant facts to light. There are recognized "privileges" against discovery, including the attorney-client privilege and the work-product privilege, which shelter certain information in the interest of safeguarding the operation of the adversarial process. There are also rules of evidence designed to enhance the fairness of the fact finding once the trial begins. At the discovery stage, however, the rules essentially favor the party seeking the information rather than the party resisting its production. ("party," as used in the Rules, refers to a party to the litigation, i.e., plaintiff, defendant or third party formally appearing as such in the suit.)

In recent years, the literature and the case law on the subject of electronic discovery ("ediscovery") have blossomed. The Federal Rules, as amended in 2006 and again in 2015, underscore the importance of safeguarding discovery with respect to stored electronic information and transmitted email messages. The fact that such data are in electronic form places in challenging contexts a number of discovery matters, such as data preservation obligations, litigant access to hard drives, backup data access, including "clouds," as well as questions relating to which party should bear the costs of retrieval and production.

F.R.C.P. 26(a)(1) requires each of the parties to most types of civil litigation, unless otherwise directed by a case-specific order, to disclose promptly to the other parties a substantial amount of pertinent information without awaiting a discovery request. This required preliminary disclosure includes, with respect to information that the disclosing party may use to support its claims or defenses, the identities of individuals likely to have discoverable information, as well as copies or descriptions of all relevant documents, electronically stored information and tangible things that the disclosing party has in its possession, custody, or control, unless the use would be solely for impeachment. A computation of each category of damages claimed must also be made available.

F.R.C.P. 26(b)(1) provides generally that parties "may obtain discovery regarding any non-privileged matter that is relevant to any party's claim or defense and proportional to the needs of the case, considering the importance of the issues at stake in the action, the amount in controversy, the parties' relative access to relevant information, the parties' resources, the importance of the discovery in resolving the issues, and whether the burden or expense of the proposed discovery outweighs its likely benefit. Information within this scope of discovery need not be admissible in evidence to be discoverable."

This complex articulation represents a significant retreat from some prior incarnations of the Rule, but the last sentence—allowing discovery of categories of information which may not include any admissible evidence—contrasts starkly with the position of many foreign legal systems which allow discovery only with respect to identified, specific documents meeting the standards of admissible evidence. The US approach to pretrial discovery is thus often described derogatorily abroad as allowing "fishing expeditions." The fact that the lawyers for the parties can launch and press the discovery against their adversaries as they see fit, until they are reined in by the court, also contrasts sharply with the procedure in civil law legal systems in which the court tightly controls and, indeed, manages discovery from the outset.

Under subsection (c) of Rule 26, the court may enter a protective order on behalf of the party from whom discovery is sought, barring or limiting the discovery in some way. Protective orders are often sought and granted when the discovery requests seek business trade secrets or other sensitive commercial data, such as customer lists. If the information in question is relevant to the dispute, the protective orders typically allow the discovery but limit disclosure so that the sensitive data are received only by the outside lawyers and experts for the party seeking the information. These individuals are placed under strict admonitions, subject to sanctions, precluding them from circulating the sensitive data to others, including their client.

Rules 27–30 provide for depositions upon oral examination, whereby one party may require a person to appear at an appropriate location to give answers to relevant questions. The testimony, which is turned into a deposition transcript by a stenographer (and may also be recorded by camera) will assist the lawyers in their ongoing trial preparation. It will also be available for possible use at trial, perhaps in place of the live testimony or to impeach the witness. Depositions of parties to the litigation are normally initiated by written notice, without need for a subpoena. The attendance of a party or nonparty witness for a deposition may be compelled by subpoena as provided in Rule 45. The notice of deposition may request that the deponent produce documents or other relevant tangible things at the deposition, and such production may be ordered by a subpoena (in which case it is called a subpoena *duces tecum*). Under F.R.C.P. 30(b)(6), a party may, in its deposition notice and by subpoena, name as the deponent a corporation or other organization, describing the matters on which examination is sought. The named organization must then designate an officer, director, managing agent or other person who will testify on its behalf "about information known or reasonably available to the organization."

When the deposition is taken within the US, its territories, and possessions, the deposition is usually conducted by the lawyers for the various parties at an agreed office location and, pursuant to F.R.C.P. 28(a), is "taken before an officer authorized to administer oaths by the laws of the United States or of the place where the examination is held, or before a person appointed by the court in which the action is pending." This "officer" is, in practice, usually a stenographer employed by a court reporting service, who administers the oath and then transcribes the deposition testimony. The deponent is generally accompanied by a lawyer, who may object to questions put to the deponent on grounds of relevance, privilege or other appropriate grounds. After stating the objection, the lawyer either allows the deponent to respond subject to the objection, or else advises the deponent not to respond. The disputes in this regard are reflected in the deposition transcript and may subsequently be submitted by the lawyers for resolution by the court.

When a party to a US civil suit is contemplating taking the deposition by oral examination of a person abroad who, by choice or physical inability, will not travel to the US, a number of additional questions are posed. Will the person voluntarily appear or must compulsory process be obtained? Will the host country assist in the conduct of the deposition, be indifferent to it, or forbid it, even on a voluntary basis? What "officer" will preside over the deposition? These legal questions are posed in addition to the practical concerns, which relate to the substantial expense of sending lawyers a considerable distance for several days and, perhaps, the need of hiring translators. Often, conducting the deposition overseas of an individual who is a foreign citizen and resident will prove practicable only if the witness will voluntarily participate or if the foreign jurisdiction is willing to compel his or her testimony or document production.

F.R.C.P. 28(b)(1) provides that depositions may be taken in a foreign country: "(A) under an applicable treaty or convention; (B) under a letter of request, whether or not captioned a 'letter rogatory'; (C) on notice, before a person authorized to administer oaths either by federal law or by the law in the place of examination; or (D) before a person commissioned by the court to administer any necessary oath and take testimony."

In those many situations where the overseas deposition can be arranged and carried out on a voluntary basis not requiring compulsory process, and assuming no objection from the host country, there are no legal obstacles. The lawyers and the deponent travel to an agreed office or hotel location in the host country, having arranged for a suitable person or persons to administer the deponent's oath and to transcribe the deposition. Moreover, when the prospective deponent is a national or resident of the US living abroad, Section 1783 of the Judicial Code authorizes the US courts to issue subpoenas requiring such a person to produce documents and ordering him or her to appear as a witness before the US court or "before a person or body designated by it." The imposition of US jurisdiction in this context has been upheld by the Supreme Court as constitutional.

To obtain, on a compulsory basis, the deposition testimony outside of the US of a person who is neither a US national or a US resident, it is necessary to secure the assistance of the foreign country concerned. F.R.C.P. 45 provides for the issuance of subpoenas to compel testimony or production of documents, either for discovery or for trial. (it should be noted that Rule 45 was amended a few years ago to include compulsion of the production of electronically stored information) Such subpoenas may only be served within the US, however, except in the circumstances addressed by Section 1783. Accordingly, as indicated by Rule 28(b), the help of the foreign government can be sought to get this government to use its powers of compulsory process to induce the prospective witness to appear to be "deposed" in the foreign country in question. The request to the foreign government may be in the traditional form of a letter of request or "letter rogatory" transmitted by the US authorities to the foreign authorities. Or the request can be made under the terms of the multilateral Hague Evidence Convention, which we will shortly be discussing in greater detail.

We should also mention here 28 U.S.C. § 1782, a statutory provision of procedures for federal courts to give assistance to foreign and international tribunals and to the litigants before such tribunals. Section 1782(a) provides that, upon receiving an application therefor from a foreign or international tribunal or "any interested person," "[t]he district court of the district in which a person resides or is found may order him to give his testimony or statement or to produce a document or other thing for use in a proceeding in a foreign or international tribunal, including criminal investigations conducted before formal accusation." A dispute over interpretation of the phrase "proceeding in a foreign or international tribunal" was resolved by the US Supreme Court in 2004 in the case of *Intel Corp. v. Advanced Micro Devices, Inc.* Prior to this ruling, the lower federal courts generally had construed the provision somewhat narrowly, holding, for example, that it does not authorize providing assistance to assist discovery in private international commercial arbitration. Some appellate courts had construed the provision as including a "foreign discoverability" requirement, namely that any documents sought would have been discoverable in the foreign proceeding had those documents been located within that jurisdiction.

In the European *Intel* dispute (which we will be discussing in a subsequent chapter), Advanced Micro Devices ("AMD") had filed an antitrust complaint against Intel with the Directorate-General for Competition of the European Commission, charging abuse of a dominant position in violation of Article 82 of the EC Treaty. In pursuit of that complaint and invoking Section 1782, AMD applied to a federal court in California for an order requiring Intel to produce documents previously discovered in Intel's US antitrust litigation with Intergraph Corporation. The district court denied the application as unsupported by applicable authority, but the Ninth Circuit reversed for the case to be considered on the merits. The Supreme Court granted review and held that (1) AMD qualified as an "interested person" for purposes of Section 1782, (2) the European Commission qualified as a § 1782 "tribunal," because the Commission is a first-instance decision maker, (3) the "proceeding" for which discovery is sought under the statute must be in reasonable contemplation, but need not be pending or imminent, and (4) § 1782 (a) contains no threshold requirement that evidence sought from the federal court would be discoverable under the law governing the foreign proceeding. The Court concluded that whether the assistance requested was appropriate was for the district court to consider on remand, taking certain factors pertinent to the case before it into account.

Returning to the Federal Rules, F.R.C.P. 31 provides another discovery device, entitled "depositions by written questions," whereby any person, including a party, may be required to provide written answers to written questions, as distinct from appearing in person for an oral examination. This device is little favored by litigators seeking discovery because the rigidity of the format, particularly the inability to ask follow-up questions, enables a skillful deponent and his or her lawyer to evade critical questions by construing them narrowly and providing short, unhelpful responses. F.R.C.P. 33 entitled "Interrogatories to parties" is similar, but it applies only to one party serving written interrogatories on another party, to be responded to fully in writing and under oath. This device suffers from the same weakness as the Rule 31 device, namely the rigidity of the format enabling evasion. However, written interrogatories are frequently served by one party on another as a means of obtaining preliminary information which can be subsequently followed up by more searching discovery, including oral depositions. Finally, F.R.C.P. 34 provides for any party to serve on another party a request to produce or allow inspection of relevant designated documents, electronically stored information and tangible things which are in the possession, custody or control of the party upon whom the request is served. Rule 34 also authorizes requests by a party to permit entry upon designated land or other property in the possession or control of the other party.

F.R.C.P. 37 is critical to an understanding of federal court discovery procedure because it provides the procedures and sanctions for compelling discovery where a party fails to make a requested disclosure or otherwise does not cooperate in the discovery process. Any party may move the court to compel another party to comply with discovery requests that have previously been made, but not complied with. The motion must include a certification that the movant has in good faith conferred or attempted to confer with the other party in an unsuccessful effort to resolve the matter without court action. As a practical matter, disputes between lawyers for the parties over discovery are commonplace. Federal judges are usually loath to referee these time consuming and frequently petty disputes on procedural matters, and they often refer the matter to a court officer known as a "magistrate judge" to review the discovery dispute in detail and make a recommendation on its resolution. The court will then grant or deny the motion to compel, in whole or in part, and it may require one party to pay the other party's expenses related to the dispute over the motion. F.R.C.P. 37(e) authorizes the court to take appropriate measures if electronically stored information is lost because a party failed to take reasonable steps to preserve it and the information cannot be restored or replaced through additional discovery.

If the court enters an order directing a party to comply with certain discovery requests, and the party fails to comply with it, the court may impose on that party one or more of the sanctions provided by subsection (b) of Rule 37. The sanctions, the appropriateness of which depend upon the nature and significance of the noncompliance, include: entry of an order of contempt of court, accepting certain facts adverse to the noncomplying party to be deemed established for the purposes of the litigation, prohibiting the noncomplying party from utilizing certain arguments or evidence at trial, striking certain pleadings of a party, or—the most damaging from the viewpoint of the lawsuit—dismissing the plaintiff's case or rendering a judgment by default against the defendant or other disobedient party.

Similarly, the Federal Rules of Criminal Procedure govern, with exceptions for some kinds of specialized proceedings, the procedure in all criminal proceedings in the US district courts, the US Courts of Appeals, and the Supreme Court of the US. Under Rule 15, depositions of prospective witnesses may be taken to preserve testimony for trial. Pursuant to Rule 16, the government is required to make available to the defendant certain relevant information. Rule 17 allows the issuance of subpoenas requiring persons to testify or produce relevant documents. If the prospective witness is in a foreign country, service of a subpoena on him is controlled by the terms of 28 U.S.C. § 1783.

[C] The Hague Evidence Convention

For many years, international discovery in national court proceedings was heavily dependent on the traditional letter rogatory. This document constitutes a formal request sent through diplomatic channels which asks the courts of the receiving country to assist the courts of the requesting country in performing a specified judicial act, usually related to the obtaining of evidence. The historic record of letters rogatory is an uninspiring one, as nations have often either failed to honor such requests, or else, by reason of bureaucratic apathy and inertia, have provided the requested assistance only after delays lasting for months or even years. The US therefore took the lead in bringing about, under the auspices of the Hague Conference on Private International Law, the negotiation and adoption of a multilateral convention designed to improve mutual judicial cooperation in this area. It was necessary, in reaching consensus, to find ways to bridge the significant gap between the legal philosophies of the common law and civil law systems on the subject of discovery. An acceptable agreement entitled the Hague Convention on the Taking of Evidence Abroad in Civil and Commercial Matters ("Hague Evidence Convention") emerged, to which the US became a party in 1972.

As in the case of the Hague Service Convention, the structure of the Hague Evidence Convention starts with each contracting nation's designation of a Central Authority, which is charged with receiving requests for assistance coming from other contracting nations and taking steps toward the execution of the request within the receiving country. This normally involves passing the request on to a local court, which is obligated under the Convention to apply the "appropriate measures of compulsion" available under national law for purposes of executing the request. A letter of request may seek the obtaining of evidence or the performance of some other judicial act. Any evidence requested must be intended for use in judicial proceedings, either commenced or contemplated. As the Convention's title indicates, it is applicable only in connection with civil or commercial matters. The Convention seeks to correct two key deficiencies in the traditional letter rogatory system by requiring both that the receiving state execute the request, albeit subject to some important exceptions, and that it be "executed expeditiously." Articles 15–22 of the Convention provide rules and procedures for the taking of evidence, with or without compulsion, by diplomatic officers, consular agents, or persons appointed as "commissioners" for that purpose.

A Central Authority may object to the execution of a letter of request directed to it on the ground that the request fails to comply with the detailed provisions therefor in the Convention (including the translation requirement), or if the request seeks performance of nonjudicial functions, or if the receiving state considers that execution of the request would prejudice that state's sovereignty or security. In addition, Article 23 of the Hague Evidence Convention permits contracting states to declare that they will not execute "Letters of Request issued for the purpose of obtaining pre-trial discovery of documents as known in Common Law countries." This exception is, of course, of particular concern from the perspective of US civil litigation, including antitrust litigation, given the critical role of pretrial discovery in the process.

A majority of the contracting states under the Convention, excluding the US and a few other countries, have, in fact, lodged Article 23 declarations. Some of these declarations bar entirely the execution of requests for pretrial discovery, while others are more limited in that they allow pretrial discovery requests which identify specific documents or categories of documents. Article 23 was obviously aimed by the non-US negotiators at the phenomenon of so-called fishing expeditions under the US system of discovery. It is true that many, if not most, document requests served by one party on another in complex US civil lawsuits call for the production of large quantities of documents, often described only by reference to general subject matter and time period. This system is highly susceptible to abuse and, as we noted earlier, frequently gives rise to unproductive squabbles among the lawyers. On the other hand, it can be persuasively argued that a legal system which permits pretrial discovery only as to specific, identified documents is not conducive to a full and unbiased development of the factual record and, therefore, to an equitable resolution of the dispute.

The Hague Evidence Convention regime, providing for the transnational collection of evidence through international cooperation, and the regime of the Federal Rules of Civil Procedure, which bases the discovery power largely on US concepts of personal jurisdiction, co-exist for purposes of US civil litigation. It was inevitable that legal questions about the exclusivity of the Convention procedures and the primacy of the US domestic procedures would arise in US cases involving foreign nationals of the other contracting states to the Convention. Indeed, before the Supreme Court resolved the issue in 1987 in the case of *Société Nationale Industrielle Aérospatiale v. U.S. District Court* ("*Aérospatiale*"), a number of federal and state courts took different positions on the application of the Convention procedures in US civil litigation in which evidence from abroad is sought. It was unclear whether the Convention procedures were to be deemed (a) exclusive, (b) optional, or (c) procedures of "first resort", i.e., to be utilized by US litigants in the first instance before initiating any discovery pursuant to the provisions of the Federal Rules of Civil Procedure.

Aérospatiale was a product liability case arising from an airplane crash in Iowa. The suit was filed in federal court in that state against two corporations owned by the Republic of France. Plaintiffs alleged that the defendants, having manufactured and sold a defective aircraft, were liable for negligence and breach of warranty. The defendants resisted plaintiffs' discovery requests as to information located in France, a country which is a signatory to the Hague Evidence Convention. They argued that the French "blocking statute" precluded them from complying with the US discovery requests and also that, in any event, the Hague Evidence Convention provided the exclusive means for obtaining discovery of evidence located in France. After the district court and the Court of Appeals had rejected these arguments, the Supreme Court granted review to resolve the relationship between the Federal Rules of Civil Procedure and the Hague Evidence Convention, both constituting "the law of the United States."

The Court divided on a 5-4 basis. The justices all agreed that the Convention does not provide the exclusive means for discovery involving signatory countries. They also all rejected the plaintiffs' position that the Convention applies to discovery sought from third parties but is inapplicable to discovery sought from a foreign litigant that is subject to the personal jurisdiction of a US court. They held the Convention applicable to discovery from litigants, as well as from third parties. The justices split, however, as to the proper application of the Convention as a nonexclusive regime. Justice Stevens' opinion for the majority rejected a "first resort to convention procedures" approach, observing that, in many situations, "the Letter of Request procedure authorized by the convention would be unduly time consuming and expensive, as well as less certain to produce needed evidence than direct use of the Federal Rules." The majority opinion declared that the Federal Rules procedures are the "normal methods" for federal litigation involving foreign parties, while the Convention procedures are "optional" or "supplemental." The majority opinion concluded that the trial courts must, in each case, undertake a "particularized analysis" of the needs of the situation to determine which discovery procedures should be applied. This analysis should take into account, the court's "knowledge of the case and of the claims and interests of the parties and the governments whose statutes and policies they invoke." The majority opinion also stated that:

> American courts, in supervising pretrial proceedings, should exercise special vigilance to protect foreign litigants from the danger that unnecessary, or unduly burdensome, discovery may place them in a disadvantageous position. Judicial supervision of discovery should always seek to minimize its costs and inconvenience and to prevent improper uses of discovery requests. When it is necessary to seek evidence abroad, however, the District Court must supervise pretrial proceedings particularly closely to prevent discovery abuses .... .American courts should ... take care to demonstrate due respect for any special problem confronted by the foreign litigant on account of its nationality or the location of its operations, and for any sovereign interest expressed by a foreign state. We do not articulate specific rules to guide this delicate task of adjudication.

The Court refused to give any importance to the French "blocking statute," disposing of it in a footnote as irrelevant to the powers of the US courts to order discovery from parties subject to their jurisdiction. The Court considered the French statute as relevant to the required "particularized comity analysis" only "to the extent that its terms and its enforcement identify the nature of the sovereign interests in non-disclosure of specific kinds of material."

The minority opinion, written by Justice Blackmun, strongly took issue with the majority's "relegation" of the Convention to an "optional" status. The opinion urged that, ordinarily, "first use" should be made of the Convention procedures, consistently with principles of comity. Notably, the minority opinion also expressed the "fear" that:

> The Court's decision means that courts will resort unnecessarily to issuing orders under the Federal Rules of Civil Procedure in a raw exercise of their jurisdictional power to the detriment of the United States' national and international interests. The Court's view of this country's international obligations is particularly unfortunate in a world in which regular commercial and legal channels loom ever more crucial.

Many federal and state trial courts have, since, tried to apply the difficult directive given them by the majority opinion in the *Aérospatiale* case. Some of the pertinent decisions reflect a conscientious effort to conduct the "particularized analysis" described by the Court and others confer "first resort" status on the Convention discovery procedures. Many, if not most, of the federal district courts seem content simply to apply the procedures of the Federal Rules with respect to discovery on litigants, leaving the Convention regime for use in connection with discovery on foreign third parties over whom the US courts lack personal jurisdiction and subpoena power.

The Supreme Court's decision in *Aérospatiale* rejected a first resort rule in favor of the Convention in a situation where personal jurisdiction was not contested and the discovery sought involved the merits of the case. This ruling left open the question of what procedure should be applied by the court when the discovery sought against a foreign party implicates the threshold question of whether personal jurisdiction on that party exists. A number of federal district courts and state trial courts have differed on this issue, with the majority subjecting jurisdictional discovery to the same approach as merits discovery. In the case entitled *In Re: Automotive Refinishing Paint Antitrust Litigation*, the district court extended the ruling of *Aérospatiale* to jurisdictional discovery and refused to require the plaintiffs to pursue their jurisdictional discovery first under the Hague Convention procedures. On appeal, the Court of Appeals for the Third Circuit agreed with the trial court that the balancing test articulated in *Aérospatiale* should be applied equally to jurisdictional discovery, there being no persuasive rationale for making the distinction urged by the foreign defendants.

[D] Foreign "Blocking" Legislation and US Discovery

We have noted the Supreme Court's summary disregard of the French "blocking statute" in the *Aérospatiale* decision. Nonetheless, special concerns relating to issues of international comity and conflicts of laws do arise when the contrary demands of foreign legislation are invoked by a party resisting compliance with a US discovery obligation. Indeed, some of the blocking legislation enacted by foreign nations has been expressly generated by the reach of US antitrust enforcement into the international sphere.

The earlier US decisions showed a tendency to defer to foreign laws barring or limiting disclosure of various types of commercial information. This deference was principally based on conflict of laws principles, but it might also have been reflecting the fact that the foreign laws in question reflected general policies protecting the confidentiality of certain types of information, such as bank secrecy laws, as distinct from the later "blocking statutes" directed more specifically against US proceedings.

For example, in the case of *Application of Chase Manhattan Bank*, in the 1960s, the US Government was seeking enforcement of a grand jury subpoena *duces tecum* which sought to direct the bank, a New York corporation, to produce records in the possession of a branch located in the Republic of Panama. The bank presented evidence of a Panamanian law making it a criminal violation to produce bank documents in an action abroad. The district court stayed the enforcement proceedings while the government petitioned the Panamanian authorities for permission to obtain the records. The Second Circuit affirmed, citing the obligation of the US courts "to respect the laws of other sovereign states even though they may differ in economic and legal philosophy from our own."

However, the argument that the US courts lack jurisdiction to require production of documents located abroad was repeatedly rejected in cases in which the court had personal jurisdiction over the party concerned. In 1947, in the *Canadian International Paper Co.* case, the officers of a Canadian company contended that they were unable to produce documents sought by a US grand jury subpoena because a quorum of the board of directors, all residents of Canada, had passed a resolution forbidding the removal of the corporate records from Canada. The district court rejected this contention as an attempted evasion of the subpoena. It ruled that, since the Canadian company was "found" in New York and had possession of the documents in question, it was required to comply. The court made the following statement of general principle:

"The fact that a corporation's records are physically located beyond the confines of the United States does not excuse it from producing them if they are in its possession and the court has jurisdiction of the corporation. The test is control—not location of the records."

Five years later, during a grand jury investigation of an alleged worldwide oil cartel, several oil companies moved to quash subpoenas insofar as they called for the production of documents located in foreign countries. In addition, the foreign governments complained to the US Department of State that the subpoenas constituted an invasion of their sovereignty. The court did not accept these jurisdictional contentions, but the grand jury was dismissed on the motion of the government which cited "existing world tensions." A civil suit was instituted instead. A degree of Supreme Court guidance on how the courts should address confrontations between US discovery and foreign laws prohibiting disclosure was forthcoming in 1958 in *Société Internationale pour Participations Industrielles et Commerciales v. Rogers* ("*Société Internationale*"). The Court's opinion provided only limited advice for the purpose of future cases, particularly since the party resisting disclosure on the basis of foreign law in *Société Internationale* was a plaintiff, rather than, as is usually the case, a defendant. Nonetheless, as the Court has not substantially revisited the applicable issues since, this decision still lays down a number of governing principles to which the lower courts adhere.

The case arose from the US government's seizure of assets during World War II pursuant to the Trading with the Enemy Act. After the war, a Swiss company named I.G. Chemie brought suit against the government, asserting that the confiscated property had belonged to it, a Swiss neutral, rather than to an enemy national. The government responded that I.G. Chemie was owned and dominated by an enemy national, I.G. Farbenindustrie, and it sought discovery from the plaintiff, under F.R.C.P. 34, of banking records to support its defense. I.G.

Chemie argued that it could not produce these documents without violating Swiss penal law. The district court ordered production and, after I.G. Chemie failed to comply fully, the court entered sanctions under F.R.C.P. 37, dismissing the complaint. The Court of Appeals affirmed.

The Supreme Court upheld the district court's discovery order as proper. However, it reversed that court's dismissal of the complaint, noting the district court's finding that I.G. Chemie "had not been in collusion with the Swiss authorities to block discovery, and had, in good faith, made diligent efforts to execute the production order." The Court reasoned that F.R.C.P. 37 did not permit the extreme sanction of dismissing a complaint where the failure to comply with a discovery order "has been due to inability, and not to willfulness, bad faith, or any fault of petitioner." The Court held that the district court had wide discretion to impose other sanctions, such as by drawing adverse inferences from the failure to make disclosures. This decision has led to US courts usually following a two step process in dealing with discovery confrontations involving foreign law. First, the court determines whether the foreign stricture should cause it to refrain from exercising its power to order the foreign discovery. Second, where the court has ordered the discovery and the party has not complied with the order, the court considers what action to take on the matter of sanctions.

Société Internationale was also important in confirming the principle that a party resisting disclosure on the basis of foreign law cannot expect to escape sanctions if the party has been lacking in "good faith" in resisting discovery, such as "colluding" with the foreign authorities. However, from the practical viewpoint, the Supreme Court's decision created as many new questions as it put old ones to rest: If a party is in good faith in complying with foreign law, so that an extreme sanction like dismissing its complaint or entering default against it is not appropriate, what is the justification for imposing on it an only slightly less severe sanction—such as making critical findings of fact against it? Is a foreign party in bad faith and in "collusion" with the foreign government if it merely advises the foreign government of the US discovery order? Is a foreign national in bad faith with its own government if, in seeking to avoid being found guilty of bad faith under US law, it ignores its own government's directive to report promptly US court "extraterritorial" discovery demands?

Section 442(2) of *The Restatement of Foreign Relations Law of the United States (Third)* largely follows the approach laid out in *Société Internationale.* (1) If disclosure of information located abroad is prohibited by foreign law, the court may require the party to whom the disclosure order is directed to make a good faith effort to secure permission for disclosure from the foreign authorities, (2) Except where there has been a lack of good faith in this regard, a US court or agency should not ordinarily impose sanctions of contempt, dismissal, or default for failure to comply, and (3) Even where there has been made a good faith, unsuccessful effort to secure permission from disclosure from the foreign authorities, the court may, in appropriate cases, make findings of fact adverse to the noncomplying party. According to the *Restatement*, this sanction is not deemed to be a penalty, but is designed to induce compliance by the party and to enhance the willingness of the other state to permit compliance.

Different cases have played out in different ways under these guidelines for resolution of confrontations between US discovery and foreign nondisclosure requirements. Many potential confrontations never reach the final stage of sanctions. The US courts generally uphold litigants' bona fide discovery requests for the production of records, wherever located, even in the face of foreign "blocking statutes." This puts the party subject to the discovery order and the foreign government in a severe dilemma: if they insist on nondisclosure, the resisting party is likely to suffer a significant sanction, such as entry of adverse findings of fact, even if it can pass the good faith test. This sanction is often tantamount to an adverse decision on the case as a whole. The foreign state's interest in preventing disclosure is seldom strong enough to justify this risk, and the tendency, therefore, is to yield to the United States' position.

In antitrust proceedings, as we have seen, the past pattern of combating foreign blocking regimes has been largely replaced by agreements to cooperate among national competition authorities. The *International Guidelines* state that the Agencies benefit greatly from sensitive nonpublic information received from parties and foreign authorities (at p. 40) and that they "protect the confidentiality of all such information received, be it from businesses or consumers located domestically or abroad, or from foreign authorities, under applicable provisions of U.S. law."

[E] Federal Trade Commission Procedures

Investigations by the FTC are originated by a variety of methods, including action on the Commission's own initiative, or following a complaint from the public, or on request from the Congress, government agencies or other officials. There are two basic forms of FTC investigation. One comprises general investigations of conditions in, or practices affecting, certain industries or segments of the economy. These are primarily undertaken to provide information for the Congress and the public, rather than to implement remedial processes. The other category of investigation stems from the law enforcement functions of the Commission, these investigations being undertaken to ascertain whether there have been violations of the statutes administered by the Commission. After the Commission has issued a complaint charging that one of the statutes which it administers has been violated, an administrative adjudicative proceeding ensues.

The FTC's Rules of Practice for Adjudicative Proceedings provide for any party to obtain discovery "to the extent that it may be reasonably expected to yield information relevant to the allegations of the complaint, to the proposed relief, or to the defenses of any respondent." The available devices for discovery on respondents or on third parties are similar to those provided for the courts by the Federal Rules of Civil Procedure, including depositions, written interrogatories, requests for document production and for admission. The information obtained by parties may include the existence, description, nature, custody, condition, and location of any books, documents, other tangible things, electronically stored information, and the identity and location of persons having any knowledge of any discoverable matter. Information may not be withheld from discovery on grounds that the information will be inadmissible at the hearing if the information sought appears reasonably calculated to lead to the discovery of admissible evidence.

After the hearing, the ALJ issues a ruling and opinion called the "initial decision." Any party to the proceeding may appeal the initial decision to the Commission, sitting as a five person adjudicative body. If the respondent is unsuccessful before the Commission, it may obtain review in the appropriate circuit Court of Appeals. Under Section 13(b) of the FTC Act, the Commission may go directly to federal court by filing a complaint to obtain a temporary restraining order or preliminary injunction where a person, partnership or corporation is violating or about to violate any provision of law enforced by the FTC.

Various forms of compulsory process are available to the Commission in the course of its investigations and proceedings. Persons, corporations and partnerships may be required to file with the Commission reports or answers in writing in response to specific questions. The Commission is also entitled to have access to and copy any documentary evidence of any person, partnership or corporation being investigated or proceeded against. In addition, the Commission or a member thereof can issue subpoenas requiring testimony or production of documents relating to any matter under investigation. The FTC must apply to the US district courts when enforcement of its subpoenas is necessary.

Section 9 of the FTC Act provides that the attendance of witnesses and production of documents "may be required from any place in the United States, at any designated place of hearing." Nonetheless, some years ago, the Commission construed its statutory authority as allowing it to serve its investigatory subpoenas even abroad. The 1980 case of *Federal Trade Commission v. Compagnie de Saint-Gobain-Pont-a-Mousson* arose from the Commission's service of a subpoena *duces tecum* on a French company by registered mail directed to the company's headquarters in Paris. Noting the delicate issues of international law and comity involved, the Court of Appeals for the District of Columbia found an absence of any indication in the statutory language or elsewhere that the Congress meant to confer on the FTC the authority to serve its compulsory process in foreign countries. The court admonished the Commission that "*the act of service itself* constitutes an exercise of American sovereign power within the area of the foreign country's territorial sovereignty." (emphasis in original)

The court's opinion noted that Congress had enacted the Antitrust Civil Process Act, which provides for extraterritorial service through CIDs. The lesson that the court drew from this enactment was that, when Congress wishes to take the internationally sensitive step of authorizing the service of US compulsory process abroad, it will express that intent expressly—as in the Antitrust Civil Process Act. In fact, the Federal Trade Commission Improvements Act of 1980 gave the Commission CID powers similar to those given to the Department of Justice, but only for investigations of "unfair or deceptive acts or practices" and not for its antitrust jurisdiction, "unfair methods of competition." Congress has since broadened the Commission's CID authority under Section 20 of the FTC Act to cover investigation of antitrust violations, allowing service "upon any person who is not found within the territorial jurisdiction of any court within the United States, in such manner as the Federal Rules of Civil Procedure prescribe for service in a foreign nation."

§4.05 ENFORCEMENT OF US ANTITRUST JUDGMENTS

In the US, there are a number of methods for enforcing a money judgment, including an antitrust judgment, when the defendant in a case has not voluntarily complied with the court's order awarding damages. Treble damage awards meet no special resistance in being enforced in the US. Property of the defendant within the country can be attached and sold, with all or part of the sale proceeds paid out to the judgment creditor. A garnishment action, involving attachment of an intangible asset of the debtor, such as a debt or income entitlement, can likewise be used to satisfy the money judgment. Issuance of a civil contempt order is the third enforcement technique. An order of civil contempt, unlike one of criminal contempt, does not reflect an offense against the dignity of the court but is essentially a remedial process used to bring about relief for the party in whose behalf the mandate of the court was issued. If and when the "contemnor" complies with the court order, the punishment will be terminated. The latter is usually in the form of a court-ordered fine, which increases over the period that the original order is not satisfied. It is also possible for the court to order imprisonment of an individual defendant until she agrees to comply with the original judgment.

Despite the existence of these remedies, there may be problems posed in their pursuit, and these may be dramatically compounded when the party acted against is a foreign entity. The fact that a US court has valid personal jurisdiction over a foreign corporation does not, of course, necessarily mean that the corporation possesses or controls substantial tangible or intangible assets in the US. Even if the foreign defendant owns a US subsidiary with substantial assets, the mere fact of the ownership will normally not be sufficient to "pierce the corporate veil" of the subsidiary to satisfy a claim against the parent, where extensive control is not maintained by the parent. Accordingly, with a foreign defendant, it may often be wise for the plaintiff to attempt to attach assets early, before they can be shifted abroad or otherwise disposed of. However, it is far easier to obtain a court order authorizing the seizure of assets after a judgment has been entered than at the commencement of the litigation.

Where the holder of a damage award is unable to benefit from any of these enforcement methods against a foreign party in the US, he must consider instituting an action in the courts of a country that has control over the judgment debtor or over a sufficient amount of the latter's assets. Whether one country will give effect to another's judgments will vary from nation to nation, and often from case to case. Every country perceives every other country's legal system differently, and factors such as reciprocity, public policy, or the nature of the judgment may determine whether recognition and enforcement of a foreign judgment will be accorded.

Many nations act in accordance with the reciprocity rule, whereby Country A will give the same type of treatment to enforcement of a judgment from Country B that the latter gives to a judgment from Country A. However, the courts in foreign countries have often had difficulty in weaving their way through the tangled web of federal and state decisions in the US in trying to determine what effect the US gives their nation's judgments. As a result, although American courts have tended to grant conclusive effect to foreign judgments, the same treatment has not always been afforded in return.

There is one additional problem, of particular relevance to US antitrust judgments, which may preclude their enforcement in foreign nations, even where reciprocity exists as a general matter. Most countries will refuse to enforce a country's judgments that are either penal in nature or contrary to the public policy of the foreign court. A US antitrust judgment, particularly one that has awarded the plaintiff three times his provable damages, will often be viewed outside of the US as fitting into one or both of these categories. Indeed, as we have previously discussed, statutes have been enacted in a number of countries which were expressly designed to, among other things, bar enforcement of US treble damage antitrust judgments.

The worldwide uncertainties over the transnational enforcement of judgments have led to the negotiation of a maze of bilateral and multilateral treaties and conventions on the subject. For example, the EC has issued the Brussels Regulation which sets forth rules on jurisdiction and enforcement of judgments that are directly binding on all of the member countries. In the US, the full faith and credit clause of the Constitution requires that the US state courts recognize and enforce the judgments of their sister states, subject to some limited exceptions. However, the US has not as yet entered into any international treaties to ensure enforcement of US judgments in foreign countries.

While many countries do enforce US judgments, obstacles to such enforcement exist in various countries and circumstances. For many years, the US, the Europeans and others attempted, under the auspices of the Hague Conference on Private International Law, to negotiate an international convention on international jurisdiction and the recognition and enforcement of judgments in civil and commercial matters. This effort failed to obtain consensus after several drafts. The Conference did reach agreement on a more limited "Choice of Court Convention" whereby parties under the Convention recognize a choice of court agreement between parties in the field of civil law and thus courts not selected in the agreement will stay all proceedings (unless the chosen court refuses to uphold the jurisdiction).

US treble damage judgments resulting from antitrust cases are particularly difficult to enforce abroad. Under international law, a State is generally entitled to refuse to recognize or enforce a foreign judgment incompatible with its public policy, and many States tend to view treble damage awards as inherently grossly excessive inasmuch as they include noncompensatory elements.

§4.06 INTERNATIONAL ARBITRATION

International arbitration has emerged in recent years as a preferred mode for the resolution of international disputes, primarily where contractual relations already exist between the disputing parties. When properly designed and implemented, an arbitration agreement provides the parties with the benefits of a mutually acceptable forum and of reasoned decision-making by one or more impartial arbiters applying the governing law selected by the parties. Much of the business community perceives arbitration as capable of affording a relatively inexpensive and speedy recourse for resolving a controversy.

The modern development and expansion of the arbitration process in the US and, indeed, throughout the world, is an interesting story. Following the path already taken by the English common law from which US law evolved, the US judiciary initially took an inhospitable view against the enforceability of arbitration agreements. This hostility came from the view that agreements to arbitrate were contrary to public policy inasmuch as they sought to deprive the courts of their lawful jurisdiction and to place the adjudication of disputes in unreliable, and perhaps even incompetent or corrupt, private hands. Over time, however, the establishment of strong arbitration institutions in the 1920s, including the International Chamber of Commerce and the American Arbitration Association, led to the adoption of the Geneva Protocol and the Geneva Convention which provided an international framework for the enforceability of arbitration agreements. National legislation designed to recognize arbitration also began to take hold, including the Federal Arbitration Act ("FAA") enacted in the US in 1925.

The cornerstone of modern international commercial arbitration was laid in 1958 with the signing of the United Nations Convention on the Recognition and Enforcement of Foreign Arbitral Awards, generally referred to as the "New York Convention." That treaty requires national courts, subject to certain exceptions, to recognize the validity of arbitration agreements and to enforce foreign arbitral awards. It also requires national courts to refer parties to arbitration when those parties have entered into a valid agreement to arbitrate that is subject to the Convention. In the US, the FAA, which had been drafted to deal with domestic arbitration, was subsequently amended to add implementing legislation for the New York Convention and the Inter-American Arbitration Convention. It is not our aim here to detail the extensive case law that has since emerged on the subject of international commercial arbitration in the US. The salient points, for our purposes, are that the US courts, with the Supreme Court in the lead, have articulated doctrine which is very pro-arbitration, which is applicable in both federal and state courts, and which, among other things, makes antitrust law enforcement a potential subject of the arbitration process.

Article II of the New York Convention states that each Contracting State shall recognize an arbitration agreement if it concerns "a subject matter capable of settlement by arbitration." Under Article V(2), among the grounds on which recognition and enforcement of an arbitral award may be refused are when "the competent authority in the country where recognition and enforcement is sought finds that: (a) the subject matter of the difference is not capable of settlement by arbitration under the law of that country; or (b) the recognition or enforcement of the award would be contrary to the public policy of that country." These treaty provisions clearly provide national authorities with significant discretion to declare that matters inherent in a private dispute impinge on matters of public policy and hence are not arbitrable. Nonetheless, in the 1974 decision in *Scherk v. Alberto-Culver Co.*, the Supreme Court noting that the FAA reversed "centuries of judicial hostility to arbitration" and, citing also concerns of international comity, gave effect to the parties' agreement to arbitrate their international commercial dispute, notwithstanding that the dispute involved questions under the federal securities laws.

Another landmark Supreme Court decision in this area came in 1985, in *Mitsubishi Motors Corp. v. Soler Chrysler-Plymouth*, which raised the question of the arbitrability under the FAA and the New York Convention of claims arising under the Sherman Act. The dispute was one between a Japanese auto manufacturer (Mitsubishi) and its Puerto Rican distributor (Soler). The distribution agreement between them provided for disputes to be "finally settled by arbitration in Japan in accordance with the rules and regulations of the Japan Commercial Arbitration Association." When a dispute arose in the course of which Mitsubishi withheld shipment of vehicles to Soler and brought suit in federal court to compel arbitration of the controversy, Soler counterclaimed on a number of legal grounds, including the claim that Mitsubishi and another of its distributors had conspired to divide markets in violation of Section 1 of the Sherman Act. The trial court ordered that all of the issues be submitted to arbitration pursuant to the agreement between the parties, but the Court of Appeals reversed, reasoning that the federal antitrust claims were not arbitrable.

In a majority opinion written by Justice Blackmun, the Court held that the antitrust claims raised by Soler were subject to the agreement to arbitrate. Applying what it described as "a healthy regard for the federal policy favoring arbitration," the Court first determined that the language of the parties' arbitration agreement was sufficiently broad to cover the antitrust issues raised by Soler. The majority opinion concluded that "concerns of international comity, respect for the capacities of foreign and transnational tribunals, and sensitivity to the need of the international commercial system for predictability in the resolution of disputes require that we enforce the parties' agreement, even assuming that a contrary result would be forthcoming in a domestic context." The Court voiced confidence that international arbitrators could be selected who would adjudicate fairly and capably the complexities that antitrust issues might present. As to the fundamental importance to "American democratic capitalism" of the antitrust regime, including the private treble damage remedy, the Court remarked that "so long as the prospective litigant effectively may vindicate its statutory cause of action in the arbitral forum, the statute will continue to serve both its remedial and deterrent function." Citing Article V(2) of the New York Convention, the Court observed that, in any event, "the national courts of the United States will have the opportunity at the award enforcement stage to ensure that the legitimate interest in the enforcement of the antitrust laws has been addressed." However, there is reason to question this assumption by the Court that a faulty arbitral handling of the US antitrust issues presented in such an international case will necessarily later find its way to the scrutiny of the US judicial system.

Justice Stevens wrote a strong dissent to the Court's opinion, in which he was joined by two Justices. This opinion disagreed with the Court's reading of the parties' arbitration clause as encompassing antitrust claims, and, moreover, it forcefully rejected the suggestion that Congress intended to authorize the arbitration of statutory, as distinct from purely contractual, claims. In the view of the dissent, Congress intended the protections afforded by statute to be administered by the judiciary and not by private arbitrators, a legislative desire supported by profound policy reasons applying with special force to antitrust law, "the Magna Carta of free enterprise" in the US. The dissenting opinion brushed away the majority's invocation of international comity, pointing out that the New York Convention expressly authorizes contracting nations to declare that some subject matters are not capable of arbitration because of the public policy considerations involved.

The *Mitsubishi* decision majority opinion is the law of the land as of this writing, and it thrusts into the lap of arbitrators the obligation of adjudicating US antitrust law claims when the issues are covered by the arbitration agreements defining the arbitrators' jurisdiction. The courts' thus conferring on arbitrators the responsibility, in selective instances, of enforcing the US antitrust laws raises a number of perplexing questions. Among them are: is the arbitrator, whose traditional role is to adjudicate only those issues which are placed before him/her by the parties, now also a sort of private attorney general who is duty bound to bring forth and resolve lurking antitrust questions which the parties have not presented by their arguments? How do the arbitrators effectively obtain market data for this purpose not only from uncooperative parties but also from nonparties who are in the pertinent industry? Which antitrust laws should the arbitrators apply where several nations' laws potentially apply to a commercial transaction, perhaps doing so on what has traditionally been labeled as an "extraterritorial" basis? And will international arbitrators, generally persons chosen for their skill and experience in areas of commercial law, be sufficiently trained or suited to put on the hats of regulators, applying such concepts as the "rule of reason" and shaping competition law remedies available under statutory law? There are more questions than answers in these areas nowadays, but this has not deterred the courts from continuing to adhere to the rule laid down by *Mitsubishi*.

Notwithstanding *Mitsubishi*, litigants unhappy with the prospects or results of leaving their antitrust disputes in the hands of arbitrators have not hesitated to knock on the courthouse doors. *Baxter International, Inc. v. Abbott Laboratories*, a case decided in 2003 by the Seventh Circuit, was such a case. In a dispute over the selling of an anesthetic in the US, Abbott initiated an arbitration against Baxter under an agreement specifying dispute resolution by a multinational arbitral tribunal, the latter consisting of a US lawyer, a Spanish lawyer and a Japanese law professor. The arbitrators ruled for Abbott, rejecting Baxter's reading of the patent license in question and its argument that a contrary reading would result in a violation of § 1 of the Sherman Act. On cross suits filed by Abbott and Baxter, the district court directed Baxter to comply with the arbitration award, rejecting Baxter's contention that the arbitrators' reading of the license violated the Sherman Act as a *per se* unlawful territorial allocation.

A divided panel of the Seventh Circuit affirmed. The majority opinion observed that the argument pressed by Baxter concerned the arbitrators' correctness on a point of law, and a mistake of law is not a ground on which an arbitral award can be set aside under the New York Convention. The court also relied on the Supreme Court's holding in *Mitsubishi* that international arbitration of antitrust claims is appropriate. Accordingly, as between Baxter and Abbott the arbitrators' decision was to be deemed conclusive, the court adding that, if the arrangement in question "really does offend the Sherman Act, then the United States, the FTC, or any purchaser of [the anesthetic] is free to sue and obtain relief."

One member of the panel, Judge Cudahy, dissented on the ground that the arbitral panel, with its lone American member dissenting, had reached an unlawful result to the dispute by reading the agreements as granting Abbott a monopoly in the US, thus effecting a "horizontal allocation of markets, a clear violation of the Sherman Act." Lamenting the "growing fondness for arbitration" which has come to "pervade the legal culture," Judge Cudahy pointed out that the New York Convention permits courts to refuse to confirm awards that are against public policy and yet the panel majority was here denying the court's "prerogative to refuse to enforce awards that command unlawful conduct." With the public interest in a competitive market at stake, the courts could not, in Judge Cudahy's view, simply allow arbitrators to command unlawful conduct, thus excising antitrust arbitration from the general framework of judicial review.

Baxter filed a petition for rehearing *en banc* but a majority of the judges of the Seventh Circuit voted to deny such rehearing. Three judges dissented from the denial of the rehearing *en banc*. Their dissenting opinion criticized the position taken by the panel majority as capable of being read as giving arbitrators the unreviewable authority to decide for themselves whether they are commanding the parties to violate the law, adding that:

> Arbitration is an ever-expanding means of resolving conflicts without incurring the increased expenditure of time and funds often associated with litigation. With due respect to the parties' choice of decision makers and also to legislative policies favoring arbitration, the role of the courts to interpret and uphold the law should not be dismissed casually. The opinion of the panel majority clouds the authority of the court to review arbitration agreements of private parties that violate public policy—an authority repeatedly acknowledged by the Supreme Court ... .

Nonetheless, the Supreme Court denied Baxter's petition for review, leaving this issue without a definitive resolution.

In a subsequent case, *JLM Industries, Inc. et al. v. Stolt-Nielsen S.A. et al.*, decided in 2004, a group of shippers of bulk chemicals filed antitrust and other claims in federal court against large ocean carriers who, it was alleged, dominated the international parcel tanker service industry. The individual shipping transactions at issue were each governed by a standard form of contract which provided that any disputes arising from the shipment were to be submitted to arbitration in either London or New York. When some of the tanker owners moved to compel arbitration pursuant to these contracts, the shippers sought to distinguish *Mitsubishi* and other precedents by arguing that *Mitsubishi* concerned antitrust issues involving a single manufacturer in a vertical context, whereas the instant case involved a more far reaching scenario of a horizontal conspiracy broadly restraining competition. The shippers' essential point was that such an antitrust case threatening "monstrous" proceedings and widespread injury would likely be too complex for an arbitration panel to handle successfully.

The Court of Appeals for the Second Circuit was unimpressed by this contention and offered its reading of *Mitsubishi* as "explicitly [rejecting] the argument that the complexity of any sort of antitrust claim is a reason to reject arbitration." The court also "[declined plaintiffs'] invitation to speculate as to the substantive law that will be applied by a British arbitral panel and, as the Supreme Court directs in *Mitsubishi*, [we] assume that [a plaintiff] 'effectively may vindicate its statutory cause of action in the arbitral forum.'"

The US courts have confirmed that the arbitrators' adjudicative and remedial powers in antitrust cases are great. In a 2004 decision, *American Gas Central Eastern Texas Gas Co. v. Union Pacific Resources Group Inc.*, the federal district court and the Court of Appeals for the Fifth Circuit affirmed an arbitrator's award upholding monopolization claims under § 2 of the Sherman Act. The complainant, known as "ACET," a natural gas "gatherer," asserted that Duke Energy was monopolizing the local gas processing market and refusing to deal with it in order to exclude it from competition. The arbitrator accepted ACET's claims and ordered Duke to offer ACET a new processing contract. The district court denied Duke Energy's motion to vacate and confirmed the award. The Court of Appeals affirmed, citing the presumption in favor of arbitration, and concluded that none of the grounds for *vacatur* of the award was applicable, including manifest disregard of the law. In particular, the Fifth Circuit refused to overturn the arbitrator's conclusions that (1) ACET suffered antitrust injury, (2) Duke Energy held monopoly power in the local gas market, (3) Duke Energy had engaged in exclusionary conduct as described in Supreme Court precedents, (4) the award remedy was suitable to restore competition in the market, and (5) it was within the arbitrator's authority to grant injunctive relief.

The pro-arbitration bent of US law now extends to important procedural issues as well. In *Green Tree Financial Corp. v. Bazzle et al.*, decided in 2003, a plurality of the Supreme Court decided that the arbitrator's authority to decide issues of contract interpretation meant that an arbitrator (and not a court) had the responsibility of deciding whether disputes arising from separate contracts between a commercial lender, Green Tree, and its customers could be administered through "class arbitration proceedings." The Court's conclusion was largely premised on its reading of the arbitration clause in each case as a broad one indicating the parties' agreement that "an arbitrator, not a judge, would answer the relevant question [whether the arbitration contracts forbade the use of class arbitration procedures.]" Three Justices dissented, reasoning that the majority had misconstrued the intent of the parties, inasmuch as Green Tree "had the contractual right to choose an arbitrator for each dispute with the ... 3,734 individual class members, and this right was denied when the same arbitrator was foisted upon [it] to resolve those claims ... ."

In recent years, the Supreme Court has granted review and rendered decisions (often split decisions) in many cases involving arbitration agreements, Cases have come to the courts on the part of individuals and small businesses seeking to shed themselves of arbitration commitments imposed on them by credit card companies and other large businesses. Agreed waivers of class action procedures that are one sided favoring the more powerful party have also been unsuccessfully attacked in the courts.

Private antitrust claims are often litigated by plaintiffs joining in a class action because the individual claims are each too small in amount to bear the expense of a large litigation against a well financed corporate opponent. If a plaintiff is unable to join in a class action with others who are similarly situated, he/she may simply have no effective remedy for his/her claim. This made the Supreme Court's 2013 decision in *American Express Co. v. Italian Colors Restaurant* a particularly important one.

That case concerned the agreement between American Express and the merchants honoring its credit card which provided that any disputes between them would be settled by arbitration and that there would be no right or authority for any claims to be arbitrated on a class action basis. (this negation is called a "class action waiver") The aggrieved merchants nonetheless filed an antitrust class action in court alleging an unlawful tying arrangement and arguing that the class action waiver should be deemed unenforceable because, given the costs of retaining the necessary experts in antitrust cases, individual prosecution of their claims was impossible. A majority of the Supreme Court rejected this argument. The majority opinion relied on the fact that arbitration is a matter of individual contract, and that the antitrust laws grant no unwaivable right to class actions. In the majority's view, the Federal Arbitration Act, which governed here, grants no right to invalidate a class action waiver on the grounds asserted. A strong dissent argued that it has been settled since *Mitsubishi* that an arbitration clause will not be enforced if it prevents the vindication of federal statutory rights. Moreover, monopoly power was used to force this class action waiver on the merchants. The three Justices dissenting urged therefore that, because the economics of antitrust cases requires obtaining expert economic analysis (an expensive undertaking), a class action waiver is the equivalent of a contract foreclosing antitrust liability and should not be permitted. Of course, the majority opinion, written by Justice Scalia, established the prevailing law.

CHAPTER 5
Conspiracies, Joint Ventures and Monopolization in US Commerce

§5.01 THE SHERMAN ACT § 1

In Chapter 3 we discussed the general principle that the US courts have subject matter jurisdiction to apply the US antitrust laws when certain practices in international commerce have a direct, substantial, and reasonably foreseeable effect on the commerce of the US. In this and succeeding chapters we will be discussing particular types of practices in domestic and international trade that have been held to violate the US antitrust laws. The present chapter will deal with agreements among competitors and potential competitors, as well as the subject of monopolization, matters governed from the antitrust viewpoint primarily by Sections 1 and 2 of the Sherman Act.

[A] Contracts, Combinations, and Conspiracies

Under US antitrust law, so-called hard core or naked anticompetitive agreements, such as price fixing, bid rigging, allocation of customers or territories, and boycotts, are proscribed in international commerce as well as in interstate commerce as *per se* illegal when they have the requisite effect on US commerce. A substantial number of the US antitrust cases brought in the international setting have involved cartels—secret agreements among dominant world firms in an industry to divide up global markets among themselves and/or fix prices. As will be discussed, many instances of these hard core restraints of trade have been uncovered as the twenty-first century has unfolded. This is somewhat surprising, considering that vigorous US antitrust enforcement against such practices has long been established, that the potential criminal penalties and civil suit exposure have become truly momentous in scope, and that tough anti-cartel measures have also been taken in Europe, Canada, and elsewhere.

Other forms of collaboration among competitors and potential competitors, which have justifiable and redeeming economic value, are subject to evaluation under the rule of reason under the antitrust laws. Among these types of agreement which we shall consider are bona fide joint ventures, group efforts at standardization, and cooperative purchasing arrangements.

Because Section 1 of the Sherman Act is addressed to "every contract, combination ... or conspiracy, in restraint of trade ...," one person acting alone cannot violate that statutory provision. An agreement, understanding, or concert of action between two or more parties is thus a prerequisite to a violation of this provision. As the Supreme Court stated as early as the *Eastern States Retail Lumber Dealers Association* case in 1914: "An act harmless when done by one may become a public wrong when done by many acting in concert, for it then takes on the form of a conspiracy ... ."

Under the Sherman Act, "contract" normally means a formal written agreement entered into by the parties. "Combination" more generally refers to a union of activity on the part of two or more persons. "Conspiracy" has been defined in law as a combination designed to accomplish an illegal purpose or to carry out a legal purpose by illegal means.

As we have previously noted, for US antitrust purposes, the existence of a "contract, combination ... or conspiracy" is not dependent upon there being a written or even what used to be called a "gentleman's" agreement between the parties, and one may be inferred from a pattern of conduct. The true test remains whether the conduct of the parties stemmed from an agreement, tacit or express, as distinct from independent decision. As a practical matter, the question of when a tacit agreement can fairly be inferred from parallel conduct remains an elusive one. It is often said that parallel conduct "plus" some other evidence indicating the existence of an agreement, such as identical pricing which obtains an unusually high profit, are sufficient to permit the inference of unlawful conspiracy to be made.

In the 1969 case of *United States v. Container Corporation of America*, the Supreme Court held that an agreement on the part of certain corrugated container manufacturers, who accounted for approximately 90% of the shipments in a certain area, to exchange price information concerning specific sales to identified customers constituted an unlawful combination or conspiracy in violation of Section 1 of the Sherman Act. Although characterizing the agreement as "somewhat casual," and notwithstanding the absence of any formal agreement to adhere to a price schedule, the Court nevertheless concluded that: "Each defendant on receiving [a] request usually furnished the data with the expectation that it would be furnished reciprocal information when it wanted it. That concerted action is of course sufficient to establish the conspiracy, the initial ingredient of a violation of Section 1 of the Sherman Act."

It should be noted that in 2009 the Supreme Court decided the case of *Bell Atlantic Corp. v. Twombly*, in which the Court appreciably stiffened the pleading requirements for plaintiffs by insisting that factual allegations be specific if a case is to survive a motion to dismiss. In that case, bare allegations of parallel conduct and conspiracy were held insufficient.

We have previously mentioned that the Supreme Court established the rule of reason in the 1911 *Standard Oil* case as a limitation on the application of Section 1 of the Sherman Act. Illegal restraints are those that are "unreasonably restrictive" of trade. As we have also observed, there is a category of agreements that are considered *per se* violations of the antitrust laws in that they are deemed inherently unreasonable, regardless of their context or of any claimed justification.

[B] Cartels: Price Fixing, Production Limitation, and Market Allocation

Many of the early important Sherman Act cases involved price fixing agreements between or among US competitors which affected US interstate commerce, rather than foreign commerce. This was the context, for example, of the *Electrical Equipment* cases in the 1960s which resulted in large fines, prison sentences, and civil damage cases.

As international commerce has flourished, so have illegal international conspiracies. They represent, if you will, an undesirable form of international business cooperation. Conspiracies among competitors to fix prices often include other illicit agreements designed to further the anticompetitive design of the parties, such as commitments to limit production, or allocations of territories and/or customers among the parties. Such agreements among competitors of different nationalities have been features of the classic "cartel" arrangement. The word "cartel," identical to the French word and very similar to the German word "kartell," generally connotes an international conspiracy to restrain trade. The opportunities to enforce competition law against international cartels have been plentiful over the years, and today such cartel activity continues to be a fertile source of antitrust proceedings around the world.

The Supreme Court has held many times, including in the landmark cases of *United States v. Topco Associates, Inc.* and *Palmer v. BRG of Georgia*, that agreements between competitors to allocate territories to minimize competition are illegal even if styled as joint ventures.

One of the main thrusts of US antitrust enforcement involving foreign trade has been against international agreements that fix import prices or allocate territories among the competitors, limiting US imports. The US Government considers that import competition often provides a needed stimulus for the more concentrated and complacent US domestic industries and that, therefore, the protection of competition coming from abroad is an essential element in the maintenance of the competitive system generally. International cartel arrangements mandated or participated in by foreign governments, such as the oil production limitations implemented by the Organization of Petroleum Exporting Countries ("OPEC"), raise challenging antitrust enforcement problems. The OPEC cases and the special issues raised by them were discussed in previous chapters.

In 1911, the same year that it decided the *Standard Oil* case, the Supreme Court condemned an international cartel arrangement under Sections 1 and 2 of the Sherman Act in the *United States v. American Tobacco Co.* case. Several corporations engaged in the tobacco trade, some American and some English, had entered into agreements in England allocating world markets in that trade, including the US market. The Court determined that the purpose of the combination was, from the beginning, to acquire control of the tobacco trade and to monopolize it by dividing markets and driving out competitors.

Another leading case in the field, the 1947 case of *United States v. National Lead Co.* involved the division by the dominant producers of titanium compounds of the world market into exclusive territories. An American company was granted all of North America as its domain. The Supreme Court had no difficulty finding this a violation of Section 1 of the Sherman Act, stating that "[n]o citation of authority is any longer necessary to support the proposition that a combination of competitors, which by agreement divides the world into exclusive trade areas, and suppresses all competition among the members of the combination, offends the Sherman Act." The defendants had cross-licensed patents to help effectuate the market allocation. They argued that this was a proper exercise of IP rights, justifying the restrictive agreements. In rejecting this argument, the reviewing courts emphasized that IP rights cannot be utilized to implement unlawful market allocations. This is still the law.

In the *Timken* antifriction bearings case, decided in 1951, world market allocation agreements among American, British, and French companies were sought to be justified on the grounds that these were part of a legitimate joint venture among the parties. The Supreme Court held the arrangements unlawful under the Sherman Act.

It observed that the district court had found that the dominant purpose of the agreement was to avoid competition. The Court also reasoned that agreements between legally separate entities to suppress competition among themselves and others cannot be justified by labeling the project a "joint venture."

In the 1970s an indictment and civil proceedings were brought in the US alleging a conspiracy by a number of US and European corporations and individuals to control the world supply of the important medicinal drugs, quinine and quinidine, and of cinchona bark, the material from which quinine is derived. The international cartel agreements allegedly included bid rigging on the purchase of quinine supplies from the US Government, fixing the prices of quinine in the US and elsewhere, and control of the world supply of cinchona bark. These US proceedings resulted in fines in the criminal case, consent decrees, and settlements. In a development foreshadowing modern international antitrust enforcement, in which cartels must face attacks from multiple authorities, the Commission of the European Communities brought a proceeding against the European quinine producers under Article 85 of the Treaty of Rome. This case also led to the imposition of fines.

Obtaining definitive evidence concerning international cartel activity is often difficult since individuals and documentation may escape by crossing national boundaries, and government to government cooperation, at least in the past, was not always operating at optimal levels. The US Government had been pursuing the DeBeers company since at least the 1940s for allegedly monopolizing the US foreign trade in African source diamonds. In that early case, the Justice Department sued nine foreign defendants, including DeBeers and the other major diamond producers in Africa, charging that they had caused all diamonds produced in Africa to be sold through a single selling agency. The Supreme Court reversed the district court with respect to an injunction issued by that court and later the lower court dismissed the complaint on the ground of lack of jurisdiction over the defendants.

Fifty years later, an antitrust indictment was filed by the Department of Justice in 1994 alleging that the General Electric Co. and DeBeers Centenary AG, a Swiss

Chapter 5: Conspiracies, Joint Ventures and Monopolization §5.01[B]

company affiliated with the DeBeers group, had conspired to fix the price of industrial diamonds worldwide. The Justice Department argued that General Electric passed price information in advance to a person who acted as agent for DeBeers. The case against General Electric was tried, and the company was acquitted. DeBeers, headquartered in Switzerland, was not tried on the charge because the US court lacked jurisdiction over the company. At her press briefing on the litigation, Attorney General Janet Reno commented that the Department had encountered difficulty in obtaining foreign-based documents on the matter.

However, a company's need to be a successful participant in the US market can be a powerful magnet. Ten years later, in a 2004 plea agreement with the federal prosecutors to resolve the 1994 indictment, DeBeers pleaded guilty to having violated Sherman § 1 by entering into agreements to raise prices for industrial diamond products sold worldwide, as charged in the indictment. It was sentenced to pay a USD 10,000,000 fine, the statutory maximum at the time the offense was committed.

The "corporate leniency policy" conducted by the Division, whereby the first company advising the Antitrust Division of its participation in illegal activity is spared from criminal enforcement, has provided significant motivation causing antitrust violators to turn themselves and their co-conspirators in to the authorities. As we have noted, there is a similar leniency policy applicable to individuals who approach the Division on their own behalf to confess participation in activity illegal under the antitrust laws. A large number of the government's antitrust investigations have been initiated or advanced by information received from a leniency applicant. The Antitrust Division has described its leniency program as its "most effective generator of international cartel cases," as well as a model for similar programs by antitrust authorities around the world.

As we noted earlier, the Antitrust Criminal Penalty Enhancement and Reform Act of 2004 which increased the maximum fines and jail sentences for antitrust criminal offenses also brought about a reduction in a major disincentive for amnesty applicants, namely, the impact of the private treble damage suits which generally follow on the heels of each government prosecution. The detrebling feature of the Act limits the damages recoverable from a corporate amnesty applicant that also gives full cooperation to private plaintiffs with respect to their damage actions against the cartel members to the actual damages inflicted by the amnesty applicant's own conduct.

In the final years of the last century, the Antitrust Division, acting on information from an executive employed by Archer Daniels Midland Co. ("ADM"), a large US "agribusiness" firm, began an investigation of price fixing and sales allocation among ADM and other producers of lysine, an additive for agricultural feed. This led the Department to a second investigation, this one into alleged worldwide price fixing and market allocation among ADM and other producers of citric acid, a food flavor additive and preservative used in many consumer products, including soft drinks and detergents. In October of 1996 ADM agreed to plead guilty to the two conspiracies and to pay a USD 100 million fine, at that time the largest criminal antitrust fine ever imposed. Two Japanese companies, a Korean company, a US-based Korean subsidiary, and various executives pleaded guilty and agreed to pay fines in connection with the lysine conspiracy. Two Swiss companies, a Dutch firm, the US-based subsidiary of a German company, and various executives also pleaded guilty and paid fines for participating in the citric acid conspiracy.

The Government made full use of its informant in the lysine cases. It was able to play for the jury, in one of the cases that went to trial, audio and video excerpts of price fixing meetings held by the conspirators in hotel rooms. It caught a senior executive of a US company telling a foreign competitor that, "... our competitors are our friends. Our customers are the enemy." The Antitrust Division had dressed an FBI agent as a hotel "bellhop" to deliver a briefcase to the meeting rooms with a hidden recording device.

Working closely with the US officials, the Canadian antitrust authorities were also able to collect record fines from ADM and other international producers of lysine, citric acid, and sodium gluconate. In June 2000 the European Commission announced that it had fined ADM, two Japanese companies, and two South Korean firms a total of EUR 110 million (USD 105.4 million) in connection with their fixing of lysine prices worldwide. Because the firms here were engaged in multiple cartels, the investigations had a serial effect. For example, the investigation and prosecution of the international citric acid cartel led to the investigation and prosecution of the international sodium gluconate cartel, which resulted in prosecution of the international sodium erythorbate cartel, which led to prosecution of the international maltol cartel.

Exposure and prosecution of another cartel, this one involving vitamin products, represented a signal victory for the antitrust enforcement authorities. The Antitrust Division brought a number of criminal indictments alleging a worldwide conspiracy, lasting from 1990 into 1999, to raise prices and allocate market shares for the sales of vitamins C and E, and other important nutritional supplements. The asserted leader of the conspiracy, F. Hoffman-La Roche Ltd. of Switzerland, agreed to pay a USD 500 million fine, the largest fine to be imposed in a US criminal case at that time, and BASF of Germany agreed to pay a USD 225 million fine. A Swiss executive agreed to pay a fine and serve a four-month prison sentence in the US for having previously lied to Department investigators in an attempt to cover up the conspiracy. Three Japanese companies committed themselves to paying USD 137 million for their role in the cartel. Joel Klein, the head of the Antitrust Division of the Justice Department, told an antitrust conference that the government's anti-cartel actions had "transformed the world" in that, "[i]n Europe, there was a kind of de facto understanding that cartel arrangements were tolerated ... [this perception] has changed dramatically." The European Commission subsequently imposed fines on eight companies amounting to a total of more than EUR 850 million for participation in the vitamin products cartel.

The defendants in the cartels who were successfully prosecuted by the Justice Department were also sued in the US in civil class actions seeking treble damages for purchasers of the subject products. These cases generally resulted in the payment of large settlements. For example, the defendants in the private class action litigation brought on behalf of direct purchasers of vitamins agreed to settle for USD 1.05 billion, a record for a private antitrust price fixing case settlement. (This amount was significantly reduced after the largest direct purchasers decided to opt out of the class action settlement and file separate cases.) Additional large settlements were announced in private class action and *parens patriae* cases brought against the vitamin producers by twenty-four state attorneys general on behalf of indirect purchasers, including the states themselves.

In another major cartel case, the Antitrust Division's graphite electrode investigation led to the conviction of seven corporations and three individuals, including the imposition of a fine of USD 134 million on Mitsubishi Corporation. Mitsubishi did not manufacture graphite electrodes, but it was charged with aiding the price fixing cartel in which its 50% US subsidiary was a participant. This was also the first case in which a Japanese business executive agreed to face a possible jail sentence for a violation of US antitrust law. The Antitrust Division also discovered that between 1999 and 2002 the rival makers of dynamic random-access memory chips ("DRAM chips") met to agree on DRAM chip prices and exchanged information to monitor sales volumes.

Micron Technology Inc. was the first to abandon the cartel and cooperate with the government. As a result, it escaped government fines. Other participants pleaded guilty, including Samsung Electronics Ltd. of South Korea which agreed in October 2005 to pay a USD 300 million fine, the second largest antitrust fine ever paid in the US at that time.

As the present century unfolded, the percentage of corporate defendants in criminal cases that were foreign-based firms surged from approximately half to nearly 70% and then returned to around 44%. The pressure on foreign individual defendants to give themselves up to US custody heightened. In 2001, the Antitrust Division adopted a policy of placing indicted fugitives on a "wanted" notice list maintained by INTERPOL, serving as a request that the subject be arrested with a view toward extradition. Several fugitive defendants were, in fact, apprehended through INTERPOL's "Red Notice" watchlist. Foreign defendants from Canada, Sweden, Germany, Switzerland, France, the Netherlands, Norway, the United Kingdom, and Japan served prison sentences in US jails for violating the US antitrust laws. In fiscal year 2005, the average jail sentence rose to an all-time high of twenty-four months.

Cooperation with foreign authorities intensified. The US and other countries took turns hosting an annual International Cartels Workshop, and, in 2001, the ICN of competition law officials was launched. This informal cooperation was accompanied by more case-specific cooperation featuring "dawn raids" (drop-in interviews and searches) and the service of subpoenas which were conducted in multiple jurisdictions simultaneously. In the investigation into the bid rigging of US funded water treatment contracts in Egypt, over 100 German police officers assisted the Antitrust Division in the simultaneous execution of search warrants on multiple companies at locations across Germany. In February 2003, the Antitrust Division, the EC Directorate-General for Competition, the Canadian Competition Bureau, and the Japan Fair Trade Commission ("JFTC") simultaneously launched searches and dawn raids investigating cartel activity on three continents.

In discussing the vigorous ongoing enforcement effort against international cartels, the subject of the extradition of antitrust law violators bears some mention. The US antitrust authorities pursuing criminal offenders long had difficulty obtaining physical custody of foreign individuals who did not set foot in the US after they were indicted. Antitrust law violations, including those criminalized under US law, were generally not deemed "extraditable" offenses under applicable treaties. Indeed, the

UK-US Mutual Legal Assistance Treaty (MLAT) was accompanied by a "side letter" which expressly excluded antitrust matters from the cooperation provisions of that treaty. However, after the British Government adopted legislation creating a new criminal offense for individuals who engage in hard core cartel activity (*see* Chapter 14), and also as a result of the 2001 terrorist attacks on the US, a new and more ambitious UK-US Extradition Treaty was agreed and came into effect. The side letter to the MLAT was removed. The new agreement described an extraditable offense on a pure "dual criminality" basis, rather than in terms of listed extraditable offenses.

This new cooperation was quickly fruitful. In 2007 the Antitrust Division announced that an independent consultant and two executives of Dunlop Oil & Marine, a manufacturer of marine hose located in Grimsby, United Kingdom, had pleaded guilty and agreed to serve prison sentences for participating in a conspiracy to rig bids, fix prices, and allocate market shares of marine hose sold in the US. Under the terms of their plea agreements, the individual defendants agreed to plead guilty to the US charges, then be escorted in custody back to the UK to cooperate with the Office of Fair Tradings (OFTs) investigation of the UK's Enterprise Act of 2002 and to allow them to plead guilty to violating the Enterprise Act.

Also in 2007, British Airways (BA) PLC, Qantas Airlines, and Japan Airlines (JAL), as well as other airlines and executives, pleaded guilty to participating in a conspiracy to fix rates charged to customers for international air cargo shipments. The following year, a British citizen agreed to plead guilty, serve eight months in jail and pay a criminal fine for participating in that conspiracy.

In the previous edition of this book, we reported on the case of Mr. Ian Norris, the former head of the British firm, Morgan Crucible plc, who was indicted in 2004 by a US grand jury for fixing prices on carbon products and organizing a conspiracy to obstruct justice. After much effort to avoid extradition to the US, including a trip to the House of Lords, Mr. Norris lost his application and in December 2010 was sentenced to prison in the US. He was not extraditable to the US on the antitrust charges since price fixing was not a criminal offense in the UK at the time in question (it is now). He was, however, extraditable on the obstruction charge.

As we described in Chapter 3, in 2012 and for several years thereafter the Antitrust Division successfully pursued its criminal case against a worldwide scheme to fix prices in liquid crystal display ("LCD") panels.

The Antitrust Division began in 2011 an investigation into price fixing, bid rigging and market allocation in the global auto parts industry. The investigation resulted in charges being brought, over several years, against ninety individuals and corporations with billions of dollars in fines being collected. For example, in 2015 a federal grand jury returned an indictment against two Japanese executives with conspiring to fix the price to automobile manufacturers in the US and elsewhere of spark plugs, standard oxygen sensors and air fuel ratio sensors. NGK Spark Plug, a Japanese company and the employer of the executives, had earlier pleaded guilty for its role in the conspiracy and agreed to pay a USD 52.11 million criminal fine. Other indictments against Japanese auto parts firms, their subsidiaries, and executives were returned in 2016. The massive collusion involved was believed to have begun in 2000 and continued until at least 2010.

As noted, the Justice Department also secured guilty pleas of violations of the Sherman Act in the world marine hose industry. In 2014, it obtained the extradition from Germany of an Italian national, Romano Pisciotti, on charges of participating in the conspiracy to suppress and eliminate competition by rigging bids, fixing prices and allocating market shares on sales of marine hose sold in the US and elsewhere. This represented the first successful extradition on a US antitrust charge. Extradition has historically been a challenge because it generally requires that the conduct be criminal in both of the countries involved.

In 2015, US Deputy Attorney General Sally Q. Yates issued the so-called Yates Memo which sought to formalize the policy on the prosecution of individuals responsible for corporate misconduct. This directive did not alter the practices in the Antitrust Division's Corporate Leniency Program, but, among other things, required prosecutors to focus on individual wrongdoers at the inception of investigations.

Also in 2015, five major banks agreed to plead guilty to conspiring to manipulate the price of US dollars and euros exchanged in the foreign currency exchange (FX) spot market. The banks agreed to pay criminal fines totaling more than USD 2.5 billion.

In other recent cases, indictments have also been returned against firms and executives for conspiring to fix the prices of electrolytic capacitors and for participating in a long running conspiracy to fix prices and allocate customers for international ocean shipments of roll-on, roll-off cargo.

In October 2016, the Antitrust Division secured the extradition from Bulgaria of an Israeli national, Yuval Marshak, for allegedly participating in schemes to falsify bid documents involving the US Foreign Military Financing program. Mr. Marshak pleaded guilty to those violations in 2017.

[C] Antitrust Scrutiny of the Tech Industry

As the importance of the tech industry in the economy has grown, so too has the level of antitrust scrutiny fixed upon its leading firms. We discussed in Chapter 2 the extended Microsoft antitrust litigation commencing in 1994.

In 2010 the Antitrust Division filed a complaint against Apple, Inc., Google, Inc., Intel Corp., Adobe Systems, Inc. and others alleging that these firms had violated the Sherman Act by entering into agreements to prevent each other from attempting to recruit their employees through "cold calls." The defendant firms accepted a settlement whereby they agreed more broadly not to enter into noncompete agreements. In 2015, these firms settled the follow on class action antitrust lawsuit which was brought by the firms' technical employees.

A bitterly fought lawsuit with Apple, Inc. and the electronic book ("e-book") market at its core was initiated in 2012. The Department of Justice, along with thirty-three States and Territories, brought a suit alleging that Apple and five leading book publishing companies had conspired to raise the prices of e-books in violation of Section 1 of the Sherman Act. Amazon was by far the leading seller of e-books in the US, and its maintenance of a USD 9.99 "price point" presented a problem for the publishers' sales of their more profitable hardcover books. It was established that the publishers met privately on a regular basis in the dining rooms of New York restaurants without counsel, when they would discuss this common problem. The publishers used different strategies to address their situation, including withholding books from Amazon. It was also established that Apple executives met with the publishers and that the publishers began to sell e-books for use with Apple's new iPad device through Apple's e-bookstore at higher prices than the Amazon price point.

The defendant publishers having settled their cases with the government, only Apple went to trial. Apple argued that it had participated in a legitimate vertical business arrangement that should be upheld under the rule of reason. The district court disagreed and concluded that Apple had orchestrated and participated in a horizontal price fixing arrangement that represented a *per se* violation of Section 1 of the Sherman Act. On Apple's appeal, the Circuit Court of Appeals for the Second Circuit affirmed the district court's ruling by a 2-1 vote. The majority agreed with the district court that Apple had orchestrated a horizontal conspiracy to raise the prices of e-books in a *per se* violation of Section 1 of the Sherman Act. The dissenting judge urged that the lower court and the majority erred in treating Apple as a participant in a horizontal price fixing conspiracy rather than as a vertical enabler of such a conspiracy, which would require a more appropriate rule of reason test under the Supreme Court's decision in *Leegin Creative Products, Inc. v. PSKS, Inc.* (discussed here earlier). In 2016, the Supreme Court denied review. The Supreme Court's decision triggered an obligation by Apple to pay USD 400 million to e-book purchasers under a settlement agreement it had earlier entered into.

The search giant, Google, a unit of holding company Alphabet, Inc., has been heavily fined by the European Commission following a full blown antitrust investigation, as we will be discussing later. There is also antitrust concern in the US (and in other nations) over Google's alleged monopoly in the online search market. In 2013 the Federal Trade Commission dropped a two-year investigation, concluding that Google had not manipulated search results to the injury of its rivals. Google had to agree to make certain changes in its search practices. Then, in 2015, the FTC opened a preliminary investigation into whether Google uses its popular mobile Android operating system to exclude competitors as more consumers turn to mobile use.

In the next chapter, we describe a lawsuit recently instituted by the Federal Trade Commission against the chip maker, Qualcomm, alleging that the company is extracting elevated royalties from its customers unlawfully.

[D] **Collective Boycotts and Refusals to Deal**

A business normally has full discretion concerning with whom it deals, particularly in its choice of suppliers and of customers. Nevertheless, refusals to deal can, in some contexts, have significant antitrust implications under US antitrust law. In particular, antitrust problems are raised by group decisions not to deal with a party and by refusals to deal on the part of a business in a monopoly or dominant position. Because refusals to deal exclude parties from business transactions and also limit the number of parties participating in the relevant marketplace, they have the inherent characteristic of

Chapter 5: Conspiracies, Joint Ventures and Monopolization §5.01[D]

restraining trade. An agreement of several corporations, partnerships or persons to engage in a concerted refusal to deal—commonly designated as a group boycott—is therefore tantamount to a combination or conspiracy in restraint of trade, to use the language of Section 1 of the Sherman Act. Such exclusions by joint action have been deemed so pernicious that so-called naked group boycotts are held to constitute *per se* violations of Section 1. Here also, an express agreement need not necessarily be shown. Where several parties refuse to deal with the same entity or individual, an agreement can sometimes be inferred from the conduct of the parties, as in the case of other Section 1 violations. On the other hand, because a refusal to deal by a single party does not involve concerted action, it cannot be construed as violating Section 1.

As we shall see later in this Chapter, if, by reason of the market power of the firm concerned and the other attendant facts, the individual refusal to deal can be characterized as an improper effort to create or maintain a monopoly, the refusal will be deemed a violation of Section 2 of the Sherman Act. Alternatively, as we will also be discussing, a powerful seller's insistence on dealing only on a prescribed basis, such as an exclusive arrangement or tie-in sale, may raise challenges under Section 3 of the Clayton Act and Section 5 of the Federal Trade Commission Act. A refusal to accord nondiscriminatory pricing or promotional benefits can be a violation of Section 2 of the Robinson-Patman Act. In this chapter, we now turn to consideration of group boycotts and other collective refusals to deal.

In 1914, the Supreme Court condemned under § 1, in *Eastern States Retail Lumber Dealers' Ass'n. v. United States*, an agreement among lumber retailers to refuse to purchase the products of wholesalers who dealt directly with consumers. Much later, in a 1941 landmark Supreme Court decision, *Fashion Originators' Guild of America v. Federal Trade Commission*, the Court established the principle that, since a group boycott is *per se* illegal, its purpose is irrelevant. That case concerned an agreement among manufacturers of original design dresses to refuse to sell such dresses to retailers who also handled dresses copied or "pirated" from such original designs. The Court upheld the FTC's refusal to hear evidence on the injurious effects of "style piracy." It observed that, even if style piracy were an acknowledged wrong, joint private coercive action was not the appropriate remedy. In *Klor's, Inc. v. Broadway-Hale Stores, Inc. et al.*, in 1959, the Court reiterated that group boycotts are *per se* illegal and are not to be tolerated, whatever the justification, or "merely because the victim is just one merchant whose business is so small that his destruction makes little difference to the economy."

Many boycott arrangements have, in fact, resulted from an industry's efforts to "protect" itself from alleged malefactors, such as price-cutters or defaulting customers. Both of these concerns, among others, were present in the *United States v. Watchmakers of Switzerland Information Center, Inc.* case. In a series of private agreements, several American and Swiss manufacturers and trade associations combined to inhibit the manufacture of watches and watch parts in the US, to the benefit of the Swiss watch industry. The "Collective Convention," to which these parties adhered, embraced some refusals to deal. Thus, the parties agreed not to deal in products made or sold by firms who were not parties to the Convention. They agreed not to sell watch parts for manufacturing purposes or to sell certain watchmaking machines to US watch manufacturers. In addition, the parties maintained and circulated "blacklists" in an effort to boycott firms who violated the agreements, firms in the US who engaged in price cutting on Swiss watches, and customers with a history of financial irresponsibility.

The US District Court for the Southern District of New York held all of these agreements illegal under Section 1 of the Sherman Act, on the authority of *Fashion Originators' Guild* and related cases. The court observed that, "[t]he illegality of defendants' actions cannot be cured by a showing that compliance with the blacklist was not always rigidly enforced."

An agreement to refuse to sell to certain customers may be an ingredient of an illegal conspiracy to divide markets among the conspirators. Then it is both a market allocation agreement and a group boycott for purposes of applying § 1. An indictment in 1940 under Section 1 against a German firm, Carl Zeiss, Inc., included a count that the company had refused to sell military optical instruments for use in the US. The firm protested that it had never dealt in such instruments, but the district court upheld the indictment in *United States v. Bausch & Lomb Optical Co. et al.* because the refusal to sell might prove to be an element of a conspiracy to divide markets. In *Carpet Group Int'l. v. Oriental Rug Importers Assn.*, the Court of Appeals for the Third Circuit held an agreement entered into by rug wholesalers which boycotted rug makers who sold directly to retailers to be unlawful *per se*.

The *per se* illegality rule applies to what are generally called "naked" boycotts, those situations in which the joint refusal to deal is not arguably ancillary to some bona fide business interest of the group. Where the concerted refusal to deal seems to be genuinely intended and fashioned so as to achieve a legitimate objective, it may instead be evaluated under the rule of reason for § 1 purposes.

Joint ventures often pose questions in this context. When a self-selected group of competitors agrees to cooperate on aspects of their business activities in order to implement an unlawful objective, such as price fixing, the arrangement is easily condemned on a *per se* basis under the Sherman Act. Where, however, the group's cooperation is designed to promote efficiencies or reduce costs is it bound to offer membership in the group to every competitor who requests it? Often, offering open membership enhances, or at least does not detract from, the group's valid business objectives. Indeed, the group may desire that all competitors in the market join the effort and pay a share of its costs, rather than sitting outside as "free riders" who get the benefit of the group's program. But the group may wish to exclude nonmembers or discriminate against them in some fashion. In *Associated Press v. United States*, the Supreme Court struck down under the Sherman Act by-laws adopted by a joint venture of some 1,200 newspapers—which was acknowledged to be an efficient joint venture—because those by-laws restrained the access of nonmembers to the AP-gathered news.

A few years ago, the Department of Justice brought a Sherman § 1 case against VISA and MasterCard, alleging that these two payment card systems conspired to restrain trade by enforcing exclusionary rules against their competitors. Specifically, it was alleged that the two systems prohibited their 20,000 bank members from issuing the competitive American Express and Discover cards. The district court found a violation of § 1, ordered the exclusionary rules revoked, and enjoined the defendants from adopting such rules. The Court of Appeals for the Second Circuit affirmed in 2003. The appellate court upheld the lower court's finding that general payment cards were a distinct product market in which VISA and MasterCard had market power. The Second Circuit held that the total exclusion of American Express and Discover from a segment of the market for network services caused harm to competition in that market. The court also rejected the defendants' argument that the arrangement had redeeming procompetitive effects.

[E] Standardization Efforts

Industry standardization efforts raise group boycott issues in a more difficult setting. In many industries, some degree of product standardization is beneficial from the viewpoint of distributors, consumers, and other users of the product by reducing costs and facilitating purchasing decisions. Such standardization is generally achieved on a voluntary basis, by industry sponsored programs, rather than through government regulation. However, a product that is deemed "nonstandard," as the result of such a process, tends to be excluded from the marketplace. The company making that product may justifiably believe that it has been the victim of an illegal group boycott and bring antitrust litigation itself or complain to the government.

Industries seek to avoid antitrust exposure on standards matters by taking a number of precautions. First, they try to ensure that standards are objective and performance-based in nature rather than subjective and design-based. Second, in developing the standards, they employ open procedures under the auspices of an independent professional organization, such as the American National Standards Institute ("ANSI"). Third, they seek to have the standards, once developed, formally promulgated by an objective body like ANSI. Industry "seal of approval" programs have invited charges that they are the equivalent of a group boycott, arbitrarily excluding would-be competitors from access to the marketplace.

The classic case of *Radiant Burners, Inc. v. Peoples Gas Light and Coke Co.*, involved the challenge to a program of the American Gas Association which awarded a seal of approval to gas burners meeting the association's tests for safety, utility, and durability. The plaintiff brought an action under Section 1 of the Sherman Act against the association and some of its members, charging that their unwillingness to accord its burners a seal was arbitrary and capricious. The suit further alleged that the utility members of the association had refused to provide gas for the plaintiff's burners because these had no seal and that the pattern of conduct of the defendants represented a conspiracy to exclude plaintiff from the market. The Supreme Court ruled that the plaintiff had stated a valid claim under the Sherman Act, specifically a conspiratorial refusal to provide gas for use in plaintiff's "Radiant Burners," barring plaintiff from the market.

It should be noted that an element of the plaintiff's claim was that the association's seal program was not based on objective standards. This is one factor that, in a different case, might distinguish a product approval or standardization case from the group boycott situation of *per se* illegality. If there are objective standards for product discrimination established which are related to a genuine public need for such discrimination, the program may well pass antitrust muster under a rule of reason approach.

An exclusionary program in the international context was successfully challenged by the Justice Department in a 1972 case involving the American Society of Mechanical Engineers ("ASME"). Because of the safety hazards presented by boiler and pressure vessel explosions, ASME had promulgated a Boiler and Pressure Vessel Code ("the Code") establishing minimum construction specifications. ASME issued a stamp for American manufacturers of boilers and pressure vessels to place on their products to indicate conformity with the Code. The Justice Department brought an action under the Sherman Act alleging that, inasmuch as many safe foreign products could not obtain the ASME stamp, the implementation of the code and stamp programs represented a conspiracy "to discriminate against and exclude from sale in the United States qualified boilers and pressure vessels manufactured outside the United States and Canada."

This arrangement was dissolved by a consent decree directing ASME to put into effect a "fair, reasonable and nondiscriminatory procedure enabling foreign manufacturers who meet the requirements of the ASME to qualify for and receive ASME Certifications of Authorization and Symbol Stamps on an equal basis with domestic manufacturers ... ." The thrust of the antitrust challenge was not directed at the safety program, the need for which was not questioned, but at the arbitrary and discriminatory way in which it was implemented.

ASME's Code was again the focus of an antitrust dispute in 1982, this case reaching the US Supreme Court as *American Soc'y of Mech. Eng'rs v. Hydrolevel Corp.* The dispute developed because an ASME subcommittee charged with interpreting the Code was dominated by the personnel of a company, "M & M," which manufactured heating boilers. This subcommittee took the position that the boilers made by a competitor of M & M, Hydrolevel Corp., failed to satisfy the technical requirements of the Code, and this action was subsequently approved by ASME itself. After Hydrolevel's boilers encountered market resistance because potential customers viewed them as nonstandard, Hydrolevel sued ASME and others, alleging violations of Sherman §§ 1 and 2. The district court and the Court of Appeals upheld the jury's finding that ASME was liable under § 1 for the actions of its "agents," the company personnel serving on the ASME standards committees. The Supreme Court affirmed, holding that ASME could be held liable in a private antitrust action, under the tort law principle of apparent authority, for the misdeeds of the standards committee officials. The Court considered that it was ASME's responsibility to prevent the persons acting on its behalf from exploiting its codes and procedures in such a manner as to injure their competitors in violation of the antitrust laws.

Sherman § 1 is not the only antitrust statute which may be utilized to challenge misconduct in the standards development process. Standard-setting efforts can also be attacked, in some circumstances, as component acts of actual or attempted monopolization in violation of § 2. The FTC has several times brought FTC § 5 cases on monopolization theories against firms which were seeking improperly to incorporate their patent rights into industry standards.

The 1988 decision of the Supreme Court in *Allied Tube & Conduit Corp. v. Indian Head, Inc.* concerned the code requirements for the design and installation of electrical wiring systems maintained by the National Fire Protection Association. During the relevant period, the code approved only electrical conduit made of steel, but the plaintiff, a manufacturer of plastic conduit, initiated a proposal before the Association to extend code approval to plastic conduit as well. The proposal was approved by one of the Association's professional panels and needed for adoption only a majority vote of the Association's members attending the annual meeting. However, the defendant, the nation's largest manufacturer of steel conduit, and others collectively agreed to defeat the proposal by packing the meeting with new Association members recruited to vote against the proposal. When the proposal was voted down at the meeting, plaintiff brought a suit against the defendant under Section 1 of the Sherman Act alleging that it had unreasonably restrained trade in the electrical conduit market.

The Supreme Court first rejected the defendant's argument that the Association was a "quasi-legislative" body and that defendant was therefore entitled to antitrust immunity under the Noerr-Pennington doctrine which protects bona fide collective efforts to influence government officials. The Court said that, even though the Association's code was routinely adopted into law by state and local governments, the "relevant context is ... the standard-setting process of a private association," and the defendant's actions should be viewed as commercial, not legislative activity. The Court held that, while the defendant could vigorously argue its position before the Association through the use of "accurate scientific evidence," it could not, without exposing itself to possible antitrust liability, "bias the process by, as in this case, stacking the private standard-setting body with decision makers sharing their economic interest in restraining competition."

In *Broadcom Corp. v. Qualcomm Inc.* the Third Circuit in 2007 reversed a trial court dismissal and held that deceptive conduct by members of a standard setting association during the process can be anticompetitive conduct subject to the antitrust laws. Broadcom and Qualcomm were both companies selling chips that operate cell phones. Broadcom alleged that Qualcomm was seeking to monopolize the market for the necessary technology by inducing the standards organizations to incorporate Qualcomm technology into the relevant standard and then refusing to license the technology on fair and reasonable terms as required by the guidelines of the standards organization.

An illustration of boycotts in the international field has been provided by certain US associations who have conducted industry trade shows at which only the association members can display their products, while excluding foreign companies from membership. Sherman Act challenges to such discrimination have been brought when access to the industry trade show is an important avenue to sale of the products in the US. US trade associations normally are free to limit their membership to US companies. However, when the association controls a "facility" critical to effective competition, such as an important trade show, the association must afford access to that facility for imports.

The government's recognition of the value of legitimate standardization activities, as well as of their potential antitrust vulnerability, led to the enactment of the

Standards Development Organization Advancement Act of 2004. This legislation, the purpose of which is to "encourage the development and promulgation of voluntary consensus standards," was enacted as an amendment to the National Cooperative Research and Production Act of 1993. As we previously mentioned, this legislation extends antitrust protections to standard development organizations (SDOs) by providing that their standards development activities are to be evaluated, for antitrust purposes, under the rule of reason. In addition, the legislation provides that an SDO which files written notification with the Attorney General and the Federal Trade Commission of its ongoing standardization activity may limit its potential antitrust liability therefor in a private suit against the SDO to actual, as opposed to treble, damages. Special rules for attorneys' fees in any case challenging the SDO's activity are also provided.

[F] Joint Ventures

Earlier in this Chapter we considered cooperative activity by companies in the nature of cartels, i.e., hard core conspiracies designed and implemented to curtail competition among the participants by fixing prices, allocating markets or reducing production. These have been held *per se* illegal under Section 1 of the Sherman Act even where the participants attempted to defend them as "joint ventures." Legitimate joint ventures do exist in great numbers, however, in both the domestic and the international setting and these may, if properly conceived, lawfully involve cooperation between or among companies who are competitive in some respects.

The utility and versatility of this approach to doing business in the international arena can be readily appreciated. A corporation that wants to expand its activities in overseas markets can benefit from enlisting a foreign co-venturer who will share in the capital investment and risk, while contributing valuable knowledge of the local market and economy. In addition, the use of the joint venture form is very suitable for use in countries, such as developing nations, who either require or look more favorably upon businesses that are, at least in part, locally owned and managed. Strategic alliances among major firms play an important role in the context of the new global economy, in which investments and risks are huge, and innovation is essential to success or survival.

Joint venture arrangements very often involve the creation by the joint venturing parents of a new corporation, which they agree to jointly own according to an allocation of the stock holding. On the other hand, the endeavor may involve one co-venturer acquiring a portion of the stock of the other venturer without creation of a third company. These structural formulations are commonly referred to as equity joint ventures. Joint ventures may, alternatively, be purely "collaborative," i.e., involving agreements by companies to cooperate without affiliation through stock ownership. Under US antitrust law, the formation of equity joint ventures is evaluated under the statutory provisions governing mergers and acquisitions. This feature will be addressed in Chapter 8. At this point we will discuss more generally the antitrust issues pertinent to both equity and collaborative joint ventures.

US antitrust jurisprudence has generally applied a rule of reason analysis to joint ventures that are ostensibly established for a legitimate purpose, recognizing that the cooperative arrangement is likely to bring benefits to both the venturers and the economy at large. The antitrust assessment will also, however, consider whether the joint venture may eliminate areas of potential competition between the venturers, may injure other parties who are denied access to the joint venture benefits, and/or be accompanied by "collateral" or "ancillary" agreements between the parties which are anticompetitive.

As we noted in Chapter 2, Congress has enacted the National Cooperative Research Act of 1984 and the National Cooperative Research and Production Act of 1993, codified together at 15 U.S.C. §§ 4301-06. This statute, as amended by the Standards Development Organization Advancement Act of 2004, clarified the substantive application of the federal and state antitrust laws to certain joint ventures and to SDOs. It requires US courts to appraise the competitive effects of a challenged joint venture or SDO covered by the Act under a rule-of-reason standard. The *International Guidelines* state that this approach is consistent with the Agencies' general analysis of joint ventures. If the venture is registered with the Agencies in advance, any private antitrust exposure by the participants is limited to actual, rather than treble, damages. The protections of the 1993 law apply only if the principal production facilities of the joint venture are located in the US and if the parties concerned are either US companies or companies coming from countries whose laws treat US participants in joint production ventures at least as favorably as they do domestic participants.

The antitrust agencies recognize that there are situations in which it is necessary for competitors to collaborate in some fashion. On April 7, 2000, the Federal Trade Commission and the Department of Justice issued *Antitrust Guidelines for Collaborations Among Competitors ("Collaboration Guidelines")* to explain the Agencies' approach toward such dealings. These guidelines were a governmental response to requests from the business community for more antitrust guidance in this area. The *Collaboration Guidelines* first discuss the types of agreements among competitors which will be held *per se* illegal. Not surprisingly, these include agreements to fix prices or outputs, rig bids, or share or divide markets by allocating customers, suppliers, territories, or lines of commerce. Other types of agreements will be analyzed under the rule of reason to determine their overall competitive effects. If an initial examination of the nature of the agreement discloses no potential for anticompetitive harm, the Agencies will end the investigation without considering procompetitive benefits. If investigation indicates anticompetitive harm, then the Agencies will examine whether the relevant agreement is reasonably necessary to achieve procompetitive benefits that likely would offset the anticompetitive harm.

Mergers, because of their permanence, will be scrutinized differently from competitor collaborations.

Under the Agencies' approach, the rule of reason analysis will focus on examining what the state of competition likely will be if the relevant joint venture goes forward, as compared to the competitive situation in its absence. "The central question is whether the relevant agreement likely harms competition by increasing the ability or incentive profitably to raise price above or reduce output, quality, service, or innovation below what likely would prevail in the absence of the relevant agreement." In evaluating possible competitive concerns, the Agencies will typically define relevant markets and calculate market shares and concentration. The business purpose of the agreement is taken into account, but anticompetitive intent alone does not establish a violation and procompetitive intent does not preclude a violation.

The *Collaboration Guidelines*, which are quite detailed, go on to discuss the different types of collaborations and how they may be analyzed. Special "safety zones"—competitor collaborations that the Agencies will normally not challenge—are granted by the Agencies with respect to some collaborations accounting for no more than 20% of a relevant market and to others relating to "innovation markets." An innovation market consists of the research and development directed to particular new or improved goods or processes and the close substitutes for that research and development. Finally, an Appendix to the *Collaboration Guidelines* posits and discusses various hypothetical joint venture situations.

The case law providing guidance on rule of reason evaluation of bona fide joint ventures is sparse compared to the many cases finding *per se* violations based on agreements to suppress competition. Joint ventures in the international context are very common, and these are seldom challenged under US antitrust law absent the previously discussed "hard core," conspiracy situation.

However, there have been some noteworthy challenges of claimed legitimate joint ventures. In a 1967 case, the Justice Department brought suit under Section 1 of the Sherman Act and Section 7 of the Clayton Act to break up a joint venture entered into between a US firm, Monsanto, and a German company, Farbenfabriken Bayer A.G. The two firms, both giant chemical companies on the world scene, had formed Mobay Chemical Co., a Delaware corporation with offices in Pittsburgh, to produce isocyanates, a new product used in the production of flexible urethane (plastic) foam. Prior to the joint venture, both Monsanto and Bayer had been producing isocyanates and selling them in the US and elsewhere. The two parents were thus already competitors in the product for which they had become joint venturers. The court entered a consent decree requiring Monsanto to sell to Bayer all of its interest in Mobay.

As was the case in the *Mobay* case, where a joint venture threatens to eliminate existing or potential competition between the venturers, it is vulnerable from the antitrust viewpoint. The elimination of existing competition is generally more critical than if the competitors are only potential competitors. However, where the market shares in the relevant product and geographic markets are highly concentrated and new entrants face high technological, financial or other barriers, the joint venture's elimination of potential competition will raise significant antitrust concerns. The focus of the antitrust scrutiny will be on the likely effect of the joint venture on competition in the US market, including whether competition in that market by foreign firms will be suppressed or enhanced.

Even where the formation of a joint venture passes antitrust review on the basis that it will not be anticompetitive, the reasonableness of any "ancillary" restraints agreed to by the co-venturers will also be scrutinized. For example, if Companies A and B, who were not existing or potential competitors in the manufacture of Product Y, established a new company to make and sell Product Y in the US, A and B could presumably agree not to compete with the new company as to Product Y for a limited period of time. This would assure the integrity of the joint venture and give the new company an opportunity to get launched without being damaged by its parents. If on the other hand, Companies A and B were to undertake not to compete with each other or the new company as to any product lines whatsoever, this agreement would clearly be overbroad and not legitimately ancillary to the conduct of the otherwise lawful joint venture.

This was a pertinent consideration in the dissolution of another joint venture between chemical giants in *United States v. Hercules, Inc.*, a 1973 case. The Justice Department alleged that a joint venture between Hercules, Inc., a US company, and Mitsui Petrochemical Industries, Ltd., a Japanese company, for the manufacture and sale in the US of high-density polyethylene, was in violation of Section 1 of the Sherman Act and Section 7 of the Clayton Act. The complaint was based on the theory that actual and potential competition between Hercules and Mitsui in the sale of another chemical, polypropylene, had been eliminated by the arrangement. The agreement included commitments by the parties to exchange patents and other technology relating to the manufacture of polypropylene, as well as other obligations on the part of Mitsui relating to the licensing of its technology to others.

The Federal Trade Commission has also had occasion to challenge international joint ventures. *In re Brunswick* was a proceeding brought by the FTC under both Section 7 of the Clayton Act and Section 5 of the FTC Act. Brunswick, a US maker and seller of outboard motors, purchased 38% of the stock of Sanshin, a Japanese subsidiary of the Japanese company, Yamaha. Sanshin also manufactured outboard motors, some of which it had been selling into the US market. Brunswick and Yamaha agreed on exchanges of technical information in the manufacture of outboard motors, but each stipulated that information so received would not be used to compete with the other company. The Commission held that the joint venture, although well intended, was unlawful in that it eliminated likely entry by Yamaha into the highly concentrated US outboard motor market. As to the collateral agreements, the Commission acknowledged that the parents would not be expected to compete with their jointly owned subsidiary, but it considered that the restraints agreed to went far beyond what would be needed to make the joint venture effective. On review, the Court of Appeals for the Eighth Circuit substantially upheld the FTC's ruling, including the latter's reliance on the potential competition doctrine.

In 1984, the FTC approved, subject to a number of stringent conditions, a joint venture agreement between two of the largest automobile manufacturers in the world, General Motors and Toyota, for the production of cars in Fremont, California. Two of the five commissioners dissented from the approval of the consent order, and the Chrysler Corporation filed an antitrust suit which sought to enjoin the joint venture as tending to create a monopoly in violation of Section 7. That case was settled by General Motors and Toyota agreeing to shorten the life of the joint venture to eight years. In 1993, acting on a motion by the joint venturers to reopen the matter, the FTC vacated the consent order on a finding that significant new entry in the North American automobile market rendered the restrictions on the duration and output of the joint venture unnecessary.

In 1999, the Supreme Court decided the case of *California Dental Ass'n v. Federal Trade Commission*, which involved a complaint brought by the FTC against the association, a voluntary group of local dental societies. The FTC alleged that the association had adopted a code of ethics which restricted truthful advertising, in violation of Section 5 of the FTC Act. The Commission held the restrictions on advertising to be violations of the Sherman and FTC Acts, applying a "quick look" rule of reason analysis designed for restraints that are not *per se* unlawful but are sufficiently anticompetitive on their face that they do not require a full-blown rule of reason inquiry. The Court of Appeals for the Ninth Circuit affirmed, finding the truncated rule-of-reason analysis to be in order.

The Supreme Court, by a majority of the Supreme Court reversed. The Court upheld the Commission's jurisdiction over the association notwithstanding the latter's nonprofit status. However, it held the "quick look" or abbreviated approach to analysis of anticompetitive conduct, which it had approved in some earlier cases, to be inaposite in the situation here presented. "It seems to us, said the majority opinion, that the [association's] advertising restrictions might plausibly be thought to have a net pro competitive effect, or possibly no effect at all on competition." Accordingly, the Commission's analysis was held to be flawed because there should have been a greater inquiry into the circumstances, details, and logic of the advertising restraint.

In a laborious opinion beginning with the warning "Nessun Dorma!" (None must sleep!), the FTC struck down in 2003, under FTC § 5, a side agreement relating to a joint venture by two major recording organizations to market jointly a new "Three Tenors" CD containing recordings by Placido Domingo, Luciano Pavarotti, and Jose Carreras (Polygram Holding, Inc.). The PolyGram group of companies and Warner Communications Inc. had entered into a joint venture to collaborate in the distribution of the recordings of a 1998 concert by the Three Tenors and, some months thereafter, they also entered into a side agreement not to discount or advertise their previous Three Tenors products for a period of time. The Commission's complaint did not challenge the establishment of the joint venture but attacked the side agreement as an unreasonable restraint of trade. A major concern of the joint venturers was the fact that the repertoire of the 1998 concert substantially overlapped with that of the previous Three Tenors recordings. The companies sought to justify the side agreement restraining the marketing of the older recordings as an ancillary restraint which was necessary to a successful marketing of the new records.

The Commission noted at the outset that this case represented the agency's first adjudicative opportunity to revisit the issue of competitor collaboration since the Supreme Court's decision in *California Dental Ass'n*, as well as since the issuance of the *Collaboration Guidelines*. The Commission's opinion reviewed in detail the case law discussing the rule of reason and *per se* violation modes of analysis, culminating in the *California Dental Ass'n* decision. The latter, said the Commission, left "no doubt that [the Court] views Section 1 analysis as a continuum, rather than a series of distinct boxes (per se, quick look, full rule of reason)." The FTC then stated that the *Collaboration Guidelines* follow the *California Dental Ass'n* approach by providing a structure for analysis of the restrictive agreement, including such factors as likelihood of competitive harm, the plausibility of the proffered justifications, and any public benefits accruing from the restraint.

Turning to the Three Tenors case, the Commission characterized the agreements not to discount and not to advertise as presumptively anticompetitive. These restraints were not justifiable as legitimate ancillary restraints because they did not relate to products within the joint venture. The Commission thus held that, "the Respondents' 'free-riding' argument is simply an attempt to shield themselves from legitimate interbrand competition. As such, the proffered justification is not cognizable under antitrust law (footnote omitted)." This conclusion "could be characterized as a finding of per se illegality," said the Commission, although it recognized that "the label matters less than the analysis," since the analysis had in fact evaluated the proffered justifications at some length.

This decision of the FTC was sustained by the Court of Appeals for the District of Columbia Circuit in 2005. The court observed that, "... the Supreme Court has steadily moved away from the dichotomous approach—under which every restraint of trade is either unlawful per se, and hence not susceptible to a pro-competitive justification, or subject to full-blown rule-of-reason analysis—toward one in which the extent of the inquiry is tailored to the suspect conduct in each particular case." The introduction of the "quick look" mode of analysis was not a movement by the Supreme Court from a dichotomy to a trichotomy, said the Court of Appeals, but a retreat from fixed categories "toward a continuum." The Court of Appeals rejected PolyGram's contention that the FTC had conflicted with Supreme Court precedent by applying a *per se* approach and thus failing to show that the restraint in question actually harmed competition. The court accepted the Commission's analytical approach of presuming this restraint unlawful based upon economic learning and market experience, with the burden shifting to the respondent to identify reasons why the restraint was unlikely to harm consumers or else offered countervailing benefits. The court also accepted the Commission's conclusion that PolyGram's agreement with Warner in all likelihood had a deleterious effect upon consumers and that PolyGram had failed to identify a procompetitive justification for the restraint.

These cases involving joint ventures, and others not discussed here, each reflect US antitrust enforcement efforts designed to maintain or to stimulate a competitive US market in the products affected. While some of the earlier cases took into account the potential effect that a particular joint venture involving one or more US companies might have with respect to US exports, the enactment of the Foreign Trade Antitrust Improvements Act of 1982 ("FTAIA") and the *Empagran* decision (as discussed in Chapter 3) have eliminated the issue of potential effects in foreign markets for purposes of most cases. The reasoning in this regard is that, if the only antitrust injury which a joint venture may cause will be to foreign parties in foreign markets, there can be no violation of US antitrust law. If, on the other hand, the activities of US exporters or of foreign parties injure a US exporter not participating in those activities, the FTAIA provides the wrongdoers with no shield against the antitrust laws.

Among the aspects of joint venture analysis receiving significant attention in domestic cases is the issue of who must be given access to the benefits of the joint venture. The question of when participation in a joint venture must be offered to all competitors, because the venture is so important that it constitutes an "essential facility" or "bottleneck," was raised in the Associated Press ("AP") litigation in 1945. That case involved the agreement of AP member newspapers to share news stories with each other. The government challenged the feature of the venture which entitled AP members to veto their rivals' bids for membership under the Sherman Act. Apparently using a rule of reason approach, the Supreme Court struck down the membership restriction as giving AP members a competitive advantage. The Court noted that AP members controlled 83% of daily newspaper circulation, providing them with a market power that enabled them to deny equality of economic opportunity to excluded competitors.

The fact that what one person views as a legitimate joint venture another sees as an unlawful conspiracy was amply illustrated in the case of *Dagher et al. v. Saudi Refining Inc. et al.*, decided by the US Court of Appeals for the Ninth Circuit in 2004. The plaintiffs represented a class of 23,000 Texaco and Shell Oil service station owners who alleged that the two oil companies and others violated Section 1 of the Sherman Act by creating a national alliance consisting of two joint ventures. The creation of the joint ventures ended competition between Shell and Texaco by combining their downstream refining and marketing of gasoline. Shell and Texaco agreed not to compete with their joint ventures. At about the same time, they also agreed that the Shell and Texaco brands would have the same price in the same market areas, so that a single individual at each joint venture was responsible for setting a coordinated price for the two brands. The Federal Trade Commission and several state Attorneys General had approved the formation of the joint ventures subject to some modifications.

The trial court granted the defendants' motion for summary judgment. It applied the rule of reason standard, rather than the *per se* or "quick look" rules, and decided that the joint ventures were valid. The trial court held that the joint ventures were substantial joint ventures which produced sufficient efficiencies and were adequately integrated to constitute indisputably legitimate joint ventures. As valid joint ventures, the court reasoned, they were entitled to set the prices for their various brands.

However, the Court of Appeals reversed, holding that the plaintiffs had presented sufficient evidence to create a triable issue of fact as to whether the alliance's unified pricing scheme was a *per se* violation of Section 1 of the Sherman Act. The defendants had, in effect, urged the Ninth Circuit to find an exception to the *per se* prohibition against price fixing where two entities have established a joint venture that unifies their production and marketing functions, and yet continues to sell their formerly competitive products as distinctive brands. The Ninth Circuit declined to do so here, emphasizing that defendants had made no showing that unifying the pricing of the distinct Texaco and Shell brands of gasoline was a necessary ancillary restraint for furthering the ventures' legitimate efforts to produce better products or capitalize on efficiencies. One member of the three-judge panel dissented on this point. He pointed out that Shell and Texaco, former competitors, had created a bona fide joint venture in which all of the two companies' assets and operations in segments were combined, with the two oil companies ceasing their refining and marketing operations.

The Supreme Court granted review in this case and, in February 2006, reversed in a brief, unanimous opinion. The US had filed an *amicus curiae* brief supporting the position of the oil companies. The Court held that the situation was not one calling for application of the *per se* liability standard "because Texaco and Shell did not compete with one another in the relevant market—namely, the sale of gasoline to service stations in the western United States—but instead participated in that market jointly through their investments in [the joint venture] ... In other words, the pricing policy challenged here amounts to little more than price setting by a single entity—albeit within the context of a joint venture ... ." The ancillary restraints doctrine relied on by the Ninth Circuit was inapposite here, said the Court, because the business activity being challenged was the core of the joint venture. The Court presumed that the joint venture itself was technically a lawful one, it having been approved by federal and state regulators, and no rule of reason contention relating to the joint venture had been raised by the plaintiffs.

American Needle, Inc. v. National Football League, a 2010 case, involved as a defendant the National Football League ("NFL"), an unincorporated association of thirty-two separately owned professional football teams. The teams had formed National Football League Properties ("NFLP") to develop, market and license their individual team color products and other properties. At first, NFLP granted nonexclusive licenses to the plaintiff and other vendors to manufacture and sell the team-labeled apparel. However, NFLP subsequently granted an exclusive license to Reebok and did not renew American Needle's license. The latter brought a Sherman Act Section 1 case against the group, alleging an illegal conspiracy. The respondents argued that they were incapable of conspiring within the meaning of Section 1 because the NFL and its teams were a single entity with respect to the conduct challenged. The district court ruled in favor of the defendants, and the Seventh Circuit affirmed.

The Supreme Court unanimously reversed and remanded. It reasoned that the alleged conduct was not beyond Section 1's coverage inasmuch as the NFL teams do not constitute a single economic entity. The teams are separate profit maximizing entities who are engaging in concerted activity potentially covered by Section 1. Rule of reason analysis should be undertaken, the Court held. The case was dormant on remand for a while and then settled.

The Supreme Court had occasion in 2015 to consider in the case of *North Carolina State Board of Dental Examiners v. FTC* to what extent the "state action" doctrine might shield industry members' joint anticompetitive conduct from antitrust challenge. In its Dental Practice Act, the State of North Carolina had declared the practice of dentistry to be a matter of public concern requiring regulation. Under the Act, the North Carolina State Board of Dental Examiners ("Board")—of which Board six of the eight members were required to be licensed dentists—was declared as the State agency for the regulation of the practice of dentistry.

In the 1990s dentists in North Carolina had started whitening teeth, but by 2003 they began to encounter competition from non-dentists who were charging lower prices for that service than the dentists. The Board issued at least forty-seven cease-and-desist letters on its official letterhead to non-dentist teeth whitening service providers and product manufacturers, many of these communications warning that the unlicensed practice of dentistry was a crime. The Board also sent out other similar missives, and eventually non-dentists ceased offering teeth whitening services in North Carolina.

In 2010, the Federal Trade Commission filed an administrative complaint charging the Board with violating Section 5 of the Federal Trade Commission Act. The FTC alleged that the Board's concerted action to exclude non-dentists from the market for teeth whitening services in North Carolina constituted an anticompetitive and unfair method of competition. The Board moved to dismiss, raising the defense of state action immunity. The FTC rejected the Board's defense and also noted that a wealth of evidence suggested that non-dentist provided teeth whitening was a safe cosmetic procedure. The Court of Appeals for the Fourth Circuit affirmed the FTC's rulings in all respects.

The Supreme Court granted review and affirmed the decision below, with three justices dissenting. The Court acknowledged the existence of the state action doctrine as enunciated in *Parker v. Brown*, whereby the antitrust laws are interpreted to confer immunity on anticompetitive conduct by the States when acting in their sovereign capacity. But here, the Court concluded, the doctrine was inapposite because there was no showing that the anticompetitive conduct carried on by nonsovereign actors met the essential prerequisite that the State actively supervise the policy being carried out. It stated that "[w]hen a State empowers a group of active market participants to decide who can participate in its market, and on what terms, the need for supervision is manifest." The State had not adopted a clear policy to displace competition in this market, and this responsibility over policy could not be delegated to the private industry market participants. The three dissenting justices responded that the majority had misunderstood the state action doctrine as, in effect, requiring a "good government" seal on the policy carried out. Under *Parker*, all that is required is that the party taking the anticompetitive action be a "state agency," which the Board was in the view of the dissenters.

[G] Cooperative Purchasing Arrangements

As the Supreme Court stated in the 1985 *Northwest Wholesale Stationers* case, cooperative purchasing agreements involving competitors are not *per se* illegal under the Sherman Act because many purchasing cooperatives are "designed to 'increase economic efficiency and render markets more, rather than less, competitive.'" In that case, the plaintiff, who had been excluded from membership in a purchasing cooperative, argued that the exclusion represented a group boycott and, as such, was *per se* illegal. The Court rejected the group boycott analogy as inapplicable. A rule of reason analysis was applied under which an important issue was whether the exclusion was motivated by efficiency concerns or by anticompetitive animus. The Court also considered relevant the issues of whether the joint venture from which the plaintiff was excluded was dominant in the marketplace and whether plaintiff's being excluded would put it at a severe competitive disadvantage. The Court held that, lacking aggregate market shares which would constitute market power, the joint purchasing could lawfully take place even if it excluded the competitor who wanted to participate.

This rule of reason approach to joint purchasing has prevailed. Particularly where the firms acting together are relatively small and the market in which they operate is not concentrated, their cooperation in obtaining scale economies or quantity discounts is viewed as enhancing efficiency and competition. On the other hand, as the *Collaboration Guidelines* indicate, some purchasing collaborations may be anticompetitive by unduly increasing the market power of the buyers over the sellers, depressing the prices of the purchased products, or by facilitating collusion through exchanges of sensitive data among competitors.

Some years ago, the Federal Trade Commission reviewed a number of proposed business to business ("B2B") agreements for carrying out joint purchasing through electronic commerce. The Commission then stated that each venture will be reviewed from the antitrust viewpoint on its own merits, but it also observed that B2B ventures have "a great potential to benefit both business and consumers through increased productivity and lower prices."

In a recent development bearing on the general subject of collusion, the EU, on the one hand, and the US DOJ and FTC, on the other, have published papers about how the use of pricing algorithms by market participants is to be analyzed under their respective competition laws. More and more companies are using algorithms to adapt their prices to changing market conditions. Not surprisingly, competition law issues are viewed as mainly triggered where reliance on algorithms is employed as part of an anticompetitive collusive scheme such as a cartel activity.

§5.02 THE SHERMAN ACT § 2

[A] What Constitutes Monopolization

We have seen that, expressed in simplified terms, Section 1 of the Sherman Act deals with agreements in restraint of trade, and Section 2 is concerned with monopolization and attempts to monopolize. Specifically, Section 2 makes the commission of each of the following separate offenses a felony: (1) to monopolize, (2) to attempt to monopolize, or (3) to combine or conspire to monopolize, "any part of the trade or commerce among the several States, or with foreign nations ... ." As explained in Chapter 2, "monopoly" or "monopoly power" has been defined as the "holding of such dominance within an industry as to command the power to fix or control prices in or exclude competition from the industry." Section 2 does not prohibit monopoly status. What it prohibits is the act of monopolization or the conspiratorially planned or attempted act of monopolization. Therefore, neither the mere size of a firm in relation to its competitors nor the virtual absence of competition within an industry are illegal in and of themselves. For a Section 2 violation, it must be shown that the firm in question possesses monopoly power in the relevant market and that it willfully acquired or maintained that power. A Section 2 private plaintiff must also establish resulting antitrust injury.

To establish that a defendant is guilty of attempted monopolization, it is necessary to show that (1) the defendant engaged in predatory or otherwise anticompetitive conduct, (2) it had a "specific intent" to monopolize, and (3) there exists a "dangerous probability" that the defendant will succeed in attaining monopoly power. A claimant must also show causal antitrust injury. The question of dangerous probability generally focuses on the defendant's market share.

The guiding principle that mere monopoly status is lawful, while the act of monopolization is unlawful, has created difficulties in the jurisprudence which persist to this day. As previously mentioned, in the 1945 case of *United States v. Aluminum Co. of America*, ("Alcoa") case, Judge Learned Hand's opinion for the US Court of Appeals for the Second Circuit reasoned that a defendant who had a monopoly "thrust" upon it or who had acquired its monopoly power through "superior skill, foresight and industry" would not be violating Section 2. He concluded, however, that Alcoa was guilty of monopolizing because, in its determination to maintain control of the aluminum ingot market, it "effectively anticipated and forestalled all competition" by "doubling and redoubling its capacity before others entered the field." Since this activity could also have been described as engaging in vigorous competitive conduct, the line drawn by the court's opinion between acceptable and unacceptable behavior on the part of a dominant firm was a thin one.

In *United States v. Grinnell Corp.*, the Supreme Court confirmed the view that a Section 2 violation requires (1) the possession of monopoly power in the relevant market, and (2) "the willful acquisition or maintenance of [that monopoly] power as distinguished from growth or development as a consequence of a superior product, business acumen, or historical accident." That standard also was imprecise because of the ambiguity of the word "willful." Later case law authority has tended to interpret Section 2 as allowing a firm to gain or preserve market power through purely competitive means, even though the latter may involve aggressive behavior. This approach retains incentives for monopolists to develop new products and efficiencies. Very occasionally, a market is recognized as a "natural monopoly market," which is not unlawful but requires regulation by the State.

The Supreme Court again confirmed the rule of the *Grinnell* decision in 2004 in *Verizon Communications Inc. v. Law Offices of Curtis V. Trinko, LLP*. The Court stated:

> The mere possession of monopoly power, and the concomitant charging of monopoly prices, is not only not unlawful; it is an important element of the free-market system. The opportunity to charge monopoly prices—at least for a short period—is what attracts "business acumen" in the first place; it induces risk taking that produces innovation and economic growth. To safeguard the incentive to innovate, the possession of monopoly power will not be found unlawful unless it is accompanied by an element of anticompetitive conduct. (emphasis in original)

The degree of market power that must be evidenced to establish the existence of monopoly power has not been definitively established in the case law. The *Alcoa* decision indicated that 90% of a market would constitute a monopoly, 60% or 64% would be doubtful and 33% would be insufficient. In the *Grinnell* decision, 87% of the market was sufficient to constitute a monopoly. The cases have generally involved companies with a 70% to 100% position in the market. It follows that, in Section 2 cases, the definition of the relevant product and geographic markets are critical issues.

[B] Market Definition

The product market definition entails, in the language of the Supreme Court's 1956 decision in the *du Pont Cellophane* case, the making of a determination as to which commodities are "reasonably interchangeable" by users for the same purpose. This economic concept of cross-elasticity of demand measures the extent to which consumers will switch from one product to another in the event of a price or quality change in the first product. In *Cellophane*, the Supreme Court held that cellophane and other flexible packaging materials were in the same relevant product market because there was a high degree of cross-elasticity among these products. Since du Pont had only 17% of the broader market, the government's claim that du Pont was a monopolist because it controlled 75% of the market for cellophane was unsuccessful.

In its 1992 decision in *Eastman Kodak Co. v. Image Technical Services, Inc.*, which we consider below in detail, the Supreme Court explained that, "[i]n determining the existence of market power, and specifically 'the responsiveness of the sales of one product to price changes of the other,'" the correct approach is to examine closely the "economic reality of the market at issue."

The process of defining the relevant geographic market focuses on the question of which sellers can effectively service a particular geographic area. Whether and to what extent foreign markets and foreign suppliers should be taken into account in defining a relevant geographic market and the suppliers who serve it are special issues which must be considered on a case by case basis. Foreign suppliers often face significant problems in penetrating the US market, such as high transportation costs, import duties, or quotas, trade law requirements including those under the antidumping and countervailing duty laws, and "Buy American" rules or consumer biases. Having a disadvantage in one or more of these regards may make a foreign supplier a less than formidable competitor in the US market. This issue will come up again in Chapter 8 in the context of merger analysis.

Considering the lack of precise standards in the jurisprudence relating to monopolization, it is not surprising that Section 2 cases have usually been brought in situations in which the firm in question has an indisputably dominant position in one or more markets and, in order to attain, maintain, or extend its dominance, has engaged in behavior which was manifestly injurious to its rivals or potential rivals. Such behavior has included the acquiring of significant rivals or the use of market practices clearly designed to discourage competitors or drive them out of business.

[C] Remedial Action for Monopolization

The remedy in monopolization cases may be structural, i.e., requiring a breakup of the offending firm, with some of its assets being sold or a new company being created and spun off. For example, two monopolization cases resolved in 1911, which involved

Standard Oil of New Jersey and American Tobacco, led to splits of those giants into thirty-four and sixteen pieces, respectively. The various pieces became the companies who are leaders of their industries today, including Exxon and Mobil (since reunited), Chevron, and Amoco in the oil industry. The remedy for monopolization may also be behavioral in nature, with the offending company under an order to observe or avoid particular conduct. In the *Microsoft* case, the trial judge initially assigned to the case concluded that only a structural remedy could curb Microsoft's improper use of its monopoly power. However, after the appellate reversal and the assignment of a new trial judge to the case, the litigation was settled with the imposition of behavioral constraints only, with the efficacy of this remedy long remaining a subject of debate.

[D] Types of Monopolistic Practices

[1] Predatory Pricing and Predatory Bidding

It is not possible to label as necessarily "predatory," and hence improper, conduct by a dominant firm such as cutting prices or introducing new products in response to competition because these acts may also be consistent with vigorous competitive behavior. Almost all of the predatory pricing cases brought over the years have been filed by competitors, not by the government, and few of these suits have prevailed. In 1993, in *Brooke Group Ltd. v. Brown & Williamson Tobacco Corp.*, the Supreme Court resolved some of the core issues presented by predatory pricing claims. The Court's opinion reiterated that Section 2 of the Sherman Act condemns predatory pricing when it poses a dangerous probability of monopolization. Moreover, the Court confirmed that a plaintiff seeking to establish competitive injury by reason of a rival's low pricing "must prove that the prices complained of are below an appropriate measure of its rival's costs." Therefore, said the Court, "above-cost prices that are below general market levels or the costs of a firm's competitors [do not] inflict injury to competition cognizable under the antitrust laws." The Court did not, however, resolve the conflict among the lower courts over the appropriate measure of cost, because the parties in the case agreed that the relevant measure was "average variable cost" (AVC). Some of the courts have selected, as the correct measure of cost, "average total cost," (ATC) which includes fixed costs and is therefore higher than AVC.

However, the Court's decision in *Brooke Group* did make it clear that a predatory pricing plaintiff under Section 2 of the Sherman Act must demonstrate not only that the defendant's below-cost pricing caused damage to its rival, but also that the alleged predator had a reasonable expectation of recovering, through the later collection of monopoly profits, a sum greater than the losses it had suffered. Unless there is such later recoupment, the Court stated, "predatory pricing produces lower aggregate prices in the market, and consumer welfare is enhanced."

In 2003, the US Court of Appeals for the Tenth Circuit affirmed the dismissal of a Sherman Act § 2 case brought by the government alleging that American Airlines was engaged in a scheme of predatory pricing against low-cost airlines. According to the complaint, American's predatory scheme was designed to monopolize routes centered on the Dallas airport, where American was the dominant carrier, and to later recoup, through "supra-competitive pricing," the losses sustained. The Tenth Circuit's opinion reviewed the *Brooke Group* formulation of the two prerequisites to recovery on a predatory pricing claim, and it observed that "[d]espite a great deal of debate on the subject, no consensus has emerged as to what the most 'appropriate' measure of cost is in predatory pricing cases." Since the government did not rely on the usual test—pricing below AVC—the court examined the four tests that the government proffered as proxies to AVC to measure the incremental costs associated with the capacity additions at issue. Following this examination, the court concluded that:

> all four proxies are invalid as a matter of law, fatally flawed in their application, and fundamentally unreliable. Because it is uncontested that American did not price below AVC for any route as a whole, we agree with the district court's conclusion that the government has not succeeded in establishing the first element of Brooke Group, pricing below an appropriate measure of cost. (Footnotes omitted)

The question of "monopsony," a market situation in which a dominant buyer has control over a large part of the market came up in the Supreme Court's 2007 decision in *Weyerhaeuser Co. v. Ross-Simmons Hardwood Lumber Co., Inc.* Ross-Simmons, a sawmill, filed a suit under § 2 of the Sherman Act against Weyerhaeuser Co. alleging that the latter drove it out of business by bidding up the price of sawlogs to a level that prevented the plaintiff from being profitable. The jury returned a verdict against Weyerhaeuser, and the Ninth Circuit Court of Appeals affirmed, rejecting Weyerhaeuser's argument that the Brooke Group standard should be applied. The Ninth Circuit reasoned that predatory bidding does not necessarily benefit consumers or stimulate competition in the way that predatory pricing does.

The Supreme Court granted review and reversed in a unanimous decision. It pointed out that monopoly and monopsony—predatory pricing and predatory bidding—are economically similar. "Both claims involve the deliberate use of unilateral pricing measures for anticompetitive purposes. And both claims logically require firms to incur short-term losses on the chance that they might reap supra competitive profits in the future." (footnote omitted) Therefore, the two tests articulated in *Brooke Group* are apposite: "First, a plaintiff seeking to establish competitive injury resulting from a rival's low prices must prove that the prices complained of are below an appropriate measure of the rival's costs ... Second, a plaintiff must demonstrate that 'the competitor had ... a dangerous probabilit[y] of recouping its investment in below-cost prices." The Court's opinion also noted that the plaintiff firm, unlike Weyerhaeuser, appeared to have engaged in little efficiency-enhancing investment.

Predatory pricing issues may come up in the context of a regulated industry, in which the members of the industry are given limited lawful monopolies. The Justice Department's case against the American Telephone and Telegraph Company ("AT&T") in the 1980s demonstrated to the court that AT&T was setting unprofitable rates in markets in which it faced possible competition, excluding any rivals, while recouping monopoly profits from its other markets. The court found AT&T to have predatory intent because the evidence showed that the company's pricing for services had no relationship to the cost of those services. This case was settled by a consent decree under which AT&T agreed to spin off its local phone companies.

[2] Refusals to Deal

Given the antitrust vulnerability of a company that achieves a monopoly position, it must watch its marketplace tactics with particular care and restraint. Even actions that would be completely unobjectionable if committed by a nondominant competitor may be adjudged improper if engaged in by a monopolist. For example, a business is normally entitled unilaterally to refuse to deal with any other business. However, monopolists may not refuse to deal in a variety of situations where this will further entrench or extend their monopoly position.

One such case, the 1985 Supreme Court decision in *Aspen Skiing Co. v. Aspen Highlands Skiing Corp.*, concerned a suit under Section 2 by the operator of one of Aspen's four main ski slopes against its dominant rival who operated the other three ski slopes. The defendant had canceled a cooperative arrangement with the plaintiff offering consumers a four slope ticket as a package. The Supreme Court held that, although a monopolist does not have a general obligation to cooperate with its competitors, Aspen Skiing Co.'s behavior here was illegal in that, without a valid business justification, it was using its dominance to injure a smaller competitor and deprive consumers of a useful option. Aspen Skiing was ordered to pay damages and later resumed the cooperation with Aspen Highlands.

In *Verizon Communications Inc. v. Law Offices of Curtis V. Trinko, LLP*, the law firm, a local telephone service customer of AT&T, filed a class action against Verizon alleging that the latter had filled rivals' orders on a discriminatory basis as part of an anticompetitive scheme to discourage customers from being customers of competitive local carriers in violation of Section 2 of the Sherman Act. The district court dismissed the complaint but the Second Circuit reinstated it. The Supreme Court held that the complaint did not state a claim under Sherman § 2. The Court reaffirmed the principle of *Aspen Skiing* that, under certain circumstances, a refusal to cooperate with rivals can constitute anticompetitive conduct and violate § 2. In doing so, the Court included the observation that "Aspen Skiing is at or near the outer boundary of § 2 liability." The Court then proceeded to distinguish the situation before it in *Trinko* on the basis that Verizon was not acting unlawfully in withholding services which had not been previously marketed or otherwise made available to the public, whereas Aspen Skiing had crossed the line inasmuch as its "unilateral termination of a voluntary (and thus presumably profitable) course of dealing suggested a willingness to forsake short-term profits to achieve an anticompetitive end." (Emphasis in original)

The question arises whether a firm's refusal to license important IP rights may be a violation of Section 2 of the Sherman Act where use of the rights is arguably an "essential facility" enabling successful competition in a particular field. In 1908, the Supreme Court held in *Continental Paper Bag Co. v. Eastern Paper Bag Co.* that a patent holder that does not employ the patent itself may nonetheless enjoin others from using

Chapter 5: Conspiracies, Joint Ventures and Monopolization §5.02[D]

it. The question has recurred in recent years, in light of the importance of access to technology and innovation for participation in many industries.

The 1999 case of *Intergraph Corp. v. Intel Corp.* involved a claim by Intergraph that Intel had an obligation to continue to license rights to certain technical data to Intergraph, which the latter had used to develop its graphics and workstation products. The Court of Appeals for the Federal Circuit refused to order such licensing since the two companies were not competitors in any relevant market and a desire to exclude others from use of one's intellectual property (IP) was presumptively valid. On the other hand, in *Image Technical Services, Inc. et al. v. Eastman Kodak Co.*, in 1997, the Ninth Circuit Court of Appeals held that: (1) unlawful exclusionary conduct by a monopolist can include its unilateral refusal to license a patent or copyright, although, (2) the monopolist's desire to exclude others from its protected work is a presumptively valid business justification.

As we shall see in our discussion of the EU rules, this general question has also arisen under EU competition law. In the *Magill* case, the European Court of Justice (ECJ) concluded that a denial of the right to use IP can, in exceptional circumstances, constitute an abuse of a company's dominant position.

[3]   Tying and Other Exclusionary Conduct

A "tying" arrangement—when a seller conditions its sale of one product (the "tying" product) on the purchase of a second product (the "tied" product)—can be challenged as a contract which may substantially lessen competition under § 3 of the Clayton Act, as an unfair method of competition under § 5 of the Federal Trade Commission Act, or as a contract in restraint of trade under § 1 of the Sherman Act. It may also be challenged as a component of monopolization under § 2 of the Sherman Act. The essence of the violation in each case is the seller's exploitation of its market power with respect to the tying product to unfairly disadvantage its competitors with respect to the tied product. We will be discussing these violations in a variety of contexts in Chapter 6.

In the previously mentioned case of *Image Technical Services, Inc. et al. v. Eastman Kodak Co.*, which the Supreme Court considered in 1992, a number of issues were presented relating to tie-ins and other exclusionary acts on the part of dominant firms. Kodak's business included the manufacture and sale of complex business machines, including photocopiers and micrographics equipment, which utilized unique parts and software programs not compatible with competitors' machines. Kodak provided after-sales replacement parts and service to its customers, accounting for 80% to 95% of the service on Kodak machines. Eighteen independent service organizations ("ISOs"), which had been servicing Kodak equipment for some years, complained that Kodak had adopted new policies which limited the availability of replacement parts to the ISOs and made it more difficult for them to compete with Kodak in servicing the equipment. The ISOs filed a suit alleging that Kodak had unlawfully tied the sale of service for Kodak machines to the sale of parts, in violation of Section 1 of the Sherman Act, and had unlawfully monopolized and attempted to monopolize the sale of service for Kodak machines, in violation of Section 2 of the Sherman Act.

The district court granted summary judgment in favor of Kodak. This decision was reversed by the Court of Appeals for the Ninth Circuit, by a divided vote, on the ground that the case could not be decided on summary judgment. The Supreme Court affirmed the reversal by a 6-3 vote, concluding that the factual record was too sparse on the key issues to permit resolution as a matter of law. The Court reasoned that, first, the trier of fact would have to determine whether service and parts were two distinct products, since a tying arrangement is, by definition, an agreement by a party to sell one product on the condition that the buyer also purchases a different product. Second, Kodak was not entitled to summary judgment because it had failed to demonstrate that it was unreasonable to infer that it had market power in the service and parts markets. Third, there was also a factual issue as to whether Kodak possessed monopoly power in service and parts for Kodak equipment. In this regard, the Court held that, "[b]ecause service and parts for Kodak equipment are not interchangeable with other manufacturers' service and parts, the relevant market from the Kodak-equipment owner's perspective is composed of only those companies that service Kodak machines." Fourth, there were triable issues of fact as to whether valid business reasons could explain Kodak's exclusionary policies or whether those policies were part of a scheme of willful acquisition or maintenance of monopoly power.

The dissenting justices reasoned that finding a manufacturer's inherent power over its own brand of equipment to constitute monopoly power for purposes of applying Section 2, as the majority opinion had done, "makes no economic sense." Moreover, stated the dissenters, in the absence of any evidence of interbrand market power on the part of Kodak, it was erroneous to apply the essentially *per se* rule against tying arrangements to Kodak's domination of the parts and service "aftermarket" for Kodak equipment. They noted:

> We have never before accepted the thesis the Court today embraces: that a seller's inherent control over the unique parts for its own brand amounts to "market power" of a character sufficient to permit invocation of the per se rule against tying.

On the remand, the ISOs withdrew the Section 1 tying claims and proceeded on their Section 2 claims that Kodak used its monopoly in the market for Kodak equipment parts to create a second monopoly in the service markets. A jury awarded the ISOs USD 71.8 million in damages after trebling, and the district court entered a ten-year injunction requiring Kodak to sell all parts to the ISOs on reasonable and nondiscriminatory terms. On the appeal, the Court of Appeals for the Ninth Circuit affirmed on the liability issues, modified the injunction, and remanded for a new trial on some of the damage issues. It held that Section 2 "prohibits a monopolist from refusing to deal in order to create or maintain a monopoly absent a legitimate business justification." The Supreme Court's decision in the case has been severely criticized by commentators as ill conceived insofar as it is premised on the "locked-in" customer theory.

Chapter 5: Conspiracies, Joint Ventures and Monopolization　　　　§5.02[D]

In Chapter 2, we described the Sherman Act cases filed against Microsoft Corporation in 1998 by the US and various plaintiff states. These cases were premised on Microsoft's holding of a more than 90% market share in the worldwide market for Intel-compatible personal computer operating systems, coupled with Microsoft's alleged use of that market power to exclude and injure firms that threatened to compete against its core products. As we indicated in Chapter 2, District Judge Thomas Penfield Jackson, who first heard the case, held that Microsoft had violated both Sections 1 and 2 of the Sherman Act, as follows:

> the court concludes that Microsoft maintained its monopoly power by anticompetitive means and attempted to monopolize the Web browser market, both in violation of Section 2. Microsoft also violated Section 1 of the Sherman Act by unlawfully tying its Web browser to its operating system. The facts found do not support the conclusion that the effect of Microsoft's marketing arrangements with other companies constituted unlawful exclusive dealing under criteria established by leading decisions under Section 1.

Microsoft's appeal was heard by seven judges of the US Court of Appeals for the District of Columbia Circuit. This appellate panel upheld the district court's conclusion that Microsoft possessed monopoly power in the relevant operating systems market and that it maintained this power through anticompetitive means, in violation of Section 2 of the Sherman Act. It remanded the district court's finding that Microsoft unlawfully tied its browser to its operating system, for assessment under a rule of reason, rather than a *per se*, analysis (observing that "the nature of the platform software market affirmatively suggests that per se rules might stunt valuable innovation"). As described in Chapter 2, on remand, the case was assigned to a new trial judge who approved the entry of a settlement judgment which did not require the restructuring of Microsoft but prohibited it from carrying out certain practices

Under the "Tunney Act," the proposed settlement was duly published for public comment, following which more than 30,000 comments were submitted on the matter, and Judge Kollar-Kotelly undertook to make the required statutory determination of whether the proposed consent decree was in the public interest. The judge concluded in November 2002 that, while the decree was not exactly what the court would have crafted itself, it adequately set forth restrictions on Microsoft's conduct which would prevent the company from utilizing its market power as a means of protecting its monopoly was approved. Subsequently, the district court entered final judgments in some of the nonsettling states' cases that closely paralleled the earlier consent decree, rejecting demands for structural remedies as distinct from restrictions on Microsoft's practices. The district court's approval of the consent decree was subsequently approved by the Court of Appeals as consistent with the public interest.

As the tortuous history of the Microsoft case in the US indicates, the question of whether the behavioral remedy accepted by the courts would be sufficient to prevent a recurrence of monopolistic conduct by Microsoft was very controversial. It is noteworthy that, as we will discuss in Chapter 12, in its 2004 judgment, the European Commission insisted on dealing with Microsoft's "abuse of its dominant position" through the more severe remedies of ordering the company to "unbundle" other products from its operating system and to disclose interface documentation to potential makers of those products. In 2005, the Korean Fair Trade Commission announced a similar decision in its antitrust case against Microsoft, directing the company to sell in South Korea versions of its Windows operating system that did not include certain other products including the Windows Media Player.

Exclusionary conduct by a monopolist was also the subject of a § 2 case decided *en banc* in 2003 by the Court of Appeals for the Third Circuit, entitled *LePage's Inc. v. 3M* (Minnesota Mining and Manufacturing Company). This was a private action brought by LePage's asserting that 3M used its monopoly position over Scotch tape brand to gain a competitive advantage in the private label tape portion of the market. LePage's alleged that 3M's unlawful actions included the use of a "bundled rebate" structure, which offered customers higher rebates when they purchased from 3M's different product lines virtually on an exclusive basis. 3M did not contest the allegation that it had a monopoly in the US transparent tape market with a 90% market share. It also conceded that it offered the alleged rebates, but it argued, in reliance on the *Brooke Group* decision of the Supreme Court, that its conduct was proper as a matter of law because it never priced its transparent tape below cost.

The district court upheld a jury verdict in favor of LePage's and, while this ruling was reversed by an appellate panel, it was reinstated by the full bench of the Third Circuit. The *en banc* opinion rejected 3M's reading of *Brooke Group*, distinguishing it as a Robinson-Patman Act case rather than a Sherman Act § 2 case like the present one. The opinion stated, "[a]ssuming arguendo that Brooke Group should be read for the proposition that a company's pricing action is legal if its prices are not below its costs, nothing in the decision suggests that its discussion of the issue is applicable to a monopolist with its unconstrained market power." The opinion also reviewed the Supreme Court's "consistent holdings that a monopolist will be found to violate § 2 of the Sherman Act if it engages in exclusionary or predatory conduct without a valid business justification." The Third Circuit upheld the jury's finding that 3M's exclusionary conduct had no legitimate business justification.

Two years later, the Third Circuit considered an antitrust action brought by the government against Dentsply International Inc. and found both the fact pattern and the legal analysis in that case to closely resemble those developed in *LePage's*. Dentsply, the dominant seller of prefabricated artificial teeth in the US, enjoyed a 75%–80% share of that market on a revenue basis, a share which the Third Circuit deemed sufficient to constitute a monopoly position, given the additional fact that Dentsply maintained supremacy over the market's dealer network. Dentsply's maintenance of that supremacy by the imposition of exclusive dealing agreements on its authorized dealers was held by the court to be an unlawful exclusion of competition in preservation of Dentsply's monopoly and hence a violation of Sherman § 2. The Supreme Court denied review.

Chapter 5: Conspiracies, Joint Ventures and Monopolization §5.02[D]

[4] International and Other Settings

In the international context, a single firm will seldom be able by itself to monopolize or attempt to monopolize all or a large part of world trade in a product. In many cases, however, a number of firms, dominant in their own countries, have been found guilty of conspiring together to monopolize trade on an international scale. The cartels that we considered earlier in this chapter often involved such conspiracies, and, to the extent that they affected the commerce of the US, incurred charges under both Section 1 and Section 2 of the Sherman Act. However, US antitrust law has not developed the separate principle of joint or collective dominance that, as we shall see, has been fashioned under the EU competition rules.

In the previously mentioned 1911 Supreme Court decision in *United States v. American Tobacco Co.*, various American firms and two English corporations engaged in the tobacco trade were charged with monopolization and attempted monopolization under Section 2, as well as with a conspiracy in restraint of trade under Section 1. There was involved a division of markets restricting, among other things, sales into and from the US. The Court held that the defendants had monopolized interstate and foreign commerce, finding that they had obtained "dominion and control over the tobacco trade." The factual record was sufficient to "justify the inference that the intention existed to use the power of the combination as a vantage ground to further monopolize the trade in tobacco ... either by driving competitors out of business or compelling them to become parties to the combination ... ."

Much later, in the 1946 case involving American Tobacco, in which the primary American cigarette manufacturers were found to have fixed prices and excluded competition in the purchase of tobacco, the Court described Section 2 as making it a crime for parties:

> to combine or conspire to acquire or maintain the power to exclude competitors from any part of the trade or commerce among the several states or with foreign nations, provided they also have such power that they are able, as a group, to exclude actual or potential competition from the field and provided that they have the intent and purpose to exercise that power.

The 1949 General Electric incandescent lamp case likewise contained counts under both Sections 1 and 2 in an international market-sharing setting. General Electric was found, by reason of its dominant position in the industry, its restrictive agreements with other firms, its use of foreign subsidiaries to eliminate foreign competition, and other activities to have monopolized the US incandescent lamp industry in violation of Section 2. Philips, a Dutch firm, was found to have also violated Section 2, by aiding General Electric to maintain the latter's monopoly.

The Justice Department brought a Sherman Act Sections 1 and 2 case in 1952 against Sisal Sales Corp. based on monopolization of imports of a product into the US. The allegation was that two US corporations and a Mexican company had jointly seized control over the supply of Mexican twine, making the Mexican firm the sole exporter of the product to the US. This stranglehold on imports of sisal was condemned by the Supreme Court as a "successful plan to destroy competition and to control and monopolize the purchase, importation and sale of sisal," in violation of Sections 1 and 2.

Other Sherman Act cases involving the import setting have included (1) the *International Nickel* case in which a Canadian company, which was the primary world supplier of nickel, combined with foreign nickel producers to allocate markets, while also utilizing its American subsidiary to monopolize US imports and production; and (2) the *De Beers* cases in which foreign defendants, who produced abroad 95% of the world's diamonds, allegedly monopolized US foreign trade by restricting production and causing all African source diamonds to be sold through a single agency.

The *Continental Ore* case, decided by the Supreme Court in 1962, was a private treble damage case brought under Sections 1 and 2. It alleged that Union Carbide & Carbon Corporation and the other defendants had conspired to monopolize the US trade in vanadium and also excluded one of the plaintiffs, a partnership operating in the US, from the Canadian vanadium market. Electro Met, Union Carbide's Canadian subsidiary, had been appointed by the Canadian government as the exclusive wartime agent to purchase and allocate vanadium for the Canadian industries. Plaintiff claimed that Electro Met had, pursuant to the conspiracy, refused to purchase from plaintiff, excluding it from the Canadian market.

The Supreme Court reversed a ruling by the Court of Appeals that the export commerce allegations were outside the purview of the Sherman Act because they challenged Electro Met's conduct as an arm of the Canadian government. The Court pointed out that the plaintiff was not questioning the validity of any action taken by the Canadian government, since its position was that Electro Met's wrongful actions were taken within the area of the discretionary powers given the company by the Canadian government. The Court sent the case back for a jury resolution of the factual allegations. It appears from the Court's opinion, including its reference to the unlawfulness of a conspiracy to monopolize the "foreign commerce of the United States," that it considered that the US exports of a product can be deemed the relevant market for purposes of a monopolization claim.

In 2005, the Court of Appeals for the Ninth Circuit held, in *Confederated Tribes of Siletz Indians of Oregon v. Weyerhaeuser Company*, that predatory buying by a dominant competitor can constitute unlawful monopolization. In that case, Weyerhaeuser was found to have denied its competitors access to necessary raw materials by paying excessive prices for sawlogs and purchasing more sawlogs than it needed.

Efforts by a single firm or by a conspiracy to control transportation facilities of significance to US commerce have been held to be subject to the monopolization proscriptions of Section 2. Various activities of the transportation industries are regulated by the US, as well as by foreign governments, and reference should be made to those regimes in considering issues pertaining to monopoly and the lawfulness of particular practices.

We mentioned earlier that the Federal Trade Commission had completed in 2013 its investigation of alleged anticompetitive conduct by Google Inc. without taking enforcement action. While it did not doubt the proposition that Google was dominant in the online search market, the FTC did not find evidence that Google unfairly preferred its own content on the Google search results page and selectively demoted its competitors' results. It stated, "[t]he totality of the evidence indicates that, in the main, Google adopted the design changes that the Commission investigated to improve the quality of its search results, and that any negative impact on actual or potential competitors was incidental to that purpose." As we shall see, the EU, following its review, did not accept the proposition that no unfair competitive actions were being taken by Google.

CHAPTER 6
Relationships with Customers or Licensees in US Commerce

§6.01 VERTICAL AGREEMENTS

The relationship between seller and purchaser, whether formalized by a written agreement or simply reflected in a course of dealing, is at the heart of commerce. Although a single sales transaction between businesses may be manifested only by a purchase order and an invoice, where the dealings are at all complex or the relationship of the parties a continuing one, there are likely to be obligations undertaken by one or more of the parties which go beyond the individual sales transaction. Some of the obligations contemplated by the parties may affect competition, and these fall within the realm of the antitrust and trade regulation laws.

A manufacturer, for example, may desire that its distributors will commit not to buy from the manufacturer's competitors, or will purchase the manufacturer's entire range of products, or will resell only to certain types of customers. The distributor may, for its part, have expectations that the manufacturer will not sell to other distributors in the same geographic area or will supply it with all of his requirements of his products. Such commitments are, in many commercial settings, justifiable or even necessary incidents of a successful distribution relationship. In some cases, however, the commitments present antitrust questions.

In the exploitation of IP, such as patents, trade secrets, trademarks, and copyrights, the licensor-licensee relationship also often entails obligations which are in the nature of restraints on one or the other of the parties. The licensor may wish to restrict the licensee's use of the IP, by field or by territory, or commit the licensee to license back improvements in the technology that are discovered by the licensee, or to require the licensee to pay for additional technology. The licensee may desire that it be the exclusive licensee as to particular territories or types of customers. In the "franchise" relationship, which normally involves licensing of a trademark or service mark associated with the conduct of a successful business, franchisor and franchisee typically look for each other to carry out obligations which may affect competition. Here also, depending on the factual context and the restraint in question, antitrust law concerns may be highly pertinent.

These restraints are, in antitrust parlance, referred to as "vertical," inasmuch as they typically are not entered into between competitors but between links in the chain of distribution of a product or service. Restraints agreed to in such vertical relationships are generally subject to antitrust evaluation under the rule of reason.

§6.02 US ANTITRUST LAW ON VERTICAL RESTRAINTS

Among the types of vertical restraints that raise antitrust questions, and that we will examine, are exclusive dealing arrangements, limitations on resale relating to price, customer or territory, and "tying" arrangements. As we discussed in the previous chapter, a tying arrangement is one in which a seller, lessor, or licensor conditions sale, lease, or license of one good, service, or technology (the tying product) on the buyer, lessee, or licensee also taking a different good, service or technology (the tied product) from the supplier or his designee. The pertinent US antitrust laws are Sections 1 and 2 of the Sherman Act, Section 3 of the Clayton Act, and Section 5 of the Federal Trade Commission Act. The Sherman Act and FTC Act provisions are, as we have previously observed, in the nature of broadly stated prohibitions against trade restraints. Section 3 of the Clayton Act, however, was designed specifically to deal with distribution restraints.

Section 3 provides as follows:

> It shall be unlawful for any person engaged in commerce, in the course of such commerce, to lease or make a sale or contract for sale of goods, wares, merchandise, machinery, supplies, or other commodities, whether patented or unpatented, for use, consumption, or resale within the United States or any Territory thereof or the District of Columbia or any insular possession or other place under the jurisdiction of the United States, or fix a price charged therefor, or discount from, or rebate upon, such price, on the condition, agreement, or understanding that the lessee or purchaser thereof shall not use or deal in the goods, wares, merchandise, machinery, supplies, or other commodities of a competitor or competitors of the lessor or seller, where the effect of such lease, sale, or contract for sale or such condition, agreement, or understanding may be to substantially lessen competition or tend to create a monopoly in any line of commerce.

This lengthy sentence is not Shakespearean in its grace, and it is reproduced here in full only because it defies easy description or summarization. The gist of the prohibition is that it is unlawful for a person to lease or sell goods for use or resale in the US on the condition that the lessee or purchaser will not deal in the goods of the person's competitor, where the effect may be substantially to lessen competition or tend to create a monopoly in US commerce.

The provision applies primarily to exclusive dealing or tying arrangements. It applies to "goods," "commodities," etc., and hence not to services or intangibles. Territorially, the prohibition applies to sales in US domestic or import commerce, and it does not cover export transactions unless the export is a US territory. It should be kept in mind that, while the reach of Section 3 has these various limitations which may permit a practice to escape Section 3 in a given case, the more generally stated prohibitions of Section 1 of the Sherman Act or of Section 5 of the FTC Act may nonetheless be applicable to the same practice.

Section 3 is not in the nature of a *per se* prohibition but applies only where the effect of the restriction may be substantially anticompetitive. The use of the word "may" provides an incipiency standard for the showing of a violation. That is, a finding of illegality under Section 3 of the Clayton Act (or under Section 5 of the FTC Act), unlike the one under Section 1 of the Sherman Act, does not require a showing of actual adverse effects on competition. It requires only the showing of a probability that the substantial adverse effects will occur if the particular arrangement is allowed to continue.

The degree of severity with which the various types of vertical restraints have been viewed for antitrust purposes has fluctuated somewhat over the years in terms of both Supreme Court jurisprudence and government enforcement philosophy. In 1985, during the Reagan Administration, the Department of Justice issued *Vertical Restraint Guidelines* covering enforcement policy regarding non-price vertical restraints (since vertical price fixing was viewed as *per se* illegal). The general attitude of these Guidelines toward vertical restraints was benevolent on the ground that such restraints tend to be procompetitive in facilitating distribution and risk allocation. However, these Guidelines were withdrawn by the Department after the Democratic Administration took power in 1993. We will now turn to the current law in this area.

[A] Exclusive Dealing

A manufacturer will often designate a particular distributor or dealer as the "exclusive" one for a particular territory. The manufacturer is binding itself not to sell the same product to other distributors or dealers in the same territory. From the business viewpoint, this arrangement may well be necessary to ensure that the distributor or dealer will commit to expending sufficient resources and effort to the sales and service of the manufacturer's product within the territory. For this reason, this exclusivity restraint is generally viewed benevolently by the courts. It reflects the manufacturer's right to determine with whom it will do business and is ancillary to the parties' legitimate business purpose of obtaining effective distribution in the marketplace.

Nonetheless, the exclusivity given to the distributor or dealer by the manufacturer does foreclose other parties from obtaining the manufacturer's product and thereby competing with the favored distributor or dealer in the latter's territory. Where the supplier's product faces little "interbrand" competition in the territory—i.e., competition by products made by other manufacturers—the elimination of "intrabrand" competition within the territory may also harm consumers who will have to purchase their product in a noncompetitive environment. Accordingly, a rule of reason assessment of the restraint will have to be made, focusing on the extent to which, in light of the nature of the restraint and the industry circumstances, competing distributors and products will be foreclosed from the marketplace.

It is the substance and not the form of the exclusive relationship that governs the antitrust analysis. For example, where each of two competitors appoints the other as the exclusive distributor for a specified territory, affecting US commerce, this will be found to be an illegal "horizontal" agreement to divide the market in violation of the Sherman Act. Thus, in *United States v. Imperial Chemical Industries, Ltd.*, the district court found that a British company and an American company had unlawfully conspired to divide the world market and monopolize world trade by jointly establishing an exclusive distributorship for selling sporting arms and ammunition. The court declined to strike down other distributorship arrangements unconnected with the conspiracy, leaving the American manufacturer free to designate proper foreign distributors as the supplier's exclusive representatives for their respective countries.

The agreement obligating a supplier to sell to only one customer within a specified territory represents only one of several types of exclusive dealing commitment. Another form of an exclusivity commitment involves a customer agreeing not to deal in the products of a competitor of her supplier. The customer may make a straightforward agreement not to carry a competitor's products or else the customer may enter into a "requirements" contract with the supplier, obligating him to purchase all of his needs for a product from the particular supplier. Both such forms of agreement may raise antitrust questions, again because of the resulting foreclosure of competitors from market access, this time the competitors of the favored supplier. Where the customer undertaking exclusivity is a significant factor in the marketplace as, for example, a major wholesaler or a chain of retail outlets, the anticompetitive impact of the exclusive arrangement in foreclosing other suppliers may be significant.

In the previous chapter, we discussed exclusive dealing practices in the context of monopolistic conduct in violation of Section 2 of the Sherman Act. The general antitrust standard for evaluating exclusive dealing arrangements in the context of Section 3 of the Clayton Act was laid down by the Supreme Court in 1961 in *Tampa Electric Co. v. Nashville Coal Co.*, in which the Court declared that a violation of Section 3 takes place when the exclusivity significantly forecloses the opportunities of competitors to enter into or remain in the market. In that case, a requirements contract obligating Tampa Electric to buy from one coal company all of the needs of one of its generating stations was upheld as lawful because Tampa Electric's purchases accounted for less than 1% of the coal market. Under the rule of reason approach enunciated in the Tampa Electric decision, the relevant market must be defined, and then the share of that market which is foreclosed must be determined.

A number of decisions have held foreclosure of 30% to 40% of the relevant supply or purchase market to constitute a sufficient foreclosure of competition to be unlawful. A former FTC Chairman, Robert Pitofsky, observed that, "U.S. case law suggests a safe harbor for exclusive dealing contracts that foreclose less than 20 per cent of the market, and probably even 30 per cent." When the market share exceeds 40%, the exclusive dealing has ordinarily been condemned. The consideration that exclusive arrangements are common in the particular industry may be an important factor in the determination. In *FTC v. Motion Picture Advertising Service Co.*, the Supreme Court struck down the defendant's exclusive advertising contracts with

Chapter 6: Relationships with Customers or Licensees in US Commerce §6.02[A]

theaters, pointing out that four firms with a combined market share of 75% used exclusive dealing contracts, affecting competing ad agencies.

Section 5 of the Federal Trade Commission Act has a potentially even greater breadth of application to exclusive dealing arrangements than Section 3 of the Clayton Act. Section 5, unlike Section 3, is not limited to transactions in tangible products like "goods" or "commodities." In addition, the Supreme Court indicated in *FTC v. Brown Shoe Co.* that the competitive effects standard of Section 5 can be lower than that of Section 3 because the "Commission has power under [Section 5] to arrest trade restraints in their incipiency without proof that they amount to an outright violation of [Section 3] of the Clayton Act or other provisions of the antitrust laws." In the *Brown Shoe* case, the Court sustained, without any reference to the percentage of foreclosure, the Commission's challenge of contracts between a large manufacturer of shoes and hundreds of independent retail shoe outlets that barred the retailers from carrying competitive shoe lines.

Some years ago, the Commission brought a case under Section 5 against the then giant toy retailer Toys "R" Us ("TRU"), charging that TRU had acted as the coordinator of a horizontal agreement among several toy manufacturers. This scheme, the Commission found, was accomplished by TRU entering into vertical agreements with the individual manufacturers wherein each of the latter agreed to limit the ability of certain discounters to obtain their products, on the condition that the other manufacturers would do likewise. The Commission found a violation of Section 5, and the Seventh Circuit Court of Appeals affirmed. The court's opinion observed that TRU represented a critical outlet for toy manufacturers, and that there was substantial evidence to support the Commission's finding "that there was a horizontal agreement among the toy manufacturers, with TRU in the center as the ringmaster, to boycott the warehouse clubs." The Commission could permissibly infer from the factual record the existence of a horizontal agreement to boycott the discounters, a *per se* violation.

Recently, the Commission resolved another Section 5 case involving anticompetitive practices in its *McWane* decision. McWane, Inc., the dominant national producer of domestic pipe fittings, which carried a full line of the product, announced to its distributors that (with limited exceptions), unless they purchased all of their domestic fittings from McWane, they would lose their rebates and be cut off from purchases for twelve weeks. The FTC brought an enforcement proceeding under Section 5 of the Federal Trade Commission Act and found that McWane's actions constituted an illegal exclusive dealing policy used to maintain McWane's monopoly power in the domestic fittings market. As the reviewing court subsequently noted, the Commission acknowledged that violations of Section 2 of the Sherman Act relating to monopolization also constitute "unfair methods of competition" under Section 5 of the Federal Trade Commission Act, and it therefore relied on Section 2 case law in its analysis. The Court of Appeals for the Eleventh Circuit affirmed the Commission's order in a detailed decision. The court agreed with the Commission that the record established that McWane's exclusive dealing arrangement foreclosed its competitors' access to distributors and harmed competition. The Supreme Court denied review in 2016.

Accordingly, a loyalty or incentive program offered by a supplier to its customers may have an anticompetitive effect in dissuading the customers from dealing with other suppliers. This does not mean that incentive programs are necessarily bad, however. In *Virgin Atlantic Airways Ltd. v. British Airways PLC*, Virgin Atlantic brought a private action against BA under §§ 1 and 2 of the Sherman Act alleging predatory practices by BA in attracting passengers to its transatlantic flights. It was undisputed that BA offered incentive agreements to travel agencies and corporate customers in the form of commissions or discounts when specified levels of purchases were reached. The district court granted summary judgment for BA, and the Second Circuit affirmed. The appellate court held that the § 1 claim failed because there was no showing of concerted action since there was no allegation that the receivers of the incentives had agreed to do anything. BA's program required no mandatory minimum purchases for participating. Moreover, under the rule of reason, Virgin Atlantic had not shown an actual adverse effect on the relevant market or harm resulting to consumers. As to the § 2 claim, the court stated that this was based on a predatory pricing theory and Virgin Atlantic had failed to establish the two necessary elements, either below cost pricing or a possibility of recoupment as required by the *Brooke Group* decision. Moreover, monopoly leveraging had not been established. As we shall see in Chapter 12, Virgin Atlantic brought essentially the same charges against BA under EU competition law, where it was more successful.

In addition to the market share factor, consideration in assessing exclusive dealing contracts will also be given to scrutinizing the validity of any business justifications offered in justification of the exclusive feature. Where the structural test of substantiality of effect is inconclusive, the business considerations are more likely to be given weight. As in the case of any other restraint tested under the rule of reason, if an exclusive dealing arrangement is motivated by a legitimate business objective, and the restraint goes no further than necessary to achieve that legitimate goal, a court will be more inclined to sustain the arrangement as lawful.

In the context of international business, the US antitrust implications of exclusive dealing agreements must, of course, be examined in terms of their effect on US commerce. Let us consider some hypothetical situations. In Case 1, we have a Swiss watch manufacturer which markets its watches in the US through a US importer who then resells the products to US retailers. The manufacturer agrees not to market its watches in the US other than through this importer/distributor. Section 3 may apply to this agreement because the products are being sold in the US, and Section 5 may apply as well. This agreement will foreclose other US watch distributors from obtaining that Swiss manufacturer's watches to sell in the US market. We do not have detailed market information about the significance of this watch manufacturer's distribution in the US market or the extent to which other manufacturers similarly give exclusive commitments to distributors. However, the chances are that the foreclosure involved is not substantial because competing US distributors will have ample alternative suppliers of watches of similar quality. Accordingly, Case 1 will likely not present an antitrust problem.

Case 2 involves the US distributor for the same Swiss manufacturer agreeing that it will not carry competitive watches. This creates a degree of foreclosure of access to the US market for competing foreign and US watch manufacturers. Again, application of Section 3 of the Clayton Act and Section 5 of the FTC Act would require a rule of reason evaluation. The outcome of this evaluation would depend on the extent of the foreclosure of distribution channels effectuated which would, in turn, be determined by the market significance of the distributor subject to the contract. Chances are that there would be many other distributors available to carry competing watches for resale and thus no antitrust problem. Indeed, the business argument for exclusivity arrangements is normally particularly persuasive in the international context. A foreign supplier may well need the fully engaged help of its own exclusive distributor to import the product successfully, get it accepted in the domestic market, and otherwise make the foreign product competitive in that market against what may be entrenched domestic suppliers.

In Case 3, we will postulate an American manufacturer of machine tools which retains a distributor for its products in Australia, agreeing that it will not sell to other Australian distributors. Here it is US export trade that may be affected in the very limited sense that other Australian distributors will be unable to obtain that US manufacturer's product for resale. Section 3 of the Clayton Act will be inapplicable because the products in question are not being sold in the US. However, Section 5 of the FTC Act and Section 1 of the Sherman Act, as illuminated by the 1982 Foreign Antitrust Improvements Act, still have some application to exports where a restraint substantially affects domestic or import commerce or the export trade of a US company not involved in the arrangement. Conceivably, US export trade will be somewhat restrained because other Australian distributors who would sell the US firm's products are unable to obtain them and, theoretically, the US supplier's export trade might be decreased because of that fact. Nonetheless, this scenario would not meet the jurisdictional requirement of the modified Section 5 and Section 1 since there would be no adverse effect on other US exporters.

Finally, we will postulate Case 4, in which the Australian exclusive distributor agrees that it will not carry the products of competitors of its US machine tool supplier. Section 3 will not apply in this export situation, but Section 5 and Section 1 might conceivably apply if other US exporters are adversely affected. Whether the exclusivity agreement creates a substantial foreclosure restraining other US machine tool manufacturers from effectively getting their products sold in Australia will depend on the extent to which there are other significant Australian distributors available to those competing US manufacturers.

A US party, which sells abroad through foreign distributors and asks the latter to pledge not to carry competing goods, may have more cause for concern with the applicable foreign law than with US law. The competition law and other rules of the applicable foreign country should be reviewed with competent counsel before drafting or entering into the distributorship agreement.

Exclusive and nonexclusive dealing contracts between a US export association and its foreign distributors were upheld in *United States v. Minnesota Mining & Manufacturing Co.* That case involved an association trading under the Webb-Pomerene Act, and some aspects of the association's activities were held to go beyond the Act's grant of immunity. The distribution contracts, however, were upheld under traditional Sherman Act analysis. Although the European distributors had agreed to limitations on carrying the products of the association's competitors, the court found that there were an ample number of foreign distributors available, so that competition was not substantially affected. It is interesting that in this case the contracts permitted the foreign distributors to handle the products of any American supplier. It would seem that this feature would create a safe harbor from a charge of restraint of US foreign commerce.

While requirements contracts are in the nature of exclusivity commitments, they may qualify for different treatment, especially where the purchasing party is the user of the product. The valid business justifications may be obvious in such cases. For the buyer, the seller's commitment may assure supply and price and thus facilitate long-term planning. For the seller it may offer a reliable market, a known price, and a consistent pattern of trade. Of course, requirements contracts are subjected to the same tests for foreclosure as are other exclusive dealing arrangements. The courts and enforcement agencies may simply find the valid business justification to be more apparent.

Accordingly, absent special market circumstances, exclusive distributorship situations of the types postulated in our hypothetical cases will not raise significant US antitrust concerns. It is to be noted that antitrust concern relating to exclusive vertical arrangements in the international area has generally focused on the issue of whether firms who are competitors or potential competitors may be utilizing exclusive distribution commitments as devices for implementing unlawful market allocation or price fixing conspiracies.

[B] Tying Agreements

Tying arrangements take on different forms, each of them geared to restricting the freedom of choice of the party on the receiving end of the "tie." One form, for example, which is called "full line forcing," involves the seller's conditioning the sale of a desired item on the purchaser's taking on the seller's full line of items. Another variant is the "package" or "block" license of technology in which the licensor insists that the licensee acquire rights to multiple patents or other IP as a condition of obtaining a desired IP right. The theory in each case is that the seller is using his coercive power and leverage in one market to block out his competitors in another market. The early Supreme Court decisions condemning tying arrangements were decided on the Court's assumption that such arrangements served hardly any purpose beyond the suppression of competition. As the Court pointed out in an important decision in a tying case, *Illinois Tool Works Inc. et al. v. Independent Ink, Inc.*, handed down in 2006, over the years "[the] Court's strong disapproval of tying arrangements has substantially diminished" and a more analytical approach has been followed. We will be taking up this recent decision in detail later in this chapter in the separate discussion concerning IP rights and tying arrangements.

Tying agreements are addressed directly by Section 3 of the Clayton Act. As we noted with respect to exclusive dealing, however, Section 3 applies only to transactions

Chapter 6: Relationships with Customers or Licensees in US Commerce   §6.02[B]

involving products in the nature of commodities and is also limited to sales made within the US and its territories. As in the exclusive dealing situation, Sections 1 and 2 of the Sherman Act, as well as Section 5 of the FTC Act, may be applied in a proper case to tie-in sales without these particular limitations. The standard to be applied in assessing whether a certain tie-in sale is sufficiently anticompetitive to be deemed unlawful has shifted somewhat over the years. In any event, the fundamental elements of an unlawful tying agreement are: (1) that there are separate tying and tied products, (2) that the buyer is given no choice of whether to buy the tied product, (3) that the seller holds sufficient economic power in the tying product market to be able to coerce the tie-in, (4) that there be anticompetitive effects in the tied product market, and (5) that a "not insubstantial" amount of commerce in the tied product market be affected by the tie.

In 2008 the Court of Appeals for the Seventh Circuit considered the case of *Sheridan v. Marathon Petroleum Co.* This was a private antitrust suit brought by a Marathon dealer against the oil company under Section 1 of the Sherman Act charging Marathon with tying the processing of credit card sales to the dealership contract. The court explained that the tying arrangement was obviously being challenged under Section 1 of the Sherman Act rather than Section 3 of the Clayton Act because the items alleged to be tied, the franchise and the processing service, were services rather than commodities. In any event, stated the court, "[t]hough some old cases say otherwise, the standards for adjudicating tying under the two statutes are now recognized to be the same."

Continuing its analysis, the court pointed out that, in *Illinois Tool Works, Inc.* and other decisions, the Supreme Court has modified the tying rule by requiring proof that the seller has "market power" in the market for the tying product. The court held that the entire suit had been rightly dismissed, since there was no showing that Marathon had monopoly or market power in any local gasoline markets nor was there a showing of any illegal "tying."

The first significant Supreme Court decision applying Section 3 to a tying agreement came in *United States v. United Shoe Machinery Corp.* in 1922. The defendant had imposed restrictions on the lessees of its shoe-making machinery prohibiting the use of that machinery if competitors' machines were used to perform certain operations on the same shoes. In addition, rental rates on the machinery included a royalty on all shoes made by the lessee, whether or not the shoes were produced by United Shoe machines. The Court held these restrictions unlawful under Section 3. Subsequently, the Supreme Court ruled in *Northern Pacific Railway Co. v. United States* in 1958 that a plaintiff could establish a violation of either Section 3 of the Clayton Act or Section 1 of the Sherman Act simply by showing that the defendant controlled sufficient economic power in the tying product to "impose an appreciable restraint on free competition in the tied product." For the purposes of tie-in cases, this merged the standard applied under Section 1 with that applied under Section 3.

In the *Fortner* case, the plaintiff challenged a "tie" based on the extension of a line of credit on the condition that the borrower purchase prefabricated houses from the defendant. In its second Fortner decision, in 1977, the Court rejected this claim on the ground that the plaintiff had failed to prove that the lender had market power and had shown "nothing more than a willingness to provide cheap financing in order to sell expensive houses."

In 1984, the issue of tying arrangements was again considered by the Supreme Court. *Jefferson Parish Hospital District No. 2 v. Hyde* was a suit by an anesthesiologist directed against East Jefferson Hospital's requirement that all surgery patients use a designated firm for anesthetic services. The Court of Appeals held that this requirement involved a tying arrangement on the reasoning that the users of the hospital's operating rooms (the tying product) were being compelled to purchase the hospital's chosen anesthesia service (the tied product). The Court of Appeals condemned the arrangement as one that was illegal *per se* under Section 1 as applied in the Northern Pacific case. The hospital possessed sufficient market power in the tying market to coerce purchase of the tied product, and the purchase of the latter constituted a "not insubstantial amount of interstate commerce." The Supreme Court disagreed. It held that a *per se* rule could not be applied on the facts of the case inasmuch as East Jefferson Hospital's market share was not large enough to permit an inference that it enjoyed market power. The Court thus rejected the principle that all tying arrangements are *per se* unlawful. Moreover, a violation of the Sherman Act could not be established under the rule of reason in *Jefferson Parish* since the record was insufficient to show that the hospital's policy unreasonably restrained competition for anesthesia services in the area.

The critical issue in tie-in cases is often whether two products are truly separate, reflecting two competitive markets. In *Jefferson Parish,* the majority of the Supreme Court found that general surgical services and anesthetic services were separate products, with patients entitled to competition in both areas. Four of the justices, however, took the position that no tie-in sale was involved because patients did not seek one service without the other. The single product/separate products dispute was more recently waged in the *Microsoft* case, with the plaintiffs arguing that Microsoft's operating system product was a tying product and its browser software a tied product that it was forcing on the consumer. Microsoft argued, to the contrary, that only a single product was involved and that, indeed, the company created efficiencies by integrating browser technology in the operating system. This issue was not definitively resolved before the case settled.

In its 1992 decision in *Eastman Kodak Co. v. Image Technical Services, Inc.,* the Supreme Court reaffirmed that a violation of Section 1 for tying is established by proof that: (1) two separate products are involved, (2) the customer is given no choice but to take the tied product in order to obtain the tying product, (3) the defendant has appreciable economic power in the tying product, and (4) a substantial volume of commerce in the tied product is affected.

Tie-in selling involving price discrimination, rather than a flat conditioning of the purchase of one product on the purchase of a second product, has also been a cause of litigation. The area is a difficult one. A party, of course, normally retains full rights to price its products, but the price of one product can be manipulated to induce purchase of a second product, causing harm to competition. Tie-in arrangements have occasionally been upheld on the basis of their business justifications where these were apparent, and the "tie" was not overbroad in terms of the valid purpose to be served. In *Mozart Co. v. Mercedes-Benz of North America, Inc.*, the plaintiff challenged Mercedes' requiring its franchised dealers to use only replacement parts supplied by Mercedes. The Court of Appeals held that Mercedes could lawfully protect its reputation and consumers' expectations of high quality by insisting on the use of authorized parts. In *United States v. Jerrold Electronics*, one of the first sellers of cable television was upheld in requiring the "package" purchase of all of the components necessary for cable reception. The court was persuaded that, because the product was a new one in the marketplace, consumers would consider Jerrold to be responsible for any problems in their cable television reception.

Similarly, "bundling" of products by a seller can raise interesting antitrust questions in the tie-in context. *Brantley v. NBC Universal Inc.* involved a suit based on § 1 of the Sherman Act brought by a class of retail cable and satellite televise subscribers against television programmers and distributors, complaining of the latter's insistence on selling cable channels in packages as distinct from selling each cable channel separately. The district court dismissed the case on the ground that it did not allege cognizable injury to competition. Plaintiffs argued that competition among distributors was injured because the distributors could offer consumers only the prepackaged channels which they were being offered.

The Ninth Circuit Court of Appeals, in a 2012 decision, affirmed this lower court ruling, also citing the plaintiffs' failure to make out a case of injury to competition. The court pointed out that plaintiffs did not allege a horizontal conspiracy on the part of the defendants and that, applying the rule of reason to the conduct alleged, a tying arrangement could well be consistent with procompetitive behavior.

In the international setting, tie-in selling into the US by a foreign company will be subjected to the antitrust analysis outlined in the US domestic cases discussed above. The key questions are: Are there separate products, one tied to the other? Does the seller have significant market power as to the tying product? Is a significant amount of commerce in the tied product being affected by the tie? Is there injury to competition?

Where the seller is a US party and the market a foreign one, jurisdictional questions come to the fore. A tie-in of products in a foreign market may injure foreign consumers and, generally, will be felt competitively primarily by the foreign companies that are also seeking to serve those consumers. Section 3 will not apply in this case involving sales to foreign markets. Section 1 and Section 5 will apply only in the situation where there are other US exporters being injured by the tie-in practice. To show a violation, it would presumably also have to be established that the US exporter utilizing the tie-ins enjoys significant control in the market for the tying product and is foreclosing a significant amount of US export commerce in the tied product. Foreign competition laws may pose a concern, however.

[C] Restraints on Resale

[1] Resale Price Maintenance

Vertical restraints agreed upon between a seller and a buyer which limit the latter's freedom to resell the product are potentially subject to the prohibitions of Section 1 of the Sherman Act or Section 5 of the FTC Act. However, the law on vertical price restraints was sharply recast by two Supreme Court decisions. The first was *State Oil Co. v. Khan* in 1997 and the second was *Leegin Creative Leather Products Inc. v. PSKS, Inc.* in 2007. It is worth tracing the history of this jurisprudence.

Vertical price fixing, also known as RPM, was first declared a *per se* violation of Section 1 of the Sherman Act in the Supreme Court's 1911 decision in *Dr. Miles Medical Co. v. John D. Park & Sons Co.* In that case, the Court first rejected Dr. Miles' claim that the company's wholesalers and retailers were consignment "agents" rather than purchasers and resellers of Dr. Miles' home medicines. Then, the Court analogized vertical price fixing to horizontal price fixing and concluded that RPM represented an unreasonable restraint on the freedom of a reseller to price as he sees fit. The rule of the *Dr. Miles* case, establishing that an agreement fixing the reseller's minimum resale price was *per se* illegal, endured for many years.

In the 1919 case of *United States v. Colgate & Co.*, the Supreme Court confirmed the right of a (nonmonopolist) seller unilaterally to refuse to deal and held that no conspiracy within the reach of Section 1 occurred when a manufacturer refused unilaterally to do business with a would-be purchaser who was a discounter of merchandise. In another early case, the Court held that the Sherman Act did not bar a producer's fixing the price on goods delivered by it to an agent on a consignment basis (i.e., where title to the goods remains with the producer).

The Congress subsequently enacted the Miller-Tydings and McGuire Acts to provide a limited antitrust exemption to protect "fair trade." Under that exemption, where state law permitted, no antitrust liability attached to a RPM contract involving a trademarked or brand-name product in competition with similar products. In 1975, Congress repealed these antitrust exemptions related to state fair trade laws. This left the *per se* rule of Dr. Miles in place. A seller might lawfully suggest a resale price to the purchaser, but the seller could not obtain agreement on or coerce the desired resale price.

A narrowing of Dr. Miles resulted, however, from the Supreme Court's 1984 decision in *Monsanto Co. v. Spray-Rite Service Corp.* and its 1988 decision in *Business Electronics Corp. v. Sharp Electronics Corp.* In *Monsanto*, the Court announced that a plaintiff had a significant burden of proof to show that a supplier's action in terminating a discounting dealer was the product of an agreement with others and not a unilateral act. It was not sufficient proof of a conspiracy that rival dealers had complained about the plaintiff's price cutting. Sharp was another dealer termination case where the dealer alleged that his termination was the product of a price fixing agreement between the manufacturer and a rival dealer. Although the rival dealer had warned Sharp that it would drop the Sharp line unless the plaintiff dealer was terminated, the Court held that the plaintiff had failed to demonstrate a conspiracy embracing an agreement on pricing. These decisions placed on potential plaintiffs in the RPM area a substantial burden with respect to establishing conspiracy.

In 1997, the Supreme Court reversed the long standing rule which also applied the *per se* standard to vertical maximum price fixing. In *State Oil Co. v. Khan*, the Court unanimously determined that agreements fixing the highest price at which a reseller could resell were not necessarily pernicious and hence were within the domain of the rule of reason.

Then the rule of *Dr. Miles* itself was overturned in 2007 in *Leegin Creative Leather Products, Inc. v. PSKS, Inc.* The case began when Leegin, in keeping with its policy of refusing to sell to retailers who discounted its goods below suggested resale prices, stopped selling to PSKS' store. PSKS filed suit, alleging that Leegin had violated Sherman Act § 1 by entering into vertical agreements with its retailers to set minimum resale prices. The district court refused to let Leegin present expert testimony about the proclosee up...competitive effects of its pricing policies. The district court and the Firth Circuit Court of Appeals ruled for PSKS on the basis of the *Dr. Miles per se* rule and refused to apply the rule of reason in the case.

The Supreme Court granted review and, by a 5-4 vote, overruled Dr. Miles, holding that all vertical price restraints are to be judged by the rule of reason. The majority determined that *Dr. Miles* was ill advised and that vertical price restraints should not be subject to a rule of *per se* unlawfulness. The majority reasoned that the justifications for vertical price restraints are similar to those for other vertical restraints in that they may serve to stimulate interbrand competition by reducing intrabrand competition. In any event, it cannot be concluded, the majority noted, that retail price maintenance always tends to restrict competition and restrict output. The dissenters pointed out that there is no economic consensus on the implications of RPM and, therefore, there existed no reason for abandoning the *per se* rule that had been in place for so many years.

[2]   *Territorial and Customer Restraints*

It has long been held that, in a proper case, vertical restraints limiting a customer's freedom to resell in terms of territory or customer may be reached under Section 1 of the Sherman Act or Section 5 of the FTC Act. *United States v. Topco Assoc., Inc.* and other Supreme Court precedents have established that horizontal agreements which allocate the sales competition among the parties geographically or by customer categories are subject to the *per se* illegality rule. However, agreements as to resale territory or customer type are not necessarily anticompetitive when they are undertaken in the context of a vertical relationship, i.e., between supplier and purchaser. The argument in favor of the arrangement is generally that the restrictive feature is conducive to an orderly marketing of the product, i.e., it motivates each distributor to serve a designated territory or type of trade to the fullest level of his ability, while protecting him from forays by neighboring distributors who might "cherry-pick" the most desirable accounts. On the other hand, such agreements may also be highly anticompetitive, especially where there is little interbrand competition in the sale of the product. The effect of insulating a distributor or dealer from competition is to narrow the buyers' choice of suppliers and probably thereby to raise prices.

When the issue of territorial and customer restrictions came before the Supreme Court in the *White Motor Company* case in 1963, the Court sent the case back to the trial court for a full exploration of the facts, on the ground that too little was known of the impact of such restrictions to conclude that they were *per se* violations of the Sherman Act.

An important test for development of the law in this area came in 1967 when the Supreme Court considered a challenge by the government under the Sherman Act against Arnold, Schwinn & Co., one of the nation's best known bicycle producers. Schwinn required that wholesale distributors resell its bicycles only within designated territories and only to franchised Schwinn dealers in those territories. The government also challenged Schwinn's requirement that the franchised dealers not resell to unfranchised dealers. Although Schwinn's market share had eroded to 13% over the years, the Supreme Court struck the restraints down, stating that it was "unreasonable without more for a manufacturer to seek to restrict and confine areas or persons with which an article may be traded after the manufacturer has parted dominion with it." This ruling placed vertical territorial and customer resale restrictions firmly in the per se illegality category.

The *per se* rule created by *Schwinn* persisted until 1977 when the Court overruled it in *Continental T.V. Inc. v. GTE Sylvania Inc.* Sylvania, the defendant, having a share of only 1% or 2% of the television market, had begun to include dealer location clauses in its distribution agreements to stimulate sales and to compete more effectively against the larger television manufacturers. The Supreme Court refused to find this conduct to be *per se* unlawful, since the decrease in intrabrand competition permitted among Sylvania dealers could stimulate interbrand competition between Sylvania retailers and retailers of other brands. The Court directed that a scrutiny of the benefits and harms posed by the restraints would have to be undertaken under the rule of reason.

Accordingly, since the decision in the *Sylvania* case, vertical territorial and customer restraints have been subject to evaluation under the rule of reason standard. Among the issues which have been weighed in the rule of reason analysis are whether the defendant enjoys significant market power, the degree to which intrabrand competition will be prevented, the extent of market concentration and of entry barriers, and the degree to which vertical restraints are employed in the industry.

Restraints on resale agreed to between foreign suppliers and US distributors involving imports into the US are subject to the rules that we have discussed above. Accordingly, a foreign supplier's agreement with a US distributor which imposes minimum price requirements on the latter is subject to a rule of reason evaluation from the antitrust viewpoint. Other restraints on resale will also be assessed on the facts under the rule of reason, assuming that a horizontal relationship between the parties does not exist. The rule of reason requirement has created an uphill situation for plaintiffs complaining of vertical restraints.

The analysis is different in the context of a US supplier selling in a foreign market through one or more foreign distributors. Assuming that there is no attempt made to restrict the foreign distributors in any way with respect to their possible resale of the products back into the US, agreements by the latter relating to their resale prices, territories or customers in foreign markets will not affect the US market and hence will not violate US antitrust law. Such arrangements must, of course, be carefully reviewed with respect to the applicable rules under foreign antitrust laws. As we will see, resale restrictions are severely scrutinized under the competition law of the EU.

The antitrust cases brought by the US enforcement agencies which have related to the designation of distributor territories in an international setting have generally included elements of horizontal market allocation and/or price fixing affecting the US market.

§6.03 LICENSING OF IP RIGHTS

The laws of the US and of many other countries establish IP rights recognizing the importance of scientific invention, artistic creation, and literary works. The intellectual "property" includes patents and copyrights, trademarks and industrial designs. The laws of various countries, including the US, also provide for the protection of trade secrets, which do not involve patented products or processes but nonetheless cover commercially valuable technology or "know-how." Some rights pertaining to IP are protected internationally by treaty regimes such as the Paris Convention for the Protection of Intellectual Property, the Berne Convention for the Protection of Literary and Artistic Works, the Universal Copyright Convention, the Madrid Agreement Concerning the International Registration of Marks, and the WTO Agreement on Trade-Related Aspects of Intellectual Property Rights ("TRIPS"). The commerce in these intangibles is enormous in amount and exists in a network of private agreements that traverse the globe. The maturing of the information revolution and of the era of the computer have greatly expanded the scope and importance of this massive sector of commerce.

There exists what sometimes is called a conflict, but might better be described as a tension, between the IP laws, on the one hand, and the antitrust or competition laws, on the other. The grant of IP rights is designed to motivate and to reward invention and creation through the granting of limited monopolies or other rights of exclusivity. Competition law endeavors to deter and punish actions which exclude competitors or otherwise injure the competitive process. The interplay between these important interests that has developed in US antitrust jurisprudence deserves significant attention here. We will also come upon it in the course of our review of the competition law in Europe and elsewhere.

[A] Subject Matter of IP Rights

Article 1, Section 8, of the US Constitution expressly grants the Congress the power to promote the progress of science and the useful arts by according for a limited time to authors and inventors the exclusive right to their respective writings and discoveries. Accordingly, the US Patent Act provides that a patent may be obtained by whomever "invents or discovers any new and useful process, machine, manufacture or composition of matter, or any new and useful improvement thereof." Conditions for patentability, such as the novelty and nonobviousness of the invention, are also set forth in the statute. The patent grant begins on the date that the patent issues, and it ends twenty years from the date on which the patent application was filed in the US. It gives the patentee the right to exclude others from making, using, or selling the invention throughout the US. If the invention is a process, the patentee has the right to exclude others from using, selling, or importing into the US products made by that process.

Under the Patent Act, patents are designated as having the attributes of personal property, so that they can be transferred by the patentee either completely by assignment or partially by license. A license may be nonexclusive, which simply permits the licensee to practice the invention free from suit by the patentee, or it may be exclusive, which precludes others from receiving similar licenses. A license may authorize the licensee to grant other parties, known as sublicensees, rights to practice the invention. A provision of the Patent Act specifically authorizes the patentee to grant exclusive rights under his patent "to the whole or any specified part of the United States." As US patents do not operate abroad, and foreign patents likewise do not operate outside of their respective territories, an inventor must seek patents in individual countries. The treaty regimes provide certain priorities and other protections in this regard.

There are, of course, many techniques, processes, formulas, devices, and compilations of data that constitute valuable business know-how and yet are not patented, either because they fail to meet the statutory requirements for a patent or because the owner chooses not to seek patent protection. Where this information is maintained confidentially, it may be recognized as a "trade secret" and protected under contract law, tort law or by statute.

However, the value of a trade secret is lost if the secret is independently discovered by a third party. Although some early federal decisions had questioned whether the recognition of a property right in trade secrets was inconsistent with the US patent system, a 1974 Supreme Court ruling settled that the state laws protecting trade secrets are enforceable. The very recent Defend Trade Secrets Act of 2016 creates a federal private cause of action for the misappropriation of trade secrets. Under the US Copyright Act, copyright protection is accorded to original works of authorship fixed in any tangible medium of expression, including literary, dramatic, or musical works, sound recordings, motion pictures, and other works. The copyright protection in works created after January 1, 1978 is generally for a term consisting of the life of the author and seventy years after the author's death.

Trademarks and service marks represent another important sector of IP in the business world. When combined with a marketing concept and licensed as part of a complete business regime, the trademark or service mark can constitute the essence of an international franchise operation, beckoning the consumer to a known brand and product. The trademark or service mark (collectively referred to here as trademarks) can consist of any words, symbols, devices, or the like, capable of identifying and distinguishing the goods or services of a business.

The Lanham Act provides for the federal registration of trademarks. A person's trademark is infringed whenever another party markets goods or services using a mark that is so similar to the protected trademark that there results a likelihood of confusion as to the source of the goods or services. The Lanham Act includes a civil action remedy for the infringement of such registrations. Even if a trademark has not been federally registered, the owner may still prevent infringement of the mark in an action for common law trademark infringement. Like other IP rights, trademark rights are transferable, in whole or in part, by assignment or license. Since the continuing value of the trademark is dependent on the preservation of the reputation of the goods or services offered in connection with the mark, the trademark owner must take the necessary steps to monitor the nature and quality of those goods and services. If the owner licenses the mark, as in the franchise situation, this responsibility for assuring quality control extends to the licensor' overseeing, to some degree, the licensees' activities.

[B]   Relationship with Antitrust Law

The US antitrust points of reference for agreements concerning IP rights are usually Sections 1 and 2 of the Sherman Act (although it should not be forgotten that Section 3 of the Clayton Act refers to tie-ins involving goods, etc., whether "patented or unpatented"). These Sherman Act provisions, as we have seen, prohibit contracts in unreasonable restraint of trade or acts of monopolization where either the interstate or foreign commerce of the US are involved. Analytical problems in enforcing antitrust law in this setting arise from the fact that the IP rights give the owner the entitlement to exclude competition within the context of the limited monopoly which he has been accorded. However, the lawful boundaries of the monopoly may be difficult to ascertain.

The *Microsoft* case that we have previously discussed is a good illustration of the analytical issues that may be posed. The Antitrust Division alleged, and the district court agreed, that Microsoft was overstepping the bounds of its lawful monopoly in personal computer operating systems by utilizing that monopoly position to seize a monopoly over another "product," Internet browsers. Microsoft maintained that two separate products were not involved and that, hence, the company could not be guilty of attempting to extend its lawful monopoly from one product to the other. The Court of Appeals subsequently reversed the finding of attempted monopolization.

When the IP owner simply uses the "property" in his own business (i.e., by manufacturing and distributing his own product, using his patented or trade secret process to manufacture a commercial item, or by using his trademark to identify the products that he makes and sells), he is not likely to encounter antitrust problems. This is because the only provision of the Sherman Act that can be violated by a person acting singly is the prohibition against monopolization or attempted monopolization in Section 2, and the limited monopoly allowed to IP owners is not in and of itself a violation of that section. There are some situations in which illegal monopolization can pertain even within this context, such as where the patent holder is attempting to enforce a fraudulently obtained patent, but such situations are not commonplace.

In contrast to this situation in which the IP owner is simply using his rights "in-house," antitrust issues are much more likely to arise once the owner decides to transfer to others limited authority to exploit his property rights. This principle surprises some owners of IP rights who reason that, since they have the exclusive legal right to the exploitation of the property, they should be entitled to attach any conditions that they choose to a license of the right. This is not the law, however. Because the policy of free and open competition embodied in the Sherman Act is a powerful one, once the owner decides to transfer a part of the rights to the property, many of the antitrust rules which are generally applicable to agreements come into play. As we shall see, however, the government's current antitrust enforcement policy in the area of IP rights is much more permissive than it was some years ago, because of increased emphasis on supporting innovation through the development and transfer of technology.

Patent licensors must be aware of the antitrust limitations on licensing and also of the equitable prohibitions which comprise the "misuse" doctrine. The patent misuse doctrine has been generally described as prohibiting a patent owner from illegally expanding the scope of the patent monopoly. The effect of a finding of patent misuse is to cause the patent to become unenforceable until the misuse is "purged." A finding of misuse does not, however, necessarily expose the patent owner to liability, including treble damage claims, under the antitrust laws, even though some of the licensing activities considered to constitute misuse are similar in their substantive aspects to activities that may create antitrust exposure. For example, in its 2015 decision in *Kimble v. Marvel Ent't*, the Supreme Court adhered to the patent law principle it established in *Brulotte v. Thys* in 1964 that a claim by a patentee for royalties for sales made after his patent expired is unenforceable *per se*.

Finally, although it is not technically an antitrust law, Section 337 of the Tariff Act of 1930 warrants consideration here because it is an important "unfair competition" remedy utilized to exclude imported products that are found to infringe the IP rights of US companies. This statute is in the nature of a detailed prohibition against unfair methods of competition and unfair acts in the importation of articles into the US, or in their sale after importation. Section 337 is administered and enforced by the US ITC.

Section 337 contains specific provisions which are targeted at imports which infringe US IP rights. Thus, the importation or sale within the US of articles which infringe a US patent (including a process patent) or copyright, registered trademark, registered mask work, or protected design is unlawful if an industry in the US relating to the protected articles exists or is in the process of being established. Injury to a US industry need not be shown for a violation where the infringement of IP rights is concerned. The ITC can issue a cease and desist order against the offending importer or exclude the articles from import. The President is given sixty days to disapprove the ITC's determination for policy reasons. The Section 337 remedy has proven to be an important one for US parties to invoke in international IP disputes, particularly because of the exclusion remedy.

A number of US' major trading partners have criticized the Section 337 regime on the ground that it is discriminatory and fails to accord "national treatment" to imported articles, inasmuch as it confers on US domestic interests a special remedy not available to foreign parties. There is, of course, a generally available remedy for patent infringement in the federal district courts. A 1994 amendment to Section 337 intended to reconcile the two remedies provides that a district court considering the same patent issues between the same parties is, on request, to stay its proceedings until the ITC determination becomes final, at which time the ITC record is transmitted to the district court. Notwithstanding the amendments, the statute has remained under attack in the WTO as allegedly failing to accord national treatment to imported goods.

In the 1970s, the antitrust enforcement agencies took a relatively severe position toward restrictions in licensing agreements, viewing them as largely anticompetitive in design and effect. This policy was championed in a number of speeches made by Antitrust Division officials which enunciated what came to be known as the "nine no-nos" of patent licensing, consisting of nine types of license restrictions that the Division would normally challenge as *per se* unlawful under the Sherman Act. These restrictions included tie-ins, "package" licenses, "grant backs," and price limitations. The nine no-nos were expressly repudiated by the appointees of the Reagan Administration, beginning in 1981. Charles F. Rule, the last Reagan appointee as Assistant Attorney General for the Antitrust Division, summed up the reversal of enforcement position in a 1986 speech in which he stated that:

> the nine no-nos no longer represent our policy. We are much more sympathetic to intellectual property licensing, including restrictions in such licenses, because we recognize its economic benefits. We also recognize that licensing, rather than being in conflict with the purposes of the antitrust laws, is consistent.

This view has argued that there exist procompetitive reasons for such restrictions in many cases, and that the practices could not be universally condemned under the *per se* rule. This softened attitude toward licensing restraints has, on the whole, survived the subsequent changes in political power.

In 1995, the Department of Justice and the Federal Trade Commission jointly issued *Antitrust Guidelines for the Licensing of Intellectual Property ("IP Guidelines")*. These original *IP Guidelines* were replaced by a revised version on January 12, 2017. The *IP Guidelines* deal with the licensing of IP protected by patent, copyright, and trade secret law and of know-how (but not trademarks). They largely reflect the existing case law and thus declare a neutral position on the IP/antitrust interplay, stating:

> 2.0 These Guidelines embody three general principles: (a) for the purpose of antitrust analysis, the Agencies apply the same analysis to conduct involving intellectual property as to conduct involving other forms of property, taking into account the specific characteristics of a particular property right; (b) the Agencies do not presume that intellectual property creates market power in the antitrust context; and (c) the Agencies recognize that intellectual property licensing allows firms to continue complementary factors of production and is generally pro-competitive.

We have seen that a firm which enjoys "market power" may be held to a demanding standard of conduct. As noted above, however, the *IP Guidelines* state that the Agencies will not presume that IP creates market power in the antitrust context. Whether such market power exists and, if it does, what antitrust implications arise, will depend upon the situation presented. Under the *IP Guidelines*, restraints in licensing agreements still generally be evaluated under the rule of reason. This approach reflects the decision of the Supreme Court in *Illinois Tool Works Inc. et al v. Independent Ink Inc.* in 2006.

Among the licensing restraints that have been held *per se* unlawful where horizontal relationships are involved have been naked price fixing, output restraints, and market division, as well as certain group boycotts. The *IP Guidelines* state (at p. 17):

> If [as a result of the restraint in a particular licensing agreement] there is no efficiency-enhancing integration of economic activity and if the type of restraint is one that has been accorded per se treatment, the Agencies will challenge the restraint under the per se use. Otherwise, the Agencies will apply a rule of reason analysis.

IP generally brings procompetitive benefits for consumers by permitting a broader and more efficient exploitation of the property. In particular, field-of-use, territorial and other forms of exclusivity give licensees the incentive to invest in the commercialization and distribution of the products by protecting the licensees against "free riding" on their investments by other licensees or by the licensor itself, The *IP Guidelines* use the concept of "technology markets" consisting of the licensed technology under review and its close substitutes. The likely competitive effects of the agreement are evaluated, using market share data if available. "Research and development markets" may also be posited for purposes of analysis. The greater part of the *IP Guidelines* is devoted to a series of hypothetical examples and to discussion of how the Agencies would address each.

The Agencies provide an antitrust "safety zone" by advising that, absent extraordinary circumstances, they (at p. 24, footnotes omitted):

> will not challenge a restraint in an intellectual property licensing arrangement if (1) the restraint is not facially anticompetitive and (2) the licensor and its licensees collectively account for no more than twenty per cent of each relevant market significantly affected by the restraint. This "safety zone" does not apply to those transfers of intellectual property rights to which a merger analysis is applied ... .

In the final section of the *IP Guidelines* the Agencies discuss the application to particular licensing restraints of the general principles which they espouse. This includes: (1) applying the *per se* illegality rule to RPM provisions in licenses, such as the licensor's fixing of the licensee's resale price of products made under a licensed patent; (2) challenging tying arrangements if the seller has market power in the tying product, the arrangement has an adverse effect on competition in the tied product, and efficiency justifications for the arrangement do not outweigh the anticompetitive effects; (3) evaluating exclusive dealing arrangements under the rule of reason, taking into account various factors including the degree of foreclosure in the relevant market and the duration of the exclusivity; (4) evaluating "grantback" provisions under the rule of reason, but favoring nonexclusive grantbacks over exclusive ones (a grantback arrangement is a commitment by the licensee of an IP right to transfer to the licensor the right to use improvements to the licensed technology subsequently developed by the licensee); and (5) challenging the enforcement of invalid IP rights, such as patents obtained by fraud on the US Patent and Trademark Office, as antitrust violations.

Disputes over patent claims are common and their resolution through settlement agreements may encounter antitrust concerns. The Supreme Court addressed one such situation in its 2013 decision in *FTC v. Actavis, Inc.* The question was whether "reverse payment" settlement agreements can sometimes violate the antitrust laws. Solvay Pharmaceuticals obtained a patent for a brand-name drug called Androgel. Actavis, Inc. and another company filed new drug applications for generic drugs modeled after Androgel, certifying that Solvay's listed patent was invalid. Solvay initiated patent litigation against the two firms, which litigation then settled. Solvay agreed to pay millions of dollars to each generic firm, allegedly as compensation for services. The FTC filed a lawsuit against all of the settling parties, contending that the alleged services had little value and claiming a violation of Section 5 of the FTC Act whereby the parties had agreed to share unlawfully in Solvay's monopoly profits. The district court and the Court of Appeals for the Eleventh Circuit ruled in favor of the respondents, reasoning that such a reverse payment settlement was a lawful means to settle a patent litigation.

The Supreme Court reversed, with three dissenters, directing the lower courts to conduct a rule of reason appraisal of this reverse payment settlement. The Court declined to hold that such settlements are presumptively unlawful. But it reasoned that the specific restraint at issue had the potential for genuine adverse effects on competition. The settlement potentially continued the full patent—related USD 500 million monopoly return, dividing that return between the settling parties, and "the consumer loses." Such a resolution of the patent litigation must be explained and justified on a rule of reason basis, said the Court.

On May 30, 2017, the Supreme Court decided an important case involving the extent of the patent grant in the litigation entitled *Impression Products, Inc. v. Lexmark International Inc.* That case involved Lexmark International Inc. ("Lexmark"), a company which manufactured and sold patented toner cartridges which it sold to consumers in the US and abroad. In exchange for a lower price, customers who purchased through Lexmark's "Return Program" were required to sign contracts agreeing to use the cartridge only once and to refrain from transferring the cartridge to anyone but Lexmark. However, companies known as remanufacturers acquired empty Lexmark toner cartridges, including Return Program cartridges, from purchasers in the US and abroad, refilled them with toner and then resold them. Lexmark sued a number of these remanufacturers, including defendant Impression Products, Inc., for patent infringement as to Return Program cartridges that Lexmark had sold both in the US and abroad, with the latter having been imported into the US. Impression Products moved to dismiss on the grounds that Lexmark's sales, both in the US and abroad, exhausted its patent rights in the cartridges, so Impression Products was free to refurbish them and resell them.

The district court granted the motion to dismiss as to the domestic Return Program cartridges but denied the motion as to the cartridges that Lexmark had sold abroad. The Court of Appeals for the Federal Circuit then ruled for Lexmark with respect to both groups of cartridges in a split decision. The court ruled that Lexmark's sales had not exhausted its US patent rights, even as to the cartridges that Lexmark had sold abroad which were subsequently reimported into the US by Impression Products. That court reasoned that a patentee may sell an item and retain the right to enforce, through patent infringement lawsuits, clearly communicated lawful restrictions as to post-sale use or resale. The appellate court also ruled that a patentee's decision to sell a product abroad did not terminate its ability to bring an infringement suit against a buyer that imported the article and sold it in the US.

The Supreme Court reversed, holding in favor of Impression Products on both issues. The Court concluded that "a patentee's decision to sell a product exhausts all of its patent rights in that item, regardless of any restrictions the patentee purports to impose or the location of the sale." As to the Return Program cartridges sold by Lexmark within the US, the Court cited the patent exhaustion doctrine, over 160 years old, which gives the purchaser of a patented product all of the rights and benefits that come along with ownership regardless of any restrictions that the patentee may have sought to impose.

The question of international exhaustion, raised as to the Lexmark products, that were sold abroad and then imported into the US, posed a somewhat different question. But the Court held that "[a]n authorized sale outside the United States, just as one within the United States, exhausts all rights under the Patent Act." The Court noted the kinship that exists between patent law and copyright law and the Court's precedents which hold that the first sale exhaustion rule applies to copies of a copyrighted work lawfully made and sold abroad. While a patentee has the right to decide whether to make a sale that exhausts its patent rights in an item, in the US or abroad, once it authorizes a sale those rights are exhausted.

Justice Ruth Bader Ginsburg was the lone dissenter in this decision. She agreed with the Court majority on the issue of domestic (i.e., US) exhaustion but disagreed with the Court's ruling on international exhaustion. Patent law is territorial, she opined, which means that foreign law, not US law, governs the patent rules regarding manufacture and sale of patented inventions in foreign countries. Therefore, it makes little sense to hold that a sale abroad can exhaust an inventor's US patent rights. Justice Ginsburg pointed out that she had also dissented in the holding that a foreign sale can exhaust US copyright protections. For those reasons, Justice Ginsburg agreed with the Federal Circuit's judgment with respect to foreign exhaustion.

[C]   Territorial Restrictions in International Licenses

The US Supreme Court opinion in the *Lexmark* case brings us neatly to the issue of territorial limitations in international licensing agreements. A major concern of the parties engaged in the negotiation of an international licensing agreement is often the territorial scope to be given the license. The prospective licensor may be enthusiastic about licensing the use of her technology or trademark abroad, but be unwilling to create a new competitor in her home market. In another scenario, the potential licensor may have a desire to retain certain established foreign markets for herself, while offering to the licensee only geographic markets which are as yet undeveloped. For his part, the licensee may be anxious to obtain as broad a potential market as possible, as well as a commitment in which the licensor agrees not to use the licensed technology in competition with the licensee.

Since IP rights, such as those granted by the patent, copyright, and trademark laws, are ordinarily national in scope, the territorial limitation concern can generally be addressed in the first instance by the licensing of rights under some national regimes and not others. For example, US Company A may grant UK Company B rights under A's UK patents for the manufacture of Product Y, while withholding rights under A's US patents relating to Y. If B tries to ship the resulting products to the US, A will be able to sue for patent infringement in the US courts and will also be able to move to exclude the products by bringing a Section 337 case in the US ITC. Except in the situation where A and B were in an actual or potential competitive relationship with respect to the manufacture of Y before the license was given, and the selective licensing is part of a scheme to divide world markets, the selective licensing feature should be unobjectionable from the antitrust viewpoint.

Accordingly, Example 1 of the *IP Guidelines* describes as unobjectionable from the antitrust viewpoint a situation in which a US firm licenses its new copyrighted software program for use only in specified portions of the US and in specified foreign countries. Similarly, a non-US party can, for example, generally grant a license under its US IP rights and withhold the licensing of foreign rights.

We now know from the *Lexmark* decision, however, that once an authorized sale of the protected product has been made outside of the US (as well as within the US), any US IP right cannot be asserted to control the further disposition of the product.

We spoke in Chapter 5 about the *du Pont Cellophane* antitrust case of the 1950s. The case involved the grant by a French firm, which was eminent in the cellophane field, to du Pont, which was in the early stages of developing its cellophane business, of the exclusive right to manufacture cellophane in North and Central America under the French secret process. In addition, the French company agreed not to compete in du Pont's territory. On a challenge by the government under the Sherman Act, the district court rejected the argument that a "territorially limited license under a trade secret process is per se illegal." The court held the territorial limitations in question to be a reasonable ancillary restraint to the license agreement "since the participants were not in fact competitors" and since the beneficial result of the agreement was the creation of the American cellophane industry.

The antitrust cases challenging territorial limitations in licensing agreements have usually concerned cartels. In the *National Lead* case, which involved the cross-licensing of patents on a territorial basis, the court struck down the arrangement as a system of territorial allocation not justifiable as ancillary to the grant of patent licenses. In the landmark *Timken Roller Bearing Co.* case, the government's complaint asserted that American Timken's plan to dominate the world market for its product had been furthered by its dividing territories through registration of the Timken mark in different countries, coupled with the requirement that its foreign licensees not manufacture or sell antifriction bearings except under the Timken mark. American Timken responded that its alleged territorial allocations were merely the taking of valid measures to implement a trademark licensing system. The Supreme Court concurred with the lower court that the trademark provisions in the agreements could not support the allocations, inasmuch as they were subsidiary and secondary to the central purpose of dividing trade territories. The Court stated that a trademark "cannot be legally used as a device for Sherman Act violation."

Trademark licenses which are restricted to particular nations may also give rise to US legal concerns in another context, referred to in US parlance as the issue of "gray market" goods. While this issue is not technically within the antitrust sphere, the reader should be aware of its existence, including its legislative and regulatory background. Section 42 of the US Lanham Act denies entry into the US of imported merchandise which copies or simulates the name or registered trademark of a US manufacturer or trader. This statute clearly bars products carrying "pirated" or counterfeit marks. In addition, following litigation over the question of whether such a provision would also bar, on request of the US trademark owner, the importation of genuine goods identified by a trademark properly applied abroad, the Congress enacted statutory language which is presently Section 526 of the Tariff Act of 1930. This provision makes it unlawful, in the absence of written consent from the US trademark owner, to import into the US merchandise of foreign manufacture bearing a trademark owned by a US citizen, association, or corporation if the US trademark is properly registered in the Patent Office and with the Secretary of the Treasury.

The main purpose for the enactment of Section 526 was the limited one of providing protection for US trademark owners against fraud by foreign parties who had transferred US businesses to the US parties. However, the breadth of the statutory language allowed the owner of a US trademark on a product to bar the identical products from importation, subjecting US consumers to a diminution in intrabrand competition and higher prices. The Department of Justice tried to address this problem by bringing four antitrust suits in 1954 alleging that the US distributors for foreign manufacturers of various brand name perfumes had improperly used Section 526 to monopolize the trade in their respective perfumes by unlawfully excluding from the US the identical products manufactured and sold by the foreign manufacturers. Although the district court ruled for the government, adopting a narrow construction of Section 526, the government moved to vacate the district court's judgment and to dismiss the cases because of an intra-governmental conflict over the proper interpretation of Section 526.

Clarification of the legislation by the Congress was not forthcoming, but the Bureau of Customs adopted relevant regulations. These regulations, as presently set out in 19 C.F.R. 133.23 relate, in pertinent part, to "restrictions on importation of gray market articles." Such articles are defined as "foreign-made articles bearing a genuine trademark or trade name identical with or substantially indistinguishable from one owned and recorded by a citizen of the United States or a corporation or association created or organized within the United States and imported without the authorization of the U.S. owner."

Under the regulations, where the specified degree of commonality between US and foreign trademark owners does not exist, the gray market product can be excluded. In addition, the gray market product can be excluded, even though there is commonality, where the goods sought to be imported are determined to be physically and materially different from the articles authorized by the US trademark owner for importation or sale in the US. Following various lawsuits over the validity of these regulations, the Supreme Court in 1988, in *K-Mart Corp. v. Cartier, Inc.*, upheld the principles of the regulations described above as authorized by Section 526 of the Tariff Act of 1930. Critics assert that this decision did not clear up all of the issues surrounding gray market goods.

The *Addison-Wesley Publishing Co.* case in the 1970s involved an international division of territories in the context of copyrights, with both horizontal and vertical aspects. That was a Sherman Act case brought against a number of major US book publishers, in which the government alleged that the defendants were unlawfully dividing national territories with major British book publishers. The suit alleged that the defendant publishers would give copyright licenses to the British publishers for English language books only for the entire "British Traditional Market" ("BTM"), comprising some seventy countries. The British publishers, in turn, allegedly agreed not to sell the books in question in the US and several other countries. In a sense, the real target of the government's US antitrust suit was the British publishers, who allegedly had agreed through their trade association that they would accept publication rights from foreign publishers only if these included the exclusive rights for publication in all of the countries in the BTM. The British publishers argued that this agreement was essential to their successfully publishing the books in question because distribution in the UK market itself was inadequate to support the publication. (The author discloses that he was the US counsel for the British book publishers.)

The case was settled by a consent decree. The British publishers, under pressure from both the Department of Justice and the defendant US publishers, gave up their adherence to the BTM agreement. Under the consent decree, the US publishers agreed to refrain from entering into agreements with groups of UK publishers to allocate, divide, or assign territories or customers for the publication, sale or distribution of English language books, where the foreign or domestic commerce of the US was affected. The consent decree also provided that nothing therein would prevent the defendant publishers from exercising their rights under the copyright law of any country, including the US. This would preserve for the publishers their legal rights to exclude books from the US under US copyright law.

[D] Field-of-Use Restrictions

A licensor may desire to limit the use to which the licensee puts the licensed technology, perhaps to assign different fields of use to different licensees, based upon their capabilities, or to retain certain fields for himself. As we have noted, the *IP Guidelines* state that field-of-use limitations in licenses often serve procompetitive ends. Nonetheless, such restrictions sometimes raise antitrust problems. In particular, the distinction must be kept in mind between a patentee's authorizing of a licensee to utilize the patented technology in a limited field and an effort to limit the use or other disposition of a patented article after it has been sold. The Supreme Court held in the *General Talking Pictures* case that a restriction in the licensing of a US patent limiting the licensee's field of manufacture was valid as a permissible benefit of the patent right. The provision considered in that case involved Western Electric's licensing the manufacture and sale of patented vacuum tube amplifiers only as to amplifiers made for noncommercial use. A majority of the Court upheld the restriction, holding that a licensee's manufacture and sale of amplifiers for commercial use constituted infringement of the patent. Accordingly, where the field-of-use restriction exists in a manufacturing license, it will generally pass muster unless the restriction is employed to extend the patent monopoly or otherwise to cartelize trade.

A patentee may not, however, rely on the monopoly granted by the patent to justify his efforts to place restrictions on purchasers of the patented article, including members of the public, regarding their use, resale, or other disposition of the article. In the 1942 *Univis Lens Co.* ruling, relied upon by the Court in its very recent *Lexmark* decision discussed above, the Supreme Court held that sale of an article embodying the patented invention "exhausts the monopoly in that article and the patentee may not thereafter, by virtue of his patent, control the use or disposition of the article."

[E] Tying Agreements

As we discussed previously, tying arrangements may be attacked under several of the US antitrust laws where they have the requisite adverse effect on US interstate or foreign commerce. Because there may be a strong temptation on the part of a patentee or owner of other IP to take advantage of the monopoly by conditioning a license under the IP on the licensee's also taking additional technology from the licensor or purchasing goods from him, tie-ins in the licensing context are scrutinized particularly closely from the antitrust viewpoint. As in the case of other types of tie-ins, tying arrangements involving IP rights may violate Section 1 or 2 of the Sherman Act or Section 5 of the FTC Act. They may also violate Section 3 of the Clayton Act where they involve sales or leases of goods for use, consumption, or resale within the US. In addition, the use of tie-ins where patent rights are concerned may subject the licensor to the patent misuse doctrine and also afford a defense to a claim of patent infringement.

It is a key prerequisite to the illegality of a tie-in under the case law that the party imposing the tie-in enjoys market power as to the tying product. The Supreme Court's 1947 decision in *International Salt Co. v. United States* and other early precedents established a rule that it was presumed that a supplier enjoyed market power in the tying product when it was patented or copyrighted. This presumption arose largely out of the patent misuse doctrine and was imported by the Supreme Court into the antitrust jurisprudence. In the *International Salt* case, the Supreme Court invalidated leases that required lessees of patented salt machines to purchase from the patentee-licensor the unpatented salt tablets used in the machines.

The Supreme Court observed in *United States v. Loew's, Inc.* in 1962, in a case which involved "block booking" of movies, that "[t]he requisite economic power is presumed when the tying product is patented or copyrighted." However, exceptions could exist. One such case was *Dehydrating Process Co. v. A.O. Smith Corp.*, involving the insistence by the manufacturer of a patented silo unloader that the unloader be sold only for installation in the manufacturer's patented silos. The First Circuit upheld the practice because the evidence showed that purchasers of the unloader had experienced considerable difficulty in using the unloader with silos made by others. Therefore, in this situation, the tie-in was deemed reasonable. The rule that a patent is presumed to equal market power eroded over the years. In 1988, Congress amended the Patent Code to eliminate the presumption in the context of patent misuse, making proof of market power a prerequisite for a party claiming misuse. In 1995, the Department of Justice and the FTC issued their *IP Guidelines* which announced that the Agencies would not presume that the owner of a patent or other IP right necessarily is given market power thereby. The situation was ripe for the Supreme Court to reconsider the presumption issue when the Court agreed to review the case of *Illinois Tool Works Inc. v. Independent Ink, Inc.* in the 2005–2006 term. In that suit, the plaintiff, Independent Ink, claimed that Illinois Tool was engaged in illegal tying by demanding that customers who purchased its patented printheads also buy its unpatented ink. The US Court of Appeals for the Federal Circuit held on the basis of the precedents, by which it felt bound, that Illinois Tools' patent created a presumption of market power without any need for the plaintiff to prove this element of its case.

The Supreme Court granted *certiorari* and reversed, holding that the mere fact that a tying product is patented does not support a presumption that the patentee holds market power for purposes of the assessment of a tying arrangement. The Court noted the diminished status of the doctrine and concluded that "Congress, the antitrust enforcement agencies, and most economists have all reached the conclusion that a patent does not necessarily confer market power upon the patentee." Since "[m]any tying arrangements ... are fully consistent with a free, competitive market," henceforth "in all cases involving a tying arrangement, the plaintiff [will be required to] prove that the defendant has market power in the tying product." The recent case law has assumed that the Court's reasoning as to patents in *Illinois Tool Works* extends to copyright and trademarks as well.

Many of the past decisions have turned on the question of whether, for purposes of making sure that the licensor's product or a technology would function properly or to assure quality control, it was necessary to insist on the use of a particular product or source of supply. As the case law has emphasized, it is often possible for the seller or licensor to establish objective specifications for the proper operation of his device or technology without designating a particular brand or supplier of necessary components. This principle applies also to the situation of the owner of a trademark (including a franchisor) who wishes to commit the trademark licensee (the franchisee) to maintaining the high quality level associated with the mark in the mind of the public. The licensor's laying down of detailed technical and other specifications for maintaining quality standards is preferable to the requirement of the use of specified suppliers or product brands, which invites antitrust scrutiny under the tie-in rule. It should be noted that, were a US firm to grant a license under its foreign patent rights to a foreign party on the condition that the latter purchase unpatented components from the former, it would be possible to find a violation of US antitrust law only on the theory that the tie-in has unreasonably foreclosed other US sellers of the components.

"Package" licensing of IP rights raises the same antitrust questions as are pertinent to tie-ins. A forced package license exists when the IP right owner insists on licensing an entire group of patents, copyrights or other rights, although the licensee is interested in less than the entire package. The licensing of a broad array of rights as an undivided grant for a set remuneration has great practical appeal, for it avoids problems such as determining which of the licensee's sales are covered by which license rights, the need for differentiated royalty rates, the extensive bookkeeping involved, and similar administrative sources of cost and irritation. Nonetheless, package licensing may constitute an antitrust violation where the "package" is coercively imposed by the licensor on the licensee, rather than freely embraced by both parties for purposes of convenience. As the Supreme Court pointed out in *Ethyl Gasoline Corp. v. United States*, "[t]he patent monopoly of one invention may no more be enlarged for the exploitation of a monopoly of another, ... than for the exploitation of an unpatented article ... or for the exploitation or promotion of a business not embraced within the patent."

The key question therefore is the difficult and often subjective one of determining whether in a particular case the licensee sought only some of the rights conferred and was coerced into accepting the entire package, or whether the licensee voluntarily contracted for all of the rights conferred. The heart of many license negotiations is verbal discussions between the parties, and insufficient documentary history is generated for future reference. Moreover, coercion can be a subtle process that is not later easily reconstructed in a court of law. The safest way for a licensor of various rights to preclude a later charge of package coercion is to make it clear that each of the rights is available to the licensee on an individual basis or in a less than total package and that the terms offered are fairly commensurate with the more limited rights in question. It has been suggested, for example, that it would be proper to license individual patents at rates the sum of which is greater than the package rate so long as the rates for individual patents are not so disproportionate to the package rate as to amount to economic coercion to force the taking of the package.

[F]   Improper Royalty Formulas

The improper formulation or imposition of royalties in a license agreement is one ground for application of the patent misuse doctrine and a possible element of an antitrust violation. The reasoning once again is that a patent or other IP right cannot be utilized to exercise leverage on the licensee so as to extract compensation from him in an area beyond the licensed subject matter. Royalty questions can arise in a number of ways. A US patentee may license the patent to another party for its full term or for a shorter period. He may also license a patent application but this arrangement carries only the protection of a trade secret until the patent issues. Royalties may not be extracted, however, for use of the patent after it has expired.

In *Brulotte v. Thys Co.*, a license agreement covering a patented machine provided for the payment of royalties on use of the machine both before and after the expiration date of the patent. The Supreme Court held the imposition of a royalty obligation for post-expiration use of the machine to be an unlawful effort by the patentee to extend the term of his monopoly beyond that granted by the law. It is clear from the Court's decision that it would not have objected to the post-expiration payments had they been deferred payments of royalties which had accrued during the life of the patent. The royalties were improper only by reason of the fact that they were based on post-expiration use of the invention. In a decision in 2015, *Kimble v. Marvel Ent't*, the Supreme Court adhered to *stare decisis* and reaffirmed the rule in *Brulotte* against royalties payable for a post patent expiration period.

The question of applying a royalty formula that is based, in whole or in part, on the licensee's sales of products not embodying the licensed patent arose in two cases involving Hazeltine Research, Inc. In *Automatic Radio Manufacturing Co. v. Hazeltine Research, Inc.*, the Supreme Court ruled that a license agreement obliging the licensee to pay a percentage royalty based on the selling price of its radio receivers, whether or not any of the licensed patents were used with respect to these receivers, was not patent misuse. The Court determined that the payment of royalties according to an agreed percentage of the licensee's sales was here reasonable because "[s]ound business judgment could indicate that such payment represents the most convenient method of fixing the business value of the privileges granted by the licensing agreement."

In the second case, involving another licensee, *Zenith Radio Corp. v. Hazeltine Research, Inc.* the Court held that Hazeltine had unlawfully conditioned the grant of the patent license upon payment of royalties on products which did not use the teaching of the patent, and that this was misuse. The Court distinguished the first case on the basis that there the royalty formula had served as a convenient payment method designed by both parties whereas in the second case the license had been conditioned by Hazeltine on the adoption by the licensee of the royalty formula. As Justice Harlan's opinion in dissent indicated, the Court was fashioning a difficult test, requiring in each case a determination of whether the royalty provision was formulated at the instance of both parties or only at the will of the licensor.

Although the licensor is normally free to set any rate of royalty that he wishes, including differing royalties for different licensees, there can be situations in which setting differing royalties is improper. Royalty discrimination cannot be practiced so as to cripple certain competitors or exclude new entrants. Royalty differentials are also impermissible when they are used as a device to exclude competition or to allocate markets among potential competitors. For example, the *La Peyre* case involved a company which held patents giving it a monopoly on the manufacture and distribution of the processing machinery used in shrimp canning. The company was also itself engaged in shrimp canning on the Gulf Coast. The company charged a substantially higher rental rate for leasing the patented machinery to shrimp canners in the Northwest section of the US than for leasing it to canners in other parts of the country.

The Federal Trade Commission determined that the discriminatory rental constituted an unfair method of competition forbidden by Section 5 of the FTC Act, inasmuch as it protected the lessor and the other Gulf Coast shrimp canners from the competition of the Northwest area canners. The Court of Appeals for the Fifth Circuit upheld the Commission, characterizing the violation as "the utilization of monopoly power in one market resulting in discrimination and curtailment of competition in another."

In January 2017, the FTC filed a complaint in federal court under Section 5 against Qualcomm Inc. Qualcomm is the world's dominant supplier of modem chips, devices that manage cellular communications in mobile products. The Commission alleges that Qualcomm will supply its modem chips only if the cell phone customers agree to pay elevated royalties to Qualcomm on the latter's patents. The FTC alleges that the risk of losing access to Qualcomm's modem chips is too great for a cell phone manufacturer to bear because it would preclude the manufacturer from selling phones for use on other important cellular products. The FTC also alleges that Qualcomm's customers are forced to accept royalties that are higher than a fair, reasonable and non-discriminatory ("FRAND") royalty. Allegedly, Qualcomm precluded Apple from sourcing modem chips from Qualcomm's competitors from 2011 to 2016. The FTC seeks a permanent injunction. The FTC action was by a 2-1 vote, with Commissioner Ohlhausen dissenting and citing "extreme circumstances" for the dissent on the ground that the "enforcement action [is] based on a flawed legal theory ... that lacks economic and evidentiary support, that was brought on the eve of a new presidential administration, and that, by mere issuance, will undermine U.S. intellectual property rights in Asia and worldwide." In May 2017 Samsung and Intel filed amicus briefs supporting the FTC's lawsuit. In June 2017 the district judge denied Qualcomm's motion to dismiss the case. As we shall discuss, Qualcomm is facing similar antitrust challenges elsewhere around the world.

[G] Multiple Licenses, Cross-Licenses and Pooling

An IP owner's conferring of licenses on a number of licensees, even if they are competitors, is by itself not objectionable from the antitrust viewpoint. As long as the terms of each license agreement are fixed between the licensor and each individual licensee, with no collusive agreement or conduct among licensees concerning prices, territories, or customers, the multiple aspect of the licensing program should be unassailable. It is also quite proper, and indeed common, for one licensee to insist during the negotiations with the licensor that a "most favored nation" clause be included in the agreement, entitling the licensee to receive from the licensor, both now and in the future, terms no less favorable than those offered by the latter to other, comparable, licensees.

Cross-license agreements—i.e., agreements between two or more parties providing for reciprocal licensing—or agreements in which companies agree to "pool" their IP rights for common use by them are also permissible, provided that they are not designed to serve an anticompetitive conspiracy or otherwise to restrain trade. Nonetheless, such arrangements have often figured in antitrust cases as devices being employed for the purpose of allocating sales territories, excluding competitors or fixing prices. The *IP Guidelines* declare that when "cross-licensing or pooling arrangements are mechanisms to accomplish naked price fixing or market division, they are subject to challenge under the per se rule." Moreover, under the essential facilities doctrine, where the parties participating in a pool of rights possess market power, they may be barred from excluding competitors from the pool.

An interesting situation concerning foreign trade was presented in *United States v. Singer Manufacturing Co.* Singer, the sole US manufacturer of household "zigzag" sewing machines, and two competitors who were also selling in the US, Gegauf of Switzerland and Vigorelli of Italy, had entered into cross-licensing agreements covering patents on a new improved machine. Although an intention of the parties was to avoid possible patent infringement of each other, they had also discussed the question of Japanese competition in the US, and Gegauf thereafter assigned to Singer its US patent rights. Singer subsequently filed patent infringement and Tariff Commission proceedings under Section 337 of the Tariff Act directed against imports of Japanese sewing machines. The government brought suit under Section 1 of the Sherman Act, alleging that this course of action, including the cross-licensing and the assignment of Gegauf's US patent, was an illegal conspiracy designed to exclude competitive Japanese sewing machines from the US. The district court held that the cross-licenses were valid as part of an effort by the parties to settle their patent conflict issues. This decision was reversed by the Supreme Court, which sustained the government's basic position that the three parties' main design was to take unlawful concerted action for the purpose of excluding the Japanese machines from the US. This concerted action included the placing of the Gegauf patent in Singer's hands and the bringing of the Section 337 action.

Patent pooling was involved in *Zenith Radio Corp. v. Hazeltine Research, Inc.*, mentioned above. The important electronics companies in England, Canada, and Australia had set up a patent pool into which they funneled many of the patents owned or controlled by the pool members, including patent rights in those countries which they had been granted by Hazeltine. When Hazeltine sued Zenith for infringing its US patents, Zenith counterclaimed with the charge that Hazeltine was engaging in conspiratorial conduct with the foreign patent pools, impairing Zenith's export sales to the countries involved. The pools' trustees had been granting only package licenses, restricted to local manufacture, which inhibited Zenith and other US manufacturers from shipping into those countries. The Supreme Court concluded that the "clear purpose [of the Canadian pool] was to exclude concerns like Zenith from the Canadian market unless willing to manufacture there" and that this purpose had been effectuated, resulting in a Sherman Act violation causing damage to Zenith. As to the English and Australian markets, the Court reasoned from the record that factors other than the activities of the pool had led to Zenith's failure to enter.

However, the Department of Justice stumbled when it brought a Sherman Act complaint in 1970 against Westinghouse Electric Corporation and two of the Mitsubishi companies, based on extensive cross-licensing of patents and unpatented technology in the electrical equipment field between the US and the Japanese companies. The Department asserted that the effect of these agreements was to prevent the Mitsubishi companies from selling in the US and Westinghouse from selling in Japan. The district court dismissed the case, and the Court of Appeals affirmed, on the ground that the government had failed to prove that the cross-licensing, in fact, had created restraints affecting US import or export trade.

§6.04 FRANCHISING

The franchise form of commercial relationship plays an important part in the distribution of goods and services, both domestically and internationally. We are accustomed to seeing familiar trade names and obtaining familiar products and services around the world in establishments that look much the same, whether we are in Oklahoma, Budapest or Jakarta. Some of these local establishments—fast-food restaurants, motels, gas stations, car dealerships, etc.—may be owned by the originator of the product or service through vertical integration. In many cases, however, the ownership and the operation of the business are in local hands and conducted under the franchise form of doing business. In these cases, the right to carry on the distinct business on a local basis has been contracted out by the originating party (the franchisor) to an independent business person (the franchisee) who owns the outlet. This relationship is normally created by the execution of an agreement whereby the franchisor confers on the franchisee a nonexclusive license of the trademark or service mark associated with the business, along with the appropriate know-how and other instructions for conducting the business, including quality control requirements. Fees, including periodic payments, are generally paid by the franchisor to the franchisee.

In its ideal form, the franchise relationship produces happy and prosperous franchisors and franchisees, along with many satisfied consumers. The franchisor, having developed a proven successful "product" and reputation, is able to maximize distribution through the efforts of strategically dispersed independent proprietors who are willing to make their own investments and efforts to promote the product's success. For his or her part, the franchisee can look forward to the near certainty of receiving significant returns on the distribution of an established product or service. Meanwhile, the consumer, even when far from home, is able to identify and patronize an establishment offering a familiar product of predictable quality. A recent Hollywood film, celebrating the founder of the McDonald's chain, showed this model, and indeed there are many examples of successful franchising.

But there are also ample opportunities for the franchise relationship to go awry. The franchisor may be unhappy with the franchisee's performance in producing, distributing or promoting the product or service. The franchisee may make the required payments slowly or not at all. The franchisee, who has made a substantial investment in the outlet and in product promotion, may feel that the product or service is performing badly, through no fault of his. The local franchisee may also chafe at the extensive degree of control and other limitations which the franchise relationship imposes on his running of his business. Accordingly, disputes frequently arise between the two parties in the franchise relationship, some of which involve antitrust issues. The disagreements may be resolved by arbitration, as is generally provided by the franchise contract, or they may become the subject of litigation. State and federal laws have stepped in to regulate aspects of the franchise relationship, usually to protect the franchisee on the presumption that he or she is "small business" and needs the protection from abuse which may result from the greater market power of the franchisor.

The Federal Trade Commission issued an original franchise rule which went into effect in October 1979. The FTC approved amendments to that Franchise Rule on January 22, 2007. The amended Rule, like the original Rule, requires franchisors to give franchisees material information about the franchisor, the costs of entering the business, the legal obligations of each party, statistics on franchised and company-owned outlets and audited financial information. Substantiation of any financial performance representations must be made. The amended Rule provides some updates, including references to the Internet.

The interest of the franchisor in the franchisee's compliance with quality specifications—and the former's possible overreaching in this respect—has given rise to significant antitrust litigation. The federal Lanham Act contemplates trademark licensing in which the licensee is controlled "in respect to the nature and the quality of the goods and services in connection with which the mark is used." This provision has been interpreted by the courts as placing an affirmative duty on the licensor of a registered mark to take reasonable measures to detect and prevent misleading use of his mark. Inasmuch as a trademark or service mark owner will often discharge this duty by including mandatory quality control provisions in the trademark license, the franchisee's freedom of action in running his or her business may, as a practical matter, be severely constricted. The favored way to avoid antitrust issues in this context is for the franchise agreement to set out minimum objective quality specifications, restricting the franchisee's freedom only in a general way. This approach has not always been followed, for good reason or not, and litigation has ensued. The case law in the area has not been uniform.

In the 1964 decision of the Second Circuit in *Susser v. Carvel Corp.*, a majority of the court held that contracts obligating franchisees to purchase from Carvel or Carvel-designated sources all ingredients of the ice cream products sold to consumers were reasonable. Applying tying clause principles, with the trademark itself as the tying product, the majority reasoned that the latter lacked the prominence necessary to establish market dominance and also that the tied products were both necessary to protect goodwill and not susceptible of advance objective specification without imposing an "impractical and unreasonable burden" on the franchisor. Seven years later, however, the Ninth Circuit in *Siegel v. Chicken Delight, Inc.* found a *per se* violation of the Sherman Act in contracts requiring franchisees to purchase exclusively from the franchisor "essential cooking equipment, dry-mix food items, and trade-mark bearing packaging." The court reasoned that the Chicken Delight trademark had public acceptance and conferred sufficient economic power on the franchisor to injure competitors seeking to sell the tied products. The court also rejected Chicken Delight's contention that the needed dip, spice mixes, and cooking machinery were not susceptible to objective specification.

The decision in *Chicken Delight* has been much criticized for assuming that a prominent trademark necessarily confers significant market power. The decision has also been criticized for evaluating the franchisor's market power in terms of the post-contract situation, i.e., after the franchisee has already committed himself to the relationship. Indeed, as we discussed in Chapter 5, the Supreme Court's 1992 decision in *Eastman Kodak Co. v. Image Technical Services, Inc.* addressed the question of how the impact of tying arrangements should be measured in the case of "locked-in" customers. That case concerned Kodak's policy of selling the replacement parts for its photocopying machines only to customers who purchased their repair service from Kodak. Independent firms that serviced Kodak photocopiers and wanted to purchase repair parts from Kodak challenged the policy as a tying arrangement in which the replacement parts were the tying product and the service the tied product. The Court suggested that, with respect to those customers who were "locked in" because they had already purchased a Kodak photocopier, there might be a relevant market consisting of Kodak-brand parts and service (of which Kodak might have a 100% market share).

In the franchise context, most courts have adjudged the franchisor's market power in terms of the precontract stage, when the potential franchisee is free to choose among all franchisors in the same field, or even among a variety of franchise investments in different fields. These decisions have reasoned that tying claims should not be upheld as long as, at the precontract stage of the franchise relationship, there is vigorous competition for the franchise commitment and the contemplated post-contract franchise requirements have been disclosed. For example, in its 1997 decision in the leading case of *Queen City Pizza, Inc. v. Domino's Pizza, Inc.*, the Court of Appeals for the Third Circuit held that pizza franchisees whose contracts required them to take the franchisor's pizza dough could not claim monopolization by the franchisor of a relevant market for Domino's pizza dough on the grounds that, post-contract, they were locked into this narrow market. The court distinguished the Kodak decision of the Supreme Court as concerning a dissimilar factual situation involving unique machine parts. *Queen City Pizza* has proven to be a highly persuasive decision at least where tying claims in the franchising field are concerned.

CHAPTER 7
The Federal Trade Commission and Robinson-Patman Acts

§7.01 THE FTC AND R-P STATUTES

As the previous chapters have indicated, the Federal Trade Commission plays an important part in US antitrust enforcement. We have observed that Section 5 of the Federal Trade Commission Act gives the Commission a broad mandate for such enforcement activity, allowing the agency to take action against unfair methods of competition in their incipiency, i.e., before they reach the stage of full-blown restraints of trade. The FTC Act, while constituting the primary grant of enforcement jurisdiction to the Commission, does not comprise its sole authority to act with respect to activities in interstate and foreign commerce. Under Section 11(a) of the Clayton Act, the Commission is given authority to enforce Sections 3, 7 and 8 of that Act, dealing with exclusive dealing and tying agreements, mergers, and interlocking directorates, respectively. The agency is also granted enforcement authority as to Section 2 of the Clayton Act, as amended by the Robinson-Patman Act, a statute concerning the discriminatory treatment of purchasers. Finally, the Commission also enforces a number of specialized consumer protection statutes. Much of the Commission's present activity is devoted to merger cases, an area discussed in the next chapter.

In this chapter, the focus of our examination will be, first, on the unique nature of the agency's powers under the Federal Trade Commission Act and, second, on the provisions and enforcement of the Robinson-Patman Act.

§7.02 THE FEDERAL TRADE COMMISSION ACT

[A] Jurisdictional Reach

Section 5 of the FTC Act charges the Commission with the enforcement of the statutory prohibition against "unfair methods of competition in or affecting commerce, and unfair or deceptive acts or practices in or affecting commerce." The scope of this prohibition, which was originally confined to unlawful activity "in" commerce, was expanded by a 1975 statutory amendment to cover also unlawful activity "affecting commerce." The word "commerce," as used in the FTC Act, includes "commerce among the several States or with foreign nations."

The Webb-Pomerene Act of 1918, which provides an antitrust exemption for certain export trade associations, contains a provision to the effect that the phrase "unfair methods of competition" appearing in the FTC Act "shall be construed as extending to unfair methods of competition used in export trade against competitors engaged in export trade, even though the acts constituting such unfair methods are done without the territorial jurisdiction of the United States." The reach of Section 5 of the FTC Act to export transactions is further defined by the 1982 amendments to both that statute and the Sherman Act, discussed earlier, which essentially limit the coverage of the prohibitions in the export context to actions adversely affecting US exporters.

Since the definition of "commerce" in the FTC Act clearly encompasses US foreign commerce, the question arises why it was deemed necessary to include new jurisdictional authority in this regard in the Webb-Pomerene Act. The reason is that the Commission had been construing its mandate under the FTC Act narrowly insofar as activity abroad was concerned. As explained in the legislative history of the Webb-Pomerene Act:

> [T]he Trade Commission would not have anything to do with unfair competition between two American exporters in China .... This act preserves the power of the Trade Commission over the two American exporters, wherever they are in all the world, and if one acts unfairly toward the other in any portion of the world, that one can be brought before the Trade Commission and enjoined.

An early case concerning jurisdiction over exports arose in 1919, *FTC v. Nestle's Food Co.* In that case, a US corporation that produced condensed milk in the US and exported it to Mexico was ordered by the Commission to cease using labels on its cans which implied that the product originated in Europe. It was ruled by the Commission that such labeling and sales constituted an unfair method of competition in that the company gained an undue preference over other US producers by causing purchasers to be misled as to the origin of the milk. The agency concluded that this decision concerning practices in export trade was authorized by Section 5 of the FTC Act as extended by the Webb-Pomerene Act.

In another early case, *FTC v. Caravel Co.*, an American export house sold admittedly inferior California Newtown apples as and at the price of Oregon Newtown Pippins, considered a superior and more expensive apple for export purposes. The

Chapter 7: The Federal Trade Commission and Robinson-Patman Acts §7.02[A]

Commission held that this substitution of goods, which was to the prejudice of the public and of the respondent's competitors, was an unfair method of competition pursuant to the amended Section 5.

The major court case in this area came in 1944 and served to confirm the early agency rulings, while also shedding some light on the extent to which the jurisdiction over foreign commerce under the FTC Act had been affected by the Webb-Pomerene Act. In this case, *Branch v. FTC*, respondent Branch was charged with engaging in both unfair methods of competition and unfair and deceptive acts in commerce. He offered, from his headquarters in Illinois, by advertising in Latin American countries, correspondence courses in thirty-seven different subjects, including architecture, engineering, law, and medicine. Branch represented that he maintained a university, that the courses were approved by the State of Illinois, and that the school was authorized to confer degrees, all of which were untrue representations. Upon these facts, the Commission ordered Branch to cease and desist from making fraudulent representations in the operation of his "diploma mill." The Commission indicated that this action was intended to compel Branch to use fair methods in competing with his US competitors, other US correspondence schools, rather than to protect his foreign customers.

On appeal, Branch argued that the Commission had no jurisdiction to issue its order because the acts complained of took place abroad. The Court of Appeals for the Seventh Circuit, however, rejected this argument. The court deemed the key consideration to be the locations of the competitors. As they were in the US, and as Branch himself had directed his activities from the US, the court saw no problem with the extraterritorial aspects of the situation. In concluding that the power granted to the Commission by Congress through Section 5 of the FTC Act was ample to support the agency's actions in this case, the court pointed out that:

> The United States may protect its commerce from the wrongful acts of its own citizens who remain, as the petitioner did, within the United States and whose wrongful acts are prejudicial to other citizens of the United States who are in competition for that commerce.

The court also found the Webb-Pomerene Act to constitute another and separate source of jurisdiction for the FTC with respect to foreign commerce in general, and export trade in particular.

In 1999, the Court of Appeals for the Eleventh Circuit considered the *Branch* decision in *Nieman v. Dryclean U.S.A. Franchise Co., Inc.*, and disagreed with *Branch's* view that Congress intended the FTC Act to apply extraterritorially. *Nieman* was a case brought by an Argentine citizen who claimed that the defendant US franchisor had unlawfully failed to make the disclosures required by the FTC's Franchise Rule in negotiating with plaintiff the possible opening of dry cleaning franchises in Argentina. In holding that the FTC Act did not authorize extraterritorial application of the Franchise Rule, the Eleventh Circuit cited the Supreme Court's 1991 holding in the *EEOC v. Arabian American Oil Co.* decision that, unless a contrary intent appears, Congressional legislation is presumed to apply only within the territorial jurisdiction of the US. The court also pointed out that *Branch* could be distinguished on the ground that, in that case, the FTC had asserted extraterritorial jurisdiction to protect domestic competitors, whereas here there was no evidence that the defendant's nondisclosure affected domestic competition in any way. The court did not discuss the Foreign Trade Antitrust Improvements Act of 1982, which amended Section 5 of the FTC Act to limit its jurisdictional scope in the context of export commerce.

[B] Acts and Practices in Violation

Prior to 1938, Section 5 dealt only with unfair methods of competition. In a deceptive advertising case, for example, this meant that the Commission had to prove both that the advertising was deceptive and that it injured competitors. The 1938 Wheeler-Lea amendments to the Federal Trade Commission Act broadened the thrust of the statute to protect the consumer as well. The Commission can thus proceed against unfair or deceptive acts that injure consumers without reference to any competitive effects. Among the unfair or deceptive acts or practices against which the Commission has moved are deceptive advertising, commercial bribery, product and name simulation, lottery schemes and shipment of unsolicited goods. With the recent advent of the Internet as a fertile medium for sales deception, the FTC's receipt of complaints alleging deceptive practices has boomed.

As we have previously noted, the Supreme Court has several times made it clear that the FTC has broad discretion to give the phrases "unfair methods of competition" and "unfair or deceptive acts or practices" specific content. In *FTC v. Motion Picture Advertising Service Co.*, for example, the Court remarked that, "Congress advisedly left the concept [of fairness] flexible to be defined with particularity by the myriad of cases from the field of business." Although Section 5 is not limited in scope to the antitrust principles established by other statutes, these are important elements of its sweep. Violations of the Sherman and Clayton Acts, for example, such as price fixing, boycotts, anticompetitive exclusive dealing, tie-ins and mergers are also violations of Section 5. In addition, Section 5 can reach acts or practices which, although not proscribed by the other antitrust statutes, are so closely related to such expressly prohibited conduct that they violate the policies sought to be carried out. In 2015, the FTC issued a Statement of Enforcement Principles Regarding "Unfair Methods of Competition" under Section 5 of the FTC Act, which stresses promotion of consumer welfare and protection of the competitive process.

For example, the Robinson-Patman Act prohibits the granting of discriminatory advertising allowances by suppliers but has no supplementary provision prohibiting the inducement of such allowances by powerful buyers. The Commission sought to close this gap by bringing an inducement proceeding under Section 5 against a large chain store and was sustained by the appellate court. The court reasoned that, while this use of Section 5 went beyond the "technical confines" of the Robinson-Patman Act, it was justified so as "fully to realize the basic policy of the [Act], which was to prevent the abuse of buying power."

As we noted in Chapter 6, in *FTC v. Brown Shoe Co.*, the Supreme Court upheld the Commission's condemnation of a coercive practice under Section 5 as a trade restraint in its incipiency without proof that it amounted to an outright violation of Section 3 of the Clayton Act or other provisions of the antitrust laws.

Section 13(b) of the Federal Trade Commission Act authorizes the federal district courts to issue injunctions against violations of the Act and, in the exercise of the courts' equitable jurisdiction, to order other ancillary equitable relief to remedy the injury caused by the defendant's violations. The Commission invoked this provision in 1999 and subsequently obtained a USD 100 million settlement from Mylan Laboratories, Inc., this being the largest monetary settlement then in the Commission's history. The Commission had alleged that Mylan violated Section 5 of the FTC Act through monopolizing and conspiring to monopolize the markets for certain anti-anxiety drugs, by denying competitors the ingredients necessary to manufacture those drugs. Mylan agreed to pay USD 100 million in disgorged profits into a fund to compensate injured consumers and state agencies. One commissioner opposed the financial remedy of the Mylan settlement, referring to it as "a backdoor approach under a statute (Section 13(b) of the FTC Act) that nowhere specifically authorizes monetary recoveries in antitrust cases and that was never so employed until very recently." Nonetheless, the Commission's authority to seek monetary remedies was upheld by the federal court.

On the heels of *Mylan*, the Commission obtained a consent judgment including a USD 19 million disgorgement against the Hearst Corporation for an alleged anticompetitive acquisition and violation of merger filing requirements. In 2004, in *FTC v. Perrigo Company and Alpharma Inc.*, the FTC filed another settlement providing for disgorgement of unlawfully obtained profits from a market-division agreement.

In 2003, after having received public comments on the issue, the Commission issued a *Policy Statement on Monetary Equitable Remedies in Competition Cases*. This statement declared that, while "the Commission continues to believe that while they can play a useful role in some competition cases, complementing more familiar remedies such as divestiture, conduct remedies, private damages, and civil or criminal penalties," the Commission would not apply disgorgement and restitution as "routine remedies." However, the Commission withdrew this Policy Statement in 2012, stating that it "had created an overly restrictive view of the Commission's options for equitable remedies." The withdrawal of the statement was objected to by one of the Commissioners and has been criticized as ill advised, since its laudable objective was to educate the business community about the Commission's policy on disgorgement. The Commission has continued to seek monetary remedies in various cases.

The Commission has brought many interesting antitrust cases under Section 5 over the years. In Chapter 5, we described the Commission's decision in the "Three Tenors" case (*Polygram Holding, Inc.*) holding a side agreement entered into in connection with a joint venture to be an unreasonable restraint of trade because it restrained the marketing of older recordings by the joint venture parties. In Chapter 6, we discussed the Commission's success in the *Actavis* case, a case brought under Section 5 in which the Supreme Court remanded for a rule of reason evaluation the challenge of a reverse payment settlement in a patent case. In 2016 the FTC issued a report announcing that pharmaceutical companies had entered into substantially fewer "pay-for-delay" patent dispute settlements since the *Actavis* decision was laid down. Also, since the *Actavis* decision, the Commission announced a USD 1.2 billion settlement resolving its antitrust case against Cephalon, Inc. for allegedly illegally blocking generic competition against Cephalon's sleep disorder drug, Provigil.

In a novel dispute involving environmental standards, the Commission filed a complaint against the Union Oil Company of California ("Unocal") under Section 5 for monopolizing the technology market for the supply of gasoline sold in California pursuant to the state emission regulation program. The complaint alleged that Unocal, through knowing and willful misrepresentations, induced California to adopt low-emission reformulated gasoline standards that substantially overlapped with Unocal's patents, thus enabling Unocal to claim hundreds of millions of dollars in royalties from refiners following the state standards. The ALJ hearing the case issued an Initial Decision which concluded that the *Noerr-Pennington* doctrine (which exempts from liability actions taken in the course of petitioning government officials) immunized Unocal's efforts to induce the California Air Resources Board and the refineries to accept Unocal's proposed gasoline standards.

On complaint counsel's appeal, in 2004 the Commission reversed the presiding officer's ruling and held that the *Noerr-Pennington* exemption could not be applied if the complaint's allegations of misrepresentation were to be established at trial. After reviewing the applicable case law in detail, including that relating to the "sham" exception to the exemption, the Commission stated:

> Whether we view misrepresentation as a distinct variant of sham petitioning or as a separate exception to Noerr—Pennington, the fabric of existing law is rich enough to extend antitrust coverage, in appropriate circumstances, to anticompetitive conduct flowing from deliberate misrepresentations that undermine the legitimacy of government proceedings.

Unocal agreed to settle the claims in a settlement that was related to Chevron's acquisition of Unocal.

Recently the FTC has taken up under Section 5 a number of "pay-for-delay" cases. These involve pharmaceutical companies settling patent disputes so as to eliminate the risk of generic competition by agreeing not to compete with an authorized generic version of a drug for a period of time. In one notable case, Teva Pharmaceuticals ("Teva") sought to make a generic version of a drug used to treat epilepsy ("Lamictal") which prompted GlaxoSmithKline ("Glaxo") to file a patent infringement lawsuit against Teva. When the court presiding over the patent litigation found the patent's main claim to be invalid, Glaxo and Teva agreed to settle the case. The parties reached a settlement in which Glaxo agreed to allow Teva to sell generic versions before the Glaxo patent expired and also agreed not to sell its own authorized generic version of the drug (the "no-AG agreement").

In 2012 a putative class of direct purchasers of Lamictal brought suit against Teva and Glaxo contending that the no-AG agreement violated Sections 1 and 2 of the Sherman Act. While the case was pending, the Supreme Court decided the *Actavis* case (discussed here in Chapter 6). The Court of Appeals for the Third Circuit remanded the case to the district court for further consideration in light of *Actavis*. The district court dismissed the complaint, holding that the *Actavis* rule applies only to reverse payments of money and that the agreement would in any event most likely survive scrutiny under the *Actavis* rule of reason test. On appeal, in the 2015 opinion styled *King Drug Co. of Florence, Inc. v. SmithKlineBeecham Corp.*, the Third Circuit vacated and remanded, holding that *Actavis* cannot be limited to reverse payments of cash. The appellate court held that the complaint adequately pleaded a case under the rule of reason. The two drug companies petitioned the Supreme Court for review, arguing that they had engaged in the routine settlement of a patent dispute. The Solicitor General filed an *amicus curiae* brief arguing that agreements of the kind at issue were on the same footing as the payment considered in *Actavis*. On November 7, 2016, the Supreme Court denied the petition for review.

The Federal Trade Commission, which had also filed an *amicus* brief, has pursued an aggressive course in these patent settlement cases in the drug industry, which are numerous. It has filed a number of administrative complaints alleging antitrust violations through pay-for-delay settlements.

[C] Activity in International Cases

The FTC's capacity to take action against anticompetitive conduct "in or affecting commerce," and to do so when the damaging effects are in their incipiency, would appear to endow the Commission with formidable potential powers to act in the international, as well as the domestic, antitrust sphere. Nonetheless, the Commission's involvement in international enforcement matters has historically been relatively modest, certainly as compared to the role played by the Antitrust Division of the Department of Justice in arresting cartel activity. The Commission's co-equal position with the Division in reviewing proposed merger and acquisition transactions has necessarily augmented its international role in recent years. The merger cases will be discussed in the next chapter.

In the area of unfair competition, we have noted the early cases which involved misrepresentations directed to foreigners which were deemed to harm American competitors. There have also been FTC cases in the realm of foreign commerce that involved acts in the nature of the traditional trade restraints barred by the Sherman Act. One such case was the *Luria Brothers & Co.* case, in which the Commission attacked under Section 5 a series of exclusive supply contracts on the ground that they unlawfully restrained trade and tended to create an incipient monopoly in the scrap metal market which, if undeterred, would have violated Sections 1 and 2 of the Sherman Act. An agreement between a central buying office for European steel mills and a three-company US scrap broker group, including Luria, provided that the three would supply all metal scrap to be purchased by the buying office over a period of several years. In the early 1950s, Luria controlled about 80% of the scrap metal market in the North Atlantic area. With only 20% of the domestic market available, Luria's competitors were forced to dispose of their scrap abroad. Because the central buying office purchased between 66% and 84% of the total scrap exported to Europe in the relevant period, Luria's competitors were effectively foreclosed from both the domestic and foreign scrap markets. The Commission concluded that Luria's practices during the years under investigation showed its unlawful effort to monopolize the scrap brokerage business in the foreign market. This conclusion was upheld on appeal.

In 2000, the FTC announced settlement of allegations under Section 5 that FMC Corporation and Asahi Chemical of Japan had engaged in a conspiracy to monopolize the world market for microcrystalline cellulose, a pharmaceutical chemical. The FTC alleged that, in or about 1984, the two companies divided the market for the product, with FMC being given the North American and European markets and Asahi Chemical the markets of Japan and East Asia. FMC was charged with also seeking agreements with smaller manufacturers to maintain its monopoly position.

In Chapter 5, we discussed the *Brunswick, General Motors-Toyota*, and *Three Tenors (Polygram)* cases, in which the Commission addressed joint ventures having antitrust implications. Many of the Commission's efforts to stamp out deceptive advertising and other practices injuring the US consumer have related to the distinction between foreign-origin and domestic products. One category of unfair or deceptive practice in this regard involves the selling, or offering for sale, of a foreign product in the US without disclosing the country of its origin. It is unfair as a general rule to sell a product without disclosing the specific country of its origin where it is not domestic. The underlying theory here is that a substantial portion of the purchasing public prefers domestic products and that the purchaser assumes that a product is of domestic origin unless he is advised to the contrary. Consequently, the reasoning goes, the purchaser is deceived if not informed of the foreign origin before he makes his purchase. Certain exceptions, however, have been established or indicated. If the foreign product is of a type that is not produced in the US, such as cultured pearls, natural pearls, or diamonds, disclosure of the product's foreign origin is not required. Likewise, if it is possible to prove that there is no public preference for a US counterpart of the foreign product, nondisclosure of the product's foreign origin will probably be defensible.

In fact, the converse problem also exists, the deceptive labeling of domestic products to create the false impression that the product is imported. There is, of course, a marked preference by many consumers for certain imported items, e.g., wine, fashion, or perfume, and therefore the risk exists that American or foreign producers will seek to deceive as to the country of origin. This area has also been the subject of significant enforcement activity by the FTC, which barred, for example, the use of the word "English" in the designation, advertising, labeling or description of soap and various other products unless the product was manufactured in England.

In this day and age when the raw material of a product may originate in one country, be incorporated into a component in a second country, and then be assembled into a finished product in a third country, labeling by country of origin is not always a straightforward matter. The Commission has often applied the test that, if the foreign component has retained its "essential characteristics of function or appearance," the foreign origin must be disclosed, whereas disclosure is not needed if the foreign component has "lost its identity" in the process of manufacture.

In April 2016 the FTC issued a report prepared by its Office of International Affairs which outlines the Commission's significant role in international antitrust matters. The report points out that building strong bilateral relationships with foreign agencies is critical to the Commission's enforcement program because many of the FTC cases now involve foreign parties, evidence located abroad and/or parallel review with foreign agencies. In fiscal year 2015, for example, the FTC coordinated with foreign agencies in three investigations, thirty merger and five nonmerger investigations. This cooperation included coordination with competition agencies from Australia, Belgium, Brazil, Canada, China, the EU, Japan, Korea, Mexico, New Zealand, Pakistan, South Africa, Taiwan, Ukraine, and the United Kingdom. The FTC cochairs the ICN's Agency Effectiveness Working Group.

§7.03 THE ROBINSON-PATMAN ACT

[A] The Scope of the Statute

In the Depression era, a subject that concerned Congress was the market power wielded by large buying groups, particularly the chain grocery stores. Investigation had shown that the chains were able to secure favored pricing treatment from suppliers by virtue of their large volume purchases. The smaller, independent grocery stores—sometimes called "Ma and Pa" stores—were thus placed in an unfavorable competitive position, and there was apprehension for their future. Public support for legislation that would compel suppliers to treat all buyers on a fair and equal basis, in order that the small independents would not be prejudiced by their lack of purchasing power, led to enactment of the Robinson-Patman Act in 1936. The two primary objectives of the Act are: (1) to prevent unscrupulous suppliers from attempting to gain an unfair advantage over their competitors by discriminating among buyers, and (2) to prevent unscrupulous buyers from using their economic power to exact discriminatory prices from suppliers to the disadvantage of less powerful buyers.

Throughout its history, the Robinson-Patman Act has encountered opposition from critics who have assailed the statute as a piece of social legislation designed to protect small and inefficient businesses from the harsh winds of competition. The essence of antitrust policy, as embodied in the Sherman Act, the critics say, is to maximize general economic good by requiring every business to be fully engaged in the competitive process. The Robinson-Patman Act, in contrast, creates a rigid structure that stabilizes prices and fails to reward efficiency. Nonetheless, the Act has survived the attacks upon it. The FTC which, in practice, has primary responsibility for the enforcement of the Robinson-Patman Act, has continued to enforce the statute from time to time, although not with the zeal with which it did so in the 1970s. Private enforcement of the Act, through treble damage actions, such as those brought by disfavored distributors or retailers against their suppliers, has also kept the statute from falling into desuetude. The AMC, in its 2007 Report, recommended that Congress repeal the Robinson-Patman Act in its entirety, but this has not occurred.

The application of the Robinson-Patman Act requires the seller to be "engaged in" interstate commerce and that one of the discriminatory sales be made in interstate commerce, i.e., that one of the two transactions must have crossed a state line.

The Act has several distinct provisions, each aimed at prohibiting a type of discrimination in the terms which a seller makes available to a buyer. Section 2(a), the most important provision, prohibits sellers from discriminating in price between purchasers of commodities of like grade and quality, where the effect of the discrimination may be substantially to lessen competition. Under Section 2(a) and Section 2(b), certain limited defenses to this nondiscrimination requirement are permitted. These defenses include a showing of "cost justification" for the discriminatory lower price, i.e., that the seller incurred lower costs in serving the favored purchaser, or a showing that the better price was offered in good faith to meet the equally low price offered by a competitor to the same buyer. The standards for establishing the cost justification defense or the meeting competition defense have been developed in the case law and are demanding in nature.

The Robinson-Patman Act also provides that it is not intended to "prevent price changes from time to time where in response to changing conditions affecting the market for or the marketability of the goods concerned, such as but not limited to actual or imminent deterioration of perishable goods, obsolescence of seasonal goods, distress sales under court process, or sales in good faith in discontinuance of business in the goods concerned."

The Act applies only to "purchasers" of "commodities," and therefore does not apply to nonsale transactions, such as leases or licenses, and it is also inapplicable to sales of services or of intangible property rights. The discrimination is barred only as between commodities "of like grade and quality," which the courts have defined in terms of the objective physical characteristics of the goods. Thus, in the case of *Borden Inc. v. FTC*, the Supreme Court held that a nationally advertised brand of milk was of the same grade and quality, for purposes of the statute's nondiscrimination requirement, as identical milk sold under a house brand. The case law highlights three types of competitive injury on which a Robinson-Patman claim may be based: (1) primary-line injury, in which competition is injured at the level of the discriminating seller and its direct competitors; (2) secondary-line injury, involving discrimination that injures competition among the discriminating seller's customers; and (3) tertiary-line injury, injury to competition at the level of the purchaser's customers.

The Act's requirement that there be a showing of price discrimination as between two purchasers has caused some conceptual difficulty in competitive bidding situations in which the unsuccessful bidder does not "purchase" because it does not get the contract but still may suffer loss because of the price discrimination against him. The US Supreme Court, in its most recent pronouncement in a Robinson-Patman case, addressed this issue in 2006 in its opinion in *Volvo Trucks North America, Inc. v. Reeder-Simco GMC, Inc.* (hereinafter "Reeder" and "Volvo"). Reeder was a franchised dealer for the sale of Volvo's trucks, but it made most of its purchases from Volvo, as well as its resales to its customers, only after a retail customer had solicited bids from several dealers and accepted Reeder's bid as the most favorable. Reeder filed Robinson-Patman Act claims against Volvo on the basis that Volvo granted other dealers more favorable price concessions than Volvo granted Reeder, which reduced Reeder's profits on successful bids and increased the number of Reeder's unsuccessful bids. Volvo argued that much of Reeder's proof involved situations in which Reeder did not buy trucks from Volvo in head-to-head competition with another dealer because only that other dealer got the contract and hence purchased trucks from Volvo. Thus, Volvo asserted, the Act's two-purchase requirement was not satisfied in those cases.

The trial court allowed a jury verdict for Reeder, and the Eighth Circuit affirmed. The latter court acknowledged that there was a split of opinion on the question of whether price discrimination in the competitive bidding process violates the Robinson-Patman Act, given that only the winning competitor actually makes a purchase. By a 2-1 vote, the reviewing panel decided that, while an unsuccessful bidder was technically not a "purchaser" within the meaning of the Act, here Reeder had actually purchased some trucks from Volvo following successful bids that it had made on contracts, and it should therefore be considered a "purchaser" from Volvo even as to those instances in which it had been an unsuccessful bidder and not made a purchase. The Supreme Court granted *certiorari* and, after hearing, reversed on a 7-2 vote. The Court held that the Eighth Circuit had erred in deciding that a manufacturer could be held liable for secondary-line price discrimination under the Robinson-Patman Act where there had been no showing that the manufacturer discriminated between dealers competing to resell the manufacturer's product to the same retail customer. Reviewing the evidence offered by Reeder at trial, the Court emphasized that in none of the discrete instances on which Reeder relied did it compete with beneficiaries of the alleged discrimination for the same customer. Absent actual competition with a favored Volvo dealer, Reeder was unable, in the Court's view, to establish the competitive injury required under the Act. The Court stated that it did not need to reach the question of whether the Act can be applied to competitive bidding and special order situations since "Reeder did not establish that it was *disfavored* vis-à-vis other Volvo dealers in the rare instances in which they competed for the same sale—let alone that the alleged discrimination was substantial." (Emphasis in original)

Interestingly, the Court's opinion went on to declare that the Robinson-Patman Act should, in any event, not be given a broad interpretation, but should be construed consistently with the "broader policies of the antitrust laws" which focus on interbrand (not intrabrand) competition. The Court would resist, the opinion said, an interpretation of the Act which would help give rise to a price uniformity and rigidity in the market which would be in open conflict with the purposes of other antitrust legislation. Such an interpretation would also be "geared more to the protection of existing *competitors* than to the stimulation of *competition*." (Emphasis in original) The Court's opinion was carefully worded but its narrow construction of the statute's reach, including its pointing out that there had been no showing of market power on the part of the purchasers here, can easily be read as supportive of the Act's many critics.

Justices Stevens and Thomas joined in a dissent from the Court's opinion. They pointed out that the jury had found price discrimination to exist and that the favored dealers at issue were competitive players in the same geographic market as Reeder. Yet the Court had found no liability under the Act "by adopting a novel, transaction-specific concept of competition" and ignoring the decades-old rule of the *Morton Salt Co.* case that juries may infer the requisite injury to competition from the fact that a manufacturer sells goods to one retailer at a higher price than to its competitors. Whether or not, as some assert, the Robinson-Patman Act represents "wholly mistaken economic theory," this was a case of "exceptional quality," said the dissenters, for enforcing the Act's prohibition against discrimination.

[B] Other Provisions of the Robinson-Patman Act

Section 2(c) of the Act is a self-contained provision prohibiting the seller from paying any brokerage fee, commission, or an equivalent to a buyer or the buyer's agent. It also prohibits a buyer from accepting any such fee or commission. Section 2(c) is aimed at the practice whereby a seller attempts to disguise the price discrimination given a favored buyer by labeling a rebate to the buyer as a "brokerage fee" or "commission." Sections 2(d) and (e) prohibit a seller from granting discriminatory promotional or merchandising allowances, services, or facilities to a buyer unless such assistance is made available to other competing buyers on "proportionally equal terms." This means, for example, that, if the seller gives a large buyer an advertising allowance equal in dollars to 10% of the buyer's purchases from the seller, the seller must also give a smaller buyer an allowance amounting to not less than 10% of his purchases from the seller. The dollar amounts paid the two buyers may not be identical, but the two must have been treated on proportionally equal terms.

Section 2(f) of the Act declares it unlawful for a buyer to knowingly induce or receive a price discrimination forbidden by Section 2(a). Section 3 of the Act declares it unlawful for persons to participate in the granting of certain discriminatory discounts, rebates, allowances, or advertising service charges. Section 3 also forbids territorial price reductions or sales at unreasonably low prices where the seller's purpose is to destroy competition or to eliminate a competitor. Section 3 is a criminal statute which has been little used, largely because of its vagueness. Moreover, the Supreme Court has held that it is not an "antitrust statute" and therefore does not provide a cause of action for private litigants seeking treble damages.

[C] Competitive Injury

Under Section 2(a), the price discriminations rendered unlawful are only those whose effect may be: (1) "substantially to lessen competition," or (2) "tend to create a monopoly in any line of commerce," or (3) "to injure, destroy, or prevent competition with any person who either grants or knowingly receives the benefit of such discrimination, or with customers of either of them ... ." Competitive injury must therefore be established as a prerequisite for a violation of Section 2(a). In contrast, Section 2(c), relating to illegal brokerage payments, is in the nature of a per se violation. No competitive injury need be established. Sections 2(d) and (e), which relate to the granting of discriminatory advertising and promotional allowances, services or facilities, likewise may be violated without a showing of competitive injury. Moreover, the seller has no defense of cost justification. The defense of meeting competition, however, is available to rebut a claim that a seller has violated Section 2(d) or (e).

Notwithstanding the *Morton Salt* inference, the plaintiff seeking to establish secondary-line injury and recover damages must normally establish that it competes

Chapter 7: The Federal Trade Commission and Robinson-Patman Acts §7.03[C]

with the favored purchaser and has lost business by reason of the defendant's lower priced sales to that competitor. As the Court of Appeals for the Fifth Circuit held in a 2003 decision, *Infusion Resources, Inc. v. Minimed, Inc.*, the plaintiff "must first prove that as the disfavored purchaser, it was engaged in actual competition with the favored purchaser(s) as of the time of the price differential."

Definition of the type and degree of injury that must be shown for a violation has proven particularly elusive in the context of primary-line injury. The question that arises when a seller's rival claims injury by reason of the seller's discriminatory sales prices is: at what point does injury inflicted on one or more of the discriminating seller's competitors constitute or threaten substantial damage to the competitive process and hence competition itself? In *Utah Pie Co. v. Continental Baking Co.*, a 1967 Supreme Court decision, the Court appeared to set a low standard for a finding of primary-line injury under Section 2(a), reasoning that injury to a competitor coupled with evidence of predatory intent was a sufficient showing. The Court failed to address otherwise whether the discrimination had brought about a substantial lessening of competition. Subsequently, a number of lower federal courts indicated their lack of confidence in this precedent by setting a very high threshold for an injury showing in the primary-line context, often requiring showings of predatory intent and below-cost pricing to establish liability, equating the standard to that under Section 2 of the Sherman Act.

The Supreme Court revisited the issue in 1993 in the case of *Brooke Group, Ltd. v. Brown & Williamson Tobacco Corp.*, which we discussed in Chapter 5 in connection with the issue of predatory pricing. *Brooke Group* was a Robinson-Patman case, although, as we have noted, the Court's opinion also discussed low pricing in the context of Section 2 of the Sherman Act. The plaintiff cigarette company (formerly Liggett & Myers) claimed that volume rebates by the defendant cigarette company to wholesalers amounted to price discrimination in violation of Section 2(a), as part of a predatory pricing scheme to pressure plaintiff to raise its list prices on generic cigarettes. The Court held that the defendant was entitled to judgment as a matter of law because the plaintiff's allegations of injury were insufficient to establish liability under Section 2(a). It dismissed the injury to competition standard set forth in *Utah Pie* as an insignificant "early judicial inquiry in this area." The Court declared that, in a primary injury case brought under the Robinson-Patman Act, the plaintiff can only recover if it establishes that: (1) "the prices complained of are below an appropriate measure of its rival's costs," and (2) the competitor had a reasonable prospect of subsequently recouping its investment in below-cost prices. The Court thus set a high threshold for primary injury claims under the Robinson-Patman Act.

As the Supreme Court emphasized in *Reeder-Simco*, the enactment of the Robinson-Patman Act was primarily spurred by a congressional desire to provide a remedy for "secondary-line injury," the victimization of small purchasers who are forced to pay more for identical goods than their larger competitors. Indeed, the case law on secondary-line injury developed advantageously for aggrieved parties. The landmark case of *FTC v. Morton Salt Co.*, concerned Morton's sales of its best brand of table salt under a quantity discount system, under which the purchaser's price was dependent on the amount of its purchases. Only five companies purchased at a sufficient volume to obtain the lowest price, and the FTC held the system to be an unlawful discrimination under Section 2(a). The Supreme Court upheld the Commission, rejecting Morton's argument that the quantity discounts were equally available to all, since, as a practical matter, they were usable only by the larger purchasers. The Court also reasoned that it was not necessary to show that the pricing discrimination had injured competition generally, because Section 2(a) also prohibits discriminatory pricing where the effect may be to "injure, destroy, or prevent competition with any person who ... knowingly receives the benefit of such discrimination." In the Court's view, this injury to competition requirement could be met simply by showing that the disfavored buyer had paid more than its favored competitor(s).

As the dissent in the *Reeder-Simco* case indicated, it has therefore been generally considered that, under *Morton Salt* and its progeny, injury to competition at the secondary level will be inferred where there exists evidence of a sustained price discrimination taking place under highly competitive conditions with respect to a price sensitive product. The Court's opinion in *Reeder-Simco* indicates, however, that a plaintiff seeking to recover damages will henceforth also likely have to show that it suffered discrimination and competitive injury on what the dissenters called a "transaction-specific" basis.

Section 2(a)'s prohibition of injurious price discrimination may be applied not only with respect to injury occurring at the level of the seller's competitors (primary line) or at the level of the disfavored purchaser (secondary line), but also at the levels of other purchasers further down the distribution chain who feel the negative effect of the discrimination. In *Perkins v. Standard Oil Co.*, the Supreme Court refused to limit the reach of the prohibition in a case involving a claim of injury by a buyer who was several levels down in the distribution chain from the level at which the price discrimination had taken place. It should be kept in mind that, even apart from the specific defenses in the statute, the Robinson-Patman Act does not require that a given seller charge the identical price on goods of like grade and quality to all of his customers, but only that this be done where necessary to avoid injury to competition. Therefore, for example, a lower price may be given—and usually is given—by a manufacturer to a wholesaler than to a direct buying retailer. The price differential enjoyed by the wholesaler is often referred to as a "functional discount," which is justified by the additional distribution functions and expenditures taken on by the wholesaler.

The functional discount argument should be invoked with care. Note, for example, *Texaco, Inc. v. Hasbrouck*, in which the Supreme Court held that Texaco's giving of lower gasoline prices to wholesalers than to direct buying retailers was not a legitimate functional discount where the bulk of the wholesalers' purchases was resold directly to consumers in competition with the retailers.

Congress enacted Section 2(c), the Robinson-Patman Act's brokerage provision, primarily to curb the practice of large chain stores of requiring their suppliers to pay "dummy" brokerage fees to persons employed by the buyers, as a means of extracting price rebates. It is settled that a § 2(c) plaintiff does not have to prove competitive injury to establish a § 2(c) violation. However, under the Supreme Court precedents, a § 2(c) case plaintiff, like any other party seeking treble damages under § 4(a) of the

Clayton Act for an antitrust violation, must prove that he has suffered "antitrust injury." The Court of Appeals for the Third Circuit held in 2003, in the case of *2660 Woodley Road Joint Venture v. ITT Sheraton Corporation*, that, although the plaintiff's complaint based on its having to pay artificially inflated prices by reason of commercial bribery was encompassed by the prohibitions of § 2(c), the plaintiff lacked antitrust standing to pursue the § 2(c) claims. The court reasoned that the plaintiff's claimed injury was not based on anticompetitive effects but on harm allegedly arising from breaches of contract and of fiduciary duty.

Section 2(f), which makes it illegal for a buyer knowingly to induce or receive a discrimination in price which is prohibited by the Act, was considered by the Supreme Court in *Great Atlantic & Pacific Tea Co. v. FTC*. The Court held that a buyer could not violate this provision unless the seller was violating it as well, meaning that the buyer could assert the affirmative defenses available to the seller. As to the cost justification and "meeting competition" defenses provided by the statute, the courts have tended to apply them strictly because the defendant has the burden of proof.

[D] The Robinson-Patman Act in Foreign Commerce

The Supreme Court held in *Gulf Oil Corp. v. Copp Paving Co.* that the requirement that one of the purchases be "in" commerce means that either the goods sold to the favored purchaser or those sold to the disfavored purchaser must cross state lines in moving from the seller to the buyer.

In *Able Sales Company, Inc. v. Compania De Azucar De Puerto Rico*, a decision of the First Circuit in 2005, the court held that the plaintiff's complaint concerning the defendant's alleged primary-line violations of § 2(a) in the selling of refined sugar did not satisfy the "in commerce" requirement of the statute, inasmuch as the defendant's sales of refined sugar did not cross state lines. The court rejected as insufficient the plaintiff's arguments that the defendant imported the raw sugar that was transformed into refined sugar and that defendant knew that one of its customers planned to export the purchased sugar.

It is plain from the language of § 2(a) that, insofar as international commerce is concerned, the prohibitions extend to discriminatory transactions in import trade, but not to such transactions in export trade. Thus, if a foreign seller discriminates in price between competing US purchasers, the statute will apply. A practical problem may, of course, exists in this situation with respect to obtaining personal jurisdiction over the foreign seller, so as to enforce effectively the law's mandate.

Price discrimination by a US seller among or between foreign purchasers is not covered by § 2(a). In *General Chemicals, Inc. v. Exxon Chemical Co. USA*, the Act was held inapplicable because the allegedly favored importer exported the commodities which he had purchased. In contrast to § 2(a), various of the limitations, including that referring to sales "within the United States" are not found in subsections (c), (d), and (e), which deal with brokerage payments, promotional allowances, services and facilities. A couple of district court decisions considered this difference in the language of the provisions to be significant and applied § 2(c) in some export contexts, as well as in the case of imports. However, in a 2003 decision, the Court of Appeals for the Ninth Circuit rejected a plaintiff's effort to apply § 2(c) broadly in international commerce.

That case, *Rotec Industries, Inc. v. Mitsubishi Corp.* concerned Rotec's sales of equipment, including tools from the US, to the Chinese Government for use in the construction of a dam on the Yangtze River. Mitsubishi was competing with Rotec for sales of such equipment and had some success, allegedly because it paid the Chinese company a "commission." Rotec brought suit in the US against Mitsubishi claiming violations of § 2(c) and other provisions of law. Rotec argued that § 2(c)'s commerce requirements were satisfied because the alleged wrongful conduct affected US foreign commerce. The district court ruled in favor of Mitsubishi, and the appellate court affirmed. The Third Circuit's opinion relied on the *Copp* decision, considering the import of that decision to be that the Robinson-Patman Act's various jurisdictional provisions are "coextensive in scope." Accordingly, it said, "[t]he reach of Section 2(c) extends only to persons and activities which are themselves within the flow of commerce among the states or with foreign nations, but does not extend to all activities which affect such commerce." The court pointed out that the allegedly wrongful payments occurred completely outside the US between a Japanese corporation and a Chinese corporation, activity which could not be considered to have occurred within the flow of commerce among the several US states or with foreign nations.

In short, the day-to-day relevance of the Robinson-Patman Act concerns commodities sold for use, consumption or resale within the US, including domestic and import commerce. As noted earlier, foreign corporations selling their products into or within the US are fully subject to the Robinson-Patman Act prohibitions. For those marketing their products within the US, the implications of the Act warrant advance planning. An enforcement proceeding by the Federal Trade Commission may bring about a significant sanction, and a private treble damage suit brought by an aggrieved competitor or customer can prove financially very damaging. While the Federal Trade Commission has initiated very few cases under the Robinson-Patman Act in recent years, private litigants have been more active in enforcing the statute. In addition, some of the states have laws that are similar in purpose and content to the Robinson-Patman Act.

CHAPTER 8
US Antitrust Aspects of Mergers and Acquisitions

§8.01 ANTITRUST TREATMENT OF MERGERS AND ACQUISITIONS

In this era of globalized trade and investment, the marriage of corporate giants of different nationalities has become commonplace. Businesses whose reputations formerly stemmed from and reflected their unique nationalities and cultures now have been joined with interests emanating from wholly different nationalities and cultures. The mergers facilitate needed access to new geographic markets and customers. They also enable the achievement of economies and efficiencies of scale, and the accumulation of greater capital, technological resources, and talented personnel.

This process of agglomeration has intensified as the national barriers to commerce continue to fall. The liberalization of trade and investment rules, the greatly enhanced speed of communication and transportation, and the linking of the continents of the world enabled by the dazzling new information technologies have all contributed to the globalization of commerce. Accordingly, in our twenty-first century setting, there are great incentives and pressures leading inexorably to international corporate mergers and acquisitions. Foreign competition, likewise, is a spur to mergers of firms operating in the same nations.

However, in industries with high entry barriers which are already concentrated, the primary allure of a corporate merger for a firm may be the prospect of diminishing competition. Here the usual antitrust concerns come into play. A vigorous competition among a variety of firms in terms of product availability, price, quality, and innovation best serves international markets, just as it serves domestic markets. Clearly, competition rules must apply in this context, but, in the absence of an international regime on the subject, both the shaping of national rules to govern international mergers and acquisitions and their enforcement raise special problems.

The successful application of national antitrust prohibitions to anticompetitive international mergers is a more daunting task than challenging international price fixing cartels. Unlike price fixing cartels, corporate mergers tend to carry a strong presumption of respectability and legal propriety. A particular merger may, indeed, be fully consistent with the national policies of one or more of the countries involved.

Yet a merger that is favored by one country may be vehemently opposed by another. Or one country may oppose one aspect of the transaction while another country opposes a different feature. The corporate parties may, therefore, be forced to respond to two or more regulatory views which are irreconcilable with each other and ultimately may find it impossible to consummate the merger in the form which they had envisioned. As we will see in a subsequent chapter dealing with European merger control law, the awkward situation that arose in connection with some mergers of leading US companies, which were not opposed by the US authorities but encountered difficulties before the European Commission, well illustrates the special obstacles posed for the consummation of megamergers in the international setting. In this chapter, we will consider the US antitrust rules applicable to mergers and acquisitions. Our discussion will cover merger enforcement policy, some leading case law precedents, as well as the special issues raised by international mergers.

§8.02 RELEVANT US LAWS

Section 7 of the Clayton Act is the principal US statute under which mergers, acquisitions and equity joint ventures are evaluated from the antitrust viewpoint. Section 7 was originally enacted in 1914. Since 1950, assets as well as stock acquisitions have been covered by the law. The statute provides, in relevant part, as follows:

> No person engaged in commerce or in any activity affecting commerce shall acquire, directly or indirectly, the whole or any part of the stock or other share capital and no person subject to the jurisdiction of the Federal Trade Commission shall acquire the whole or any part of the assets of another person engaged also in commerce or in any activity affecting commerce, where in any line of commerce or in any activity affecting commerce in any section of the country, the effect of such acquisition may be substantially to lessen competition, or to tend to create a monopoly.

The Supreme Court has settled that whether or not this prohibition is violated requires a finding based on probabilities, not certainties. Thus, the words "may be" are to be interpreted as meaning that a substantial lessening of competition is "sufficiently probable and imminent" to warrant relief, according to *United States v. Marine Bancorporation*, a 1974 case.

Section 1 of the Sherman Act, relating to combinations in restraint of trade, and Section 2 of the Sherman Act, relating to monopolization, may also be applied, in some circumstances, to strike down merger transactions of large proportions. However, while Section 7 of the Clayton Act allows the challenge of merger transactions under an "incipiency" standard, i.e., where their effect may be substantially to lessen competition, the Sherman Act prohibitions have traditionally been construed as involving the higher threshold of a showing of a substantial restraint of trade. Accordingly, the

Chapter 8: US Antitrust Aspects of Mergers and Acquisitions §8.02

Clayton Act has long assumed preeminence as the primary instrument for merger control on antitrust grounds.

The Federal Trade Commission and the Antitrust Division of the Department of Justice have concurrent jurisdiction to enforce Section 7 of the Clayton Act. Since Section 5 of the Federal Trade Commission Act may also be used to attack anticompetitive mergers, commentators have speculated as to whether the standards of this provision differ from those under Section 7 of the Clayton Act. This question has been essentially an academic one inasmuch as the Federal Trade Commission has usually applied the established Section 7 standards even where it has seen fit to proceed under Section 5.

In 1980, Section 7 was amended by the Antitrust Procedural Improvements Act, causing the jurisdictional scope of the statute to become coextensive with Congress' power under the Commerce Clause. The application of Section 7 had been limited to cases in which both the acquiring and the acquired firm were "engaged in commerce." The amendments significantly expanded the reach of the statute by inserting the phrase "or in any activity affecting commerce" after the word "commerce" in three places.

For purposes of antitrust analysis, mergers are classified as either horizontal, vertical or conglomerate. A "horizontal" merger is one that involves two firms which manufacture the same product, or a close substitute, and which operate in the same geographic market. A "vertical" merger is one involving two firms which are at different levels of a particular supply chain, e.g., production of Product A and distribution of Product A. A "conglomerate" merger is one that is neither horizontal nor vertical.

The reach of Section 7 extends to stock and asset acquisitions affecting the interstate commerce of the US, as well as that with foreign nations. Therefore, the statute can be applied even in the case of mergers between two foreign corporations, based on potential anticompetitive effects in the US or on US imports resulting from the merger.

Since the Antitrust Division and the FTC have joint authority for enforcement of the Clayton Act, including Section 7, in theory a particular merger or acquisition may be reviewed by either of the two enforcement bodies. In 2002, the officials of the Antitrust Division and the Federal Trade Commission announced an agreement which they had worked out to divide between the two agencies the various industries for merger review responsibility. However, this explicit division of labor was short-lived, since it immediately met congressional opposition and hence was abandoned after a few months. Which of the two agencies will, in fact, undertake the review in a particular case is decided through a process of consultation. The responsibility is usually assigned to whichever agency has the greater familiarity with the industry or companies concerned, so that it can often be predicted which agency will scrutinize a merger in a particular industry. The "clearance" period, the time during which the Agencies officially determine by consultation which one will conduct a merger investigation, can nonetheless be a cause of delay in some cases.

Before the law was amended to require that parties planning large merger transactions notify the two government agencies in advance of consummation, the principal remedy available to the enforcement authorities was to seek, after the transaction had already taken place, a divestiture of the business or portion of the business deemed obtained in violation of the antitrust laws. Since the enactment of the Hart-Scott-Rodino Antitrust Improvements Act of 1976 ("HSR Act"), imposing pre-merger notification requirements, the antitrust enforcement authorities have enjoyed much greater flexibility in addressing remedies. Often, the agency concerned will negotiate a settlement with the parties with respect to the features of the proposed transaction that the agency considers objectionable. After agreement has been reached, the parties will enter into a consent order in which the acquiring company agrees to divest itself of certain of its preexisting assets or of certain assets that it was proposing to acquire in the transaction. The consent order will set a time schedule for the completion of the required divestiture. The agency may require the parties to identify, in advance of its approving the settlement, an acceptable purchaser for the assets to be divested.

Under § 4 of the Clayton Act, it is possible for a private party, such as a competitor of the merging parties who considers itself threatened or damaged by a merger, to bring a private suit for an injunction or damages, based on the impending or consummated violation of Section 7. However, under the "antitrust injury" requirement for private enforcement that we have previously discussed, the courts have imposed strict requirements for such a private plaintiff to establish that it has "standing" to attack the merger. The plaintiff must be able to show not only that the transaction is likely to injure competition in the marketplace generally but also that the plaintiff will suffer antitrust injury itself. In consequence, successful attacks by private parties are relatively difficult. A merger may also be challenged by state authorities under either federal or state antitrust law. In *California v. American Stores Co.*, the Supreme Court upheld the authority of state or private plaintiffs to obtain injunctive relief under the Clayton Act against a takeover. In recent years, federal and state authorities have worked closely together in merger investigation and law enforcement.

Mergers in regulated industries may also be statutorily subjected to the scrutiny of the agencies overseeing those industries. For example, mergers and acquisitions involving the sale or transfer of telecommunications and broadcast licenses granted by the Federal Communications Commission (the "FCC") are subject to that agency's jurisdiction, as well as that of the Antitrust Division. The FCC applies a broad public interest standard in making its evaluation, including an assessment of any likely anticompetitive effects.

The enforcement policy taken under Section 7 by the Agencies has changed over the years, as has the jurisprudence set out by the court decisions. For example, as we shall see, in the 1960s, the Agencies filed a number of merger cases which today would be viewed as untenable, given the small size of the merging firms and the low concentration levels in the markets in which they competed. Mergers involving competitors holding combined market shares of less than 7% were successfully attacked by the government on the ground that market concentration had to be deterred in its incipiency.

By the 1980s, notably after a Republican Administration took office, there was far less inclination to view the "bigness" of a US firm as a threat to the national economy. In keeping with the economic philosophy advocated by the "Chicago School," a US multinational company's enhancing its size and capabilities through a merger or acquisition became regarded as, more likely than not, an acceptable step designed to enable the firm to become more efficient and hence a better competitor in the world market. This trend has continued to the present, regardless of the political coloring of the Administration. In general, only horizontal mergers have tended to evoke significant antitrust interest, and many horizontal transactions have gone unmolested, some of which involved very large companies. In sum, enforcement philosophy has never returned to the severity of the 1960s, and there is little prospect that it will ever do so. As one distinguished commentator and critic, Herbert Hovenkamp, has written, "the dubious legacy ... of the [Earl] Warren [Supreme] Court in the 1960s [was that] it condemned mergers because they created certain efficiencies."

The reader should also be aware of Section 8 of the Clayton Act which deals with interlocking directorates. This provision prohibits, with certain exceptions, one person from serving as a director or officer of two competing corporations if two thresholds are met. The 1990 amendment requires the Federal Trade Commission to revise these thresholds annually based on the change in the level of gross national product. Accordingly, the Commission revises and announces the new thresholds each year.

§8.03 PREMERGER NOTIFICATION

As noted above, before the enactment of the HSR Act, antimerger enforcement faced significant obstacles. The government authorities often learned of a merger only after it had occurred or else shortly before its consummation, providing no time or insufficient time to review the transaction and, if necessary, to take steps to block it. In consequence, many mergers were reviewed by the government only after they had already taken place. In those cases, if the agency viewed the merger as unlawful, its only recourse was to try to undo the merger after the fact, which meant initiating a full enforcement proceeding. Appellate review of lower court or FTC rulings often extended the litigation process by months or even years. If the government finally prevailed in its challenge of the already completed transaction, the final order in its favor was often issued years after tangible and intangible assets of the merging parties, including their personnel, had long been intermingled or discarded. The government's unhappy task in this context was to try to fashion an order which would hopefully "unscramble the eggs" through a divestiture or other remedial action designed to undo, to the extent possible, the anticompetitive damage wrought by the merger.

The rules of the game shifted dramatically in the government's favor in 1976 when the HSR Act was passed, becoming Section 7(A) of the Clayton Act. The HSR Act requires parties proposing to engage in acquisitions of assets or voting securities which are above certain specified thresholds of magnitude to notify the Antitrust Division and the FTC in advance and to wait a specified number of days before consummating the transaction so as to permit antitrust review. The legislation also provides for the applicable amounts to be adjusted and published for each fiscal year to reflect percentage changes in the gross national product.

On January 19, 2017, the FTC announced its annual revisions to the HSR jurisdictional thresholds, increasing key thresholds approximately 3.3% to reflect changes in the gross national product. Transactions valued at more than USD 323 million are made subject to the HSR Act without regard to the size-of-person involved, unless exempt. Transactions valued at USD 323 million or less will be subject to the HSR Act if the parties also meet the size-of-person thresholds. The size-of-person test is generally met where a "person" with annual sales or total assets of USD 161.5 million makes an acquisition where the target or the target's parent has annual sales or total assets of USD 16.2 million, or vice-versa.

The *International Guidelines* describe the international reach of the HSR ACT as follows:

> Transactions are subject to [the notice and waiting requirements] only if they meet certain conditions, including minimum size thresholds. Some transactions are explicitly exempted from these requirements by the statute's text. The HSR Act and the Hart-Scott-Rodino Premerger Notification Rules ... exempt from the notification requirements certain international transactions (typically those having little nexus to U.S. commerce) that otherwise meet the statutory thresholds. (at p. 8, footnotes omitted)

When required to make notification of a proposed merger or acquisition transaction, the parties must submit to the two Agencies the initial filing of information and documents required by the regulations and then observe a waiting period. This means that the parties must delay the transaction for a thirty-day period (a fifteen-day period in the case of a cash tender offer or a bankruptcy), or until the Agencies grant early termination of the waiting period, while one of the Agencies reviews it. If, before the end of that waiting period, the responsible Agency issues a request to the parties for additional information (generally called a "Second Request"), the companies cannot complete their deal until they have substantially complied with the Second Request and observed an additional thirty-day waiting period (a ten-day period for cash tender offers or a bankruptcy). The length of time for this review may be extended by agreement. Unless the agency takes action that results in a court order stopping the merger, the parties can close their deal at the end of the waiting period. Given the cost, uncertainty and burden of complying with HSR Act notification, on the one hand, and the formidable potential liability incurred for failure to comply with the Act, on the other, an awareness of the threshold standards for the application of the statutory notification requirement is crucial.

Failure to comply with the HSR Act is punishable by substantial civil monetary penalties. In August 2016, the limit on those penalties was adjusted upward to USD 40,000 for each day a violation continues. The government has warned that premature integration, also known as "gun jumping," before the merger closes may lead to civil or even criminal antitrust enforcement. Multimillion dollar fines have, in fact, been imposed on parties who completed their transactions without fully complying with the Act.

The HSR Act requirements also apply to the formation of joint ventures which involve the acquisition of assets or joint ventures. There are a number of general exemptions which, if applicable, will excuse from notification an otherwise reportable transaction. These include, among others, the acquisition of nonvoting securities, acquisitions of some securities solely for the purpose of investment, and acquisitions of goods or realty in the ordinary course of business. Some industries, such as banking, telecommunications, and transportation, are covered by special legislation entrusting review of their transactions to other federal agencies, and these are exempt from the HSR Act requirements.

It can be seen from the content of the different tests that many transactions involving non-US companies which affect US commerce will be caught by the reporting requirements. However, the implementing regulations contain a special set of exemptions to exclude from the notification requirements certain foreign-related merger or acquisition transactions involving foreign or US persons where little impact on US commerce is to be anticipated. Rule changes must be carefully monitored.

The reader will probably have gleaned from the above summary of the threshold requirements of the HSR Act that the filing and exemption rules are very detailed. The job of determining whether the reporting requirements apply to a specific acquisition or merger transaction of a substantial nature is not one for an amateur. There are, in fact, lawyers in many US firms who earn a good part of their keep as specialists on the fine points of HSR Act compliance practice.

After the agency has decided to issue a Second Request, the chances are that the waiting period will prove to be a lengthy one. Such follow-up requests usually contain numerous detailed interrogatories and document demands requiring time consuming responses on such issues as market structure, the reasons for the transaction, and market strategy. In addition, with respect to companies having foreign operations, it should be kept in mind that all documents submitted in response to a Second Request must be in English, whatever their original language. The information supplied to the government in compliance with the HSR Act is confidential and may be disclosed only to Congress or in connection with an administrative or judicial proceeding. While a merger transaction is awaiting Agency clearance, the companies planning to consolidate must carefully monitor their relationship and avoid "gun jumping." In 1999, the Antitrust Division cleared a merger between Computer Associates International and Platinum Technology International. On subsequently discovering that the two companies had been coordinating pricing and other matters before the approval of the merger, the Division brought a lawsuit against Computer Associates International in 2001, alleging illegal premerger coordination in violation of the Sherman and HSR Acts. This case was settled in April 2002 with the company agreeing to pay the maximum USD 638,000 fine.

§8.04　ANTITRUST ANALYSIS OF MERGERS

Merger review occupies a major part of the resources of both the Federal Trade Commission and the Antitrust Division. These governmental authorities assess the legality of a corporate merger or acquisition in the light of its functional impact on competition within the context of the market structure of the particular industry. Since the Supreme Court has given little guidance in recent years regarding the substantive standards under Section 7, and most cases are resolved by consent decrees rather than litigation, the guidelines issued by the government agencies have assumed more and more importance in postulating the rules for merger analysis.

Merger Guidelines outlining the government's enforcement policies were issued by the Department of Justice in 1968, 1982, and 1984. In 1992, the FTC joined the Department of Justice in issuing *Horizontal Merger Guidelines* and, in 2010, the two Agencies issued revised *Horizontal Merger Guidelines*. The Department issued *Non-Horizontal Merger Guidelines* in 1984, which have not been revised since then. The Guidelines do not represent law as such, but they are authoritative and comprehensive statements of enforcement policy.

The central theme of the 2010 *Horizontal Merger Guidelines ("Horizontal Guidelines")* is that "mergers should not be permitted to create, enhance, or entrench market power or to facilitate its exercise." A merger is deemed to enhance market power "if it is likely to encourage one or more firms to raise price, reduce output, diminish innovation, or otherwise harm customers as a result of diminished competitive constraints or incentives." It should be noted that both the Antitrust Division and the FTC have published separate Guides that identify effective remedies to deal with anticompetitive mergers.

In assessing the likely competitive effects of a horizontal merger, market definition is critical. It helps to specify the line of commerce and section of the country which will be the subject of study. It also allows the Agencies to identify the market participants and to measure market shares and the degree of market concentration.

In identifying the relevant product market, the Agencies use the "hypothetical monopolist test" to identify a set of products that are reasonably interchangeable with a product sold by one of the merging firms. "Specifically, the test requires that a hypothetical profit-maximizing firm, not subject to price regulation, that was the only present and future seller of those products ('hypothetical monopolist') likely would impose at least a small but significant and non-transitory increase in price ('SSNIP') on at least one product in the market, including at least one product sold by one of the merging firms." The Agencies most often use a SSNIP of 5% of the price paid by customers for the products or services to which the merging firms contribute value. The purpose of defining the market and measuring market shares in this fashion is to "illuminate the evaluation of competitive effects." (*Horizontal Guidelines*, Paragraph 4.1.1)

In identifying the relevant geographic market, the scope of the market often depends on transportation costs. In addition, "[o]ther factors such as language, regulation, tariff and non-tariff barriers, custom and familiarity, reputation, and service availability may impede long-distance or international transactions. The competitive significance of foreign firms may be assessed at various exchange rates, especially if exchange rates have fluctuated in the recent past ... In the absence of price discrimination based on customer location, the Agencies " normally define geographic markets based on the location of suppliers ... ." (*Horizontal Guidelines*, Paragraph 4.2)

Once the relevant product and geographic markets have been defined, the market shares of the firms concerned and the level of concentration of the market shares generally become the critical issues in the determination of the lawfulness of the amalgamation. In most contexts, each firm's market share is based on its actual or projected revenues from the targeted customers. Among the other factors that may be pertinent to the determination are the ease and likelihood of entry by new competitors into the market and whether any significant efficiencies will be generated by the merger. Defensive arguments may be raised where applicable, including the failing company doctrine. The failing company defense, which is seldom successful, is based on the rationale that a merger involving a company which is in failing health cannot be viewed as a threat to competition because the failing company will cease to be a competitive factor in the industry in any event.

As noted, market concentration is often one useful indicator of the likely competitive effects of a proposed merger. In determining market concentration, the Agencies often use the Herfindahl-Hirschman Index ("HHI"). The HHI is calculated by summing the squares of the individual firms' market shares, a formula which gives proportionately greater weight to the larger market shares. The Agencies consider both the post-merger level of the HHI and the increase in the HHI resulting from the merger. Markets are generally classified into three types: (1) Unconcentrated; (2) Moderately Concentrated; and (3) Highly Concentrated. The higher the post-merger HHI and the increase in the HHI, the greater the likelihood that the Agencies will request additional information to conduct their analysis. Markets in which the post-merger HHI is below 1,500 are viewed as "unconcentrated." If the post-merger HHI is between 1,500 and 2,500, the market is viewed as "moderately concentrated." If the post-merger HHI is over 2,500, the market is considered "highly concentrated."

In considering the likely impact of the merger, the Agencies also take into account the "unilateral effects" of the merger (the elimination of competition between the two merging firms), the pricing of the products, the role of negotiations in pricing, capacity factors, and whether the merger is likely to curtail innovation in the industry. The Agencies also consider whether the merger may diminish competition in the industry and foster collusion by enabling or encouraging post-merger coordinated interaction among firms that harms customers. Whether powerful buyers exist in the industry, and the possible post-merger role of these customers, are examined. Do other firms plan to enter the market as suppliers and, if so, what will the effect of the merger be on the entry plans? Will the merger spur the development of significant efficiencies in the market?

If there is a claim that the merger is not likely to enhance market power in the industry because one of the merging firms is facing imminent failure (known as the failing company defense), the Agencies will insist that all of the following circumstances apply: "(1) the allegedly failing firm would be unable to meet its financial obligations in the near future; (2) it would not be able to reorganize successfully under Chapter 11 of the Bankruptcy Act; and (3) it has made unsuccessful good-faith efforts to elicit reasonable alternative offers that would keep its tangible and intangible assets in the relevant market and pose a less severe danger to competition than does the proposed merger (*Horizontal Guidelines*, para 11, footnote omitted)."

The Agencies will also examine mergers of competing buyers that may enhance market power on the buying side of the market ("monopsony power"). Do suppliers have numerous attractive outlets for their goods or services? Will the merger lead to a beneficial reduction in prices or foster efficiencies not arising from the enhancement of market power? As for claimed resulting efficiencies from the merger, the *Horizontal Guidelines* state (at paragraph 10): "[t]he Agencies credit only those efficiencies likely to be accomplished with the proposed merger and unlikely to be accomplished in the absence of either the proposed mergers or another means having comparable anticompetitive effects."

The Guidelines are not binding on the reviewing courts, but they have frequently been viewed as persuasive. The Agencies' reliance on the SSNIP and the HHI have likewise been accepted by the courts. As to the weight of the efficiency counter-argument, the Supreme Court's 1967 ruling in the *Procter & Gamble* case indicated that efficiency was not a defense, and the Court has not revisited that position since. The Court of Appeals for the Eleventh Circuit declared in 1991 in *FTC v. University Health, Inc.* that "in certain circumstances, a defendant may rebut the government's prima facie case with evidence showing that the intended merger would create significant efficiencies in the relevant market."

Accordingly, a number of lower court decisions have considered efficiency benefits in their analyses, but the defense has seldom succeeded. For example, in 2001 the Court of Appeals for the District of Columbia Circuit cited high industry concentration levels requiring "proof of extraordinary efficiencies, which the [companies] failed to supply" in rejecting the efficiency defense in *FTC v. H.J.Heinz Co.* The Court of Appeals for the Sixth Circuit ruled in 2014 in *ProMedica Health Sys., Inc. v. FTC* that the defendant had not made a convincing consumer welfare or efficiencies argument.

With respect to another proposed merger involving health providers, the Court of Appeals for the Ninth Circuit stated in 2015 in *Saint Alphonsus Medical Center-Nampa, Inc. v. St. Luke's Health Sys., Ltd.* that, even in those Circuits that have recognized the possible availability of the defense, "[n]one of the reported appellate decisions have actually held that a § 7 defendant has actually rebutted a prima facie case with an efficiencies defense." However, while court decisions upholding the defense are lacking, the likelihood of significant post-merger efficiencies has sometimes influenced the merger assessments made by the authorities.

The 2010 Guidelines contain an emphasis on the importance of "innovation competition" which was lacking in the earlier version. The issue thus posed with respect to each merger is whether post-merger the incentives for the merged firm's development of innovation will be lower than existed for the two firms premerger.

Non-Horizontal Merger Guidelines were originally issued in 1984 as part of the Antitrust Division's Merger Guidelines. When, subsequently, the Department of Justice and the FTC issued their *Horizontal Merger Guidelines*, the *Non-Horizontal Merger Guidelines* were left behind to stand alone as a guide to "conglomerate merger" antitrust law. While the latter regime, such as it is, focuses on potential competition as a key issue, there have been few cases brought on that basis in recent years.

The *Non-Horizontal Merger Guidelines* observe that, although a merger between a firm that is in a market and another firm that is only potentially in that market is not a horizontal merger, such a merger may have anticompetitive consequences by removing one of the merger partners from "the edge of the market." Such an anticompetitive effect may occur if one of the firms in the merger is a "perceived" potential competitor, i.e., a "significant competitive threat that constrains the behavior of the firms already in the market." Alternatively, the merger may remove an "actual" potential competitor from entry into the market. The Department of Justice states that it will analyze both situations in the same way by considering such factors as the extent of market concentration, the conditions of entry generally and for the potential competitor, and efficiency considerations.

The *Non-Horizontal Guidelines* also discuss the special circumstances in which the Department will challenge a vertical merger, i.e., one involving backward or forward integration. Factors to be taken into account include the creation of entry barriers, the facilitation of collusion, the elimination of a disruptive buyer, the possible evasion of rate regulation, and efficiency considerations.

In 2011, the Department of Justice issued a revised "Policy Guide to Merger Remedies," replacing the 2004 version of this Guide.

In *Polypore Int'l, Inc. v. FTC*, a decision in 2012 by the Eleventh Circuit Court of Appeals, the court confirmed that the FTC has broad discretion in formulating remedies for unlawful practices, including in merger cases. Hence, the court upheld the Commission's decision to order divestiture of a plant located in Austria.

§8.05 JOINT VENTURE POLICY

As we discussed in Chapter 5, a cooperative endeavor between competitors, whether styled as a joint venture, a strategic alliance or something else, can run afoul of the Sherman Act or of Section 5 of the FTC Act if the collaboration is anticompetitive in nature. It has long been settled that a joint venture can also violate the prohibitions of Section 7 of the Clayton Act where the collaboration involves an acquisition of stock or assets. *United States v. Penn-Olin Chemical Co.* involved a joint venture launched by Pennsalt Chemicals Corporation and Olin Mathieson Chemical Corporation to produce and sell sodium chlorate in the southeastern US. Each of the parent companies had purchased 50% of the stock of the joint venture company, Penn-Olin Chemical Co. Neither of the parent companies was in the sodium chlorate market prior to the joint venture, but both appeared to have the inclination, know-how and resources to enter the market.

The Supreme Court ruled first that Section 7 of the Clayton Act may be applicable to a joint venture where two companies form a third to engage in a new enterprise. The Court then held that a violation could be established by a showing that, in the absence of the joint venture, one of the companies involved would have entered the market, with the other company presenting a substantial incentive to competition by remaining poised on the sidelines as a potential entrant.

As we previously noted, the competitive implications of a joint venture must be analyzed in several respects. The initial inquiry is whether the formation of the joint venture will affect competition adversely within the relevant market or markets by eliminating actual competition, or potential competition (as in *Penn-Olin*), or by facilitating undesirable "spill over" collaboration between the parties. Conversely, the formation of a joint venture may be procompetitive where it enables entry into a market that neither of the parent companies could have entered alone or introduces efficiencies not otherwise achievable. If the joint venture is justifiable in formation, the second inquiry is whether it, nonetheless, contains objectionable features because the parties have adopted unnecessary anticompetitive ancillary restraints in their agreement. Third, in those infrequent situations in which the joint venture will be controlling an essential facility for participation in an industry, it must be determined to what extent the venturers may have a duty to provide access to the benefits of their endeavor to other competitors. The broader subject of competitor joint endeavors is well covered in the Agencies' *Antitrust Guidelines for Collaborations Among Competitors*.

§8.06   MERGER CASE LAW

[A]   The Earlier Precedents

The change in enforcement philosophy that has occurred in the US with respect to merger control since the first edition of this Primer came out in 1974 has been truly startling. The trend has been one of a liberalization of enforcement policy prompted in significant part by the recognition that, in many industries, technology is changing, economies of scale are appropriate and, moreover, competition must be appraised in a global context.

We observed in our first edition that "smaller and smaller combined market shares [have] been deemed sufficient to presume anticompetitive effects." Some fifty years ago, the Supreme Court was active in shaping the standards of legality under Section 7. In its seminal 1963 decision in *United States v. Philadelphia National Bank*, the Court held the merger of two large banks in Philadelphia illegal where the combined bank would have held a 30% market share. This magnitude of market share did not create a *per se* finding of illegality, the Court stated, but a post-merger share of 30% or higher did give rise to a presumption of illegality, shifting the burden to the proponents of the merger. A year later, in *United States v. Aluminum Co. of America (Rome Cable)*, the Court emphasized the significance of market concentration and the aggressive competitive nature of the acquired firm.

In a 1966 Supreme Court decision, *United States v. Von's Grocery Co.*, the Court, observing an increase in concentration among grocery store chains in Los Angeles, held unlawful a merger of two chains that would have resulted in a combined market share of only 7.5% of the market.

Such a challenge and such a result are not conceivable today. We have had an era of megamergers in a host of industries, including oils (e.g., Mobil and Exxon, BP Amoco and Arco), autos (e.g., Chrysler and Daimler-Benz, Ford and Volvo), aerospace (Boeing and McDonnell Douglas), pharmaceuticals (e.g., Pfizer and Warner Lambert, Glaxo Wellcome and SmithKline Beecham), airlines (e.g., American Airlines and US Airways, Air France and KLM) and media (e.g., Viacom and CBS, America On Line and Time Warner—this last one labeled by some to have been the most foolish transaction in business history). The law firms in the major cities of the world, formerly used to operating on a national scale, have overseen a burst of international merger activity.

Antitrust jurisprudence as applied to non-horizontal mergers was, in the past, also more stringent. One of the important potential competition cases was the Supreme Court's 1967 decision in *FTC v. Procter & Gamble* mentioned above. P & G manufactured a wide variety of household cleansers but not bleach, and it sought to acquire Clorox, which manufactured only bleach. Notwithstanding the evidence that P & G never intended to enter the bleach market on its own, the Court condemned the merger because it viewed P & G as the most likely entrant into the bleach market.

Subsequently, the Supreme Court's 1973 decision in the *Falstaff Brewing Corp.* case took the potential competition doctrine to new heights. Disregarding evidence that Falstaff's management had expressly decided against entry into a regional beer market other than by acquisition of a substantial brewery already in that market, the Court reversed the district court's decision that Section 7 had not been violated by Falstaff's acquisition of Narragansett, a regional brewer. The Court reasoned that the real issue to be probed was whether Falstaff was perceived in the industry as a company which might enter the regional market by the creation of a new brewery. This was an articulation of the "perceived potential entrant" doctrine.

However, one year later, in *United States v. Marine Bancorporation, Inc.*, the Supreme Court declined to adopt an "actual potential entrant doctrine" in a case where the government did not establish that the acquiring firm could and would have entered the target market competitively.

Sometimes, even "pure" conglomerate mergers were thought to be vulnerable to antitrust attack. The theoretical basis for this view was often the "deep pocket" rationale, i.e., the fear that the resulting combination's great financial resources might entrench the market power of an already leading firm or create insurmountable barriers to entry into an industry. In actual fact, many of the conglomerate empires failed to achieve the "synergies" which they envisioned, and they foundered by reason of their own weight and the lack of any rapport among the parts. The 1984 *Non-Horizontal Merger Guidelines* indicate that conglomerate mergers will seldom present grounds for a challenge under present doctrine.

It is worth noting, however, that, in their 2017 *Antitrust Guidelines for the Licensing of Intellectual Property*, the Agencies offer the intriguing concepts of "technology markets" and "research and development markets," concepts which could be incorporated into Section 7 merger analysis.

In any event, the tide began to turn in 1974 when, in *United States v. General Dynamics Corp.*, the Supreme Court expanded the arguments that defendants could make to rebut the prima facie case created by the market concentration numbers, and, since then, defendants have been able to urge the consideration of such factors as ease of entry and efficiency. In *General Dynamics*, the Court also emphasized that reliance on historical market share data to assess the future impact of a merger may have to be tempered by a recognition that market conditions may change those data in critical respects in the future, such as by the expiration of patents or through the exhaustion of mineral reserves.

In 1990, the Court of Appeals for the District of Columbia Circuit summed up the state of merger analysis in its opinion in *United States v. Baker Hughes Inc.* as follows: "The Supreme Court has adopted a totality-of-the-circumstances approach to the statute, weighing a variety of factors to determine the effects of transactions on competition ... Evidence of market concentration provides a convenient starting point for a broader inquiry into future competitiveness." Defendants have thus succeeded in some cases in showing that the market share data give an inaccurate picture of the likely future competitive situation. Ease of entry into the industry has constituted an important argument in this regard. On the other hand, the existence of significant entry barriers, where there already exists high market concentration, has provided a strong argument for defeating a merger. Entry barriers can include "physical" barriers, such as capital requirements and technology, or such intangibles as brand loyalty. In the *Baker Hughes* case, the court rejected the Justice Department's challenge, despite the high market shares involved, noting that the market featured "few suppliers, sophisticated buyers, and competitive prices—a market in which entry was likely, especially if the newly merged firm tried to raise its prices."

FTC Chairman Robert Pitofsky characterized the change in US merger policy thus in 2000:

> At one time, United States enforcement officials were comfortable challenging mergers that may have reduced concentration in a properly defined relevant market from as many as 10 to 9 firms. Today the market shares reflected in the DOJ-FTC guidelines suggest that the threshold for undue concentration is much higher. Unless there are exceptional circumstances, U.S. enforcement initiatives these days usually involve concentration among leading firms reducing the number of competitors from no more than 6 to 5 firms.

Despite the above discussion, which would seem to signal a relaxed antitrust view toward merger activity, the merger scrutiny function has remained vital and important. The federal agencies, in particular, have been able to step in to assess every significant transaction because of the HSR Act premerger notification requirements. Few merger cases go to court but many transactions are "fixed," through a partial divestiture or other remedy, before they are approved by the Agencies.

[B] Some More Recent Cases

One horizontal merger case, the 1997 district court decision in *FTC v. Staples, Inc.*, helped to revive the concept of the relevant product "submarket" for purposes of merger analysis. The term describes a well-defined segment of product use existing within a broader definable market. In the *Staples* case, involving a merger of Staples, Inc. and Home Depot, the nation's two largest chains of office supply stores, the district court enjoined the transaction in reliance on a submarket analysis. The court recognized a broad market consisting of consumable office supplies sellers (in which the merging firms totaled only 5.5%) but it also found a relevant smaller market for evaluating anticompetitive effects—a submarket consisting of office supply "superstores" in which the merging firms were dominant. The court also rejected the defendants' argument that entry into the office supply superstore market was easy. However, the reference to the term "submarket" has been characterized by some commentators as "useless" for analytical purposes.

The force of the efficiency defense was tested at the appellate level in 2001 in a case in which the FTC sought a preliminary injunction from the federal courts to block a proposed merger between the nation's second and third largest producers of prepared baby foods, the H.J. Heinz Co. and the Beech-Nut Nutrition Corp. The two companies enjoyed, respectively, a 17.4% and a 15.4% market share, and the market leader, Gerber Products Co., had a 65% market share. The Commission urged that the merger would tend to substantially lessen competition in the already concentrated industry and create a duopoly situation which would facilitate collusion and other anticompetitive interaction between the two dominant firms. The district court denied the injunction, finding it "more probable than not" that the merger would actually increase competition in the industry by mounting a challenge to Gerber's market dominance. The court considered the structural arguments against the merger outweighed by "powerful evidence in the record about the efficiencies realized by the merger and about the enhanced prospects of the merged entity to introduce innovative products to compete with Gerber."

On the Commission's appeal, the Court of Appeals for the District of Columbia Circuit reversed this ruling and directed the entry of a preliminary injunction against the merger. The appellate court reasoned that, "the high market concentration levels present in this case require, in rebuttal, proof of extra-ordinary efficiencies, which the [companies] failed to supply." For example, although Heinz argued that the merger would enable it to achieve product improvements through acquisition of Beech-Nut's better recipes, Heinz had made no showing that it could not itself obtain better recipes by investing more money in product development and promotion. The appellate court observed that the high industry concentration levels established by the FTC indicated that the government would probably succeed on the merits of the case, possibly precluding assertion of an efficiencies defense.

While court decisions upholding the defense are lacking, the presence of significant efficiencies has sometimes influenced the prosecutorial decisions reached by the authorities.

Many cases are settled on the basis of divestitures of assets for the purpose of maintaining competition. For example, in 2003 the FTC entered into a settlement agreement with Pfizer Inc., the largest pharmaceutical company in the US, enabling it to consummate its USD 60 billion deal to acquire Pharmacia, another large drug manufacturer. The consent agreement required the companies to divest pharmaceutical products in nine separate product markets to different third parties.

Vertical merger cases have been brought from time to time, with foreclosure effects the issue as a company proposes to acquire a large supplier or a large customer. These challenges have been resolved largely through consent orders. For example, when Time Warner acquired Turner Broadcasting in 1995, the Federal Trade Commission was concerned that the transaction would foreclose: (a) other providers of programming from obtaining adequate cable television distribution, and (b) other distributors of television programming from having favorable access to Time Warner programming. The consent decree entered into by the parties with the FTC contained a number of conduct provisions, such as requiring Time Warner to protect the access of unaffiliated programmers to its cable distribution and prohibiting Time Warner from engaging in price discrimination in selling programming to distributors.

The foreclosure issue came up again in 2000, when America Online, Inc. ("AOL") announced its plan to acquire Time Warner. Time Warner was dominant in cable service in many major US cities, second only to AT&T. It was also the owner of a large array of news and entertainment properties, including CNN, Warner Brothers, the HBO cable network, and many leading magazines. AOL was a major force on the Internet, with some 29 million subscribers to its online services. Critics perceived AOL as trying to create a "walled garden," in which it steered its subscribers to AOL-affiliated content and services. The primary focus of the FTC, which reviewed the transaction and conditionally approved it at the end of 2000, was to ensure that rival Internet service providers would have access to the combined firm's cable lines.

Accordingly, in order to win the Commission's approval of this merger, the parties were forced to agree to accept a number of compliance obligations. Most importantly, the parties had to agree that the merged company would open up its high speed cable lines to competing Internet services and would submit to continued governmental monitoring of its compliance in this regard. AOL Time Warner undertook to offer service on its cable lines to at least one competing Internet service before offering service to AOL and, subsequently, to offer such access to other competing providers. The merged company was bound by other commitments as well, including an obligation to refrain from interfering with content passed along its cable lines.

A number of large mergers were approved in 2005 by the Department of Justice and the FTC with conditions attached. The Department required significant divestitures in connection with two large mergers in the telecommunications industry. One was the proposed acquisition by Verizon Communications Inc. of MCI, Inc., a merger which the government alleged would be likely to lessen competition substantially for local private lines and related services in eight metropolitan areas in violation of Section 7 of the Clayton Act. The companies entered into a settlement agreement with the government stipulating that they would divest themselves to viable competitors of the "last-mile connections" to hundreds of buildings. If they did not dispose of these divestiture assets within the time set, the court would appoint a trustee selected by the US to effect the divestiture. The other merger was SBC Communications Inc.'s proposed acquisition of AT&T, which also would eliminate competition for facilities-based local private line service to certain buildings in metropolitan areas. This case also was settled, with SBC agreeing to divest wireline connections to a large number of buildings in the territory, to a single buyer in each city.

In the fall of 2005 the FTC conditionally approved the USD 57 billion acquisition by the Procter & Gamble Company (P&G) of another major consumer products manufacturer, the Gillette Company. The merged entity promised to be a giant with the largest advertising budget of any US company. The Commission's antitrust concerns included the fact that the companies had a variety of competing consumer products and the possibility that the merged entity might exclude competitors by claiming premium retailer shelf space. After analysis, the Commission staff concluded that the loss of competition between P&G and Gillette in broad consumer categories was unlikely to cause competitive harm, so it entered into a consent agreement with the companies designed to divest specific overlapping assets including toothbrushes and deodorants. An outside accountant was appointed as the interim monitor to ensure the companies' maintaining the competitive viability of the assets until they were transferred to Commission-approved buyers.

The FTC announced that this merger had also been reviewed by the European Commission's Directorate-General, the Canadian Competition Bureau, and the Mexican Federal Competition Commission, and that these officials had consulted and cooperated with one another pursuant to their respective international cooperation agreements and the "Best Practices" procedures adopted in 2002 by the US and the EC for cooperation in merger investigations. The Best Practices were jointly promulgated after serious differences in merger policy between the officials in the US and Europe were revealed in the General Electric-Honeywell case which is discussed below.

In 2007, organic marketer Whole Foods Market Inc. attempted to acquire a smaller rival, Wild Oats Market Inc. The FTC challenged the merger under Section 7, alleging that the two firms were the two largest operators in a relevant market that the Commission defined as "premium, natural and organic supermarkets ['PNOS markets']." The district court dismissed the case, defining the relevant market for antitrust purposes to be all supermarkets. Subsequently, however, the Court of Appeals for the District of Columbia reversed and remanded the case to the lower court. Relying on a submarket theory, the appellate court observed that "[t]he district court's error of law led it to ignore FTC evidence that strongly suggested Whole Foods and Wild Oats compete for consumers within a PNOS market, even if they also compete on individual products for marginal consumers in the broader market." In a settlement with the FTC in 2009, Whole Foods agreed to divest thirty-two stores of the two companies, as well as the "Wild Oats" brand name.

In 2014, Comcast Corporation, the largest video and wired broadband Internet access provider in the US announced plans to acquire Time Warner Cable, the fourth largest video and the third largest wired broadband Internet access provider. After the Department of Justice announced that it would file suit to block the merger on antitrust grounds, Comcast abandoned the transaction.

In 2015, Staples and Office Depot, two leading office supply companies, once more tried to consolidate in a merger. The FTC filed a complaint to enjoin the merger, alleging that it would reduce competition nationwide in the market for consumable office supplies sold to large business customers for their own use. After the district court entered an order enjoining the merger, the companies abandoned their merger plan.

The airline industry has been rocked by financial instability in many countries, including in the US following deregulation, and a long list of mergers has taken place, most of them not objected to by regulators. In the US, American Airlines and its parent, AMR, filed for Chapter 11 bankruptcy in 2011 and emerged therefrom in 2013. Subsequently, the reorganized American Airlines merged with US Airways, creating the world's largest airline. The Department of Justice and several States filed an antitrust complaint against the merger, claiming that it would reduce consumer choices and raise fares. Subsequently, the district court approved a settlement whereby the merged company would divest itself of certain slots, gates, and ground facilities in seven airports around the US. Nonetheless, the US was left with only four major airlines, creating an ever more dismal service situation for passengers which have recently been publicized following several unfortunate incidents.

With changes taking place in the US health care system, both the Federal Trade Commission and the Antitrust Division have sought to thwart anticompetitive combinations in that industry. Some of the challenged mergers have been relatively small in size but the theory of the Agencies has been that competition among health care providers serving particular communities must remain vital.

The case known as *St. Alphonsus Medical Center-Nampa, Inc. v. St. Luke's Health Sys., Ltd.*, arose from the 2012 merger of two health care providers in Nampa, Idaho. The FTC and the State of Idaho sued, alleging that the merger violated § 7 of the Clayton Act and state law, and two local hospitals filed a similar complaint. The district court believed that the merger was intended to improve patient outcomes and might well do so, but nonetheless found that the merger violated § 7 and ordered divestiture.

The Court of Appeals for the Ninth Circuit affirmed in 2015. It stated that "the job before us is not to determine the optimal future shape of the country's health care system, but instead to determine whether this particular merger violates the Clayton Act." The court found such a violation because the resulting high market concentration as demonstrated by the HHI would create a substantial lessening of competition in the area and there was no proof that any resulting efficiencies from the merger would mitigate that situation.

In two federal appellate decisions in 2016, the Third Circuit in *FTC v. Penn State Hershey Medical Center* and the Seventh Circuit in *FTC v. Advocate Health Care Network*, reversed district court decisions which had denied the Commission's requests to enjoin hospital mergers. In the Seventh Circuit case, on reconsideration, the district court concluded that Chicago's North Shore area comprised the relevant geographic market because patients prefer to receive hospital services close to their homes.

In an Antitrust Division case, the US Court of Appeals for the D.C. Circuit in April 2017 affirmed the decision by the District Court to block health insurer Anthem Inc. from acquiring Cigna Corp. The majority of the Court of Appeals held that Anthem had failed to show the requisite "extraordinary efficiencies necessary to offset the conceded anticompetitive effect" of the consolidation. This was the largest proposed transaction in the history of the health care industry, which would have affected dozens of US health insurance markets.

Earlier in the year, a district court also ruled in favor of the Justice Department and blocked health insurer Aetna Inc.'s acquisition of rival insurer Humana Inc. The court ruled that the proposed merger was likely to substantially lessen competition in the sale of Medicare coverage in 364 counties in the nation.

AT&T has had a rich antitrust history. Created in 1885 as the AT&T by Alexander Graham Bell, the inventor of the telephone, the firm acquired the Bell Telephone Company and became the primary telephone service in the US as a monopoly. In 1982 it settled an antitrust suit brought by the Department of Justice and divested itself of seven local "Baby Bell" phone companies. One of the former Baby Bells, Southwestern

Bell Co., changed its name to SBC Communications Inc. ("SBC") in 1995. In 2005 SBC purchased former parent AT&T, and the resulting firm became AT&T Inc. The corporation made a number of acquisitions over the next few years, including the purchase of Cellular One. In 2011, it sought to acquire T-Mobile USA Inc. from Deutsche Telekom. The Department of Justice promptly brought suit under Section 7, alleging that the USD 39 billion acquisition would substantially lessen competition for mobile wireless telecommunications services across the US. The deal would have made AT&T Mobility the largest mobile phone provider in the country. The proposed merger was very controversial with advocates on both sides. AT&T decided to end its merger bid after reviewing the opposition and its options.

In 2015, AT&T purchased DirecTV, and in 2016 the company announced a USD 85.4 billion deal to buy the media company, Time Warner. The two giant firms do not compete but the size of the deal was indicative that it would draw careful scrutiny from regulators. It would be a vertical merger. AT&T is the second largest wireless carrier, one of the leading broadband providers and also a major pay-TV provider. Time Warner is currently a media conglomerate which includes CNN, HBO, the Warner Bros. studio and other assets. In short, one firm is a content distributor and the other a content supplier. The owners of mobile devices have been demanding more and more premium content. One of the key antitrust issues posed is whether the consolidation would lead AT&T to restrict the distribution of Time Warner's content to the merged firm's benefit. This proposed acquisition is still under regulatory review in the US. It has cleared review by the European Commission.

§8.07 INTERNATIONAL ASPECTS

One nation's efforts to control, or simply to review, the consummation of mergers and acquisitions by multinational corporations in the global setting can give rise to international friction for a number of reasons. Nationalism has always been a primary cause of friction. Not surprisingly, Nation A does not look kindly on Nation B when the latter interferes with the efforts undertaken by Nation A's "national champion" to expand its assets or markets through acquisitions or joint ventures. Fortunately, in recent years there has developed internationally a widespread acceptance of the need to foster competition, whatever the nationality of the competitors, and of the role of antitrust law in providing nondiscriminatory rules for attaining that competitive model. However, antitrust enforcement policies may and do differ between countries and between regions, and these conceptual differences may themselves be sufficient to generate considerable friction between merger control regimes. We will consider these problem areas by looking at cases that have given rise to disputes, as well as some that have been the subject of harmonious cooperation.

We have observed that, given the wide jurisdictional scope of Section 7 and the other applicable US laws, antimerger enforcement and premerger notification can apply not only to mergers between US companies, but also to transactions in which a US firm acquires a foreign firm, or a foreign firm acquires a US firm, or even in the case of a merger between two foreign firms. The key issue on the merits in each situation is the likely effect of the transaction on competition in US markets.

International mergers and consolidations with antitrust implications are commonplace nowadays. For just one example as to the scope of this commerce, one has only to look at a recent narrative in the beer market. In 2008, the company InBev, with headquarters in Belgium, acquired a major US brewer, Anheuser-Busch, thereby expanding on InBev's position as the world's largest brewer. In 2013, InBev attempted to consolidate with Grupo Modelo, a Mexican brewery in which InBev already owned a substantial stake and which was the third largest brewer of beer sold in the US. The Department of Justice filed an antitrust suit against the two companies, alleging that InBev's acquisition of the remaining interest in Modelo would substantially lessen competition in the market for beer in the US as a whole and in at least twenty-six metropolitan areas across the nation. The companies settled the suit by agreeing to divest Modelo's entire US business. The Department said that the proposed settlement would maintain competition in the beer industry nationwide. Beer consumers brought a separate antitrust action attacking the merger but they were unsuccessful.

Still more recently, the combined company, Anheuser-Busch InBev NV ("AB InBev") acquired another major brewer, SABMiller Plc, after obtaining US antitrust approval by agreeing to give up ownership of the Miller brand (a competitor of InBev's Budweiser). The company also agreed with the Chinese Government to give up the brand, Snow Beer, and agreed with the EU to give up almost all of SABMiller's brands in Europe. AB InBev also agreed to continuing reporting obligations, including the need to notify US antitrust officials if it acquires a craft brewer.

Many of the US merger cases involving international amalgamations have been in the context of a US firm acquiring a foreign firm which was an actual or potential competitor in the US market. Here, the impact on the US market is clear, personal jurisdiction over at least the acquiring party readily exists, and problems of comity are relatively unlikely. In some situations, the foreign firm to be acquired or its US subsidiary owns production or other US facilities. Economically, the effects of this acquisition are not different from the effects of a purely domestic transaction. Accordingly, the same antitrust evaluation will be made.

This setting was presented in the 1966 case of *United States v. Jos. Schlitz Brewing Co.* Schlitz, a Wisconsin corporation, had acquired a controlling interest in John Labatt Ltd., a Canadian corporation, which, in turn, controlled a majority interest in the General Brewing Co., a California corporation. The government filed suit against Schlitz and General Brewing, alleging that the Schlitz-Labatt transaction, when coupled with Schlitz's earlier acquisition of another brewer, Burgermeister, threatened competition in the production and sale of beer in various US markets, including the State of California, in violation of Section 7 of the Clayton Act.

The district court first made the jurisdictional findings which were requisite under Section 7 prior to its 1980 expansion, namely, that Schlitz and General Brewing were both "engaged in commerce" within the meaning of the Act, and that Labatt was also so engaged inasmuch as the "continuous flow of Labatt beer from Canada to Labatt's distributors in the United States constitutes an engagement in foreign and interstate commerce ... ." The court then designated beer as the appropriate product market and the US as a whole, plus various regions thereof, as the relevant geographic markets. It concluded that the reasonable probable effect of the transaction would be to lessen competition substantially in those markets. Its basic reasoning was that Schlitz was already one of the nation's largest brewers, that the beer industry was trending toward concentration, and that, absent the merger, "Labatt had the desire, the intention and the resourcefulness to enter the United States markets and to make General Brewing a stronger competitor in those markets." Other than viewing Labatt as a likely source of invigorating competition from outside that should be preserved, the court evaluated the proposed merger with the same analysis as if a purely domestic merger had been involved.

Traditionally, effective relief from the anticompetitive effects of an international merger was more easily obtained by national authorities where one or both of the merging parties maintained local subsidiaries. For example, in 1969-1970, two large, diversified Swiss chemical companies, CIBA Ltd. and J.R. Geigy, S.A., agreed to merge their worldwide operations. CIBA and Geigy each maintained subsidiaries in the US which competed with each other in the manufacture and sale of various products, including dyestuffs and optical brightening agents. The Department of Justice brought suit under Section 7 against the parent corporations and their US subsidiaries, alleging that a merger of the parents would unlawfully eliminate actual competition in the US between the two subsidiaries. The government's request for relief made it clear that it was the coming under joint control of the subsidiaries that it was seeking to enjoin.

Asserting that they were voluntarily submitting to the US district court's jurisdiction, the two Swiss corporations entered into a consent settlement of the case. Under the agreement, the companies were required to establish a new corporation that was to be sold by them within two years and that was to be the recipient of the dyestuffs and optical brightening agents business of CIBA's US subsidiary. Other provisions were also included to bring about divestiture with respect to the competing product lines—including necessary patents, trademarks, ingredients, know-how, and customer lists.

As regards the "voluntary" submittal of the two Swiss corporations to the jurisdiction of the US court, it was undoubtedly in the interest of those companies because their US subsidiaries were effectively hostages to a successful resolution of the matter. The key to the government's effective assertion of jurisdiction and fashioning of the remedy here was, in fact, the existence of the two US subsidiaries. This factor enabled the Department of Justice readily to assert personal jurisdiction, avoid major difficulties with Switzerland over comity concerns, and design a mechanism for shaping an appropriate and limited remedy for purposes of the US market. Nowadays, the large multinational corporations generally acknowledge that they are subject to the jurisdiction of the US—as well as of the other countries in which they do business—and divestiture orders agreed to by the companies to obtain US approval of their mergers and acquisitions may well involve the disposition of some of their foreign assets.

Indeed, in 1997, CIBA-Geigy Ltd. agreed to merge with another Swiss corporation, Sandoz Ltd., into a third Swiss corporation, to be known as "Novartis." The two merging companies, including their US subsidiaries, had competed in the US markets for gene therapy development, corn herbicide and flea control products, which the

Federal Trade Commission found to be three relevant lines of commerce for antitrust analysis. All three markets were highly concentrated and difficult to enter. While neither of the two firms had a commercialized gene therapy product, the FTC determined the existence of an innovation market for the development of gene therapies. (The European Commission did likewise in its review of this merger.) The FTC concluded that the merger would violate Section 7 of the Clayton Act and Section 5 of the FTC Act and approved the transaction only when the parties accepted strict divestiture and licensing remedies affecting the businesses in the three markets.

Evaluation of the competitive effects of a merger involving a foreign party will take into account whether the foreign party or parties have American subsidiaries or otherwise operate physical facilities on US soil. Let us assume that a foreign firm which an American firm seeks to acquire has substantial exports to the US, through sales to independent importers, and that these products compete with those of the American firm. Since the same economic effect is to be feared from the merger—elimination of an existing substantial competitor and increased concentration—the antitrust analysis will be conducted in much the same fashion as if it were wholly domestic. There will, however, have to be an additional inquiry to determine whether the foreign firm's products face special disadvantages such as high transportation costs, import tariffs or quotas, or a consumer preference for US products. If the imports do have such an handicap, the argument can be made, in favor of permitting the acquisition to proceed, that the foreign competition is not a substantial competitive factor in the overall picture. Of course, the usually critical issues of market shares, the level of concentration in the market, and entry factors will also play important roles in the analytical process.

Potential competition from abroad may also be the subject of inquiry under Section 7, particularly where the US industry is highly concentrated. For example, in 1976, the Justice Department challenged the acquisition by the Gillette Company, the leading American manufacturer of safety razors, of Braun Aktiengesellschaft, a large German manufacturer of electrical appliances, including electric razors. The US shaving instrument industry was very concentrated. Braun had eyed the US market, but had precluded itself from it for a period of time under a licensing agreement it had entered into with another firm. The case was settled by a consent decree under which Gillette was to create a new US entity, later to be divested, to sell Braun shavers in the US market. Gillette attempted in 1989 to acquire the non-European operations of Wilkinson Sword, a leading British razor blade producer. The Department of Justice again stepped in and obtained a consent decree under which Gillette agreed not to acquire Wilkinson's US business.

In situations in which a foreign firm is proposing to acquire a US firm, the competitive analysis relating to the US market is much the same. The central question is whether the merger will eliminate an existing or potential competitor in that market. The politics of the situation are different, however, primarily because the issue of foreign investment in the US is implicated. A challenge to the transaction by the US authorities might be misconceived by the acquiring firm and by its government as an exercise in US economic protectionism, rather than as the nondiscriminatory administration of regulatory legislation. The need to be seen as observing the principles of

Chapter 8: US Antitrust Aspects of Mergers and Acquisitions §8.07

comity may lead the US authorities to conduct the matter more cautiously, albeit not differently in substance.

A merger challenge falling generally into this category occurred in 1969–1970 involving the proposed acquisition by the British Petroleum Company Ltd. ("BP") of 54% of the stock of a US petroleum company, Standard Oil Co. of Ohio ("Sohio"). BP, alleged by the government to be the second largest foreign industrial company and the world's third largest crude oil producer, had previously begun integrated oil operations in the US as a result of an acquisition of assets from Atlantic Richfield Co. The Antitrust Division challenged the Sohio transaction under Section 7, relying upon competition and potential competition theories relating to US regional markets. The case was settled by a consent decree under which BP and Sohio agreed to divest themselves of certain retail outlets in the affected regions. The Justice Department's intervention prompted a strong adverse reaction in Europe, where it was regarded by many as an unwarranted American effort to inhibit investment from abroad, notwithstanding years of takeovers of foreign companies by American multinationals. From the antitrust standpoint in the US, however, the case was a straightforward one.

Since then, there have been many other instances in which the Justice Department or the FTC have objected to the efforts of foreign companies, often European ones, to acquire US companies with which they were in competition or potential competition. These cases have frequently been resolved through the entry of consent orders, with the acquisitions being permitted on the condition that specified units or assets be divested in such a way as to enable these operations to be effective competitors.

One of these cases involved the proposal by British Telecommunications plc ("BT") in 1994 to pay USD 4.3 billion for 20% of the stock of MCI Communications Corp. ("MCI") for the purpose of forming a joint venture to provide global telecommunications services. The Department of Justice challenged the transaction, largely because it was concerned that the new relationship would disadvantage MCI's competitors by denying them fair access to the British firm's UK network. The purchase was permitted after the parties entered into a consent order prohibiting, among other things, any discrimination against US carriers with regard to multinational communications. Three years later the Justice Department cleared BT's acquisition of the remainder of MCI's stock, subject to some modification of the existing consent order. The merged entity agreed to report periodically on its interconnections and on other matters to enable the Department to monitor whether the company was engaging in discrimination against competing US carriers.

The globalization of the economy and the emergence of many regimes for merger review around the world have brought about an internationalization of the review process where large transactions are concerned. Even when the two merging companies share the same nationality, if the scope of their operations is international, they will likely be required to comply with a significant number of national and/or regional advance or post-merger notification requirements. The notification forms that must be filled out are numerous and disparate, prompting the legal professions of many nations to burn the midnight oil, with the attendant cost burdens for the companies. The enforcement authorities around the world are now well aware of this burden on the merging parties, as well as of the desirability of the various officials' reaching consistent merger review conclusions, and they are increasingly cooperating and coordinating their efforts in international cases, subject to constraints relating to confidentiality of information.

The existence of a good international working relationship between regulators does not, however, necessarily insure that they share a commonality of interest or of perspective. This point was vividly illustrated in some high profile cases involving US and European antitrust authorities. The difficulties first became apparent in a major case in 1997 in connection with the Boeing Company's acquisition of McDonnell Douglas Corporation. The two were both American companies and manufacturers of commercial aircraft. Their only significant competitor was Airbus Industrie, a European consortium. In the US review of the transaction, the FTC voted 4-1 not to challenge the merger, on the ground that, although McDonnell Douglas was not technically a failing company, it no longer constituted a meaningful competitive force in the commercial aircraft sector. In an interesting initiative, the four Commissioners issued a statement emphasizing that their decision was based on the merits and that the agency did not clear the transaction for the purpose of establishing a "national champion" in the commercial aircraft industry. As we discuss in Chapter 13, the European Commission also reviewed the transaction in detail, and then expressed concern that the merger of the two US companies would enhance Boeing's dominant position in various aircraft markets, disadvantaging Airbus. The European Commission ultimately approved the merger only on the condition that Boeing agree not to enforce the exclusive supply contracts which it had entered into with a number of US airlines.

A serious divergence of views, also involving the merger of two US firms, arose between these enforcement authorities in 2001 when General Electric Co. ("GE") proposed a USD 45 billion acquisition of Honeywell International, Inc. GE occupied the leading position in the world aircraft engine market while Honeywell was an important producer of avionics and other aircraft components. Following review, the deal was cleared by the US Department of Justice's Antitrust Division subject to some conditions. On the other hand, the European Commission disapproved and blocked the transaction, concluding that the merger would create or strengthen dominant positions in several markets and that the remedies proposed by the parties were insufficient to resolve the competition issues presented. In particular, the European Commission expressed concern that GE's existing dominance would be strengthened "through the extension of GE's financial power and vertical integration to Honeywell activities and of the combination of their respective complementary products." (The European Commission's decision is further discussed in Chapter 13.)

In the US, the Antitrust Division, which had not objected to the transaction, made a submission in October 2001 to the OECD Roundtable on Portfolio Effects in Conglomerate Mergers taking issue with the European Commission's analysis of the merger. The Antitrust Division described the Commission's approach in GE-Honeywell as being based on flawed theories of competitive harm related to "range effects." These flawed theories were stated to be: (1) that the merger would create economies of scale and scope that other firms would be unable to match, (2) that the merged firm would gain a decisive advantage over its competitors by virtue of its greater size and financial resources, and (3) that the merger would facilitate the tying or bundling of complementary products. The Commission's reliance on range effects, said the Antitrust Division, placed the interests of competitors ahead of those of competition generally and would lead to the likely blocking or deterring of procompetitive, efficiency-enhancing mergers. The Division asserted that the first two theories noted above were rejected in the US Merger Guidelines on the reasoning that "challenging a merger because it will create a more efficient firm through economies of scale and scope is at odds with the fundamental objectives of the antitrust laws. And there is no empirical support for the notion that size alone conveys any significant competitive advantage that is not efficiency related." Moreover, said the Antitrust Division, the bundling theory should not be applied to block a merger that will facilitate efficient bundling—that is, voluntary bundling through discounts or otherwise that benefits customers by offering them the improved products, lower prices and lower transaction costs they desire.

In 1991, the EU and the US had entered into an Agreement between the European Communities and the Government of the USA regarding the application of their competition laws. The purpose of that Agreement was "to promote cooperation and coordination and lessen the possibility or impact of differences between the Parties in the application of their competition laws." With the friction generated by GE-Honeywell in mind, in October 2002 the US-EU Merger Working Group, representing the US and European antitrust agencies, issued a set of "best practices," in an effort to coordinate more effectively the respective enforcement regimes' merger review processes and policies in merger investigations. The document recited, at the outset, that "both jurisdictions have an interest in reaching, insofar as possible, consistent, or at least non-conflicting outcomes." The "best practices" are "intended to promote fully-informed decision-making on the part of both sides' authorities, to minimize the risk of divergent outcomes on both sides of the Atlantic, to facilitate coherence and compatibility in remedies, to enhance the efficiency of their respective investigations, to reduce burdens on merging parties and third parties, and to increase the overall transparency of the merger review processes."

In October 2011 the three involved enforcement agencies adopted "revised Best Practices on Merger Cooperation in cases where a U.S. agency and the Competition Directorate-General of the European Commission are reviewing the same merger." The revised Best Practices build on the experience gained by the agencies in a significant number of cases in the intervening years. The revised "best practices" include: (1) the reviewing agencies are to contact one another promptly upon learning of a merger that appears to require review in both the US and the EU and agree on a tentative timetable for regular inter-agency consultations; (2) coordination on timing, especially with regard to the key decision-making stages; (3) discussion and coordination on the agencies' respective analyses, on such matters as market definition, assessments of competitive effects and efficiencies, theories of competitive harm, economic theories and empirical evidence; (4) discussion and coordination of information on discovery requests to the merging parties; and (5) cooperation on remedies where they need to be considered in both jurisdictions and reaching a compatible outcome where the agencies seek different remedies or settlements.

Recent US Government actions have led to the abandonment of some major merger plans. In 2016, US drug maker Pfizer, Inc. and Ireland-based Allergen Plc decided to walk away from their USD 160 billion merger deal, after the US Treasury altered tax rules to discourage such deals called "inversions." Also in 2016, two US corporations, Halliburton Company and Baker Hughes, Inc., gave up their merger plans after the Department of Justice filed a civil antitrust suit to block it. The Department stated that the acquisition "would combine two of the three largest oilfield services companies in the United States and the world, eliminating important head-to-head competition in markets for 23 products or services use for on- and off-shore exploration and production in the United States." Baker Hughes was subsequently acquired by General Electric.

In 2017, the Justice Department approved the merger of Dow Chemical and DuPont on the condition that the companies sell certain crop protection products and other assets. With the key antitrust positions not yet fully filled by the new US Administration, a number of merger proposals are still under review. They include, as earlier mentioned, AT&T's proposed acquisition of Time Warner, as well as Bayer's proposal to acquire Monsanto. Sprint and T-Mobile are said to still be engaging in merger discussions.

We should leave this chapter with the observation that merger law itself is undergoing some fresh evaluation because of the digital revolution. Once powerful traditional retail firms are going out of business or seeking shelter with each other because of the inroads made on their business by online sellers, particularly by Amazon. Amazon itself has announced plans to acquire Whole Foods Market Inc., giving Amazon a network of physical grocery stores to go with its giant online business. Traditional retailers are, for their part, seeking acquisition avenues to take part in the online business. Perhaps it is time to do some new thinking about conglomerate mergers.

Part II   European Union Competition Law

CHAPTER 9
Overview of the Competition Law of the European Union

§9.01 THE EU

The European Common Market was the result of the post-World War II efforts of Jean Monnet, Robert Schuman, Winston Churchill, and others to revitalize the 100-year-old dream of a "United States of Europe." These statesmen hoped that, if the European countries could move toward the goal of political and economic integration, another war in Western Europe could be prevented and recovery from the devastation of World War II would be facilitated. For the same reasons, the US encouraged this idea through the Marshall Plan.

The first major step toward this goal was the establishment in 1951 by the Treaty of Paris of a new legal entity, to be under supranational control and known as the European Coal and Steel Community ("ECSC"). The original six Member States were Belgium, France, Italy, Luxembourg, The Netherlands, and West Germany. They agreed, with respect to coal and steel, to eliminate import and export duties, discriminatory measures, subsidies or state aids, and restrictive practices. Accordingly, one of the responsibilities of the new Community was to ensure the maintenance of normal competitive conditions, which meant identifying and eliminating anticompetitive practices.

The ECSC was so successful that the six Member States decided to expand the effort to comprise a common market for nearly all goods and services. Thus, the Treaties of Rome were signed in 1957 to create the "EEC" and the European Atomic Energy Community ("Euratom"). By virtue of the Merger Treaty of 1965, the separate ECSC, EEC, and Euratom administrations were combined into a single Council of Ministers, Commission, European Parliament, and ECJ. A Court of First Instance ("CFI") was added in 1989 to reduce the workload of the ECJ. The Single European Act, which entered into force in 1987, brought major revisions to the EEC Treaty designed to eliminate nontariff barriers and enable free movement, leading to a Europe "without internal frontiers" by the end of 1992.

Subsequently, the EEC Treaty was substantially amended by the Treaty on European Union, also called the Maastricht Treaty, which came into force in 1993 and changed the name of the EEC to simply the "EC". The regime was ambitiously expanded to include economic and monetary union, including environmental, social, health, education, and other broad policy concerns. After being in force for fifty years, the Treaty of Paris expired in 2002, and the ECSC was disbanded.

As can be seen, the history of the EU is one of evolution by treaty. The Amsterdam Treaty, which was signed in 1997 and came into force in May of 1999 brought about a number of additional changes, including a significant extension of the European Parliament's legislative powers. The Amsterdam Treaty also renumbered the provisions of the EC Treaty, which it amended, including those relating to competition law. In particular, the provisions which we will be studying in detail, which were formerly Articles 85 and 86 of the EC Treaty, became Articles 81 and 82 of the new amended Treaty. But there was more change to come.

In June 2004, the European Council agreed on a Draft Treaty Establishing a Constitution for Europe which would have created a fully integrated European entity. It required ratification by the twenty-five Member States. A number of countries ratified the Draft Treaty but referenda in France and the Netherlands resulted in "no" votes.

The next treaty, the Treaty of Lisbon, came into force as of December 1, 2009, ending the "EC" appellation and bestowing all legal personality on the "European Union." The Lisbon Treaty is divided into two parts: the Treaty on European Union and the Treaty on the Functioning of the European Union (TFEU). The provisions relating to competition law became Articles 101 and 102 of the TFEU. We will be referring to the competition law provisions by these numbers, except in discussing case law which was decided under the prior numbering systems.

The number of nations joining the regime and thereby ceding substantial sovereignty to it has grown from six to twenty-eight. Denmark, Ireland, and the United Kingdom joined in 1973, Greece in 1981, Portugal and Spain in 1986, and Austria, Finland, and Sweden in 1995. The Treaty of Nice, which entered into force in 2003 laid the institutional groundwork for the further enlargement of the EU. On May 1, 2004, the EU expanded to twenty-five member countries, adding Poland, the Czech Republic, Hungary, Slovenia, Estonia, Latvia, Lithuania, Slovakia, Malta, and Cyprus. Bulgaria and Romania joined in 2007 and Croatia in 2013. The EU has its own currency, the euro, which is used by nineteen of the member countries. The United Kingdom gave notice in March 2017 that it intends to depart from the EU. The severance process known colloquially as "Brexit" is to be negotiated over a two-year period.

In addition, some but not all of the EU member countries have signed the Schengen Agreement which allows the free movement of citizens without passport controls within the Schengen area.

Even before the UK gave notice of its intention to leave the EU, the group faced a daunting challenge as it sought to continuously integrate successfully into a single regime an ever-growing number of nations of diverse social, economic and political make-ups. The rejection of the proposed Constitution by the voters in two of the original member countries, followed by a need to deal with an influx of refugees from outside the EU and rising political opposition to the union in a number of key member nations, have all spurred questions concerning the future of the Union and of the Eurozone.

Nonetheless, in bringing together in harmony and cooperation many European nations whose relations with each other led to some of the darkest events in human history, the EU represents an impressive and hopeful achievement. In particular, it currently constitutes one of the largest, most dynamic and sophisticated centers of global commercial activity. It also comprises the largest market for US exports. Of special interest to us here, of course, is the operations of the EU competition laws that provide valuable insights into how an ambitious supranational antitrust regime can be designed to function effectively. Notably, EU competition law continues to serve as an influential model for those nations which are still developing their approaches to the problems posed by restraints of trade.

It should be kept in mind that there is a two-tiered system of competition law enforcement in the EU. The Member States are authorized to maintain their own national systems of competition law so long as the legislation is compatible with the provisions of EU law. The role of the Member States in enforcing EU competition law was significantly augmented by Council Regulation 1/2003, effective May 1, 2004, which empowered the competition authorities and courts of the Member States to apply directly what are now Article 101(3) of the Treaty on the Functioning of the European Union ("TFEU", hereafter), as well as Articles 101(1) and 102.

When the competition authorities in a Member State are enforcing EU law in a matter, they may pursue it until such time as the European Commission opens an investigation on the same matter. In the event of conflict between the EU and the national law, the EU law takes precedence. The national laws thus coexist with Articles 101 and 102 of the EU regime. For example, the fact that a contract violates Article 101 can be used as a defense to a suit for breach of contract in a national court.

Before we commence our study of the substance of the EU's competition laws, however, it is desirable that we have an understanding of the pertinent EU institutions and their respective roles within the Union. They are reflected in the Treaty on European Union, which consists of the provisions of the Maastricht Treaty as amended by the later treaties.

§9.02 THE EU INSTITUTIONS

[A] The Council of Ministers

The Council of Ministers ("Council"), operating in Brussels, Belgium, is the chief political institution of the EU, whose duties include coordinating the economic policies of the Member States in fulfillment of the treaty objectives. (It should not be confused with the Council of Europe, which is an international organization, or the European Council, which is made up of the heads of State.) The Council of Ministers is composed of one minister from the government of each Member State who has responsibility for the particular policy area under discussion. He/she is designated by the national government in power. The Council exercises legislative powers and, on a wide range of issues, these powers are exercised in co-decision with the European Parliament. The presidency of the Council is rotated among the Member States for six-month period. The Treaty provides for action to be taken by unanimous vote of the Council on some matters and by a "qualified majority" on others. The qualified majority provisions of the Treaty give each Member State a number of votes based primarily on its population. For our purposes, it should also be noted that Article 103 TFEU provides that the appropriate regulations or directives to give effect to the principles set out in Articles 101 and 102 (the competition rules) "shall be laid down by the Council on a proposal from the Commission and after consulting the European Parliament."

[B] The Commission

The Commission, also located in Brussels, acts as the executive body for the EU and as guardian of the Treaties. Its twenty-eight Commissioners (known as the College of Commissioners) are appointed by the twenty-eight Member States with the approval of the European Parliament. The President of the European Commission is elected by the European Parliament for a five-year term. He allocates the separate portfolios to the members of the Commission.

Commissioners serve five-year terms and may be reappointed. The Commissioners are committed to acting in the interests of the Union as a whole. Therefore, they do not represent individual Member States, do not take instructions from them, and swear an oath of independence from any partisan influence. Each Commissioner is charged with responsibility for a specific policy area designed to carry out the treaty objectives and oversees a particular Directorate-General (department). The Directorates-General and specialized services cover a wide variety of activities, including competition, agriculture, and external relations. The staff of each Directorate-General is headed by a top civil servant and has a significant body of civil servants who have been drawn by the Commission from the Member States and who have developed specialized experience and skills relating to the sector or industry in question. These persons also enjoy independence from the Member States and are responsible only to the Commission. The Directorate-General for Competition is also referred to as DG COMP.

At the heart of the Commission's duties is the responsibility to assure that the free movement of goods, services, capital, and persons throughout the territory of the EU takes place, to the extent mandated by the treaties. The Commission is authorized to investigate violations of the treaties and to issue law enforcement decisions. It also formulates legislative proposals, in the form of regulations or directives. The Commission is the only body which can propose EU legislation. The Council decides what action to take on these proposals in co-decision (or, in some cases, consultation) with the Parliament. In some cases, the Commission, while exercising powers given to it by the Council, has asserted the power to act without express Council authorization. Furthermore, in its proposals, the Commission is required to take the principle of "subsidiarity" into account. Under this principle of the treaties, supranational activity is to be limited to those areas in which results are best achieved at the European, as distinct from the national, level.

The Commission also functions as the EU's representative in international trade relationships, including WTO matters, and in cooperation with foreign antitrust officials. The Commission negotiates most of the trade and cooperation agreements on behalf of the EU, with Council authorization. For example, as we discussed in previous chapters, the Commission has worked closely on antitrust matters of mutual interest with US officials, under the cooperation agreement entered into by the respective EU and US enforcement agencies. EU competition policy is carried out by the Commission's Directorate-General for Competition (DG COMP) and the Commissioner in charge of competition policy.

The Commission's Directorate-General for Competition is headed by a Director General and there are three Deputy Directors General with special responsibility for, respectively, antitrust, mergers, and state aids. A Chief Competition Economist has been added because of the Commission's desire to apply increased economic analysis in the handling of cases.

[C] The Parliament

The European Parliament, with places of work in Brussels and in Strasbourg, France, has evolved as an institution over the years. Prior to 1979, its members were nominated by the national legislatures of the Member States, and it performed an advisory and supervisory role. The original Parliament was, accordingly, a weak body. As the need for it to become a more democratic and effective institution within the EU was recognized, the role of the Parliament was strengthened. Since 1979 its members have been elected directly by the citizens of the Member States to serve five-year terms. The number of representatives elected from each Member State is based on the population of the latter. The elected representatives sit not as national delegations but in political groups that cut across national lines and run the gamut of European politics.

The majority of European laws are adopted jointly by the European Parliament and the Council in a process called co-decision, which was introduced by the Maastricht Treaty, extended by the Amsterdam Treaty and included in the Lisbon Treaty. The Parliament is empowered to put questions to the Commission and the Council, including the setting up of committees of inquiry (as was done, for example, in the case of "mad cow disease"). In the legislative process, depending on the area of legislation under consideration, the powers of the Parliament may be "consultative", "cooperative," or "co-decisional." This means that, depending on the subject matter involved, the Parliament may have the right to be consulted on a piece of legislation and to give an opinion on it, or to offer proposed amendments, or even to make a "co-decision" which gives it a veto on the matter if conciliation with the Council is not feasible. Since the changes made by the Treaty of Amsterdam, co-decision, whereby joint Council and Parliament acts are adopted, has become the most significant legislative process. The Parliament is given power also to appoint the Commission by a vote of confidence, and it may censure the Commission, an act which requires the Commissioners all to resign. The Commission did, in fact, resign as a body in 1999 amidst charges of mismanagement, under the threat of such a censure.

[D] The EU Courts

The European Court of Justice (hereinafter "Court of Justice" or "ECJ"), located in Luxembourg, is the supreme judicial authority of the EU. It is comprised of one judge from each Member State, currently twenty-eight, selected by common accord. These judges are appointed for six-year terms but are regularly appointed for longer service. The function of the ECJ is simply stated in Article 220 of the TEU as "ensur[ing] that in the interpretation and application of the Treaty the law is observed." Since the great majority of the judges have been trained in the civil law tradition, rather than in the common law, civil law procedures have predominated. The Court may sit as a full Court (in very exceptional cases), but usually sits as a Grand Chamber of thirteen judges or in chambers of three or five judges. The judges select one of their number to be President of the Court for a renewable term of three years. The Court determines what type of presentation may be made to it. Member States and institutions of the EU may intervene in cases before the ECJ. The Statute of the Court of Justice of the EU sets out procedures for the Court to observe. The judges hearing a case must all agree on one judgment and opinion. These opinions are relatively brief, and there are no dissenting opinions.

The ECJ presently has eight Advocates-General who are appointed to advise the Court, reflecting a position derived from the French legal system. The role of an Advocate-General is to assist the Court, with complete impartiality and independence, by submitting a public opinion on the matter at hand. The opinion of the Advocate-General often serves as a learned and very valuable summary of the state of EU law on a particular issue. The Court, which also receives written and oral arguments from counsel for the parties, is free to adopt or reject the opinion given by the Advocate-General.

The ECJ's authority is broad. In the first place, it has jurisdiction to review the legality of acts of the Council, the Commission, and the European Parliament. Second, it has jurisdiction to give preliminary rulings, on reference from courts of the Member States, and on issues involving interpretation of the EU Treaties and Community legislation. Third, the ECJ may be asked to consider whether a Member State has failed to fulfill an obligation under the EC Treaties. The judgments of the General Court (see below) are appealable to the ECJ on points of law. The ECJ's jurisdiction is spelled out in the Statute of the Court of Justice.

The General Court ("GC"), formerly called the Court of First Instance ("CFI"), was created under the Single European Act and began to operate in 1989. It was established because of the heavy caseload burden of the ECJ. The GC is "attached" to the ECJ, sharing its building and facilities in Luxembourg. The GC consists of one judge from each Member State, and they are appointed for renewable six-year terms. The GC normally sits in chambers composed of three or five judges each. The Treaty of Nice, effective February 1, 2003, provided for the creation of "judicial panels" in certain specific areas.

The creation of this lower court was thought necessary, in part, because the ECJ was expending a great deal of time in the process of reviewing factual matters. Broadly speaking, the GC has jurisdiction to hear at first instance all direct actions brought by individuals and the Member States, with the exception of those to be assigned to a judicial panel and those reserved for the ECJ. As we shall see, this jurisdiction has given the GC an important role in reviewing Commission decisions on competition law matters. The GC can review factual issues, legal issues, and any fine imposed by the Commission. The jurisdiction of the GC also includes all direct actions brought by private parties against EU institutions.

The GC procedure provides for written submissions followed by an oral argument in open court. As noted, appeal of GC decisions to the ECJ is permitted on points of law only and not on points of fact. The right to appeal on issues of law applies, however, in all cases. The ECJ may also consider appeals asserting that the GC lacked jurisdiction, committed a breach of procedure adversely affecting the appellant, or infringed Community law.

It should be kept in mind that the courts of the Member States also function as EU courts in that they may review the administrative implementation of that part of the EU law for which the Member States have responsibility. The national courts are also responsible for upholding those rights of the nationals of the Member States that are conferred on the individuals by EU law.

[E] The Application of EU Law

As we have seen, the law governing the EU is fundamentally derived from a number of treaties into which the Member States have entered. The most important of these is the EC Treaty, including the amendments which have been made to the original Treaty of Rome. Article 288 TFEU (formerly Article 249 of the EC Treaty) provides that, "to exercise the Union's competences, the institutions shall adopt regulations, decisions, recommendations and opinions."

A regulation is a rule issued by the Council or by the Commission based on a Council enabling regulation which has general application throughout the EU without going through any implementing procedures in the Member States. As Article 288 TFEU states, a regulation is "binding in its entirety and directly applicable in all Member States." This means that regulations issued in the EU which are not designed to require further implementing legislation become part of the national legal system of each Member State. Where a self-executing regulation creates individual rights for private parties, the national courts must protect those rights. Regulations are pertinent to competition law, as well as to agricultural policy and other matters.

A directive of the Council, the Parliament, or the Commission is binding on each Member State to which it is addressed as to the result to be achieved, but the State is permitted to determine the form and method for fulfilling the obligation. The Member States must enact or amend their laws or regulations in order to implement the directives. Every directive has a time scale for implementation by the Member States. The EU has held that damages are available against a Member State for failure to implement an EU directive which was designed to confer identifiable rights for the benefit of individuals. The EU determines which Treaty provisions, international treaty commitments and Council directives are "directly effective," meaning that they confer rights on the citizens of the Member States which may be invoked by those individuals. For example, equal pay for equal work has been held a directly effective Treaty provision, pushing aside all national laws allowing discrimination on the basis of sex or union membership with respect to pay. The EU has held that the supremacy of EU law over national law must be implied from the EU Treaties.

A guideline or notice issued by the Commission does not have the force of law but is administratively binding on the Commission itself. Law enforcement decisions may be rendered by both the Council and the Commission, and they are binding on the individuals or entities addressed. Most of the law enforcement proceedings are brought by the Commission, and these may be against Member States, enterprises or other bodies. A decision, regulation, or directive must provide the reasons for which it was taken. The parties addressed may seek judicial review by the EU courts. A Council or Commission action may be held void for lack of competence, for infringement of a rule of law or of essential procedure, or for misuse of powers. These grounds for appeal are largely derived from French administrative law.

§9.03 OVERVIEW OF THE COMPETITION LAW RULES AND THEIR ENFORCEMENT

[A] The Competition Law Rules

The EU competition law rules cover all sectors of the economy, including, since July 2002, the coal and steel sectors. There are narrow exceptions in the areas of agriculture and certain transport. The competition rules also apply to banking, financial services, and insurance. The Commission has given detailed attention to the activities in each of these specialized sectors, including grants of exemption as appropriate. There are also group or block exemptions for certain types of agreements which we will be discussing in the pages ahead.

The Council has issued special regulations for the various transport sectors. Under Council Regulation 4056/86, there was established a block exemption allowing liner shipping conferences to fix prices and regulate capacity jointly. This exemption was ended in 2008 and the European liner shipping industry was thus subjected to the competition rules.

The basic competition rules are found in Article 101 TFEU (formerly Article 81 and, earlier, Article 85, of the EC Treaty) and Article 102 TFEU (formerly Article 82 and, earlier, Article 86, of the EC Treaty) of the TFEU. Generally, these two articles prohibit, as incompatible with the common market, certain anticompetitive agreements, practices and abuses by "undertakings" insofar as they "may affect trade between Member

States." Undertakings are essentially business enterprises, broadly defined, and whatever their form, e.g., corporations, associations, partnerships, or sole proprietorships. While a natural person may be an "undertaking" if he/she is personally engaged in business activities as an economic unit, an individual working for someone else, like a company executive or commercial agent executing orders of a principal, is not an "undertaking" covered by the prohibitions. The Articles 101 and 102 prohibitions apply to undertakings which are established in the EU countries. The competition rules also apply, as determined by the jurisprudence of the Court of Justice, to the activities of any undertakings established in non-EU countries to the extent that their anticompetitive conduct is implemented within the EU and produces prohibited effects.

In understanding the territorial scope of the EU competition law regime, it should be noted that the concept of protected commerce covers not only trade involving the current twenty-eight EU Member States but also trade within the broader European Economic Area ("EEA"). The EEA came into being in 1994 by an agreement between the EC and the members of the European Free Trade Association ("EFTA"), which was designed to enable EFTA countries to participate in the European Single Market without having to join the EU. With Austria, Finland and Sweden having since become EU members, three of the remaining four EFTA members—Iceland, Norway and Liechtenstein—have remained in the EEA along with the EU countries. The fourth remaining EFTA country, Switzerland, failed to ratify the EEA Agreement, and it has become linked to the EU scheme by bilateral agreements distinct from the EEA Agreement. Pursuant to the EEA Agreement, competition rules similar to those of EU Treaty Articles 101 and 102 bind the EU nations in the context of the EEA as a whole.

It should also be kept in mind that the EU competition rules fulfill both an antitrust function—the maintenance of a competitive market regime—and the fundamental Union objective of insuring the integration of the Member State economies. For this reason, as we shall see when we discuss the EU competition case law, trade restraints which seek to carve out market divisions along national lines are particular targets of enforcement action.

Article 101(1) TFEU (and Article 53 of the EEA Agreement) broadly prohibits agreements between undertakings, decisions by associations of undertakings, and concerted practices "which may affect trade between Member States and which have as their object or effect the prevention, restriction or distortion of competition within the internal market ... ." Article 101(1) enumerates a number of activities which are "in particular" the object of this prohibition, including price fixing, production limitations, market-sharing, discrimination among parties, and tie-ins. In articulating a prohibition which applies only to joint conduct, and not to conduct by a single actor, Article 101(1) is akin—but certainly not identical to—Section 1 of the Sherman Act under US law. Article 101(2) provides that the agreements prohibited under the first clause are automatically void. However, the broad prohibitions are counterbalanced by a broad possibility that an agreement, decision or concerted practice may be exempted from the Article 101(1) prohibition if it is determined to meet certain conditions listed in Article 101(3).

Article 102 TFEU (and Article 54 of the EEA Agreement) provides that "any abuse by one or more undertakings of a dominant position within the internal market or in a substantial part of it shall be prohibited as incompatible with the internal market in so far as it may affect trade between Member States." Four examples of such abuse are listed in the text of the article: (a) directly or indirectly imposing unfair purchase or selling prices or other unfair trading conditions; (b) limiting production, markets or technical development to the prejudice of consumers; (c) applying dissimilar conditions to equivalent transactions with other trading parties, thereby placing them at a competitive disadvantage; and (d) making the conclusion of contracts subject to acceptance by the other parties of supplementary obligations which, by their nature or according to commercial usage, have no connection with the subject of such contracts.

On its face, Article 102 differs in two important respects from Article 101. First, although Article 101 requires an agreement, decision, or concerted practice involving at least two independent enterprises, one enterprise acting alone may violate Article 102 by abusing its dominant position. Second, unlike Article 101, Article 102 contains no provision for an exemption.

Article 102 prohibits only the abuse of a dominant economic position by an enterprise, not the creation or acquisition of such a position, whether by merger or otherwise. Accordingly, although Article 102 is similar to Section 2 of the Sherman Act in prohibiting abusive practices by a single dominant firm, the two provisions differ inasmuch as Section 2 also targets the actions of monopolization and attempts to monopolize. In short, the creation of a dominant position, by merger or other "monopolistic" activity, may be attacked under Section 2 but not under Article 102. However, as we shall discuss, the EU's merger control regime fills in this gap with respect to mergers and acquisitions, and the differences between Section 2 and Article 102 are less significant than may at first appear.

Articles 101 and 102 can both be applied against an undertaking in a single proceeding based on a pattern of conduct, providing that the elements of both prohibitions are made out. The CFI (now the "GC") held in the *Italian Flat Glass* case that the Commission cannot simply "recycle" a set of allegations to make out a violation of both provisions but must address the specific elements of each Article that it invokes.

Article 103 TFEU provides that the "appropriate regulations or directives to give effect to the principles set out in Articles 101 and 102 shall be laid down by the Council, on a proposal from the Commission and after consulting the European Parliament."

Article 106 TFEU addresses the important subject of public undertakings and undertakings to which the Member States seek to grant special or exclusive rights, such as monopoly positions. The Member States retain the right to strike their own balances between private and public ownership, including the establishment and maintenance of state monopolies for particular activities. However, Article 106(1) specifies that this reserved power should not derogate from the Community competition regime. Pursuant to this provision, the Member States have an obligation, in so far as they create public companies or grant private companies exclusive or other special rights, to neither enact nor maintain measures contrary to the Treaty competition rules. Paragraph (2) contains a narrow exception to the general principle of paragraph (1) to the effect that entities "entrusted with the operation of services of general economic interest or having the character of a revenue-producing monopoly" shall comply with the competition law rules "in so far as the application of such rules does not obstruct the performance, in law or fact, of the particular tasks assigned to them." The importance of adherence of the Member States to their obligations under these provisions is underlined by Article 106(3), which provides that "[t]he Commission shall ensure the application of the provisions of this Article and shall, where necessary, address appropriate directives or decisions to Member States."

We will also be discussing in detail the implementation of the EU Merger Regulation, Council Regulation 139/2004, effective May 1, 2004, which prohibits "concentrations" (which may involve mergers, acquisitions and joint ventures) which are likely to significantly impede effective competition within the EU or a substantial part of it, particularly as a result of the creation or strengthening of a dominant position.

[B] Council Regulation 1/2003

For many years, the primary EU legislative instrument implementing the competition law provisions of the EC Treaty was Council Regulation 17 of February 6, 1962. That document provided that agreements, decisions, and concerted practices covered by Article 81(1) and abuses of a dominant position covered by Article 82 were prohibited, with no prior decision to that effect required. It also provided a "negative clearance" procedure whereby parties seeking the benefit of the exemption provision of Article 81(3) were to apply to the Commission therefor by "notifying" the Commission of the agreement, decision or concerted practice for which exemption to Article 81(1) was sought. While, under the case law of the ECJ, the competition authorities and courts of the Member States, as well as the Commission, had the power to enforce Articles 81(1) and 82, Regulation 17/62 authorized only the Commission to make the determination of exemption under Article 81(3). However, after a lengthy period of study and consultation, a new Council Regulation superseding Regulation 17/62 was adopted and has been in effect since May 1, 2004. (This Regulation known as Council Regulation (EC) No. 1/2003 of December 16, 2002, is reproduced in Appendix II of this volume.) As this Regulation states in its introduction relating to Article 81(3):

> 2) in particular, there is a need to rethink the arrangements for applying the exception from the prohibition on agreements, which restrict competition, laid down in Article 81(3) of the Treaty. Under Article 83(2)(b) of the Treaty, account must be taken in this regard of the need to ensure effective supervision, on the one hand, and to simplify administration to the greatest possible extent on the other.
> 3) The centralised scheme set up by Regulation No 17 no longer secures a balance between those two objectives. It hampers application of the Community competition rules by the courts and competition authorities of the Member States, and the system of notification it involves prevents the Commission from concentrating its resources on curbing the most serious infringements. It also imposes considerable costs on undertakings.
> 4) The present system should therefore be replaced by a directly applicable exception system in which the competition authorities and courts of the Member States have the power to apply not only Articles 81(1) and Article 82 of the Treaty, which have direct applicability by virtue of the case-law of the

Court of Justice of the European Communities, but also Article 81(3) of the Treaty.

We will discuss the past and present applications of what is now Article 101(3) in greater detail in the next chapter.

In replacing Regulation 17/62 as the comprehensive procedural regulation, Council Regulation 1/2003 provided some rules which were new and also continued others which had been laid down in Regulation 17/62. In summarizing the Regulation, we will update by substituting Articles 101 and 102 TFEU for Articles 81 and 82 of the EC Treaty. Note also that the term "NCAs," standing for national competition authorities, will sometimes be used in place of "competition authorities of the Member States."

The highlights of this regulation include the following principles:

(1) **The Prohibitions and Article [101(3) TFEU] Reform:** As before, agreements, decisions and concerted practices caught by Article [101(1) TFEU] which do not satisfy the conditions of Article [101(3) TFEU] are prohibited, no prior decision to that effect being required. However, such agreements, decisions and concerted practices satisfying the conditions of Article [101(3) TFEU] are not prohibited, no prior decision to that effect being required. Also, as before, the abuse of a dominant position referred to in Article [102 TFEU] is prohibited, no prior decision to that effect being required.

(2) **Member State Authority to Enforce EU and National Laws**: The competition authorities of the Member States are authorized to apply Articles [101 and 102 TFEU] in individual cases, including the power to require that infringements be brought to an end and imposing fines, periodic penalty payments or any other penalty provided for in their national law. Indeed, pursuant to Article 3(1) of Regulation 1/2003, when the competition authorities and courts of the Member States apply national competition law to agreements, decisions by associations of undertakings and practices which may affect trade between Member States, they are obliged also to apply Articles [101 and 102 TFEU] of the Treaty. Alternatively, in such instances, the NCAs and courts may apply these EU provisions only, and not their national laws. In any event, the application of national law to decisions, agreements and concerted practices covered by Article [101(1) TFEU] may not lead to prohibition if they are not also prohibited under EU competition law.

As was the rule before, the initiation by the Commission of proceedings against an infringement of Article [101 or 102 TFEU] relieves the competition authority of the Member State of its competence to apply those Articles in the same matter. However, if a competition authority of a Member State is already acting on a case, the Commission will only initiate proceedings after consulting with that national authority.

There are respects in which national law may be applied more strictly than EU competition law. Thus, Member States are not precluded from adopting and applying on their territory stricter national competition law which prohibits or imposes sanctions on *unilateral* conduct engaged in by undertakings. Also, national laws may impose criminal sanctions on natural persons, unless this is a means of enforcing competition rules relating to undertakings. Note the logic of this limitation seeking to establish the point that there is no inconsistency between the national and EU systems in this regard: While the EU competition rules, Articles 101 and 102 TFEU, do not provide for criminal sanctions, these EU prohibitions are directed only against undertakings, i.e., business enterprises, and not against natural persons.

(3) **Commission Remedial Powers**: The Commission is entrusted with broad authority in making decisions and shaping remedies. It may order interim measures, accept binding commitments from undertakings about ending infringements, and it may impose:

> any behavioural or structural remedies which are proportionate to the infringement committed and necessary to bring the infringement effectively to an end. Structural remedies can only be imposed either where there is no equally effective behavioural remedy or where any equally effective behavioural remedy would be more burdensome for the undertaking concerned than the structural remedy ... (Article 7 (1)).

This provision eliminates any doubts about the extent of the Commission's authority to impose structural relief to bring an infringement to an end.

(4) **Network of Public Authorities**: The Commission and the competition authorities of the Member States are directed to form together a network of public authorities for the purpose of applying the EU rules in close cooperation. Notwithstanding any national provision to the contrary, the exchange of information and the use of that information in evidence is allowed between the members of the network even when the information is confidential.

(5) **Role of the National Courts**: The courts of the Member States are also given the power to apply Articles [101 and 102 TFEU] in full in cases brought before them. The Member State courts, like the national competition authorities, must apply Articles [101 and 102 TFEU] where they apply national competition law to agreements and practices which may affect trade between Member States, and they may not prohibit such agreements and practices if they are also not prohibited under EU competition law. The national courts cannot rule in such cases in a manner counter to decisions adopted or "contemplated" by the Commission in proceedings it has initiated. To assure consistency in the application of the competition rules, arrangements are mandated to bring about cooperation between the national courts and the Commission. This is to include exchanges of information, documentation and views, including prompt submittal to the Commission by the Member States of the pertinent written judgments of their national courts, and, where appropriate, submission by the Commission and/or the national competition authorities of observations to the national courts.

(6) **The Advisory Committee**: The Advisory Committee on Restrictive Practices and Dominant Positions which was established by Regulation 17 as a

mandatory consultation body for the Commission is found to have functioned in a very satisfactory fashion and to be well suited to the new system of decentralized application of the competition rules. It will also be used as a forum for discussing cases that are being handled by the competition authorities of the Member States. For the discussion of individual cases, the Advisory Committee will be composed of representatives of the competition authorities of the Member States. When issues other than individual cases are being discussed, an additional Member State representative competent in competition matters may be included. The Commission must consult the Advisory Committee before making decisions in a number of key matters, and the Commission must take "utmost account" of the opinion delivered by the Advisory Committee.

(7) **Uniformity of Application**: Where national courts or competent authorities of the Member States rule on agreements, decisions, or practices under Article [101 or 102 TFEU] which are already the subject of a Commission decision, these authorities and courts cannot take decisions which run counter to the decision adopted by the Commission. The national courts must also avoid taking decisions which would conflict with a decision contemplated by the Commission in proceedings it has initiated. To that effect, the national court may consider whether it is necessary for it to stay its proceedings.

(8) **Commission Powers of Investigation**: The Commission's existing powers of investigation are confirmed, and additional authority which it has been seeking is provided. Thus, the Commission remains empowered throughout the EU to require, by simple request or by decision, that undertakings and their associations provide any information necessary to detect any agreement, decision or concerted practice prohibited by Article [101 TFEU] or any abuse of a dominant position prohibited by Article [102 TFEU]. Undertakings cannot be forced to admit that they have committed an infringement, but they are obliged to answer factual questions and to provide documents, even if the supplying of this information is incriminating.

The Commission also retains the power to conduct on-site inspections at business sites to investigate possible violations of Articles [101 and 102 TFEU], and the competition authorities of the Member States are to actively assist the Commission officials in these efforts. Such "inspections" include entering premises, examining records, taking copies or excerpts, and asking business persons and staff to provide explanations regarding pertinent facts or documents. The persons authorized by the Commission to conduct the inspection must produce a written authorization at the time specifying the subject matter and purpose of the inspection and the penalties provided for the production of incomplete records or the giving of incorrect or misleading answers to questions. "In good time before the inspection," the Commission must give notice of the inspection to the competition authority of the Member State in whose territory it will be conducted.

The Council Regulation also notes that "[t]he detection of the infringement of the competition rules is growing ever more difficult, and, in order to protect competition effectively, the Commission's powers need to be supplemented." Thus, the Commission will be able to conduct interviews of persons who may be in possession of useful information and to record the statements made; officials are permitted to affix seals as to any business premises or records for the time needed for the inspection, normally for not more than seventy-two hours; and, in particular, given the fact that experience has shown that business records are sometimes kept in the homes of directors or other people working for an undertaking, Commission officials are empowered to enter any premises, including means of transport and private homes, where reasonable suspicion indicates that relevant business records may be kept. Such inspections of "other premises," however, require a prior "decision" by the Commission ordering the inspection and indicating the right to have the decision reviewed by the Court of Justice. There must also be prior authorization from the national judicial authority of the Member State concerned for this type of inspection decision.

(9) **Commission Public Interest Finding**: "Where the [Union] public interest relating to the application of Arts. [101 and 102 TFEU] so requires, the Commission, acting on its own initiative, may by decision find that Art. [101 TFEU] is not applicable to an agreement, a decision by an association of undertakings or a concerted practice, either because the conditions of Art. [101 TFEU] are not fulfilled, or because the conditions of Art. [101 (3) TFEU] are satisfied. The Commission may likewise make such a finding with reference to Art. [102 TFEU]." (Article 10)

(10) **Member State Investigations**: The competition authority of a Member State may carry out in its own territory any inspection or other fact-finding measure under its national law on behalf of the competition authority of another Member State, in connection with establishing whether Article [101 or 102 TFEU] has been infringed. At the request of the Commission, the Member State competition authorities shall undertake inspections which have been authorized by the Commission.

(11) **Penalties and Periodic Penalty Payments**: Compliance with Articles [101 and 102 TFEU] and with the obligations of the Regulation by undertakings and associations of undertakings will continue to be enforceable by the Commission's imposition of fines and periodic penalty payments. Thus, the Commission may by decision impose the following on undertakings and associations for procedural or substantive infringements:

(a) For, intentionally or negligently, violating a procedural requirement, by, e.g., supplying incorrect, incomplete, misleading, or untimely information in response to a request, or refusing to submit to an inspection ordered by a Commission decision, fines not exceeding 1% of the total turnover in the preceding business year.

(b) For infringement of a rule of substance, such as a violation of Article [101 or 102 TFEU] or failure to comply with a binding commitment, fines not exceeding for each undertaking and association of undertakings participating in the infringement 10% of its total turnover in the preceding business year; where the infringement of an association relates to the activities of its members, the fine shall not exceed 10% of the sum of the total turnover of each member active on the market affected by the infringement of the association.

In fixing the amount of a fine, the Commission is to give regard to both the gravity and the duration of the infringement. Where a fine is imposed on an association based on its members' turnover and the association is not solvent, the association is required to call on its members for contributions to the amount of the fine.

(c) In order to compel an undertaking or association to comply with a previous Commission decision, including one ordering the end to an infringement of Article [101 or 102 TFEU], or ordering interim measures, or ordering compliance with a binding commitment, or ordering the supply of complete and correct information or submission to an inspection, the Commission may, by decision, impose on undertakings or associations of undertakings periodic penalty payments not exceeding 5% of the average daily turnover in the preceding business per day.

The Commission's power to impose fines and periodic penalty payments is subject to the following limitation periods: (a) three years in the case of infringements of provisions concerning requests for information or the conduct of inspections; and (b) five years as to all other infringements.

(12) **Hearings and Rights of Defense**: The burden of proving an infringement of Article [101(1) or 102 TFEU] rests on the party or authority alleging the infringement. Undertakings and associations of undertakings which are the subject of proceedings conducted by the Commission are entitled to the opportunity to be heard on the matters to which the Commission has taken objection. The rights of defense of the parties concerned include a right of access to the Commission's files, subject to the protection of business secrets and with the proviso that this access shall not extend to confidential information and internal documents of the Commission or the competition authorities of the Member States. The Commission may base its decisions only on objections to which the parties concerned have been able to comment. Complainants have the right to "be associated closely with the proceedings." As to proposed commitments by undertakings or findings of inapplicability of the Articles, the Commission must first publish a summary of the matter so as to allow interested third parties to submit their observations.

The Commission has issued a number of supporting statements necessary for the application of Regulation 1/2003, including the "Implementing Regulation," Commission Regulation 773/2004 relating to the conduct of proceedings under Articles 101 and 102. In 2012, DG COMP published an *Antitrust Manual of Procedures: Internal DG Competition working documents on procedures for the application of Articles 101 and 102 TFEU.*

[C] Overview of Commission Enforcement

As one can see, the Commission combines administrative and judicial functions. Its powers and procedures with respect to the enforcement of the prohibitions in Articles 101 and 102 are set forth in the above-described Council Regulation 1/2003 ("the Regulation"). Pursuant to Article 7 of the Regulation, the Commission may institute proceedings to determine the existence of alleged violations of Article 101 or 102 TFEU, either on its own initiative or upon the complaint of a Member State or of any "natural or legal persons who can show a legitimate interest." If it finds an infringement of these provisions, the Commission "may by decision require the undertakings or associations of undertakings concerned to bring such infringement to an end."

The European Commission and the national competition authorities in all EU Member States cooperate and communicate with each other through the European Competition Network or "ECN." This mechanism allows information sharing on companies engaged in cross-border illegal conduct and for consultation on proposed enforcement actions. The members of the ECN have also established an EU Merger Working Group for cooperation and application of best practices in the area of merger control.

[1] Fines and Penalties

As has been noted above, the Commission is authorized to impose fines upon undertakings or associations of undertakings for either procedural or substantive infringements. For a violation of a procedural rule, such as the providing of incorrect information or refusal to submit to an investigation ordered by a decision, the fine may not exceed 1% of the firm's total turnover in the preceding business year. For infringement of a rule of substance, such as a violation of Article 101(1) or 102, or failure to comply with a binding commitment, the Commission may impose fines not exceeding 10% of the total turnover for the preceding business year. An infringement must have been committed intentionally or negligently to be subject to a fine. The fines are stated by the Regulation to be not of a "criminal law nature." Other than directing the Commission to take into account the gravity and duration of the infringement, the Regulation gives the Commission discretion to take into account the individual case in setting the amount of the fine.

In 2006, the Commission published in the Official Journal a new version of its *Guidelines on the method of setting fines pursuant to Article 23 (2) (a) of Regulation 1/2003*. They are binding on the Commission but do not limit the Court of Justice's power to assess fines. The Guidelines indicate a "basic amount" for each fine according to the gravity and duration of the infringement, and this number is adjusted to take into account the economic capacity of the offender, whether there are aggravating circumstances (like instigating the conduct or repeated infringements) or attenuating circumstances (such as cooperation). These fines may be imposed on undertakings or associations of undertakings. As we have noted, there is no provision, such as there is, for example, under US law, for attaching personal liability by way of fines or other punishment to those individual executives or employees within an undertaking who actually engaged in the proscribed conduct.

As we have also seen, periodic penalty payments, as distinct from fines, may be imposed by the Commission on undertakings or associations of undertakings to compel them to comply with earlier Commission decisions, such as a direction to terminate an infringement of Article 101 or 102 or to submit to an investigation.

Finally, there is a formal requirement derived from Article 5 TEU which is known as the "principle of proportionality." This requirement, as interpreted by the Court of Justice, means that any remedy imposed by the Commission with respect to an infringement must not go beyond what is appropriate and necessary to achieve the regulatory objective pursued. The principle of "subsidiarity," also derived from Article 5 TEU, refers to the circumstances where it is appropriate for action to be taken by the Union, rather than the Member States.

[2] Leniency for Cooperation by Undertakings

In 1996, the Commission issued a Notice describing its leniency program by which cooperation by an undertaking would affect the imposition of a fine. As in the case of the US leniency program, the EU program's purpose was and is to provide an incentive for firms participating in secret cartels to put an end to that activity and step forward to advise the authorities about the existence of the illegal arrangements. In February 2002, the Commission issued a new Notice on its leniency program, and then, on December 6, 2006, the Commission adopted the current revised *Notice on Immunity from fines and reduction of fines in cartel cases* (the "2006 Leniency Notice"). The modified program is intended to be stronger than its predecessors in providing more guidance to applicants and increasing the "transparency" of the procedure.

First, the 2006 Leniency Notice promises full immunity from fines to a company which submits a request to the Commission therefor and is the first firm to provide evidence of a cartel hitherto unknown to the Commission or, if the Commission is aware of the cartel, if the firm is the first to provide the Commission with crucial information enabling the Commission to establish the cartel's existence.

To obtain immunity or a reduction in fines, the "whistleblower" must give genuine, continuous and expeditious cooperation; terminate any involvement in the cartel (unless the Commission deems that continuing involvement might be useful to the investigation); and the whistleblower must not have destroyed, falsified or concealed any relevant evidence when contemplating its application for immunity.

A firm which cannot claim total immunity may nevertheless request a reduction in fines if it supplies evidence which represents significant added value with respect to the evidence already held by the Commission. Evidence which does not need to be corroborated will have more value to the Commission than evidence which has to be confirmed or backed up. The first firm meeting these conditions will be granted a 30%–50% reduction in the fine which would otherwise have been imposed, the second 20%–30%, and the others up to 20%. The amount of the reduction given within these parameters depends on when the evidence was supplied and the extent to which it represents added value.

The 2006 Leniency Notice also establishes a procedure to protect corporate statements from having to be disclosed in civil damage proceedings. To avoid such a statement falling into the hands of a would-be private plaintiff, the statement may be made orally to Commission staff rather than in writing. The staff may convert the oral statement to writing, but the latter is not discoverable from the whistleblower firm when in the hands of the Commission.

The Commission considers that the leniency program has proven to be very successful in meeting its purposes.

[3]   Complaints

Article 7 of Regulation 1/2003 speaks of the Commission, "acting on a complaint or its own initiative," in determining that there has been an infringement of Article [101 or 102 TFEU]. A "complaint" may be filed by a natural or legal person who can show a legitimate interest or by a Member State.

In 2004, the Commission published two pertinent documents, Commission Regulation 773/2004 (the "Implementing Regulation") on the conduct of proceedings, as well as a *Notice on the handling of complaints by the Commission under Articles [101 and 102 TFEU]*. An Annex to the Regulation, Form C, lists the information which must be supplied when making a complaint, including details of the alleged infringement and evidence, the Commission finding or action sought, the grounds on which a legitimate interest is claimed (i.e., how the activity affects the complainant) and whether proceedings on the subject are pending before national competition authorities or national courts. The complainant is entitled to access to certain nonconfidential information, to participate in the proceedings to a limited extent, and to appeal to the EU courts any decision addressed directly to the complainant, including a decision rejecting the complaint. The Notice points out, however, that the procedural rights of complainants are "less far reaching" than the right to a fair hearing of the companies which are the subject of an infringement proceeding.

The Notice is largely intended to help potential non-State complainants "to make an informed choice about whether to address themselves to the Commission, to one of the Member States' competition authorities or to a national court." It does not address complaints filed by or against Member States. The Notice points out that national courts can both decide on the nullity or validity of contracts and grant damages to an aggrieved individual for violations of Articles [101 and 102 TFEU]. Moreover, Member State competition authorities (cooperating with the Commission within the ECN) may be well placed to deal effectively with activities within and/or affecting their territories.

The Notice provides details about the form in which complaints should be filed, in keeping with the requirements of Form C annexed to the Regulation. It also explains how the "legitimate interest" requirement is interpreted under the case law. A party meeting this requirement may include, for example, a party to an agreement or practice, or an injured competitor or other business entity, but it may also be a consumer association or trade union. The Notice also explains that it is settled that the Commission is not required to conduct an investigation simply because there has been a complaint, and that it has discretion to consider the EU interest (broadly defined) involved. The Commission must, in any event, decide on complaints within a reasonable time and give the complainant its reasons for rejecting the complaint, as well as an opportunity to comment on the rejection within a given time period. Finally, it is also possible for one to file an "informal" complaint with the Commission, by supplying information without satisfying all the formalities or even revealing one's identity, but the procedural rights given complainants are not available in this situation.

[4] Investigation

If the Commission decides that an investigation is warranted, it can employ the broad powers provided it for that purpose in Regulation 1/2003. These measures include, pursuant to Article 17: conducting investigations into sectors of the economy and into types of agreements where it appears that there may be a restriction or distortion of competition; requiring, by simple request or by decision, that undertakings or associations of undertakings provide all necessary information (Article 18); interviewing persons who consent to be interviewed and taking statements from them (Article 19); and conducting inspections of premises and means of transport to examine and, if necessary, seal books and records, take extracts, and to ask representatives or staffs of the undertakings or associations for explanations of relevant facts or documents. The Commission staff conducting the inspection must produce a written authorization and notice of the penalties provided for supplying incomplete, incorrect or misleading information. The Member State concerned is entitled to be given prior notice by the Commission and obligated to afford any necessary assistance to the Commission (Article 20).

Article 21 of Regulation 1/2003 empowers the Commission, on the basis of reasonable suspicion and with prior authorization from the national judicial authority of the Member State concerned, to order by decision that an inspection be conducted in any premises other than the business premises of undertakings or associations, "including the homes of directors, managers and other members of staff of the undertakings and associations of undertakings concerned ... ."

The unannounced "on-the-spot" inspection visits to company premises by Commission personnel are colloquially referred to as "dawn raids" by the people subjected to them and in the press. The company is entitled to the assistance of counsel during the Commission staff's visit, providing the company's attorney can get to the premises within a reasonable amount of time. The Commission has increased fines for infringements where the undertaking concerned failed to cooperate during an inspection visit.

In *Deutsche Bahn and others v. European Commission*, the question came before the European courts whether, where the Commission discovers, during a dawn raid, documents which are not within the scope of its decision but which suggest that the undertaking may be guilty of a different infringement, the Commission may adopt a second decision and investigation targeting the new infringement. In 2013, the GC upheld the Commission's position in this regard. However, in 2015, the ECJ upheld the Commission's power to conduct dawn raids without judicial authorization but also ruled that the company's rights of defense had been infringed by the Commission's obtaining documents which had been improperly discovered. So the ECJ annulled the second and third inspection decisions since these were triggered by documents improperly discovered during the first inspection.

The Commission's investigative powers may be directed at third parties, as well as against the parties under investigation. Commission requests for information are usually made initially on the basis that response is voluntary. If an undertaking receiving a request fails to comply on a voluntary basis or provides incomplete information, the Commission may issue a decision ordering compliance. Noncompliance with such an order can be punished by fines or penalty payments. The decision ordering compliance is reviewable by the GC. Fines may also be imposed for providing misleading or incorrect information in response to either a request or an order.

The information received by the Commission from businesses is often supplemented by research into press reports, and review of specialized industry publications and statistics. In addition, if the Commission desires information from an undertaking which is based outside of the EU, it first requests that information indirectly, from a subsidiary, sales office or branch within the EU if possible. It may require the production of documents or other information outside the EU. If the firm has no office within the EU, the Commission will send its request directly to the headquarters of the foreign firm.

There is a limited privilege against self-incrimination which has been recognized by the EU courts. The extent of this privilege is that, while an undertaking under investigation is not entitled to refuse to provide documents or factual information requested by the Commission, as one of its rights of defense it cannot be compelled by the Commission to admit that it has violated Article 101 or 102 TFEU.

The matter of attorney-client privilege deserves special discussion here, particularly since there is currently no universal international standard on the existence and scope of the privilege. The ECJ held in 1982, in *AM & S v. Commission* that correspondence and communications between an undertaking and its independent—i.e., "outside"—counsel, who is entitled to practice law in one of the Member States (and now the EEA), are entitled to be kept confidential to the extent necessary to the undertaking's defense. This privilege was extended to papers directed by the company to outside counsel or from outside counsel to the company, for the purpose of asking for or providing advice or defense with respect to the matters under investigation or prosecution. The scope of this "professional privilege" was subsequently extended by the CFI to protect internal memoranda reflecting outside legal advice. However, this formulation has excluded from privileged status communications to or from in-house counsel or to or from outside counsel not authorized to practice law in a Member State, for example, a US lawyer. Correspondence between an undertaking's outside lawyer and a lawyer acting for a third party is not privileged. The privilege beings to the client, not the lawyer.

In the case of *Akzo Nobel Chemicals* and its subsidiary, Akros Chemicals, the undertakings argued for privilege relating to advice given by in-house counsel on the ground that the in-house lawyer in question was subject to the legal professional rules of the Dutch Bar Council. On the appeal, the President of the GC noted (at paragraph 126) that "increasingly in the legal orders of the Member States and, possibly, as a consequence, in the Community legal order, there is no presumption that the link of employment between a lawyer and an undertaking will always, and as a matter of principle, affect the independence necessary for the effective exercise of the role of collaborating in the administration of justice by the courts if, in addition, the lawyer is bound by strict rules of professional conduct, which where necessary require that he observe the particular duties commensurate with his status." However, the GC declined to depart from the *AM & S* case, as did the ECJ which observed that, as an employee of the undertaking, the lawyer necessarily lacked independence from his employer.

Investigations may also be conducted by the national authorities in their own territories, either for their own enforcement proceedings or on the Commission's behalf. Article 12(1) of Regulation 1/2003 provides that, for purposes of applying Articles [101 and 102 TFEU] "the Commission and the competition authorities of the Member States shall have the power to provide one another with and use in evidence any matter of fact or law, including confidential information." All of the authorities concerned must take the necessary steps to protect the confidentiality of such information, although it may be used to prove infringements.

[5] Statement of Objections, Hearing, and Decision

Article 10 of Commission Regulation 773/2004 provides that, when the Commission determines, after investigation, that it will initiate an enforcement proceeding, it will inform the parties concerned by issuing a Statement of Objections. This statement sets forth the Commission's objections to the agreement or practice under review and the action it proposes to take by way of orders or fines. The undertaking concerned is given a specified amount of time in which to file a written reply stating its position, a period which normally covers a number of weeks. Other persons showing a sufficient interest in the matter are also given the opportunity to submit their views in writing to the Commission. The language of the proceeding will vary, depending upon the nationality of the addressee or its jurisdiction. The Commission will give the parties to whom the Statement of Objections is addressed an opportunity to be heard, including an oral hearing if the parties so request in their written submissions (Articles 11 and 12).

Article 27(1) of the Commission Regulation provides that, before the Commission takes a decision under Article 7 or 8 (infringement and interim measure decisions) or under Article 23 or 24 (fines and periodic penalty payments), the undertakings concerned have a right to be heard. The Commission is bound to use the information which it obtained during its investigation only in connection with the proceeding and must protect business secrets and other confidential information. Article 27(2) of Regulation 1/2003 and Article 15 of Commission Regulation 773/2004 continue the prior practice in requiring that the Commission must provide access to its files to the extent necessary for the maintenance of the defense. This generally means that those defending the undertaking under scrutiny have access to the documents of importance to the case, except for business secrets of other undertakings, internal documents of the Commission or of the competition authorities of the Member States and correspondence between the enforcement authorities.

If an oral hearing takes place, it is primarily an opportunity for the respondent to supplement orally its written submissions, rather than in the nature of a trial, although the Commission may also afford the complainant an opportunity to express its views. The oral hearings are not public but persons with sufficient interest or necessary to the hearing may attend. The oral hearing takes place before "a Hearing Officer in full independence" (Article 14 of Commission Regulation 773/2004). This hearing officer is responsible for the conduct of the hearing and, among other things, fixes its time, place and duration, and decides what fresh documents may be admitted and witnesses heard. The hearing officer reports to the competent Commissioner on the hearing and the conclusions he has drawn from it with respect to the right to be heard, with a copy of the report given to the Director-General for Competition. The Commission has issued a number of relevant papers on the subject of the hearing procedures, including *Best Practices for the conduct of proceedings concerning Articles 101 and 102 TFEU*, and a *Notice on the rules for access to the Commission's files*.

In May 2001 the Commission issued a Decision outlining and strengthening the role of the hearing officer as a guardian of the parties' basic procedural protections, and particularly their right to be heard. The office of the hearing officer was moved from the premises of the Directorate-General for Competition to the office of the Commissioner in charge of competition policy. This step and others were reaffirmed in a Decision of the Commission of October 13, 2011 intending to further strengthen and clarify the independence of the hearing officer position.

In recent years, some complaints about the Commission's alleged maladministration of a proceeding have been taken by the undertakings concerned to the European Ombudsman. For example, in the case involving Intel, the company claimed that the Commission had committed several procedural errors in its investigation. The Ombudsman conducted a thorough inquiry and, in 2009, concluded with a detailed opinion, dismissing many of Intel's points but finding that the Commission had infringed good principles of administration by failing to compose agreed minutes of a meeting.

After the oral hearing, DG COMP prepares a draft decision. Pursuant to Article 14 of Regulation 1/2003 the Commission is then required to consult the Advisory Committee on Restrictive Practices and Dominant Positions, which consists of representatives of the Member States' competition authorities, before rendering a formal decision. The Committee is given access to the Statement of Objections, the written defense and other key documents, as well as the Commission's draft decision.

The consultation takes place via a meeting or by written procedure. When the Committee formulates a written opinion on the matter, it is attached to the draft decision, and the documents are circulated to the Commissioners. The Committee's opinion is not binding on the Commission, but Article 14(5) of Regulation 1/2003 specifies that the Commission is to take "utmost account" of the opinion and to "inform the Committee of the manner in which its opinion has been taken into account."

The Commission may close a case out without issuing a formal decision or it may issue a decision on any one or more of a variety of substantive or procedural grounds, including rejection of a complaint, deciding that Article 101 or 102 is inapplicable, accepting a commitment and making it binding on the undertakings, issuing cease and desist orders and/or sanctions, and interim orders. Article 9 of Regulation 1/2003 authorized the Commission, for the first time, to settle investigations formally by decisions accepting commitments which meet the Commission's concerns and are binding on the undertakings, without the need for making infringement findings.

The staff of the Directorate-General for Competition drafts the decisions, consulting with the Legal Service of the Commission and other interested units. Decisions of a substantive nature must be approved by a majority vote of the full Commission. Some procedural decisions may be made by an individual member of the Commission. After their adoption, the formal decisions are served upon the addressees and published in the Official Journal.

[D] Judicial Review

Commission decisions are reviewable by the EU courts and must comply with the prescribed procedural requirements, including a satisfactory address of the main factual and legal aspects supporting the decision taken. The GC has jurisdiction to review all decisions taken by the Commission. A party to such a decision is entitled to appeal, as is any person affected by a decision which, although addressed to another person, is of direct and individual concern to the third party. In principle, the GC may annul, increase or decrease any fine or periodic payment set by the Commission. The Commission's failure to make a decision can also be appealed. The GC's review of the Commission's decision is on both the facts and the law. The GC will not, however, substitute its own judgment on factual matters, but will essentially determine whether the Commission's findings are justified on the record. On procedural matters, the GC reviews whether the party charged received its rights of defense, such as appropriate access to the Commission's file. The GC can also grant interim relief, such as suspending, pending the hearing of the appeal, an obligation which the Commission has imposed. After the GC has rendered a decision on the appeal, its ruling can be appealed to the ECJ, but only on issues of law.

The procedures before the two EU courts are established by the Statute of the Court of Justice of the EU and the Rules of Procedure of the GC and the ECJ. In 2015 the GC adopted revised Rules of Procedure. Proceedings in the GC usually take place in a three or five judge chamber. One judge of the chamber is appointed to be the reporting judge, and his/her clerks prepare a preliminary report based on the documents and the applicable law. An oral hearing follows, and a judgment is then rendered by the court.

After the GC has rendered a decision on an appeal, its ruling can be appealed to the ECJ, but only on issues of law. Appeals may be taken by parties directly affected by the decision of the GC, as well as by Member States and the EU's governing institutions.

Article 263 TFEU empowers the ECJ to review the legality of acts of the Council or the Commission, on grounds including lack of competence (jurisdiction), infringement of an essential procedural requirement, infringement of the Treaties or of any rule of law relating to their application, and misuse of powers. Under Article 31 of Regulation 1/2003, as under Article 264 TFEU, the Court of Justice has unlimited jurisdiction to review decisions involving substantive or procedural matters whereby the Commission has fixed a fine or periodic penalty payment. Like the GC, the ECJ may cancel, reduce, or increase the fine or penalty payment imposed.

[E] Private Enforcement of EU Competition Law

The European Commission has continued to provide strong enforcement of Articles 101 and 102 TFEU at the EU level. Since the adoption of Regulation 1/2003, the national enforcement authorities have, in general, also been active in challenging infringements of those provisions which take place within their jurisdictions. The ECN has proven to be successful as a forum for consultations between the Commission and the national authorities, as well as among the latter, including exchanges of information and coordination of responsibility. The Commission has invited a public discussion on how the NCAs can become even more effective enforcers of the EU antitrust rules.

The Commission has also made it plain that an optimal enforcement regime must, in addition, include significant private enforcement on the national level. Commission officials have expressed the view that more private enforcement should lead to even greater compliance with EU competition rules. They have cited a number of important benefits that can accrue from private enforcement, including the awarding of compensation to the victims of illegal anticompetitive behavior, the availability of the sanction of nullity in contractual disputes, and the ability to pursue claims that the Commission, in its discretion, might not assert.

In its judgment in *Courage v. Crehan* in 2001, the ECJ recognized a right to recover damages for breaches of EU competition law. The Court stated that "[t]he full effect of Article 81 of the Treaty and, in particular, the practical effect of the prohibition laid down in Article 81(1) would be put at risk if it were not open to any individual to claim damage for loss caused to him by a contract or by conduct liable to restrict or distort competition ... actions for damages before the national courts can make a significant contribution to the maintenance of effective competition in the Community." The availability and importance of the private damage remedy have been underscored by the ECJ several times since.

Recital (7) of Regulation 1/2003 proclaims that "[n]ational courts have an essential part to play in applying the Community competition rules," for example by awarding damages to the victims of infringements. Article 6 of the Regulation 1/2003, accordingly, declares that the national courts have the power to apply Articles [101 and 102 TFEU], confirming that those courts are competent to apply EU competition law in private lawsuits. Indeed, with Articles 101 and 102 being directly applicable to private commercial relationships, the national courts are obligated to give effect in the private litigation before them to these aspects of the EU law. In particular, the elimination of the Commission's "exemption monopoly" under Article 81(3) by Regulation 1/2003, which became effective May 1, 2004, has permitted national judges to rule on Articles 101 and 102 issues in their entirety. Previously, the fact that only the Commission was authorized to grant exemptions under Article 81(3) enabled defendants in private actions in national courts to delay that litigation by filing a notification with the Commission seeking an exemption under that provision.

However, what procedures and remedies the national courts will apply in the actions brought before them remain matters of national law. These are by no means uniform within the EC Member States, and few helpful precedents exist in the national courts in the context of competition law on such critical issues as causation of injury, "pass-on" and the computation of compensation. EU competition law has often been applied in private actions as a means of giving effect to a defense that a contract is void or conduct illegal under Article 101 or 102. In some cases, injunctions have been issued by national courts, enjoining behavior illegal under the EC law, such as a refusal to deal or boycott. Damage actions have often been premised on general principles of contract or tort liability rather than directly on competition law rules.

As we discussed earlier in this book, in the US there exist special incentives for private antitrust plaintiffs and their counsel in the form of class action procedures, treble damage awards, and generous contingency fees. These incentives generally do not exist in the Member States to fuel private damage litigation, although some of the countries have now authorized higher damage awards for violation of competition laws.

A study undertaken by a law firm under a contract with the Commission confirmed that levels of private enforcement through damages claims in Europe were very low. The study found both a "total underdevelopment" and an "astonishing diversity" in approach with respect to the maintenance of actions for breaches of EU competition law in the Member States. Following up these findings, in December 2005, the Commission published for public consultation a Green Paper and a Commission Staff Working Paper discussing how damages actions for breach of the EC antitrust rules might be facilitated. The Commission continued to advocate more complete and effective use of the private damages remedy.

In 2013, the Commission issued a document entitled *Communication from the Commission on quantifying harm in actions for damages based on breaches of Article 101 or 102 of the Treaty on the Functioning of the European Union*. The *Communication* addresses "Compensation For Victims of Competition Law Infringements: The Challenge of Quantifying the Harm Suffered." It counsels that "Parties injured by an infringement of directly effective EU rules should ... have the full real value of their losses restored: the entitlement of all compensation covers the actual loss (*damnum emergens*), as well as compensation for loss of profit (*lucrum cessans*) suffered as a result of the infringement; and entitlement to interest from the time the damage occurred (footnotes omitted)." The Commission at the same time issued a Staff Working Document which provided detailed advice on the same subject.

Observers have noted that, in recent years, there has been significantly expanded private damages litigation in some EU countries, often stimulated by competition law lawyers. This has been the case notably in England and Wales, the Netherlands and

Germany. Other Member States have been less receptive to private damage claims based on competition rules. As we will discuss in Chapter 14, acceptance of the private action remedy has been particularly spurred in the United Kingdom since the coming into force in June 2003 of the Enterprise Act 2002 which expressly allows the award of damages in competition cases by a new body, the Competition Appeal Tribunal (CAT).

After many years of debate on the subject, on November 26, 2014, the European Parliament and the Council issued Directive 2014/104/EU "on certain rules governing actions for damages under national law for infringements of the competition law provisions of the Member States and of the European Union," a document known as the "Damages Directive." The crux of that directive is that (at paragraph 4) "the right in Union law to compensation for harm resulting from infringements of Union and national competition law requires each Member State to have procedural rules ensuring the effective exercise of that right." The Damages Directive required implementation by the Member States by December 27, 2016.

Only a few of the Member States met that deadline. The Commission sent letters out in January 2017 to those nations which had not complied. By early 2017, a significant number of the Member nations had adopted legislation designed to comply with the Damages Directive. The measures incorporated in these national laws included provisions empowering national courts to order disclosure of relevant evidence from defendants, claimants or third parties; making final infringement decisions of national competition authorities binding on their national courts; recognizing the passing-on defense; setting limitation periods; introducing a rebuttable presumption that cartels cause harm; and codifying the joint and several liability of co-infringers. The Damages Directive is intended to apply only in cases where there is a breach of EU competition law and not when only domestic law applies.

CHAPTER 10
Article 101 TFEU: Agreements, Decisions, and Concerted Practices – Activity Involving Competitors

§10.01 INTRODUCTION

Article 101 of the Treaty on the Functioning of the European Union ("TFEU") has three major clauses. For ease of reference, we reproduce the Article in full below:

> **Article 101 TFEU**
> 1. The following shall be prohibited as incompatible with the internal market: all agreements between undertakings, decisions by associations of undertakings and concerted practices which may affect trade between Member States and which have as their object or effect the prevention, restriction or distortion of competition within the internal market, and in particular those which:
>   (a) directly or indirectly fix purchase or selling prices or any other trading conditions;
>   (b) limit or control production, markets, technical development, or investment;
>   (c) share markets or sources of supply;
>   (d) apply dissimilar conditions to equivalent transactions with other trading parties, thereby placing them at a competitive disadvantage;
>   (e) make the conclusion of contracts subject to acceptance by the other parties of supplementary obligations which, by their nature or according to commercial usage, have no connection with the subject of such contracts.
> 2. Any agreements or decisions prohibited pursuant to this Article shall be automatically void.
> 3. The provisions of paragraph 1 may, however, be declared inapplicable in the case of:—any agreement or category of agreements between undertakings,—any decision or category of decisions by associations of undertakings,—any concerted practice or category of concerted practices,

which contributes to improving the production or distribution of goods or to promoting technical or economic progress, while allowing consumers a fair share of the resulting benefit, and which does not: (a) impose on the undertakings concerned restrictions which are not indispensable to the attainment of these objectives; (b) afford such undertakings the possibility of eliminating competition in respect of a substantial part of the products in question.

In this chapter we will consider each of these sections of Article 101 individually. We will then see how they are applied in the context of activity involving actual or potential competitors—so-called horizontal relationships. In the next chapter, we will discuss the application of Article 101 in the "vertical" context, i.e., to relations with suppliers, customers or licensees.

§10.02 ARTICLE 101(1): PROHIBITED ACTIVITY

[A] Undertakings

As we have noted previously, the prohibitions of Article 101(1) are addressed to actions by "undertakings," a word which appears several times in the TFEU but is not defined. The rulings of the Commission and the ECJ establish that an undertaking may be an individual, a corporation, a limited liability company, partnership, sole proprietorship or other forms of legal entity. It may also be a body that does not have legal personality, if it carries on economic activity and is autonomous. Nonprofit or public entities performing economic functions, such as production or distribution, are also considered undertakings subject to Article 101. In the case of public bodies, therefore, it is necessary to distinguish between their conduct of economic activity, which is subject to the competition law rules, and their exercise of public authority, which is exempt from the application of these rules. Moreover, an "undertaking" must enjoy economic independence, so that an individual operating in a wage-earning capacity in a corporation or other business would not himself or herself be an undertaking. However, self-employed individuals, such as lawyers or accountants, have been held to be "undertakings" for purposes of Article 101(1).

The Commission and the ECJ have reasoned that, where companies in a group are not legally and economically autonomous and are a single economic unit under common control, they constitute a single undertaking. Therefore, agreements between a parent company and its wholly owned subsidiaries or between those subsidiaries have been held not to violate Article 101. Such agreements are merely a distribution of tasks within a single economic unit. However, where effective common control does not exist, one company's ownership of a majority interest in another company does not suffice to make the two into a single undertaking.

Similar reasoning has applied to distinguish the situations where a manufacturer enters into agreements with independent distributors of his products from those situations where a manufacturer integrates the distribution of his products by appointing commercial agents. The former agreement may be covered by Article 101(1) while the latter generally is not. There is no geographical delimitation of "undertaking" in the Treaty. Therefore, the Court of Justice has held that, in a proper case, the concept is broad enough to cover companies which are incorporated outside of the EU and have their facilities outside as well.

The question of the liability of a parent company for the competition law infringements of its subsidiaries came up before the ECJ recently in the case of *Akzo Nobel NV and Others v. European Commission*. Article 25(1)(b) of Regulation 1/2003 provides that the powers conferred on the Commission to impose fines with respect to an infringement expire after five years. Akzo Nobel's subsidiaries, which had been found to have violated Article 81 EC by participating in price fixing and market allocation agreements, had their fines for the first infringement period annulled by the GC because of that time limitation. However, Akzo Nobel, as the ultimate parent company of companies which had participated directly in the cartels, was held liable for the entire infringement period. Akzo Nobel appealed this ruling.

In its opinion of April 27, 2017, the ECJ first pointed out that it is the settled law of the Court that:

> the unlawful conduct of a subsidiary may be attributed to the parent company in particular where, although having a separate legal personality, that subsidiary does not determine independently its own conduct on the market, but essentially carries out the instructions given it by the parent company, having regard especially to the economic, organisational and legal links between those two legal entities (citing cases). That is the case because, in such a situation, the parent company and its subsidiary form a single economic unit and therefore form a single undertaking for the purposes of EU competition law.

Here, held the Court, the unlawful actions of the two wholly owned subsidiaries were attributed to the ultimate parent company who "exercised decisive influence over them, with the result that, during that infringement period, the three companies formed one and the same undertaking for the purposes of EU competition law." Moreover, the GC was "fully entitled to find" that the time bar applying to the subsidiaries did not preclude the parent from being held liable for the first infringement period.

[B]   Prohibited Agreements, Decisions, and Concerted Practices

The essence of a violation of Article 101(1) is the existence of a prohibited agreement between undertakings, or a decision by an association of undertakings, or a concerted practice between undertakings. The prohibitions apply to trade in services, as well as in products. Accordingly, agreements and concerted practices between undertakings are potentially covered, as are "decisions" by associations. An association covered by the provision is not necessarily an undertaking itself and may be an association of undertakings. In *MasterCard Inc. v. Commission*, the Court of Justice in 2014 upheld the Commission's determination that the reorganized MasterCard organization had continued to be an institutionalized form of coordination by the participating banks and thus was an association of undertakings for purposes of Article 101(1).

An "agreement" involves a meeting of the minds between the parties that they will coordinate their behavior, which may be expressed in writing or orally. The behavior of one or more of the parties may also be cited as evidence that an agreement exists. Moreover, as the Court of Justice held in the *Sandoz Prodotti Farmaceutici* case, so long as it reflects the will of the parties, an agreement (including a so-called gentlemen's agreement) can be covered by Article 101(1) even if it is not a valid and binding contract under national law. As the CFI stated in 2003, in *Marlines SA v. Commission*, "[e]ven tacit acceptance may, where the person concerned does not distance itself, be treated as acceptance of and participation in a prohibited agreement ... " (at paragraph 21).

However, whether characterized as an agreement or a concerted practice, the conduct can only be unlawful under Article 101(1) if it involves collusion between or among the parties, as distinct from independent parallel behavior. Since more than unilateral conduct must be established, there must be a showing, at least, of acquiescence by the other partners, express or implied, in the attitude taken by the one party. In *Bayer AG v. Commission*, the Commission found that the Bayer subsidiaries in France and Spain were violating Article [101(1) TFEU] imposing an export ban in the course of selling pharmaceuticals to their respective wholesalers. The Commission reasoned that, in adjusting the way in which they presented their orders to the Bayer subsidiaries, the wholesalers were showing that they understood the export ban and would comply with it. On review, the CFI ruled that the Commission had erred in finding an infringement in that "acquiescence of the wholesalers in Bayer's new policy has not been established and the Commission has therefore failed to prove the existence of an agreement."

The ECJ affirmed the CFI's decision in a 2004 decision. It noted with favor the CFI's application of "the principle that the concept of an agreement within the meaning of Article 81(1) of the Treaty centers around the existence of a concurrence of wills between at least two parties, the form in which it is manifested being unimportant so long as it constitutes the faithful expression of the parties' intention ... it is sufficient that the undertakings in question should have expressed their common intention to conduct themselves on the market in a specific way." The ECJ held that the CFI did not err in holding that the Commission had failed sufficiently to establish that Bayer had imposed an export ban, that the supply of products to wholesalers was conditional on the latter's compliance with such a ban, or that the wholesalers had the intention of joining with Bayer to prevent exports.

As previously noted, a "decision" by an association entails an expression of the will of a group to follow a particular course of conduct, whether or not the expression is binding on the group members. The concept of an "association" is broadly construed, so as to cover many forms of groups composed of entities engaged in the same business who have subjected aspects of their activities to coordination. The decision is tantamount to an agreement between those association members who approved it. While the other members may be bound by the decision so far as the association is concerned, nonapproving members who do not abide by the dictates of the decision are not considered to have violated Article 101(1).

It may be difficult to distinguish between an "agreement" and a "concerted practice" in some cases. In the *Dyestuffs* case (*Imperial Chem. Indus. v. Commission*), the Court of Justice explained that a "concerted practice" is a form of coordination between undertakings which, while lacking some of the elements of a true contract, "in practice, consciously substitutes a practical cooperation for the risk of competition." This interpretation has since been reiterated in several rulings. The evidence in the *Dyestuffs* case was that, following meetings among the ten manufacturers of dyestuffs, the companies had issued three price increases that were nearly identical in coverage, amount, and timing. The Court upheld a Commission ruling that the conduct of the ten manufacturers constituted a concerted practice. The Commission argued successfully that, although parallel behavior alone does not constitute a concerted practice, "it is nevertheless liable to constitute strong circumstantial evidence when it leads to conditions of competition which do not match the normal conditions of the market ... ."

A pattern of behavior which does not amount to an agreement may nonetheless constitute a concerted practice. More recently, in the *Asnef-Equifax* case, the ECJ stated, in the context of a credit information exchange system, that it was not necessary for purposes of applying Article 101(1) to make "a precise characterization of the nature of the cooperation ... " as an agreement, concerted practice or decision of an association of undertakings. The point is to look for a shared purpose and design.

As is the case in the context of US law with respect to the application of Section 1 of the Sherman Act, every instance of parallel behavior among competitors does not amount to unlawful coordination of action under Article 101(1). The Court of Justice stated in *Woodpulp II* and other judgments that parallel behavior can be viewed as evidence of concerted activity only where coordination is the only plausible explanation for the common conduct. For example, a company's raising its prices to equal those of a higher priced competitor can be explained innocently as reflecting the company's unilateral decision to take advantage of a market situation in which it can increase its profits. When parallel conduct can be regarded as a sign of coordination is often difficult to determine.

As we shall see in the next chapter, the Article 101 prohibitions may be applied to vertical, as well as horizontal, restraints, such as restrictions imposed by a manufacturer on its distributors. Given the EC Treaty's dedication to ensuring that there exists an economic integration of the Community, featuring the free movement of goods and services across national boundaries, much Commission enforcement attention has been devoted to vertical restraints attempting to limit distribution along national lines.

[C] May Affect Trade Between Member States

Another requisite of a violation of Article 101(1) is that the agreement, decision, or concerted practice must be of such a type that it "may affect trade between Member States" of the EU.

This language is viewed as setting down the jurisdictional standard for the application of EU competition rules, as distinct from application of national law. It raises conceptual issues similar to—but not necessarily identical to—the jurisdictional issues that we previously considered in assessing the reach of the Sherman Act and the other US antitrust laws in the international setting.

The Court of Justice held in its landmark 1966 *Consten and Grundig* decision that a restraint satisfies the jurisdictional test of Article 101(1) TFEU if it is "capable of constituting a threat, either direct or indirect, actual or potential, to freedom of trade between Member States in a manner which might harm the attainment of the objective of a single market between States." Accordingly, restrictions of potential, as well as actual, competition between undertakings are deemed covered by the prohibitions.

The ECJ has, however, also ruled that Article 101(1) can only be invoked as to agreements, concerted practices and association decisions which have an "appreciable" impact on trade between Member States (as well as on competition). The national competition authorities may be able to pursue under their laws those situations in which there is actual or potential harm to competition but where the impact involved falls short of causing or threatening appreciable injury to trade between the EC States.

The ECJ reaffirmed the applicable standard in its judgment in 2004 in the *British Sugar* case:

> for an agreement between undertakings or a concerted practice to be capable of affecting trade between Member States, it must be possible to foresee with a sufficient degree of probability and on the basis of objective factors of law or fact that it may have an influence, direct or indirect, actual or potential, on the pattern of trade between Member States, such as might prejudice the realisation of a market between the Member States ... the fact that a cartel relates only to the marketing of products in a single Member State is not sufficient to exclude the possibility that trade between Member States might be affected. Since the market concerned is susceptible to imports, the members of a national price cartel can retain their market share only if they defend themselves against foreign competition.

In 2004, the Commission published *Guidelines on the effect on trade concept contained in Articles 81 and 82 of the Treaty,* setting out the principles developed by the EU courts on the subject and offering some quantitative criteria in defining what is an "appreciable" effect on trade within the common market. These *Guidelines* state that this concept contemplates a significant level of cross-border effects within the EU as indicated by such factors as the nature of the agreement and practice, the nature of the products covered, and the position and importance of the undertakings concerned. As to this latter factor, whether an effect is appreciable can be measured both in absolute terms (turnover) and in relative terms, comparing the position of the undertaking(s) concerned to that of other players on the market (market share). It is not a prerequisite for establishing an appreciable effect that trade be reduced but simply that an appreciable change is capable of being caused in the pattern of trade between Member States.

These *Guidelines* include a negative rebuttable presumption of nonappreciability, where the aggregate market share of the parties on any relevant market within the EU affected by the agreements does not exceed 5% and the parties' turnover is below EUR 40 million. There is also a positive rebuttable presumption of appreciability which arises where the turnover thresholds cited are exceeded and the parties' market shares exceed 5%.

Under the case law, the "trade" protected encompasses not only transactions involving goods or services but also the other types of economic cross-border interactions covered by the EU Treaties including investment, movements of capital and cross-border payments. These *Guidelines* also point out that, for the purposes of establishing Community law jurisdiction, it is sufficient that an agreement or practice involving third countries or undertakings located in third countries is capable of affecting cross-border economic activity inside the Community. Thus Articles 101 and 102 potentially may be applied "irrespective of where the parties concerned are located or where the agreement has been concluded, provided that the agreement or practice is either implemented inside the Community or produces effects inside the Community."

Moreover, agreements between or among EU undertakings relating to their exports (i.e., to "third countries") can affect trade between Member States within the meaning of Article 101(1) even though the primary effects of the agreement are felt in third countries. An agreement as to exports from the Union may, for example, affect the prices or volumes of the sales made by the undertakings within the EU or affect possible resales ("re-imports") of the products from third countries into the EU.

In fact, various agreements, decisions of associations, or concerted practices which involved, in whole or in part, undertakings who were headquartered in third countries have been held in important EU court decisions to be subject to the application of Article 101(1). The Commission has brought proceedings against firms based in non-Community countries who are engaged in anticompetitive arrangements affecting the volumes or prices of imports entering the Union. In this regard, the Commission has long inclined to an "effects test" similar to that which has been applied under US antitrust law.

The Court of Justice has been more cautious on the subject and has not expressly adopted this standard. In deciding the *Dyestuffs* cartel case in 1972 (*ICI & others v. Commission*), the Court reasoned that the non-Community manufacturers involved had violated Article 101(1) TFEU because the conduct of their subsidiaries (who had no real autonomy) within the Common Market, could be imputed to the parent companies. As was recently reaffirmed in the *Akzo Nobel* decision, it is well settled in EU law that the conduct of a subsidiary may be regarded as attributable to the parent company where the subsidiary is dependent on the parent. This was an expression by the Court of what has been called "the single economic unit doctrine."

The *Woodpulp* case (*Ahlström & Others*), which the Court considered in 1988 ("*Woodpulp 1*") and again in 1993 ("*Woodpulp 2*") involved concerted pricing arrangements engaged in by Swedish, Finnish, Canadian, and US producers with respect to their sales into Europe. Some of the sales of pulp made by these producers into Europe were made through subsidiaries or branches which the companies had in Europe, but others were made directly to buyers through independent sales agents. The US producers made their sales through a Webb-Pomerene Association, which was duly authorized under US law. The Commission found all of the parties to be in violation of Article [101(1) TFEU]. The companies argued to the Court that this case presented different facts from the *Dyestuffs* case, and that jurisdiction could be found here only under the "effects" doctrine, which the Court had never accepted.

The Court, while still not embracing the "effects" doctrine, held in *Woodpulp I* that Article [101(1) TFEU] could nonetheless be applied, as the Commission had done here, because the anticompetitive activities had been "implemented" within the Community. The Court stated that, when the producers established outside of the Community engaged in price competition to win orders from purchasers in the Community, that constituted competition within the Common Market. The non-Community producers thus implemented their illegal pricing agreements within the Community, and it was "immaterial in that respect whether or not they had recourse to subsidiaries, agents, subagents, or branches within the Community in order to make their contacts with purchasers within the Community." The Court also stated that the Community's jurisdiction to apply its competition rules to such conduct was covered by the territorial principle, "as universally recognized in public international law."

The US companies had also argued that, under international law principles of "noninterference," the Community competition rules should not be applied against conduct authorized by the US under the Webb-Pomerene legislation. The Court responded that, if such a principle existed, it was not applicable because the Webb-Pomerene Act simply exempted US export cartels from the US antitrust laws and did not require the formation of the cartels. Moreover, the US authorities had raised no claim of conflict of jurisdiction when they were advised of the EU proceedings by the Commission pursuant to the OECD consultation procedures.

The territoriality issue arose in 1999 in the *Gencor Ltd.* case, this time in the context of the Community Merger Regulation. Gencor, a South African company, and Lonrho, a UK company, notified the Commission under the Merger Regulation of their proposal to acquire joint control of some South African platinum metals firms. The Commission objected to the transaction, one of its main concerns being that the concentration might result in a restriction of platinum output leading to an upward pressure on prices in the Community. On appeal to the CFI, Gencor argued that the Merger Regulation applied only to concentrations which are carried out within the Common Market, whereas this case involved activities conducted within the territory of a third country (South Africa), which had been approved by the authorities of that country.

The CFI held that the Merger Regulation applied to the transaction since Gencor and Lonrho both had sales in the Community sufficient to meet the "Community dimension" requirement of the regulation. There was no prerequisite that the undertakings in question be established in the Community or the activities carried out in the Community. The CFI considered this ruling consistent with the ECJ's ruling in *Woodpulp* because: "According to *Woodpulp*, the criterion as to the implementation of an agreement is satisfied by mere sale within the Community, irrespective of the location of the sources of supply and the production plant."

The CFI's opinion also determined that the application of Community competition law in the *Gencor* case was consistent with international law. Interestingly, it used the language reminiscent of the US effects doctrine in making this determination. The court's ruling stated that: "[a]pplication of the Regulation is justified under public international law when it is foreseeable that a proposed concentration will have an immediate and substantial effect in the Community."

As a practical matter, it is difficult to see much difference between the effects doctrine applied under US antitrust law and the implementation standard that the ECJ adopted. In the case of price fixing and the other usual cartel arrangements, the conclusions reached in applying the two standards will presumably be the same. It would be possible to postulate a hypothetical situation in which the effects doctrine would apply but there would be no "implementation" of an unlawful scheme within the Community, such as a collective total boycott of the Community market by outside producers—not a very likely scenario.

On another aspect of the territorial issue, it is well settled that an anticompetitive arrangement involving only undertakings within a single Member State and limited to the territory of that State can be held to be prohibited under Article 101(1) if it is found to affect trade between Member States. In the *Vereeniging van Cementhandelaren* decision in 1972, the Court of Justice held that pricing rules imposed by the association of cement dealers in The Netherlands on its member companies relating to the Dutch market violated Community law by having the effect of "reinforcing the compartmentalization of markets on a national basis ... ." The Court reasoned that the extent of regulation imposed by the association reduced penetration of the market.

The international law principles of comity or noninterference with other nations' important interests have been given some deference by the European Commission in special situations. The active cooperation in which the different enforcement authorities have in recent years engaged can help smooth the way for the application of these principles.

[D]   Object or Effect of Restricting Competition Within the Internal Market

The last essential element of a violation of Article 101(1) is that the agreement, decision, or concerted practice has as its "object or effect the prevention, restriction or distortion of competition within the internal market ... ." Where the object is established, the effect need not be shown. In the *Consten and Grundig* case, the Court of Justice said "[f]or the purpose of applying Article [101(1) TFEU] it is superfluous to take into account the concrete effects of an agreement once it appears that it has the object of restricting, preventing, or distorting competition."

In the *Montecatini* and *ANIC Partecipazioni* cases, in 1999, the ECJ again stated that, for the purposes of applying Article 101(1), there is no need to take account of the concrete effects of an agreement or of a concerted practice once it is established that the agreement or practice has as its object the prevention, restriction or distortion of competition. Since the prohibition in Article 101(1) is directed against anticompetitive actions that "may" affect trade between Member States, proof of actual effects is not required for an infringement of the provision. Accordingly, even where the prohibited effect has not been felt, for example where an anticompetitive agreement has been entered into but not yet implemented, it may be prohibited by reason of its unlawful objective.

More recently, in a 2014 decision in *Expedia Inc. v. Autorité de la Concurrence*, the Court of Justice stated as settled law that (1) for the purposes of applying Article 101(1) there is no need to take account of the concrete effects of an agreement once it appears that it has as its *object* the prevention, restriction or distortion of competition; (2) an agreement that may affect trade between Member States and that has an anticompetitive object constitutes, by its nature and independently of any concrete effect that it may have, an appreciable restriction on competition; and (3) an agreement of undertakings falls outside of the prohibition if it has only an insignificant effect on the market.

An effect on competition within the Common Market, for purposes of Article 101(1), need only be an effect on a substantial part of the Common Market. Moreover, in some situations, a single Member State can constitute a substantial part of the Common Market in this context, as can a significant component within the Member State, such as a port or an airport.

There is no specific "rule of reason" test in EU competition law as there is in US antitrust law. Nonetheless, where the restraint presented does not involve a hard core restriction from which an adverse competitive impact may be presumed, the analysis is very similar. The fact-finder must examine the industry market setting, as well as the purpose and likely impact of the restraint, in order to ascertain whether the restraint poses a reasonable risk of an appreciable adverse effect on Community trade.

The Commission has issued a number of Notices providing its views on the application of Article 101(1) to different types of agreements. As we will be discussing, there are also guidelines on vertical restraints and on horizontal cooperation agreements. One of the notices covers a *de minimis* doctrine which the Commission first described in a "notice on agreements of minor importance" in 1970. This rule has since been modified, most recently in June 2014. Citing the *Expedia* decision, the *Notice on agreements of minor importance which do not appreciably restrict competition under Article 101 (1) TFEU* states at the outset that the *de minimis* doctrine does not apply to "agreements which have as their object the prevention, restriction or distortion of competition within the internal market." This Notice also does not address the question of what constitutes an appreciable effect on trade between Member States. It only provides the Commission's view that agreements between undertakings do not appreciably restrict competition within the meaning of Article 101(1) if (a) the aggregate market share held by the parties does not exceed 10% "on any of the relevant markets affected by the agreement where the agreement is made between undertakings which are actual or potential competitors"; or (b) "if the market share held by each of the parties to the agreement does not exceed 15% on any of the relevant markets affected by the agreement, where the agreement is made between undertakings which are not actual or potential competitors on any of these markets ... ." Moreover, the Commission believes that agreements between small and medium sized enterprises rarely affect trade between EU countries to a significant degree.

However, even if they meet the *de minimis* thresholds provided in the Notice, the parties will not enjoy a safe harbor if the object of their agreement is to fix prices, limit output, allocate markets or customers, or otherwise create anticompetitive hard core restrictions.

[E] Relevant Markets

Market shares are, therefore, an important factor in the evaluation of the likely effect of an agreement, decision, or concerted practice. In 1997, the Commission issued a *Notice on the definition of relevant market for the purposes of Community competition law*. The Notice provides guidance on the approach taken by the Commission in applying the concepts of relevant product and geographic markets in enforcement of Community competition law.

A relevant product market comprises all those products and/or services which are regarded as interchangeable or substitutable by the consumer by reason of the products' characteristics, their prices and their intended use. A relevant geographic market comprises the area in which the firms concerned are involved in the supply of products or services and in which the conditions of competition are sufficiently homogeneous.

Before making the final relevant market determinations the Commission carries out an assessment of demand-side substitutability (customers) and supply-side substitutability (suppliers). In the first case, the question is whether customers for the product in question can switch readily to a similar product in response to a small but permanent price increase (between 5% and 10%). In the second case, the question is whether other supplies can readily switch production to the relevant products and sell them on the relevant market.

Other factors considered are recent past data, the undertaking's specific economic and statistical studies, views of customers and competitors, studies of consumer preferences, barriers, and costs in market switching, and customer and price discrimination possibilities. We will be discussing the relevant market issues concerning Articles 101(1) and 102 subsequently.

§10.03 ARTICLE 10(2) NULLITY

Provisions of agreements or decisions that are unlawful under Article 101(1) are rendered "automatically void" by Article 101(2). Whether the remainder of the agreement or decision survives is a matter of national law. Concerted practices are not covered by Article 101(2) because there is no legal transaction to which the void status could apply. The ECJ has ruled that the void status applies only when there has been a specific ruling that (a) the agreement or decision falls afoul of Article 101(1) and (b) there is no basis for an exemption under Article 101(3). The void status or nullity of an agreement or a decision means that it cannot be enforced against a party thereto in the civil courts of the Member States and also that third parties may rely on the nullity.

§10.04 THE APPLICATION OF ARTICLE 101(3)

The broad prohibitions contained in Article 101(1) are qualified by the possibility that those prohibitions may be "declared inapplicable" pursuant to Article 101(3). Article

101(3) states that this declaration applies when the agreement, decision, or concerted practice is one which:

> [1] contributes to improving the production or distribution of goods or to promoting technical or economic progress [and] [2] allows consumers a fair share of the resulting benefit, [and which does not] [3] (a) impose on the undertakings concerned restrictions which are not indispensable to the attainment of these objectives; [or] [4] (b) afford such undertakings the possibility of eliminating competition in respect of a substantial part of the products in question.

The Commission may exempt a particular type or category of agreement or practice under Article 101(3) through the issuance of a "block exemption" which has been authorized by a Council regulation. Exemptions under Article 101(3) may also be granted in individual cases.

Article 101(3) does not specify who is authorized to make the determination that its listed conditions for exemption are satisfied in a given case, providing for the inapplicability of Article 101(1). Before it was replaced by Regulation 1/2003, Regulation 17 governed this matter and stated in Article 9(1) that only the Commission was empowered to make such a declaration of inapplicability. Member State authorities were authorized to declare that a particular agreement was not covered by Article [101(1) TFEU], but they were not permitted to take the additional step of ruling that the agreement, although covered by Article [101(1) TFEU], should nevertheless be granted an individual exemption pursuant to Article [101(3) TFEU]. Under the new regime, which became effective on May 1, 2004, Article 101(3) became "directly applicable," so that the Member States competition authorities and the national courts were henceforth permitted to make the assessment contemplated by Article 101 as a whole in individual cases. Before moving on to a discussion of the current regime of decentralization, however, let us take a brief look at the notification and exemption regime which previously controlled.

[A] The Past Regime: Notification

Under Regulation 17, the parties to an agreement, decision or concerted practice were allowed to ask the Commission for a declaration that their arrangement met the standards listed in then Article 81(3) and was therefore not prohibited by then Article 81(1). The grant of an exemption was binding on the national authorities and courts of the Member States. An exemption under Article 81(3) was for a finite period of time. The procedures for obtaining an exemption under Article 81(3) were outlined in Regulation 17 and required parties seeking an individual exemption for an agreement, decision, or concerted practice to "notify" it to the Commission. After examining the circumstances, the Commission might grant the exemption request, either by adoption of a formal decision or by issuance of a "comfort letter," or it might reject the exemption, or grant it only after obtaining modification of the notified agreement. Certain kinds of agreements did not have to be notified as a result of Article 4(2) of Regulation 17, so that the Commission could grant an exemption whether or not the agreement had been notified.

The favorable effects of notification differed somewhat depending on whether the agreement notified was an "old" agreement (i.e., it existed as of March 13, 1962) or a "new" agreement (it was concluded after this date, the coming into force of Regulation 17). As to old agreements which were timely notified, the Commission was authorized to grant an amnesty for the past ("erase the dirty past"), and no fines could be imposed on the participants for activity described in the notification taking place before the Commission ruled on the exemption. New agreements did not have provisional validity when notified, but no fines for violation of Articles 81 and 82 could be imposed for actions taking place after the notification and before the Commission's ruling on the exemption application, so long as the actions fell within the limits of the activity described in the notification.

The vast flow of paper generated by this regime and the need for a detailed examination of each matter notified pursuant to it burdened the Commission and led it to concentrate its limited resources on the most important cases. In April 1999, the Commission adopted a White Paper proposing modernization of the rules implementing Articles 81 and 82 of the Treaty. The White Paper pointed out that, in a Community of fifteen Member States, the centralized system for notification established by Regulation 17 at the beginning of the 1960s, which gave the Commission the exclusive power to grant exemptions under Article 81(3), was no longer effective. The notification system no longer ensured adequate surveillance of industry practices by Community authorities, and it constituted an excessive bureaucratic constraint for firms wishing to comply with the rules.

As the White Paper put it:

> [t]he procedure set out in Regulation 17 rapidly proved too cumbersome to be followed systematically. Under the Regulation, each time a restrictive practice is notified to it, the Commission should examine the case, publish a notice in the Official Journal in the eleven languages to allow third parties to submit their comments, present a draft decision to the Advisory Committee and lastly, adopt the decision and publish it in all the languages. Given the large number of cases, the Commission quickly came to reserve this complex procedure for the most important ones, adopting on average less than ten or so formal decisions each year. More than 90 per cent of cases are closed informally, in particular by sending "comfort letters."

With the Community facing in the future a further enlargement of its membership, the Commission considered the system designed by Regulation 17 to be no longer appropriate for Europe at the start of the twenty-first century. The White Paper therefore proposed the adoption of a "directly applicable exception system" which would entail abolition of the notification system and allow the Article 81(3) exception to be applied, like Articles 81(1) and 82, by any national competition authority or court, as well as by the Commission. This decentralization proposal drew widespread debate and criticism, as well as support. In particular, business groups and other critics voiced their concerns that the needed uniformity in the interpretation and application of European competition law might not be preserved if these additional powers to apply Community law were to be conferred on fifteen or more sets of national authorities and courts. The "one stop shop" of Commission enforcement would, it was feared, be replaced by a "regulatory lottery" of diverse national viewpoints and rulings. In addition, doubts were expressed about the fundamental ability of many of the national courts to deal with the sophisticated issues of competition law presented.

Nonetheless, on September 27, 2000, the Commission issued a proposal for a Council Regulation designed to reform the Regulation 17 rules largely along the lines recommended by the Commission's White Paper by creating a directly applicable exception system. Council Regulation 1/2003 to this effect was subsequently adopted on December 16, 2002, with an effective date of May 1, 2004.

[B] The Present Regime: Decentralization

As we have noted, under the new rules, agreements, decisions or concerted practices which fall under Article 101(1) but do not meet the conditions of Article 101(3) are automatically prohibited, with no prior decision on that point needed. The Commission, national competition authorities and national courts each have the power to determine whether the Article 101(3) conditions are met in a given case. The national bodies must respect the interpretations of Article 101(3) laid down by the EU courts and also take due account of the precedents of the Commission.

Only the Commission, acting under a Council Regulation, can adopt a block exemption for a specified type of agreement, concerted practice or decision of an association of undertakings. However, as provided by Article 29 of Regulation 1/2003, the benefit of such an exemption can be withdrawn in an individual case either (1) by the Commission where it finds that there are effects incompatible with Article 101(3) of the EU Treaty, or (2) by the competition authority of a Member State where the particular agreement, concerted practice or decision has "effects which are incompatible with Article 101(3) of the Treaty in the territory of [that] Member State, or in a part thereof, which has all the characteristics of a distinct geographic market ... ."

As we observed above, there are four separate conditions which must all be met before an exemption can be granted under Article 101(3). In effect, the Commission or national body presented with the case must be able to find: (1) that the agreement, decision or concerted practice improves the production or distribution of goods or promotes technical or economic progress; and (2) if so, it allows consumers a fair share of the resulting benefit; and (3) it does not impose restrictions on the undertakings concerned unless those restrictions are indispensable to the attainment of the objectives in question; and (4) it does not afford the undertakings the possibility of eliminating competition in respect of a substantial part of the products. As the Commission states in its *Guidelines* discussed below, "[g]iven that these four conditions are cumulative it is unnecessary to examine any remaining conditions once it is found that one of the conditions of Article [101(3) TFEU] is not fulfilled." The Commission also states that "the balancing of anticompetitive and pro-competitive effects is conducted exclusively within the framework laid down by Article [101(3)]."

The basic question for the Commission's consideration is whether the adverse impact of the anticompetitive restraint included in the agreement, decision or concerted practice is outweighed by the benefits claimed by the parties to result from the arrangement. The maintenance of effective competition in the relevant industry and the emergence of public benefits as a result of the proposed activity provide the keystones of the analysis. Thus, any improvement in the production or distribution of goods or promotion of technical or economic progress brought about by the agreement, decision, or concerted practice must also be accompanied by substantial benefits for consumers. And the competitive restrictions imposed must be determined to be "indispensable" to the attainment of the improvements sought.

For an agency or court to conduct a satisfactory analysis of these complex issues in a given case requires, among other things, access to considerable economic data, the ability to assess these market data accurately, and great skill in foreseeing future market effects. There has been some cause for concern, therefore, as to whether the disparate national competition agencies and the courts of the (now twenty-eight) Member States, many of them inexperienced in economic fact-finding, can be expected soon to muster the information-gathering and analytical skills necessary to bring about successful, let alone uniform, resolutions of the Article 101(3) issues that are presented to them. The Commission, anticipating this problem, issued, on April 27, 2004, as part of its modernization package, a set of *Guidelines on the application of Article [101(3)] of the Treaty*. These *Guidelines* provide an instructive, detailed point-by-point explanation of the prohibition rule of Article 101(1) and the exception rule of Article 101(3), with references to the case law and other authority.

A decision by the Commission that an agreement falling under Article 101(1) cannot be exempted under Article 101(3) is reviewable by the GC and then, on points of law, by the ECJ. For example, in *Van den Bergh Foods Ltd.*, the Commission found that the ice cream company's supply of freezer cabinets to retailers on the condition that they be used exclusively for Van den Bergh's products restricted competition in the relevant market in Ireland in violation of then Article 85(1). The Commission also determined that the agreements containing the exclusivity clause could not be exempted under then Article 85(3) because they did not contribute to an improvement in the distribution of the product, did not allow consumers a fair share of the resulting benefit, were not indispensable to the attainment of the cited benefits and afforded the company the possibility of eliminating a substantial part of the competition in the relevant market. The Commission also found that the company violated then Article 86 by abusing its position in the relevant market.

Van den Bergh brought an action in the CFI for annulment of the Commission's decision. The court, in a 2003 decision, rejected all of the company's arguments. It first rejected the argument that there had been no violation of Article 81(1), particularly the assertion that a rule of reason test should be applied in this regard. The court stated that the existence of "such a rule in Community competition law is not accepted" and that, therefore, the procompetitive and anticompetitive aspects of a restriction may be weighed only within the specific framework of the Article 81(3) provision. In considering the Commission's ruling under Article 81(3), the court first laid out the proper standard for its review:

> It is settled case-law that the review carried out by the Court of the complex economic assessments undertaken by the Commission in the exercise of the

discretion conferred on it by [Article 81(3)] of the Treaty in relation to each of the four conditions laid down therein must be limited to ascertaining whether the procedural rules have been complied with, whether proper reasons have been provided, whether the facts have been accurately stated and whether there has been any manifest error of appraisal or misuse of powers .... It is not for the Court of First Instance to substitute its own assessment for that of the Commission.

The CFI further noted that, if any one of the four conditions laid down in Article 81(3) for an exemption was not satisfied, the exemption must be refused. The court concluded that the Commission had conducted a detailed analysis in light of the four conditions and that, since it properly found the first of the specified conditions (based on the improvement of distribution) to be unsatisfied, it was not necessary for the court "to consider whether the Commission committed a manifest error in regard to its assessment of the other conditions laid down by [the] provision." The CFI also upheld the Commission's finding that the company abused its dominant position.

Article 101(3) provides that the prohibition of Article 101(1) may be declared inapplicable in the case of any agreement, decision, concerted practice or "category" of such an arrangement. Most of the block or group exemptions are fashioned by the Commission acting under authority conferred by the Council.

The principal block exemptions issued over the years by the Commission have related to research and development agreements, specialization agreements, insurance, consortia between liner shipping companies, technology transfer agreements, and certain categories of vertical agreements. Exemption regulations are adopted for a specified period of time. Some block exemptions have been withdrawn, modified, or replaced over the years. When the Commission seeks to adopt an exemption regulation, it must publish the draft in the Official Journal of the European Communities to allow public comment, and it must consult with the Advisory Committee on Restrictive Practices and Monopolies. We will discuss the most significant block exemptions shortly.

Before a particular agreement, decision, or concerted practice has been challenged, parties may seek advice from the Commission as to whether, in the Commission's view, the conditions for exemption under Article 101(3) will be met in this case. Recital 38 of Regulation 1/2003 states that "[w]here cases give rise to genuine uncertainty because they present novel or unresolved questions for the application of these rules, individual undertakings may wish to seek informal guidance from the Commission." The national competition authorities may be also asked for such guidance. These informal guidance letters are not binding on the Commission or any of the national authorities, but they are viewed as persuasive authority should the same matter be subsequently raised.

The Commission issued on April 27, 2004, a *Notice on Informal Guidance Relating to Novel Questions Concerning Articles [101 and 102 TFEU] of the Treaty That Arise in Individual Cases*. This Notice acknowledges that "[u]ndertakings are generally well placed to assess the legality of their actions in such a way as to enable them to take an informed decision on whether to go ahead with an agreement or practice and in what form." Where cases give rise to genuine uncertainty because they present novel or unresolved questions ... "undertakings may wish to seek informal guidance from the

Commission," and "where it considers it appropriate and subject to its enforcement priorities, the Commission may provide such guidance on novel questions concerning the interpretation of Articles [101 and/or 102 TFEU] in a written statement (guidance letter)." The issuance of a guidance letter will only be considered, however, where certain conditions are met, including a lack of clarification in the existing EU legal framework (including case law) and that the matter has sufficient economic significance. The Commission will not consider purely hypothetical questions, but questions raised by a transaction which has reached a "sufficiently advanced stage" may be raised before a contemplated agreement or practice has been implemented.

[C] Comparison with US Law

As we have seen, under EU law all of the restraints of trade described by Article 101(1) are declared to be prohibited but the prohibition may nonetheless be held inapplicable if the challenged agreement, decision, or concerted practice is able to meet the specific criteria listed for an Article 101(3) exemption. The reader will recognize that the EU competition rules therefore differ from US antitrust law in that they do not isolate at the outset certain business agreements or practices as being invariably "*per se*" unlawful. Nor does the EU apply a general rule of reason in order to determine whether a questionable agreement, association decision, or concerted practice should, on balance, be deemed acceptable. Moreover, while EU competition philosophy focuses on consumer welfare expressly and directly by making it a precondition to a merchant's obtaining an exemption under Article 101(3) for a restrictive agreement or practice, US law merely assumes generally that the maintenance of effective competition among merchants will bear economic fruit which will include consumer benefits.

In practice, however, the difference between the US and EU competition law rules is not so great. As the EU Commission and the EU courts have made clear, agreements or concerted practices involving hard core restraints, such as price fixing or absolute market allocation, have always been deemed covered by the Article 101(1) prohibition with scant chance of qualifying under the Article 101(3) criteria. Moreover, the weighing process undertaken under Article 101(3), which balances the benefits claimed for a non-hard core restraint as against its anticompetitive effects, is, in principle, if not in name, reminiscent of a US rule of reason evaluation. The decentralization regime, in providing for the evaluation of all of the Article 101 issues at the same time, rather than separating out the Article 101(3) benefits assessment, further brings the EU practice into an approximation of US Sherman Act § 1 practice, in which the anticompetitive and procompetitive implications of an agreement or practice are assessed by the same enforcement authority as of one piece.

§10.05 ARTICLE 101(1) IN THE HORIZONTAL CONTEXT

Five types of agreements, decisions, or practices are specifically enumerated in Article 101(1). Even these activities are not prohibited unless they are such that they may affect trade between Member States. On the other hand, conduct which is not specifically enumerated in one of the five categories may nonetheless fall within the prohibition of Article 101(1). As we have discussed, Clause (3) of Article 101 sets out the conditions under which conduct prohibited by Clause (1) may be declared inapplicable, i.e., exempted.

The prohibitory language of Article 101(1) is broad enough to encompass both horizontal and vertical restraints. The first three prohibitions involve: (a) directly or indirectly fixing purchase or selling prices or any other trading conditions; (b) limiting or controlling production, markets, technical development, or investment; and (c) sharing of markets or sources of supply. In this chapter we will focus on the application of these prohibitions in the horizontal setting. In the next chapter, we will consider their application in vertical settings, as well as the application of the two other prohibitions of Article 101(1), which relate to: applying dissimilar conditions to equivalent transactions; and requiring acceptance of supplementary obligations, both of which involve situations which appear primarily in the vertical context.

[A] Price Fixing and Market Allocation

The Commission has consistently condemned, under Article 101(1)(a), agreements between competing undertakings to fix prices. This enforcement activity has extended along the broad swath of competitive business conduct including joint setting of prices for goods or services, the setting of minimum resale prices, the rigging of public bids, the prohibition of discounts, the fixing of minimum commissions, etc. All forms of price fixing have generally been treated as hard core violations, and the Commission has been prompted to grant exemptions in these cases only in the most rare instances. Joint fixing of rates may be permitted by the Commission in particular fields enjoying limited exemptions.

Much of the European Commission's enforcement of the prohibition against price fixing in the horizontal context has been directed against cartels—competitors engaging in agreements or concerted practices for the purpose of avoiding the competitive process through the fixing of noncompetitive price levels and/or other terms of trade within the EU or a part of it. The Commission has persistently rejected arguments offered to justify horizontal price fixing agreements, such as an industry's purported need to take measures to protect itself from facing ruinous competition. The setting of "recommended" prices has also not been allowed in the horizontal setting. Moreover, national regulation of prices has been deemed to justify price uniformity only when the national law left no discretion to the undertakings in fixing their prices.

Agreements to limit output or sales or to allocate markets are also considered to constitute hard core restrictions on competition which are seldom considered for an exemption. Allocations by competitors among themselves of sales by volume, by quota or by territory fall into this category. In particular, agreements to allocate Member State national markets outright, or by export or import limitation, or by reciprocal exclusive dealing arrangements, have all been struck down by the Commission as restrictions of competition inconsistent with the EU's commitment to the creation of a common market. Cartel market divisions accomplished by allocation of individual customers to particular suppliers have been similarly treated.

In a case which had its counterpart in the US, the Commission, in the early years of the Community, brought proceedings under then Article 85 against French, German, and Dutch companies engaged in the sale of quinine and synthetic quinidine, ingredients used for making various medicines, including those used to treat malaria. Both products were derived from cinchona bark, which was grown in various developing countries. Faced with increased supplies of the bark and lower prices for their products, the companies organized a cartel. The cartel arrangement included agreement on the prices to be paid for the bark, allocation of bark purchases, and allocation of particular domestic and export markets among the participants. The common market was supposedly excluded from the export agreement, but the companies based their common market prices in relation to their export prices, so that the pricing agreement had an impact within the Community. The Commission imposed significant fines on the participants, which fines were somewhat reduced by the Court of Justice on appeal. The Court indicated that it would not recognize the technical distinctions urged by the companies to attempt to differentiate between formal export agreements and "gentlemen's agreements." All were prohibited either as agreements or concerted practices.

The *Quinine Cartel* case was followed in 1972 by the *Dyestuffs* cartel case mentioned earlier. In the classic cartel mode, the manufacturers of dyes in the Community sought to protect their national markets from outside competition and to keep prices at desired levels. This was an oligopolistic market involving a relatively small number of substantial producers. The evidence showed similar price increases and price increase retractions which, the companies argued, reflected not concerted activity but simply the existence of price leadership. The Court of Justice did not accept the companies' explanations that the many parallel price movements had been caused by unilateral responses to market conditions and found that the companies had engaged in conduct designed to substitute for the risks of competition. This was cooperation, said the Court, "which amounts to a concerted practice prohibited by Article 85(1) of the Treaty." The concert of action among the companies was largely inferred by the Court.

We have previously mentioned the 1972 *Verineeging Cementhandelaren* case, which involved an association of Dutch cement dealers ("VCH"), whose members accounted for two-thirds of the sales of cement in Holland. VCH adopted regulations requiring mandatory resale prices for deliveries of less than 100 tons and a system of recommended prices for deliveries of 100 tons or more. The Court of Justice upheld the Commission's decision that both the fixed-price and the recommended price system violated then Article 85(1). The Court observed that:

> While a system of "fixed prices" is clearly contrary to that provision, the "recommended price" system is equally so ... Indeed the fixing of a price simply recommended affects competition by the fact that it permits all the participants to foresee with a reasonable degree of certainty what the price policy of the competitors will be.

As we noted, the Court also rejected VCH's contention that Article 85(1) did not apply because the agreement was among undertakings in only one Member State and applied only to prices within that national market. The Court stated:

> An agreement which extends to the whole of the territory of a Member State has, by its very nature, the effect of consolidating a national partitioning, thus hindering the economic interpenetration to which the Treaty is directed and ensuring a protection for the national production. More particularly, the restrictive provisions by which the members of the applicant association are bound as well as the exclusion by the association of all sales to re-sellers who are not authorized by it make more difficult the activity or the penetration on the Dutch market of producers or sellers from the other Member States.

A 1984 cartel case involved a producers' group established by the major Western companies producing zinc. They agreed on set prices for their products and also agreed not to sell zinc on the LME (*Zinc Producer Group*) but to engage in support buying of zinc on the LME. They further committed to selling zinc only to so-called bona fide customers for the latter's own consumption, forbidding any resale. The Commission determined that these actions were in violation of then Article 85(1), and it imposed substantial fines on the participants. A British company was held liable for its participation in the group even before the UK's accession to the EC Treaty, since the principal effects of the cartel activity were felt within the Community.

Several cases were brought by the Commission in the late 1980s against large chemical companies whose list prices and price increases for particular chemicals showed a marked uniformity. It was established that the leading producers met regularly and exchanged information. The producers in the *Polypropylene Case* agreed on initiatives featuring target prices for each grade and national currency effective from an agreed date. Substantial fines were imposed on the participants.

Exchanges of information by direct competitors are not necessarily barred under Article 101(1) but, particularly where the data exchanges convey precise information on pricing or other sensitive matters, they will invite antitrust scrutiny in Europe (as in the US). Such exchanges by competitors which are calculated to stabilize their market conduct have been regularly condemned by the Commission and the EU courts.

For example, in *UK Agricultural Tractor Registration Exchange*, the CFI and the Court of Justice upheld the Commission's condemnation of an agreement among UK tractor suppliers to exchange information concerning the origin of tractors sold in the UK. The ECJ emphasized that the exchange of this kind of information, by reducing or removing the degree of uncertainty of the operation of this concentrated market, was "liable to have an adverse influence on competition between manufacturers."

In its 2003 judgment in *Thyssen Stahl AG v. Commission*, the ECJ affirmed a CFI ruling which sustained a Commission decision finding that members of the European steel industry had participated in a series of agreements, decisions, and concerted practices designed to fix prices, share markets and exchange information in breach of Article 65(1) of the European Steel and Coal Community Treaty (a provision tracking then EC Treaty Article 81(1)). The ECJ declared that an information exchange system may constitute a breach of competition rules even where the relevant market is not a highly concentrated oligopolistic market insofar as the exchange system reduces market uncertainty and affects the participants' decision-making independence.

Not all industry exchanges or compilations of market data are improper, particularly if they are restricted to historical aggregate data. Thus, trade associations and other bodies may conduct programs which involve the collection of statistical information from individual companies and the dissemination of compilations of industry statistics. The aggregate figure released should not reveal detail which permits the identification of specific company prices or transactions.

Where exchanges of competitive information take place in industry meetings which coordinate future market activity, they are highly vulnerable to the enforcement agencies. In 1994 the Commission successfully challenged the *Cartonboard* cartel. Cartonboard is sold by mills to converters who manufacture folding cartons for industry use. The Commission ascertained that the European producers had been meeting for several years as the Product Group Paper Board to discuss market shares and other confidential information. The minutes of this group amply documented the concerted nature of the producers' activity, which led to regular price increases and a stability in the competitors' market shares. The Commission imposed substantial fines on the participants.

Another important case concerned a European cement cartel, implemented through information exchanges made under the auspices of the industry trade association, the *European Cement Association, Cembureau*. The scheme was designed to enable the cement producers in each nation to protect their domestic market by determining what imports would be allowed into that market. In particular, a producer task force was created to make sure that exports from Greece would not penetrate the European market. The cement producers and their trade association also arranged for the exchange of information on prices applicable in the various Member States. The Commission imposed large fines on forty-two companies and trade associations.

The decision by the Court of Justice in June 2005 in *Dansk Rørindustri*, sustaining the Commission's rulings in striking down a cartel by producers of pre-insulated pipes, outlined useful advice for companies which have been put in compromising situations:

> Where participation in [cartel] meetings has been established, it is for that undertaking to put forward evidence to establish that its participation in those meetings was without anti-competitive intention by demonstrating that it had indicated to its competitors that it was participating in those meetings in a spirit that was different from theirs ... In that regard, a party which tacitly approves of an unlawful initiative, without publicly distancing itself from its content or reporting it to the administrative authorities, effectively encourages the continuation of the infringement and compromises its discovery.

The European Commission's revised *Leniency Notice*, issued in 2006 (see the discussion earlier in this chapter), is now playing an important role in the Commission's enforcement program, as large numbers of immunity applications have flowed into the Commission since the Notice's adoption. The Commission also revised its *Fining Guidelines* in 2006 to increase the deterrent effect of fines. While Council Regulation 1/2003 limits the fines for companies to 10% of their total annual turnover, the Commission is able within this limit to base fines on up to 30% of the company's annual sales to which the infringement relates, multiplied by the number of years of participation in the infringement. Moreover, the mere fact that a company enters into a cartel can cost it an "entry fee" of at least 15% to 25% of its yearly turnover in the relevant product. Between 2010 and 2014, the Commission imposed fines in twenty-one decisions totaling EUR 7,355 billion.

We will shortly be discussing the revised *Guidelines on the applicability of Article 101 of the Treaty on the Functioning of the European Union to horizontal co-operation agreements* which the Commission issued in 2011. Among the observations made in these *Guidelines,* following up on the decision in *Expedia,* is that "[i]t is not necessary to examine the actual or potential effects of an agreement on the market once its anti-competitive object has been established."

Decisions by the Commission in recent years ordering significant fines following cartel investigations have extended to many industries, including vitamins, carbonless paper, graphite electrodes, sorbates, citric acid, sodium gluconate, lysine, French meats, plasterboard and industrial copper tubes, animal feed phosphates, and organic peroxides.

Among the largest fines imposed were those assessed for the members of the *vitamins cartel* in the amount of EUR 855 million and those imposed on the participants in the *plasterboard cartel* totaling EUR 478 million. The companies fined for cartel activity included European firms, non-European firms with European bases, and non-European firms lacking a European base. Jurisdiction over the latter was premised on the fact that these companies had "implemented" the cartel in Europe with respect to products sold directly into the EU.

In these cases, companies cooperating with the Commission received substantial reductions in their fines, with full immunity granted by the Commission in some instances. The CFI reduced the amount of the fines imposed by the Commission in some cases. Members of the vitamins cartel, involving Roche, BASF and others, were also subjected to fines in the US, Canada, Australia and South Korea.

A number of these cartels were essentially global conspiracies to fix prices and allocate markets in the major regions of the world. These were major matters on which the competition authorities shared information. US, Canadian and Japanese authorities were among those taking action against the global cartel participants, along with the European Commission. This cooperation against cartel activity has been continuous. For example, in 2003, antitrust authorities of the EU, the US, and Japan coordinated simultaneous "dawn raids" of unannounced inspections on three chemical manufacturers for price fixing, with the Japan Fair Trade Commission "raiding" the corporate headquarters and the US authorities calling on the US corporate offices.

As the above EU precedents indicate, horizontal price fixing activity in violation of the prohibition of Article 101(1) has normally involved collusion designed by competitors to keep prices above competitive levels. Nonetheless, the Article 101(1) prohibition against price fixing can also be applied to agreements fashioned by competitors to distort the competitive process by maintaining prices at very low levels. This type of conduct, known as predatory pricing, is motivated by the participants' desire to injure other competitors or to exclude potential competitors from the market.

In recent years, among the important cartel cases brought by the Commission have included the following. In 2008, fines reduced to EUR 715 million by the GC on appeal, were imposed on the *St. Gobain* companies for anticompetitive agreements and concerted practices in the car glass sector in violation of Article 101. In 2009, the Commission imposed a substantial fine which was reduced later on appeal in *E.ON Ruhrgas and E.ON AG* for sharing the French and German markets for natural gas. In 2010, large fines were imposed by the Commission on a number of air cargo carriers for fixing fuel and security surcharges. The GC annulled the Commission's decision against the eleven cartel participants that appealed, citing a procedural error. In March 2017, the Commission re-adopted the cartel decision against the air cargo carriers and imposed fines.

In 2012, the Commission imposed fines on seven undertakings for operating cartels to fix prices, share markets and customers in cathode ray tubes (CRT) in violation of Article 101, with the appeal dismissed in 2015. In 2013, the Commission fined banks for participating in cartels in the Euro interest rate derivatives industry by manipulating Euro and Yen LIBOR. In 2014, cartel participants were fined in the paper envelope, smart card, canned mushrooms, and other industries. In 2015, the Commission fined suppliers of optical disc drives, retail food packagers, and parking heater producers for their cartel infringements. In 2016, there were more fines levied on participants in the euro interest rate derivatives cartel, fines of EUR 2.93 billion for the participants in a truck producers cartel, and also fines for car parts producers and steel abrasives suppliers. In 2017, fines were levied against six car air conditioning and engine cooling supplies in a cartel settlement. In April 2017, the ECJ upheld the Commission's actions against the banana cartel, ruling that the Commission could rely on and use as evidence documents that were legally transmitted to the Commission by national authorities other than competition authorities.

There are precedents making it clear that, as the language of Article 101(1)(a) suggests, horizontal agreements or concerted practices which avoid competition with respect to trading conditions other than price levels may also be caught by the provision. Thus, the Commission has challenged collusion by competitors to fix terms of payment including credit, the length of the warranty period, the amount of interest charges, and the inclusion of delivery costs in the selling price, as well as agreements regarding the terms for providing services.

[B] Concerted Refusals to Deal (Boycotts)

As under the US law relating to "naked" anticompetitive boycotts, agreements among competitors to refuse to deal with another enterprise are condemned in the EU under Article 101(1). Often these agreements are shaped not as outright boycotts but as exclusive dealing arrangements.

For example, in the 1974 *Belgian Wallpapers* case, the wallpaper manufacturers were found by the Commission to have developed regulations detailing to whom they would sell and the terms of resale. The manufacturers refused to sell to wholesalers whose customers did not comply with the resale restrictions. The Commission stated that such a "collective boycott" is "traditionally considered one of the most serious infringements of the rules of competition" and thus "constitutes an intentional infringement of Article 85(1)." Although this decision was subsequently quashed by the ECJ on the ground that the Commission had not sufficiently established that the agreement resulted in an effect on trade between Member States, the Commission's reasoning on the boycott issue was not overruled.

In the 1983 case of *NV IAZ International Belgium v. Commission*, the association in Belgium of manufacturers and affiliated importers of washing machines and dish washers adopted a scheme whereby only the affiliated firms could receive the necessary labels attesting to the conformity of the product to established drinking water standards. The Commission successfully challenged this scheme as a violation of Article 85(1) to exclude "parallel imports" from the Belgian market.

Agreements among firms falling short of boycotts, such as concerted action requiring the imposition of discriminatory terms in dealings with particular suppliers, purchasers, or other parties, have also been condemned as infringements of Article 101(1). Note that the Article 101(1)(d) prohibition expressly refers to agreements, decisions, and concerted practices which "apply dissimilar conditions to equivalent transactions with other trading parties, thereby placing them at a competitive disadvantage."

[C] Limitation or Control of Production

Horizontal agreements to limit or otherwise control the production of the competitors are often features of a cartel. While the ultimate goal of the cartel participants' collusion is generally to raise or maintain their prices, and hence their profits, the path to that goal often entails commitments to limit or otherwise coordinate the amount of product that is available for the market. The form of the agreement may be to limit investment, or production capacity or production itself. Such agreements have been regularly struck down by the Commission and the EU courts. For example, in the 1994 *polyvinylchloride (PVC)* producers' case, fines were imposed by the Commission under Article 85(1) on parties who had engaged in a concerted practice involving the acceptance of production quotas and sales limitations.

Alleged justifications urged by the participants for what they may characterize as a "defensive" cartel, such as the claimed need to reduce their industry's significant production overcapacity, have generally not been accepted as excuses for the anticompetitive conduct. However, a test of this enforcement principle of the EU has come in the context of so-called crisis cartels. These have involved agreements by competitors in an industry to close down a portion of their productive capacity in the event that the industry capacity so far outstrips demand for the product as to threaten the viability of many in the industry. In effect acknowledging the economic and political realities in such cases, the Commission, in past years, showed some flexibility in dealing with crisis cartels, notwithstanding that the production controlling activity was clearly covered by Article 85(1) (now Article 101(1)) and that the language of the subsection (3) exempting provisions could not be readily applied to immunize this conduct. In the early years of the Treaty, when the iron and steel, glass, cement and other European industries were suffering through significant recessions, the Commission dispensed with or reduced fines that could have been imposed on the firms in those industries on the basis of the agreements and concerted practices they had engaged in to deal with their "crises." The Commission also imposed mandatory production quotas as to some products under the ECSC Treaty.

The Commission has given guidance in its Annual Reports as to the conditions that will have to be met by an industry attempting to restructure itself in an effort to rectify its structural overcapacity. Under this policy, agreed reductions in capacity and output would qualify for an exemption under Article 101(3) only if: (a) the reduction in overcapacity is permanent and irreversible and will enable the existing participants in the industry to compete at that lower level of capacity; (b) the reduction in capacity will facilitate moves to specialization by the companies affected; and (c) the reduction in capacity is timed in such a way as to minimize the social dislocation caused by the resulting loss of employment.

This policy has been reflected in various Commission decisions allowing agreements which met this standard. One such decision involved the companies which manufactured synthetic fibers, who had been struggling for some time with an industry production capacity that greatly exceeded the demand for the products. In its 1985 *Synthetic Fibres* decision, the Commission noted that market forces had failed to bring about the reduction in overcapacity necessary to achieve an effective competitive structure and exempted an agreement whereby each company committed itself to reducing its capacity by a specified date. Increases of capacity after 1985 were permitted by the commitments and there were no restraints on the participants' levels of production from the reduced capacity.

In the *Dutch Bricks (Stichting Baksteen)* case, the Commission considered a series of agreements among the Dutch brick manufacturers which was intended to "rationalize" production by closing some capacity, fixing production quotas and acquiring production facilities with a view to eliminating them. The Commission opposed this scheme, and the producers subsequently notified a new plan to dismantle what they considered surplus production capacity. In a 1994 decision, the Commission found that this plan would restrict competition in the common market within the meaning of Article 85(1), but it also found that the "restructuring" of the Dutch brick industry proposed would restore the health of the industry as regards its overcapacity, providing the consumer and other benefits required for exemption under Article 85(3). The Commission limited the period of exemption for this activity to a five year window of time.

Accordingly, some forms of cooperation by actual or potential competitors in preproduction activity or even in production activity are not necessarily anticompetitive and may, in fact, enhance competition and efficiency within an industry. The Commission has continued to recognize this principle, particularly through its exemption rulings and decisions under the standards of Article 81(3). The Commission's *Guidelines on Horizontal Cooperation Agreements*, discussed below with reference to joint purchasing, also address production cooperation agreements, including specialization agreements. Indeed, there is a distinct block exemption devoted to specialization agreements.

§10.06 PERMISSIBLE COOPERATION AMONG COMPETITORS

Where hard core practices such as price fixing, market allocation, and boycotts are not involved, cooperative activities on the part of competitors may, depending on the circumstances, be deemed to be fully acceptable, indeed beneficial, under the EU competition laws. The Commission's *Guidelines on Horizontal Cooperation Agreements* which were issued in 2011, replacing the version published in 2001, address these situations. In addition, guidance applicable to particular industries and situations has been implemented by the Commission largely through sector-specific rules and block exemptions.

[A] The Guidelines on Horizontal Cooperation Agreements

The *Guidelines on Horizontal Cooperation Agreements* state that they relate to cooperation agreements between actual or potential competitors. The Commission recognizes that horizontal cooperation agreements can lead to substantial economic benefits but affirms that any anticompetitive effects from them must be addressed within the framework of Article 101 TFEU. The *Guidelines* apply to six forms of agreements: information exchange, research and development (R & D), joint production, purchasing, commercialization and standardization. In the case of R & D agreements, reference should also be made to the block exemption, discussed below.

If there is a question about how to categorize an agreement for purposes of analysis, that is accomplished with reference to the cooperation agreement's "centre of gravity." Moreover, the principles in the *Guidelines* are based on the factual assumption that trade between Member States is affected by the agreement in question. Agreements are analyzed in two stages: (1) whether the agreement has as its object or effect the restriction of competition in the sense of Article 101(1) and, if so, (2) whether there are procompetitive effects pursuant to Article 101 (3). There may be concern about anticompetitive effects arising in the marketplace with respect to price, to output, or to product quality, variety or innovation.

The parties' market power is an important focus in the analysis of the competitive effects of a cooperative activity. The *Guidelines* explain that "[m]arket power is the ability to profitably maintain prices above competitive levels for a period of time or to profitably maintain output in terms of product quantities, product quality and variety or innovation below competitive levels for a period of time." Where the parties have a low combined market share, their agreements are unlikely to create restive effects on competition. Some "safe harbors" in the form of low market shares are provided in this regard in various chapters of the *Guidelines*. We will be referring again to these *Guidelines*.

[1] Joint Purchasing

The prohibition of Article 101(1) includes a reference to the direct or indirect fixing of "purchase" prices. This raises the question of the extent to which agreements among competitors regarding their purchasing practices, including possible joint purchasing, are deemed caught by Article 101(1) as anticompetitive and not redeemed by the exemption of Article 101(3). As occurred in the cases of the aluminum and zinc cartels challenged by the Commission in the 1980s, anticompetitive schemes designed to fix sales prices sometimes also included commitments by the companies to coordinate their purchasing activities. This feature of the conspiracies was intended to enable the cartel participants to control the availability and price of the product at its source in the marketplace. Coordination of purchasing in the context of such cartel activity has been viewed as blatantly anticompetitive and condemned by the Commission and the EU courts.

In addition, coordinated or collective purchasing by significant competitors can also prove anticompetitive when the companies use their collective market power to coerce the suppliers into offering uncompetitive low prices, exclude other competitors unfairly from the joint activity, or utilize the collective activity to exchange information for the purpose of collusion.

The fact that coordinated purchasing arrangements have been improperly utilized by cartels does not mean, however, that such arrangements are always prohibited under Article 101(1). Coordinated purchasing agreements among competitors, including joint purchasing of items on an aggregate basis, may be wholly legitimate depending on the circumstances. As we discussed in the context of the US antitrust law rules applicable to joint purchasing, it is considered that collective buying activities can have beneficial effects for consumers, as well as for the participants, in permitting economies of scale and other efficiencies. This same viewpoint is reflected in EU competition law. In the 1994 *Gottrup-Klim* case, the Court of Justice observed that the pooling of purchases through a cooperative association could enhance competition by, among other things, allowing buyers to offset the market power of large producers.

In determining whether Article 101(1) is applicable to a joint buying agreement and, if so, whether an exemption under Article 101(3) can be granted, the Commission has taken into account the aggregate market share of the participating competitors, whether they are free to make their purchases individually, the effect of the activity on nonparticipating competitors, and the nature of any ancillary agreements among competitors.

In the 1968 *SOCEMAS* case, the Commission granted a negative clearance, signifying that Article 85(1) was inapplicable, to collective purchasing by seventy-seven food stores established in France. The Commission took into account that the combined market shares for the items purchased were not large, that the purpose of the agreement was not anticompetitive, and that the participants remained free to purchase from abroad independently. In the 1980 *National Sulphuric Acid Association* case, the Commission granted an exemption permitting the primary manufacturers of sulphuric acid in the UK to pool their purchasing of sulphur. One justification for the joint purchasing was that the sulphuric acid manufacturers were dealing with a sulphur industry that was very concentrated. The grant of the exemption was conditioned on the member of the pool remaining free to purchase up to 75% of their needs from outside the pool and to resell to nonmembers the sulphur obtained from the pool.

Chapter 5 of the 2011 *Guidelines on Horizontal Cooperation Agreements* addresses joint purchasing agreements. Three possible concerns are identified with respect to these agreements: (1) if the purchasers have a significant degree of market power in their *selling* market, they may be unwilling to pass on to consumers the benefits of any lower prices; (2) if the parties have significant market power in their *purchasing* market, they may force their suppliers to reduce the range or quality of the products they produce; and (3) powerful buyers may be able to shut out competing purchasers by cutting of or limiting their access to sellers. The *Guidelines* also state that, in most cases, anticompetitive market power is unlikely to exist if the parties have a combined market share not exceeding 15% on the purchasing market as well as a combined market share not exceeding 15% on the selling market.

The Commission has granted approval to business-to-business (B2B) marketplace joint ventures, such as the "Covisint" endeavor formed by the major auto manufacturers in 2001. The car makers and auto parts suppliers engaged in a purchaser-managed electronic marketplace designed to reduce costs and improve efficiency in their purchases in the supply chain. In approving the project, the Commission noted that participation in Covisint would be open to all firms in the industry on a nondiscriminatory basis.

[2] Standardization Agreements

As we discussed previously in the context of US antitrust law, joint efforts by competitors in the development and promulgation of technical or quality standards for their industry's products are wholly legitimate when carried out under proper legal safeguards and oversight. The assured interchangeability of products reduces costs, enhances competition and facilitates consumer use and choice. In Europe, as in the US, the competition law recognizes these benefits of standardization. In both systems, the obverse proposition is also acknowledged: that standardization activities are capable of injuring competition by excluding legitimate products and competitors and by reducing consumer choices. An approach must therefore be utilized which encourages the development of fair standards through fair procedures, while preventing or striking down the abuses to which the standardization process is susceptible.

In 1971, the EC Council adopted Regulation 2821/71 empowering the Commission to grant group exemptions to agreements applicable to "standards or types," as well as to specialization and R & D agreements. In addition, Article 4.2(3) of Regulation 17 exempted from notification agreements having as their sole object the development or uniform application of standards or types, although actual exemption would depend on whether the Article 85(3) conditions were met by a particular endeavor. However, the Commission did not address the issue broadly until the issuance in 2001 of the

Guidelines on Horizontal Cooperation Agreements, which included a section on standardization agreements. The subject is again treated in Chapter 7 of the 2011 replacement version of the *Guidelines*, with added sophistication.

Paragraphs 277–291 of the *Guidelines* explain that standard setting activities that comply with four basic principles will normally not be violative of Article 101(1). These principles are: (1) participation in the standard setting must be unrestricted; (2) the procedure for adopting the standard must be transparent; (3) there is no obligation to comply with the standard; and (4) the standard can be effectively accessed on fair, reasonable and non-discriminatory ("FRAND") terms. If any of these principles is not met, the standards program is to be evaluated on an effects basis. A detailed assessment of the situation must be made where the widespread use of standard terms limits product variety and innovation or where the use of standard terms is a decisive part of the transaction with the customer.

The *Guidelines* also focus on standards involving "IP rights". In particular, participants wishing to have involved their IP rights included in a standard should provide an irrevocable commitment in writing to offer to license the IP rights to all third parties on fair, reasonable and nondiscriminatory terms (i.e., a "FRAND commitment").

A number of cases involving the Commission and the EU courts have concerned standard setting scenarios. One recent proceeding, *EMC Development v. Commission*, involved a claim by a cement producer that a standard for the European cement market had been discriminatorily designed to favor the major existing producers. The complainant's product did not fit within the standards that had been developed. The GC upheld the Commission's conclusion that the standard in question, which was nonbinding, had been adopted through an open, nondiscriminatory and transparent process. The further appeal to the ECJ was dismissed.

The requirement that, in certain cases, IP rights owners must negotiate FRAND commitments with would-be licensees has prompted a number of disputes, including some in the so-called smartphone patent wars. In the case of *Motorola – Enforcement of GPRS standard essential patents*, Motorola Mobility had committed to license on FRAND terms two patents declared by it to be essential to telecommunication standards. Apple Inc., seeking a license, proposed to submit the dispute about the FRAND terms to a national court for a binding decision. Motorola countered by seeking an injunction against Apple in a German court. The European Commission adopted a decision finding that this action by Motorola constituted an abuse of a dominant position in violation of Article 102 TFEU since Motorola had willingly given a FRAND commitment to license the patents and Apple had indicated a willingness to enter into a licensing agreement on FRAND terms.

At the same time, the Commission engaged Samsung in an enforcement proceeding in *Samsung – Enforcement of UMTS standard essential patents*, also concerning that company's commitment to license on FRAND terms certain of its standard essential patents covering mobile telecommunications. Samsung sought injunctions against Apple from national courts on the basis of its patents, notwithstanding that the Commission considered Apple to be "not unwilling" to enter into a license agreement on FRAND terms. Thus the Commission preliminarily concluded that Samsung's seeking of the court injunctions constituted an abuse of a dominant position (as in *Motorola*). However, Samsung offered the Commission a commitment of a licensing framework whereby it would agree to negotiate on FRAND terms for twelve months and, if no licensing agreement was reached, the matter would be submitted to arbitration or court adjudication for decision. After comments were submitted by interested parties, Samsung made final commitments which were accepted by the Commission as satisfactory.

The 2001 *Guidelines on Horizontal Cooperation Agreements* included a separate chapter on "environmental agreements," i.e., endeavors through which competitors jointly undertake to achieve pollution abatement or some other environmentally friendly goal. The 2011 *Guidelines* have no such separate chapter, but Chapter 7 of the new *Guidelines* relating to standardization agreements also refers to environmental agreements. Paragraph 329 of Chapter 7, for example, offers the case of an industry whose members agree to replace their existing product lines with products which are more environmentally friendly (e.g., energy efficient) but are also more expensive. These improved products are, in fact, more cost efficient for the purchasers of the products. After analysis, the example concludes that the exempting criteria of Article 101(3) would appear to be fulfilled.

[3] Commercialization Agreements: Joint Marketing

Chapter 6 of the *Guidelines on Horizontal Cooperation Agreements* addresses "commercialization agreements." Such an agreement involves cooperation between competitors in the selling, distribution or promotion of their products. Distribution agreements which do not involve actual or potential competitors are covered by the Block Exemption Regulation on Vertical Restraints and the *Guidelines on Vertical Restraints* (discussed in our next chapter). The *Guidelines on Horizontal Cooperation Agreements* observe that the principal concern under Article 101 about joint selling by competitors is the price fixing that results from the competitors' coordination of their pricing policies. Market partitioning by the parties is another major concern.

If Article 101(1) is deemed applicable, any efficiencies arising from the agreement will be analyzed under Article 101(3). Price fixing will generally not be considered justifiable. Paragraph 240 grants a safe harbor for commercialization agreements. It provides that it is unlikely that market power exists if the parties to the agreement have a combined market share not exceeding 15%. In any event, if the parties' combined market share does not exceed 15%, it is likely that the conditions of Article 101(3) are fulfilled. The Commission has authorized joint selling arrangements in a number of situations on the basis that the Article 101(3) criteria were fulfilled.

[4] Joint Production

Chapter 4 of the *Guidelines on Horizontal Cooperation Agreements* addresses joint production agreements. These can vary in form and scope, including coproduction as a joint venture or by subcontracting the production to one of the parties. However, "vertical" subcontracting arrangements, where the undertakings operate at different levels of the market are not covered by these *Guidelines*. The *Guidelines* note a number of concerns about joint production agreements. In particular, they may lead to a direct limitation of competition between the parties as to output levels, prices or other matters, even if they market the product independently. In addition, joint production can be used to raise the costs of competitors ultimately forcing them out of the market.

However, if the production agreement enables the parties to enter a market that they would not otherwise have been able to enter, the agreement will not be viewed as restricting competition. The market power of the parties is also the key to whether their cooperation will be deemed to restrict competition. Paragraph 169 of the *Guidelines* points out that joint production agreements may be covered by the Specialisation Block Exemption if they are concluded between parties with a combined market share not exceeding 20% in the relevant market. Moreover, it is unlikely that market power exists if the parties to the agreement have a combined market share not exceeding 20%.

[5] Information Exchange

Chapter 2 of the *Guidelines on Horizontal Cooperation Agreements* addresses exchanges of information in the marketplace. As we have seen, where an information exchange concerns prices or territories or other features of competition and takes place in the context of cartel activity among competitors, it will be condemned as part and parcel of a violation of Article 101(1) TFEU. However, more innocent exchanges of information among industry members are often beneficial in enabling efficiencies and other valuable byproducts of the gained knowledge.

The *Guidelines* warn that "[i]nformation exchanges may generate various types of efficiency gains, but may also lead to restrictions of competition in particular in situations where it is liable to enable undertakings to be aware of market strategies of their competitors." Thus, seemingly simple steps like an undertaking disclosing strategic information to a competitor or attending a meeting where a competitor discloses its pricing plan in the presence of its competitors can have serious consequences under Article 101.

[B] The Block Exemptions

We spoke above of the "block exemptions" adopted by the Commission which provide that Article 101(1) is inapplicable to certain categories of agreements. As the Commission explains in paragraph 2 of the *Guidelines on the application of [Article 101(3) TFEU]*:

> All existing block exemption regulations remain in force and agreements covered by block exemption regulations are legally valid and enforceable even if they are restrictive of competition within the meaning of Article [101 (1) (3)]. Such agreements can only be prohibited for the future and only upon formal withdrawal of the block exemption by the Commission or a national competition authority

(footnote omitted). Block exempted agreements cannot be held invalid by national courts in the context of private litigation.

Article 29 of Regulation 1/2003 authorizes the Commission and NCAs to withdraw the benefit of a block exemption in certain individual cases and situations.

The principal block exemptions presently in force are discussed below.

[1] Research and Development Agreements

On December 14, 2010 the Commission adopted Regulation 1217/2010, a block exemption regulation applicable to research and development agreements ("R & D"), replacing Regulation 2659/2000 which was expiring. The new regulation will expire on December 31, 2022. Reference on R & D issues should also be made to Chapter 3 of the *Guidelines on Horizontal Cooperation Agreements* which deals with agreements which have R & D agreements as their "centre of gravity." The Commission's *Technology Transfer Guidelines*, which we will be discussing later, may also be relevant.

The Commission's attitude toward R & D agreements is essentially benevolent because such agreements normally focus on developing new products rather than on restricting trade. The second introductory clause to Regulation 1217/2010 recites that: "Article 179(2) of the [TFEU] calls upon the Union to encourage undertakings, including small and medium sized undertakings, in their research and technological development activities of high quality, and to support their efforts to cooperate with one another. This Regulation is intended to facilitate research and development while at the same time effectively protecting competition." The benefit of the exemption is intended to be limited to those agreements as to which it can be assumed that they satisfy the conditions of Article 101(3) TFEU.

Joint R & D can take different forms such as manufacture, the exploitation of IP rights that substantially contribute to technical or economic progress, or the marketing of new products. The parties involved should stipulate in the R & D agreements that they will all have full access to the final results of the joint R & D, including any arising IP rights and know-how, for the purposes of further R & D and exploitation. Where the parties are not competing undertakings, the exemption from Article 101(1) will apply for the duration of the R & D. Where the results are jointly exploited, the exemption will continue to apply for seven years from the time the contract products or contract technologies are first put on the market within the internal market. If, however, two or more of the parties are competitors, the length of the exemption will depend on the size of the combined market shares of the parties involved.

The parties should take into account that the block exemption will cease to apply if the parties' combined share of the market for the products, services or technologies arising out of the joint R & D becomes too great, although a period will be allowed for the market shares to stabilize after the commencement of joint exploitation.

The *Guidelines* address market definition which can be challenging in the R & D context. Where an R & D agreement relates to improvement of existing products, they and their close substitutes comprise the relevant market. If new products are contemplated, they may form a new relevant market. However, where the focus is on innovation, it may not be possible to frame the market in terms of existing product or technology markets. The *Guidelines* point out that, while most R & D agreements will not cause concerns about anticompetitiveness, anticompetitive effects caught by Article 101(1) may occur where the arrangement reduces or slows down innovation, where there are brought about restrictions in markets outside of the scope of the R & D agreement, or where at least one party has significant market power to bring about foreclosure of access to the market.

[2] Specialization Agreements

A "specialization" agreement is one in which two or more enterprises (i.e., undertakings) agree on a division of effort with respect to the production and/or sale of various products. This relationship often involves each party agreeing to supply the other with the products which the latter does not manufacture, enabling both to sell the full range of products in designated territories. Such agreements often include reciprocal supply clauses, promises not to compete with one another's "specialties" or commitments not to enter into similar agreements with other enterprises.

On December 14, 2010, the Commission adopted Regulation 1218/2010, a block exemption for specialization agreements which will expire on December 31, 2022. This Regulation replaced the expiring Regulation 2658/2000. Paragraph (3) of the introduction states that: "[b]elow a certain level of market power it can in general be presumed, for the application of [Article 101(3) TFEU], that the positive effects of specialisation agreements will outweigh any negative effects on competition." It is also stated that agreements for specialization in production are most likely to contribute to improving the production or distribution of goods if the parties have complementary skills, assets or activities.

"Specialisation agreements" are defined in Article 1 of the Regulation to include a "unilateral specialisation agreement," a "reciprocal specialisation agreement" or a "joint production agreement." A "unilateral specialisation agreement" is one "between two parties which are active on the same product market by virtue of which one party agrees to fully or partly cease production of certain products or to refrain from producing those products and to purchase them from the other party, who agrees to produce and supply the products." A "reciprocal specialisation agreement" is one "between two or more parties which are active on the same product market, by virtue of which two or more parties on a reciprocal basis agree to fully or partly cease or refrain from producing certain but different products and to purchase these products from the other parties, who agree to produce and supply them." A "joint production agreement" is one "by virtue of which two or more parties agree to produce certain products jointly." The block exemption declares that, pursuant to Article 101(3), Article 101(1) TFEU shall not apply to specialization agreements as provided.

The exemption granted is conditional on the combined market share of the parties not exceeding 20% on any relevant market. Moreover, the exemption provided does not apply where the object of the agreement is "(a) the fixing of prices when selling the products to third parties with the exception of the fixing of prices charged to immediate customers in combination in the context of joint distribution; (b) the limitation of output or sales with the exception of: (i) provisions on the agreed amount of products in the context of unilateral or reciprocal specialisation agreements or the setting of the capacity and production volume in the context of a joint production agreement; and (ii) the setting of sales targets in the context of joint distribution; (c) the allocation of markets or customers."

Of course, as the block exemption recognizes, divisions of activities by undertakings are not always innocent. For example, the previously discussed *Quinine Cartel* case and the *Rolled Zinc* case in 1982 both involved Commission challenges to allocations of production activities among the participants. In the *Quinine Cartel* case, the ECJ stated that, since they were entered into among significant competitors, the agreements "clearly have as their object the restriction of competition within the Common Market and are capable of affecting trade between Member States." On the other hand, in the 1973 *Prym-Beka* case, where the parties were not significant competitors, the Commission granted an individual exemption where Prym agreed to give up the manufacture of needles for sewing machines and transferred its needle manufacturing equipment to a much smaller company, Beka, on the condition that Beka agreed to supply all of Prym's needle requirements.

The 2001 *Guidelines on Horizontal Cooperation Agreements* included a separate chapter on "environmental agreements," i.e., endeavors through which competitors jointly undertake to achieve pollution abatement or some other environmentally friendly goal. The 2011 *Guidelines* have no such separate chapter, but Chapter 7 of the new *Guidelines* relating to standardization agreements also refers to environmental agreements. Paragraph 329 of Chapter 7, for example, suggests the case of an industry whose members agree to replace their existing product line with products which are more environmentally friendly (e.g., energy efficient) but are also more expensive. These improved products are also more cost efficient for the purchasers of the product. After analysis, the example concludes that the exempting criteria of Article 101(3) would appear to be fulfilled.

[3]   Insurance

A new block exemption for the insurance industry was adopted by the Commission in 2010 through Regulation 267/2010. The Commission also published contemporaneously a *Communication on the application of Article 101 (3) of the TFEU to certain categories of agreements, decisions, and concerted practices in the insurance sector.* Regulation 267/2010 ("IBER") granted block exemption to agreements in the insurance sector for the joint conduct of studies on mortality tables and on other risk issues, as well as for setting up pools of insurance or reinsurance for certain common coverage. Regulation 267/2010 expired on March 31, 2017 and was not renewed. The types of cooperation that it covered thus fell under the general rules of the competition law.

The block exemptions relating to vertical agreements generally (Regulation 330/2010), to vertical agreements relating to the motor vehicle aftermarket (Regulation

461/2010), and to technology transfer agreements (Regulation 316/2014) are discussed in the next chapter.

[4] Banking

The Commission has addressed a number of horizontal cooperation agreements in the banking sector. Some are related to issues of facilitating cross-border or credit card transactions. In 2002, for example, the Commission decided that Visa Internationals' "multilateral interchange fee" agreed upon between banks met the requirements of Article 101(3). However, in its 2007 decision in *MasterCard* the Commission concluded that Master Card's interchange fee system restricted competition in violation of Article 101(1) while not meeting the standard of Article 101(3). This ruling was upheld by the GC. The Commission has published a *Notice on Cross-border Credit Transfer*s which discusses the compatibility of cross-border credit transfers with the EU competition rules.

[5] Agriculture

Title III of the TFEU sets out special provisions for agriculture and fisheries, providing for the Union to define and implement a common policy in these two areas. Article 42 declares that the "rules on competition shall apply to production of and trade in agricultural products only to the extent determined by the European Parliament and the Council ... ." The detailed Common Agricultural Policy ("CAP") is an outgrowth of the agreed policies, including import levies and quotas. Commodity prices are maintained and subsidies are paid to farmers.

[C] Cooperation on Exports

Agreements among firms within the EU to cooperate on matters involving their exports from Europe which restrict the terms of their competition may or may not fall afoul of Article 101(1). If the cooperation affects only exports to nonmember countries so that it does not affect trade between Member States either directly or indirectly, it will not infringe Article 101(1). In some instances, cooperation affecting trade between Member States may provide benefits so as to qualify it for exemption under Article 101(3). However, the Commission has determined in a number of cases of export cooperation that the agreements had the effect of preventing or limiting sales from a Member State to one or more other Member States and thus infringed Article 101(1).

In the 2006 case involving *General Motors BV*, the Commission determined that an auto manufacturer's use of dealership bonus contracts which excluded export sales from the system had a restrictive objective from the viewpoint of Article [101 TFEU]. The Commission ruled that the export ban "had as its object to obstruct the cross-border trade in cars between Dutch dealers and dealers in other Member States, and to partition the different markets." This decision was upheld by the CFI and the ECJ. The Court of Justice pointed out that the "case-law shows that an agreement concerning distribution has a restrictive object for the purposes of Article [101 TFEU] if it clearly manifests the will to treat export sales less favorably than national sales and thus leads to a partitioning of the market in question."

In the 1975 *Suiker Unie (Sugar Cartel)* case, it was established that the parties' cooperation on sugar exports to the world markets had the improper effect of limiting competition among them within Europe by reducing sugar supplies available for the common market.

[D] Case Law Involving Joint Ventures

There have been a great many EU cases involving joint ventures, both under the standards of Article 101 and under the Merger Regulation, and, for purposes of this Primer, we will be able only to go over a few highlight points and cases. So-called full function joint ventures, featuring entities which are separate and have operational autonomy are not evaluated under Article 101 but under the merger control rules. As we have seen, the *Guidelines on Horizontal Cooperation Agreements* provide analysis as to the competition law aspects of joint venturing agreements in the areas of research and development, production, purchasing, information exchange, commercialization and standardization. The block exemptions for R & D and specialization agreements may also be relevant.

One important early case involving a joint venture was the *DeLaval/Stork* decision in 1977. DeLaval, a US company, and Stork, a Dutch company, both manufactured turbines. They formed a joint venture to manufacture and sell turbines, compressors, and other equipment. The joint venture made significant sales in the Community, while Stork and DeLaval continued to sell products not covered by the joint venture in the Community. The Commission granted and later renewed an exemption under Article 85(3) on the reasoning that the venture made it easier for DeLaval to penetrate European markets and also allowed Stork to develop its business more quickly. There was significant competition in the joint venture's product lines in Europe, and the Commission considered that neither DeLaval nor Stork could have entered those markets as effectively without sharing the risk and the investment.

Similarly, in the 1977 *Vacuum Interrupters* case, the Commission granted an exemption to a joint venture by two British electrical equipment manufacturers which sought to develop a new circuit breaker. The Commission determined that neither manufacturer would have undertaken alone the technical and financial demands presented by the endeavor.

Where a joint venture of this sort has been considered valid, the Commission has also approved, usually for a limited duration, the maintenance of ancillary restrictions limiting the freedom of action of the undertakings concerned. These restrictions have related to such matters as exclusive distribution, supply and purchase obligations, and noncompetition clauses. For example, where the parents have established the joint venture to open up a new type of production, the Commission has approved ancillary obligations limiting the territory or field of technical application of the joint venture.

In the 1986 *Optical Fibers* case, Corning Glass Works, a US company specializing in glass technology, entered into parallel joint ventures with a UK and a German cable manufacturer for the production and sale of optical fibers. The Commission did not consider that Corning and the European companies were actual or potential competitors. Nonetheless it was concerned that the "network effect" of the parallel joint ventures involving Corning could lead to a reduction of competition down the road, implicating Article 85(1). The Commission granted an exemption under Article 85(3) because the creation of the joint venture was indispensable to attainment of the worthwhile high-tech objectives, but it also required amendments to the joint ventures to reduce the risks presented.

In a particularly controversial case in 1992 the Commission granted an exemption to a joint venture by Ford and Volkswagen *(Ford/Volkswagen)* to develop and manufacture a multi-purpose passenger vehicle ("MPV") in Portugal. The new facility was a 50/50 joint venture, with Ford taking the lead in manufacture and plant operation, while Volkswagen did the product development. The Commission rejected the argument made by rival auto manufacturers that both parent companies were capable of economically developing their own MPVs. The Commission concluded that, for at least a limited period of years, the joint effort was indispensable for serving effectively the needs of European consumers in a relatively new product sector.

However, the Commission reached the contrary conclusion that same year in the context of the *Astra* case. In that case, SES, a Luxembourg company which owned the Astra satellite, had entered into a joint venture agreement with British Telecom ("BT") under which operators of television programs originating in the UK would be "up-linked" to the Astra satellite. The Commission determined that BT was in a position to offer space on other satellites, while SES offered uplinking signals which could compete with those of BT. Thus, the cooperation agreement unnecessarily restricted competition between the parties in both respects.

In 1994, Shell Petroleum NV and Montedison Nederland NV *(Shell/Montecatini)* notified under the Merger Regulation the establishment of a proposed joint venture company in the polyolefins chemicals sector. The Commission determined that the transaction, as notified, would eliminate the competition between the two main technologies licensed for the production of polypropylene, leading to the creation of a dominant position in the polypropylene technology product market. The US Federal Trade Commission also was concerned that the cooperation would lead to the establishment of a monopoly position in the technology for the manufacture of polypropylene. The European Commission approved the cooperation subject to commitments excluding activities in the polypropylene field from the venture.

Five years later, General Electric and Pratt & Whitney applied to the Commission for a negative clearance or an exemption to enable them to form a 50/50 joint venture to develop, manufacture, sell and support a new jet engine intended for future, very large commercial aircraft. The Commission found that, although the cooperative effort might be more efficient economically, it would be feasible for the two large parent companies involved to develop the product independently, given that both were active in jet engine production already. Moreover, permitting the joint venture would reduce the number of potential suppliers of these products from three (the two parties plus

Rolls Royce) to two (the joint venture and Rolls Royce). While this meant that the proposal was caught by Article 81(1), the Commission also concluded that an exemption under Article 81(3) was justified. Permitting the cooperation would lead to the development of a new, technologically advanced engine which was less expensive and with lower emissions at lower cost, within a shorter time. A number of conditions were attached to the exemption: the parent companies were to stay at arm's length from the joint venture, the latter was to be strictly limited to development and sale of the particular engines specified, and servicing manuals on the new engine were to be made available to third parties. The exemption granted was for a period of fifteen years, this being the period in which the investment might be recouped by the parties.

The Commission has recognized that, in some industries, there is a clear need for a degree of competitor cooperation, with public benefits resulting therefrom. We mentioned above the "Covisint" joint purchasing venture of the auto manufacturers. In addition, the Commission has cleared under the European competition rules as applied to the aviation sector a number of alliances between Europe's national airlines on the ground that some consolidation is a necessity for the companies' survival. While, for years, the Commission was limited to enforcing competition rules in the air transport sector to services between EU airports, Council Regulation 411/2004 now provides that the Commission's powers under Regulation 1/2003 apply to all routes. Council Regulation 487/2009 gives the Commission the authority to exempt certain air transport practices, but there are at present no block exemptions relating to air transport.

In 2003, the Commission approved an alliance between BA and Iberia, noting that the parties' networks were largely complementary but also making sure that passengers would have sufficient competitive alternatives on the routes which the two airlines dominated. Similarly, in 2004 the Commission approved an alliance between Air France and Alitalia, determining that, although the two airlines' networks were highly complementary, competing services between France and Italy would have to be safeguarded. In *British Airways/American Airlines/Iberia* in 2010, the Commission accepted airline commitments to divest airport slots to facilitate expanded air routes between London and US cities. The Commission has also reviewed cooperation agreements involving Lufthansa, Austrian Airlines, and SAS. The Commission has kept a watchful eye on the cooperation undertaken within the various airline "alliances." In 2015, it extracted passenger friendly commitments while allowing cooperation under a transatlantic joint venture involving *Air France/KLM, Alitalia and Delta,* members of "the SkyTeam" alliance, We will be discussing other joint venture cases in the context of the Merger Regulation in Chapter 13.

In recent years, the stunning new developments in technology have spurred many joint ventures in the EU. In particular, the globalization of the telecommunications industry has led to alliances seeking to offer new state-of-the-art national and international communications services. The Commission has attempted to cope with these developments consistently with its policy of encouraging both innovation and competition in the industry. As we have seen, the determination of whether a particular joint venture will pass antitrust muster requires a detailed study of the proposed venture's economic setting, as well as of the nature of the understandings between the parties.

CHAPTER 11
Article 101 TFEU: Agreements, Decisions and Concerted Practices – Suppliers, Customers and Licensees

§11.01   ARTICLE 101 TFEU: VERTICAL RESTRAINTS GENERALLY

Supply contracts, distribution agreements, and licenses of trademarks and of technology constitute essential and routine components of everyday domestic and international trade. As we discussed in Chapter 6, in antitrust parlance these arrangements are described as "vertical" because they normally entail relationships between business parties at different levels of trade, not between competitors. Nonetheless, these vertical agreements may impose constraints on one or both of the parties, such as exclusive buying or supply commitments, territorial restrictions, or limitations on the use of licensed IP. Just as such vertical constraints are tested under US law to determine to what extent they restrain competition, so are they evaluated under European law against the prohibition in Article 101(1) TFEU of certain restrictive agreements, concerted practices, and decisions. The Court of Justice earlier held that Article 101 applies to all agreements between undertakings which distort competition within the common market, regardless of whether the relationship is characterized as horizontal or vertical.

A producing firm may utilize independent distributors to get its goods to market, or it may integrate vertically by incorporating a distribution network which is wholly owned, or it may sell directly through the Internet and thus engage in "disintermediation," an elegant word for a process more commonly called "cutting out the middleman."

It is generally agreed among lawyers and economists that, in many contexts, non-price vertical restraints enhance market efficiency and the competitive process, while in some other contexts these restraints impair healthy competition. Market structure and market power play important roles in indicating the competitive effect of a particular restraint. We have seen that, in the US, the balancing process is usually carried out through application of the rule of reason analysis, taking into account such factors as the purpose of the restraint, the market power of the parties, and the degree of foreclosure of competition. Under the European system, a somewhat similar type of analysis has been employed by the Commission, which has factored into its analysis both the prohibition of Article 101(1) and the countervailing benefits provision of Article 101(3). Broadly put, while suppliers and customers, as well as licensors and licensees, are normally free to deal with each other on any terms they may desire, the Article 101(1) prohibition against anticompetitive agreements and concerted practices does come into play in some instances. It should also be kept in mind that, as we will discuss in the next chapter, the Article 102 prohibition against abuse of a dominant position limits the terms on which a dominant party may seek to do business.

For many years, where the Commission considered that a particular type of vertical agreement satisfied all of the conditions of Article [101(3) TFEU], notwithstanding its inclusion of certain restrictive clauses bringing the agreement within Article [101(1) TFEU], it issued a block exemption applicable to that category of agreement. This approach led to the issuance of block exemptions for certain agreements involving exclusive distribution, exclusive purchasing, technology licensing and franchise agreements, among others. These block exemptions tended to follow a general pattern by listing both permissible restrictions ("white list") and impermissible restrictions ("black list"), along with conditions that had to be met for agreements to qualify for the block exemption.

In the late 1990s the Commission undertook an extensive study of its approach to vertical restraints. In 1997, it published a Green Paper and in 1998 a Communication on the issue of the application of the EC competition rules to vertical restraints. The primary conclusion reached by the Commission was that the previous block exemption regulations were flawed in being overly legalistic and form-based in nature, so as to allow exemption to some injurious restraints while imposing an unnecessary compliance burden on many firms which lacked significant market power. In particular, the Commission's emphasis on white lists of permitted restraints had created regulatory "straitjackets" for company trade practices. What was needed, the Commission concluded, was a new policy relying on an economics-based approach, making the analysis turn on the actual or likely effect of the vertical restraint on the market. The Commission proposed to replace a number of block exemption regulations with a single regulation covering all types of vertical agreements.

Accordingly, on December 22, 1999, the Commission issued Regulation 2790/1999, a block exemption on the application of Article 81(3) of the Treaty to categories of vertical agreements and concerted practices which entered into force on June 1, 2000. On October 13, 2000, the Commission published *Guidelines on Vertical Restraints ("Vertical Guidelines")* in the Official Journal, to be read with that Regulation.

On April 20, 2010, Regulation 2790/1999 was replaced by Regulation 330/2010 (the "BE Regulation"), which will expire on May 31, 2022. The 2000 *Vertical Guidelines* were replaced in 2010, and it is to these current versions of the two documents that we will be referring. (Motor vehicles and spare parts are subject to a separate Regulation, No. 461/2010).

It should be noted here that the Court of Justice held in *Viho v. Commission* in 1996 and in other decisions that, where firms are part of a single economic entity, as is the case with a parent firm having wholly owned subsidiaries, the joint action strictures of Article 101(1) do not apply. As the Court put it, "... where there is no agreement between economically independent entities, relations within an economic unit cannot amount to an agreement or concerted practice between undertakings which restricts competition within the meaning of Article [101(1) TFEU]." However, such vertical integration may be considered in the context of whether a firm holds a dominant position for purposes of Article 102 TFEU.

Similarly, an agreement between a principal and a commercial agent will typically not be subject to Article 101(1) because the agent does not bear risk of loss as an independent actor and he/she is simply acting on the principal's behalf.

§11.02   THE BE REGULATION

No. 330/2010, the BE Regulation provides a block exemption from the application of Article 101(1) for vertical agreements meeting certain conditions. The benefit of the block exemption is intended to be limited to those vertical agreements which can be assumed to satisfy the conditions of Article 101(3), i.e., they will improve economic efficiency within a chain of production or distribution, reducing costs and optimizing sales and investment levels.

The BE Regulation's presumption that the likelihood that such efficiency enhancing effects will outweigh any anticompetitive effects of the contract restrictions varies in relation to the extent of the market power of the undertakings concerned. Where the market share held by each of the undertakings party to the agreement does not exceed 30%, there is a presumption in favor of the propriety of the agreement, providing that it does not contain certain types of severe restrictions of competition. Above the market share threshold of 30%, there is no presumption either in favor of or against the validity of the arrangement. Individual review of the agreement is necessary. However, irrespective of the market shares of the undertakings concerned, the Regulation is not intended to benefit vertical agreements containing certain types of severe restrictions on competition such as minimum and fixed resale prices or certain types of territorial protection. In the case of these hard core restraints individual exemption of the agreement is also unlikely.

It is permissible for the supplier to impose a maximum resale price or to uncoercively "recommend" a resale price. Territorial restrictions on resale are permitted in certain specific contexts, such as where a territory has been allocated by the supplier exclusively to another party.

The exemption also does not apply to noncompete commitments exceeding five years or of indefinite duration, certain post-termination obligations imposed on a buyer, and obligations causing the members of a selective distribution system not to sell the brands of particular competing suppliers. These types of obligations are not necessarily unlawful under Article 101, but they do not get the benefit of the block exemption. Vertical agreements entered into between competitors are excluded from the block exemption although there are some exceptions to this exclusion. In addition, Article 2(3) of the BE Regulation includes within the scope of the block exemption vertical agreements containing certain provisions relating to the assignment of IP rights to a buyer or user of such rights by a buyer in those situations where the main object of the agreement is the purchase or distribution of goods or services. This limited inclusion has the effect of excluding from the BE Regulation all other vertical agreements containing IP rights provisions. The BE Regulation, therefore, does not cover pure licensing agreements. We will be addressing such agreements separately in this chapter.

If the Regulation does not prohibit a particular type of vertical agreement, it is permitted, assuming that it is a genuine vertical agreement between parties not in competition. In addition, the possible applicability of the Commission's 2014 Notice on Agreements of Minor Importance (the *de minimis* Notice) should be kept in mind. With respect to vertical agreements, the Notice provides that, so long as the market share held by each of the parties does not exceed 15% in any of the relevant markets, the agreement will not be considered as falling within Article 101(1).

The BE Regulation is to be viewed as having a much broader scope of application than the three expired block exemptions discussed above combined. It covers, in general, all purchase and distribution agreements for goods and services.

§11.03 THE GUIDELINES ON VERTICAL RESTRAINTS

The *Vertical Guidelines* first describe the types of vertical agreements which generally fall outside of Article 101(1). These include agreements which are of "minor importance" because the noncompeting undertakings' market shares do not individually exceed 15% in the relevant market (without prejudice to the application of the standards set by the *de minimis* Notice) and "genuine" agency agreements, where the agent is acting on behalf of a principal who bears the risk of the selling or purchasing functions.

The *Vertical Guidelines* then describe the application of the BE Regulation in exempting vertical agreements, particularly the safe harbor created by the 30% market share threshold. The *Vertical Guidelines* also explain the application of the block exemption in those situations in which it applies to IP rights, i.e., as part of a vertical agreement involving the buying or selling of goods or services. It is explained that licensing contained in franchise agreements is covered by the BE Regulation under certain conditions, and "[t]hose conditions are usually fulfilled as under most franchise agreements, including master franchise agreements, the franchisor provides goods and/or services, in particular commercial or technical assistance services, to the franchisee." In addition, "[w]here the franchise agreement only or primarily concerns licensing of IPRs, it is not covered by the Block Exemption Regulation, but the Commission will, as a general rule, apply the principles set out in the Block Exemption Regulation and these Guidelines to such an agreement."

The *Vertical Guidelines* point out that the BE Regulation does not apply to vertical agreements falling within the scope of the block exemptions on technology transfer, or in the motor vehicle sector, or to those agreements entered into which are in the nature of specialization agreements or R & D agreements. Subcontracting is covered by a Notice issued by the Commission on December 18, 1978. According to that Notice, subcontracts whereby the subcontractor undertakes to produce certain products exclusively for the contractor generally fall outside of Article 101(1) provided that the technology or equipment is necessary to enable the subcontractor to make the products. However, other restrictions, such as the subcontractor's committing not to conduct or exploit its own R & D or not to produce for third parties in general may fall within Article 101(1).

The *Vertical Guidelines* provide extensive guidance regarding the nature and scope of the hard core restrictions, which, under Article 4 of the BE Regulation, will lead to the exclusion of an entire vertical agreement from the block exemption.

As we have discussed, the prohibition of Article 101(1) extends to certain agreements, decisions by associations and concerted practices insofar as they "may affect trade between Member States." Hard core restrictions may be objectively necessary and thus acceptable in exceptional situations for an agreement of a particular type or nature, such as ensuring compliance with a public ban on selling certain substances. In discussing the jurisdictional scope of the block exemption for vertical agreements, the *Vertical Guidelines* indicate that the hard core restrictions will be unacceptable: (i) if they are found in vertical agreements concerning trade within the EU; and (ii) pursuant to the judgments in various court decisions, if they appear in agreements which involve trade with non-Member States but which nonetheless have an appreciable effect on trade between Member States, such as affecting imports or re-imports into the Union.

These Guidelines observe that vertical agreements implemented in several Member States are normally capable of affecting trade between Member States if they cause trade to be channeled in a particular way, such as through networks of selective distribution. Vertical agreements covering the whole of a Member State may be capable of affecting patterns of trade between Member States when they make it more difficult for undertakings from other Member States to penetrate the market in question. As to agreements between undertakings in two or more Member States that concern exports and imports, they are by their very nature capable of affecting trade between Member States.

The *Vertical Guidelines* provide that, in the case of "genuine" agency agreements, the obligations imposed by the principal on the agent with respect to the latter's power to negotiate and/or conclude contracts do not fall within the scope of application of Article 101(1) TFEU. An agency agreement is genuine for this purpose only if the agent does not bear any risk or only an insignificant risk in relation to: (a) the contracts on which he is acting for the principal; and (b) market-specific investments for that field of activity. In this context of a genuine agency, it will generally be considered to be an inherent part of the agency agreement for the agent to have obligations concerning the restricting of sales by territory or customer, as well as to the prices and conditions on which the agent sells or purchases on the principal's behalf. If, on the other hand, the agreement constitutes a nongenuine agency agreement, it may be caught by Article 101(1) subject to the conditions of the BE Regulation and the other provisions of the Guidelines.

§11.04 POLICIES IN THE VERTICAL CONTEXT

From the BE Regulation, the *Vertical Guidelines*, and the relevant case law, one can discern the principal policies that animate the rules to be as follows.

[A] Export Restraints

Where an "object" of a vertical agreement is the restraint of exports from the EU or to or from a Member State, it constitutes an infringement of Article 101(1). So, may a producer, for example, set up one independent distributor for France and another for Germany and require each not to sell under any circumstances outside of its designated national territory? It appears that this will be considered a violation of Article 101(1) and will, in the usual case, not be permitted under Article 101(3). The European courts and the Commission have generally held that this pattern will not be permitted unless there are unusual circumstances.

For the EU, the concept of "parallel trade" goes to the heart of the single market idea. The Commission has defined parallel trade as:

> a lawful trade in goods between Member States of the European Union. Parallel trade is based on the principle of the free movement of goods within the Internal Market. It is known as "parallel" to the extent that it takes place outside and—in most cases—in parallel with the distribution network that the manufacturers or original suppliers have established for their products at a Member State, while it concerns products which are in every respect similar to the ones marketed by the distribution networks.

We discussed earlier the *General Motors Nederland BV* case in 2006 in which Opel Nederland BV, a 100% owned subsidiary of General Motors Nederland BV, was held to have violated Article [101(1)] by denying bonuses to dealers with respect to their export sales. Similarly, in the case of *GlaxoSmithKline Services Unlimited*, the Court of Justice upheld the Commission in 2009, ruling that "[W]ith respect to parallel trade, the Court has already held that, in principle, agreements aimed at prohibiting or limiting parallel trade have as their object the prevention of competition." The Court added:

> Thus on a number of occasions the Court has held agreements aimed at partitioning national markets according to national borders or making the interpenetration of national markets more difficult, in particular those aimed at preventing or restricting parallel imports, to be agreements whose object is to restrict competition within the meaning of Article [101(1)].

In sum, there are many ways in which producers in the EU have sought to prevent export sales on the part of their distributors or dealers from occurring. The Commission has regularly struck these devices down as improper attempts to partition the single market and these actions have been upheld by the EU courts. Some export restrictions, for example, those relating to unsafe products or involving the testing of new products, may be permitted.

[B]   Resale Price Maintenance

In the vertical context, pricing arrangements may involve various scenarios, e.g., a supplier's obtaining the agreement of its purchaser that the price at which the latter will resell the product to third parties will be: (i) at a specified level; or (ii) above a specified level (minimum resale price); or (iii) below a specified level (maximum resale price). As we earlier observed, such a practice engaged in by a supplier, particularly under (i) or (ii), is commonly referred to as RPM.

The EU law on RPM is clearly stated at Article 4(a) of the BE Regulation and in the Vertical Guidelines: agreements or concerted practices which have as their direct or indirect object the establishment of a fixed or minimum price level to be observed by the buyer constitute hard core restraints which are generally prohibited by Article 101(1) TFEU. Undertakings have the possibility to plead an efficiency defense under Article 101(3) in an individual case.

The Vertical Guidelines point out that prohibited RPM sometimes is achieved through indirect means, such as fixing the distributor's margin or the maximum level of discount that the distributor can grant from a price level. Measures taken by manufacturers to identify price-cutting distributors are also suspect, such as the implementation of a price monitoring system or requiring resellers to report other members of the distribution network who deviate from the price level. A supplier's imposing a maximum resale price or recommending a resale price to the buyer do not constitute prohibited RPM measures, except where they amount to the imposition on the reseller of a fixed or minimum resale price as a result of pressure applied or incentives offered.

The *Vertical Guidelines* also state (at paragraph 226):

> The practice of recommending a resale price to a reseller or requiring a reseller to respect a maximum resale price is covered by the Block Exemption Regulation when the market share of each of the parties to the agreement does not exceed the 30% threshold, provided it does not amount to a minimum or fixed sale price as a result of pressure from or incentives offered by any of the parties.

When a supplier's market share is above the 30% threshold, assessment of the particular situation must be made with respect to the setting of maximum and recommended prices. The practices can pose competition risks by becoming a focal point for resellers to follow and also by facilitating collusion between suppliers. The most important factor for the assessment is the market position of the supplier involved, because the more important the supplier the more likely that its pricing preferences will be followed. The second most important factor is the market position of competitors, especially in a narrow oligopoly where an industry practice of using or publishing maximum or recommended prices is most likely to facilitate collusion on pricing by suppliers.

The Court of Justice confirmed in its 2006 holding in *Volkswagen v. Commission* that "non binding recommendations" made by the auto company to its dealers as to resale prices did not create an agreement within the meaning of Article 101(1) TFEU. In 2008, the ECJ held in *CEPSA Estaciones de Servicio SA v. LV Tobar e Hijos SL* that the fact finder must ascertain whether the seller's fixing of a maximum sales price in this case "does not remain, in reality, a fixed or minimum sales price, account being taken of all the contractual obligations and the conduct of the parties ... ."

[C] Single Branding

The Vertical Guidelines devote significant attention to a practice which they call "single branding," consisting of an obligation or incentive scheme applied by a supplier which leads the buyer to agree not to buy and resell or incorporate competing goods or services. It is a form of exclusive dealing. Three possible negative effects on interbrand competition stemming from this practice are cited: foreclosure of the market to other suppliers, facilitation of collusion between suppliers in case of cumulative use, and, where the buyer is a retailer selling to final consumers, a loss of in-store inter-brand competition. According to the Vertical Guidelines, a so-called English clause, requiring the buyer to report any better offer and allowing him to accept it only when the first supplier does not match it, can be expected to have the same effect as a noncompete obligation.

Single branding is exempted by the BE Regulation when the supplier's and buyer's market share each do not exceed 30% and the agreement is subject to a limitation in time of five years for the noncompete obligation. Above the 30% threshold or beyond the time limit of five years, assessment must be made of the individual case. The stronger the market position of the supplier and the greater the scope of the noncompete obligation, the more significant the foreclosure of other suppliers is likely to be. Noncompete obligations exceeding five years are not necessary for most types of investments.

Where the block exemption standards are not met, the applicability of Article 101(1) must be assessed in terms of the economic context in which the parties operate. The market position of the supplier, the length of the commitment, whether the supplier's competitors use similar arrangements, entry barriers, and buyer countervailing market power are to be considered. Single branding obligations shorter than one year entered into by nondominant companies are generally not considered to give rise to significant anticompetitive effects.

The Vertical Guidelines also discuss "quantity forcing," which involves the imposition of a weaker form of noncompete obligation, with the buyer concentrating his purchases to a large extent with one supplier. The arrangement may, for example, entail minimum purchase requirements or a loyalty rebate scheme. Quantity forcing, which has similar but weaker foreclosure effects than a noncompete obligation, will be assessed in terms of the specific market situation.

There is significant EU case law discussing the issues in this area. For example, in its decision in 2000 in *Neste Markkinointi v. Yötuuli,* the ECJ articulated the applicable law thus:

> It should be recalled that, even if exclusive purchasing agreements do not have as their object the restriction of competition within the meaning of Article [101 (1)], it is nevertheless necessary to ascertain whether they have the effect of preventing, restricting, or distorting competition. The effects of an exclusive purchasing agreement have to be assessed in the economic and legal context in which the agreement occurs and where it may combine with other agreements to have a cumulative effect on competition.

[D]   Restriction on Resale Territory or Customer

The placing by a seller within a Member State of "absolute" restrictions on a purchaser limiting his resale territory or range of customers potentially strikes at the heart of the common market concept that binds the EU. The Commission and the courts have often stressed this principle, and it is again early stated in the *Vertical Guidelines*: "Market integration enhances competition in the European Union. Companies should not be allowed to re-establish private barriers between Member States where State barriers have been successfully abolished."

Accordingly, "market partitioning," whereby a seller restricts the buyer as to the territory into which or the customer to whom the buyer may resell the contract goods or services, is, under Article 4(b) of the BE Regulation, a hard core restriction precluding the application of the block exemption to the vertical agreement as a whole. The hard core restriction exists, according to the *Vertical Guidelines*, not only where a direct obligation is placed on the distributor to refrain from selling in certain territories or to certain customers but also where indirect measures are applied to reach the same objective. These measures may include, for example, refusals to supply, or to grant the regular bonuses or discounts, or to provide warranty service where resales in certain territories or to certain customers are involved.

There are a number of exceptions spelled out in the BE Regulation and in the *Vertical Guidelines* to this general principle. Distributors may be prohibited from selling to certain end users if there is an objective justification related to the product, such as a general ban on selling dangerous substances to certain customers for reasons of safety or health. More broadly, Article 4(b) of the BE Regulation describes four exceptions to the treatment of territory and customer limitations on resale as hard core restraints: First, a supplier may restrict active sales by his direct buyers to a territory or a customer group which the supplier has reserved to itself or allocated to another buyer. However, passive sales to such territories or customer groups must be allowed, This means, for example, that a distributor can agree to refrain from actively approaching customers inside another distributor's assigned territory or establishing a warehouse in that distributor's assigned territory.

On the other hand, the distributor cannot be required to refrain from responding to unsolicited requests from individual customers outside of his assigned territory, including delivering goods or services to such customers. The *Vertical Guidelines* specify too that use of the Internet is not considered a form of active selling for purposes of these principles, and that every distributor must be free to use the Internet to advertise or to sell products. Therefore, if a customer visits the website of a distributor and the contact leads to a sale, including delivery, then that is considered passive, not active, selling.

The three other exceptions to hard core restrictions enumerated in Article 4(b) allow for the restriction of both active and passive sales. They allow: (i) restricting a wholesaler from selling to end users; (ii) restricting the members of a "selective distribution system" from selling to unauthorized distributors; and (iii) restricting a buyer of components supplied for incorporation from reselling them to competitors of the supplier. It should be kept in mind in considering these principles that it is a prerequisite to a finding of a violation of Article 101(1) that there be found the existence of either a restrictive agreement between undertakings, a decision by an association, or a concerted practice. This prerequisite is as fully applicable in the vertical context as it is in the horizontal context.

As we discussed in the previous chapter, the *Bayer* case involved the subsidiaries of a drug manufacturer reducing their sales to their wholesalers in two Member States, allegedly because the wholesalers were reselling some of the product into a third Member State. The Court of First Instance ruled that the Commission had not established a violation of Article 81(1), inasmuch as it had not sufficiently established either that the Bayer companies had imposed an export ban or that the wholesalers buying from Bayer had an intention to comply with such a ban. There was no showing by the Commission of the existence of an agreement, express or implied, between the manufacturer and the wholesalers. The decision of the CFI in *Bayer* was affirmed by the ECJ. In some other cases, the Commission has been able to show a pattern of conduct by distributors constituting their acquiescence in a trade restrictive policy of their suppliers. Of course, unilateral conduct, including the imposition of restrictions on purchasers, may constitute abuse of a dominant position in violation of Article 102.

The EU jurisprudence striking down under the competition rules contractual and other arrangements between a supplier and his exclusive distributors which would create absolute territorial protection for each distributor goes back many years. The landmark 1966 *Consten & Grundig* case involved an agreement between Grundig, a German manufacturer of radios, tape recorders and other products bearing its name, and a French company, Consten, whom Grundig made its sole distributor in France. The agreement provided that Consten could not sell Grundig products outside of France, and Grundig agreed not to sell to other persons in France. In order to bolster Consten's territorial protection, Grundig permitted Consten to register in its own name in France the "GINT" brand name which was carried on all Grundig appliances. All other Grundig purchasers, German and foreign, were similarly prohibited from selling the Grundig products outside of their assigned national territories.

Consten brought a suit for unfair competition and infringement of the GINT trademark against a French company which had been able to obtain Grundig appliances in Germany for resale to French retailers. The French competitor complained to the Commission in Brussels, and the latter, following an investigation, issued a decision concluding that the agreement between Grundig and Consten violated Article 85(1) and was void. The Commission reasoned that the distribution and licensing agreements impermissibly restricted competition within the Community insofar as they precluded the possibility of "parallel imports" from one Member State into another. According to the Commission, the possibility of parallel imports "should constitute a corrective factor for excessive prices imposed by an exclusive concession holder and should be an element of price harmonization in a unified market having the same features as a single domestic market."

On the appeal to the ECJ, the Court largely upheld the views of the Commission and rendered a decision which set the course for the jurisprudence in this area. Accordingly, Article 101(1) protects parallel imports, and distributorship arrangements cannot be established which impair the integration of the Union. Moreover, national laws protecting IP rights, such as patents, trademarks and copyrights may not be applied to defeat the EU law in this area.

The Commission fashioned a strict policy against agreements imposing "export bans" on distributors, but it also articulated conditions for exemption so as to allow exclusive distributorships a limited degree of territorial protection. Efforts to confer absolute territorial protection, preventing parallel imports between Member States, were challenged, sometimes with high fines being imposed. Some exclusive distributorship systems, however, satisfied the conditions for an improvement in the distribution of goods and also benefitted consumers by making products readily available. Exemptions were granted in some of these cases where the arrangement allowed for a possibility of parallel imports in the products concerned.

[E] Noncompete Obligations

Article 5 of the BE Regulation excludes certain obligations from the benefit of the block exemption even though the safe harbor market share threshold is not exceeded. The first such exclusion relates to noncompete obligations, the duration of which are indefinite or exceed five years. Noncompete obligations are defined in Article 1(1)(d) as obligations which require the buyer to purchase from the supplier, or from an undertaking designated by him, more than 80% of the buyer's total purchases during the previous year of the contract goods and services and their substitutes. The five-year duration limit does not apply in certain cases. Paragraph 66 of the *Vertical Guidelines* states that, in general, noncompete obligations are exempted under the BE Regulation where their duration is limited to five years of less and no obstacles exist that hinder the buyer from effectively terminating the noncompete obligation at the end of the five-year period.

The second exclusion from the block exemption, in Article 5(1)(b), is where the buyer is obligated not to manufacture, purchase or sell certain goods or services after termination of the agreement between seller and buyer. An exception to this exclusion is in Article 5(3) which applies where the buyer has entered into a noncompete obligation which is indispensable to protect know-how transferred by the supplier to the buyer, is limited to the property from which the buyer operated during the contract period and the obligation is limited to one year after termination of the agreement.

The third exclusion from the block exemption, in Article 5(1)(c), concerns the sale of competing goods in a selective service system. While the dealers in such a system can be obligated not to resell competing brands in general, the obligation does not enjoy the benefits of the block exemption where it is directed against buying from specific competing suppliers (in the nature of a boycott).

It should be remembered that vertical agreements falling outside of the BE Regulation are not presumed to be illegal but may need individual examination. The *Vertical Guidelines* advise companies to undertake their own assessments. Of course, the impermissibility of the hard core restrictions is clear.

Article 29(1) of Regulation 1/2003 gives the Commission the power to withdraw the benefit of the block exemption where it finds in any particular case that a vertical agreement, considered either in isolation or in conjunction with similar agreements enforced by competing suppliers or buyers, has effects which are incompatible with Article 101(3). Article 29(2) of the same Regulation confers power on the competition authorities of the Member States to withdraw the benefit of the block exemption where agreements to which the block exemption applies have effects incompatible with Article 101(3) in the territory of a Member State, or in a part thereof, which has all of the characteristics of a distinct geographic market. Paragraph 78 of the *Guidelines* provides that the Commission has the exclusive power to withdraw the benefit of the BE Regulation in respect of vertical agreements restricting competition on a relevant geographic market which is wider than the territory of a single Member State. When the territory of a single Member State, or a part thereof, constitutes the relevant geographic market, the Commission and the Member State concerned have concurrent competence for withdrawal.

[F]   Exclusive and Selective Distribution

The *Vertical Guidelines* describe an "exclusive distribution agreement" in paragraph 151 as one in which the supplier agrees to sell his products only to one distributor for resale in a particular territory. Moreover, in such agreements the distributor is usually prevented from actively selling into other exclusively allocated territories. The possible competition risks from such arrangements, the *Guidelines* note, are mainly "reduced intra-brand competition and market partitioning, which may facilitate price discrimination in particular. When most or all of the suppliers apply exclusive distribution, it may facilitate collusion, both at the suppliers' and distributors' level."

The block exemption applies to exclusive distribution arrangements as long as both the supplier's and the buyer's market share each do not exceed 30%, even if combined with other non-hard core vertical restraints, such as a noncompete obligation limited to five years, quantity forcing or exclusive purchasing. Article 4(b) of the BE Regulation provides an exception to the block exemption and then an exception to the exception: (1) (aside from the RPM issues previously discussed), the agreement may *not* restrict the territory into which, or of the customers to whom, a buyer party to the agreement (without prejudice to a restriction on its place of establishment) may sell the contract goods or services, except (2) there *may be* (a) restriction of active sales into the exclusive territory or to an exclusive customer group reserved to the supplier or allocated by the supplier to another buyer, where such a restriction does not limit sales by the customer of the buyer; (b) a restriction of sales to end users by a buyer operating at the wholesale level of trade; (c) the restriction of sales by the members of a selective distribution system to unauthorized distributors within the territory reserved by the supplier to operate that system; and (d) the restriction of the buyer's ability to sell components, supplied for the purposes of incorporation, to customers who would use them to manufacture the same type of goods as those produced by the supplier.

"Selective distribution" is a system established by a producer in which the products can be purchased and resold only by authorized distributors and retailers. It is defined in Article 1(e) of the BE Regulation as "a distribution system where the supplier undertakes to sell the contract goods or services, either directly or indirectly, only to distributors selected on the basis of specified criteria and where these distributors undertake not to sell such goods or services to unauthorised distributors within the territory reserved by the supplier to operate that system." It is primarily used to distribute branded final products. The purpose of the supplier may be to preserve its brand image, to ensure proper service, to speed up distribution, or for a variety of reasons. The resellers typically agree with the supplier in advance to resell only to other resellers meeting the specified criteria or to the final consumer.

Selective distribution differs from exclusive distribution in that the former is linked to the nature of the product and is also a restriction on any sales to nonauthorized distributors without regard to territory. A combination of exclusive distribution and selective distribution is only exempted by the BE Regulation if active selling in other territories is not restricted (without prejudice to the possibility of prohibiting a member of the system from operating out of an unauthorized place of establishment).

The *Guidelines* indicate that selective distribution systems may have anticompetitive effects by restricting intrabrand competition, foreclosing access to the market, softening competition and facilitating collusion between suppliers or buyers. In making this assessment, the *Guidelines* at Article 75 point out the difference between "quantitative selective distribution" and "purely qualitative selective distribution." The latter selects dealers only on the basis of objective criteria required by the nature of the product such as training of sales personnel, the service provided at the point of sale, a certain range of the products being sold, etc. When legitimately carried out, purely qualitative selective distribution generally falls outside of Article 101(1) for lack of anticompetitive effects.

Qualitative and quantitative selective distribution are both exempted by the BE Regulation as long as the market share of both supplier and buyer each do not exceed 30%, even if combined with other non-hard core vertical restraints, such as noncompete or exclusive distribution, provided active selling by the authorized distributors to each other and to end users is not restricted. Where appreciable anticompetitive effects occur, the benefit of the block exemption is likely to be withdrawn. The market positions of the supplier and its competitors are of central importance in assessing possible anticompetitive effects, as the loss of intra-brand competition can only be problematic if inter-brand competition is limited.

Restrictions on "passive sales" in vertical agreements are generally considered to be hard core restrictions that fall outside of the of the block exemption. Examples of "passive" sales would include responding to unsolicited requests from individual customers including business generated by advertising in media or on the internet.

The early cases in this area involved such products as perfume, automobiles, and electrical equipment. An important early decision was the *Metro/SABA (No. 1)* case in 1977, which involved a German company specializing in electrical and electronic equipment. SABA created a distribution network in Germany by appointing wholesalers who would purchase the SABA products and resell them to approved specialist dealers who had to be dealing primarily in this type of equipment. The dealers had to commit to specified locations, to stocking a full range of products, and to maintaining a level of technical expertise. SABA's agreements also included prohibitions on particular types of dealing within the approved chain of distribution and on exports to other Community countries. Metro, a wholesaler who had been unable to join the SABA system, challenged a decision by the Commission which had approved only SABA's prohibition against direct sales by wholesalers or direct distributors to consumers.

The Court of Justice rejected Metro's attack on the selective distribution system. It pointed out that SABA's market share of the products concerned was 10% or less and that consumers had a valid interest in having access to a network of specialist dealers in the context of purchasing high quality, technically advanced goods. The Court took the position that a number of restrictions did not fall under Article 85(1) in that they were appropriate requirements in the distribution of consumer durable products. It also recognized that price competition was not the only form of competition deserving protection. The Court stated that selective distribution represented a legitimate form of maintaining competition provided that resellers were chosen according to objective criteria of a qualitative nature relating to their technical qualifications and that these conditions were applied uniformly and nondiscriminatorily to all potential resellers.

In *Metro/SABA (No. 2)*, in 1986, when Metro again challenged a Commission decision granting an exemption to SABA, the Court of Justice again rejected the challenge. Metro argued that competition in the electronic sector by independent operators was being threatened by the fact that an increasing number of producers were utilizing selective distribution systems based on qualitative criteria. In this second decision, the Court stated that the existence of a large number of selective distribution systems in an industry did not by itself lead to the conclusion that competition was being restricted or distorted or that an exemption should be denied. Accordingly, the principle of selective distribution systems being justified by their reliance upon objective "qualitative" criteria became established. The qualitative criteria for approval of parties in a selective network have covered, as the *Vertical Guidelines* have noted, such matters as the technical qualifications of the staff, maintenance of sufficient stock, maintaining suitably equipped premises, committing to providing before or after sales service, and keeping appropriate opening hours.

In its decision in *L'Oréal v. PVBA* in 1980, the Court of Justice ruled that inquiry into the propriety of a system of selective distribution should also concern whether the characteristics of the particular product necessitated such a system to preserve quality and ensure proper use, whether those objectives were already satisfied by national rules governing sale, and whether the criteria laid down went beyond what was necessary.

The case of *Vichy v. Commission* involved a distribution system used by a French company limiting the sale of its cosmetics outside of France to retail stores in which a qualified pharmacist was present. The company maintained that this restriction enhanced interbrand competition and that it was necessary to assuring quality control and proper customer service. The Commission denied Vichy an exemption, reasoning that the claimed benefits could be pursued without the restriction, which the company did not apply in its sales within France. The Commission's ruling was upheld by the CFI.

[G]   **Franchising**

The *Vertical Guidelines* also discuss the application of the BE Regulation to franchising agreements. As we have observed, franchise agreements typically contain licenses of trademarks and/or know-how for the use and distribution of goods or services. The franchisor also usually provides the franchisee with commercial or technical assistance during the life of the agreement. In addition to paying a fee for these benefits, the franchisee generally is required to agree to a number of vertical restraints, such as noncompete obligations, which are calculated to protect the franchise network as a whole and to enhance its chances for success.

As the *Vertical Guidelines* note, licensing contained in franchise agreements will normally be covered by the terms of the BE Regulation since the IP rights provisions are incidental to and directly related to the use, sale or resale of goods or services. The BE Regulation applies up to the 30% market share threshold with respect to vertical restraints within a franchise agreement relating to the purchase, sale and resale of goods and services, such as selective distribution, noncompete obligations or exclusive distribution. Similarly, exclusive supply agreements, whereby the supplier is obliged to sell the contract products only to one buyer, will fall under the block exemption so long as the supplier's and the buyer's market shares are not over 30%.

Paragraph 45 of the *Vertical Guidelines* sets out a list of IPR-related obligations on the part of the franchisee which are generally considered to be necessary to protect the franchisor's rights and, if these obligations should fall under Article 101(1) TFEU, are also considered to be covered by the BE Regulation. These customary terms are a noncompete obligation, and the obligations not to disclose to third parties confidential know-how provided by the franchisor; to license back, on a nonexclusive basis, any new know-how obtained; to assist the franchisor in taking action against parties who infringe the licensed IPRs; to use the licensed know-how only for the purpose of exploiting the franchise; and to refrain from assigning rights and obligations under the franchise agreement without the franchisor's consent. The franchisor, for his part, may be obligated not to compete with the franchisee in a particular area of operation and not to appoint other franchisees in a franchisee's designated territory.

A noncompete obligation by the franchisee as to goods and services purchased by him, which obligation is of any duration not exceeding the life of the franchise agreement, is deemed to fall outside of the Article 101(1) prohibition so long as the obligation is necessary to maintain the common identity and reputation of the franchised network.

Prior to the Commission's issuance of a block exemption for certain categories of franchise agreements in 1988, the ECJ had set forth substantial views on the subject in its judgment of January 28, 1986 in the *Pronuptia* case. Pronuptia de Paris, which was a leading producer of wedding dresses and accessories, had entered into franchise agreements in the German market. One of the German franchisees refused to pay the agreed fees and argued that the franchise agreement was void under Article 85(2) because a number of restrictions which it imposed were incompatible with Article 85(1) of the EC competition law. The franchisee disputed, among other things, the obligations placed upon it to advertise and sell the contract goods in ways approved by the franchisor and to purchase only from the franchisor or from suppliers approved by it. The German Supreme Court referred to the ECJ the issue of whether Article 85 applied to franchise agreements and, if so, whether the block exemption relating to exclusive distribution also applied.

The Court determined that, although the block exemption was inapplicable, franchise agreements like the one before it offered valuable benefits for both parties. Moreover, depending on the provisions and their economic context, such agreements might be compatible with competition and fall outside of Article 85(1). The Court considered that two conditions would have to be met for such a franchise system to work: first, the franchisor would have to be able to communicate its know-how to the franchisees and provide them with the necessary assistance without taking the risk that this might benefit competitors, and, second, the franchisor would have to be allowed to take the measures necessary to maintain the reputation and identity of the franchise network as a whole.

From this rationale, the Court concluded that there were certain restrictions which should be viewed as not restricting competition pursuant to Article 85(1). These included the imposition of obligations on the franchisee to refrain from competing with the network (including for a reasonable period after expiration of the agreement), to apply the know-how provided, to maintain premises in a location and in a manner set out by the franchisor, and to submit proposed advertisements for approval. However, quality control oversight by the franchisor as to the goods offered for sale needed to be circumscribed. This meant that the franchisor could require the franchisee to sell only products supplied by the franchisor or by suppliers selected by it only to the extent that it was impractical for the franchisor to lay down objective quality specifications. Moreover, clauses prohibiting the franchisee from opening a second shop in his or her territory and imposing RPM were held to be covered by the prohibition of Article 85(1). The block exemption issued by the Commission in 1988 with respect to franchise agreements drew significantly from the principles enunciated by the Court in the *Pronuptia* case, and, subsequently, the BE Regulation did as well.

[H] Tying

As we know from our review of US law, "tying" exists when the supplier makes the sale of one product (the tying product) conditional upon the buyer's also purchasing another distinct product (the tied product) from the supplier or someone designated by him. The *Vertical Guidelines* state that tying may constitute a vertical restraint under Article 101(1), as well as an abuse of a dominant position under Article 102. Indeed, both Article 101(1)(e) and Article 102(d) expressly list among the presumptively improper practices the making "of contracts subject to acceptance by the other parties of supplementary obligations which, by their nature or according to commercial usage, have no connection with the subject of such contracts." The *Vertical Guidelines* state that tying may lead to anticompetitive foreclosure effects in the tied market, the tying market, or both at the same time. It may also lead to supra-competitive prices and cause higher entry barriers in the markets for both kinds of products.

As we discussed previously, the threshold question in an alleged tying situation is often whether there are two distinct products involved, a matter which depends largely on the perspective of the buyers. The products can be considered distinct if, in the absence of the tying, the buyers would purchase them from different suppliers. In the 1986 *Windsurfing International* case, the ECJ determined that the company was violating Article 81(1)(e) by tying the sales of riggings to the purchase of boards, since the two constituted distinct products. In the 1991 *Hilti* case the CFI found that nail guns, cartridges and nails were three distinct products rather than indistinct components of a single power actuated fastening system.

The *Vertical Guidelines* state that tying is exempt under the BE Regulation when the market share of the supplier on both the tying and tied product markets and the market share of the buyer on the relevant upstream market does not exceed 30%, even where combined with other non-hard core vertical restraints such as noncompete, quantity forcing in respect of the tying product or exclusive purchasing.

Above the 30% market threshold, an assessment is made in individual cases. The market position of the supplier on the tying market is of primary importance, because that fact is vital as to whether the buyer will find it difficult to refuse the tying obligation. For the same reason, the market positions of the supplier's competitors are important factors, as is the buying power of the purchaser. Because tying obligations may help to produce efficiencies, exemption under Article 101(3) may still be possible so long as the supplier is not dominant. The *Vertical Guidelines* state that, "[f]or tying to fulfil the conditions of Article 101(3) it must, however, be shown that at least part of these cost reductions are passed on to the consumer." The effect of supra-competitive prices is considered anticompetitive in itself. We will be considering tying again in the context of Article 102 in the next chapter.

[I] Hard Core Restrictions

With a few exceptions, the hard core restrictions are not protected by the exemptions provided by the BE Regulation or the *de minimis* Notice. This is the case irrespective of the parties' market shares. Article 4 of the BE Regulation states that the exemption shall not apply to (among other restrictions): (a) "the restriction of the buyer's ability to determine its sale price, without prejudice to the possibility of the supplier's imposing a maximum sale price or recommending a sale price, provided that they do not amount to a fixed or minimum sale price as a result of pressure from, or incentives offered by, any of the parties" and (b) "the restriction of the territory into which, or of the customers to whom, the buyer may sell the contract goods or services," with certain exceptions including the restriction of active sales into a territory or to a customer group exclusively allocated by the supplier to himself or to another buyer or the restriction of sales to end users by a wholesaler. The restrictions labeled as hard core are not necessarily illegal but they require individual examination in context.

Following such individual examination, the Commission may sometimes conclude that a particular restriction is not covered by Article 101(1) because it does not appreciably restrict competition or will not appreciably affect trade between Member States. For example, in the German book price-fixing case in 2002 (*Deutsche Buchpreisbindung* case), the German book publishers and sellers terminated the Commission proceedings against them by submitting an undertaking that they would not interfere with the direct cross-border selling of German books to final consumers in Germany, in particular, via the Internet. The Commission announced that, on the basis of this undertaking, the German industry's book pricing system governing the retail price maintenance of books in Germany did not appreciably affect trade between Member States in the sense of Article 101(1).

Companies' efforts to impose territorial restrictions on distributors and to maintain resale prices continue to be a prime target of the Commission enforcement program under Article 101 because these restraints strike at the very heart of the common market concept. Despite aggressive antitrust enforcement and public education campaigns on the part of the authorities, hard core vertical restriction cases, like those unveiling international cartels, still arise on a regular basis. Many Commission proceedings, such as those involving Bayer, Glaxo, Yamaha, and Nintendo, and a number of auto companies, have involved large multinational corporations seeking to prevent "parallel trade" by using one device or another in attempting to partition the EU back into its national markets and to prevent intrabrand price competition from spreading from one EU nation to another.

[J] Discrimination in Pricing and Other Terms

The discriminatory treatment of customers does not necessarily entail any form of restrictive agreement, but it may constitute an unlawful practice. Article 101(1)(d) and Article 102(c) TFEU both contain prohibitions against agreements to apply "dissimilar conditions to equivalent transactions with other trading parties, thereby placing them at a competitive disadvantage." We saw that US antitrust law has detailed rules contained in the Robinson-Patman Act proscribing discriminations in price and in promotional benefits. The Robinson-Patman Act was adopted in 1936 as special legislation designed to protect small businesses from discrimination at the hands of their suppliers. The specific defenses of meeting competition and cost justification are provided for the supplier. In contrast, the above-quoted EU Treaty provisions on the subject of business discrimination lack elaboration, as well as the benefit of legislative history, which might have helped to illuminate their application to specific situations.

The cases under EU competition law involving the discrimination issue have come up primarily in the context of abuse of a dominant position under what is now Article 102. There has been little enforcement activity on the issue under the Article 101(1) prohibition which is directed against conduct undertaken pursuant to an agreement or concerted practice, as distinct from unilateral conduct. As the ECJ said in the *Viho Europe* case in 1996:

> The discrimination at which Article 81(1) is aimed must therefore be the result of an agreement ... or a concerted practice between separate and autonomous economic entities and not the result of unilateral conduct by a single undertaking.

One should not conclude from this situation that it is not possible to apply Article 101(1) to a nondominant company's discriminatory treatment of a particular customer or customers. Knowledgeable commentators have suggested that the Article 101(1)(d) prohibition can, in an appropriate case, be applied to an agreement between a supplier and a customer in which the supplier agrees to give favorable terms to that customer or, alternatively, where the supplier agrees with that customer to offer unfavorable terms to another customer or customers.

Moreover, the Commission has taken the position that a company's general conditions of sale can be regarded as potentially covered by Article 101 since those terms form part of the contracts the company has with its customers. On this reasoning, a seller's application of general conditions which discriminate between customers could be challenged under Article 101(1) without regard to whether or not the seller was dominant. Moreover, where a seller has utilized price discrimination to restrict exports, it has been held to be an infringement of Article 101(1). In several cases, going back as far as *Kodak* in 1970 and *Distillers* in 1977, the Commission considered that the Article 85(1) prohibition was applicable to a seller's agreements or its conditions of sale requiring purchasers to charge higher prices on export to another EC country than they charged on resale within the domestic market.

[K] Current Rules for Car Distribution and the Aftermarket

The pricing policies maintained by the manufacturers of automobiles combined with differing national tax policies in the Member States have caused high differentials to exist as between the sales prices for the same autos in different Member States. Citing these factors, as well as the special circumstances pertaining to the distribution of automobiles by the manufacturers through their dealers, the Commission, for some years, shaped a block exemption applicable just to that industry. The Commission also has published several reports on the issues raised in the distribution of motor vehicles and it has found that consumers still have difficulty taking advantage of the price differentials between Member States. The objective of the Commission's actions has been to obtain for consumers the benefits of the single market by facilitating cross-border sales and promoting competition in this context. The Commission found it necessary to retool the block exemption on a regular basis. Moreover, in a number of cases, it has levied heavy fines against a number of major European auto manufacturers for restraining parallel imports in concerted conduct with their dealers.

The original Regulation 123/85 was replaced by a slightly revised version, Regulation 1475/95 on Motor Vehicle Distribution and Servicing Agreements. When the 1995 Regulation expired in 2002, it was replaced by Regulation 1400/2002 which expired in 2010. Regulation 461/2010 is a current regulation regarding the motor vehicle sector. Article 3 of that Regulation provides that, with effect from June 1, 2013, Regulation 330/2010 (the BE Regulation) will apply to vertical agreements relating to the purchase, sale or resale of new motor vehicles. We discussed the BE Regulation above.

Article 4 of Regulation 461/2010 provides a block exemption for vertical agreements relating to the purchase, sale or resale of spare parts for motor vehicles or repair and maintenance service for motor vehicles, providing the agreements meet the requirements of the BE Regulation and do not contain hard core restrictions of the type set out in Regulation 461/2010. The hard core restrictions listed include restricting a supplier of spare parts or equipment from selling to authorized or independent parties or end users. This regulation will cover the motor vehicle aftermarket until May 31, 2023. The Commission has also published *Supplementary Guidelines* relating to distribution in the motor vehicle sector.

§11.05 ASSIGNMENTS AND LICENSES OF IP RIGHTS

[A] Introduction

The exercise of intellectual property ("IP") rights—primarily those relating to patents, know-how, trademarks, and copyrights,—is a vital element of commerce in the EU, as elsewhere in the world. The nature of each such right (sometimes referred to as an industrial property right) and the procedures for protecting it are largely shaped by the laws of the individual Member States. These laws may vary significantly, although they are subject to the obligations imposed by various international conventions to which the Member States and/or the EU have subscribed.

Among the international commitments of the EU and its Member States (as well as of the US) is the World Trade Organization Agreement on Trade-Related Aspects of Intellectual Property Rights ("TRIPS"). The TRIPS Agreement requires signatories to comply with various provisions of the Paris Convention for the Protection of Intellectual Property and the Berne Convention dealing with copyright, as well as to accord "national treatment" to the nationals of other signatories. The detailed provisions of the TRIPS Agreement include also standards for the grant of protection for copyright, trademarks, industrial designs, patents, and lay-out designs of integrated circuits. Patents, for example, are to be available for any inventions which are new, involve an inventive component and are capable of industrial application. The term of protection may not expire before the expiration of twenty years counted from the filing date. Article 40 of the TRIPS Agreement begins with the recitation of a consensus that "some licensing practices or conditions pertaining to intellectual property rights which restrain competition may have adverse effects on trade and may impede the transfer and dissemination of technology." Article 40(2) very explicitly advances the endorsement of competition law principles in the context of IP rights by stating as follows:

> 2. Nothing in this Agreement shall prevent Members from specifying in their legislation licensing practices or conditions that may in particular cases constitute an abuse of intellectual property rights having an adverse effect on competition in the relevant market. As provided above, a Member may adopt, consistently with the other provisions of this Agreement, appropriate measures to prevent or control such practices, which may include for example exclusive grantback conditions, conditions preventing challenges to validity and coercive package licensing, in the light of the relevant laws and regulations of that Member.

Despite the quickening pace of globalization, including the integration of the European nations, patent systems have continued to be largely national in scope. Under the Patent Cooperation Treaty, concluded in 1970, a procedure is provided for a single filing of an international patent application. This establishes a filing date in all contracting states but the issuance of the patent is a national or regional matter.

In Europe, patents are still granted in the individual Member States. Since the European Patent Convention went into effect in 1977, an applicant has been able to obtain a bundle of patents from the European Patent Office in Munich reflecting each Member State and non-Member State which has ratified the Convention. These patents are national patents, valid only in those countries for which they have been issued. Work on establishing a European patent with unitary effect (EPUE) pursuant to EU regulations continues.

In the EU, know-how, much of it in the nature of unpatented confidential and valuable technology, is unprotected as such by any specific IP legislation. However, national law may provide an aggrieved party with a right of action against unauthorized use or disclosure of valuable know-how. So far as EU competition law is concerned, as we will be discussing, the rules which have been fashioned with respect to the licensing of patents have largely been applied to know-how licensing as well.

[B] Trademarks

Trademarks are also granted on a national basis by the Member States. However, the effort to attain an EU regime in trademarks has moved more swiftly than that in the patent area. A directive known as First Council Directive 89/104 EC to Approximate the Laws of the Member States Relating to Trademarks was adopted in 1989 to advance the harmonization of the trademark laws of the Member States. The national laws were duly amended to comply with this directive. (This Directive was renewed on October 22, 2008.) As a result of Council Regulation 40/94 on the Community Trademark, as amended, undertakings were able since 1996 to obtain an EU trademark in parallel to the protection of trademarks available in Member States by applying for it at the Community Trademark Office in Alicante, Spain.

The EU adopted a trademark reform package in 2015. It determined that the EU trademark system had become a successful and viable alternative to the protection of trademarks at the level of the Member States. The name of the EU office in Alicante was changed to the European Union Intellectual Property Office (EUIPO), and the Community Trademark was renamed to be the European Union Trade Mark ("EU Trade Mark"). The Trade Mark Directive, No. 2008/95/EC, was replaced by Regulation 2015/2424 of December 16, 2015 and entered into force on March 23, 2016. Member States have until January 14, 2019 to incorporate the new provisions into their national laws.

These EU marks are deemed to have a "unitary character" and to be valid throughout the entire territory of the Union. Under the applicable rules, a trademark for goods or services may be licensed exclusively or nonexclusively for all or part of the territory to which it applies. We will discuss below the extent to which the placing on the market of the trademarked product by the owner of the mark or with his consent is considered, under the EU law, to "exhaust" the rights conferred by the mark. The new Regulation provides as follows as to exhaustion of the rights conferred:

(1) A trademark shall not entitle the proprietor to prohibit its use in relation to goods which have been put on the market in the Union under that trademark by the proprietor or with the proprietor's consent.
(2) Paragraph 1 shall not apply where there exist legitimate reasons for the proprietor to oppose further commercialization of the goods, especially where the condition of the goods is changed or impaired after they have been put on the market.

[C] Copyright

There exist a number of important international copyright conventions, including the Berne Convention for the Protection of Literary and Artistic Works and the Universal Copyright Convention. Although these conventions facilitate copyright protection on an international basis, there is no such thing as an international copyright grant. National law is the basis for the creation of protection against unauthorized use of literary and other copyrightable forms of expression. However, in the EU, the Council has adopted a number of directives which the Member States have incorporated into their national laws and have thus contributed to copyright protection.

In 1991, the Computer Programs Directive imposed a common standard for the copyright protection of computer programs. The Copyright Duration Directive, No. 93/98 of October 28, 1993, harmonized the term of protection for copyright and certain related rights in the Member States. It set the duration of copyright in literary, artistic, cinematographic and audiovisual works at seventy years from the death of the author and for related rights at fifty years. Another Directive, No. 2004/48/EC on the enforcement of IP rights, seeks "to approximate legislative systems so as to ensure a high, equivalent and homogeneous level of protection in the Internal Market." It provides guidance to the Member States as to their application of enforcement measures and remedies that will be fair and equitable, not unnecessarily costly or involving unwarranted delays.

Indeed, the conferring and enforcement of IP rights on a national basis can create significant legal and practical problems when the countries granting the rights are also members of an integrated common market, as in the case of the Member States of the EU. Particularly in the early years of the Community, there existed, in addition to the inherent tension existing between competition law rules and IP "monopolies," an added degree of tension resulting from the Community's need to prevent the use of IP rights as devices for partitioning the Community into its national markets. If a holder of exclusive national IP rights could utilize those rights to prevent the importation or exportation of a product from one Member State to another, the exclusion of the "parallel imports" would be a fragmentation of the Community. On the other hand, legitimately awarded national IP rights needed to be recognized. As we will see, this potential problem was effectively addressed by the Commission and the Community Courts.

§11.06 THE DIGITAL MARKET

The era of the computer is fully upon us, and its devices dominate our commercial lives (and also, perhaps, our personal lives), which now take on a different form and pace. The EU, for so long focused on creating a marketplace in which physical goods can travel unimpeded across national borders, discovered recently that only 15% of its citizens shop online from another EU country and only 7% of EU small and medium sized businesses sold cross-border. So, in 2015, the EU adopted a Digital Single Market Strategy designed to embrace the digital revolution for its citizens and businesses.

Commission President Jean-Claude Juncker announced a 16-step action plan to be fleshed out by the Commission by the end of 2016. The three "pillars" of the Strategy are as follows.

(1) Providing better access for consumers and businesses to digital goods and services across Europe. This will require, among other things, developing harmonized EU rules on contracts and consumer protection to make cross-border e-commerce easier; reducing parcel delivery costs and inefficiencies; developing a modern copyright law for Europe; and reviewing the Satellite and Cable Directive.

(2) Creating the right conditions and a level playing field for digital networks and innovative services to flourish. This will require an ambitious overhaul of EU telecom rules; reviewing the audiovisual media framework; analyzing the role of online platforms and tracking illegal content on the Internet; reviewing the e-Privacy Directive; and partnering with industry on improved cybersecurity.

(3) Maximizing the growth potential of the digital economy. This will entail launching both a European free flow of data initiative and a European Cloud initiative; defining priorities for standards and interoperability; and supporting an inclusive digital society to serve citizens, businesses, and public administrations in their interactions with each other.

The Commission has developed a large number of legislative proposals and policy initiatives to carry out this mandate. It has called on the European Parliament and the Council to act swiftly on these proposals, and "above all [on] the updated EU telecoms rules which will boost investments in high-speed and quality networks, which are critical for the full deployment of the digital economy and society."

§11.07 THE FREE MOVEMENT OF GOODS: THE EXHAUSTION DOCTRINE

Under the EC Treaty, the status of IP rights had to be evaluated not only in terms of the competition law provisions but also with reference to those provisions which sought to assure protection for the free movement of goods. Article 30 of that Treaty, now Article 36 of the TFEU, safeguarded various prohibitions or restrictions on imports or exports, including "the protection of industrial and commercial property."

The ECJ has laid down principles which protect these rights of property ownership, but interpret them narrowly when they potentially conflict with the measures needed for integrating the Community, including the rules for the protection of competition. First, in a series of cases, the Court developed the doctrine that, while the EC Treaty left undisturbed the existence of property rights, the exercise of these rights would, to the extent necessary, be circumscribed. That exercise had to be carried on in such a way that it did not impede the competitive process and the freedom of movement of goods between Member States, including the possibility of parallel imports.

In the *Consten and Grundig* case, the Court sustained the application of the Community competition law rules to nullify efforts by trademark proprietors and their licensees to exercise their national rights for the purpose of blocking parallel imports. Enjoining the use of trademark rights in that situation, said the Court, did not affect the grant of the national trademark rights, "but only limits their exercise to the extent necessary to give effect to the prohibition under Article 85(1)." In 1968, in the *Parke, Davis v. Probel* judgment, the Court adopted similar reasoning concerning the possible abuse of patent rights to partition Community markets. The principles were thus well established that the exercise of national IP rights was now limited by the requirements of Community law and that the exercise of these rights would be protected only insofar as it was necessary to safeguard the rationale which gave rise to those rights in the first place, i.e., the need to provide adequate remuneration for invention and assure the safe transfer of technology.

Establishing appropriate rules of law required a proper calibration of the "exhaustion doctrine." Under national law, an IP right is usually deemed to be "exhausted" after the product protected (by the right) has been marketed for the first time by the rights holder himself, or by another party (e.g., a licensee) with the rights' holder's consent. At that point, the anticipated remuneration for the invention or other innovation is deemed to have been earned, and it is considered that the IP right should not burden the alienation of the product further. It was thus recognized, for example, that a patentee who placed her patented product on the market in Member State A could not prevent the purchaser of the product from freely disposing of it either within Member State A or outside of it. The IP right had been exhausted. A variation of this situation was presented in the *Parke, Davis* case just mentioned above. In that decision, the ECJ held that the owner of a Dutch patent for an antibiotic process could preclude the marketing of a version of the drug in Holland in the particular circumstances presented, since the drug had been manufactured in Italy which did not confer patent protection on drugs. Given that the drug had not been placed on the market in any Community country with the permission of the patent holder, the freedom of movement issue was not presented.

It remained to be seen, however, how the freedom of movement principle would be applied in a situation in which an effort was made to bar the importation into a Member State of an IP product which had been placed in another Member State market by the rights holder or his licensee. Cases were promptly referred to the Court concerning patents, trademarks, and copyrights. The first case was *Deutsche Grammophon v. Metro*, involving an effort by Metro, which had purchased sound recordings in France produced by Deutsche Grammophon, to sell them in Germany over the objection of the latter, which held the exclusive copyrights. The Court held that, since Deutsche Grammophon had itself placed the recordings on the market in a Member State, it could not use its rights to block the import of those recordings into another Member State. In sum, once the goods had been placed on a Community market by the rights holder or by a third party with the rights holder's consent, their parallel importation into another Member State could not be blocked.

The same result obtained in the patent and trademark situations which came before the Court in 1974 in the *Centrafarm* cases. Centrafarm had purchased from the Sterling-Winthrop group, a United Kingdom drug producer, patented drugs under the trade name of "Negram" in the UK and Germany for resale in Holland. *Centrafarm v. Sterling Drug Inc.* and *Centrafarm v. Winthrop BV*, involved the drug manufacturer's efforts to prevent Centrafarm from selling the drugs in Holland, asserting the manufacturer's Dutch patent and trademark rights. In both cases, the Court of Justice held that the first sale of the drugs had exhausted the rights of the owner of the IP and that, thereafter, the purchaser of the underlying product could market it freely. Exceptions to the free movement of goods for the protection of IP were permissible only to the extent necessary to protect the specific object, i.e., the essence, of that right. That object was accomplished once the product had been manufactured and placed into circulation.

In the *Coditel I* and *Coditel II* cases, in 1980 and 1982, the ECJ confirmed that the distinction recognized between the existence of a right conferred by Member State legislation and the exercise of that right to restrict trade between Member States also applied in the context of the movement of services. Nonetheless, in the *Coditel I* judgment, the Court ruled that an exclusive copyright license in a film given for several years by the French producer to a Belgian distributor was not incompatible with Article 59 of the Treaty, protecting the freedom to provide services. Then, two years later in *Coditel II*, the Court drew an important distinction between performance rights (which can give rise to a royalty each time a work is publicly performed) and rights to sell products (which are exhausted by the product's sale with the rights' owner's consent).

The Court concluded that, in the particular context provided by the film industry, "the mere fact that the owner in a copyright in a film has granted to a sole licensee the exclusive right to exhibit that film in the territory of a Member State and, consequently, to prohibit, during a specific period, its showing by others, is not sufficient [to place the contract under the prohibition of Article 85(1)]."

By reason of the EEA Agreement, the exhaustion principle also applies to situations in which the protected product is placed on the market in an EEA Country (Norway, Iceland, and Liechtenstein). The exhaustion doctrine does not apply, however, when one seeks to import for the first time into an EEA or Community country protected goods which have been initially marketed outside of those nations. At that point, an enterprise which is the owner of the IP right in the country of import may enforce it to prevent the importation of the product.

Trademarks, unlike patents, do not promote technological progress and innovation. Their function is to identify the origin of a product or service and thereby, to protect both the proprietor of the mark and the consumer against market place confusion or deception. Trademarks, unlike patents and copyrights, are not limited in duration to a fixed period of time and can continue to exist indefinitely. The early jurisprudence of the EC did not have high regard for trademarks, viewing them as somewhat unworthy creations which involved little invention and might be utilized to partition the Community along national lines. As we discussed earlier, the Court of Justice held in the *Consten/Grundig* case that a series of bilateral exclusive distributorship agreements enabling the enforcement of national trademarks violated Article 85(1) of the Treaty insofar as they resulted in absolute territorial protection against parallel imports. In the Court's view, the registration by Consten, the French distributor, of the GINT trademark that Grundig, the German manufacturer, affixed to all its products, was designed to fortify the distributorship agreement's built-in protection against parallel imports and was therefore a disguised restriction on trade between Member States.

In the 1977 decision relating to the *Davide Campari Milano SpA Agreement* the Italian aperitif producer granted companies from other European countries exclusive licenses under its various national trademarks and its secret processes for the drinks. The Commission granted an exemption under Article 85(3) with respect to clauses in which Campari agreed to refrain from manufacturing drinks itself in the licensed territories and the licensees agreed not to deal in competing products and also not to pursue active selling, advertise, or establish branches outside the territories assigned to each. In both the *Campari* case and in the *Moosehead/Whitbread* decision, the Commission accepted commitments by the licensees to purchase certain materials only from the licensor, because this requirement was justified on quality control grounds. Also upheld were commitments to use the licensed know-how only for the manufacture of the licensed goods and only under the licensor's trademark, as well as the obligation not to disclose the secret processes to third parties.

The case of *Zino Davidoff SA* and *Levi Strauss & Co.*, decided by the ECJ in 2001, involved trademarked toiletries and trademarked jeans which third parties had obtained from authorized traders outside of the EEA and which they then sought to import into the United Kingdom over the objections of the owners of the UK registered

Chapter 11: Article 101 TFEU: Suppliers, Customers and Licensees §11.07

marks, Zino Davidoff SA and Levi Strauss & Co. The UK court referred to the ECJ the questions concerning the application of Community law in these situations. In its opinion, the Court pointed out that the effect of the Trade Mark Directive is "to limit exhaustion of the rights conferred on the proprietor of a trade mark to cases where goods have been put on the market in the EEA and to allow the proprietor to market his products outside that area without exhausting his rights within the EEA." The central question was whether the mark owners had consented to the marketing of the trademarked products within the EEA. In view of the serious effect of such consent, said the Court, "consent must be so expressed that an intention to renounce [the exclusive rights] is unequivocally demonstrated." While implied consent might be inferred in some circumstances, such consent could not be implied from mere silence on the part of the mark's proprietor or the lack of a warning label on the goods. Moreover, it was not relevant whether the importer was unaware of the owner's objections. There was no exhaustion.

The ECJ has ruled in a series of cases involving pharmaceuticals that, once a trademarked product has been repackaged, the exhaustion principle only applies in certain circumstances. Thus, if there has been a repackaging of the goods and a reaffixing of the trademark without the trademark owner's consent, the owner may successfully oppose the further marketing within the Union of the repackaged product unless certain conditions for applying the exhaustion principle apply. Among the prerequisites to applying the exhaustion rule in this context which the Court has laid down is that the original condition of the product was not adversely affected by the repackaging and that the consumer received notice concerning whom had carried out the repackaging. In addition, the trademark proprietor must be given notice of the proposed repackaging, and it has to be shown that allowing the proprietor to enforce his trademark rights against the repackager would contribute to the artificial partitioning of the Community. On the other hand, the trademark proprietor may oppose the repackaging if it is shown to be based solely on the parallel importer's attempt to secure a commercial advantage rather than being "objectively necessary" for the marketing of the product.

This complicated jurisprudence caused some confusion which the Court tried to clear up in its 2002 decisions in *Boehringer Ingelheim* and *Merck/Paranova*. In both cases, the Court emphasized that "replacement packaging of pharmaceutical products is objectively necessary within the meaning of the Court's case-law if, without such repackaging, effective access to the market concerned, or to a substantial part of that market, must be considered to be hindered as the result of strong resistance from a significant proportion of consumers to relabelled pharmaceutical products." However, the Court referred several of the key factual inquiries back to the national courts, including the determination of whether the act of repackaging was necessary to achieve effective market access for the products in question, rather than an attempt to gain a commercial advantage.

These principles relating to exhaustion address the situation in which the imported trademarked goods have been repackaged for resale using the trademark that pertained in the Member State in which the goods were originally obtained. In the case of *Pharmacia & Upjohn SA v. Paranova A/S*, a different question was put by the Danish courts to the ECJ by reference under Article 234 of the EC Treaty. The issue there was whether a parallel importer was entitled to repackage and sell the goods under the trademark which the proprietor used in the importing State for identical goods, even though the proprietor had applied a different mark when it first placed the goods on the market. The facts again involved a pharmaceutical product. Upjohn marketed the antibiotic clindamycin in the Community using various forms of the trademark "Dalacin." Paranova purchased the product in France under the name "Dalacine" and in Greece under the name "Dalacin C," and repackaged them for sale in Denmark under the name "Dalacin." Upjohn obtained an injunction under Danish law prohibiting Paranova from selling the imported goods under that mark.

The Court of Justice noted that the Trade Mark Directive did not address this situation and that the case was governed by Articles 28 and 30 of the Treaty relating to the free movement of goods. The Court concluded that, in principle, the exhaustion rule does apply where the parallel importer replaces the original trademark by that used by the proprietor in the Member State of import. However, said the Court, the exhaustion would apply only if the national court of the importing country made the finding that the replacement of one mark with the other was "objectively necessary" for the marketing of the product in the Member State of import, i.e., that there would be a legal or other significant barrier to the marketing of the product in the importing state under its original dress. The Court stated that the necessity requirement would not be satisfied if, for example, the replacement of the trademark is motivated solely by the parallel importer's desire to secure a commercial advantage in selling the product.

A trademark-related question that came up in the early years was whether the separate owners of a particular trademark in different Community countries were barred from using the mark to challenge each other where the trademark came from a common origin or common source. This issue arose in 1974 in *Van Zuylen Freres v. Hag* (known as "*Hag I*"). Van Zuylen had obtained the rights to the Benelux trademark for "Hag" coffee from the Custodian of Enemy Property after the war, while the original owner of the mark, Hag AG of Germany, had resumed the selling of coffee under the mark in the Benelux area. Van Zuylen attempted to block Hag AG from importing coffee into Luxembourg, asserting an infringement of its Hag trademark. The Court of Justice ruled against Van Zuylen, reasoning that the holder of a trademark in one Member State could not utilize it so as to prevent the marketing in that Member State of goods legally produced in another Member State, where the identical trademark had the same source or origin.

However, this decision was overruled by the Court in 1990 in *Hag II*, which involved an effort by the German Hag company to prevent the owner of the Benelux trademark (the successor to Van Zuylen) from selling coffee under the mark in Germany. The Court sustained the German company's right to bar the Belgian company from selling its coffee in Germany. The decision abandoned the notion of common origin as a basis for disregarding national trademark rights, and it acknowledged the importance of trademark rights as "an essential element in the system of undistorted competition which the Treaty seeks to establish and maintain." Trademarks were to be viewed as legitimate property rights, delineated by national law, and necessary to protect the goodwill of a manufacturer of quality products.

Confirmation that *Hag II*, and not *Hag I*, represented the state of the law came in the *Ideal Standard* case in 1994. That case involved a situation in which the ownership of the identical trademarks in France and Germany had been separated on a voluntary basis. The German rights holder subsequently attempted to block the marketing in Germany of trademarked products exported by the French rights holder. The Court upheld the position of the German company, notwithstanding the fact that the two national marks had initially shared a common origin. The Court observed that any differences in the quality of the goods sold under the two marks could not be controlled and that consumers would not be able reliably to identify the origin of the goods should the French goods be sold under the identical mark in Germany.

The *Terrapin v. Terranova* case in 1976 raised still another question. Terranova was a German manufacturer of plaster for buildings which had registered in Germany several trademarks relating to its building materials, including the words "Terra," "Terranova," and "Terrafabrikate." Terrapin was an English company which manufactured houses and components using the trademark "Terrapin," which it owned in the UK and sought to register in Germany where it was also operating. After litigation had ensued, the German Supreme Court referred to the ECJ under Article 177 the question of whether the German company could, consistently with the freedom of movement provisions of the EC Treaty, oppose the use of the name "Terrapin" by the English company in Germany. The Court determined that the German authorities could, consistently with the Treaty, refuse to register the "Terrapin" trademark, given the genuine risk of confusion. The absence of economic links or agreements between the two parties was obviously another critical factor.

§11.08 THE TECHNOLOGY TRANSFER BLOCK EXEMPTION REGULATION

In the early years of the Community, thousands of patent licenses were notified to the Commission for possible exemption. The task of working out a general approach applicable to the restrictions in such licenses was an obvious issue for the Commission's consideration, but the issues presented were complex and, under the Commission's mandate, issuance of a block exemption had to wait until sufficient experience had been obtained in individual decision-making. The first public statement by the Commission on the subject came in a Notice on Patent Licensing Agreements which was issued on December 24, 1962 and hence became known as a "Christmas Message." The first section of the Notice listed those clauses which were considered not to be covered by Article 85(1), including provisions assuring exclusivity for the licensee, and the second section stated that other clauses would be assessed individually. However, the Commission subsequently did not adhere to all of the rules which it had declared, particularly as to the exclusivity issue, and it withdrew the Notice in 1984.

A number of important individual decisions preceded the finalization of a block exemption. Among the noteworthy decisions were those rendered in the *Burroughs-Delplanque* and *Burroughs-Geha* decisions in 1971 involving requests for negative clearances for manufacturing licenses for a new carbon black paper under Burroughs'

French and German patents. In these cases, the Commission reversed the position it had taken in the Christmas Message and now took the position that, in certain situations, the grant of an exclusive license to manufacture or sell a patented product in a given territory might be covered by the prohibition of Article 85(1), since the exclusivity limited the licensor's ability to grant others licenses in the same territory. In the *Burroughs* decisions, the Commission did approve in principle the following restraints, in appropriate cases: (1) limitation of a patent license to a specific territory; (2) a prohibition against sublicensing; (3) a licensee's obligation to produce in sufficient quantities to satisfy demand; (4) a licensee's obligation to follow standards of quality and technical instructions of the licensor; (5) the obligation to pay a minimum royalty; and (6) the obligation to maintain the secrecy of confidential know-how, even after the expiration of the license.

In the *Burroughs* cases the Commission also approved the imposition of a nonexclusive "grantback" provision on the licensee, obligating him to disclose to the licensor, on a reciprocal basis, technical improvements obtained during the course of the license. Later, in the *Raymond-Nagoya* decision, the Commission insisted that a grantback obligation be made on a nonexclusive basis only, disapproving a provision which required the transfer to the licensor of any improvements developed by the licensee. The principle that an exclusive grantback license commitment might be covered by Article 85(1) was confirmed in several other cases in this era, although negative clearances or individual exemptions were issued by the Commission in some instances.

Another milestone in the development of the principles leading to the issuance of the block exemption was the *Maize Seed* case, in which the Commission and the ECJ rendered decisions in 1978 and 1982, respectively. That case involved INRA, a French state agency, which held breeders' rights in a variety of maize seeds. INRA granted to a German company the exclusive right to distribute INRA's maize seed varieties in Germany, and it agreed to a number of restrictions on competition, including a commitment to prevent other imports of those seeds into Germany. The Commission held the restrictive terms to which the parties had agreed to be in violation of Article 85(1), and it denied a request for an exemption under Article 85(3). Among the restrictions struck down by the Commission were the licensor's obligations not to itself produce or sell the INRA varieties in Germany, or authorize others to do so, or allow third parties to export the goods concerned to Germany.

On appeal, the Court did not accept all of the Commission's reasoning. The Court found not incompatible in itself with Article 85(1) the grant of an "open" exclusive license, whereby the licensor merely agreed not to grant rights to the same territory to other licensees, but without affecting the position of parallel imports from other territories. The propriety of such a license would have to be decided on its own facts. On the other hand, a "closed" exclusive license, which sought to assure absolute territorial protection by preventing parallel imports, like INRA's commitment to prevent unauthorized sales of the seeds into Germany, did violate Article 85(1).

After going through a number of public drafts, the Commission finally issued a block exemption applicable to patent licensing agreements, Regulation 2349/84 which became effective January 1, 1985. The exemption's final provisions on the subject of exclusivity were significantly shaped by the Court's *Maize Seed* decision. The Regulation applied to pure patent licenses and to "mixed" patent and know-how licensing agreements, but with the latter narrowly defined, i.e., where know-how constituted secret technical knowledge permitting a better exploitation of the licensed patents. Agreements involving "pure" know-how licenses and "mixed" know-how/patent licenses were subsequently provided for through the issuance of Regulation 556/89 granting a group exemption to such agreements and entering into force on April 1, 1989. The mixed agreements covered were those not covered by the patent license block exemption. This new approach was accomplished by the issuance in 1996 of Regulation 240/96 applicable to "certain categories of technology transfer agreements," which covered both patented and unpatented technology and replaced the two prior regulations.

Regulation 772/2004 on the Application of Article 81(3) of the Treaty to Categories of Technology Transfer Agreements was issued in 2004, repealing Regulation 240/96. In keeping with the Commission's current philosophy, Regulation 772/2004 announced the adoption of an "economics-based approach," designed to "move away from the approach of listing exempted clauses and to place greater emphasis on defining the categories of agreements which are exempted up to a certain level of market power and on specifying the restrictions of clauses which are not to be contained in such agreements." Accordingly, the lists of black and grey clauses used by the prior Regulation were eliminated and the focus for receipt of the benefit of the block exemption was placed on market share thresholds. Along with the new Regulation, the Commission issued *Guidelines on the Application of Article 81 to Technology Transfer Agreements*. This forty page document was intended to clarify the application of the new block exemption regulation to technology transfer agreements, as well as the application of Article (81)(3) to such agreements which were not covered by the new Regulation.

In December 2011, the Commission issued a questionnaire to learn of the public reaction to the block exemption and the *Guidelines*. Following this review, the Commission adopted Regulation 316/2014 conferring block exemption on technology transfer agreements pursuant to Article 101(3) of the Treaty. Regulation 316/2014 replaced the prior Regulation and will expire on April 30, 2026. There follows a brief review of this current block exemption.

Regulation 316/2014, like its predecessor, applies to "technology transfer agreements." "Agreement" is defined to include an agreement, an association decision, or a concerted practice. Among the agreements covered are patent licensing agreements, know-how licensing agreements, software copyright licensing agreements, and mixed patent, know-how or software copyright licensing agreements. Agreements in which the licensing of IP rights is not the primary object of the agreement, such as contracts relating primarily to the purchase or distribution of products, are not covered by this block exemption, although they may be covered by one of the other block exemptions. The benefit of the block exemption established by this Regulation is intended to be limited to those agreements which can be assumed with sufficient certainty to satisfy the conditions of Article 101(3) TFEU.

There are market thresholds to the exemption. Where the undertakings party to the agreement are competing undertakings, the exemption provided applies on condition that the combined market share of the parties does not exceed 20% on the market. Where the undertakings party to the agreement are not competing undertakings, the exemption provided applies on condition that the market share of each of the parties does not exceed 30% on the relevant market.

Many technology transfer agreements do not infringe Article 101(1) at all and therefore do not need the benefit of the block exemption provided here. The *Technology Transfer Guidelines* issued in connection with the new Regulation on March 28, 2014 assert at paragraph 17 that license agreements "have substantial pro-competitive potential," and that most such agreements are in fact pro-competitive and hence fall outside of Article 101(1). Moreover, even where an agreement is above the market share threshold, there is no presumption that it infringes Article 101(1) or is incapable of meeting the terms of Article 101(3).

Paragraph 6 of the *Guidelines* sets out the bedrock principle of "Union exhaustion":

> Once a product incorporating an intellectual property right, with the exception of performance rights, has been put on the market inside the European Economic Area (EEA) by the holder or with its consent, the intellectual property right is exhausted in the sense that the holder can no longer use it to control the sale of the product (principle of Union exhaustion) (footnotes omitted)

Footnote 8 of the *Guidelines* elaborates that "This principle of Union exhaustion is for example enshrined in [the Trade Mark Directive], which provides that the trade mark shall not entitle the proprietor to prohibit its use in relation to goods which have been put on the market in the Union under that trade mark by the proprietor or with its consent ... ."

The block exemption for technology transfer applies only in the case of bilateral agreements, not multilateral ones. The exemption applies for as long as the licensed technology rights have not expired, lapsed or been declared invalid or, in the case of know-how, for as long as the know-how remains secret. However, where know-how becomes publicly known as a result of action by the licensee, the exemption continues for the duration of the agreement. Licensing arrangements in R & D agreements and specialization agreements are not covered by Regulation 316/2014 since they are under the block exemptions for such arrangements.

Article 4 of the Regulation lists the hard core restrictions which are considered restrictions as to object covered by Article 101(1) TFEU and not likely to satisfy the requirements of Article 101(3) TFEU. There is one set of hard core restrictions for agreements between competing undertakings which is contained in Article 4(1) of the Regulation and another for agreements between noncompeting undertakings contained in Article 4(2). Moreover, for a number of hard core restrictions involving licenses between competitors, the Regulation makes a distinction between "reciprocal" and "nonreciprocal" licensing agreements. Because reciprocal agreements involving competitors can be utilized to allocate markets, control output and otherwise restrain competition between the parties, they are treated more severely than the situation where the licensing is nonreciprocal. Article 4(2) lists the hard core restrictions with respect to licenses between noncompetitors. When, on applying the appropriate provision, a technology transfer agreement contains a hard core restriction of competition, then the agreement as a whole falls outside the scope of the block exemption.

The following are hard core restrictions enumerated in Article 4(1) relating to licenses between competitors: (1) *restricting a party's ability to determine its prices to third parties*. Paragraph 99 of the *Guidelines* states that "[i]t is immaterial whether the agreement concerns fixed, minimum, maximum or recommended prices"; (2) *output limitations*, other than limitations on the output of contract products imposed on the licensees in a reciprocal agreement; (3) *market or customer allocations*, except in a number of specified situations; and (4) *the restriction of the licensee's ability to exploit its own technology rights or the restriction of the ability of any of the parties to the agreement to carry out research and development*, unless such latter restriction is indispensable to prevent the disclosure of the licensed know-how to third parties.

Article 4(2) of the Regulation provides that the block exemption does not apply where the parties are not competing undertakings to agreements which have as their object: (1) *The restriction of a party's ability to determine its sales prices*. It is permissible to impose a maximum price provided that this does not amount to a fixed or minimum price as a result of pressure from, or incentives offered by, any of the parties. (2) *Restricting the territory into which, or the customer group to whom, the licensee may passively sell the goods*. There are exceptions provided to this prohibition, including where there is an exclusive territory or an exclusive customer group reserved for the licensor. (3) *The restriction of active or passive sales to end users by a licensee which is a member of a selective distribution system and which operates at the retail level*, without prejudice to the possibility of prohibiting a member of the system from operating out of an unauthorized place of establishment.

Under Article 5 of the Regulation, certain obligations in a licensing agreement are deemed "excluded restrictions." These restrictions are not covered by the block exemption, and an individual assessment of their competitive effects is required (inclusion of any of these restrictions does not prevent the application of the block exemption to the rest of the agreement). The restrictions include: exclusive grant-backs to the licensor or to a third party designated by the licensor and no-challenge clauses regarding the IP rights of the licensor.

The *Guidelines* discuss the application of Article 101(1) to various common types of licensing restraints. Some restraints are generally not restrictive of competition within the meaning of Article 101(1). These include nondisclosure obligations, sublicensing prohibitions, obligations not to use the licensed technology after the expiry of the agreement providing that the technology remains valid and in force, obligations to assist the licensor in enforcing the licensed IP rights, minimum royalty payment or minimum production commitments, and obligations to use the licensor's trademark or indicate the name of the licensor on the product. Also normally acceptable are various forms of royalty arrangements, exclusive licensing between noncompetitors, certain restrictions on active sales into the territory or to the customer group allocated to another licensee, certain field of use limitations, and some captive use restrictions. It is not possible here to describe all of the different contexts in which these issues may be raised, which may render the particular restriction as anticompetitive, pro-competitive, or neutral.

Restrictions in technology licensing agreements which provide for "tying" or "bundling" of technologies and/or products present the usual antitrust concerns over such arrangements. The main restrictive effect of tying is foreclosure of competing suppliers of the tied product. Whether two or more technologies or products are by necessity linked for use or promote the successful application of the technology are important considerations which go toward justifying the arrangement, as is the effect of the tie-in on the market. The Regulation's market share thresholds for competitor and noncompetitor agreements apply here. The Guidelines advise that "[f]or tying to produce likely anti-competitive effects the licensor must have a significant degree of market power in the tying product so as to restrict competition in the tied product."

The *Guidelines* also discuss noncompete obligations and technology pools. The possible anticompetitive effects of each require careful assessment in context. Technology pools are defined as arrangements whereby two or more parties assemble a package of technology which is licensed to contributors to the pool and also to third parties. Such group arrangements are not covered by the block exemption. Technology pools may restrict competition and reduce innovation or they may be pro-competitive in reducing transaction costs and allowing for one-stop shopping of technologies.

In the *3G Patent Platform Partnership* case in 2003, the Commission addressed a plan by manufacturers of equipment for mobile technologies to bundle the different technologies in a single platform so as to give the companies access to all of the necessary patents. So that competition between the essential patents could be maintained, the parties were required to agree not to combine all of these patents in a single platform but to set up different arrangements for the separate technologies and for granting licenses on nondiscriminatory terms.

As the *Guidelines* indicate, settlement terms agreed to by parties in resolving their IP disputes are also watched carefully by the EU competition authorities. We observed in the prior chapters describing the US law that certain settlement arrangements made to resolve patent disputes may themselves create anticompetitive situations which fall afoul of antitrust strictures.

Chapter 12

Article 102 TFEU: Abuse of a Dominant Position

§12.01 INTRODUCTION

For ease of reference, we reproduce Article 102 TFEU in full below:

> **Article 102 TFEU**
>
> Any abuse by one or more undertakings of a dominant position within the internal market or in a substantial part of it shall be prohibited as incompatible with the internal market in so far as it may affect trade between Member States.
>
> Such abuse may, in particular, consist in:
>
> (a) directly or indirectly imposing unfair purchase or selling prices or other unfair trading conditions; (b) limiting production, markets or technical development to the prejudice of consumers; (c) applying dissimilar conditions to equivalent transactions with other trading parties, thereby placing them at a competitive disadvantage; (d) making the conclusion of contracts subject to acceptance by the other parties of supplementary obligations which, by their nature or according to commercial usage, have no connection with the subject of such contracts.

On its face, Article 102 differs in two important respects from Article 101. First, although Article 101 requires an agreement, decision, or concerted practice between two independent parties, one party acting alone may violate Article 102 by abusing a dominant position. Nonetheless, as the language of Article 102 indicates, the provision may also be applied to interdependent actions by more than one party. Second, unlike Article 101, Article 102 contains no provision for an exemption. It is settled that, where an agreement or practice infringes both Article 101 and Article 102, the Commission may proceed against the violation under either or both provisions.

Over time, the modernization and increasing refinement of the EU competition rules has made the enforcement of Articles 101 and 102 significantly more effective.

Moreover, we should also keep in mind that, pursuant to Article 3 of Regulation 1/2003, where the EU Member States' national competition authorities and national courts apply national competition law to any infringement prohibited by Article 101 TFEU or Article 102 TFEU, which may affect trade between Member States, they are bound to also apply the pertinent EU competition provision.

Three elements must be present for Article 102 to apply to an undertaking. It must have: (1) a "dominant position" within the common market or a substantial part thereof, (2) which the undertaking has "abused," (3) so as to potentially affect trade between Member States. The mere holding of a dominant market power is not actionable under Article 102. The principle underlying the prohibition is that a firm which enjoys a dominant position has a special responsibility not to eliminate or distort competition.

As we will be discussing in the next chapter, the EU Merger Regulation, No. 139/2004, which was first adopted in 1989 and then replaced in 2004, is broadly defined to cover mergers, acquisitions of control and the creation of full-function joint ventures. It applies to any "concentration" that is deemed to have an "EU dimension" and thus can be applied to such transactions where they significantly impede effective competition, in particular as a result of the creation or strengthening of a dominant position.

There has long been a debate about how the Commission should focus its enforcement efforts with respect to Article 102, on such questions as the extent to which the provision should be applied to protect competitors of the dominant firm as distinct from giving significant recognition to the efficiencies generated by the latter. In 2005, there was published a DG COMP staff discussion paper designed to promote a public discussion as to which policies the Commission should pursue in enforcing the provision in the future. This *Discussion Paper on the application of Article [102 TFEU] to exclusionary abuses* did in fact lead to many expressions of conflicting views over the extent to which the Commission should be pursuing litigation against dominant firms.

Then, in February 2009, the Commission published *Guidance on Article 102 Enforcement Priorities*. This led to further public debate, in part because of the difference between the Commission's stated enforcement priorities and the seemingly more strict jurisprudence of the EU courts. For purposes of this book, we will not enter into this discussion, but the reader should be aware of the disagreement that exists among the commentators and in the EU competition law community about the appropriate enforcement philosophy with respect to Article 102. In this chapter, we will consider the content of each of the components of an Article 102 infringement, and we will review the highlights of the jurisprudence that has developed on the subject of abuse of a dominant position.

Accordingly, for a violation of Article 102, there must be an abuse by one or more undertakings of a dominant position. Once again, an undertaking may be any entity engaged in commercial activity, including public, as well as privately owned businesses. In its opinion of June 28, 2005 in *Dansk Rørindustri*, the ECJ stated that "... according to settled case-law, in the field of competition law, the concept of an undertaking covers any entity engaged in an economic activity, regardless of its legal status and the way in which it is financed ... ."

§12.02 PRINCIPAL ELEMENTS OF ARTICLE 102

[A] Dominant Position

A bedrock requirement for the application of Article 102 is that there be an abuse by one or more undertakings of a "dominant position." Article 102 does not define the concept. The phrase had some early use in national laws, however, and, in Article 66 of the ECSC Treaty, it was defined in terms of an undertaking having a position so strong as to enable it to be shielded from effective competition. Several early formulations were proffered by the Court of Justice and the Commission. In the 1971 *Continental Can* case, the Commission declared that "undertakings are in a dominant position when they have the power to behave independently, which puts them in a position to act without taking into account their competitors, purchasers, or suppliers." The ECJ supplied similar definitions of dominance in its 1978 judgment in *United Brands* and again a year later in the *Hoffmann-La Roche ("Vitamins")* case.

In the landmark *United Brands* case, the integrated giant in the international fruit business had a 40%-45% market share in the four relevant Member States. The company had a large investment in plantations, an extensive distribution system, and a control over the fruit ripening process that placed its competitors at a disadvantage. In this context, the Court described a "dominant position" within the meaning of then Article 86 to be "a position of economic strength enjoyed by an undertaking which enables it to prevent effective competition being maintained on the relevant market by giving it the power to behave to an appreciable extent independently of its competitors, customers and ultimately of its consumers." Consequently, United Brands was held to have a dominant position because its market share was much greater than that of any of its competitors and because it was able to behave in the market in a strategically independent way.

In the *Hoffmann-La Roche ("Vitamins")* case, the Court found that Roche had market shares for various vitamins in Community markets ranging from 47% to 95%. The company's 47% share for Vitamin A was held sufficient for a dominant position because Roche's two main competitors jointly did not exceed that share. The Court commented that, while it was possible for a firm in a dominant to be subject to some degree of competition, the dominant company would have "an appreciable influence on the conditions under which that competition will develop." No single factor would determine whether an undertaking enjoyed a dominant position, but among the determinative factors "a highly important one is the existence of very large market shares" Very large shares are in themselves and save in exceptional circumstances, evidence of the existence of a dominant position, assuming that these shares have been held "for some time."

Market share is, therefore, an important indicator in determining dominance. In the 1991 *Akzo* case, the ECJ, after referring to the *La Roche* decision, stated that, in the absence of exceptional circumstances, a firm with a market share of 50% or more could be presumed to be dominant. In its *Guidance on Article 102 Enforcement Priorities*, the Commission states that dominance is "not likely" if the undertaking's share is below 40%.

Ascertaining a company's market share requires a determination of the relevant product and geographic markets. In the language of Article 102, for the provision to apply, the dominant position must be held "within the internal market or in a substantial part of it." The relevant geographic market in an Article 102 case may be the entire Union, one or more Member States, a substantial part of a Member State, or even an essential facility like a major port or airport. Neither the Commission nor the EU courts have specified what percentage of the internal market is "substantial" for purposes of Article 102. Keep in mind also that, in the language of the provision, the abuse must have an effect on trade between Member States.

The "substantiality" of the area covered must be assessed, not in terms of its physical territory, but in terms of the area's economic importance, often with reference to its population. At first, there was a belief that substantiality implied that, at the very least, the territory of an entire Member State had to be involved. However, in its *Sugar Cartel* decision, the Court of Justice confirmed the Commission's view that even a substantial portion of a Member State could meet the standard in an appropriate situation. In that case, the Court held that the southern region of Germany, containing a population of 22 million people and a significant part of the production and consumption of sugar in the Community, amounted to a "substantial part" of the common market.

There are many decisions deeming the requirement of substantiality to be met with respect to a single facility. For example, in the *Porto di Genova* case, the Court determined that, considering the heavy traffic which the port of Genoa generated and its considerable economic significance with respect to maritime activities throughout Italy, the port constituted a substantial part of the common market in port operations.

In determining the product market, the sales of the relevant undertakings, either in value or in volume, must be arrayed against each other. In the *Michelin I* case, the ECJ described the relevant product market as one including "the totality of the products which, with respect to their characteristics, are particularly suitable for satisfying constant needs and are only to a limited extent interchangeable with other products." On the facts in *Michelin I*, the markets for new tires for original equipment and for new replacement tires were distinguished, inasmuch as they were sold through different channels for different customers. In its *Napier Brown-British Sugar* decision in 1988, the Commission distinguished between a market for sugar sold in bulk to industry and one for sugar sold to retailers in smaller bags.

In sum, the Commission's *Notice on the Definition of Relevant Market for the Purposes of Community Competition Law* (issued in 1997 and updated) offered the following brief and useful description of the relevant market determinations:

> A relevant product market comprises all those products and/or services which are regarded as interchangeable or substitutable by the consumer by reason of the products' characteristics, their prices and their intended use. A relevant geographic market comprises the area in which the firms concerned are involved in the supply of products and services and in which the conditions of competition are sufficiently homogeneous.

The pertinent factors, in the determination of whether an undertaking is dominant may include, in addition to market share: entry barriers which might impede new competitors from arising, the financial power of the companies (the "deep pocket" factor), the ability to establish prices, production capabilities, vertical integration, presence in related markets, and the possession of key IP rights or other technological advantages. The holding of a number of copyrights, patents or trademarks does not, in itself, establish the existence of a dominant position, although it may be a factor. On the other hand, the existence of significant potential competition may be cited as an element militating against dominance.

As mentioned earlier, under the terms of the Treaty, Member States retain their powers to create statutory monopolies, subject to compliance with the EU competition rules. Entities within a Member State which are not "public authorities" and to which the State has granted monopoly or other exclusive rights in the business sphere will be considered to hold a dominant position to the extent that they control relevant markets affecting EU trade.

The principle of joint or collective dominance, for purposes of applying Article 102, has been confirmed by the Commission and the EU courts in a number of cases, as we shall see.

[B] Abuse

Although Article 102 lists four examples of abusive conduct, it does not define what other specific behavior by a dominant undertaking may fall within the prohibited behavior. The listing of abuses is not exhaustive. In the *Continental Can* case, the Court of Justice stated that the prohibition "is not only aimed at practices which may cause damage to consumers directly, but also at those which are detrimental to them through their impact on effective competition structure." Accordingly, the provision is applicable against abusive conduct by a dominant entity which impairs the market access of competitors (monopolistic or exclusionary abuse) and also against practices of the entity involving use of its market power to injure suppliers or purchasers (exploitative abuse). There have been many more cases of the former type of abuse than of the latter.

It is not unlawful for a firm to have a dominant position. What is prohibited is abuse of that position. The Court of Justice stated in *Michelin I* that a firm in a dominant position has a "special responsibility not to allow its conduct to impair genuine undistorted competition" on the common market.

The Court also stated in its judgments in the *Continental Can* and *Hoffmann-La Roche ("Vitamins")* cases that an intent to cause injury need not be shown for a violation of Article 102 because the concept of abuse is an objective one, which is irrespective of fault and of the means by which it is achieved. The question of intent can, nonetheless, become relevant in assessing whether certain conduct, such as a refusal to deal or low pricing, is abusive as being based on an exclusionary strategy or, on the other hand, is based on valid business justifications.

The delineation of the scope of Article 102 has faced the same criticism that we have seen encountered by the Robinson-Patman Act in the US: that it is applied to protect competitors, even inefficient ones, rather than the competitive process over-all. Then there are also the counter-critics who label the former as being anti-regulation. The Commission and the EU courts have steadfastly maintained that the purpose of Article 102 is to protect competition, not individual competitors, and that the consumer is intended to be the ultimate beneficiary of this regulation.

[C] Affect Trade Between Member States

The prohibition of Article 102, like that of Article 101(1), applies only if the conduct under scrutiny is likely to affect trade between Member States. The ECJ stated in the *Commercial Solvents* case that a finding on this issue requires that "all the consequences of the conduct complained of for the competitive structure in the Common Market" be taken into account. In the *Hugin/Liptons* case, the concept of effect on trade under both Articles 101 and 102 was described similarly by the Court:

> Thus Community law covers any agreement or any practice which is capable of constituting a threat to freedom of trade between Member States in a manner which might harm the attainment of the objectives of a single market between the Member States, in particular by partitioning the national markets or by affecting the structure of competition within the Common Market.

It has also been broadly stated in the case law that an abuse of a dominant position affects trade between Member States when it is capable of influencing, either directly or indirectly, actually or potentially, the pattern of trade in goods and services between Member States. In its 2003 decision in *Michelin*, the CFI reiterated that, to establish an infringement of Article 102, it is not necessary for the Commission to prove that the abusive conduct has appreciably affected trade between Member States, but only that it is capable of doing so.

[D] Remedies

Article 10 of Regulation 1/2003 authorizes the Commission to make a decision on its own initiative that Article 101 or Article 102 is not applicable to certain conduct. Businesses may seek advance guidance letters from the Commission in this regard. Article 7 of Regulation 1/2003 states that the Commission may by decision require an infringement of either provision to be brought to an end. The Commission may impose fines for infringements of Article 102, even if the abusive conduct has been discontinued. In addition, Article 7 of Regulation 1/2003 explicitly authorizes the Commission to impose "any behavioural or structural remedies which are proportionate to the infringement committed and necessary to bring the infringement effectively to an end. Structural remedies can only be imposed either where there is no equally effective behavioural remedy or where any equally effective behavioural remedy would be more burdensome for the undertaking concerned than the structural remedy." Infringements of Article 102 may also be actionable in the national courts, including damage suits.

§12.03 ABUSIVE PRACTICES BY DOMINANT FIRMS: THE PRECEDENTS

We turn now to consideration of the types of practices which have been found abusive for the purposes of applying Article 102. It is possible to trace the case law historically, with the landmark decisions at the fore. An alternative approach would be to review the Commission's decisions and the EU courts' jurisprudence analytically according to the types of abuses challenged. In this context, three types of abuse have been identified: (1) *Exploitative abuses*, including reducing output and increasing prices to the disadvantage of customers; (2) *Exclusionary abuses*, including practices preventing the development of competition; and (3) *Single market abuses*, including practices designed to partition the internal market. Much of the case law focuses on exclusionary abuses, and the Commission's 2009 *Guidance* paper limits itself to issues of exclusionary conduct.

Our approach in this first section will be primarily historic, centered on the progression of the EU competition law in the different areas of Article 102 enforcement through the court decisions. A second section will trace the important recent developments in the cases bought by the EU authorities against leading international players in the technology industries.

[A] Excessive, Predatory or Discriminatory Terms

The *United Brands* decision, which came before the ECJ in 1978, addressed a number of issues relating to a dominant firm's pricing practices. Under Article 102, a dominant firm's pricing practices can be challenged on differing theories: (1) that its prices are too high from the purchaser's viewpoint (excessive prices); or (2) that the prices are so low as to damage competitors (predatory prices); or (3) that the prices are unfair in discriminating among different customers (discriminatory prices). These issues were placed before the ECJ in the *United Brands* case. The company, a US firm, owned its own banana plantations in South America and enjoyed a large share of the banana market in the Community. It shipped its Chiquita bananas to two unloading ports, where they were resold to various national distributors at significantly different prices, notwithstanding that the purchasers paid the freight costs to the various ripening installations. United Brands' market share was in the range of 40%–45% in the geographic market at issue which consisted of Germany, Benelux, Ireland, and Denmark.

The company was found to be dominant in this market by reason of its market share, high degree of vertical integration, the existence of high barriers to entry and other factors. The Commission charged United Brands with abuse of its position based on a number of separate practices: (i) prohibiting the resale by distributors of unripe bananas; (ii) refusing to sell to a Danish distributor who had promoted competing bananas; (iii) discriminatory pricing as between different Member States; and (iv) charging of excessive prices.

The Court ruled that the prohibition on sales of green bananas was abusive because it worked as an export ban, in effect restricting distributors to selling ripened bananas in their local markets. United Brands' refusal to supply the Danish distributor because of its promoting competitive brands was also held abusive. The Court reasoned that a dominant supplier could not lawfully cut off a long time distributor which was a continuing customer at its usual levels. The Court also agreed with the Commission that United Brands' selling at different prices to its distributors in different Member States was, under the circumstances, a violation of the prohibition against dominant firms "applying dissimilar conditions to equivalent transactions ... ." United Brands appeared to be pricing bananas discriminatorily among the distributors in the different national markets so as to extract the highest price available in each territory. The Court concluded that the company's discriminatory prices were not economically justified and, therefore, "were just so many obstacles to the free movement of goods," creating a "rigid partitioning of national markets."

The Commission's charge that United Brands' pricing was excessive was based on the fact that the company's prices for Ireland were substantially lower than those for the other countries. The Court's decision confirmed that a dominant firm's extraction from purchasers of prices which have no reasonable relation to the economic value of the product could infringe then Article 86. However, the Court refused to find that an infringement had been established in this regard, because it considered that the Commission had not presented an economic analysis which was sufficient to support its charge of excessive pricing, particularly since there was only a 7% differential in the pricing of United Brands and its main competitors.

Although the Court confirmed in *United Brands* that excessive pricing on the part of a dominant firm can constitute a violation of Article 102, in practice the issue has sometimes been a problematic one. It is difficult to postulate what level of price is "excessive" in a particular situation. The Commission failed to satisfy the Court of Justice on this point in *United Brands* and also in a 1975 case that it had brought against General Motors. Nonetheless, the *General Motors* decision did confirm the principle that charging unfairly high prices is an abuse. The Court has several times stated that an undertaking abuses its dominant position where it charges fees for its services which are unfair or disproportionate to the "economic value" of the services provided.

In another important case, *Tetra Pak 2*, the Court of Justice and the Commission condemned as abusive the conduct of a dominant manufacturer of packaging cartons, finding that the company's resale restrictions on its customers and its price differences set along national lines were an unlawful attempt to partition the Community into national markets. The Commission reasoned that, since Tetra Pak's operations were Community-wide, its price differentiation "cannot be explained in economic terms" except by "the market compartmentalization policy which Tetra Pak managed artificially to maintain."

The Commission fined British Sugar in the 1988 *British Sugar* case for abusing its dominant position in the industrial sugar market in its dealings with a customer, Napier Brown. Among the findings made by the Commission was that British Sugar was pricing its sales of industrial sugar to Napier Brown at a margin which made it unprofitable for the latter to compete for retail consumers through the creation and sale of retail sugar packets.

In 1991, in the case of *AKZO Chemie*, with respect to pricing below ATC, the Court of Justice stated that "[s]uch prices can drive from the market undertakings which are perhaps as efficient as the dominant undertaking but which because of their smaller financial resources are incapable of withstanding the competition waged against them." The Court found that all but one of AKZO's prices offered to its competitor's customers were between average variable and average total costs. AKZO's intent to eliminate its competitor from the market was established from the record.

It has been established in a number of decisions that it may be a violation of Article 102 for a firm enjoying valuable IP rights or a state-granted monopoly to exploit that position by charging excessive or discriminatory prices. For example, in its 1989 decision in *SACEM 2*, the ECJ stated that it was indicative of an abuse of a dominant position for a performing rights society to charge a royalty that was many times higher in some Member States than in others. In 2001, the Commission found in *Deutsche Post* that the German postal operator had abused its near monopoly position in a number of ways, including charging excessive prices (i.e., prices having no reasonable relationship to real costs or to the real value of the service provided) for a class of incoming international mail.

In *Deutsche Telekom 2*, in 2003, the company ("DT") had a dominant position over the "local loop," the final section of the telecommunications network that linked the ultimate customer to the local switching point. DT made wholesale capacity on its local loop available to operators wishing also to provide retail services. However, it did so at a price that squeezed the margin of these would-be competitors. The Commission found this to be an abuse of a dominant position and imposed a fine. The GC and the ECJ upheld the Commission's decision. In its 2010 decision, the ECJ agreed that DT was guilty of an abusive "margin squeeze" in leaving an insufficient margin for competitors who wished to also provide retail services. The Court rejected the company's argument that its conduct was lawful because it was permitted by the German regulator of the electronic communications sector.

One year later, in the *TeliaSonera* case, the Court responded to a request for an opinion by a Swedish court and again found the existence of a margin squeeze which amounted to abuse of a dominant position aimed at competitors. Accordingly, it is the view of the Court that, while a dominant integrated firm is not violating Article 102 if it merely decides not to supply the upstream product to others, if it chooses to supply it, it may not do so at a price that will squeeze the margin of an equally efficient competitor.

[B] Limiting Production, Markets or Technical Development

Article 102(b) provides that an abuse of a dominant position may consist of "limiting production, markets or technical development to the prejudice of consumers." There have been a number of important cases involving refusals to supply or to otherwise provide market access by dominant firms.

A refusal to deal may constitute the abuse of a dominant position, as was established by the Court of Justice's 1974 decision in the *Commercial Solvents* case, as well as in the Court's decision in *United Brands*. Commercial Solvents Corporation ("CSC") held a world monopoly position as the manufacturer of products resulting from the nitration of paraffin, including nitropropane. Nitropropane was used for the production of aminobutanol which, in turn, was used for the industrial production of ethambutol, a compound used to treat tuberculosis. Zoja, an Italian producer of ethambutol, complained that CSC and its Italian subsidiary were abusing their dominant position in the production of nitropropane and aminobutanol to eliminate Zoja as a producer of ethambutol. The two companies had refused to provide Zoja with adequate supplies of ethambutol. The Court of Justice agreed with the Commission that the two companies were abusing their dominant position in the nitropropane and aminobutanol markets to restrict competition in the derivative, ethambutol. In the circumstances, they had an obligation to supply Zoja, especially since they had discontinued so doing without adequate commercial justification.

In the *Télémarketing* case, the Court applied this rule to a dominant supplier of services which reserved for itself "an ancillary activity which might be carried out by another undertaking as part of its activities on a neighbouring but separate market, with the possibility of eliminating all competition from such undertaking." As we have seen, in the *British Sugar* case, the Commission imposed a fine on British Sugar for abusing its dominant position in refusing to supply Napier Brown, a regular customer, with industrial sugar. The evidence indicated that the refusal to supply and other difficulties imposed by British Sugar on Napier Brown were motivated by the former's desire to impede the latter's efforts to compete with it for retail customers. In the *Hugin/Liptons* and *Hilti* cases, the Court of Justice confirmed that a dominant firm's abusive refusal to supply a competitor may involve the supply of needed spare parts. While a dominant firm's refusal to supply an existing customer is more likely to be deemed an abuse, there have been circumstances in which the refusal to supply a new customer was held unjustified as an effort to exclude competition.

In *British Leyland*, the British auto manufacturer was charged with refusing to renew the certifications for left-hand drive cars that it had previously been granting for the importation of Leyland cars into the United Kingdom. The conduct, which foreclosed parallel imports of the cars, was condemned as an abusive limitation of output in violation of then Article 86.

There is case law establishing that it is a violation of Article 102 for a firm having control of a facility which is essential to business participation in an industry to deny competitors access to that facility. This rule also applies where the controlling firm sets terms for the use of the facility which are so onerous that they place the actual or potential competitor at a significant competitive disadvantage. The facility may be a port terminal, an airport, a railroad or electronic network or any other structure or activity which is commercially necessary for competitors to participate effectively in a market. The principle has been applied when the dominant party both controls access to the essential facility and is itself a competitor in the market using the facility.

The *Oscar Bronner* case involved Bronner, the publisher of a daily newspaper with a 3.6% share of the Austrian daily newspaper market by circulation and Mediaprint, the publisher of two Austrian newspapers with a combined market share of 46.8%. Mediaprint also operated the only nationwide home-delivery distribution service for subscribers. When it refused to include Bronner's newspaper in its home-delivery service for a fee, although it did provide this service to another newspaper outside its group, Bronner brought suit in the Austrian courts based on national law provisions analogous to the EU's Article 102. The Austrian court, reasoning that Bronner's exclusion was capable of affecting trade between Member States because Bronner sold some newspapers abroad, referred to the ECJ under EC Article 177 for a preliminary ruling on whether Mediaprint was abusing a dominant position in violation of then EC Article 82. Mediaprint and the European Commission both argued that the Court of Justice should not hear the case inasmuch as, on the facts cited, the issue involved Austrian home-delivery and not Community trade. Nevertheless, the Court decided to review the matter, stating that "a request from a national court may be rejected only if it is quite obvious that the interpretation of Community law or review of the validity of a rule of Community law sought by that court bears no relation to the actual facts of the case or to the subject matter of the main action." On the merits, the Court held that there was here no obligation for the dominant firm to deliver Bronner's newspapers, since Bronner could create another home-delivery scheme, either alone or with other publishers, and hence access to Mediaprint's program was not "indispensable" to Bronner's ability to stay in the market.

Several of the leading EU cases in this area have involved access to facilities necessary for transportation activities, including a group of cases involving a company called Sealink, the operator of passenger ferries. In one of these cases, a competing ferry company complained that Sealink was using its ownership of the Holyhead harbor in Wales so as to schedule its runs between Holyhead and Dublin in a manner which was physically disruptive to the competitor's operations on the same route. Sealink had changed its schedules so that its ferries passed by the competitor's terminal, causing turbulence and hence disruption. The Commission found that Sealink's ownership of this important gateway between the UK and Ireland gave it a dominant position in a substantial part of the Common Market, and that Sealink was therefore not permitted to revise its schedules to disadvantage a competitor's operations on that route.

In *Aer Lingus/British Midland,* the Commission found that Aer Lingus, as the dominant air carrier on the London-Dublin route, should be required to accept, for a two-year initial period, the tickets of a new competitor, British Midland. Competitive access to such "interlining" agreements and to the inclusion of a carrier's flight schedules in a competitor's computerized reservation system have, in some circumstances, been held to be essential facilities for competition in the air transport field.

The Court of Justice has held that, when a state grants exclusive rights to an undertaking to provide a category of services and the undertaking cannot satisfy the market demand for the services in question, the exercise of the exclusive rights can be an abuse of a dominant position. This was the Court's reasoning in *Höfner and Elser v. Macrotron,* in ruling that an agency which had been given the German legal monopoly for recruiting employment abused its dominant position when it failed to meet the demand for those services, and yet insisted on its exclusive rights.

The important *Port of Genoa* case raised a number of issues relating to abuse of a dominant position by an essential facility. That case involved an Italian law which entrusted a company with exclusive rights to operate the Port of Genoa. The Gabrielli firm sought to import steel from Germany through Genoa and, although the ship it had chartered possessed the necessary equipment for unloading the steel, such direct unloading was not permitted because the use of foreign labor was prohibited and because the right to perform dock work was held by the port company which held a monopoly. After the delivery of the steel had been delayed by strikes of the port company workers, Gabrielli sued the company for damages attributable to the delay and to the excessive costs of the stevedoring company. The Italian court referred the matter to the ECJ for a preliminary ruling.

The Court held that the port represented a substantial part of the Common Market and that the port company, by reason of its exclusive rights, had a dominant position which it had abused. The Italian state was not entitled to reserve the stevedoring jobs to Italian nationals alone. Moreover, the Italian state's granting of the port monopoly was subject to compliance with the EU competition law rules. In that regard, the port company had abused its position by charging overly high prices and refusing to use modern technology in its operations.

In *Microsoft II*, the Commission found that Microsoft had abused its dominant position in the PC operating system market in a number of ways, including by refusing to supply interoperability information for the development of interoperable products. We will discuss this case shortly in greater detail.

These principles regarding market access have also been applied in the financial services industry. The *Clearstream* case concerned Clearstream Banking AG, Germany's only central securities depository, which was deemed by the Commission as holding a dominant position for providing cross-border clearing and settlement services to intermediaries situated in other Member States. The Commission found that Clearstream, "an unavoidable trading partner" had infringed then Article 82 by refusing to supply Euroclear Bank, a competitor, with settlement services and by applying discriminatory prices to the detriment of Euroclear.

In 2014, the Commission imposed fines on Slovak Telekom and its parent, Deutsche Telekom, for shutting out competitors from the Slovak market for broadband services. Slovak Telekom was found to be refusing to supply unbundled access to its local loops to competitors and also to be imposing a margin squeeze on these operators. The Commission's decision indicated that the offering by a dominant firm of desired supplies on unreasonable terms would be treated as the equivalent of a refusal to supply.

In its *Guidance on Article 102 Enforcement Priorities*, the Commission stated that, while a refusal to supply a new customer is capable of infringing Article 102, it is more likely that termination of an existing relationship will be found to be abusive (at paragraph 84).

[C] Applying Dissimilar Conditions to Equivalent Transactions

Article 102(c) declares it an abuse of a dominant position for a dominant firm to apply "dissimilar conditions to equivalent transactions with other trading parties, thereby placing them at a competitive disadvantage." This has been often applied in cases of price discrimination, where a dominant firm discriminates in the terms offered to different customers, for the purpose of maximizing profits, dividing national markets or excluding competition.

There are many such precedents. As we have discussed, in *United Brands*, one of the practices condemned by the Commission and the ECJ was the dominant firm's pricing of bananas discriminatorily among distributors in different national markets so as to recover the highest price available in each market. Again, in *Tetra Pak II*, the Commission and the ECJ held to be abusive, as an unlawful attempt to partition the Community into national markets, the imposition by a dominant manufacturer of packaging cartons of resale restrictions and price differences set along national lines. In *British Sugar*, the Commission found price discrimination between customers for bulk and packaged products to be abusive as part of a dominant firm's effort to eliminate competition.

There is a question of the extent to which a dominant supplier is permitted to offer prices selectively, as a defensive measure to enable it to meet competition from another supplier. In the *Irish Sugar* case, the Commission determined that the dominant Irish sugar producer violated then Article 82 in a variety of ways, including by offering its products through discriminatory low prices to customers of a competitor. The CFI and ECJ affirmed the Commission's conclusions. The CFI's opinion commented that "... whilst such an undertaking must be allowed the right to take such reasonable steps as it deems appropriate to protect [its] interests such behavior cannot be allowed if its purpose is to strengthen that dominant position and thereby abuse it."

In *Virgin/British Airways*, the Commission found BA guilty of violating Article 102(c) by compensating travel agents at different levels of remuneration. The GC and the Court of Justice upheld this decision. The GC pointed out that BA's rewards program applied different rates of commission to travel agents who booked identical amounts of revenue in the sale of BA tickets.

[D]   Tying

Both Article 101(1)(e) and Article 102(2)(d) provide that tying arrangements may amount to infringements. The Commission enumerated in the *Microsoft II* decision the four elements required to establish tying prohibited under Article 102: (a) the tying and the tied goods are two separate products; (b) the undertaking concerned is dominant in the tying product market; (c) the undertaking concerned does not give customers the choice of obtaining the tying product separately; and (d) the tying forecloses competition. For a violation of Article 102(d)(2), the dominant firm will presumably have sufficient market power to be able to impose the tying obligations on its customers.

Tying by a dominant firm is prohibited under Article 102(d)(2) only if the supplementary (i.e., tied) obligations have an insufficient connection with the main subject of the contract (i.e., the tying subject) and if the two sets of obligations are practicably separable from each other. Claimed business justifications for tie-ins have often been rejected by the EU courts and the Commission. For example, in the

Windsurfing International case, the company maintained that there existed only a market for complete sailboards, consisting of a windsurf board and rigging. In holding that the company was engaged in tying riggings and boards, the Court of Justice reasoned that the two were separate products. As earlier noted, in the *Hilti* case, nail guns and the consumable cartridges and nails for use with the guns were held to be three distinct products and not a single power-actuated packaging system as argued by the company. Similarly, in *Microsoft II*, the Commission rejected the company's claim that an operating system and a streaming media player were one integrated product.

In the *Tetra Pak II* case, the charges against the company under Article 102 (then Article 86) included the argument that it was tying the machines for packaging food liquids with the cartons used in those machines. The company maintained that there was a natural association between the items and that it was therefore offering a single "integrated liquid food packaging system." Neither the Commission nor the two courts accepted this argument. The ECJ and the CFI determined that, since independent manufacturers specialized in making the needed aseptic cartons, there was no legitimate basis for Tetra Pak to treat the cartons as part of an integrated service. In both this case and the *Hilti* case the companies were also unsuccessful in arguing that their tying approach was justified by considerations of protecting the public health and safety from defective products. This area of concern, the courts stated, was for the public authorities to manage, not the manufacturers. In theory, as is the case in US law, there may be cases in which it will be possible for a company to establish that it must treat two or more products and/or services as an integrated system in order to assure proper technical operation and to protect the supplier's reputation.

In the *De Post/La Poste* case, the Commission determined that the Belgian postal service's grant of preferential prices to customers for general mail covered by the postal monopoly was improperly conditioned on customers also using Belgian Post for its new business to business mail service open to competition.

In 2011, the Commission issued a press release stating that it had examined allegations that IBM was tying its sales of mainframe hardware to sales of its operating system, following complaints by rival software vendors. The Commission announced that, following an in-depth investigation of these allegations, it had decided to close the case, and the three complainants withdrew their complaints.

It has been suggested that the Commission and the ECJ have tended to apply Article 102 to abusive conduct by dominant firms so long as that behavior has *some* effect on the normal functioning of the market, on the theory that the dominance has already weakened competition in the market. On the other hand, it is a requirement under Article 102 that an appreciable effect on trade be shown for an infringement to be made out.

[E] Exclusive Dealing and Loyalty Discounts

Exclusive dealing arrangements imposed by dominant firms on their customers are generally violative of Article 102 where they are likely to affect trade between Member States. Locking in important customers is an effective way to exclude or further disadvantage competitors who are already weak because of the market power of the dominant firm. The ECJ stated in the *Hoffmann-La Roche ("Vitamins")* case that "the concept of abuse ... in principle includes any obligation to obtain supplies exclusively from an undertaking in a dominant position which benefits that undertaking."

This principle prevents a dominant firm from entering into agreements with customers requiring them to purchase all or the majority of their requirements of a particular product or products from the dominant firm. This reasoning has also been applied to dominant firms' conferring of so-called loyalty rebates and fidelity discounts, both of which involve the dominant firm's giving the customer a financial incentive to buy exclusively from it. The practice has been viewed as injurious to competitors, as well as to less important buyers who are not able to meet the quantity conditions set for participation. On the other hand, when provided by a nondominant firm, such incentives may be quite appropriate elements of competition. It should be kept in mind that the block exemption granted by the BE Regulation, No. 330/2010, to certain categories of vertical agreements does not confer an exemption with respect to Article 102 TFEU.

In the *Hoffmann-La Roche ("Vitamins")* case, the Court of Justice and the Commission held abusive La Roche's practice of entering into supply contracts with major industrial purchasers which contained rebates for exclusivity, the effect of which was to pressure the customers into concentrating their purchases from La Roche. The 1983 *Michelin I* case involved Michelin's setting of sales targets for individual tire distributors and providing of rebates linked to the attainment of those targets. The Court agreed with the Commission that the linking of discounts to the attainment of the individual targets, along with pressure placed on the customers by frequent visits from Michelin representatives, amounted to an abuse. *Michelin II*, decided by the Commission in 2001 and affirmed by the CFI in 2003, again struck down fidelity rebates by the tire company. The CFI pointed out that "the longer the reference period, the more loyalty-inducing the quantity rebate system."

Michelin France, which was the dominant supplier of both new replacement and retreaded tires in that country, gave its dealers annual quantity rebates based on their total purchases from the company. The Commission described this system as infringing then Article 82 because it was a loyalty and target rebate designed to exclude competition, rather than one based on economically justified grounds such as lower costs for the supplier. Where the rebates given are associated with transactions reflecting cost savings for the dominant supplier, as in the case of sizeable individual deliveries or prompt payment, an appropriate rebate program should be acceptable.

The Commission has for many years kept the Coca-Cola Company's practices in Europe under scrutiny, particularly the company's efforts to enter into exclusivity programs with retail outlets concerning their carbonated soft drink purchases. In 1988, the Commission forced a Coca-Cola subsidiary which had a dominant position in the Italian cola market to discontinue its system of fidelity rebates. In June 2005, the Commission adopted a decision accepting binding commitments from the company and three major bottlers concerning the distribution of these products. This decision in which the Commission accepted binding commitments without a finding of infringement was made possible by the new authority conferred by Article 9 of Regulation

1/2003. The commitments, which remained in force through 2010, included giving Coca-Cola customers the freedom to buy and sell carbonated soft drinks from any supplier of their choice, not offering rebates that reward customers purely for purchasing the same amount or more of Coca-Cola's products than in the past, not requiring or rewarding purchases of additional brands when the customer wants only the best-selling brands, and allowing retailers to use at least 20% of the coolers provided by Coca-Cola for any product of the retailer's choosing. A fine amounting to 10% of Coca-Cola's worldwide turnover would result if the company did not fulfill its commitments.

In *Van Den Bergh Foods Ltd.*, the CFI in 2003 affirmed the Commission's decision that the ice cream company's practices in supplying freezer cabinets to retailers so as to induce exclusivity infringed both then Articles 81 and 82. The court agreed with the Commission that the company had a dominant position in the relevant ice cream market and that, although the provision of freezer cabinets on the condition of their exclusive use constituted a standard practice in that market, it was nonetheless an abuse for a dominant supplier to restrict competition by engaging in the practice. The CFI also held that the Commission was not guilty of "re-cycling" the facts constituting an infringement of Article 81(1) to also find an Article 82 infringement, an approach that had been criticized by the court in its 1992 *Italian Flat Glass* judgment. The court found that in the *Van Den Bergh Foods Ltd.* case, the Commission had correctly addressed the elements required by Article 82 in the context of the company's dominant position.

In the *British Airways* case (referred to earlier as *Virgin/British Airways* when before the Commission), the CFI upheld the Commission's finding that the airline held a dominant position in the UK market for air travel agency services, and that it had abused that position by giving loyalty-based awards to travel agents with the object and effect of excluding competition. The court emphasized that, while dominance itself is not a cause for reproach, a dominant firm has a special responsibility not to allow its conduct to impair genuine undistorted competition in the Common Market. The court observed that a system of rebates by a dominant firm in which the amount of the rebate increases in relation to the volume purchased will infringe Article 102 where "the criteria and rules for granting that rebate show that the system is not based upon an economically justified consideration but tends, like a fidelity and objective rebate, to prevent customers obtaining supplies from rival producers ... ." In 2007, the Court of Justice also rejected British Airways' appeal.

The case of *Tomra Systems ASA* involved the Tomra group of European subsidiaries which produced automatic recovery machines for the collection of used beverage containers. Following a complaint, the Commission investigated Tomra's activities and then entered a decision finding that Tomra had infringed then EC Article 82 and Article 54 of the EEA Agreement by implementing an exclusionary strategy in several EU markets. The exclusivity agreements included individualized quantity commitments and individualized retroactive rebate schemes, thus foreclosing competition. The Commission also found that Tomra's market shares in Europe had continuously exceeded 70% in the years before 1997 and after 1999 they exceeded 95%. The Commission viewed Tomra's retroactive rebate scheme based on thresholds corresponding to the customer's entire requirements or a large proportion thereof as equivalent to loyalty rebates. No cost efficiencies were demonstrated to justify these practices. The Commission imposed a fine of EUR 16 million increased by 10% for each full year of the infringement.

On appeal, the GC rejected all of Tomra's arguments. In a decision in 2012, the ECJ similarly rejected the appeal in its entirety. In its opinion, the Court pointed out that abuse of a dominant position is an objective concept, with the existence of any anticompetitive intent only one of a number of facts which may be taken into account in order to determine that a dominant position has been abused. The Commission therefore was under no obligation to establish the nature of Tomra's intent. The Court also held that, to establish a violation of Article 102, it was not necessary for the Commission to determine a precise threshold of foreclosure of the market. Further, the Court held that a finding that the prices in question were below cost was not a prerequisite to a finding that the retroactive rebate scheme operated by a dominant undertaking was abusive nor was it necessary for the Commission to make an analysis of the actual effects of the rebates on competition.

In *Post Danmark A/S*, decided in October 2015, the ECJ emphasized that, "in order to determine whether a rebate scheme ... implemented by a dominant undertaking is capable of having an exclusionary effect on the market contrary to Article [102 TFEU], it is necessary to examine all the circumstances of the case, in particular, the criteria and rules governing the grant of the rebates, the extent of the dominant position of the undertaking concerned and the particular conditions of the relevant market."

[F]   Abuses of IP Rights

A dominant firm's abuse of its IP rights may constitute a violation of Article 102. In its 1978 judgment in *Hoffmann-La Roche v. Centrafarm*, the Court of Justice confirmed that the exercise of an IP right (a trademark in that case) "is not contrary to Article 86 [now Article 102] of the Treaty on the sole ground that it is the act of an undertaking occupying a dominant position in the market if the ... right has not been used as an instrument for the abuse of such a position." The key issue is at what point the IP rights owner has ventured beyond the exercise of the rights of exclusion to which it is lawfully entitled into abusive, prohibited behavior.

In this same decision, the Court also indicated that, although mere exercise by a dominant company of its IP rights to exclude others did not alone amount to a violation, such exercise could be abusive in certain circumstances, for example, if the trademark were used as a disguised restriction of trade having the purpose to artificially partition the common market. The court's statement was in answer to a reference for a preliminary ruling from a German court and involved issues concerning repackaging.

The acquisition of rights of exclusion by a dominant company can be viewed as an element of a prohibited effort to eliminate competition. In *Tetra Pak I*, the Tetra Pak company enjoyed a 90% share of the Community market for both "aseptic" filling machines and the milk cartons used with them. Tetra Pak acquired the exclusive patent license which its main potential competitor had for making the cartons and machines.

This denied the use of the main alternative to all of Tetra Pak's competitors. The Commission decided, and was upheld by the CFI, that the dominant firm's acquisition of an exclusive license in the circumstances presented was an abuse in violation of then Article 86, inasmuch as it would prevent or substantially delay the entry of new competition against the already dominant firm.

Incidentally, in November 2016, China's State Administration for Industry and Commerce ("SAIC") imposed a heavy financial penalty on Tetra Pak for abuse of its dominant position in the sale of aseptic paper packaging equipment for liquid food in violation of China's anti-monopoly law. The offenses listed included tying practices, exclusive dealing and the granting of loyalty discounts to customers.

In *Volvo v. Eric Veng* and *Maxicar v. Renault*, the Court of Justice reasoned that, since the owner of an IP right is normally entitled to exclude others from manufacturing or selling goods which infringe his valid rights, he is equally entitled to refuse to grant licenses. However, the Court also stated that it would be an abuse of a car manufacturer's dominant position with respect to its spare parts to arbitrarily refuse to sell those parts at reasonable prices to independent repairers, assuming that the model of the car was still in circulation.

The interpretation of these two decisions became an issue in the subsequent *Magill* litigation which involved the refusal by several British and Irish radio and television authorities to license Magill, an independent publisher, to reproduce the weekly broadcasting schedules for Ireland. Magill complained that, in denying the licenses, the broadcasting companies were abusing their copyrights relating to the schedules in violation of then Article 86. The CFI agreed with the Commission that the broadcasting companies enjoyed dominant positions with respect to the weekly listings. The court reasoned that the companies were here excluding competition in a manner not justified by the copyright monopoly, inasmuch as they were preventing the birth of a new product in the marketplace, a general broadcasting magazine. The CFI relied, by way of analogy, on the statements of the ECJ in the *Volvo* and *Renault* decisions that the car makers would not have been entitled arbitrarily to refuse to supply spare parts to independent repairers or for models still in significant use.

This decision was much criticized by commentators who argued that the CFI had failed to recognize that the denial of a license, even to a potential competitor, went to the substance of the enjoyment of the IP rights in question. The mere denial of a license, argued the critics, should not be considered the abuse of a dominant position and a violation of the competition rules. When the *Magill* litigation came up before the Court of Justice in 1995, the Court's opinion expressed the general principle that "the refusal by the owner of an exclusive right to grant a license, even if it is the act of an undertaking holding a dominant position, cannot in itself constitute abuse of a dominant position." But then it also stated that "the exercise of an exclusive right by a proprietor may, in exceptional circumstances, involve abusive conduct."

The Court offered a number of reasons why this should be treated as an exceptional case. One was that this new product, a comprehensive listings guide, could not be published unless this information, for which there was obvious consumer demand, was made available. Another reason was the failure to provide an objective reason for the refusal to supply. The ECJ therefore affirmed the decisions of the

Commission and the CFI mandating compulsory licensing of the right to reproduce the copyrighted program listings. The *Magill* case has since been viewed as exceptional and not as signaling a broad attack on IP rights in the EU. The Commission has attempted to give the principle declared application only in special circumstances.

The ECJ gave *Magill* a narrow scope of application in the *Oscar Bronner* case, a refusal to deal situation which did not involve intellectual property. *Magill* was raised by the complainant in the *Tiercé Ladbroke* case. This case involved the claim of a Belgian bookmaker that the French company which held the exclusive rights to transmit sound and pictures of French horse races had violated then Article 82 by refusing to allow the complainant the right to transmit the French races in Belgium for a fee. The Commission rejected the complaint and the CFI affirmed. The CFI distinguished *Magill* on the ground that, in the present case, the two companies were not operating in the same market and that, in any event, there could be no violation of the prohibition since there was not involved a product or service which was essential to carrying on the business in question.

A number of cases relating to abuses of IP rights have involved the activities of performing rights societies. These societies collect from the owner individual copyrights for musical pieces which the societies administer as a block by licensing them to broadcasters and others for royalties. Some of the restrictions applied by these societies have been challenged. In the *GEMA I* case in 1971 the Commission decided that various rules of the German Performing Rights Society violated then Article 82. The rules deemed improper included discriminations against nationals of other Member States, charging royalties for unprotected musical works, requiring higher royalties on records not produced in Germany, requiring its individual members to assign to the society all of their categories of creative work for the whole world, and making withdrawal from membership in the association overly difficult.

The Court of Justice confirmed in *BRT v. SABAM* in 1974 that such performing rights societies were likely in a dominant position and that they would be violating then Article 82 to the extent that they were imposing on their members obligations which were not essential for the achievement of the legitimate objectives of the society.

In *Greenwich Film Productions v. SACEM*, the Court of Justice stated that then Article 82 could be applied to the activities of a French performing arts society which concerned performances of musical works outside of the Community but affected trade between the Member States. In the *GVL* case the Commission and the Court of Justice determined that it was a violation of Article 82 for a German society to refuse to enter into agreements with foreign artists who were not domiciled in Germany. On the other hand, in its judgment in *Tournier*, the Court of Justice stated that such a society could refuse to give access to its works to foreign users where this could be justified by the expense involved of overseeing the activity in the other country.

The *IMS Health* litigation was a lengthy dispute in which the ECJ denied a grant of interim relief in 2002 and then responded in 2004 to a request by a German court for a preliminary ruling on the interpretation of Article 82. IMS Health ("IMS") provided studies tracking regional sales of pharmaceutical and healthcare products based on its copyrighted "1860 brick structure" corresponding to the geographic areas. NDC Health ("NDC"), a competitor, attempted to use the structure but was prohibited from doing so when IMS obtained an injunction from the German court. NDC then filed a complaint with the European Commission alleging that IMS' refusal to grant NDC a license to use the 1860 brick structure was a violation of Article 82. The Commission found "exceptional circumstances" justifying the order of a license to enable NDC to compete in the pharmaceutical sales data market but the order was suspended by the courts, the ECJ holding that there were inadequate reasons for an interim measure.

The German court then referred to the ECJ a series of questions relating to the application of Article 82. The Court reviewed the principles developed in the *Magill*, *Bronner*, and *Volvo* judgments and the general rule that, while refusal to grant a license normally does not by itself constitute abuse of a dominant position, exceptional circumstances may render the refusal abusive conduct. The Court disposed of the matter by articulating several points for decision by the national court on the basis that Article 82 would be violated in this case if the protected format was indispensable to the presentation of the regional sales data, the undertaking requesting the license intended to offer new products or services not offered by the rights owner and for which there was a potential consumer demand, the refusal was not justified by objective considerations, and the refusal to grant the license was capable of excluding all competition in the relevant market.

The *Microsoft* litigation raised a number of issues relating to refusal to supply in the intellectual property area and is discussed separately later in this chapter.

[G] Joint Dominance

So-called collective dominance, also referred to as "joint dominance" or "oligopolistic dominance," has been addressed by the EU competition authorities both under Article 102 TFEU and under the European Union Merger Regulation ("EUMR"). We will focus in this chapter on the Article 102 case law and will consider in the next chapter how the issue of joint dominance has been treated under the EUMR.

Article 102 prohibits "... abuse by one or more undertakings of a dominant position." This language raises the question of when conduct by two or more entities constitutes prohibited abusive conduct under Article 102 and how this interdiction relates to Article 101, which is directed against collusive joint anticompetitive conduct. The Court of Justice confirmed in the *Hoffmann-La Roche ("Vitamins")* judgment that, when the conditions of both Article 101 and Article 102 are met so that both provisions have been infringed, the Commission may bring proceedings under either Article.

The Commission has generally treated anticompetitive joint conduct by parties, including cartel activity, as a matter to be addressed under Article 101. On occasion, however, it has applied the notion of the collective dominant position to be addressed by Article 102. In the *Italian Flat Glass* case, the Commission found violations of both provisions (then Articles 85 and 86) on the part of three Italian producers of flat glass, representing 95% of the car glass market and 79% of the non-automotive market, who had agreed on their pricing and other policies. The Commission found that the producers' exchanges of products were so extensive as to represent "structural links" among them and not merely concerted practices. However, the CFI overruled the

Article 86 charges against the three companies in a 1992 decision, stating that, while that provision might be applicable in a suitable case in which competitors were, in fact, united by economic links, "for the purposes of establishing an infringement of Article 86, it is not sufficient ... to 'recycle' the facts constituting an infringement of Article 85 ... ." In short, the Commission had established illicit dealings among the companies in violation of Article 85 but had not shown the existence of a collective dominant position, a prerequisite to the application of Article 86.

In the *Almelo* case, in 1994, the ECJ made the statement that, "[i]n order for ... a collective dominant position to exist, the undertakings must be linked in such a way that they adopt the same conduct on the market." In its later practice, the Commission has relied not only on structural links but also on such factors as similarity of cost structures of the companies, product homogeneity, mature production technology, and high entry barriers. This approach, permitting the application of Article 102 to the collective activities of several companies sharing common characteristics in an oligopolistic industry has been approved by the EU courts.

The issue of joint dominance was addressed by the Court of Justice in a judgment rendered in 2000 in cases under the name *Compagnie Maritime Belge Transports SA and Others*, also referred to as the "*CEWAL*" or "*Fighting Ships*" cases. The shipping conferences in these cases operated a regular liner service between West Africa and certain Northern European ports, the principal conference being Associated Central West African Lines ("CEWAL"). The Commission found that three of these liner conferences had infringed then Article 85 and also that members of the conferences had abused their collective dominant position in violation of then Article 86.

The Commission considered that the conference members collectively held a significant dominant position on their routes because of their very high market shares and other factors. It based the abuse charges on three grounds: (i) the conference members had attempted to enforce agreements under which they enjoyed exclusive rights to ship goods on the route to Zaire; (ii) they established 100% loyalty arrangements with certain customers and blacklisted disloyal shippers; and (iii) they employed a system of "fighting ships," a practice which involved targeting their principal competitors with special low rates. The CFI reduced the fines imposed by the Commission but dismissed the appeals.

Only the Article 86 issues were presented to the Court of Justice. The Court confirmed the settled principle that the same practice may give rise to infringement of both Article 85 and Article 86. However, said the Court, the objectives of the two provisions must be distinguished. For a collective dominant position to exist under Article 86 there must exist economic links or other factors which give rise to a connection between the two or more legally independent entities. Moreover, from an economic viewpoint, the entities must present themselves or otherwise act together on a particular market as a collective entity. There mere fact that there exists an agreement, decision or concerted practice involving them does not itself create the necessary link, although the implementation of these relationships may bring about the requisite links.

On the merits, the Court ruled that a liner conference, by its nature, can be characterized as a collective entity which presents itself as such on the market with respect to both users and competitors. Hence, Article 86 was theoretically applicable. On the question of whether there had been abuse of the dominant position, the Court then proceeded to accept some of the arguments raised by the liners and to reject others. The court, like the CFI before it, upheld the Commission's view that the practice of "fighting ships" applied against a targeted competitor constituted an abuse of a dominant position. It also upheld the Commission's decision condemning the loyalty contracts. Even if these practices were protected for purposes of Article 85 by the block exemption issued under Article 85(3) for shipping lines, this would not bar the application of Article 86. The Court concluded, nonetheless, that fines should not have been imposed on the individual lines since the Commission's statement of objections had been directed against CEWAL.

In its decision in the *Piau* case in 2005, involving national football associations, the CFI cited the three cumulative conditions that must be met for a finding of collective dominance: (1) each member of the dominant oligopoly must have the ability to know how the other members are behaving in order to monitor whether or not they are adopting the common policy; (2) the situation of tacit coordination must be sustainable over time, i.e., there must be an incentive not to depart from the common policy; and (3) the foreseeable reaction of current and future competitors, as well as of consumers, must not jeopardize the results expected from the common policy.

§12.04 THE TECHNOLOGY CASES

In recent years, the economic power and commercial importance (here the writer is close to uttering the word "dominance") of the world class technology companies have brought their activities to the fore. This development has leapt to the attention of the EU competition authorities, and the latter have generated significant investigation and prosecution proceedings in this sphere. We will summarize below the nature and status as of this writing of these vital aspects of the competition law development.

As background, it should be noted that in 1991, the EC adopted Software Directive 91/250/EEC on the legal protection of computer programs and providing for copyright law to serve as the main basis for protecting software. In particular, the Directive recognized the right of software licensees to decompile and reverse engineer the licensed software to enable them to obtain the information needed "to achieve the interoperability of an independently created computer program with other programs … ." The Directive also made it clear that then Articles 81 and 82 of the Treaty were fully applicable if a dominant supplier refused to make available the information necessary for interoperability.

Software Directive 91/250/EC was replaced on April 23, 2009 with an amended version known as Directive 2009/24/EC. Like its predecessor, this current Directive seeks to assure that the Member States will accord protection to computer programs under copyright law as literary works. The Directive also provides (at paragraph 17) that "[t]he provisions of this Directive are without prejudice to the application of the competition rules under Articles 81 and 82 of the Treaty if a dominant supplier refuses to make information available which is necessary for interoperability as defined in this Directive."

[A] Microsoft

The European Commission, like the antitrust authorities in several countries, has kept a watchful eye on the practices of Microsoft Corporation, the dominant manufacturer of personal computer systems in Europe, as elsewhere. As we saw, in the US, the government antitrust litigation against the company resulted in an initial ruling that Microsoft possessed monopoly power in the relevant operating systems market and that it maintained that power through anticompetitive means in violation of Section 2 of the Sherman Act. The US courts then approved a settlement which set forth restrictions on Microsoft's conduct and provided for that conduct to be monitored for the purpose of enforcing the consent decree.

In the mid-1990s the European Commission looked into complaints that Microsoft's licensing practices were foreclosing participation by other companies in the European market for personal computer software. The alleged practices included Microsoft's utilization of "per-processor" licenses, which charged royalties to computer manufacturers regardless of whether or not the unit included pre-installed Microsoft software. Microsoft settled these allegations in both the EC and the US by agreeing to alter its licensing practices. It agreed that it would not enter into licensing contracts which were longer than one year in duration and that it would not impose minimum commitments on licensees or use per-processor licenses (*Microsoft Corp.*, 1994, settlement following commitments).

In 2000, the Commission began a new investigation into Microsoft's software licensing practices in the context of the company's dominance in personal computer software. Sun Microsystems Inc. and other Microsoft competitors complained that Microsoft had bundled its PC operating system with its own server software and other Microsoft products (known as "middleware") in a way which allowed only Microsoft's products to be fully interoperable. This bundling, it was alleged, disadvantaged the competitors who did not have access to the interfaces and was designed to enable Microsoft to extend its dominance in PC operating systems into the closely related markets for server operating system software and middleware. Microsoft responded that the information that it had made available, along with the possibility of reverse engineering, provided these other companies with all the information they needed to be competitive.

Shortly thereafter, the Commission issued a statement of objections, expressing its view that Microsoft was threatening to extend its existing dominance into these adjacent markets and was, at best, giving interface information only on a partial and discriminatory basis to some of its competitors. A supplementary statement of objections was issued by the Commission in 2001, including the new allegation that Microsoft was illegally tying its Media Player product with its dominant Windows operating system.

On March 24, 2004, the Commission issued a 300 page decision concluding that Microsoft had infringed Article 82 by leveraging its near monopoly in the market for PC operating systems. Microsoft was found to have abused its market power by deliberately restricting interoperability between its dominant Windows operating system and non-Microsoft work group servers and by tying its Windows Media Player, a product where it faced competition with the operating system. The Commission identified three relevant product markets: the market for client PC operating systems, the market for work group server operating systems, and the market for streaming media players. The relevant geographic markets for all three was found to be worldwide. The Commission asserted that Microsoft had over 90% of the market for personal computer operating software systems and at least 60% of the market for work group server operating systems. (*Microsoft Corp.*, decision of March 24, 2004).

The Commission determined that Microsoft had abused its market power by deliberately restricting interoperability between it Window PC systems and non-Microsoft work group servers, enabling Microsoft to acquire a dominant position in the market for work group server operating systems, the heart of corporate IT networks. Retracing the applicable case law, and emphasizing the ECJ's statement in *Magill* that "the exercise of an exclusive right by the proprietor [of intellectual property] may, in exceptional circumstances, involve abusive conduct," the Commission reasoned that "Microsoft is abusing its dominant position by refusing to supply Sun and other undertakings with the specifications for the protocols used by Windows work group servers in order to [allow these undertakings to implement] specifications for the purpose of developing and distributing interoperable work group server operating system products." The Commission also found that Microsoft was improperly tying its Windows Media Player to its dominant operating system, with the effect of significantly weakening competition in the media player market. In this connection, the Commission rejected Microsoft's arguments that the operating system and the media player were a single integrated product and that the tying was justified by the "benefits" which it provided.

The Commission imposed a fine of EUR 497.2 million on Microsoft. In addition, as a remedy regarding interoperability, the Commission ordered Microsoft to disclose complete interface documentation to enable makers of non-Microsoft work group servers to achieve full interoperability with Windows PC's and servers. (Microsoft being entitled to reasonable remuneration for IP rights.) The interface documentation would not, however, need to include the Windows source code. As regards tying, Microsoft was ordered to offer to PC manufacturers a version of its Windows client PC operating system without the Windows Media Player so that they too could offer the consumer the bundle of an operating system and media player. The Commission also ordered the establishment of a suitable compliance monitoring regime, including a monitoring trustee.

In December 2005, the Commission filed its fourth statement of objections against Microsoft, threatening the company with daily penalties of up to EUR 2 million per day for failing to supply complete and accurate information on its Windows operating system in compliance with the Commission's decision. The US Government transmitted an e-mail expressing concern over whether Microsoft was being fairly treated.

In 2007, the CFI upheld the Commission's decision. It found that Microsoft had abused its dominant position by refusing to supply interoperability information. Citing *Magill, IMS Health,* and *Bronner,* the court stated that it is only in exceptional circumstances that the exercise of an exclusive right by the owner of the intellectual property may give rise to an abuse of a dominant position under Article 102 TFEU. Here the Commission did not err when it found that the information concerning interoperability with the Windows architecture was indispensable. It was not necessary for the Commission to find that the refusal to license was likely to eliminate all competition, just that the refusal at issue was liable to, or likely to, eliminate all effective competition. Microsoft's refusal to supply the relevant information, the court held, limited technical development to the prejudice of consumers within the meaning of Article 102.

On the tying issue, the court agreed with the Commission that the operating software system and the media player were separate products, at least in May 1999 when the conduct complained of was alleged to be harmful, whatever might be the situation regarding the product relationships in 2007. Microsoft was held to have a dominant position on the market for the tying product, namely the PC operating system. Microsoft's bundling was abusive, foreclosing competition with respect to the Windows Media Player, and Microsoft had shown no objective justification for the bundling.

Following this decision, there was criticism that the EU competition scheme was now protecting individual competitors rather than the competitive process as a whole. At the US Department of Justice, the Assistant Attorney General for Antitrust issued a press release which said in part: "We are, however, concerned that the standard applied to unilateral conduct by the CFI, rather than helping consumers, may have the unfortunate consequence of harming consumers by chilling innovation and discouraging competition. In the United States, the antitrust laws are enforced to protect consumers by protecting competition, not competitors."

In 2006, the Commission held that Microsoft had failed to comply with its obligation to supply full interoperability information in accordance with the decision of March 2004, and it imposed a fine of EUR 280.5 million. On February 27, 2008, the Commission adopted a decision imposing a penalty of EUR 899 million on Microsoft for charging unreasonable prices for access to interface documentation. The amount of the fine for the periodic penalty payment was reduced to EUR 860 million on appeal.

In January 2008, the Commission announced that it would be initiating two new investigations against Microsoft under Article 82. One related to a complaint received about interoperability issues and the second was on a complaint by Opera, the producer of a competing browser, who argued that Microsoft's inclusion of Internet Explorer in Microsoft's operating system constituted an illegal tie-in. The Commission announced in 2009 that it had accepted commitments from Microsoft that it would offer users of Windows choice among different web browsers. On March 6, 2013, the Commission announced a decision finding that Microsoft had failed to comply with these commitments and imposing a fine of EUR 561 million on Microsoft for failing to comply from May 2011 to July 2012.

[B]   Intel

The European Commission has for some years been overseeing the practices of the giant US chip maker, Intel Corporation. Intel described itself as the world's largest semiconductor chip maker, based on revenue. Advanced Micro Devices, Inc. ("AMD"), another US semiconductor company, submitted a formal complaint to the Commission alleging violations by Intel of the EU competition rules. In May 2004, the Commission launched a round of investigations at Intel and customer locations. On July 26, 2007, the Commission notified a statement of objections to Intel, taking the preliminary view that Intel held a dominant position and had abused it by engaging in exclusionary marketing arrangements and other improper practices. In July 2008, the Commission notified a supplementary statement of objections to Intel.

The Commission also observed that Intel's practices were receiving attention in other jurisdictions, including Japan, Korea, and the US.

The products concerned were microprocessors, also known as Central Processing Units (CPUs). The CPU is the device that interprets and executes instructions, also known as the "computer's brain." "x86 architecture CPUs" is one type of CPU, with Intel and AMD being the main manufacturers of this type of CPU. AMD and Intel had a cross-license agreement with regard to the x86 instruction set. AMD asserted that: "the x86 instruction set is subject to substantial intellectual property right protection. A potential entrant will thus require either a license from Intel, or an enormous combination of ingenuity, time and capital committed to the seemingly impossible task of creating a non-infringing x86 instruction set." The Commission found that Intel held very high market shares in excess of around 80% in an overall x86 CPU market and in excess or around 70% in the submarkets, evidence of the existence of a dominant position.

The Commission found that Intel had abused its dominant position in the worldwide x86 CPU market by: (1) foreclosing the market by providing hidden rebates to computer manufacturers on condition that they purchase all or a very high percentage of their CPU's from Intel; (2) refraining from stocking computers which did not incorporate Intel CPU's; and (3) making direct payments to computer manufacturers to prevent or delay sales of rival products and limiting the sales channels available to these products. The Commission imposed a fine of EUR 1.06 billion on Intel.

On Intel's appeal, the GC sustained the Commission in a 2014 decision. It held that the rebates granted by Intel to Dell, HP, NEC and Lenovo, computer manufacturers, were in the nature of exclusivity rebates, conditional on the customer obtaining all or most of its requirements from an undertaking in a dominant position. Except in exceptional circumstances, these rebates are incompatible with the objective of undistorted competition because they are designed to remove or restrict the purchaser's freedom to choose its sources of supply, while denying other producers access to the marketplace. The Commission is not required to show actual effect on a case by case basis, it is sufficient to demonstrate the existence of a loyalty mechanism which constitutes interference by a dominant firm with the structure of competition on a market.

The case then went on appeal to the Court of Justice. On September 20, 2017, the Court released an opinion setting aside the entire GC judgment. The GC was directed to examine whether the loyalty rebates applied by Intel were capable of restricting competition and thus formed an abuse of a dominant position.

[C] **Google**

The European Commission has initiated three major antitrust proceedings against Google. Alphabet Inc. is the parent company of Google. The cases are as follows:

(1) *Comparison Shopping*: In April 2015 the Commission sent a Statement of Objections to Google alleging that the company had abused its dominant position in the markets for general internet search services in the EEA by systematically favoring its own comparison shopping product (called "Google Shopping") in its general search results page on websites. The preliminary conclusion of the Commission's investigation, which was opened in November 2010, was that Google gave such favoritism to its shopping product called "Google Shopping" by, e.g., showing it more prominently on the screen. The Commission alleged that, since 2008 or so, Google has displayed its comparison shopping product prominently at the top of the search results, irrespective of whether it was the most relevant response to the inquiry. This disadvantaged rival comparison shopping services, hindering their ability to compete. The Commission observed that Google had a European market share above 90% for placement on general internet search services and above 80% on third party websites.

On July 14, 2016, the Commission adopted a supplementary Statement of Objections in this matter. This consisted of fresh evidence adduced by the Commission to support the allegation that Google abused its dominant position by favoring its own comparison shopping service.

On June 27, 2017, the Commission announced that it was fining Google EUR 2.42 billion (USD 2.7 billion) for abusing its market dominance as a search engine by promoting its own comparison shopping service in its search results and "demoting" those of its competitors. The Commission found that Google's comparison shopping service was made most visible to consumers in Google's search results, while rival shopping services were subjected to generic search algorithms which reduced them to lesser status. Google was directed to end the conduct within ninety days or face penalty payments of up to 5% of the average daily worldwide turnover of Alphabet, Google's parent company. The Commission will be monitoring Google's compliance closely.

A number of Google's competitors, including Oracle and Yelp, applauded the Commission's action, but much of the comment in the US criticized it as unwarranted under existing antitrust law. As we noted earlier, the US FTC investigated Google's activities some time ago and decided not to take antitrust enforcement action. An editorial in the Washington Post on July 2, 2017 argued that Google's practices did no demonstrable harm to consumers or to competition and concluded thus: "The immense size and power of all Internet giants are a legitimate focus for the antitrust authorities on both sides of the Atlantic. Brussels v. Google, however, seems to be a case of punishment without crime." A committee of the US Congress held a hearing at which witnesses opined that other countries may be using antitrust enforcement to single out US companies.

(2) *Android*: The Commission alleged that, since 2005, Google has led development of the Android mobile operating system. The majority of smartphone and tablet manufacturers use the Android operating system in combination with a range of Google's proprietary applications and services. The Commission's investigation stems from three concerns: (a) Google allegedly requiring or incentivizing smartphone and tablet manufacturers to exclusively pre-install Google's own applications or services, in particular Google's search engine, (b) alleged bundling of Google products with other apps and services; and (c) hindering manufacturers from developing other open-source versions of Android.

(3) *AdSense*: On July 14, 2016, the Commission issued another Statement of Objections against Google, this proceeding referred to as the "AdSense case." Google places search ads directly on the Google search website but also as an intermediary on third party websites through its "AdSense for search" platform, a form of search advertising intermediation. A large portion of Google's revenues from search advertising intermediation stems from its agreements with large third parties known as Direct Partners. The Commission alleged that, in its agreements with these Direct Partners, Google breached EU antitrust rules by requiring exclusivity, requiring placement of a minimum number of Google search ads, and claiming the right to authorize competing ads.

Later in 2016, Google filed its response to these charges. It denied any wrongdoing, arguing that its services were beneficial in helping consumers, advertisers, and even some competitors to find the digital information they seek online. It argued that the online shopping landscape has evolved significantly over the past decade so that now there are hundreds of shopping comparison sites. In particular, Google maintained, a rapidly increasing amount of traffic has flowed from Google search pages to popular sites like Amazon and eBay as they expanded in Europe. Amazon's emergence is a key part of Google's defense. With respect to AdSense, Google responded that it has already made some changes to its practices in the hope of resolving the Commission's objections.

As regards the charge that Google abused Android's dominance to block its competitors in the market, Google argued that rivals Apple and Microsoft had many more pre-installed apps than the typical Android smartphone. There has in fact been pending for some time in Russia a similar complaint lodged against the Android system. Decisions by the EU Commission on the other Google charges are awaited in 2017.

The European Commissioner for Competition, Margrethe Vestager, gave a speech on April 16, 2015 defending the Commission's very active involvement in the technology area. In particular, she rejected any suggestion that the Commission was targeting US technology firms, stating:

> In all our cases, we are indifferent to the nationality of the companies involved. Our responsibility is to make sure that any company with operations in the territory of the EU complies with our Treaty rules. I listen to all without prejudice or preference. We try to collect all the data that are relevant to a given case. And then we apply the law.

Commissioner Vestager added:

> It is clear that U.S. companies are strong players in the IT sector, so it is normal that they are often involved in our cases in this sector. And that can be on both sides of the argument. So one out of four individual companies that complained in the Google search case is a US company. Companies from the US also play a major role in complaining business associations.

[D] Amazon

In June 2015, the European Commission initiated an antitrust investigation directed against Amazon.com, Inc. and Amazon EU S.à.r.l ("Amazon"). The investigation was aimed at certain clauses in Amazon's contracts with e-book publishers. These clauses, sometimes referred to as "most-favored-nation" or "MFN" clauses, required publishers to inform Amazon about more favorable or alternative terms offered to Amazon's competitors and seeking to ensure that the publishers would provide Amazon with similar terms and conditions as are offered to Amazon's competitors. Amazon has been the largest distributor of e-books in Europe.

Between December 2011 and 2013, the Commission had investigated e-book practices involving Apple and some publishing houses, but these proceedings were closed after the companies offered appropriate commitments.

To address the Commission's concerns, Amazon offered a number of commitments, including the noninclusion in any new e-book agreement with publishers of the clauses objected to by the Commission. The Commission tested the proposed commitments, seeking public comment. On May 4, 2017, The Commission announced that it had accepted Amazon's commitments and adopted a decision rendering these commitments legally binding.

Amazon's commitments include: (i) nonenforcement of clauses requiring publishers to offer Amazon similar non-price terms and conditions as those offered to Amazon's competitors; and (ii) allowing publishers to terminate e-book contracts that contain a clause linking discount possibilities for e-books to the retail price of a given e-book on a competing platform (the so-called Discount Pool Provision). The commitments apply for a period of five years and to any e-book in any language distributed by Amazon in the EEA.

[E] Apple

Apple Sales International and Apple Operations Europe are two Irish incorporated companies that are fully owned by the Apple group, ultimately controlled by the US parent, Apple, Inc. Following an in-depth state aid investigation launched in 2014, the European Commission concluded that two tax rulings issued by the Irish authorities to Apple substantially and artificially lowered the tax paid by Apple in Ireland since 1991. The Commission launched a proceeding in 2016 alleging that this selective tax treatment of Apple in Ireland was illegal under EU state aid rules because it gave Apple a significant advantage over other businesses that follow national tax rules. The Commission directed Ireland to recover from Apple the unpaid taxes for the years 2003–2014 of up to EUR 13 billion plus interest.

Under the Commission's analysis, almost all sales profits recorded by the two Irish companies were internally attributed to "head offices" which existed only on paper but claimed to generate profits which were not subject to tax.

Ireland and Apple have both appealed the Commission's action. Ireland asserts that "[t]he Commission has no competence, under State aid rules, unilaterally to substitute its own view of the geographic scope and extent of the member state's tax jurisdiction for those of the member state itself." Apple argues that the Commission made basic errors in its interpretation of Irish tax law and with respect to the basis of the profits made by Apple. Apple also maintains that the investigation was improperly conducted, alleging the Commission's failure to conduct a diligent and impartial investigation.

While it was an Article 101 conspiracy case and not an Article 102 dominant position case, this is a good point to mention the charges brought by the EU Commission in 2011 against Apple Inc. and five international publishers of e-books involving the collusive pricing of e-books. We described in Chapter 5 the successful litigation brought by the US Department of Justice against these parties under Section 1 of the Sherman Act. The EU Commission and the Antitrust Division worked closely together on this matter, which was cited by the US acting Assistant Attorney General as a "shining example" of the progress achieved in international cooperation on antitrust matters. The Commission extracted commitments from the companies to eliminate their efforts to limit retail price competition in the e-book market.

[F] Qualcomm

In 2015 the Commission sent two Statements of Objections to Qualcomm. The Commission alleged that the company illegally paid a major customer for exclusively using Qualcomm's chipsets and also sold chipsets below cost with the aim of forcing a competitor out of the market. These charges were made under Article 102. Qualcomm has defended itself in the proceeding, including complaining to the General Court that the Commission's demand on the company for information was unduly onerous and financially burdensome. Qualcomm's appeal in this regard was dismissed by the GC.

CHAPTER 13
Merger Control in the European Union

§13.01 INTRODUCTION TO MERGER CONTROL

Merger control is today a significant concern of the competition authorities of the EU. This was not always the case and, indeed, neither of the twin Articles of the EU competition law regime was designed with merger scrutiny firmly in mind. It was not until the final days of 1989 that the Member States reached the final agreement which enabled the promulgation of Council Regulation 4064/89, entrusting the Commission with jurisdiction over "concentrations" having a "Community dimension." This legislation was significantly amended in the years that followed, and it was recast, in the light of the experience gained, into Council Regulation 139/2004 of January 20, 2004 on the control of concentrations between undertakings. In the words of recital (6), the Merger Regulation (now also known as the "EUMR") was designed "to meet the challenges of a more integrated market and the future enlargement of the European Union," while still meeting the principles of subsidiarity and of proportionality as set out in Article 5 of the Treaty. Therefore, the Regulation "does not go beyond what is necessary in order to achieve the objective of ensuring that competition in the common market is not distorted, in accordance with the principle of an open market economy with free competition."

The new Merger Regulation became applicable as of May 1, 2004, which was also the date of repeal of the 1989 version. Article 2(3) declares to be incompatible with the common market concentrations which "would significantly impede effective competition, in the common market or in a substantial part of it, in particular as the result of the creation or strengthening of a dominant position ... ." The Merger Regulation, like Articles 101 and 102 TFEU, is enforced by the Directorate-General for Competition of the European Commission in Brussels. Within DG COMP there is a Deputy Director General with special responsibility for mergers. DG COMP also has a Chief Competition Economist who reports directly to the Director General and provides independent advice on cases and policy. As is the case with most competition law regimes overseeing merger activity, prior notification is an important element of the regulatory scheme.

In this chapter, we will review the events that led to the adoption of the original Merger Regulation and to the shaping of the new EUMR. We will then go over the latter's main provisions, and go on to consider some of the most important cases that have been adjudicated or settled since the merger control program went into effect.

§13.02 BEFORE THE MERGER REGULATION

In the early years of the EU, the Commission operated under the assumption that then Article 85 (now Article 101 TFEU), requiring collusion between independent companies, could not be applied to a merger transaction. Then Article 86 (now Article 102 TFEU) offered a more promising avenue, assuming that the case was one in which a company already having great market power was attempting to increase that dominance by acquiring another competitor in the market. The Commission looked for a suitable test case for presenting to the Court of Justice the theory that Article 86 could be applied to conduct involving market structure, as well as market practices.

The *Continental Can* case, involving an American manufacturer of metal containers, was selected by the Commission for this purpose. In 1969 the company brought to 85% its interest in a German container manufacturer (SLW), which was the largest producer of certain types of light metal containers in continental Europe. Continental Can also invited an English company, Metal Box, a Dutch firm, TDV, and a French company, Carnaud, to participate in a plan to form a holding company to operate in the European container market. Carnaud declined to participate, but the other three agreed that Continental Can would establish a Delaware corporation, Europemballage, to which Continental Can would transfer its interests in SLW. After Europemballage was established, it offered to purchase the shares of TDV. These measures would give Continental Can a holding of more than 91% of the Dutch company, which was a leading manufacturer of packing material in Benelux, along with its control of the German company.

The Commission promptly instituted a proceeding against Continental Can and Europemballage under Article 86 on the ground that the group's acquisition of a majority of the TDV stock eliminated competition in the market for certain types of metal containers. The Commission subsequently ruled that Continental Can had a dominant position through SLW, at least on the German market, with respect to certain containers for preserved meats and fish. It also ruled that Continental Can had abused that position by taking over TDV, one of its principal competitors. On the appeal to the ECJ, Continental Can argued that Article 86 was neither intended to prohibit mergers or other structural measures for increasing market share nor to prohibit the establishment or increase of a dominant position. Rather, the provision was applicable, in the company's view, only to "abusive exploitation of a dominant position" through practices employed in the marketplace.

The Court of Justice rejected this contention. It pointed out that Article 3(f) of the EEC Treaty required the establishment of a system protecting competition within the

Common Market and reasoned that this objective would be subverted if enterprises were left free to impair competition through mergers and acquisitions. The Court stated that "... the strengthening of the position held by one enterprise can be an abuse and prohibited under Article 86 of the Treaty regardless of the methods or means used to attain it, provided it has the effects described ... ." The Court went on to accept the Commission's view that an "abuse" occurs "where an enterprise in a dominant position so strengthens its position through a merger that actual or potential competition in the relevant products would be virtually eliminated in a substantial part of the Common Market."

Nonetheless, the Court reversed the decision of the Commission because the latter had failed to establish that Continental Can had a dominant position in Germany. In particular, in simply assigning tin cans for fish and tin cans for meat to separate relevant product markets, and assuming that market power followed from the market shares attained, the Commission had failed sufficiently to take into account the possibility that producers of one type of light metal containers could provide a counterbalance to the merged enterprise by slightly adjusting their production procedures to manufacture another type of light metal containers.

Despite the reversal of the Commission's decision, its interpretation of Article 86 in the context of mergers had been upheld by the Court. As The Economist headlined its story on the case, "Battle Lost, War Won." However, as the Commission recognized, continued reliance on Article 86 for merger control would fall short in at least two critical respects. First, the *Continental Can* rationale was limited to situations in which one of the merging enterprises was already in a dominant position, and not to mergers which brought about the attainment of the dominant position. Second, the Commission would be authorized to challenge the merger transaction only after the merger had already taken place. A Council regulation with complete procedural and substantive provision for effective merger control was needed.

Accordingly, a few months after the decision of the Court in the *Continental Can* case, the Commission submitted to the Council the first draft of what eventually became the Merger Regulation. A key aspect of this first draft that drew heavy political criticism was its setting of a very low threshold for coverage of a merger transaction, thus potentially sweeping into the Community control scheme an extremely large number of mergers. Several new drafts were submitted to the Council by the Commission over the next few years, raising the turnover threshold for jurisdiction, but political opposition from the Member States persisted.

During this period of deadlock, the Commission indicated that, if a regulation was not approved, it would have no recourse but to pursue merger control under theories covered by Articles 85 and 86. In fact, the Court of Justice gave some support, in its 1987 judgment in the *Philip Morris* case, to the notion that Article 85 could be applicable "where, by the acquisition of a shareholding or through subsidiary clauses in the agreement, the investing company obtains legal or de facto control of the commercial conduct of the other company or where the agreement provides for commercial cooperation between the companies or creates a structure likely to be used for such cooperation." This judgment, portending an uncertain future for enforcement in this area, caused the Member States to refocus their attentions on the prospects for an acceptable merger regulation.

New proposals from the Commission significantly reduced the number of mergers that would be within the bounds of Community control. Some other questions were still being debated, including whether Community review would be limited to competition issues and the extent to which national competition authorities might retain a role where significant national interests were implicated. By the end of 1989, the terms of the new regime were agreed.

In 1992, the Commission directed the leading US razor manufacturer, Gillette, to give up the interest which it had acquired in its primary competitor, Wilkinson, before the merger control regulation became effective. The Commission relied on EC Treaty Article 86, reasoning that Gillette's shareholding in Wilkinson represented an abuse of its dominant position.

§13.03 MERGER REGULATION 139/2004

As previously noted, the current EUMR became applicable as of May 1, 2004. Prior to that, Merger Regulation 4064/89, which came into effect on September 21, 1990, was amended by Regulation 1310/97, which became effective on March 1, 1998. The original version of the Merger Regulation required a distinction between "concentrative" joint ventures, which were subject to the ECMR, and "co-operative" joint ventures which were not. The distinction caused much difficulty, and the need to make it was eliminated by the 1998 amendments. All "full-function" joint ventures meeting the turnover thresholds, as well as mergers, are now potentially within the scope of the EUMR. The EUMR applies to concentrations which have a "Community dimension" or, in the more recent parlance, a "Union dimension," while concentrations which are at a smaller scale are subject to the Member State merger control programs. Forms of cooperation between enterprises which do not fall under the EUMR may, of course, be prohibited by TFEU Article 101(1) or 102.

The Merger Regulation covers all industries, including the coal and steel sectors, now that the ECSC Treaty has expired. It applies to both privately owned and state owned firms, except to the extent that application of the Merger Regulation would jeopardize public service obligations. Special rules apply in the calculation of the turnover thresholds in the case of state owned businesses.

There were a number of reasons militating for the adoption of a new Merger Regulation in 2004. These included the need to redefine the substantive standard for merger control, to amend the timing of notification, to revise the referral procedure to and from the Commission, and to provide additional time for the consideration of proposed remedies. The Merger Regulation regime now extends to the twenty-eight Member States of the EU. The EUMR is premised on the concept of the "one-stop shop," with the Commission that "shop" for mergers of a Union dimension. The Member States are not permitted to apply their national competition laws to concentrations with a Union dimension, except in certain limited circumstances.

The preamble to the EUMR recites that, while the existing competition law articles are, according to the case law of the Court of Justice, applicable to certain concentrations, these provisions are "not sufficient to control all operations which may prove to be incompatible with the system of undistorted competition envisaged in the Treaty." The provisions adopted by the EUMR are intended to apply to significant structural changes, the market impact of which goes beyond the national borders of any one Member State. The scope of the EUMR is therefore defined in terms of the geographic area of activity of the undertakings concerned and is limited by quantitative thresholds in order to cover those concentrations which have an EU dimension. Concentrations not covered by the Merger Regulation remain, in principle, within the jurisdiction of the Member States.

Article 3 of the EUMR defines a "concentration" as either (1) a merger of two or more previously independent undertakings or parts of undertakings, or (2) the acquisition by one or more undertakings or by persons controlling at least one undertaking, of direct or indirect control of the whole or parts of one or more other undertakings, whether by purchase of securities or assets, by contract or by any other means. Under Article 4, the latter includes, but is not limited to, the creation of a joint venture which performs on a lasting basis all the functions of an autonomous economic entity. The regulatory scheme created by the original Merger Regulation was based on the principle of prohibiting concentrations with a Community dimension which created or strengthened a dominant position in the common market. The new EUMR prohibits concentrations which are likely to impede effective competition in the common market whether or not they create or strengthen a dominant position.

Under the principle of subsidiarity a merger is examined by the judicial authority best placed to do so. However, as a general rule, concentrations with a Union dimension must be notified to the Commission prior to their implementation and following the conclusion of the agreement, the announcement of the public bid or the acquisition of a controlling interest. A "pre-notification" procedure allows the companies or persons concerned to file a "reasoned submission" with the Commission in advance of formal notification, which allows the Commission to carry out coordination with any competent national authorities. Where a merger has a Union dimension, the Commission has sole jurisdiction over it. The Commission has extensive powers, including the power to prohibit a merger. This has been rarely done, and objections are often resolved by the merging parties offering binding commitments to address competition concerns. The Commission's application of the Merger Regulation is subject to judicial review.

The Commission has issued an Implementing Regulation, No. 802/2004, which fleshes out the requirements of the Merger Regulation. This Regulation has been amended several times. The Commission has also published a number of guidelines and notices on both substantive and procedural issues to aid in the interpretation of the EUMR. These materials include:

(1) *Notice on the definition of the relevant market* (December 1997);
(2) *Guidelines on the assessment of horizontal mergers* (February 2004);
(3) *Guidelines on the assessment of non-horizontal mergers* (October 2008);

(4) *Notice on remedies acceptable under the EUMR* (October 2008);
(5) *Consolidated jurisdictional notice* (April 2008);
(6) *Best Practices on the conduct of EC merger control proceedings* (January 2004);
(7) *Notice on a simplified procedure for treatment of certain concentrations* (March 2005);
(8) *Notice on case referral in respect of concentrations* (March 2005);
(9) *Notice on restrictions directly related to and necessary to concentrations* (March 2005);
(10) *Best practices on cooperation between EU national competition authorities in merger review;*
(11) *Cooperation between the European Union and the United States: Best practices on cooperation in merger cases;*
(12) *Best Practice Guidelines: the Commission's model texts for divestiture commitments and the trustee mandate* (December 2013).

Let us consider in greater detail some of the salient aspects of the EUMR.

[A] Concentrations Having a Union Dimension

The determination as to whether a concentration is one of EU dimension, and hence subject to the EUMR, depends on the "turnover" within the EU of the undertakings involved. Except for financial institutions and insurance undertakings, "turnover" refers to sales of goods and provision of services in the preceding financial year, excluding value added and sales taxes. As provided in Article 1(2) of the EUMR, a concentration has an EU dimension if: (a) the combined aggregate worldwide turnover of all the undertakings concerned (in the preceding financial year) is more than EUR 5,000 million; *and* (b) the aggregate Union-wide turnover of each of at least two of the undertakings concerned is more than EUR 250 million, *unless* each of the undertakings concerned achieves more than two-thirds of its aggregate Union-wide turnover within one and the same Member State (this is known as the "two-thirds rule").

Even if these thresholds are not met, a concentration will be deemed to have an EU dimension under Article 1(3) if: (a) the combined aggregate worldwide turnover of all the undertakings concerned exceeds EUR 2,500 million; and (b) in each of at least three Member States, the combined aggregate turnover of all the undertakings concerned exceeds EUR 100 million; and (c) in each of the three Member States included for purposes of point (b), the aggregate turnover of each of at least two of the undertakings concerned exceeds EUR 25 million in each of the three Member States included in (b); and (d) the aggregate EU-wide turnover of each of at least two of the undertakings concerned exceeds EUR 100 million, unless each of the undertakings concerned achieves more than two-thirds of its aggregate EU-wide turnover within one and the same Member State.

The Commission has been considering additional threshold tests to overcome possible shortcomings in the present turnover-based system. This could involve the introduction of a complementary threshold based on the value of the transaction, a "deal size threshold."

The Commission must be notified of any merger with an EU dimension prior to its implementation. The Commission has pointed out that, if the merging firms are not operating in the same or related markets, or if they have only very small market shares not reaching specified market share thresholds, the merger will typically not give rise to significant competition problems. In such cases the merger review is done by a simplified procedure involving a routine check. The market share thresholds for this simplified procedure are 15% combined market shares on a market where they both compete, or 25% market shares on vertically related markets. Above these market share thresholds, the Commission carries out a full investigation.

It should be noted that mergers and acquisitions involving companies based outside of the EU, including foreign to foreign mergers, are covered if they have sufficient turnover within more than one Member State. The CFI pointed out in the *Gencor/Lonrho* case that the Merger Regulation does not require that, in order for a concentration to have an EU dimension, the undertakings in question must be established in the EU or that the production activities covered by the concentration must be carried out within EU territory. Further, the CFI confirmed that this "extraterritorial" application of the Merger Regulation is permitted under public international law when it is "foreseeable that a proposed concentration will have an immediate and substantial effect in the Community."

The turnover attributed to an undertaking comprises that of its entire family, including the turnover of any parent and of any subsidiaries forming part of the same group. The rules for combining the turnovers of related undertakings are set forth in Article 5(4) of the EUMR and depend on such factors as ownership, the power to exercise voting rights, and the right to manage the other undertaking's affairs. The relevant turnover for joint ventures is the turnover of the parents, including their groups, and thus joint ventures are often caught. There are special rules for defining the turnover of financial and insurance institutions.

The EUMR may be triggered by one undertaking acquiring direct or indirect "control" of another undertaking. Whether "control" is being obtained by a transaction is defined in terms of the presence of "rights, contracts, or any other means which, either separately or in combination ... confer the possibility of exercising decisive influence on an undertaking ... ." Each case is to be decided on its own facts through consideration of such factors as share ownership and rights, board representation and provisions in shareholder agreements. Acquisition of a minority interest may or may not be found by the Commission to confer "decisive influence" over a company, depending on how widely dispersed the other shareholdings are and on who will hold the power to manage and oversee the course of the business. In the *Anglo American/Lonrho* case, the Commission confirmed its view that effective control exists for purposes of the EUMR where a minority shareholder has sufficient voting power to control shareholders' meetings of the target company.

Where the EU dimension exists, the Commission has exclusive jurisdiction to review the concentration. Subject to the referral process, the Member States are not permitted to apply their national competition laws to any concentration that has an EU dimension. They do have a limited participatory role, including receiving a copy of each notification and having the opportunity to consult with the Commission.

The standards for determining which mergers have a Community dimension, and are therefore within the exclusive competence of the Commission, have not worked entirely to the Commission's satisfaction. For one thing, the two-thirds rule has allowed the Member States to claim authority over some large mergers and put them in the position to create "national champions" for themselves, to the detriment of EU-wide competition. The Commission rejects the concept of national champions where the Member States are concerned. Some of the national authorities have been aggressive in striking down large proposed mergers within their territories while others have been permissive in reviewing the transactions.

In 2005, the Spanish enterprise Gas Natural SDG, SA announced its proposed hostile takeover of its national rival, the Endesa, SA energy group. This merger promised to create one of the largest energy groups in Europe. However, the European Commission determined that the matter had to be referred to the Spanish competition authorities because, since both enterprises made less than one-third of their turnover outside Spain, the transaction was not one having a Community dimension. Endesa applied to the CFI for annulment of the Commission's decision as a matter of urgency, asserting that the Commission had erroneously calculated its turnover figures, but the President of the CFI dismissed the request for review. The Spanish Government then approved the proposed takeover subject to conditions, including the forced sale of generation capacity by the merged group. Subsequently, the giant German utility company, E. On AG, topped Gas Natural's offer by making an all-cash offer bid for Endesa.

When the Commission was unable to review Gas Natural's bid, the EU's Competition Commissioner, Neelie Kroes, criticized the two-thirds rule and called for the Commission to be given fresh powers to review certain large mergers even if the companies conducted the bulk of their business in one Member State. In June 2009, the Commission published a *Report on the functioning of Regulation No. 139/2004* in which it observed that "the present form of the two-thirds rule merits further consideration."

In 2014, the Commission launched a public consultation on proposals to improve EU merger control. The Commission's key proposals, outlined in its White Paper, were: (i) establishing a "light and tailor-made" review of acquisitions of noncontrolling shareholdings that could be harmful to competition; (ii) making case referrals between Member States and the Commission more "business-friendly" and effective; (iii) simplifying procedures; and (iv) fostering greater coherence and convergence between Member States In the application of merger control. The public consultation period has continued.

[B] Case Referral and Consultation

The referral process enables the Member States to deal with cases having a primarily national or local impact although they may meet the Community dimension thresholds. On the other hand, there is also provision for referrals by the Member States to the

Commission of concentrations not having Union dimensions. Several provisions of the ECMR provide for such eventualities.

Article 4(4) of the Merger Regulation allows the parties to a transaction to make a reasoned submission to the Commission that a concentration will significantly affect competition in a market within a Member State which presents all the characteristics of a distinct market and should therefore be examined, in whole or in part, by that Member State. (The parties are not thereby required to demonstrate that the effect on competition will be adverse.) The Commission then transmits the request to all Member States. The Member State in question must within fifteen working days express its agreement or disagreement with the request. Unless the Member State in question disagrees, the Commission, where it considers that such a distinct market exists, and that competition in that market may be significantly affected by the concentration, may decide to refer the whole or part of the case to the competent authorities of that Member State with a view to the application of that State's national competition law. In July 2014, the Commission proposed that the self-incrimination aspect of Article 4(4) be eliminated with parties only having to show that the transaction was likely to have its main impact in the Member State concerned.

Article 9 of the EUMR allows a Member State to make a request to the Commission that a certain concentration, although having a Union dimension, should be referred to that Member State. The first such situation, under Article 9(2)(a), is where a concentration threatens to affect significantly competition within a Member State that presents all the characteristics of a distinct market. The second situation, under Article 9(2)(b), is where a concentration affects competition within a Member State which presents all the characteristics of a distinct market and which does not constitute a substantial part of the internal market: usually a narrow geographical market within a single Member State.

A significant number of cases have, in fact, been referred wholly or partially by the Commission to the Member States under these provisions. There have been occasional disputes over these referrals, including the two cases in 2003 of Royal Philips Electronics and Cableuropa SA in which the Commission's decisions to make referrals to the national authorities were unsuccessfully challenged in the CFI.

The Commission noted in a 2007 report that there were at least 100 transactions that were notified in three or more Member States. The EUMR provides for concentrations not having a Union dimension being referred to the Commission in certain situations, thereby affording the benefit of one-stop merger control. Article 4(5) of the EUMR allows the parties to a concentration that is capable of being reviewed by at least three Member States to make a reasoned submission that it should instead be reviewed by the Commission. A single Member State can disagree with such referral. If there is no disagreement, only the EUMR, and not national law, becomes applicable.

Under Article 22 of the EUMR, a Member State may refer a concentration that does not have a Union dimension to the Commission for investigation if the concentration affects trade between Member States and threatens to affect competition significantly within the territory of the Member State making the request. In 2010, the Commission accepted a request from six Member States to investigate the acquisition by Procter & Gamble of Sara Lee's air freshener. Referrals have taken place under both of the provisions discussed above.

Article 21(4) of the Merger Regulation provides a "legitimate interests exception," whereby the Member States may take appropriate measures to protect valid national interests with respect to a concentration, such as in cases involving public security, plurality of the media, and prudential rules. There have been few decisions allowing a Member State to proceed on this basis, since it derogates from the one-stop shop principle.

The Commission has several times clashed with national authorities who wished to carry out their own policies in merger situations. In two cases, *BSCH/Champalimaud* and *Secil/Holderbank/Cimpor*, the Commission clashed with the Portuguese Government, which had prohibited, on the basis of national economic policies, proposed mergers between Portuguese companies and non-Portuguese banks. The Commission, in both cases, negated the decisions of the Portuguese Government as incompatible with Community law. In the second case, the ECJ sustained the Commission's decision in a June 2004 judgment, holding that Portugal's actions were not justified by any legitimate national interests recognized by Article 21 of the Merger Regulation.

To illustrate further how this system works in practice, this would be a good place to mention the BSkyB saga which begins with Rupert Murdoch's News Corporation owning 39.1% of the pay-TV operator British Sky Broadcasting ("BSkyB"). In 2010, in the case of *News Corp/BSkyB*, the European Commission approved under the EUMR the proposed acquisition by News Corporation of the shares of BSkyB which News Corporation did not already own. However, the UK Secretary of State for Business Innovation and Skills had filed a European "intervention notice," so the Commission's decision also stated that the UK remained free to decide whether or not to take appropriate measures to protect its legitimate interest in media plurality as permitted under Article 21 of the EUMR. Following the phone hacking scandal which implicated Murdoch's News of the World paper in the UK, the bid for the remaining shares of BSkyB was withdrawn.

BSkyB was renamed Sky plc ("Sky") and became the leading pay-TV operator in Austria, Germany, Ireland, Italy, and the UK. In 2017 Murdoch's Twenty-First Century Fox, Inc. ("Fox") renewed the bid for the remaining shares in Sky. On April 7, 2017, the Commission approved unconditionally under the EUMR the proposed acquisition by Fox, concluding that the transaction would raise no competition concerns in Europe because the transaction would lead to only a limited increase in Sky's existing share of the markets for the acquisition of TV content as well as in the market for the wholesale supply of TV channels in the relevant Member States. However, the Commission also noted the relevance of Article 21 of the EUMR and the fact that the UK Secretary of State for Culture, Media and Sport had issued a European intervention notice indicating that the UK wished to make its own public interest review of the proposed transaction. The Commission, accordingly, cleared the transaction "without prejudice to the UK's ongoing media plurality review" of the deal. As of this writing, the transaction, which is very controversial in the UK, is under review by the nation's media watchdog, Ofcom, and by the Competition and Markets Authority (CMA).

In another point of deference to the Member States, Article 346(1)(b) TFEU permits Member States to take measures to protect their national security, a power which enables Member States to assert jurisdiction over the military aspects of proposed mergers. The UK Government was able to invoke this provision in 1994 when British Aerospace proposed to take over VSEL, where both companies produced military equipment for the British military.

The Commission has, as earlier noted, made guidance available regarding its case allocation policies and procedures in its Notice on Case Referral, published March 5, 2005. In addition to cooperating with the Member States, the Commission consults on mergers of international significance with the interested foreign authorities. The ICN has been previously discussed, including the *ICN Merger Guidelines Workbook*, with an emphasis on recommended enforcement techniques. There are many bilateral and multilateral agreements fostering cooperation among competition authorities in which the EU is actively engaged. The formal mechanisms already in place for this purpose include the 1991 US-EU competition law cooperation agreement, a similar 1999 EU-Canada cooperation agreement, a cooperation agreement entered into with Japan in 2003, one with South Korea signed in 2009, and one with Switzerland signed in 2014. There are also EU cooperation agreements with competition agencies in China, Russia, and India.

[C] Notification and Review Procedure

Article 4(1) of the Merger Regulation provides that concentrations with a Union dimension must be notified to the Commission prior to their implementation and following either the conclusion of the agreement, the announcement of a public bid, or the acquisition of a controlling interest. Article 4(1) also allows the concerned undertakings to make notification of a proposed concentration with a Union dimension before one of these events, where they can demonstrate to the Commission a good faith intention to conclude an agreement or, in the case of a public bid, that they have publicly announced an intention to make such a bid. The notification must be made by the buyer in the case of an acquisition of sole control or jointly by the parties in the case of a merger which creates a new undertaking or results in acquisition of joint control.

A concentration which is to be examined by the Commission may not be implemented before notification and until the Commission has reached its decision following investigation. The Commission may grant a derogation from this requirement, and the suspension rule accords more flexibility in the case of public takeover bids. The EUMR authorizes the Commission to impose fines of up to 10% of the aggregate worldwide turnover of the undertakings concerned if they fail, intentionally or negligently, to notify a concentration prior to implementation. Where misleading or incorrect information is supplied by the parties in the merger review process, the Commission is empowered to impose fines of up to 1% of aggregate worldwide turnover. Periodic penalty payments not exceeding 5% of the average daily aggregate turnover of the undertakings concerned can be imposed for each day of delay in supplying information, submitting to an ordered inspection, or in complying with other obligations imposed by decision. The Commission has shown its willingness to utilize this authority, including the fining of Tetra Laval in 2004, and more recently Facebook, for the supply of false or misleading information.

The Commission's Directorate-General for Competition encourages parties to meet with its staff before notification to discuss such matters as jurisdiction and the information to be included in the notification form. The notification is to be submitted either on the Form CO, which requires extensive information about the transaction and the markets involved, or on the Short Form CO, which requires much less information but can be used only where the low market shares involved indicate little need for competition law concerns. The Short Form procedure was amended with effect from January 1, 2014 and is included in the Commission's *Notice on a simplified procedure for treatment of certain concentrations*. The Commission staff and the officials of the Member States are bound by obligations of professional secrecy with respect to the information that they receive during the process. The Commission's decisions are publicly announced and made available.

Completion of Form CO can involve a sizeable effort, depending on the transaction. The task may call for preparation and submittal of detailed market information on the parties, their competitors and customers, and the Commission may reject the notification on grounds of incompleteness. The Commission has the same types of powers to investigate concentrations that it has with respect to Article 101 or 102 investigations. Thus, it may examine books and records, carry out "dawn raids" and ask for oral explanations. When a concentration having a Union dimension has been notified, that fact is published in the Official Journal of the EU, and the Commission may invite third parties to submit their views on the transaction.

The Merger Regulation provides for a first phase and a second phase inquiry, and it sets out time limits. The Commission must reach a Phase I decision within twenty-five working days from the effective date of notification on whether the notified concentration falls within the scope of the Regulation and, if so, raises serious doubts about its compatibility with the common market. This period may be increased by ten working days where the parties submit commitments to remedy the competition law problems perceived in the transaction. If the transaction is not within the scope of the Merger Regulation, the Commission must issue a reasoned decision to this effect. A Phase I review may involve requests for information from the merging parties or third parties. It may also involve sending questionnaires to competitors or customers or other market participants to seek their views about the transaction. If the Commission finds the concentration to fall within the Merger Regulation, it must issue a reasoned decision stating either (1) that the transaction does not present serious doubts as to its compatibility with the internal market or that it can be approved subject to conditions, or (2) that there are serious doubts as to the compatibility of the notified concentration with the internal market, at which point the Commission must initiate Phase II proceedings. More than 90% of all cases are resolved in Phase I, generally without remedies.

The Phase II proceedings, which are initiated when the Commission has concerns that the transaction could restrict competition in the internal market, may consume up to ninety working days. These concerns may involve a detailed market investigation.

The period can be extended for various reasons, including the need to consider commitments which may be offered by the parties. This is when the Commission will examine claimed efficiencies for consumers which could outweigh the merger's negative effects. The proceedings during Phase II may involve the Commission's seeking additional information from the parties or from third persons, conducting market analysis, giving the parties access to the Commission's file, and the Commission's issuance of a Statement of Objections. The notifying parties may make written reply to the latter and, if they so request, are entitled to present their case orally at a formal hearing in which other interested parties, including complainants, may participate. After this phase of the investigation the Commission may either unconditionally clear the merger, approve it subject to remedies, or prohibit the transaction.

Following the CFI's criticisms in some appeal proceedings that the Commission's analysis lacked sufficient rigor in some of its merger reviews, the Commission created the mechanism of a "devil's advocate panel," a team made up of lawyers and economists from DG Competition and from other Directorates-General who were independent of the main case team. This peer review panel functioned to scrutinize the views of the DG Competition case team for their soundness during Phase II. In the *Sony/BMG* merger case, in July 2004, the then Competition Commissioner, Mario Monti, upheld a decision by this panel to the effect that the Commission had failed to establish that the proposed combination would enhance the ability of the major record companies to collude to set prices tacitly.

[D] Remedies

In rendering its decision after the Phase II inquiry, the Commission may attach conditions and obligations to the clearance of the concentration, including requiring the parties to comply with the commitments that they have proposed. The Commission may, alternatively, state that the concentration is incompatible with the internal market and block it, without stating any conditions.

The parties can offer undertakings (commitments) on a timely basis during either Phase I or Phase II in an effort to remedy the perceived competition issues presented by a concentration. The Commission stands ready to accept such a remedy if it is adequate to ensure effective competition in the relevant market. The remedy may be in the form of the divestiture of a business, through creation of a new competitive entry, or by another approach suited to the situation, such as the granting of licenses. The Commission prefers structural remedies, such as divestitures, over behavioral commitments which may be difficult to monitor.

In 2005, the Commission published a *Merger Remedies Study* in which it reviewed the effectiveness of remedies accepted in past cases. This study preceded the revision in 2008 of the *Notice on remedies acceptable under the EUMR*. That year the Commission also adopted Regulation 1033/2008 which amended the merger Implementing Regulation to provide for a new form, Form RM, which merging firms must submit to the Commission when offering remedies. The Regulation also made it clear that independent trustees could be appointed to assist the Commission in overseeing compliance with parties' commitments. These changes also foreshadowed the issuance in 2013 of the Commission's document entitled *Best Practice Guidelines: The Commission's Model Texts for Divestiture Commitments and the Trustee Mandate under the EC Merger Regulation*.

The *Notice on remedies* lists the types of acceptable remedies in suitable cases. First mentioned is divestiture of particular business activities to a suitable purchaser. It is critical that the business activity be a viable one which can compete effectively with the merged entity on a lasting basis. The Commission will determine whether a proposed purchaser is suitable in this sense. The Commission does not favor "carving out" a business from the merged entity to try to create a viable operation, in the sense of putting together assets that did not operate together in the past. The purchaser must be independent of the merging parties and have sufficient resources. The divestiture process is described, including the approval of purchasers, the obligations of the parties during the interim period and after divestiture, and the roles of monitoring and divestiture trustees.

Another set of remedies involves commitments to make available access to infrastructure and technology, including patents. These remedies have been applied in a number of cases. The Notice also makes the point that behavioral remedies as to future conduct by the parties will be acceptable only in exceptional circumstances.

The CFI ruled in *Petrolessence SA v. Commission* in 2003 that the Commission has the discretion to approve or disapprove a proposed purchaser, subject to limited judicial review on the matter. The Guidelines on divestiture commitments indicate the time limits for the completion of the sale by divestiture. The Commission oversees compliance with any commitments given by the parties, and it may impose sanctions for noncompliance, including fines, periodic penalty payments, or even revocation of the decision.

The CFI remarked in its decision in the *Gencor/Lonrho* case that, although structural commitments such as divestiture are preferable from the viewpoint of the Merger Regulation's objective of protecting competition, "the possibility cannot automatically be ruled out that commitments which prima facie are behavioural, for instance not to use a trademark for a certain period, or to make part of the production capacity of the entity arising from the concentration available to third-party competitors, or, more generally, to grant access to essential facilities on non-discriminatory terms, may themselves also be capable of preventing the emergence or strengthening of a dominant position."

Structural remedies are not always well suited or feasible to remove dominance concerns, so the Commission has imposed behavioral remedies in resolving a number of merger cases. The merged firm's obligations in complying with these remedies may well run over a lengthy time period. A key question at the outset of fashioning a behavioral remedy is how the monitoring of the firm's compliance with its commitments will be accomplished. This kind of in-depth, long-term oversight of a company's activities is not something that the Commission is itself always well positioned to undertake. In a number of cases, the Commission has left the matter of a firm's compliance with the commitments which it has accepted to monitoring by experts or to review by independent arbitrators. In cases where the protection of third parties will be necessary, such as to assure that the merged firm will keep any supply commitments given, the Commission has often relied on the inclusion of the condition that any future disputes over the commitment will be submitted to resolution by independent arbitrators. The Commission may retain the power to approve the nature of the arbitration process, including the appointment of the arbitrator or arbitrators.

[E]   Judicial Review

Pursuant to Article 263 of the TFEU and Article 16 of the EUMR, Commission decisions can be appealed on both substantive and procedural grounds to the GC by the parties and also by third parties who are able to show that they are directly and individually concerned by the decision. The EU courts have upheld the standing in this regard of employees or competitors of the companies concerned. GC judgments can be appealed to the ECJ on points of law. The GC's review results either in the Commission's decision being upheld in whole or in part, or in annulment of the decision in whole or in part. The lengthy time required for the appeal process has created situations in which the delay itself kills the merger deal, and both EU courts have instituted fast-track review procedures in an effort to expedite the appellate process. Nonetheless, particularly in view of the extended and uncertain time-table posed by the appeal process, parties tend to make a strenuous effort to reach a negotiated outcome with the Commission.

The task of the Commission under the Merger Regulation is to determine whether a proposed concentration is incompatible with the internal market in that it would significantly impede effective competition in that market or in a substantial part of it, in particular as a result of the creation or strengthening of a dominant position. Article 263 permits any natural or legal person to start proceedings against a decision which is addressed to it or which is addressed to another person but which is of direct and individual concern to it.

In *Sun Chemical Group BV and others v. Commission* in 2007, the GC indicated some leeway for the Commission in conducting review, by stating, ["a]ccording to settled law, review by the [EU] judicature of complex economic assessments made by the Commission in the exercise of the power of assessment conferred on it by the Merger Regulation is limited to ascertaining compliance with the rules governing procedure and the statement of reasons, the substantive accuracy of the facts and the absence of manifest errors of assessment or misuse of powers ... ."

§13.04   MERGER ANALYSIS

As will be recalled, when conducting merger analysis from the antitrust viewpoint, the authorities look for anticipated adverse competitive effects. The primary concern will be anticipated *horizontal* effects, when the merger is to take place between actual or potential competitors operating in the same product and geographical markets. Less common are concerns about *vertical* effects, where a merger involves firms operating at different, but related, levels of the market. One company may be a producer at one level of the distribution chain (typically "downstream") who sells to producers at the next level of the distribution chain (typically "upstream"). Finally, there may be concern about *conglomerate* effects, raised by special factors such as the great market power brought to the merger by one or both parties. There has been little or no interest in the antitrust implications of conglomerate mergers in the US in recent years, but the European Commission has not totally abandoned the subject matter.

The task of the Commission under the Merger Regulation is to determine whether a proposed concentration is incompatible with the internal market in that it would significantly impede effective competition in that market or in a substantial part of it in particular as a result of the creation or strengthening of a dominant position. Article 2(1)(b) of the EUMR provides that, in making its appraisal, the Commission shall take into account:

> the market position of the undertakings concerned and their economic and financial power, the alternatives available to suppliers and users, their access to supplies or markets, any legal or other barriers to entry, supply and demand trends for the relevant goods and services, the interests of the intermediate and ultimate consumers, and the development of technical and economic progress provided that it is to consumers' advantage and does not form an obstacle to competition.

The Introduction to the *Horizontal Guidelines* (the *Guidelines*) observes that:

> 4. The creation or strengthening of a dominant position held by a single firm as a result of a merger has been the most common basis for finding that a concentration would result in a significant impediment to effective competition. Furthermore, the concept of dominance has also been applied in an oligopolistic setting to cases of collective dominance. As a consequence, it is expected that most cases of incompatibility of a concentration with the common market will continue to be based on dominance.

In providing guidance as to how the Commission assesses concentrations when the undertakings concerned are actual or potential competitors in the same relevant market the *Guidelines* address: market share and concentration thresholds; the likelihood of anticompetitive effects; countervailing buyer power; the possibility of competitive market entry; efficiencies; and failing firms.

[A] Market Shares and Concentration Levels

The *Guidelines* observe that well-established case law holds that very large market shares of 50% or more may in themselves be evidence of a dominant market position. The Commission has thus considered mergers resulting in firms holding market shares between 40% and 50% and, in some cases, even below 40%, to be leading to the creation or strengthening of a dominant position. Recital 32 of the Merger Regulation states that, where the market share of the undertakings concerned does not exceed 25% either in the internal market or in a substantial part of it, this is an indication that the concentration is not likely to impede effective competition.

In order to measure concentration levels, the Commission often applies the HHI which, as we discussed earlier in the context of US antitrust, is calculated by summing the squares of all the firms in the market. The Commission notes that the post-merger change in the HHI, known as the "delta," is a useful proxy for the change in concentration directly brought about by the merger. It is unlikely that horizontal competition concerns will be identified in a market with a post-merger HHI below 1,000. Furthermore, the Commission is unlikely to identify such concerns in a merger with a post-merger HHI between 1,000 and 2,000 and a delta below 250, or a merger with a post-merger HHI above 2,000 and a delta below 150, except where special circumstances apply such as new entry, innovation not reflected in market shares, a history of coordination, or one of the merging parties has a premerger market share of 50% or more.

In *Sun Chemical Group BV and others v. Commission*, the GC held that "the greater the margin by which those thresholds are exceeded, the more the HHI values will be indicative of competition concerns."

[B] Possible Anticompetitive Effects

The possible anticompetitive effects posed by horizontal mergers are stated in the *Guidelines* to be: (1) unilateral effects, such as the removal of rivals or of other competitive constraints on a firm's conduct in the relevant market, and (2) coordinated effects, where the merger leads to or facilitates coordinated anticompetitive behavior by the firms in the market. The CFI's judgment in the *Airtours* case in 2002 laid down the standards for a finding of coordinated effects to be sustainable. These are contained in the *Guidelines*, namely (a) sufficient transparency in the relevant market so that the firms are able to monitor whether coordination is being adhered to, (b) the presence of discipline in the form of a credible deterrent mechanism that can be activated if deviation is detected, and (c) the reaction of outsiders, such as actual and potential competitors or customers, should not be able to jeopardize the results expected by the firms from their coordination.

The job of predicting the likelihood of future coordinated effects following a merger can be a difficult one. For example, in two cases in 2014 involving the cement industry, *Holcim Cemex West* and *Cemex/Holcim assets*, the Commission ventured that, while certain features of the grey cement industry (including past cartel activity) made the industry prone to coordination among the competitors, on balance the notified transaction was unlikely to make coordination easier, more stable or more effective.

The *Guidelines* also point out that a firm's merger with a potential competitor can generate horizontal anticompetitive effects, whether coordinated or unilateral, if the potential competitor has been significantly constraining the behavior of the firms in the market.

The *Guidelines* further state that the Commission will consider any vertical effects that the merger is likely to have in terms of foreclosure of the market. With respect to upstream markets, the Commission may analyze to what extent the merged entity will be able to increase its buyer power so as to reduce its purchases of inputs or to foreclose its rivals. On the other hand, increased buyer power may be beneficial for competition in bringing about cost reductions which are likely to be passed on to consumers. Whether the merger will have anticompetitive effects in downstream markets may depend on the extent to which there exists countervailing buyer power, enabling customers to have bargaining strength towards the seller due to the buyer's size, its commercial importance and its ability to switch to alternative suppliers.

[C] Entry Barriers

Entry assessment also constitutes an important component of the Commission's merger evaluation. The Commission examines whether entry by new competitors is likely or whether the fact of potential entry is itself likely to constrain the post-merger behavior of the market incumbents. Barriers to entry may include regulatory barriers, technological factors, and commitments by the market incumbents to building large excess capacity. The incumbent firms may also be benefitted by their experience or reputation, a status which may have created brand loyalty or other advantages favoring the incumbents.

[D] Efficiencies

Recital 29 of the EUMR provides that, when assessing the impact of a merger on competition, it is appropriate to take into account any substantiated and likely effects put forward by the undertakings concerned. Accordingly, the *Guidelines* state that "[i]t is possible that efficiencies brought about by a merger [will] counteract the effects on competition and in particular the potential harm to consumers that it might otherwise have ... ." The Commission will, therefore, consider any substantiated efficiency claims, and it may decide that the merger is not incompatible with the internal market when there is sufficient evidence that the efficiencies generated by the merger are likely to enhance the ability and incentive of the merged entity to act procompetitively for the benefits of consumers. For this result, it is necessary that the efficiencies benefit consumers, are merger-specific and are verifiable. For example, costs savings in production or distribution may give the merged entity the ability and incentive to charge lower prices following the merger. In this regard, cost efficiencies that lead to reductions in variable or marginal costs are more likely to be relevant to the assessment of efficiencies than reductions in fixed costs.

Parties urging that claimed efficiencies should favor the approval of a merger have had, at best, mixed success with the Commission. For example, in *Deutsche Börse/NYSE Euronext* in 2012, two companies in the financial markets proposed to merge and argued that this would result in significant efficiency gains. The Commission determined, and was upheld by the GC, that the merger would lead to a significant impediment to effective competition in various European financial markets which would not be effectively counteracted by the claimed efficiency gains. In *Ryanair Holdings plc*, Ryanair sought to justify its acquisition of Air Lingus by claiming resulting cost savings related to staff costs, aircraft ownership costs, maintenance costs, airport charges and other alleged resulting efficiencies. The GC upheld the Commission's rejection of this argument essentially by tracking the Commission's compliance with the efficiency standards set by the *Guidelines*.

[E] Failing Firms

The *Guidelines* further provide that the Commission may decide that an otherwise problematic merger is nevertheless compatible with the common market if one of the merging parties is a failing firm. The following three criteria are especially relevant to the consideration of such a failing firm defense: (a) the alleged failing firm would in the near future be forced out of the market because of financial difficulties; (b) there is no less anticompetitive alternative purchaser than through the notified merger; and (c) in the absence of the merger, the assets of the failing firm would inevitably exit the market.

The Commission applied the failing company defense in the *Kali und Salz/MDK/Treuhand* case. The Commission allowed a concentration resulting in a very large market share, on the ground that this was the only way in which the acquired producer of potash could restructure its production capacity. In the absence of the acquisition, the acquired firm would have departed the market in any event, leaving its market share to be picked up by the other firm. In *BASF/Pantochim/Eurodiol*, the Commission also applied the "rescue merger concept," or failing firm defense, to allow BASF, the large German chemical company, to acquire two Belgian chemical companies which were in receivership. The Commission reasoned that, although dominance concerns existed, no alternative purchaser was available and the production capacity of the two firms would definitely exit the market in the absence of the purchase by BASF.

The defense was accepted twice in 2013, in *Nynas/Shell/Harburg Refinery* and also in *Aegean/Olympic II*. On the other hand, the failing company defense has often been rejected as inapplicable, as the Commission did in 2002 in *Sogecable/Canalsatélite Digital/Via Digital*. It also rejected the defense in 2007 in the case of *JCI/VB/Flamm*.

[F] Vertical and Conglomerate Mergers

In 2007, the Commission published *Guidelines on the assessment of non-horizontal mergers* (the *Guidelines*), addressing the subjects of the vertical and conglomerate effects of mergers. With respect to vertical relationships, foreclosure effects, either upstream or downstream, are given particular importance. As regards conglomerate mergers, the focus is on the effects which the combination of the firms' financial resources or technical and commercial expertise are likely to have on the market.

The Commission views vertical and conglomerate mergers as less of a concern than horizontal mergers because they do not entail the loss of direct competition. Moreover, vertical and conglomerate mergers also provide substantial scope for efficiencies. But, these, like horizontal mergers, must be scrutinized for coordinated and non-coordinated effects. The *Guidelines* state that the Commission is unlikely to find concerns with non-horizontal mergers, be they of a coordinated or a non-coordinated nature, when the market share post-merger of the new entity in each of the markets concerned is below 30% and the post-merger HHI is below 2,000. Where the market shares do not reflect the likely competitive impact of a merger, the Commission may investigate transactions below these thresholds.

In the case of vertical mergers, the Commission will consider any "input foreclosure" or "customer foreclosure." Input foreclosure would entail "where, post-merger, the new entity would be likely to restrict access to the products or services that it would have otherwise supplied absent the merger, thereby raising its downstream rivals' costs ... [t]he relevant benchmark is whether the increased input costs would lead to higher prices for consumers." Customer foreclosure occurs when a supplier integrates with an important customer in the downstream market, thereby foreclosing access to a sufficient customer base to rivals in the upstream market. In assessing this possible scenario, "the Commission examines, first, whether the merged entity would have the ability to foreclose access to downstream markets by reducing its purchases from upstream rivals, second, whether it would have the incentive to reduce its purchases upstream, and third, whether a foreclosure strategy would have a significant detrimental effect on consumers in the downstream market."

The Commission has addressed vertical concerns in a number of cases, applying remedies and accepting commitments to deal with possible foreclosure issues in some of them. In *Google/DoubleClick*, Google proposed to take over DoubleClick, a leading supplier of online ad serving technology. The case was referred to the European Commission by five Member States. Reviewing the vertical aspects of the transaction, the Commission concluded that, given the existence of strong competitors like Microsoft, the merged firm would have neither the ability nor the incentive to foreclose competition.

In *Thomson/Reuters*, the Commission cleared under the EUMR in 2008 the proposed acquisition of the UK-based Reuters Group by Thomson Corporation of Canada. Reuters was best known as one of the largest international news agencies, and both of the companies were leading providers of financial information. The Commission found the horizontal aspects of the merger to be limited, but was concerned about the possible foreclosure of new products redistribution downstream. The companies secured approval of the transaction by committing to divestiture of databases and other relevant assets. This review involved close cooperation with the US Justice Department.

The *Guidelines* acknowledge that conglomerate mergers in the majority of circumstances will not lead to any competition problems. However, the merged entity may be able to leverage a strong market position from one market to another by means of tying or bundling or other exclusionary practices. These practices, based on selling products jointly, can foreclose competition to the merged firm.

Notwithstanding the statement in the *Guidelines* that conglomerate mergers will seldom raise concerns from the competition viewpoint, the Commission, going back to cases such as *General Electric/Honeywell*, *Guinness/Grand Metropolitan*, and *Tetra Laval/Sidel*, has long expressed an interest in the "portfolio effects" of mergers. This theory, reflected in the *Guidelines*, postulates that a company which has a broad "portfolio" or range of products is in a position to disadvantage its competitors by the way in which it markets its products. This may be done through pricing or promotion or through leveraging by selling its goods or services to its customers as a package or bundle.

In its 2002 decision in *Tetra Laval*, the CFI held that the Commission had not proven its case based on conglomerate concerns, but it confirmed that, in a proper case, the Commission may prohibit a merger because it will enable a firm with a dominant position in one market to use its leverage to create or strengthen dominance in another market. In its decision the same year on the appeal of the Commission's decision in the *Schneider Electric* case, the CFI made it clear that the Commission has a significant burden of proof in establishing the anticipated portfolio effects on which it relies in rejecting a merger. This caution for the Commission as to its handling of conglomerate merger cases was voiced again when the ECJ affirmed the CFI's rulings in *Tetra Laval* and when the CFI decided the *General Electric/Honeywell* case, both in 2005. We will discuss the *General Electric/Honeywell* case in detail in the latter section of this chapter.

In *Procter & Gamble/Gillette* the Commission cleared the Procter & Gamble Company's proposed acquisition of The Gillette Company. The Commission noted that both consumer product companies had a significant overlap in the powered toothbrushes market, and the parties committed to a divestiture in that product. The Commission also observed that there might be possible conglomerate effects arising from the fact that the parties had large market shares in numerous product markets where their activities did not overlap. The parties' increased "portfolio power" from the merger raised possibilities of bundling sales of products to the disadvantage of competing branded product suppliers. But the Commission concluded that there would be significant competition in this regard notwithstanding the merger.

In *Intel/McAfee*, in 2011, the Commission reviewed the acquisition by Intel, the leading manufacturer of CPUs, of McAfee, a vendor of information technology security. The Commission expressed concern that conglomerate effects might result from the possible bundling of Intel's CPUs with McAfee's security solutions, which could shut out from the market other companies' security products. The merger was cleared after Intel committed to give full access to vendors of rival security solutions.

§13.05 COLLECTIVE DOMINANCE

A question which necessarily arose with respect to the EUMR was whether its prohibition of concentrations causing the creation or the strengthening of a dominant position was applicable to situations involving collective or joint dominance of an industry, or only to sole dominance. As we saw in Chapter 12, Article 102 TFEU, which expressly applies to abuse by "one or more undertakings" of a dominant position, has been applied against joint dominance. The questions in that context have centered on the extent to which structural or other links between the pertinent companies may be needed to satisfy the concept of collective dominance. As for the EUMR, it does not expressly address the subject of collective dominance or coordinated oligopoly, but the issue has been resolved by the case law of the European Commission and courts. It is thus settled that the Merger Regulation may also be applied where a concentration would result in the significant impeding of effective competition through the creation or strengthening of a collective dominant position enjoyed by the parties to the transaction and one or more other competitors in the industry.

The Commission's concern with oligopoly is in terms of both market dominance by a small number of firms and the opportunities for collusion that such market structure facilitates. In 1992, applying the Merger Regulation, the Commission opposed Nestlé's effort to acquire Perrier. The two companies accounted for some 60% of the French bottled mineral water market, and the Commission reasoned that the resulting reduction in suppliers of bottled mineral water from three to two "would create a duopolistic dominant position on the French bottled water market which would significantly impede effective competition and would be very likely to cause a considerable harm to consumers." Nestlé agreed to divest itself of a major brand, so as to weaken the market power of the duopoly.

In the case of *Kali und Salz/MdK/Treuhand (France and Others v. Commission)*, one of the Commission's findings was that, in the Community outside of Germany, the merger would lead to a dominant duopoly made up of the merged entity and its French competitor, SCPA. In 1998, the ECJ annulled the Commission's decision in its entirety, determining that these findings as to a collective dominant position were inadequately supported. The Court's decision nonetheless confirmed that the then Merger Regulation could be applied to a concentration which creates or strengthens joint dominance. The Court pointed out that "[a] concentration which creates or strengthens a dominant position on the part of the parties concerned with an entity not involved in the concentration is liable to prove incompatible with the system of undistorted competition which the Treaty seeks to secure."

We have previously mentioned the 1999 *Gencor/Lonrho* decision in which the CFI relied on the ECJ's judgment in *Kali und Salz/MdK/Treuhand* on the collective market dominance issue. In that case, the CFI upheld a Commission ruling that a proposed acquisition, which would have created a duopoly on the platinum and rhodium markets, was incompatible with the common market. The CFI stated that mergers leading to the creation of an oligopolistic market structure may be prohibited even where no structural links between the remaining powerful companies exist. It was sufficient for the Commission to establish that there existed economic links uniting the firms in a specific market, including a "relationship of interdependence existing between the parties to a tight oligopoly" in which the parties were "strongly encouraged to align their conduct in the market." The Commission had made the necessary showing based on the envisaged alteration of the structure of the market, the similarity of the competitors' cost structures, and the presence of other economic links between these companies.

In the *Airtours/First Choice* case in 1999 the Commission moved to block a merger under the then Merger Regulation on the ground that the merger would create a situation of collective dominance in the short-haul package tour operator market in the United Kingdom. This was a situation in which the four major travel firms were vertically integrated upstream (airline operation) and downstream (travel agencies). The Commission concluded that, after the takeover of First Choice by Airtours, the combined firm and the two other companies, with a combined market share of 83%, would have a collective dominant position in the United Kingdom market for short-haul package holiday tours.

This ruling was subsequently annulled by the CFI in June 2002, beginning a series of reversals by the CFI of the Commission's merger rulings. The court held in *Airtours/First Choice* that the Commission had not provided adequate evidence to support its finding that there already was a tendency in the industry to collective dominance while there was evidence that the market was indeed a competitive one. Moreover, in the court's view, the Commission had failed to prove that a collective dominant position would be created by the merger in question. The CFI stated that the elements that must be proven in a collective dominance case are: that each member of the oligopoly has knowledge of how the other members are behaving, so that it may adopt the same policy; that there exists a deterrent preventing the participants from departing from the policy; and that the policy be able to withstand challenge by actual and potential competitors, as well as by customers. This decision sent a clear message from the CFI, according to many observers, that DG Competition had put forward a weak effort in analyzing and arguing the case and would be expected to be more thorough in its merger analysis. Following this court decision, the Commission has not sought to block many mergers on collective dominance grounds.

In 2004 the Commission considered under the then Merger Regulation the proposed acquisition by the French producer of industrial gas, Air Liquide, of the industrial gas business in certain countries of Messer, a German group (*Air Liquide/Messer*). The Commission determined that the merger would turn Air Liquide, the world leader in the industrial gases sector, into one of the two main players in Germany (together with Linde AG), raising dominance or duopoly issues. Accordingly, the Commission cleared the transaction only after it had received substantial divestiture commitments with regard to the merging firms' activities in Germany.

§13.06 FULL-FUNCTION JOINT VENTURES

On March 2, 1998, the European Commission published a Notice addressing the subject of "full-function" joint ventures in the context of the then Merger Regulation. It provided that a concentration would meet this definition and therefore fall within the scope of the Merger Regulation only if its operations would bring about "a lasting change in the structure of the undertakings concerned." Article 3(2) of the Merger Regulation similarly describes a full-function joint venture as one "performing on a lasting basis all the functions of an autonomous economic entity ... ." Article 2(4) adds that, to the extent that such a joint venture has as its object or effect the coordination of the competitive behavior of undertakings that remain independent, such coordination shall be appraised in accordance with the criteria of Articles 101(1) and (3) TFEU. However, restrictions accepted by the parent companies of a full-function joint venture that are directly related and necessary for the implementation of the concentration (ancillary restrictions) will be assessed together with the concentration itself.

Full-function joint ventures are therefore subject to the EUMR if they meet the turnover thresholds. The entire turnover of the groups intending to have joint control of the venture is taken into account for this purpose. As in the case of mergers, the substantive test under the EUMR is whether the transaction will significantly impede competition.

Article 2(5) of the Merger Regulation provides that, in making its appraisal of cooperative activities with respect to a joint venture, the Commission shall take into account, in particular: (1) whether the parent companies retain "to a significant extent, activities in the same market as the joint venture or in a market which is upstream or downstream from that of the joint venture or in a neighbouring market closely related to this market," and (2) whether the coordination undertaken "affords the undertakings concerned the possibility of eliminating competition in respect of a substantial part of the products or services in question." The Commission has found an unacceptable anticompetitive coordination in only a few cases involving full-function joint ventures, and it has tended to ask the parties to remove or lessen the coordination proposed rather than to condemn the transaction as a whole.

In *BT/AT&T*, involving a joint venture between two telecommunications firm, the transaction was approved subject to commitments to eliminate the risk of coordination between the parents. Also required was the divestiture of ACC, a wholly owned subsidiary of AT&T. In *Areva/Urenco/ETCJV* the concern was that the coordination in the joint venture would lead to a greater scope for exchange of information on uranium enrichment. This was addressed by commitments creating increased firewalls between the parties and the joint venture and between the parties themselves.

In 2007, the Commission cleared the creation of SonyBMG, a joint venture combining the recorded-music businesses of the Sony music and Bertelsmann music groups after concluding that the transaction would not create or strengthen a dominant or collective dominant position in the music markets in the EEA and EU. This transaction had been re-notified. The Commission' first approval of it had been annulled by the CFI in 2006, after it was challenged by IMPALA, an association of independent music production companies. In 2008, the ECJ annulled the CFI's ruling and upheld the Commission in *Bertelsmann AG v. IMPALA*. Subsequently the Commission approved Sony's acquisition of the whole of SonyBMG.

§13.07 ANCILLARY RESTRAINTS

The Merger Regulation provides that a decision by the Commission declaring a concentration compatible with the common market shall be deemed to cover restrictions directly related and necessary to the implementation of that concentration. On March 5, 2005 the Commission issued a *Notice on restrictions directly related and necessary to concentrations*, replacing a 2001 version. A central principle introduced is one of "self-assessment" of such restrictions, so as not to oblige the Commission to assess and individually address each ancillary restraint. The Commission exercises a "residual function with regard to specific novel or unresolved issues giving rise to genuine uncertainty ... ." For restrictions that are not directly related and necessary to the implementation of the concentration, Articles 101 and 102 TFEU remain potentially applicable.

The Notice states that agreements that are truly necessary to the implementation of a concentration are typically aimed at protecting the value transferred, maintaining the continuity of supply after the break-up of an entity, or enabling the start of a new entity. Among the restrictions that may be justifiable are noncompetition clauses which are appropriately limited in scope and duration, suitably designed license agreements, and purchase and supply obligations. The Notice also discusses when these types of ancillary restraints will be deemed "directly related and necessary" in the context of the relationship between a full-function joint venture and its parent undertakings.

The Commission has sometimes stepped in to address ancillary restraint matters where the parties have overstepped their bounds. In a case in 2012, *Siemens/Areva*, the two companies had created a joint venture and agreed on specific noncompete obligations. The Commission found that the noncompete clause was excessive as it prevented Siemens from competing in markets in which the joint venture only acted as a re-seller, raising questions under Article 101 TFEU. The Commission accepted the parties' commitments to cut back the noncompete clause.

In *Telefónica SA/Portugal Telecom SGPS SA* the Commission imposed fines totaling EUR 79 million on the two companies. The infraction resulted from a deal in which Spain's Telefónica had acquired sole control of a mobile telephone joint venture in Brazil which it had operated with Portugal Telecom. The parties had included in the deal an agreement that the two companies would not compete in the telecom business in each others' home countries. The GC in 2016 upheld the Commission's decision on the merits but directed the Commission to take a fresh look at the fairness of the fines imposed.

§13.08 SOME MERGER CASE HIGHLIGHTS

There have been too many interesting merger cases since the inception of the EUMR to cover them all here, so we will content ourselves with focusing on some highlights in that regard, including those cases having trans-Atlantic ramifications. Some of the cases have been mentioned briefly in the previous pages. Many of the merger cases decided by the Commission have been important ones in terms of the economic scope of the transactions involved. Where they have reviewed the same transactions, the US antitrust enforcement agencies and the European Commission have, in general, seen matters eye to eye, but some of the Commission's decisions have been controversial from a US viewpoint.

Of course, there has been a great deal of merger activity involving European firms and/or European commerce in the last fifty years or so. In 2007 Competition Commissioner Kroes spoke of the hundreds of mergers considered by the Commission in 2006 and 2007, calling them a tsunami of activity, but a good development because:

> It shows that the market itself is adapting to change, and that European companies are adapting to global competition. Healthy restructuring is taking place in many sectors, from energy to banking, from air transport to telecommunications. These processes—provided that they have been shown to have no negative effect on

competition—must be allowed to run their courses without undue political interference.

Mergers involving the world aircraft industry for some time posed concerns for the Commission. In 1991, it considered a concentration in the European aircraft manufacturing industry in the *Aérospatiale-Alenial de Havilland* case. Two European companies, Aérospatiale and Alenia, proposed to jointly acquire the assets of Boeing's Canadian division, de Havilland. The transaction would have given the joint venture the capacity to manufacture the whole range of commuter aircraft and enable it to significantly broaden its customer base. The Commission, however, disapproved the acquisition on the ground that it would create a dominant position which would have an adverse impact on competitors both inside and outside of the Community. The efficiency defense which had been asserted was rejected by the Commission as insubstantial. The Commission's decision to block this concentration, which would have strengthened the European aircraft industry, was much criticized within the Community. In contrast, the decision in the case was praised in a speech by the Chairman of the US Federal Trade Commission, Robert Pitofsky, who called it "an immensely important EC decision" which "signal[ed] DG-IV's and the Commission's faithfulness to competition policy over industrial policy."

On the other hand, the Commission's 1997 intervention in the merger of two US firms, Boeing and McDonnell Douglas, was criticized on the other side of the Atlantic, where the merger had cleared without objection. The two companies' combined aggregate worldwide and Community-wide turnover made their proposed transaction a concentration with a Community dimension within the coverage of the Merger Regulation. The Commission determined that the transaction was "of great significance in the [European Economic Area or 'EEA'] as it is in the world market of which the EEA is an important part." The decision found that Boeing already enjoyed a dominant position in the overall market for large commercial aircraft, as well as in the markets for narrow-body and wide-body aircraft. Boeing had a market share in the EEA of about 58%, McDonnell Douglas of about 20% and the European firm, Airbus, of about 21%. (Boeing's world market share was 60%.) The Commission concluded that the proposed concentration would lead to a strengthening of Boeing's dominant position. The Commission approved the transaction only subject to Boeing's accepting a number of remedial commitments, including an agreement not to enforce exclusivity rights that the manufacturer held with a number of large airlines.

By the turn of the century, the Commission's merger review policy was being perceived by observers as taking an increasingly antagonistic line. Commentators maintained that Mario Monti, then the Commissioner in charge of competition policy, was stiffening the policy to lead to the rejection or abandonment of many mergers. In addition, the Commission was approving many problematic merger transactions only subject to asset divestitures while expecting the merging companies to identify an "upfront buyer" for those assets.

It was at this point that the Commission made a merger decision which caused an open split in the views of the European and the US antitrust authorities, who had previously been reluctant to criticize one another. As we noted in Chapter 8, in the summer of 2001, the Commission blocked a large merger involving US firms, the planned USD 45 billion acquisition by General Electric Co. ("GE") of Honeywell International Inc. ("Honeywell"). GE was seen as having a dominant position in the markets for jet engines for large commercial aircraft and jet engines for large regional aircraft. GE was also financially powerful and vertically integrated into aircraft leasing. Honeywell was the leading supplier of avionics and non-avionics products, as well as of engines for corporate jet aircraft and of engine starters. The deal had been cleared by the US Department of Justice subject to conditions. The European Commission, however, declared the transaction incompatible with the common market and with the EEA Agreement. The Commission determined that the merger would create or strengthen dominant positions in several markets and that the remedies proposed by the parties would not resolve the competition concerns presented. The Commission reasoned that the combination of the two companies' activities would:

> have resulted in the creation of dominant positions in the markets for the supply of avionics, non-avionics and corporate jet engines, as well as to the strengthening of GE's existing dominant positions in jet engines for large commercial and large regional jets. The dominance would have been created or strengthened as a result of horizontal overlaps in some markets as well as through the extension of GE's financial power and vertical integration to Honeywell activities and of the combination of their respective complementary products. Such integration would enable the merged entity to leverage the respective market power of the two companies into the products of one another. This would have the effect of foreclosing competitors, thereby eliminating competition in these markets, ultimately affecting adversely product quality, service and consumers' prices.

General Electric and Honeywell abandoned their merger plan but filed appeals from the Commission's decision with the CFI.

As we noted earlier, the Antitrust Division in the US subsequently expressed a strong contrary view on the subject of this proposed merger in a submission made in October 2001 to the OECD Roundtable on Portfolio Effects in Conglomerate Mergers. The Antitrust Division described the European Commission's approach in *GE/Honeywell* as being based on flawed theories of competitive harm related to "range" effects. The Commission's reliance on range effects, said the Antitrust Division, placed the interests of competitors ahead of the interests of competition and would lead to the likely blocking or deterring of procompetitive, efficiency enhancing mergers. The Antitrust Division argued that "challenging a merger because it will create a more efficient firm through economies of scale and scope is at odds with the fundamental objectives of the antitrust laws" and also that bundling theory should not be applied to block a merger that will facilitate efficient bundling which benefits customers.

With *GE/Honeywell* in mind, on October 2002, the US Justice Department's Antitrust Division and the EU Competition Commissioner jointly issued a set of "best practices," in an effort to coordinate better the two enforcement regimes' merger review processes and policies toward conglomerate mergers. This document, entitled *Best Practices on Cooperation in Merger Investigations* and issued by the US-EU Merger Working Group, was discussed in Chapter 8.

§13.08

In the waning days of 2005, the CFI decided the General Electric and Honeywell appeals. The court stated that, although the Commission had made certain errors in its analysis, it had validly found the concentration to be incompatible with the common market in relation to three separate markets, and hence the contested decision should not be annulled. Thus, the court concluded:

> the Commission validly found in the contested decision that following the merger [General Electric's] pre-existing dominant position on the market for jet engines for large regional aircraft would be strengthened and that dominant positions would be created for the merged entity on the markets for engines for corporate jet aircraft and for small marine gas turbines ... . The contested decision also establishes that on each of those markets the creation or strengthening of a dominant position would have resulted in effective competition being significantly impeded in the common market.

The court further held, however, that, notwithstanding that the Commission validly held that GE was in a dominant position in the market for jet engines for large commercial aircraft, it had not sufficiently established that dominant positions would be created or strengthened for the merged entity through either (i) the vertical overlap between Honeywell's engine starters and GE's jet engines for large commercial aircraft, (ii) the combination of Honeywell's avionics and non-avionics products and the financial strength of the GE group, or (iii) the possibility of bundling the sale of GE's engines with Honeywell's avionics and non-avionics products.

In these regards, the court found that, while GE's financial strength contributed to its premerger dominance in the market for large commercial aircraft jet engines, the Commission had not established by convincing evidence that there was a likelihood that GE would, after the merger, exploit its position to promote Honeywell's products to the disadvantage of competitors or that this practice would have been likely to create dominant positions in the various avionics and non-avionics markets concerned. As to the Commission's finding that the merged entity would be in a position to "bundle" or package its complementary products for customers, with anticompetitive effects, the court ruled that the Commission did not sufficiently establish this proposition simply by showing that GE would have a wider range of products than its competitors. Thus, "the Commission made a manifest error of assessment in finding that the merged entity's future use of bundling would lead to the creation or strengthening of a dominant position on the markets for avionics or non-avionics products, or to the strengthening of GE's pre-merger dominant position on the markets for large commercial jet aircraft engines."

Both sides drew comfort from this long-awaited decision. The Commission expressed satisfaction that the CFI had sustained its condemnation of the merger, while business groups predicted that the court's rejection of the Commission's findings on "conglomerate effects" and bundling would discourage reliance on these theories to attack future mergers. But, as we have seen, the Commission has not abandoned this approach entirely.

Another important area of Commission merger control activity over the years has been the telecommunications industry, broadly defined. Given that the global communications systems and technologies have been in constant flux, and considering the resulting evolution of the industry, this is not surprising. The US and the European competition authorities have both actively overseen the merger wave involving telecommunications and other high-tech companies.

WorldCom Inc.'s 1998 takeover of MCI Communications Corporation involved a merger of two giant US-based telecommunications companies which offered a variety of international and regional communications services. The proposed merger was notified to the European Commission, as well as to the US authorities, since the transaction was of Community dimension under the Merger Regulation. At the outset of its decision on the matter, the Commission observed that there had been a considerable degree of cooperation between it and the US Department of Justice in the course of the investigation of the proposed transaction. The Commission determined that the combination of WorldCom's and MCI's Internet "backbone" networks—the high speed lines that carry most of the Internet traffic—would create a network of such size that the combined entity would be enabled to act independently in the market, to the detriment of both competitors and consumers. Accordingly, the Commission held the merger compatible with the common market only on the condition that the internet business of MCI be divested. The divestiture that subsequently took place proved untidy inasmuch as, after WorldCom had agreed to sell part of its internet services to Cable & Wireless PLC to comply with its commitment to the Commission, a dispute arose as to precisely what was included in the sale. This dispute reportedly was settled out of court by a handsome payment to Cable & Wireless PLC.

In 1999, when MCI WorldCom announced its proposed acquisition of Sprint Corp. in a USD 115 billion deal, the competition authorities gave the transaction their prompt attention. This included examination of the merger by the two authorities in parallel pursuant to the EU—US 1991 Cooperation Agreement. MCI WorldCom was anxious to obtain Sprint because the former lacked a wireless network and did not want to take the time to build its own. However, in the US, the merger would have combined the nation's second and third largest long distance phone companies, creating a market share (based on revenue) of 36%. The industry leader, AT&T, held a 43% share. A review by the Department of Justice indicated that it should block the merger under the Clayton Act, and the Department eventually filed suit for that purpose. The European Commission was also very concerned about the merger, primarily on the ground that it would create market dominance in the provision of high speed Internet backbone service. In an effort to obtain approval of the deal, MCI WorldCom offered to sell Sprint's Internet backbone and long-distance operations, which would leave it with the wireless operations.

As it became increasingly clear that the Commission would, nonetheless, object to the deal, MCI WorldCom attempted to withdraw its notification of the merger in order to avoid a prohibition decision. Since it appeared to the Commission that the parties had not abandoned the merger agreement, the Commission refused to accept the withdrawal of the notification. The Commission prohibited the merger on the grounds that the combined company would have dominance over the transmission of information over the Internet, with the ability to dictate prices and other business terms. MCI WorldCom criticized the decision on the ground that the reasoning had failed to take into account Internet market changes since the WorldCom-MCI transaction, including the impact of new entrants and new technologies. The parties then issued press releases stating that they were abandoning the merger in view of the opposition of the US Department of Justice.

MCI WorldCom nonetheless pursued an appeal of the Commission's decision. After the company and most of its subsidiaries in the US had filed a voluntary petition for reorganization under Chapter 11 of the US bankruptcy law in 2002, the CFI asked whether the company was still interested in seeking annulment of the contested decision. The company replied in the affirmative, stating that it expected to emerge from reorganization in 2003 and that current problems in the telecommunications sector gave it a greater chance than before of successfully effecting the contested concentration. The company emerged from the bankruptcy proceeding as MCI, Inc.

In a decision issued on September 28, 2004, the CFI held that MCI Inc.'s action for annulment was admissible, pointing out that the US court action had not led to an injunction and therefore the contested European decision was the only "existing and certain legal obstacle" to carrying out the transaction should the parties wish to do so. On the merits, the CFI ruled that, given that the parties had advised the Commission that they no longer intended to implement the proposed merger in the form presented in the notification and were withdrawing the notification, the Commission should have found that it no longer had the power under the Merger Regulation to adopt a decision declaring the concentration incompatible with the common market. In exercising its competence, the court said, the Commission must "rule on a real merger transaction ... ." Moreover, the Commission in this case had "unexpectedly departed from its consistent administrative practice" of accepting withdrawals of notifications by the parties concerned. The court annulled the contested decision and ordered the Commission to pay its costs and those of the company.

The proposed USD 110 billion acquisition of Time Warner Inc. by America Online Inc. ("AOL") gave both competition authorities another opportunity to consider the enormous significance of the Internet in the new global marketplace. As we discussed in Chapter 8, the US antitrust scrutiny of this merger was conducted by the Federal Trade Commission, which approved the transaction, but only subject to some important conditions. The European Commission also reviewed this merger, doing so at the same time that it was reviewing a separate joint venture deal that Time Warner had proposed to undertake with the EMI Group PLC of the United Kingdom. The planned Time Warner-EMI alliance raised concerns under the Commission's collective dominance principles in that it would cause a reduction in the number of major recorded-music distributors from five to four. European composers and songwriters warned that the combination would have a dominant position in Europe in music publishing. After the Commission indicated that it would not approve the EMI deal, the parties withdrew it.

Time Warner's merger with AOL was of less concern to the European Commission than it was to the Federal Trade Commission in the US. Time Warner had no cable television systems in Europe, and AOL was smaller than local online services in every European country. In contrast, in the US, there was substantial concern that Time Warner would be able, after the merger, to use its vast cable television operations to provide high-speed online services, while restricting access to those lines on the part of

AOL's competitors. To secure European Commission approval of their merger, AOL and Time Warner agreed to various commitments. These included their pulling out of certain European joint ventures in the music business, obligating themselves not to discriminate against competitors in certain markets for five years, and, for three years, not requiring that content providers dealing with AOL in the US enter into such deals in Europe.

It should be noted here that, on March 14, 2017, the Commission approved under its simplified procedure in a brief decision the proposed acquisition by AT&T of all of the shares of Time Warner Inc. The Commission viewed the two companies as not competing with each other in the European market. The decision describes AT&T as providing only business telecommunications services within the internal market while Time Warner provides global media and entertainment services, including television services, feature films and video games. The acquisition is still under review in the US and is controversial there where the two companies have more extensive operations.

In 2000, the Commission brought about the termination of the USD 17 billion merger of three of the world's largest aluminum companies, Alcan of Canada, Pechiney of France, and Alusuisse Lonza Group of Switzerland. It found that the combination would cause single dominance and collective dominance problems in a number of markets for aluminum products. The Commission rejected proposed remedial commitments by Alcan as inadequate.

That same year, the Commission also objected to a proposed merger by Sweden's leading truck manufacturers, Volvo and Scania, causing them to abandon the transaction. The Commission was concerned that the merged company would be dominant in the market for heavy trucks in the Nordic countries and would create an effective duopoly with DaimlerChrysler AG in some other markets. Numerous consolidations in the international auto industry have taken place in the last twenty years or so, including that involving Fiat and Chrysler in 2009, and they have been cleared by the antitrust authorities.

For some twelve years after the adoption of the EUMR, it seemed that the Commission's decisions in merger reviews were likely to constitute the last words on the matter, because appeals of the adverse Commission decision were both slow in being heard and unlikely to result in reversal. The Community courts eventually introduced fast-track review procedures, which observers estimated cut the waiting time for appeals from about three years to one year from the Commission's decision. The CFI accepted three merger cases for fast-track review in 2002 and, in that same year, the CFI annulled the Commission's rulings in several high profile merger cases. The reversals led the Commission to apply more rigorous standards to its assessment of mergers, with a greater reliance on economic analysis.

The first of the important merger cases decided against the Commission at this time was the *Airtours* case, which we have already mentioned. On June 6, 2002, the CFI annulled the prohibition which the Commission had based on collective dominance grounds of a merger of two UK suppliers of leisure travel services. The court determined that the Commission had failed properly to assess the dynamics of the market in several respects.

§13.08

On October 22, 2002, in *Schneider*, the CFI annulled another decision by the Commission blocking a merger, this one involving a transaction between two French electrical goods markers, Schneider Electrical and Legrand. The CFI stated that it found several "obvious errors, omissions and contradictions" in the Commission's economic reasoning and also that the companies had not received a fair opportunity to defend the merger. Specifically, the court reasoned that the Commission had relied too heavily on its portfolio effects analysis, given that competitors also carried a full range of brands.

Schneider subsequently brought an action against the Commission for damages under Article 288(2) of the EC Treaty which provided that "in the case of non-contractual liability, the Community shall, in accordance with the general principles common to the laws of the Member States, make good any damage caused by its institutions or by its servants in the performance of their duties." Schneider argued that the damages covered compensation for the losses that it incurred as a result of the Commission's poor management of the merger investigation. In July 2007 the CFI ruled that the Commission must compensate Schneider for some of its claimed damages. In July 2009 the ECJ set aside in part the CFI's judgment, cutting back the compensation to which Schneider was entitled. The Court's decision did, however, reaffirm the principle that parties are able to claim compensation as a result of a serious breach by the Commission such as breaching a party's right of defense. The language of Article 288 of the EC Treaty, including the damage right which it confers, has been carried over as Article 340 of the TFEU. The General Court also has been held to be liable for damages for breaches of its own.

In 2002, in *Tetra Laval*, the CFI reversed the Commission's blocking of the acquisition of Sidel SA by Tetra Laval SA, the world's largest maker of carton packaging for beverages. The Commission had determined that the merged entity would have been capable of exploiting its dominant position in the market for aseptic carton and would have been encouraged to do so in order to leverage its leading position in the plastic carton sector so as to create a dominant position. In annulling this decision, the CFI cited "insufficient evidence and some errors of assessment" on the part of the Commission, including a failure to prove a risk of leveraging by the merged entity in this conglomerate setting.

The Commission appealed to the ECJ, which affirmed the CFI's rulings in a judgment rendered on February 15, 2005. The Court held that: (a) the CFI did not exceed its powers of review in finding the Commission's evidence to be inadequate, particularly in the context of a conglomerate-type of concentration which required the making of a difficult and uncertain prospective analysis and (b) "although the CFI erred in law by rejecting the Commission's conclusions as to the adoption by the merged entity of conduct likely to result in leveraging, it was nevertheless right to hold ... that the Commission ought to have taken account of the commitments submitted by Tetra with regard to that entity's future conduct ... ." The Court noted that, to the extent that the Commission was complaining that the CFI had failed to assess the relevant evidence properly, this was not a matter subject to review by the ECJ in appeal proceedings.

It is worth observing that, in deciding the *General Electric/Honeywell* case in 2005, the CFI relied heavily on the ECJ's admonition in *Tetra Laval* that assessing the future consequences of a conglomerate-type concentration requires the marshalling of particularly sound evidence, because the chains of cause and effect following such a merger may be dimly discernible, uncertain and difficult to establish.

In April 2003, the Commission sustained another reversal from the CFI, but this time in connection with the challenge of a merger which the Commission had allowed. This merger was between two French companies, SEB and Moulinex, which were both manufacturers of small electrical household appliances which the companies sold in various of the Member States. The Commission had referred the French aspects of the case to the French authorities and found, with respect to the other markets, that either no commitments were necessary or that serious doubts about the compatibility of the concentration with the common market could be overcome by accepting commitments proposed by the parties. In *BaByliss-SEB/Moulinex*, the CFI annulled the Commission's decision as to the Member States for which no commitments had been required on the ground that the Commission's reasoning in finding no threat to competition in those countries was inadequate. In the related case of *Royal Philips Electronics*, decided at the same time, the CFI affirmed the Commission's decision to refer a part of the case to France, agreeing that the relevant markets in France constituted distinct markets within the meaning of the ECMR. The court emphasized that the Commission has broad, albeit not unlimited, discretion on the question of referral under the relevant ECMR provision.

The Commission approved a number of joint ventures in 2003. In one, two major German chemical producers, Celanese AG and Degussa AG, agreed to contribute most of their "oxo chemicals" business to a 50/50 joint venture. The Commission stated that it was initially concerned about the parties' strong position in several markets, including the high market shares achieved by the joint venture. However, it determined that market share was not a reliable indicator of market power in this case and that the main competitors of the joint venture enjoyed enough spare capacity to be able to keep in check any attempt by the joint venture to raise prices. In another case, *Accor/Hilton/Six Continents*, the Commission granted regulatory clearance to the ownership and control by several major hotel chains of a joint venture, "WorldRes. Europe," designed to operate a global Internet-based reservations system. The purpose of the joint venture was to allow the hotel industry participants to store, manage, and distribute the information on their room rates and availabilities to interested parties, allowing the making of real-time reservations. The Commission concluded that the joint venture would not be large enough in scope to foreclose competing suppliers of hotel accommodations or suppliers of online distribution services and also that there were sufficient built-in safeguards in the system to prevent the joint venture from leading the hotel chains concerned to coordinate their commercial strategies.

In 2003, the Commission also approved the acquisition of Pharmacia Corporation by Pfizer, Inc., which created the largest pharmaceutical company in the world. In the Commission's mind, there existed serious doubts about the compatibility of this transaction with the common market, inasmuch as there would have been created a very strong market position for the merged entity consisting of existing products and "pipeline" products together. However, the merger was cleared on the basis of commitments offered by the parties to divest or transfer certain products. The

Commission noted that it had closely cooperated with the US Federal Trade Commission in the analysis of this matter, notably in the product areas of urinary incontinence and erectile dysfunction where the parties agreed to divestitures on a worldwide scale. In 2004 the Commission approved another merger intended to create one of the largest pharmaceutical companies in the world, the acquisition of Aventis by Sanofi-Synthélabo. The approval was, once again, subject to many commitments to undertake sales or grant licenses as to various businesses.

One of the cases that we considered in Chapter 8 was the unsuccessful effort mounted by the US Department of Justice's Antitrust Division and a number of US states to block Oracle Corporation's acquisition, through a hostile bid, of the stock of PeopleSoft Inc. The theory of these government authorities was that the merger of these two makers of software applications for business use threatened to substantially lessen competition in an alleged product market of "high function software," but the federal trial court refused to accept their arguments and to enjoin the merger. The European Commission also received notification of this proposed merger, and it undertook an investigation which involved consulting with the Antitrust Division in the US and also reviewing the evidence which had been adduced during the trial in California.

Like the US authorities, the Commission considered that Oracle and PeopleSoft were, respectively, the second and third largest suppliers in the world of sophisticated enterprise application software, used by large corporate entities to coordinate their business functions. A German company, SAP, was the largest supplier, and all three companies operated worldwide. The Commission's investigation identified as separate markets "high function" financial planning and reporting (FMS) and human resources processes (HR) software purchased by and critical for large and complex business enterprises. The Commission issued a Statement of Objections on March 12, 2004, alleging that, in reducing the number of players in the market for high function HR and FMS software from three to two, the transaction would possibly create a dominant position as a result of which effective competition would be significantly impeded and customers would be adversely affected. The Commission also found preliminarily that the merger would have the potential for creating coordination by the two remaining players in the market. However, on September 9, 2004, before the Commission's final deadline for a decision on the merger had arrived, the US district court dismissed the Department of Justice's application for an injunction. As we noted in our earlier discussion, the US court rejected the Department's asserted relevant product market definition of "high function" software and thus its concept of a distinct three competitor market. The Department of Justice announced that it would not appeal, so there was nothing to deter the consummation of the merger in the US.

The European Commission issued its final decision on October 26, 2004, approving the proposed merger without requiring any commitments. It defined the relevant product market as the worldwide market for high function FMS and HR solutions or software for large enterprises with complex functional needs. However, as to the players in that market, the Commission determined that several companies other than the three top competitors could "not be excluded." It found that several other vendors, including Microsoft, sometimes won bids for high function FMS and HR software applications. Therefore, the Commission concluded that there was insufficient evidence that the merger would cause competitive harm. Commentators promptly speculated on the question of whether the Commission's final analysis was primarily based on careful economic analysis of the market or on a desire to avoid another split decision between the US and the European enforcement authorities.

In 2013, the Commission prohibited the proposed acquisition of TNT Express by United Parcel Service ("UPS"), finding that the merger would have restricted competition in the market for international express deliveries in fifteen Member States. UPS offered to divest TNT's subsidiaries in seventeen Member States. Nonetheless, the concentration would have left UPS as the only alternative in some markets. Although the Commission accepted that efficiencies in the form of cost savings would result from the merger, they were not deemed sufficient to outweigh the negative effects the merger would have on competition. UPS appealed the decision but then abandoned the merger. In 2015, FedEx stepped in and struck its own deal to acquire TNT Express, agreeing to sell TNT's airline operations. UPS bitterly opposed the deal in Europe. FedEx gained approval of the merger in Europe, where FedEx does not have a significant presence, and the US regulators also approved the deal. Nonetheless, TNT Express pursued an appeal, and it succeeded when the GC, on March 7, 2017, annulled the Commission's decision. The court ruled that the Commission had infringed UPS' right of defense by failing to communicate the final version of the econometric model which the Commission had used in its merger assessment. It was too late to further UPS' merger plan, but the court's ruling may enable UPS to make a damage claim against the Commission.

The Commission's actions regarding Microsoft have not all been on the negative side. On October 7, 2011 the Commission cleared under the EUMR Microsoft's acquisition of Skype. Cisco Systems filed an appeal with the GC protesting this approval. Cisco's arguments were that the acquisition would enable Microsoft to (1) incorporate Skype into a bundle with Microsoft's own products, and/or (2) tie Skype to Microsoft's products, and/or (3) degrade their interoperability. The GC upheld the Commission in a decision on December 11, 2013, noting that Microsoft, despite being powerful in the PC market, has less presence in new operating devices in the consumer communications market. In a separate matter, on December 6, 2016, the Commission approved Microsoft's acquisition of LinkedIn, subject to behavioral conditions.

On March 29, 2017 the Commission announced that it had prohibited the merger between Deutsche Börse AG and the London Stock Exchange Group. The merger would have combined the two largest European stock exchange operators who owned the stock exchanges of Germany, Italy and the UK, as well as several of the largest European clearing houses. In the Commission's view, the merger would have created a de facto monopoly in the markets for clearing fixed income instruments. The parties rejected a divestiture suggested by the Commission and offered only "a complex set of behavioural measures" which the Commission rejected.

On May 18, 2017, the European Commission announced that it had fined Facebook EUR 10 million for providing incorrect or misleading information during the Commission's investigation under the EU Merger Regulation of Facebook's acquisition of WhatsApp. The Commission stated that it had found that, contrary to Facebook's statements during the 2014 merger review process, the technical possibility of automatically matching Facebook and WhatsApp users' identities already existed in 2014 and that Facebook's staff were aware of such a possibility. Various regulators in the EU have opened investigations into Facebook's privacy policies, including the German competition authority investigating whether Facebook misused its dominant position to collect individuals' digital information.

Also in May 2017, the Commission cleared the acquisition of Baker Hughes Inc. by General Electric, notwithstanding that the two companies compete in several markets. The merger had earlier received US antitrust approval. As we go to print, the European Commission has announced that it has opened an in depth investigation into the proposed acquisition of Monsanto (US) by Bayer (Germany). The acquisition would create the world's largest integrated pesticides and seed company, in industries that are already globally concentrated. The Commission stated that its preliminary concerns were that the merger could reduce competition in a number of different markets resulting in higher prices, lower quality, less choice, and less innovation.

The European Commission continues to have a heavy workload of reviewing merger proposals, with most transactions being found unobjectionable.

Part III   Other Selected Competition Laws

CHAPTER 14
The United Kingdom

§14.01 BACKGROUND

Following a popular referendum, the United Kingdom declared its intention to withdraw from the EU (an action known as "Brexit"). Since it gave formal notice of withdrawal in March of 2017, the UK has been undertaking to negotiate with the EU the terms of a continuing relationship. The UK will remain within the EU until the break is finalized. In any event, UK individuals and businesses will continue to be subject to EU competition law to the extent that they are involved in the commerce of the continuing EU. (*See* previous Chapters 9–13.) However, after the break, EU law will no longer be directly applicable in the UK. We will be discussing here the domestic law of the United Kingdom. At the end of this segment, we will offer a brief discussion of the competition law implications of Brexit for the UK.

The United Kingdom of Great Britain and Northern Ireland joined the European Communities on January 1, 1973. The United Kingdom ("UK") consists of England, Wales, Scotland, and Northern Ireland. The Channel Islands and the Isle of Man are dependencies of the UK. The UK's preaccession competition law was contained in five statutes, with the later ones amending or expanding on their predecessors. These statutes were usually referred to by the dates of their enactment, which were 1948, 1956, 1964, 1965 and 1968. Additional legislation was added in 1973, 1976, 1977, and 1980.

The Fair Trading Act 1973 established the Office of Fair Trading (OFT), headed by the Director General of Fair Trading ("Director General" or "DGFT"). The regime created by this legislation had a number of separate components. One component authorized the Secretary of State and the Director General to refer to the Monopolies and Mergers Commission (MMC) cases in which it appeared that a "monopoly situation" existed or might exist and cases of mergers that created or enhanced market shares of at least 25% or involved assets exceeding a specified threshold.

In monopoly references, the MMC was to investigate and report whether a monopoly situation existed and, if so, whether the monopoly situation operated or might be expected to operate against the public interest, with the Secretary of State to impose a remedy. In merger cases, the MMC was to report on whether the merger operated or might be expected to operate against the public interest, with the Secretary of State having the authority to prevent or dissolve the merger. A formal voluntary premerger notification scheme became effective in 1990.

In addition, the UK legislation required certain types of restrictive agreements to be submitted to the Director General, who maintained a public register of these agreements and referred certain of them to the Restrictive Practices Court. The court considered whether a particular agreement was against the public interest or whether, on the other hand, it fell within one or more of several "gateways" identifying benefits to the public, with the benefits outweighing the adverse effects of the agreement. The Competition Act 1980 supplemented these provisions by giving the Director General authority over anticompetitive practices by single firms that did not amount to monopoly, such as tie-in selling, exclusive dealing, price discrimination and predatory pricing.

§14.02 LATER LEGISLATION

The overall approach to competition regulation put in place by these statutes was not perceived as very effective. Following much study of the subject, the decision was eventually reached to create new legislation which would harmonize UK competition law with Articles 85 and 86 (now TFEU Articles 101 and 102) of the EC Treaty. This new legislation, known as The Competition Act 1998 (Competition Act), received the Royal Assent on November 1998, and became effective on March 1, 2000. This enactment achieved a great reform of UK competition law, bringing it into line with that of the EC. The Act repealed the Restrictive Trade Practices Act 1976 and 1977, the Restrictive Practices Court Act 1976, the Resale Prices Act 1976, and many sections of the Competition Act 1980. The Act established the Competition Commission and transferred to it the functions of the MMC, which was dissolved.

The Competition Act was the first piece of UK competition legislation to be firmly based on competitive effects principles. It introduced two basic prohibitions. The first relates to agreements between undertakings, decisions by associations of undertakings or concerted practices which may affect trade within the UK and have as their object or effect the prevention, restriction, or distortion of competition within the UK (the "Chapter 1 Prohibition"). The second prohibition relates to conduct on the part of one or more undertakings which amount to the abuse of a dominant position if it may affect trade within the UK (the "Chapter ll Prohibition"). Wide powers were given to the authorities to investigate infringements and impose penalties. However, under this original Competition Act scheme, as under the EU legislation, individuals acting as such were not subject to the prohibitions and there was no criminal law regime imposed. The Competition Act also left untouched the merger control process which was established under the Fair Trading Act 1973.

On November 7, 2002 the Enterprise Act 2002 (the Enterprise Act) was passed, amending this scheme in significant respects, although the Competition Act was left largely intact. Certain parts of the Enterprise Act came into effect on April 1, 2003 and others on June 20, 2003. As of April 1, 2003, the post of DGFT was abolished and the OFT (which had been merely the administrative support for the DGFT) was elevated to the status of an independent corporate statutory body. Criminal penalties were introduced into the competition law, to be imposed on individuals who dishonestly engaged in the most serious forms of anticompetitive activity like horizontal price fixing, limiting supply or production, market sharing or bid rigging.

The Enterprise and Regulatory Reform Act 2013 ("ERRA") was the next piece of important legislation. It created the Competition and Markets Authority ("CMA") and abolished its predecessors, the OFT and the Competition Commission. Their competition law functions were transferred to the CMA. In addition, the provisions on mergers and markets were streamlined and the criminal cartel offense provision was made more effective.

The CMA has the statutory duty to promote competition for the benefit of consumers. It is divided into three Directorates: Enforcement, Mergers and Markets and Corporate Services. Its permanent staff numbers in the hundreds of persons, including specific enforcement teams for cartel and criminal investigations.

In this regard, the CMA plays the main role in enforcing the Chapter l and ll Prohibitions under the Competition Act 1998 and the Enterprise Act 2002. The Chapter l Prohibition forbids agreements, decisions by associations of undertakings and concerted practices that have as their object the restriction of competition. The Chapter ll Prohibition forbids the abuse of a dominant position. (These are modeled after the EU's TFEU Articles 101 and 102 Prohibitions.) The CMA has significant powers to obtain information, enter premises to conduct investigations, make decisions and impose financial penalties. The CMA may also bring criminal prosecutions of the cartel offense under the Enterprise Act 2002. In practice, the CMA cooperates with the Serious Fraud Office in criminal cases.

The CMA has powers under the Enterprise Act to review mergers and investigate markets. Many of the decisions of the CMA are appealable to the Competition Appeal Tribunal ("CAT") which was established by the Enterprise Act 2002. The CAT is an independent judicial body. Appeals on issues of law may be taken, with permission, from the CAT to the Court of Appeal (in England and Wales).

There are also sectoral regulators which have concurrent authority with the CMA to enforce competition law prohibitions. Accordingly, the regulators for telecommunications, electricity and gas, water and sewerage, civil aviation, and railway services, concurrently with the CMA, have jurisdiction to address the competition issues arising in some or all of the activities of the participants in the industries they regulate.

§14.03 PRIVATE ENFORCEMENT

The UK courts established in the 1980s that a private suit for damages could be brought to remedy violations of the competition law provisions of the EC Treaty. On May 21,

2004, in the first reported case of a UK court awarding damages for breach of EC Articles 81 and 82, the Court of Appeal awarded damages to the claimant in the *Crehan* case based on a violation of EC law. The court held that, as a matter of EC law as interpreted by the ECJ in its preliminary ruling in the *Crehan* case, the UK courts were bound to provide an effective remedy for such a breach of EC law.

Private actions to recover damages for breaches of the prohibitions of the Competition Act or of TFEU Articles 101 and 102 may be brought directly in the United Kingdom courts. The Consumer Rights Act 2015 expanded the jurisdiction of the CAT in this regard. A claimant seeking damages in the UK may bring a "standalone" action and prove an infringement of the competition rules without the benefit of a prior decision to that effect or else bring a "follow on" action where there has been a prior decision by an authority (the CMA, a sectoral regulator, or the European Commission) finding a violation of EU and/or UK competition law.

On May 26, 2017, for example, the CAT struck a blow against the prestigious Law Society of England and Wales by ruling that the Law Society had abused its dominant position in the market for the provision of quality certifications and accreditation services to conveyancing firms in the UK. The claimant, Socrates Training, had complained that the Law Society unfairly required law firms to purchase training sessions from the Law Society as a condition of maintaining their accreditation status.

Also in 2017, in response to the European Commission's Damages Directive to the EU Member States, the UK adopted the necessary additional implementing regulations for competition law damage cases. These were laid before Parliament on December 20, 2016 and came into force on March 9, 2017. The UK Government felt that the UK rules were largely in line with the requirements of the Directive and therefore significant changes to the UK legislation were not necessary. The regulations implement the Directive as a single regime whether under EU law or under UK domestic competition law. It is unclear whether this single regime will survive Brexit.

The pertinent UK Regulations will apply to claims relating to cartels arising on or after March 9, 2017. The primary changes are the following:

(1) The limitation period will not start until the anticompetitive behavior has ceased, the claimant knows the identity of the infringer, and he has sufficient knowledge of the breach causing his loss.
(2) Limitation periods are also suspended when a competition authority is investigating the relevant behavior, when the parties to a claim agree to enter into a consensual dispute resolution process or where the collective damages regime applies under the Consumer Rights Act 2015.
(3) The courts will have powers to order the disclosure of relevant evidence from the defendant, claimants or third parties. Leniency, settlement and other such submissions are protected from disclosure.
(4) The passing-on defense is recognized with the burden of proving that an overcharge has been passed on resting on the defendant.
(5) There is a rebuttable presumption that cartels cause harm.
(6) The joint and several liability of competition co-infringers is confirmed.

(7) Final decisions of EU Member State competition authorities or review courts may be presented as prima facie evidence before the UK courts that an infringement has occurred.

§14.04 THE PROHIBITIONS

The Competition Act's Chapter 1 and ll Prohibitions, like those under EU Articles 101 and 102, apply to "undertakings" as construed under EC law. As we have seen, this definition applies broadly to any natural or legal person engaged in economic activity. It includes corporations, partnerships, trade associations, nonprofit organizations, cooperatives, individuals operating as sole traders, and, in some circumstances, public entities that offer goods or services in the marketplace. "Undertaking" does not include an individual acting as an officer or employee of a business.

The Chapter 1 Prohibition contained in Section 2(1) of the Competition Act provides that "agreements between undertakings, decisions by associations of undertakings or concerted practices which (a) may affect trade within the United Kingdom, and (b) have as their object or effect the prevention, restriction, or distortion of competition within the United Kingdom, are prohibited [unless exempted]." Section 2(2) of the Act is a prohibition "in particular" of the same five forms of coordinated anticompetitive activity which are enumerated in TFEU Article 101(1) of the EU discussed earlier in this Primer.

Section 2(3) states that this prohibition applies only if the agreement, decision or practice is, or is intended to be, "implemented" in the United Kingdom. This language adopts the approach to extraterritoriality taken by the ECJ in the *Woodpulp I* case, rather than the broader "effects" doctrine asserted by the US. The UK Government has never been enthusiastic about the US effects doctrine which it fought with some vigor last century before the EU came close to adopting it.

As in EU law, the term "agreement" has a wide meaning as used in the Act. An agreement may result from written or oral exchanges of communications, including so-called gentlemens' agreements and need not be legally enforceable to be caught by the prohibition. As is also the case under the EU jurisprudence, the words "effect on competition" in Section 2 of the Competition Act are applied as meaning "appreciable effect on competition."

Under Section 2(4) of the Competition Act, agreements which violate the Chapter 1 Prohibitions are void. In addition, infringing undertakings may be liable to third parties for resulting losses, the infringing firm may be subject to financial penalties, and the directors responsible for the breach may be disqualified.

As under EU law, only the offending clauses are void, and the rest of the agreement remains enforceable. The Competition Act provides for certain types of agreements to qualify either for exclusion or exemption from the Chapter 1 Prohibitions. Under the Competition Act, the Secretary of State may, acting on the CMA's recommendation, make domestic block exemptions.

The Chapter II Prohibition is found in Section 18(1) of the Competition Act which prohibits "any conduct on the part of one or more undertakings which amounts to the abuse of a dominant position in a market ... if it may affect trade within the [United Kingdom]." As with TFEU Article 102, what is prohibited is the abuse, not the holding, of a dominant position. Where such an infringement is found, the undertaking can be required to bring the infringement to an end and may be subjected to a fine.

§14.05 THE CARTEL OFFENSE

The "cartel offence" instituted by Section 188 of the Enterprise Act legislation provided that "(1) An individual is guilty of an offence if he dishonestly agrees with one or more other persons to make or implement, or to cause to be made or implemented, arrangements of the following kind relating to at least two undertakings (A and B)." In 2013, Section 47 of the ERRA extracted from the provision the word "dishonestly" as applied to cartels made on or after April 1, 2014, a prerequisite which had made establishing the offense more complicated and difficult.

The activities targeted by the cartel offense are described in Section 188(2) of the Competition Act as including price fixing, market sharing, limitation of production or supply, and bid rigging. It is an offense that applies only to individuals and is distinct from the Chapter 1 Prohibition. Vertical agreements, including RPM, are not covered by the cartel offense. There are a number of detailed circumstances described in which the offense will not have been deemed committed. However, the cartel offense is committed irrespective of whether or not the agreement reached between the individuals is actually implemented.

The cartel offense is triable either in the magistrates' court for a summary trial or before a jury in the Crown Court for a trial on indictment. On conviction upon indictment, a person guilty of this offense is liable to imprisonment for a term not exceeding five years or to an unlimited fine, or to both. On summary conviction the offender is liable to a term not exceeding six months or to a fine not exceeding the statutory maximum for the court, or to both. Accordingly, this criminal offense is an indictable offense. There is a right to appeal to the higher courts.

The first case brought under the UK cartel offense law involved the international marine hose industry whose members were also fined by the European Commission as well as in the US courts through action of the Department of Justice. The UK proceedings resulted in terms of imprisonment for three individuals. In 2008 four employees of BA were charged in a cartel on fuel surcharges. They pleaded not guilty, and the OFT decided to withdraw the proceedings.

The Company Directors Disqualification Act 1986 authorizes the CMA or pertinent sectoral regulator to apply to the court for the disqualification of a company director in certain circumstances. If: (i) the court finds that the company of which the individual is a director has committed a breach of competition law (Chapter I and/or Article 101); and (ii) the court considers that his conduct as director makes him unfit to be concerned in the management of a company, then the court must make a competition disqualification order (CDO). In connection with this second finding, the court must have considered whether the director's conduct contributed to the breach of the competition law, whether he or she had reasonable grounds to suspect that the company was engaging in a breach of competition law and took no steps to prevent it, and whether, if he/she did not know that the company's conduct constituted such a breach, he/she ought to have known it.

The maximum period of disqualification under a CDO is fifteen years. Three company directors were disqualified for periods of between five and seven years as a result of their participation in the *Marine hoses* cartel.

§14.06   VERTICAL AGREEMENTS

The UK Exclusion Order, made under Section 50 of the Competition Act, excluded vertical agreements from the application of the Chapter 1 Prohibition for purposes of UK law. As this exclusion indicated, the UK scheme had scarce interest in dealing with vertical agreements. With the advent of the EC decentralization of its competition law, the UK Government decided to repeal the UK Exclusion Order in the interests of clarity and conformity with the EC scheme. This repeal took place effective May 1, 2005, with a new limited exclusion order issued in 2004 for certain land agreements. The repeal of the Exclusion Order put vertical agreements generally on the same footing as other agreements subject to the Chapter 1 Prohibition. This prohibition applies to agreements between undertakings which may affect trade within the UK but does not affect trade between Member States. Article 101 TFEU is applicable where an agreement may affect trade between Member States. However, by virtue of Section 10 of the Competition Act, the EU block exemption applies in all events, so there is no need for the UK to adopt a block exemption of its own for vertical agreements. This will presumably be altered after Brexit.

There have been a number of investigations concerning vertical agreements. In several cases, vertical agreements involving the imposition of minimum resale prices have been struck down. The CMA adopted the OFT's *Guidance on Vertical Agreements*. The *Guidance* lists as hard core restrictions for both Article 101 and the Chapter 1 Prohibition the setting of fixed or minimum resale prices, although maximum and recommended resale prices are usually permissible as not infringing competition law. Other vertical agreements, including selective and exclusive distribution arrangements, noncompete or exclusive dealing, tie-in sales and bundling, full-line forcing and quantity forcing, may potentially restrict competition and require specific assessment for their effect on competition.

§14.07   MERGERS

Ever since the UK Government instituted oversight of competitive activity in 1965, this has included scrutiny of significant mergers from the antitrust viewpoint. Until the recent reforms, the Fair Trading Act 1973 dictated the process for assessing merger situations which met certain size thresholds and yet did not fall under the EC Merger Regulation as having a Community dimension.

The Enterprise Act, which came into effect on June 20, 2003, repealed the Fair Trading Act 1973 and put in place new provisions for merger review. The OFT and the Competition Commission remained central to the operation of the system, but the Secretary of State was largely taken out of the oversight process. When the ERRA provisions went into effect on April 1, 2014 the functions of the OFT and the Competition Commission were taken over by the CMA.

Section 22(1) of the Enterprise Act provides that the CMA is required to make a Phase 2 reference if it believes that it is or may be the case that a "relevant merger situation" has been created and that the creation of that situation has resulted, or may be expected to result, in a substantial lessening of competition within any market or markets in the UK, or a part of the UK, for goods or services. For there to be a "relevant merger situation," two or more enterprises must have ceased to be distinct. The Phase 1 investigation by the CMA leads to a decision as to whether the duty to make a Phase 2 reference applies.

With respect to anticipated mergers, the CMA is required to make a reference, with some exceptions, if it believes that "(a) arrangements are in progress or in contemplation which, if carried into effect, will result in the creation of a relevant merger situation; and (b) the creation of that situation may be expected to result in a substantial lessening of competition within any market or markets in the United Kingdom for goods or services."

With some exceptions, "concentrations" that have a "Union dimension" under the EU Merger Regulation cannot be investigated under national domestic law. This matter was discussed in Chapter 13 *supra*. Under the merger control scheme, firms have no obligation to pre-notify mergers to the CMA, although they often choose to have premerger discussions with the CMA.

The ERRA separates the Phase 1 and 2 decision-making in merger and market cases. The Phase 1 decision-maker is the Senior Director of Mergers or another senior staff member. The CMA's functions in merger matters are performed by members of a specially appointed CMA panel.

A relevant merger situation may include a joint venture if it causes a change of control or influence over an identifiable enterprise and either the share of supply or turnover test is met. It can be seen also that mergers between non-UK firms may be caught by these criteria if one or more of the firms are sufficiently active within the UK. A different review regime is provided for assessment of mergers involving public interest matters, including national security.

After a Phase 2 reference has been made, the Chair of the CMA Panel appoints an Inquiry Group of at least three members of the CMA Panel to serve on a Phase 2 Inquiry Group. This group has extensive investigatory powers and can impose penalties for noncompliance. Hearings are held with third parties, as well as with the main parties. Within prescribed time limits, the CMA must make a decision about the likely competitive effects of the completed or anticipated merger and issue a reasoned report. Where the CMA has concluded that there is an anticompetitive outcome, it is required to take such action as it considers to be reasonable and practicable to remedy, mitigate, or prevent the anticipated substantial lessening of competition.

Chapter 14: The United Kingdom §14.07

The CMA may seek commitments, issue orders and impose monetary penalties as necessary remedial action. Any divestitures that are agreed to or ordered are usually scheduled within a specified time, with the purchaser subject to the CMA's approval. Any person who is aggrieved by a decision of the CMA or of the Secretary of State can apply to the CAT for review. The CAT's decision may be appealed to the Court of Appeal.

There have been many mergers involving UK companies reviewed by the responsible authorities over the years but not many disapproved. A significant number of the mergers referred for a Phase 2 investigation have been abandoned by the parties. In recent years, of course, the larger international transactions have fallen under the EU merger control legislation.

One interesting merger which the Competition Commission found would operate against the public interest in 1999 involved the proposed acquisition of Manchester United, the famous English football club, by British Sky Broadcasting Group plc ("BskyB"), the dominant provider of sports premium television channels. The CC concluded that the proposed merger would adversely affect BskyB's broadcaster competitors by making it more difficult for them to secure rights to show Premier League matches. In addition, the CC found that the merger could be expected to have the adverse effect of damaging the quality of British football by reinforcing the trend toward unequal wealth among the clubs and also by giving BskyB the power to make decisions which did not reflect the long-term interests of football.

During 2000, at the request of the UK, the European Commission referred to the UK competition authorities for review the acquisition by Interbrew SA ("Interbrew"), a Belgian company, of the brewing interests of Bass PLC ("Bass"), a British brewer. The effect of the merger, which had already taken place, was to make the combined business the largest brewer in Great Britain and to create a duopoly of Interbrew and Scottish and Newcastle plc., which would also control the largest distribution operations in the country. Operating under the earlier merger control regime, the Secretary of State, on the advice of the Director General, referred the merger to the CC. In its study, the CC considered nine possible behavioral and structural remedies which might be applied to remedy the adverse effects to be anticipated from the merger. A majority of the CC concluded that the only suitable remedy would be to require that Interbrew divest the UK business of Bass. The Secretary of State agreed with this assessment and directed the OFT to seek suitable undertakings from Interbrew to bring about the divestiture of its interest in Bass. However, the High Court subsequently ruled that the CC had acted unfairly in failing to give Interbrew sufficient opportunity to discuss alternative remedies.

A case decided by the Court of Appeal in 2004, *IBA Health Ltd. v. OFT*, involved a complaint by a third party competitor that the OFT had failed to perform its duty in not having referred to the CC a merger between two other firms, iSoft and Torex. The CAT ruled against the OFT. The Court of Appeal dismissed the OFT's appeal. The court agreed with the OFT that it is the OFT's own belief about the likely effect of a merger that controls a reference, but it held that this belief must be reasonable and objectively justified on the facts. Here, said the court, "there was genuinely room for two views" and the OFT, acting as the first-stage screening process, should have made the reference to enable the CC to make the definitive ruling.

In a long running litigation, the CMA blocked the acquisition by Eurotunnel of three sea ferries from SeaFrance, a cross-channel ferry operator which had gone into liquidation and could not be sold as a going concern. The CMA concluded that that the assets acquired by Eurotunnel constituted an "enterprise" under UK law, and therefore the agency had jurisdiction to review the deal.

The CMA's jurisdiction in the matter was upheld by the CAT and finally by the UK Supreme Court in 2015. The Supreme Court reasoned that the test for whether a collection of assets of an undertaking which is no longer a going concern is an "enterprise" for purposes of the Enterprise Act is one of economic continuity. The first question posed, said the court, is whether the buyer in acquiring the assets in question is obtaining more than might have been acquired by going to the market to buy factors of production. The second question is whether the advantage is due to the fact that the assets were previously part of the target enterprise. In this case, the capacity for the liquidated enterprise to perform the same activities as part of the same business continues to subsist.

§14.08 ANTITRUST IN THE UK AFTER BREXIT

On March 29, 2017, the United Kingdom served notice of withdrawal from the EU under Article 50 of the Treaty on European Union. Based on Article 50, the EU treaties shall cease to apply to the UK either (a) from the date of entry into force of the withdrawal agreement that the UK negotiates with the EU acting through its Council and other institutions or (b) two years after the date of notification, unless the European Council, in agreement with the UK, decides to extend this period. The current expectation is that most or all of the two-year period will be needed to negotiate the exit provisions and the UK's new relationship with the EU. Therefore, in practice, the British exit date is expected to be in 2019. Among the difficult issues to be negotiated are the future: (1) rights of EU citizens in the UK and of UK persons on the continent, (2) status of the land border between Northern Ireland and the Republic of Ireland, and (3) nature of the UK's trade relationship with its largest commercial partner.

If Britain and the rest of the EU cannot agree to the exit terms by the spring of 2019, they may agree to extend the negotiating period. An undesirable case scenario would be that no new terms are agreed and that Britain simply drops out without an agreement on its future relations with its largest trading partner. This possibility is being referred to as "dirty Brexit."

If the UK were to leave the EU but join the European Economic Area the UK would remain in the single market and much of the existing body of EU law, including the antitrust regime, would still apply. However, Theresa May, the UK Prime Minister, has announced that the UK does not seek continued membership in the single European market, but seeks a separately negotiated free trade agreement.

Of the greatest importance from the antitrust viewpoint, perhaps, is the fact that, post-Brexit, the EU competition rules, Articles 101 and 102 TFEU, will continue to apply to actions and agreements of British companies and individuals that have an effect in the EU (as, for example, is the case with respect to US businesses today). One key change, however, is that the European Commission will no longer have the power to carry out onsite investigations in the UK or to expect the CMA necessarily to assist it in this regard.

The current UK statutory requirement that the UK competition rules be interpreted in a manner consistent with the competition case law of the ECJ is unlikely to survive Brexit. But, given the similar wording of the competition law provisions, EU and UK law are likely to remain similar for some time. In sum, EU competition law will probably remain influential in the further development of UK law, at least in the short run.

However, UK courts will no longer be able to refer questions of interpretation to the ECJ. Moreover, UK jurisprudence and the policies of UK enforcement authorities may decide to diverge from the EU on such matters as exemptions from prohibitions. Under EU law, the CMA is currently required to apply EU competition law where it applies UK national competition law and cannot take action where the Commission has opened a formal investigation. With Brexit this will fall away, and there will be a risk of parallel and perhaps divergent approaches to particular conduct and activity. However, it seems likely that the EU and the UK will eventually fashion a cooperation agreement on competition law matters of the type currently in use between competition law enforcement agencies around the world.

Currently, mergers that meet the EU filing thresholds and standards must be notified to the European Commission and need not be cleared by national authorities, providing a "one-stop shop" for business. This will disappear after Brexit, and parallel reviews, including multiple filings, will doubtless take place. The CMA will have jurisdiction over more numerous and more significant transactions than at present. Businesses will have additional burdens with more regulatory filings entailed.

CHAPTER 15
Japan

§15.01 HISTORICAL BACKGROUND

The history of the Japanese antitrust laws commences with the end of World War II. The Allied Powers were determined to liberalize the Japanese economy and to prevent the rejuvenation of the "zaibatsu"—large industrial combines that had monopolized Japanese business activities before and during the war. State-supported cartels in the form of trade associations also dominated many Japanese industries. Accordingly, the US occupation authority, headed by General Douglas MacArthur, expressly directed the Japanese Government to enact a law which would eliminate and prevent private monopoly and restraint of trade. In response, the Japanese Government enacted the "Act Concerning Prohibition of Private Monopoly and Maintenance of Fair Trade" (the "Antimonopoly Act" or "AMA") in 1947. The law had been drafted jointly by the Japanese Government and General MacArthur's staff. It was modeled on the Sherman, Clayton, and Federal Trade Commission Acts of the US, but was more detailed than the American legislation. The Antimonopoly Act created the Japan Fair Trade Commission ("JFTC"), an independent five-person enforcement body patterned along the lines of the US Federal Trade Commission, and that body remains as the enforcement authority under the oft-amended law.

The 1947 Antimonopoly Act, which was substantially amended in 1949, 1953, and 1977, continued to be the subject of significant amendments in 1991, 1992, 1996–2000, 2002, 2003, 2005, 2009, and 2013.

The 1949 and 1953 changes were, in part, designed to weaken the original legislation, which many Japanese business persons viewed as unrealistically rigid, particularly for the post-war Japanese economy. Special exempting laws were also enacted at that time. The various changes in the law included deletion of a number of prohibitions, the creation of exemptions for certain kinds of cartels and limiting the enforcement powers of the JFTC. Japan's powerful Ministry of International Trade and Industry ("MITI" or "the Trade Ministry") was among those hostile to the AMA, preferring to organize much of the economy through "administrative guidance" including "kankoku sotan" (advice to limit production). MITI officials spoke about the need to expel "excess competition" in order to stabilize the economy. The combination of administrative guidance and industry cooperation resulted in the creation of MITI-sponsored export, recession and rationalization cartels, which escaped the AMA either through exemptions or circumvention. The JFTC accommodated, as best it could, to this situation.

The 1977 amendments, on the other hand, reflected an emerging viewpoint in Japan that more forceful action needed to be taken to prevent the damage being caused to the economy by the cartels. There was a public outcry against the oil companies who were seen as gouging high prices through cartel practices. Following a task force study, the AMA was strengthened, and the JFTC's enforcement powers were significantly enhanced. In particular, the Commission was authorized to impose surcharges on companies based on the sales they had made in the course of their participation in illegal cartels. Previously, the only remedy available to the JFTC was to issue a cease and desist order—a punishment which by itself provided insufficient incentive for compliance—or to seek a severe criminal penalty, a remedy that was seldom imposed. The 1977 amendments also gave the Commission the power to break up monopolistic situations and to require reports from firms when price rises indicate possible cartel activity.

Subsequent amendments have also been designed primarily to strengthen the statute and the JFTC. The perception of the Commission's effectiveness from the outside was formerly unkind. For example, a September 1989 issue of The Economist remarked that, "The law itself has teeth in plenty; the problem is that its designated watchdog has been trained not to bite."

In its efforts to gain greater access for US firms seeking to enter or further penetrate the Japanese market, the US Government continued to have frequent contacts with the Japanese Government for the purpose of urging the elimination of trade barriers and the more effective enforcement of the AMA. From the Japanese perspective, the statute had been adequately enforced, in the context of the conditions and needs of the Japanese economy. However, a bilateral agreement designed to enable greater entry into the Japanese market by US and other foreign firms, known as the Structural Impediments Initiative ("SII"), was concluded in 1990 by the two governments. The SII was an effort by the two governments to jointly identify structural barriers impeding trade and formulate approaches to rectify these situations.

One continuing concern of the US in regard to Japanese trade barriers was the existence of the "keiretsu." The term refers to special relationships among Japanese companies, based on ownership, historical ties, or other factors that create incentives for the firms concerned to deal with each other, rather than with other parties, including foreign firms. The issue of distribution keiretsu, which are networks of affiliated wholesalers and retailers used by manufacturers to distribute their products, was particularly nettlesome in the Japan-US dialogue. US critics characterized the keiretsu pattern as one designed by collusive cartels for the purpose of excluding competition. Japanese policy makers and commentators, on the other hand, generally defended keiretsu as reflecting a stable and efficient approach to economic organization, conditioned by historical factors and Japanese culture.

The SII exercise led the Japanese Government to take a number of measures to strengthen the AMA. In 1991, the JFTC sought to address the anticompetitive abuses in vertical business relationships by issuing guidelines entitled *The Antimonopoly Act Guidelines Concerning Distribution Systems and Business Practices*. That year the AMA was amended to raise the surcharge (civil penalties or administrative fines) applicable to certain cartels from 1.5% to 6% of turnover during the period in which the cartel operated. In 1992, the criminal penalty applicable to corporations was increased to JPY 100 million.

In 1996, the status of the JFTC was raised to the ministerial level. Its enforcement capability was enhanced by increases in its budget and staffing, and the agency opened an office for the purpose of receiving complaints from foreign parties directed against exclusionary practices by Japanese firms. In 1997 and 1999, many cartel exemptions were eliminated. In 2000, private parties obtained the right to file for injunctions against unfair trade practice violations.

In his inauguration speech in 2001, Prime Minister Junichiro Koizumi described the need for Japan to foster a strong competition policy as an important component of the government's program to reform the structure of the economy. In 2002, the criminal penalty for corporations was increased from JPY 100 million to JPY 500 million. Service of process procedures applicable to firms based in foreign countries were introduced.

In 2003, the oversight of the JFTC was transferred from the Ministry of Internal Affairs and Communications to the Prime Minister's Office.

Despite resistance from powerful business groups, the AMA was significantly amended again in 2005 in an effort to make it more effective. The surcharge system, which was designed as a deterrent against cartel and bid rigging activities, was strengthened by increasing the surcharge rates from 6% to 10% and enlarging the range of AMA violations subject to surcharges. Higher surcharge levels were imposed for repeat violations.

A leniency program was introduced to create an incentive for cartel participants to step forward and inform the JFTC of the unlawful activity, bringing Japan up to the developing international standard in this regard. The hearing rules before the JFTC were revised in a number of respects, including allowing the JFTC to issue elimination orders without initiating hearing procedures, after having provided the respondent with a preliminary opportunity to give its views. In addition, new powers were granted the JFTC for use in criminal investigations.

In 2009, a surcharge was introduced for exclusionary private monopolization and for certain unfair trade practice violations. A uniform filing system for all types of mergers and acquisitions was adopted.

The 2013 amendments eliminated the 2005 appeal system pursuant to which the final decisions of the JFTC were appealable to the Tokyo High Court. The new system introduced provides for appeals brought against administrative measures adopted by the JFTC to go exclusively to the Tokyo District Court, with any subsequent appeal to the Tokyo High Court and any final appeal to the Supreme Court of Japan. It was hoped that the use of judicial appellate panels as prescribed would bring about the competition law expertise desired in the review process.

Other reforms provided by this legislation included designation by the JFTC of hearing officers to preside over the administrative hearing; allowing alleged infringers to obtain explanation from the JFTC of the JFTC's likely actions; and the possibility for alleged infringers to inspect and photocopy the evidence extracted from them by the agency. The measures were intended to provide greater due process for those involved.

The Japanese Government gradually embarked on a course of deregulation of the economy. This involved the privatization of public corporations, reduction of approval requirements, and other government controls over industry, and generally making way for more market access and competition. Deregulation measures took place with respect to airlines, retail stores, post offices, banks, alcoholic beverage distribution, insurance, cosmetics, medicine, automobiles, petroleum products, telecommunications, electricity, and gas.

The JFTC continued to promulgate guidelines to encourage and clarify compliance with the AMA. Among these, in addition to the *Distribution Guidelines* mentioned above, are *Monopolistic Situations* (1978–2005); *Merger Guidelines* (1980); *Mergers and Acquisitions* (2002–2011); *Research and Development Guidelines* (1993); *Public Bid Guidelines* (1994); *Prior Consultation Systems* (2001); *Unfair Trade Practices Guidelines* (1984–2016); *Trade Association Guidelines* (1995–2001); *Professional Association Guidelines* (2001); *Franchising Guidelines* (2002); *Standard Setting Guidelines* (2005); *Business Combination Guidelines* (2004); *IP Guidelines* (2007–2016); *Exclusionary Private Monopolization Guidelines* (2009); *Sales Below Cost Guidelines* (2009); *Investigation Procedures* (2016); and *Public Support for Revitalization* (2016). We will mention other guidelines in the pages ahead.

§15.02 OVERVIEW OF THE LEGISLATION

[A] The Japan Fair Trade Commission

The JFTC is an independent regulatory agency attached to the Prime Minister's Office. Pursuant to Article 29 of the AMA the Commission consists of a chairman and four commissioners who are appointed by the Prime Minister with the consent of both Houses of the Diet. Their term of office is five years and they may be reappointed. The commissioners are expected to have knowledge and experience in law or economics. The Commission is served by a general secretariat consisting of hundreds of staff members and two operating bureaus, the Investigation Bureau and the Economic Affairs Bureau. The Commission has eight branch offices.

The JFTC has the power to undertake investigations of prohibited conduct, to conduct administrative hearings, issue remedial orders and, since 1977, to impose surcharges (civil penalties) on businesses guilty of cartel activity. The procedure for judicial review of JFTC decisions has changed since the passage of the 2013 legislation. The amendments became effective on April 1, 2015. Under the prior system, the Commission would issue an order against a party with no prior hearing. Parties that wished to contest that order could request that the JFTC conduct a hearing. Following the conclusion of that hearing, the party could challenge the order by filing a lawsuit with the Tokyo High Court (an intermediate court situated between the district courts and the Supreme Court).

Under the 2013 reforms, the only appeal from an order of the JFTC lies to the Tokyo District Court, to be heard by a panel of three or, if necessary, five judges. On a subsequent appeal to the Tokyo High Court, it assigns the case to a panel of five judges. Final appeal lies to the Supreme Court of Japan. A party may file a complaint with the Tokyo District Court without first undergoing a JFTC hearing.

Persons may complain to the Commission of violations of the Act and ask for elimination or other appropriate measures to be taken. If the JFTC believes that a violation may have occurred it will undertake an investigation. Article 47 of the AMA gives the Commission extensive posers to investigate complaints. To carry out a "dawn raid" the JFTC official needs only to show to the targeted party his investigator identification and a notice of investigation. Under Article 47(1) (iv), the Commission may enter any business office of the persons concerned with a case or other necessary sites, and inspect the conditions of business operation and property, books and documents, and other materials. Even the residence of an employee may become the subject of an on-site inspection. If parties involved in an alleged violation refuse, obstruct or evade the on-site inspection or do not submit materials without justifiable reasons, the penal provisions of Article 94 of the AMA may apply. During an on-site inspection, the party investigated may have its attorney present, but the investigator will not wait for him/her to arrive. These matters are discussed in the *Guidelines on Administrative Investigation Procedures under the Antimonopoly Act* which the Commission has issued and which became effective on January 4, 2016. The attorney-client privilege has not been recognized by the Commission.

As mentioned above, the 2013 amendments to the Act contained a number of provisions intended to assure greater due process for parties appearing before the Commission. When a respondent does not accept the views of the Commission, there is triggered a litigation type administrative hearing. If a complaint has been issued, the hearing must be conducted by a neutral "designated officer." A person who has been involved in the investigation of the case on behalf of the JFTC may not serve as the hearing examiner. The party under investigation may request, obtain from the Commission and copy certain of the information relied on by the Commission. The investigator and the respondent's representative may present witnesses and experts, and both parties may make opening and closing statements. After conclusion of the hearing process, the hearing examiner prepares a draft decision and submits it and the dossier to the JFTC for due consideration. The JFTC then issues its decision.

If the respondent is dissatisfied with the decision, he/she can file a lawsuit with the Tokyo District Court. The amended Act permits the reviewing court to undertake a de novo review of the JFTC's factual findings. Under the prior system, the factual findings of the JFTC could not be overturned if supported by substantial evidence.

Persons who are uncertain whether a particular contemplated action or practice may raise a problem under the AMA may apply to the JFTC for prior consultation in this regard. The JFTC will examine the matter and reply whether or not, in its judgment, the proposed conduct will violate the AMA. It should be noted that the JFTC has a helpful website, in both Japanese and English versions, the latter being found at www.jftc.go.jp/en.

[B] Available Remedies and Leniency

The AMA prohibits enterprises (persons carrying on any business) from engaging in any of the three types of anticompetitive conduct: (1) private monopolization, or (2) unreasonable restraint of trade, both of which are prohibited by Article 3 of the AMA, or (3) unfair trade practices, which are prohibited by Article 19. Article 2 of the AMA defines these concepts and others included in the law. Article 6 is specifically directed at international cartels and provides that an enterprise must not enter into an international agreement which contains such matters as constitute unreasonable restraint of trade or unfair trade practices.

The remedies for unreasonable restraints of trade are: (1) cease and desist orders, (2) orders of administrative surcharges, and (3) criminal penalties. The first two remedies are administrative and effected by the JFTC. The third is initiated by the JFTC for hard core cartel infractions. In a non-cartel case, the JFTC typically may, pursuant to Article 7(1), order the party to cease and desist from the unlawful acts, to transfer a part of the relevant enterprise's business, or to take any other measures necessary to eliminate the unlawful acts.

A surcharge order requires a party to an illegal cartel to pay into the National Treasury an amount that is calculated according to a prescribed percentage of the value of the sales of the products involved in the cartel during the time the cartel was in effect. The percentage of the surcharge is fixed by the legislation.

The Japanese Government's need to make enforcement of the AMA more effective, particularly against cartels, led to institution in 1977 of the administrative surcharge as a nondiscretionary administrative fine applicable to hard core restraints of trade like price fixing and bid rigging. Critics of Japanese enforcement of the AMA consistently argued that the surcharge rates, which at one time were as low as a half percent of the firm's sales affected by the unlawful activity, did not provide a sufficient deterrent against cartel activity. The business community at first resisted any increase, but progressive increases in the rates have been legislated and have been applied to different offenses under the Act.

Although enforcement of the AMA is primarily administrative in nature, the statute also contains criminal provisions. The most severe of these criminal penalties are applicable to persons who commit, in violation of the AMA, private monopolization, unreasonable restraint of trade (cartels) or substantial restraint of competition in the course of prohibited trade association activity. The AMA is directed at entrepreneurs or enterprises, (i.e., businesses). However, individuals may also be prosecuted if they participate in cartel activity. Article 89 subjects individuals who have committed one of the specified offenses to imprisonment for up to five years or to a fine of not more than JPY 5 million for individuals. Section 95 provides that, in the case of a corporation, the maximum penalty for committing one of these offenses is JPY 500 million.

Somewhat lesser penalties are imposed for other offenses under the Act, such as filing of false reports or failure to comply with a decision of the JFTC. A trade association may be sentenced to dissolution, along with other punishments. When it considers that a criminal offense under the AMA exists, the JFTC is charged with filing an accusation to that effect with the public prosecutor's office. When he receives such an accusation from the Commission, the public prosecutor makes a decision regarding whom to file an indictment against in the appropriate court. In a criminal case, the standard is that of "beyond a reasonable doubt." For the JFTC to take an administrative measure, the preponderance of the evidence standard from civil cases is applied.

In October 2005, the JFTC announced a policy of actively pursuing criminal penalties against "[v]icious and serious cases which are considered to have widespread influence on people's livings, out of those violations which substantially restrain competition in certain areas of trade such as price-fixing cartels, supply restraint cartels, market allocations, bid rigging, group boycotts and other violation[s]."

The 2005 amendments to the AMA introduced a new leniency program offering full immunity to those culprits "first in the door." The 2009 amendments added a feature, at Article 7-2(13), which allows related companies to seek leniency jointly and be treated as a single applicant.

A leniency request may seek surcharge reduction, immunity or both. After the investigation has begun, only three applicants for leniency will be considered. The first applicant accepted before initiation of the investigation receives full immunity. The enterprise must have discontinued the violation. The second enterprise to submit information about the illegal activity to the JFTC, before the initiation of an investigation, is afforded a 50% reduction in the surcharge payable. The third enterprise to report such activity to the JFTC, before the initiation of an investigation, receives a 30% reduction in the surcharge payable.

If the first, second or third informants come to the JFTC to supply information only after an investigation has been initiated, each informant can receive only a 30% reduction in the surcharge. The benefits of the leniency policy are unavailable, however, if the company supplied false information, coerced another enterprise into committing the violations, or blocked another enterprise from ceasing its involvement in the activity.

[C] Private Enforcement

A private right of action to recover indemnification is created, in certain circumstances, by Article 25 of the AMA on behalf of any entrepreneur who has been injured by another's private monopolization, unreasonable restraint of trade, or unfair trade practices. However, pursuant to Article 26, this right to claim damages in court exists only if there has been a cease and desist order, a payment order, or a final and conclusive JFTC decision under the AMA. If this condition is met, the defendant's liability in the private suit is absolute, in that the latter cannot escape it by proving that he did not act willfully or negligently. The plaintiff must prove the causal link between the illegal conduct and his injury and must also prove the amount of the claimed loss.

Under the AMA, such suits must be brought within three years of the JFTC's decision having been rendered. In addition, there are court precedents establishing that, whether or not the JFTC has issued a decision against the particular conduct, a private plaintiff can file a tort claim under Article 709 of the Civil Code seeks recovery of damages for his injury. However, for a tort suit, negligence or willful misconduct on the part of the defendant must be shown. There is no provision for class actions, and punitive damages may not be awarded.

Section 24 of the AMA gives a person whose interests are infringed or likely be infringed by an unfair trade practice and who is suffering or likely to suffer serious damage thereby the right to apply to a court for an injunction against such infringement by an entrepreneur or trade association.

In a 1987 case brought by consumers under Section 25 against oil refineries for damages allegedly suffered as a result of price fixing in petroleum products, the Supreme Court of Japan held that the plaintiffs had failed to prove the linkage between the alleged price fixing at the refinery level and any injury sustained at the consumer level. The first damage award in a private case occurred in 1993 when the Osaka High Court held that the Toshiba Elevator Co. had improperly engaged in a tie-in when it refused to supply parts and components to its customer who was under a contract with an independent repair company for servicing of elevators. In the *Shiseido* case in 1994, the Tokyo High Court reversed a lower court decision directing Japan's largest cosmetics company to resume the supply of its products under a contract with a retailer. The appellate court held that the plaintiff had not established that Shiseido's requirement that retailers engage only in "face-to-face" sales was intended to maintain the retail price of the products. The Supreme Court subsequently supported the appellate court's decision.

Private damage suits, on the heels of cease and desist decisions by the JFTC, have become more common in the last few years. Many of the cases were brought by local governments and their residents as the victims in local bid rigging situations. However, a law enacted in 2002 barring residents from suing on the government's behalf has put the burden to act on the local governments themselves.

[D] Key Terms of the AMA

As we have observed, a number of prohibitions of the AMA, including those directed at private monopolization, unreasonable restraint of trade, and unfair trade practices are directed at entrepreneurs or enterprises, as the Japanese term is sometimes translated. Article 2(1) of the AMA defines the term to mean "a person who carries on a commercial, industrial, financial or any other business." It has been broadly applied to cover any business enterprise, whether for-profit, or nonprofit, such as a trade association or public entity which is engaged in economic activities.

Private monopolization, unreasonable restraint of trade, and certain mergers are unlawful where they give rise to a substantial restraint of competition in any particular field of trade. The phrase "substantial restraint of competition" has been defined by the Tokyo High Court and the Supreme Court as describing a situation in which one entrepreneur or a group of entrepreneurs has such dominant power in a market that it is able substantially to control or manipulate the prices and other business terms in the market. The anticompetitive conduct entails the establishment, maintenance or strengthening of such market control.

The phrase "any particular field of trade" requires making a determination in each case of the particular market in which the anticompetitive conduct must be appraised. This usually involves defining the product market in terms of the reasonable interchangeability of various products and defining the geographic market in which the competition takes place. The conclusion may be in terms of markets or submarkets, according to the goods, services, geographic area, and types of customers concerned. Definition may also take into account the different levels of distribution through which transactions in an industry move. Both horizontal and vertical situations are deemed to be covered.

[E] Exemptions

Various industries and sectors have enjoyed a degree of exemption from the AMA, including insurance, maritime, and aviation. Telecommunications businesses are subject to regulation under the Telecommunications Business Law. In 2001, the JFTC and the Ministry of Internal Affairs and Communication issued *Guidelines for the Promotion of Competition in the Telecommunications Business Field*, last revised in 2002.

Electricity and gas businesses are also subject to regulation under laws applicable to those industries. The JFTC and the Ministry of Economy, Trade, and Industry have issued *Guidelines for Proper Electric Power Trade*. The last revision became effective in April 2017. There are also *Guidelines Concerning Appropriate Gas Dealings* which were last revised in 2004.

The AMA itself provides some areas of exemption. For example, Article 21 provides that the Act does not apply to actions found to constitute an exercise of rights under the Copyright Act, Patent Act, Utility Model Act, Design Act or Trademark Act. Of course, misuse of those rights can result in a violation of the provisions of the AMA. Article 22 exempts cooperatives which conform to certain requirements. Article 24-2 exempts RPM contracts for certain products under certain circumstances.

§15.03 MONOPOLIZATION

There are two substantive provisions in the AMA which address monopolization. One of these is the prohibition of "private monopolization" which has been in Article 3 of the AMA since the legislation's inception. The term is defined in Section 2(5) in behavioral terms, as individual or joint conduct by entrepreneurs which excludes or controls the business activities of other entrepreneurs so as to cause, contrary to the public interest, a substantial restraint of competition in any particular field of trade. The other provision is found in Article 8-4 of the AMA as a result of the 1977 amendments and authorizes the JFTC to take remedial measures against "monopolistic situations." This term is defined in Article 2(7) according to criteria of market structure and performance in the context of industries in which one or more firms are dominant in market share terms, new entry is difficult, and prices and profits are very high.

The elements of "private monopolization" under the AMA are very close to the principles which have developed in the US jurisprudence under Section 2 of the Sherman Act and in the EU under Article 102 of the Treaty on the Functioning of the European Union. The act of "monopolization" is prohibited, not the status of being a monopoly. Moreover, there is no illegal monopolization under Section 3 of the AMA if a dominant firm has had monopoly thrust upon it by purely technological or other objective factors not controlled by the firm or if the firm enjoys its position by reason of its greater skill, foresight or diligence. If, on the other hand, the firm has gained or preserved its dominance through improper practices, such as exclusion of competitors or other actions designed to injure or preclude competition, a violation occurs.

One reason for the relative paucity of private monopolization cases is that many of the exclusionary and predatory practices which may be cited as elements of monopolistic conduct are also among the unfair trade practices designated pursuant to Section 2(9). Given the greater difficulty of establishing monopolization in violation of Section 3, the JFTC has often decided to seek a cease and desist order against a practice through the easier route offered by the prohibition of unfair trade practices in Section 19.

However, due to the amendments to the AMA which came into effect on January 1, 2010, the exclusionary private monopolization infraction became subject to the surcharge payment regime. This prompted the JFTC to issue *Guidelines for Exclusionary Private Monopolization* in 2009. These *Guidelines* explain that the offense consists of conduct that makes it difficult for other entrepreneurs to continue their business activities or for new market entrants to commence their business activities, thereby likely causing a substantial restraint of trade.

Typical exclusionary conduct cited includes below cost selling which causes difficulty to the business of an equally or more efficient competitor; exclusive dealing; tying; and refusal to supply and discriminatory treatment "beyond a reasonable degree" concerning necessary products.

The JFTC will give priority to the investigation of cases where the share of the product supplied by the entrepreneur in question exceeds 50% after the commencement of the conduct in question, and the conduct is deemed to have a serious impact on national life. Efficiency improvements may be taken into account but not normally when the exclusionary conduct has reached a monopolistic or almost monopolistic level. It should also be noted that a firm may be found guilty of committing unfair trade practices even if its conduct does not violate the private monopolization standards.

A number of private monopolization cases took place in the 1940s and 1950s. A 1950 decision of the JFTC, the *Saitama Bank* case, established that there can be a violation of Section 3 even if the market monopolized is not a market in which the offender is primarily engaged. In that case, the bank attempted to gain control of the silk export trade in one prefecture by making loans available to silk mills on the condition that they sell their raw silk to an affiliate of the bank. The JFTC found that this effort to exclude the competitors of the affiliate and to control the silk market was a prohibited attempt to effect private monopolization.

The 1956 *Snow Brand Dairy Co.* case involved two dairy companies which together controlled more than 80% of the purchase of raw milk in the largest milk producing district. These dairy companies, acting in collusion with a financial organization, carried out a scheme whereby loans would be issued only to farmers who sold their milk exclusively to the two companies. In a formal decision, the JFTC ruled that the dairy companies had effected a private monopoly in excluding competitors from buying milk. These were cases of exclusion of competitors, in the language of Section 2(5) of the AMA.

There was also an early case of unlawful control by an entrepreneur of the business activities of a competitor, within the meaning of Section 2(5). This was the *Noda Soy Sauce* case decided by the JFTC in 1955. The industry leader, the Noda Soy Sauce Co. ("Kikkoman"), held a 34% share of the soy sauce sales in the Tokyo area and enjoyed, by far, the most prestigious product and trademark recognition. Kikkoman was the price leader for its competitors in soy sauce products and also pressured its distributors and retailers to maintain high prices on Kikkoman products. The JFTC brought a proceeding against Kikkoman and concluded that the company had violated the AMA by monopolizing the soy sauce market through controlling its competitors' pricing decisions.

The control was indirect, but effective, in that Kikkoman's conduct placed its competitors in the situation where they had to pursue similar pricing. The Tokyo High Court affirmed the JFTC's decision.

Direct control of competitors was found by the JFTC in the 1972 *Toyo Can Co.* case. Toyo had a market share of the tin can manufacturing market in Japan which exceeded 50%. Among other things, Toyo acquired the stock of competitors over the years and refused to supply cans to those customers who produced cans for their internal use. The JFTC issued a recommended decision, which Toyo accepted, requiring a partial divestiture and withdrawal of the restrictive sale conditions.

In 1997, in the *Pachinko Machine Patent Pool* case, the JFTC took action against a patent management company which was preventing companies from manufacturing pachinko machines by withholding patent rights. This involved collective action inasmuch as a patent pool had been formed by all of the manufacturers of pachinko machines and, without access to the patents, competitors could not enter the market. The Commission issued a recommended decision that this was a violation of Section 3.

In 1998, the JFTC issued a recommendation under the Section 3 prohibition against private monopolization in the *MDS Nordion Inc.* case. The Commission found that the Canadian company was preventing competitors from entering the market for sales of a material called Molybdenum-99, by concluding full requirements contracts effective for ten-year period with the purchasers of the material.

In 2000, the JFTC issued several decisions based on charges of private monopolization against dominant companies for employing exclusionary acts which blocked entry by competitors. One of these involved a warning issued against Nippon Telegraph and Telephone East Corporation ("NTT East"), the holder of a dominant position in its regional communication market. This action was directed against NTT East's imposition of restrictions on companies which sought interconnections with its subscriber cables. Only a warning was issued because the company had already taken some corrective steps. The JFTC pointed out that NTT East's actions "may have strengthened the company's market position in the area's local communication market, substantially restrained competition in the internet access services utilizing the subscriber lines and violated Section 3 of the AMA."

Indeed, the Commission has had a long running campaign against the activities of NTT East, the dominant optical fiber network operator. The Commission subsequently found that the company had tried to exclude competitors from the market for high speed internet access by charging them higher prices than it charged its own customers. The JFTC's finding that NTT East had engaged in exclusion type monopolization was upheld by the Supreme Court in 2010.

In 2004, the JFTC launched an investigation of alleged private monopolization involving Intel Kabushiki Kaisha (IJKK), a wholly owned subsidiary of Intel Corporation of California. The investigation included a "dawn raid" on the company's Tokyo office. In March 2005, the JFTC issued a recommendation to IJKK requiring that company to cease and desist in its conduct violating Section 3 of the AMA. The recommendation alleged that IJKK had caused the five major Japanese manufacturers of personal computers to refrain from using CPUs manufactured and sold by IJKK's competitors. IJKK allegedly carried out this coercion or inducement by providing the five manufacturers with rebates and certain funds referred to as "market development funds" with the purpose of maximizing the number of Intel CPUs utilized by the manufacturers. The JFTC directed IJKK to cease this conduct, not engage in any conduct designed to exclude competitors, and undertake antimonopoly training for its sales staff. IJKK accepted the Commission's decision and recommendation.

The JFTC also issued a cease and desist order for private monopolization against the Japanese Society for Rights of Authors, Composers and Publishers ("JASRAC"), a dominant copyright collection society in Japan. JASRAC maintained exclusionary pricing schemes by insisting on unlimited use "comprehensive contracts" for copyright licensing fees. The Supreme Court dismissed JASRAC's appeal in 2015.

Also in 2015, the JFTC issued a cease and desist order against the JA Fukui Prefectural Economic Federation of Agricultural Cooperatives for private monopolization. The Commission found that the respondent substantially restrained competition with respect to grain facility operations by designating bidders and managing to have these bidders win the contracts.

A "monopolistic situation," as defined in Section 2(7) of the AMA is one in which, assuming that the total annual sales of the goods or services concerned in Japan is over JPY 100 billion, (1) one firm has a 50% share or two firms have a 75% share of the particular market, (2) new market entry is very difficult, (3) there have been unusual price increases or only slight decreases in price for a considerable period of time, in the light of the circumstances, and (4) the enterprise earns an excessive profit rate or expends unusually high overhead costs.

Where such a situation exists, the JFTC may take measures to restore competition, including ordering the dissolution or partial divestiture of the firm. However, Section 8-4 further provides that the JFTC may not apply measures which "may reduce the scale of business of the said entrepreneur to such an extent that the costs required for the supply of goods or services which such entrepreneur supplies will rise sharply, undermine its financial position and make it difficult for the entrepreneur to maintain its international competitiveness, or where other alternative measures may be taken which the Commission finds sufficient to restore competition with respect to such goods or services." The Commission has published *Guidelines Concerning the Interpretation of "Specific Business Fields" as Defined in the Provisions of "Monopolistic Situation"* in the Antimonopoly Act, which were last revised in early 2006.

From time to time, the JFTC has listed the industries in which the market share standards are met, and the firms affected have therefore been put on notice that they are possible targets for the invocation of Section 8-4. They may, for the reason that they are potential targets in this regard, decide to moderate their behavior. It is not clear, however, that the existence of this structural control has resulted in lower market concentration in any industries in Japan. Knowledgeable commentators doubt the efficacy of this little used remedy given the stringency of the standards for its use.

§15.04 UNREASONABLE RESTRAINT OF TRADE

A primary purpose of the AMA was to provide effective legislation to combat cartels, which had long been a scourge in the Japanese economy. Section 4 of the original legislation, which prohibited cartels without requiring a substantial restraint of competition, was deleted by the 1953 amendments. The anti-cartel purpose of the law has since been served by the prohibition of "unreasonable restraint of trade" in Section 3.

The term is defined in Article 2(6) as business activities by which entrepreneurs, by agreement or other concerted action with other entrepreneurs, "mutually restrict or conduct their business activities in such a manner as to fix, maintain, or increase prices, or to limit production, technology, products, facilities, or customers or suppliers, thereby causing, contrary to the public interest, a substantial restraint of competition in any particular field of trade." Among the agreements and understandings covered by this prohibition are price fixing, bid rigging, production limitations, customer and market allocations, and collective boycotts.

Clauses (i) through (v) of Article 8(1) prohibit trade associations from engaging in acts involving a substantial restraint of competition, entering into international agreements prohibited by Article 6, limiting the number of entrepreneurs in a field of business, unjustly restricting the activities of member entrepreneurs, and causing entrepreneurs to employ unfair trade practices. In cases involving a substantial restraint of competition, the surcharges are levied on the companies making up the trade association. Trade associations are required to file a report with the JFTC within thirty days after they are formed and at other times. The JFTC has issued several guidelines relating to trade association activities to assist such organizations in being law abiding.

An illegal agreement may be written or oral, and its existence may be inferred from circumstantial evidence. Parallel conduct on the part of competitors, without more, has not been deemed sufficient to permit the inference that a cartel exists. The

JFTC has not announced a specific policy as to what point in the development of a cartel it will consider the price fixing, market allocation or other anticompetitive arrangement to constitute a substantial restraint of competition within the meaning of Article 2(6). The Commission has, however, brought a number of cases where full-blown cartel activity was not yet in effect, but the agreement was one which would obviously substantially restrain competition, and the participants had taken preliminary steps to carry it out. The courts have confirmed the position that the offense is completed when the cartel agreement is made.

Particularly during Japan's high growth years in the 1960s and 1970s, there was serious conflict between the procompetition provisions of the AMA and the industrial policies promoted by MITI. The latter sponsored many export cartels, recession cartels, and rationalization cartels, justifying its actions on the basis of particular exemption laws or on its powers to provide "administrative guidance" to Japanese industry. The JFTC did, on occasion, challenge cartels which were not authorized by an exemption even though the challenged industry activity had been undertaken on the advice of MITI or another government agency. Court decisions indicated that, in some situations, administrative guidance might provide a defense to a charge under the AMA against cartel activity. The ground for possible conflict in this regard has been greatly reduced in recent years.

In 1994, the JFTC issued *Guidelines Concerning Administrative Guidance Under the Antimonopoly Act*. The guidelines emphasize that activities affecting such key aspects of competition like prices, production, and market entry or withdrawal, may violate the AMA even if the activities were brought about by administrative guidance. The message is that reliance by industry on administrative guidance which affects competition is safe only where it is fully based on a specific provision of law or regulation.

The matter of export cartels deserves mention, given their prominence in the past. There are two Japanese laws which must be distinguished in this regard. One is the Foreign Exchange and Foreign Trade Law under which the Trade Ministry is authorized to control the export of commodities and technology by designating controlled items or requiring approvals. In these situations, there are no cartels, but simply compliance by exporters with the orders of the Ministry.

On the other hand, there still also exists the Export and Import Transactions Act ("Export-Import Law") which provides that, in certain circumstances, the AMA does not apply to any agreements made under the Export-Import Law. Article 5(1) of the Export-Import Law provides that exporters may enter into an agreement with regard to the price, quantity, design and other matters in export transactions of a specific type of goods to be exported to a specific destination by notifying the Minister of Economy, Trade and Industry of the agreement no later than ten days prior to the date of execution. Under Article 5(2) the Minister must then order the parties to amend or discontinue the agreement if he makes a finding that the agreement will have any injurious effects. Article 34 requires the Minister to advise the JFTC of any action in this regard. The JFTC advises that, as of early 2017, it has not received a notification in this regard from the Minister for at least ten years, indicating that export cartels are no longer in good standing in Japan.

Enforcement of the AMA against hard core cartels engaged in price fixing or bid rigging has been the JFTC's top priority since the inception of the legislation. This priority has continued into the twenty-first century, with bid rigging cases accounting for a large percentage in terms of the various types of AMA violations established. We can mention only a few of the cartel and bid rigging cases here to impart the flavor of the JFTC's enforcement efforts in these regards. The remedy sought and obtained in most cases was the imposition of the surcharge payment penalty.

The first important criminal prosecution took place in 1974 and was brought against the Petroleum Industry Federation and Japanese oil firms and their officers, for price fixing and output restrictions. No one went to jail, however. The convictions were affirmed by the Supreme Court in 1984. Subsequent criminal prosecutions have been relatively rare, even after the 2005 amendments.

In 1995, the JFTC filed criminal accusations against nine electrical equipment manufacturers, including Hitachi, Ltd., Toshiba Corporation, and Mitsubishi Electric Corporation, for rigging bids on tenders commissioned by the Japan Sewage Works Agency. In 1996, the Tokyo High Court issued judgments finding those nine companies, seventeen of their employees and one official of the above-named agency guilty. The companies were fined, and the individual offenders received prison sentences which were suspended for two years. In 1999, there were criminal proceedings brought against the ductile cast pipe manufacturers for forming a cartel and against oil products companies for bid rigging.

In 2003, the JFTC issued an elimination recommendation to Kaneka Corporation and Mitsubishi Rayon Co. for agreeing, in unreasonable restraint of trade, with Kureha Chemical Industry Co. to raise the sales prices for various "modifiers" used in plastic products. This action came as part of a worldwide crackdown against modifier producers which was highlighted by simultaneous on-site inspections carried out on February 12, 2003, by the JFTC, the US Department of Justice, the Canadian Competition Bureau, and the European Commission.

As we have noted, the rigging of public bids has been an enormous problem in Japan, particularly the "dango" system used in the construction industry to avoid the competitive bidding process. Collusion within the industry has significantly increased the companies' profits while adversely affecting the country's economy. Under dango, the bids are coordinated and the successful bidder selected. Subcontracts may be agreed to compensate the predesignated bid winner in the event that it does not have the lowest bid.

In 2002, the Act Concerning Elimination and Prevention of Involvement in Bid Rigging was passed. This legislation authorizes the JFTC to make demands on ministries and government agencies requiring them to investigate bid rigging situations and take the necessary action to terminate the situation. Nonetheless, the bid rigging tradition endures.

In 2005, the JFTC filed a criminal investigation with the Public Prosecutor General against six companies and five individuals for bid rigging with respect to steel bridge construction projects ordered by the Japan Highway Corporation (Highway Corporation). One of the individuals accused was the executive director of the Highway Corporation who, it was alleged, participated in a conspiracy with the bidding companies who agreed in advance how to bid so as to allow one to be the winner in the tender for the construction projects.

The JFTC's efforts to combat bid rigging have been supplemented in recent years by damage suits filed against offenders, on the heels of JFTC cease and desist orders, on behalf of local governments who have been victimized by the practice.

We have mentioned elsewhere in this book the international cartel discovered and prosecuted by various antitrust authorities with respect to market sharing and price fixing in the global marine hose sector (concerning rubber hose used to transport oil between tankers and facilities). In 2008, the JFTC issued a cease and desist order against the entrepreneurs manufacturing and selling marine hose and imposed a surcharge of JPY 2,380,000 on the Japanese participant, Bridgestone Corporation.

In 2009, the JFTC investigated another international cartel which had been challenged in the US and the EU, this one involving the manufacturers and sellers of cathode ray tubes for televisions ("CRT case"). The Commission found that the companies had taken part in meetings in which they set minimum target prices. The Commission imposed a surcharge of JPY 3,322,240,000 on five companies.

In early 2016, the Tokyo High Court heard the appeals from the JFTC rulings in the CRT case. This proceeding was the first in which the Commission had imposed a surcharge payment order against a foreign company in an international cartel case. This gave the court a first opportunity to rule on the "extraterritorial" aspects of the AMA regime. However, the court relied on the fact that the parent companies involved were all located in Japan and therefore did not opine on the territorial issue.

In 2014, the JFTC issued cease and desist orders and surcharge payment orders on the corrugated board manufacturers for entering into price fixing agreements. That year the Commission also issued cease and desist orders and surcharge payment orders against several firms in the business of providing international ocean shipping services for automobiles. The Commission also asked the responsible ministry to remove cartel exemptions enjoyed by the ocean shipping services.

In 2016, the Commission challenged a criminal bid rigging violation by several companies who were designating successful bidders in the paving repair work for the Great East Japan Earthquake damage. In 2017, the JFTC issued cease and desist orders and surcharge payment orders against the distributors of wallpaper who were fixing prices. On June 1, 2017, the Commission closed an investigation which it had begun concerning the activities of Amazon Japan G.K. which was suspected of restricting the business activities of the sellers in Amazon Marketplace. Amazon had agreed to take voluntary measures to terminate the challenged activities.

§15.05 UNFAIR TRADE PRACTICES

Article 19 of the AMA prohibits unfair trade practices, a term defined in Article 2(9)(i)–(v) by the enumeration of several types of practices which may tend to impede fair competition. Broadly stated, they include concerted refusals to supply, unjustly selling below cost, unjust price discrimination, RPM, and engaging in other specified acts while making use of one's superior bargaining position.

Article 2(9)(vi) gives the JFTC the authority to designate other practices which tend to impede fair competition as "unfair trade practices" under the AMA. Some of these designations apply to all industries and others apply to specific industries only. Unlike the prohibitions against unreasonable restraints of trade and private monopolization, unfair trade practices are not subject to criminal sanctions. They are subject to cease and desist orders and, only in the case of the infractions listed in Article 2(9)(i)-(v), to surcharge orders.

Within this framework, the JFTC is given the authority to designate more specifically which practices will be deemed to fall within the prohibition. In 1982, the Commission designated, with a short definition in each instance, unfair trade practices for this purpose, and the wording of these designations has since been partially revised over the years. The titles of the general designated practices are as follows: (1) Concerted Refusal to Trade, (2) Other Refusal to Deal, (3) Discriminatory Consideration, (4) Discriminatory Treatment on Trade Terms, etc. … (5) Discriminatory Treatment in a Trade Association, etc. … (6) Unjust Low Price Sales, (7) Unjust High Price Purchasing, (8) Deceptive Customer Inducement, (9) Customer Inducement by Unjust Benefits, (10) Tie-in Sales, etc. … (11) Trading on Exclusive Terms, (12) Trading on Restrictive Terms, (13) Unjust Interference with Appointment of Officer in one's Transacting Party, (14) Interference with a Competitor's Transactions and (15) Interference with Internal Operation of a Competing Company.

The JFTC has also issued specific designations and guidelines on unfair practices relating to firms in particular industries and to particular types of arrangements. Among these designations are *Designation of Specific Unfair Trade Practices by Large-Scale Retailers Relating to the Trade with Suppliers* and *Designation of Specific Unfair Trade Practices in the Newspaper Business*.

The JFTC first published in 1991 *Guidelines Concerning Distribution Systems and Business Practices Under the Antimonopoly Act ("Distribution Guidelines")*. They have been revised several times, most recently in May 2016. These *Guidelines* are helpful in understanding the Commission's views on the unfair trade practices.

The list of generally designated practices is significantly (although not entirely) concerned with restraints imposed in vertical relationships, among them being practices in distribution which have the effect of shutting out or damaging the competitors of the supplier. The alleged widespread existence of exclusionary practices in the Japanese distribution sector has long been a point of contention in the US-Japan trade dialogue. The "keiretsu" relationships issue—usually described in terms of the formal or informal bonds between Japanese manufacturers and their distributors and/or suppliers—were a significant irritant in this regard. During the SII negotiations, the US strenuously maintained that the exclusionary distribution relationships maintained by Japanese manufacturers were precluding or impairing the efforts by many US exporters to penetrate the Japanese market.

Thus, in response to a request from the US antitrust enforcement agencies, the JFTC issued its *Distribution Guidelines* in 1991, which elaborated the position of the JFTC on the various restraints practiced in distribution.

Readers who have persisted with this book thus far will be largely familiar with the nature of the above-listed activities which the JFTC has designated as unfair trade practices. Those readers also will not need another explanation of why and when the types of conduct listed may, depending on their circumstances, be either acceptable or unacceptable from the antitrust viewpoint. We will, therefore, limit our discussion here to those aspects of the Japanese treatment of the issues that are of special interest.

RPM: Under Article 2(9)(iv) of the AMA, it is unlawful to restrict another party's free decision on the selling price of the goods. This precludes one party maintaining a written or oral agreement requiring the second party to sell at a price indicated by the first party. Suggested resale prices given to distributors only as a point of reference are permitted, so long as the suggestion is not enforced.

Exclusive dealing: The *Distribution Guidelines* indicate that exclusive dealing requirements are likely to be illegal when an "influential supplier" restricts its customers from dealing with other suppliers. Since exclusive dealing is not necessarily anticompetitive, much depends on the market power of the parties and the reason and context of the restriction.

Refusal to deal: Refusals to deal are unlawful if they involve either (a) the taking of collective action, without proper justification, by competitors against another entrepreneur (i.e., a group boycott), or (b) unilaterally and unjustly refusing to deal or restricting the supply of goods or services to another entrepreneur. Concerted refusals to deal are, in principle, illegal if they cause a substantial restraint of trade in a market in violation of Section 3 of the AMA. Unilateral refusals to deal are not illegal in principle because a firm normally has freedom of choice in selecting its trading partners. However, in exceptional situations, even a refusal to deal by a single firm is illegal as an unfair trade practice. This will be the case where the refusal is by a powerful firm and for the purpose of carrying out illegal conduct or for an unjust purpose, such as excluding a competitor from the market.

Tie-in selling: Tie-in selling is, in principle, an unlawful trade practice where the obligation to purchase a second commodity or service from the supplier or his designee is coerced or otherwise unfairly imposed on the purchaser. For example, in 1998, the JFTC issued a recommendation decision for a violation of Section 19 of the AMA against the Japanese subsidiary of Microsoft Corporation for tying distinct types of software to licenses of other software to personal computer manufacturers.

Territorial restraints: Restrictions on distributors' sales territories are evaluated according to the nature of the restriction and the market context. Without more, it is unobjectionable for the manufacturer to assign areas of primary responsibility for sales and restricting the locations of the distributors' business premises as a means of setting up an effective distribution system. It is an unfair trade practice for an influential manufacturer in the market to assign exclusive territories to distributors (areas outside of which they may not sell) where this practice is likely to maintain the price level of the product in the market.

Restraints on resale: Restrictions on distributors' customers are unlawful as unfair trade practices where the purpose is to avoid resales to price-cutters or otherwise to maintain the price level of the product in question.

Below cost sales: Supplying a commodity or service continuously, without a proper justification, at a price which is excessively below cost, so as to cause difficulties to other entrepreneurs, is designated as an unfair trade practice. In 2009, the JFTC published updated *Guidelines Concerning Unjust Low Price Sales under the Antimonopoly Act.* They describe the offense as "[w]ithout justifiable grounds, supplying goods or services continuously for a consideration which is excessively below the costs required for the supply, thereby tending to cause difficulties to the business activities of other entrepreneurs ... ."

Price discrimination: Under the JFTC's designation, either supplying or accepting a commodity or service at prices which discriminate between regions or parties is an unfair trade practice where this is unjust. The few court decisions which illuminate this issue indicate that the provision will be enforced only where the price discrimination has a substantial adverse effect on competition, such as where a dominant company is selling at lower prices in one region or to particular customers with the intent of driving competitors out of business or precluding their market entry.

Abuse of Superior Bargaining Position: The 2009 revision of the AMA introduced in Article 2, paragraph (9), item (v), a form of unfair trade practice entitled "abuse of superior bargaining position." The JFTC issued in 2010 detailed *Guidelines Concerning Abuse of Superior Bargaining Position under the Antimonopoly Act.*

§15.06 LICENSING OF INTELLECTUAL PROPERTY

Section 21 of the AMA declares the statute's provisions to be inapplicable to acts recognizable as the exercise of rights under the Copyright Act, Patent Act, Utility Model Act, Design Act, or Trademark Act. In 2007 the JFTC issued *Guidelines for the Use of Intellectual Property under the Antimonopoly Act*, and it released a revised version in 2016.

A key change was the additional language relating to "FRAND" obligations, a refinement adopted recently by other enforcers around the world. A company's FRAND obligations arise when, as a patent owner, it takes part in a standard setting organization ("SSO") that sets the technical requirements for a particular technology. The SSO will typically require the holders of patents that are essential to the standard to license their patents on fair and reasonable ("FRAND") terms. This phenomenon is now taking place in several nations and, as we have seen, in the EU.

The JFTC states that companies who promise the use of their patents to an SSO on FRAND terms cannot refuse to license a willing licensee or to sue for an injunction against a willing licensee without running the risk that they may be found to be illegally excluding others.

On September 28, 2009, the JFTC issued a cease and desist order against Qualcomm Inc. for violating its FRAND obligations. The company holds several essential patents with FRAND obligations related to certain technology. It required licensees to license their patents at no royalty to Qualcomm in order to use Qualcomm's essential patents. The JFTC order determined that Qualcomm was engaging in a restrictive trade practice by trading on restrictive terms. The Tokyo High Court has stayed enforcement of the cease and desist order pending the full JFTC evidentiary hearing and final decision. Qualcomm is engaged in similar disputes around the world and in a continuing litigation with Apple Inc.

Another relevant set of guidelines relevant to intellectual property is the one issued in 2005 and entitled the *Guidelines on Standardization and Patent Pool Arrangements*. Patent pools are deemed to constitute an unreasonable restraint of trade if created in concert with competitors to mutually restrict or coordinate their business activities so as to cause a substantial restraint of competition.

In another lengthy battle the JFTC challenged Microsoft Corporation's "nonassertion clause" in the company's license agreements with PC manufacturers in Japan. The case endured for several years and involved some seventeen hearings. The JFTC, after investigating in 2004, determined that Microsoft violated Article 19 of the AMA by forcing licensed PC manufacturers and sellers to execute agreements containing a clause by which they agreed not to initiate any litigation against Microsoft or any licensee arising out of any infringement of the patent rights for the relevant PC operating system. The JFTC noted that Microsoft had a dominant position in the worldwide and Japanese markets for PC operating systems amounting to an over 90% market share. The Commission reasoned that Microsoft's "nonassertion provision" and related "survival provision" in its draft license terms for its Windows operating system was restraining PC manufacturers from enforcing their patents which might cause the manufacturers to lose their incentives to develop competitive technology.

Microsoft removed the provision from its contracts starting in August 2004 but refused to nullify it in existing contracts. It defended the provision as designed to prevent any "disruptive IP disputes."

On September 2008, the Commission issued another hearing decision on the nonassertion clause, finding again that Microsoft was trading on restrictive terms and thus committing an unfair trade practice. However, due to insufficient proof, the Commission was unable to determine whether the fair competitive environment in the PC market was adversely affected. The Commission ordered Microsoft to confirm that it had ceased the practice and would not take similar action in the future.

§15.07 MERGERS AND ACQUISITIONS

[A] Prohibitions

Articles 9-18 of the AMA deal with the competitive implications of stockholdings, interlocking directorates, mergers, and acquisitions.

Article 9(1) and (2) provides: "(1) No company may be established that would cause an excessive concentration of economic power due to share holding (including equity interest; the same applies hereinafter) in other companies in Japan. (2) No company (including a foreign company; the same applies hereinafter) may become a company that causes an excessive concentration of economic power in Japan by acquiring or holding shares in other companies in Japan."

Accordingly, Article 9 deals with "general concentration" in prohibiting companies from acquiring or holding the stock of other companies in Japan so as to cause an excessive concentration of economic power. A situation of general concentration is one in which a combination of enterprises is so large in scale and powerful that it may have a negative impact on the economy as a whole, even if it does not restrain competition in any particular field.

Article 10(1) deals with "specific concentration." It provides that "[n]o company may acquire or hold shares of any other companies if its acquisition or holding of shares substantially restrains competition in any particular field of trade, nor may any company use unfair trade practices to acquire or hold shares in another company."

Article 11 deals with acquisitions and holdings of voting rights in the banking and insurance industries. It has been said that Articles 9 and 11 are hold overs from an earlier time when concern focused on the *zeibatsu* who controlled companies in diverse markets. The rest of the merger regulation is similar to the other regimes that we have considered in this book.

Article 13 of the AMA bars officers or employees of a company from holding positions in more than one company where the effect may be substantially to restrain competition in any particular field of trade. The provision also prohibits companies from coercing their competitors into interlocking directorate situations.

Section 15 prohibits mergers which involve unfair trade practices or where the effect of the merger may be substantially to restrain competition in any particular field of trade. Section 15 also requires merger transactions meeting specific size thresholds to be notified to the JFTC before the merger is effectuated. Section 16 prohibits other transactions, including acquisitions of assets and other joint arrangements, if carried on through unfair trade practices or where the effect may be substantially to restrain competition in any particular field of trade.

[B]   Premerger Review

The AMA's premerger notification requirements differ depending on whether the transaction is one of stock acquisition, merger, demerger (a corporate restructuring in which the entity's business operations are segregated into components) share transfer, or acquisition of a business.

The general standard for notification, since the 2009 amendments, has changed from being geared to asset size to being keyed to a concept of "domestic turnover," applicable to both Japanese and non-Japanese companies. This term includes any turnover of entities within the corporate group, regardless of the location of the offices, making the sale of goods or services to consumers located in Japan. A party's failure to file a required notification, filing a false report, or failure to observe the waiting period is punishable under Article 91-2 by a fine not exceeding JPY 2 million. Article 18 empowers the JFTC to bring suit to have a merger declared null and void where the filing or waiting requirements were not observed.

Under Article 17-2(1) of the AMA, if an action in violation of the statutory prohibitions has occurred, the Commission may order the enterprise concerned to dispose of all or some of its shares, transfer a part of its business or take any other measures necessary to eliminate the unlawful acts. In practice, the JFTC has seldom used this statutory power. Through consultation with the affected parties it has often dissuaded transactions or arranged for modifications or restructurings to achieve the statutory goals.

Where the Commission decides to investigate a merger transaction, it may collect documents and other written materials, consult third parties, and summon witnesses to testify. After receiving significant criticism regarding its review process, the JFTC made substantial changes in its procedures which are reflected in a document issued June 14, 2011 entitled *Policies Concerning Procedures of Review of Business Combination*.

The procedure described by the document is briefly as follows: During the waiting period after notification (usually thirty days), the JFTC will normally either decide that the proposed business combination is not problematic or ask for more information to permit a detailed review.

The company can then submit any clarifying or justifying opinions or other materials. This will permit a "primary review" after which the Commission will determine whether still further review is needed. "Secondary review," when needed, involves requesting the company for reports and hearing third party opinions. At the end of secondary review, the JFTC will either give notification that it will not issue a cease and desist order or advise that it will take further enforcement action under the AMA. Under Article 10(9), the Commission must initiate a proceeding for a cease and desist order within ninety days after all reports have been received.

[C] Merger Analysis

The JFTC's *Guidelines to Application of the Antimonopoly Act Concerning Review of Business Combination (Merger Guidelines)* were first issued in 2004 and have often been revised, most recently on June 14, 2011.

The JFTC's merger analysis begins with definition of the product and geographic ranges of the particular field of trade under scrutiny. The product range is determined by identifying the goods which have similar functions and efficacy to the users. This includes consideration of which types of goods can prevent price increases or other changes in terms because users can turn to those goods as a substitute. The geographic range of a particular field of trade is identified similarly, by determining whether producers in one region can prevent price increases in another region because users can turn to them for substitutes.

The *Merger Guidelines* state that, for a violation of the AMA, it is not necessary to establish that a substantial restraint of competition will inevitably result from the merger or acquisition. It is enough to show that the transaction will alter the market structure in an anticompetitive way, so as to give the merged company, either unilaterally or in cooperation with other companies, the latitude to manipulate price, quality, volume and other conditions of trade. Thus, the question is whether it is probable that the business combination under review could easily lead to a substantial restraint of competition.

Among the factors which the JFTC takes into account are the market shares and rankings of the parties, market concentration, entry barriers and imports, any competitive pressures from related markets, improvements in efficiency brought about by the combination, and the financial condition of the entities involved. Likely effects resulting from both unilateral and coordinated conduct on the part of the market participants will be considered.

In market share and concentration analysis, the JFTC, like other competition authorities, utilizes the Herfindahl-Hirschman Index (HHI). The *Merger Guidelines* state, with respect to horizontal combinations, that "[i]n light of past cases, if the HHI is not more than 2,500 and the market share of the company group after the business combination is not more than 35%, the possibility that a business combination may be substantially to restrain competition is usually thought to be small." Different standards are set for vertical and conglomerate mergers, reflecting the Commission's view that they have less impact on competition than horizontal mergers except where they cause foreclosure or other exclusion of competitors.

On the subject of efficiency, the *Merger Guidelines* state that improvements in efficiency, whether brought about through economies of scale, the integration of production facilities, specialization of factories, reduction in transportation costs, or efficiency in research and development will be examined in terms of their impact on competition.

[D] Some Case Law

Before 1970 there were some significant decisions in the merger area, but, in recent years, fewer mergers have been challenged. Any competition concerns presented by a proposed transaction are usually worked out between the parties and the JFTC staff.

In an important case in 1969, which went through lengthy hearings, the JFTC challenged the proposed merger of the Yawata Iron & Steel Co. ("Yawata") and the Fuji Iron & Steel Co. ("Fuji"). These two leaders of the Japanese steel industry had been separated in 1946 in implementation of the plan to dissolve the *zaibatsu*. The merger would have given the consolidated entity the largest market share in various iron and steel products, ranging from 34% in hot rolled bars to 98% cent in steel pile. In heavy rails, the combined entity would then own a 98.3% market share. The business sector and MITI supported the consolidation as necessary to gird the Japanese industry for international competition.

However, the JFTC rejected the companies' proposals for modification of the transaction and issued a recommendation that they not merge. The companies did not accept the recommendation and extensive hearings ensued. After the hearings, the companies filed a motion for a consent decision. They proposed a large number of remedial steps, including divestitures and provision of technology assistance to competitors. The JFTC accepted the proposal and entered a consent decision, which allowed the merger to close in 1969.

Among the subsequent transactions under review there was the 1998 consolidation of Exxon Corporation and Mobil Corporation, two giant US oil companies with

Japanese subsidiaries. The JFTC determined that the sale of petroleum products as a whole constituted a particular field of trade, and it also designated sales of gasoline, kerosene and light oil each as a particular field of trade. The relevant geographic markets were determined to be both nationwide and in each prefecture. The Commission noted that the consolidated company would be the second largest seller of petroleum products nationwide, with an almost 20% market share, and, in some prefectures, would have a greater than 30% share of sales of gasoline, kerosene, and light oil. Nonetheless, the Commission cleared the merger, finding that there was no substantial threat to competition because there were plural strong competitors nationwide and keen competition at the retail level.

In 1999, the JFTC approved the acquisition by Japan Tobacco, Inc. ("JTI") of the tobacco operations outside the US (including Japan) of RJR Nabisco, the third largest tobacco company in the world. The Commission pointed out that, inasmuch as JTI had an almost 80% share in the sale of tobacco products in Japan, acquisition of RJR's 3% market share might result in restraint of competition in the Japanese market. However, the Commission approved the transaction after JTI agreed that it would not involve itself in exportation of RJR Nabisco-brand tobacco products to Japan and would not import or sell these products in Japan independently. It observed that there was ease of entry into the production of white Portland cement and that demand for the product had been steadily decreasing.

The JFTC was presented with an important merger case in 2002 when JAL and Japan Air Systems (JAS) sought clearance to establish a holding company and integrate their businesses. The companies explained that the purpose of this transaction was to rationalize their operations and promote efficiency, making them more competitive domestically and internationally. The merger was problematic from the antitrust viewpoint. The airline sector in Japan was oligopolistic, and there was only one other airline competing in the market, All Nippon Airways (ANA). The merger would give the JAL/JAS combination a domestic market share of about 50% and, moreover, the three airlines had a history of collusion on pricing and other matters. The JFTC and the Ministry of National Land and Transportation, which had jurisdiction over airlines, approved the transaction subject to the two airlines satisfying certain conditions, including giving up a number of landing/takeoff slots at Haneda Airport in Tokyo, transferring the physical facilities to new airlines, and reducing airfares.

In 2005, the JFTC reviewed the competitive impact on the Japanese medical devices market of the proposed acquisition by Johnson & Johnson of the stock of Guidant Corporation, both firms based in the US. This review was undertaken in cooperation with the US Federal Trade Commission and the European Commission who were also examining the transaction. Both of the merging parties distributed medical devices all over the world, including Japan where they sold through their Japanese affiliates or through importers, and both manufactured and distributed devices used for the treatment of coronary heart disease and other arterial diseases. Dividing these medical devices into relevant product markets, the JFTC found that two markets would be monopolized by the parties following the proposed stock acquisition. As to one of these, the JFTC determined that the presence of several possible entrants indicated that the acquisition might not substantially restrain competition.

With respect to the last product, EVH devices, the JFTC pointed out that, in light of US FTC and European Commission concerns, the parties had agreed to sell to a third party the worldwide EVH devices business owned by a Johnson & Johnson subsidiary. The JFTC therefore cleared the merger subject to the sale of the EVH devices business. All of this official activity went for naught, however, when Guidant Corporation chose, instead, to be acquired by Boston Scientific Corporation. That transaction was cleared by the Commission in 2006.

The Commission has approved a number of joint venture efforts, concluding that they were unlikely to restrain competition in any particular field of trade. For example, in March 2016 the JFTC advised Nippon Paper Industries Co., Ltd. and Tokushu Tokai Paper Co., Ltd. that it would not object to their plan to join forces in a new subsidiary and to combine their sales departments for containerboard.

CHAPTER 16
India

§16.01 THE BACKGROUND

After India became independent in 1947, it adopted a centrally planned economic structure also called the Nehruvian Socialism Model. This was a mixed model covering both private and public sectors. The government retained control over strategic industries including mining, electricity, and heavy industry. The functions of the private sector were made subject to regulation under the Industrial (Department and Regulation) Act of 1951 ("IDRA"). This gave the government control over the investment decisions of private industries. A process of economic reform began in the mid-1980s which has continued since then to usher India into a market-based economy today.

A Monopolies Inquiry Commission established in 1964 found high levels of concentration of economic power in over 85% of industry in India.

To enable the government to address concentration in Indian industry the Monopoly and Restrictive Trade Practices Act ("MRTP Act") was enacted in 1969, and it remained the controlling competition law in India until it was repealed in 2009. It was frequently amended.

The MRTP Act was designed to prevent concentrations of economic power and also to protect consumers. This involved imposing merger controls, curbing monopolies, and halting unfair and restrictive trade practices. The specific targets of the law included: (1) "monopolistic trade practices" including maintaining prices at an unreasonable level, unreasonably preventing competition, limiting technical development, permitting deteriorating quality and increasing costs of production, prices and profits; (2) "unfair trade practices" relating to consumer protection issues such as misleading advertisements, promotions, product safety standards, etc. and (3) "restrictive trade practices", known as RTPs, such as refusals to deal, tie-in sales, full line forcing, exclusive dealing, price discrimination, predatory pricing, territorial restraints, and resale price maintenance.

Under the MRTP Act, undertakings whose asset value surpassed certain financial thresholds were required to obtain prior approval of the government before expanding their operations in any manner including through mergers. In 1991, the government amended the MRTP Act by removing all preapproval requirements as to new undertakings, expansions, mergers, and appointments of directors.

The MRTP Commission, which was established along with the Act, treated the restrictive trade practices enumerated in the Act as *per se* violations of the Act. However, in 1977 the Supreme Court of India held in *Tata Engineering and Locomotive Ltd. v. Registrar of Restrictive Trade Agreements* that the rule of reason had to be applied in cases of agreements constituting restrictive trade practice violations. The Supreme Court reaffirmed that decision in 1979 in the case of *Mahindra & Mahindra Ltd. v. Union of India*.

In response to these decisions the MRTP Amendment Act 1984 was enacted to reestablish that the types of agreements listed under Section 33(1) of the MRTP Act, including RPM, area restriction, exclusive dealing, etc. would be deemed restrictive. The Supreme Court subsequently held in *Voltas Ltd. v. Union of India* that, under the general definition of RTPs in Section 2(o), (i.e., practices other than the ones listed under Section 33(1)), appraisal could be made under the rule of reason.

§16.02 COMPETITION ACT 2002

At the end of the last century, the Indian Government decided that the MRTP Act had become obsolete and did not sufficiently promote competition, particularly in the light of international economic developments. The MRTP Commission could not impose adequate penalties for infractions, there was no provision for extraterritorial jurisdiction, and the lack of definition of key terms in the law led to ambiguities and uncertainty for business compliance purposes.

The Competition Act 2002 ("the Competition Act") received the assent of the President of India on January 13, 2003. However, the validity of the Act was challenged in the Supreme Court before it became fully operational. The principal basis of the objection was that the Competition Commission envisaged by the Competition Act was in essence a judicial body, and therefore, under the Indian Constitution, the power to appoint the members of the Commission should rest with the Chief Justice of India or his nominee (an issue on which the Competition Act was incomplete). The Supreme Court decided the case primarily on the ground that the main challenge should be decided only after the promised amendment of the Act.

In the light of the order of the Supreme Court, various amendments to the Act were introduced by the government, culminating in the Competition (Amendment) Act, 2007 which went into force on October 12, 2007. These amendments included provision for repeal of the MRTP. Full repeal of the MRTP Act, including dissolution of the MRTP Commission, did not occur until September 1, 2009. The Government of India has continued to introduce proposed amendments of the Competition Act in the nature of refinements and additions. The Competition Act applies to the whole of India except for the States of Jammu and Kashmir.

In accordance with the provisions of the 2007 Amendment Act, the Competition Commission of India ("Commission") and the Competition Appellate Tribunal ("CAT") were established for enforcement of the law.

[A] The Competition Commission

Sections 7 and 8 of the Competition Act establish a Commission to be known as the Competition Commission of India. The Commission consists of a Chairperson and not less than two and not more than six other members to be appointed by the Central Government. They are appointed for a five-year term and may be reappointed. It is provided that each member shall be a person of ability, integrity and standing and who has special knowledge of, and such professional experience of not less than fifteen years in international trade, economics, business, commerce, law, finance, accountancy, management, industry, public affairs or competition matters, including competition law and policy. The upper age limit for a chairperson as well as a member is sixty-five years.

[B] Section 3: Prohibition of Anticompetitive Agreements

Section 3(1) of the Competition Act states that "[no] enterprise or association of enterprises or person or association of persons shall enter into any agreement in respect of production, supply, distribution, storage, acquisition or control of goods or provision of services, which causes or is likely to cause an appreciable adverse effect on competition within India." Section 3(2) provides that any agreement entered into in contravention of the above provision shall be void. Section 3(3) lists the types of agreements which shall be presumed to have an appreciable adverse effect on competition, including direct or indirect determination of purchase or sales prices, limits or controls of production or supply, market sharing or allocation agreements, and bid rigging. These provisions are regarded as aimed primarily at horizontal agreements and include cartels. Joint ventures are specifically excluded from the prohibition where they produce increased efficiency.

Section 3(4) is aimed at vertical agreements where a rule of reason analysis will be made. It provides that any agreement amongst enterprises or persons at different stages or levels of the production chain in different markets, in respect of production, supply, distribution, storage, sale or price of, or trade in goods or provision of services, including tie-in arrangements, exclusive supply agreements, exclusive distribution agreements, refusals to deal or RPM shall be an agreement in contravention of Section 3(1) if such agreement causes or is likely to cause an appreciable adverse effect on competition in India.

Section 3(5) provides that none of the prohibitions shall restrict the right of any person to restrain any infringement of any of his rights guaranteed under the intellectual property statutes of India.

Section 19(3) of the Competition Act provides further guidance for the Commission by stating that the latter shall give due regard, in determining whether an agreement has the prohibited effect on competition, to all or any of the following factors: (a) creation of barriers to new entrants in the market; (b) driving existing competitors out of the market; (c) foreclosure of competition by hindering entry into the market; (d) accrual of benefits to consumers; (e) improvements in production or distribution of goods or provision of services; and (f) promotion of technical, scientific and economic development by means of production or distribution of goods or provision of services.

[C] Section 4: Abuse of Dominance

Section 4 of the Competition Act addresses abuse of a dominant position. It is based on the EU prohibition contained in Article 102 of the Treaty on the Functioning of the EU (*see* Chapter 12 *supra*).

Section 4 provides that no enterprise or group shall abuse its dominant position. In summary, such an abuse is defined as including the imposing of unfair or discriminatory trading conditions or prices or predatory prices, limiting the supply of goods or services or a market or technical or scientific development relating to goods or services, denial of market access, imposing on other contracting parties obligations not related to the basic contract with them, and using a dominant position in one market to gain entry into another market or to protect that other market.

In making its appraisal of a complaint of abuse, the Commission must first determine both the relevant product and geographic markets.

Section 2(r), (s) and (t) of the Competition Act defines these terms. (We have previously described these concepts in previous chapters involving other competition law regimes and so will not repeat a description here.)

Section 19(4) directs the Commission to consider the following factors in inquiring whether an enterprise enjoys a dominant position or not: the market share, size and resources of the enterprise, size and importance of the competitors, economic power of the enterprise, any vertical integration, dependence of consumers, monopoly or dominant position, any entry barriers (regulatory, financial or technical), countervailing buying power, market structure and size, relative advantages, any other relevant factor.

As in the case of the EU regime, dominance itself is not sufficient for a violation. There must be a showing of abuse of that dominance.

[D] Enforcement of Sections 3 and 4

To explain the enforcement scheme, the existence of two more participants should be noted. First, under Section 16(1) of the Competition Act, the Central Government may appoint a Director-General for the purposes of assisting the Commission in conducting inquiries into contravention of any of the provisions of the Act and for performing such other functions as may be provided by the Act.

Second, by Sections 53A through 53U, there is created the Competition Appellate Tribunal ("CAT") to be a quasi-judicial body with adjudicatory powers. It hears appeals from any direction or order of the Commission made under certain specified sections of the law and also adjudicates certain claims for compensation. Any person aggrieved by any decision or order of the CAT may file an appeal to the Supreme Court of India within a prescribed period.

Section 26 of the Competition Act provides the procedure to be followed by the Commission in proceedings under Section 19 involving anticompetitive agreements or abuse of a dominant position. On receipt of a reference from the Central Government or a State Government or a statutory authority or on its own knowledge or information, if the Commission is of the opinion that there exists a prima facie case with respect to a matter, the Commission must direct the Director-General to cause an investigation to be made. After receipt of such a direction, the Director-General must submit a report on his findings within such period as may be specified by the Commission. If the Director-General's report recommends that there is a contravention of any of the provisions of the statute, and the Commission is of the opinion that further inquiry is called for, the Commission must inquire into such contravention. The Commission has issued regulations concerning the Director-General's investigations and reports, as well as other matters.

Under Section 41(2) of the Competition Act, the Director-General is given all of the powers that are conferred upon the Commission in Section 36(2). These powers include summoning and enforcing the attendance of any person and examining him on oath, requiring the production of documents, receiving evidence on affidavit, issuing commissions for the examination of witnesses or documents and requisitioning public documents.

The Competition Commission has recently asserted under Section 41 the power to conduct "dawn raids." In September 2014, the Director-General's office entered and searched the premises of a noncooperating company, JCB India Ltd., after obtaining a warrant to do so. The company, India's largest manufacturer of construction equipment, was being investigated for abuse of its dominant position in the market.

Before a final order is entered by the Commission, it is empowered under Section 33 to restrain a party from carrying on an act in violation of the relevant statutory section until the conclusion of the inquiry or entry of a final order.

If, after inquiry, the Commission finds that there has been a contravention of any of the prohibitions, it may ("pass") take any or all of the following steps authorized by Section 27 of the Act: (a) direct the party's discontinuance of the agreement or abuse of a dominant position; (b) "impose such penalty, as it may deem fit which shall be not more than ten percent of the average of the turnover for the last three preceding financial years, upon each of such person or enterprises which are parties to such agreements or abuse" [if such agreement is a cartel, the Commission may impose upon each participant to the cartel a penalty of up to three times of its profit for each year of the continuance of such agreement or 10% of its turnover for each year of the continuance of the agreement, whichever is higher]; (c) [omitted by the amendment]; (d) direct modification of the prohibited agreement; (e) direct that the enterprises concerned abide by such other orders as the Commission may pass, including payment of any costs; and (f) pass such other order or issue such directions as it sees fit.

Note the special treatment of orders to be imposed against "cartels." Section 2(c) of the Competition Act defines a cartel as including "an association of producers, sellers, distributors, traders or service providers who, by agreement amongst themselves, limit, control, or attempt to control the production, distribution, sale or price of, or, trade in goods or provision of services."

The Competition Act has an international reach which it claims under the effects doctrine. Section 32, entitled "acts taking place outside India but having an effect on competition in India," provides that the Commission has power to make inquiry and pass orders with respect to agreements, abuses of dominant positions or combinations which have or are likely to have an appreciable adverse effect on competition in the relevant market in India, notwithstanding that any of the parties are outside India or any agreement was entered into outside of India.

Section 53A(1)(B) and 53N of the Competition Act allow the Central Government or a State Government or a local authority or any enterprise or person to apply to the CAT for an order awarding compensation for any loss or damage caused by an enterprise as a result of the latter's contravention of any of the prohibitions.

[E] Mergers

The antitrust oversight of mergers and acquisitions (which are referred to as "combinations") is contained in Sections 5 and 6 of the Competition Act. Section 5 describes a regulated combination as an acquisition, merger or amalgamation of enterprises which meets the specified size thresholds. Or, to put it more specifically, a regulated combination as defined by Section 5 involves an acquisition of control over one or more enterprises brought about by an agreement or understanding between two or more persons (individual, company, etc.) which meets specified size thresholds in terms of asset value or turnover, either in India or outside. The asset value and turnover thresholds are stated in both rupees (and crores) and US dollars. The threshold levels are too detailed to be elaborated for our purposes, but they are considered to be quite high.

Section 6(1) states that "[no] person or enterprise shall enter into a combination which causes or is likely to cause an appreciable adverse effect on competition within the relevant market in India and such a combination shall be void."

Section 6(2) provides that any person or enterprise who or which proposes to enter into such a combination shall give notice to the Commission in the form specified within a specified time. Section 6(2A) states that no combination shall come into effect until 210 days have passed from the day on which the notice was given to the Commission under subsection 6(2) or the Commission has passed orders under Section 32, whichever is earlier.

Sections 20, 29, 30 and 31 set out the procedures for investigation of a combination and describe the orders which the Commission can pass with respect to the combinations. After determining the relevant product and geographic markets as directed by the Competition Act, the Commission must determine whether the combination would have the effect of or is likely to have an appreciable adverse effect on competition in the relevant market. Section 20 lists the factors to be considered, including competitors, barriers to entry, available product substitutes, innovation, vertical integration and other relevant competitive considerations.

When the Commission has issued a notice to show cause, based on its *prima facie* opinion that a combination has caused or is likely to cause an appreciable effect on competition within the relevant market in India, the parties to the combination have thirty days to respond why an investigation should not be conducted. The Commission may call for additional information and also for a report from the Director-General. The parties may be required to publish details of the combination to advise the public and persons affected with respect to the matter. Such persons likely to be affected are invited to file written objections with the Commission.

Under Section 31, after determining whether or not the subject combination has, or is likely to have, an appreciable adverse effect on competition, the Commission must either approve the combination or direct that it shall be void and not take effect. The Commission may propose an appropriate modification to the combination, giving the parties time to accept this modification within a specified period.

Where the Commission finally orders a combination to be void, the transaction and the parties are to be dealt with accordingly under any law in force.

These provisions dealing with review of combinations by the Commission also apply, pursuant to Section 32, to combinations taking place outside of India or where a party to the combination is outside of India where there is the requisite effect on competition in India.

In the latter part of 2016, it was made known that the Commission had approved more than 300 mergers and acquisitions without blocking a single transaction. Some transactions were approved only after divestitures were made.

§16.03 SOME CASE LAW

Some of the provisions of the Competition Act require further interpretation, of course, and one can sometimes look to the decisions of the Commission and the Indian courts for this additional understanding. For example, horizontal agreements relating to activities covered under Section 3(3) are "presumed" to have an appreciable adverse effect on competition in India. However, the Supreme Court of India ruled in 1986 in the case of *Sodhi Transport Co. v. State of U.P.* that the words "shall be presumed" provide no evidentiary weight by themselves and merely indicate who has the burden of proof.

As discussed above, vertical restraints such as RPM and exclusive arrangements are treated under Section 3(4) as not being *per se* anticompetitive, putting the onus on the parties and the Commission to debate whether, in a particular case, the practice has the requisite anticompetitive effect. The Commission has opined in some decisions that RPM is likely to have such an effect. However, in the 2015 decision in *Shri Ghanshyam Das Vij v. M/S Bajaj Corp. Ltd. & Others* the Commission stated that whether a vertical agreement like exclusive distribution by area or RPM restricts the competitive process always requires an analysis of the balance between the positive and negative factors listed under Section 19(3)(a)-(f) of the Act.

The concept of "dominant position" used in Section 4 of the Act and applied by the Commission is based on the concept as described by the European Court of Justice in the 1978 *United Brands* decision. According to that formula, dominance is a position of economic strength enjoyed by an undertaking which enables it to prevent effective competition being maintained on the relevant market by affording it the power to behave to an appreciable extent independently of its competitors, customers and ultimately of its consumers. The Commission confirmed in 2015 in *Shri Brajesh Asthana v. Uflex Ltd.* that proving a dominant position is not sufficient for a violation of Section 4 of the Competition Act and that abuse of that position must be established.

In the case of *M/S Fast Track Call Cab Private Limited v. M/S ANI Technologies Pvt. Ltd.* an information was filed against Ola Cabs by a group of auto rickshaw and taxi drivers who were plying their trade in Delhi. These complainants alleged abuse of dominance in violation of Section 4 of the Competition Act. They claimed that Ola Cabs had received huge funding and had a fleet of 320,000 vehicles plus 16,000 auto rickshaws giving it a market share of about 80% in India. In addition, it was alleged that Ola Cabs was unfairly incentivizing its drivers and providing customers with unfair discounts.

The Commission, in evaluating the matter, posited two relevant markets, one for radio taxis and the second for auto rickshaws. It took the *prima facie* preliminary view that Ola Cabs was abusing its dominant position by engaging in predatory pricing and providing unfair discounts to customers and drivers. The Commission then ordered a full investigation.

In August 2016 the Commission dismissed the case. It determined that Ola Cabs did not have dominance in either of the product markets. In particular, in the radio taxi market, the Commission found a highly competitive situation involving Uber, with no dominant player. Ola Cabs was also found to have no dominance in the number of auto rickshaws operating in Delhi.

There have been a number of investigations of alleged cartel activity. After prices of steel suddenly spiked, the Director-General conducted an investigation of four major steel producers for the period April 2007–March 2010. The inquiry found that five major players produced about 90% of the total domestic production of HR coil, that the production of four main steel products was concentrated among these producers and that their pricing of four main products was moving in tandem.

Although the Commission agreed with the DG that the market was oligopolistic, it concluded that the pricing policies followed by the major players did not reveal the presence of a prior agreement. Since it could not make a finding of a contravention of the Competition Act, the Commission ordered closure of the case, known as *In Re: Alleged cartelization by Steel Manufacturers*.

The provision in Section 3(5) of the Act safeguarding the right of persons to restrain infringement of, or to impose reasonable conditions, for the purpose of protecting statutory IP rights has been at the center of some cases. In *Shamsher Kataria v. Honda Siel Cars Ltd and others* (known as the *Automobiles Spare Parts Case*) the dispute pertained to agreements entered into between the car manufacturers and their suppliers of spare parts. For some of the spare parts, technical specifications were provided by the car companies to their suppliers. Under the agreements the parts suppliers were prohibited from selling the spare parts in the aftermarket unless they received the prior consent of the car companies. The Commission challenged these restrictions.

The car companies argued that the restrictions were permitted pursuant to Section 3(5) of the Act because of the technical specifications involved. The Commission responded that the companies had not been able to identify particular statutory IPR mentioned in Section 3(5) that would justify their restrictive agreements. This decision by the Commission was upheld in a decision of the CAT in December 2016. The auto manufacturers were found guilty of abusing their dominant position and entering into anticompetitive agreements with their original equipment suppliers and others.

In 2013, the Commission fined the state-run mining giant Coal India Ltd. INR 1,773 crore for leveraging its dominant position in the market for noncooking coal to force buyers into one-sided fuel supply agreements. This was one of the largest penalties levied on a public sector enterprise in such a case. In 2016, the CAT vacated that judgment on procedural grounds. The tribunal stated that the Commission's order violated natural justice inasmuch as the enforcement decision was improperly made by a panel which included members who did not hear the oral arguments in the case. On March 24, 2017 the Commission reduced the company's fine to INR 591 crore, citing mitigating circumstances.

On May 8, 2017, the Supreme Court of India upheld a decision by the Competition Appellate Tribunal to the effect that the penalty for anticompetitive practices found to be in violation of the Competition Act 2002 should be based on "relevant" turnover relating to a particular product and not on the total turnover of the multi-product company's products. The case entitled *Excel Crop Care Ltd. v. Competition Commission of India* involved bid rigging in the supply of aluminum phosphide tablets.

CHAPTER 17
South Korea

§17.01 HISTORICAL BACKGROUND

The Republic of Korea (henceforth "ROK" or "Korea"), constituting the southern portion of the Korean Peninsula, was established as a republic in 1948 and continued in that status after the end of the Korean War in 1953. It has a population of over 50 million people and is an economic powerhouse, constituting one of the world's largest economies. About half of its population is concentrated in the Seoul Capital Area. The ROK is technologically extremely advanced and has been described as having the world's fastest Internet speed and highest smartphone ownership.

However, in recent years the nation has been both financially and politically troubled. Its economic growth slowed after the 2008 global financial crisis. In 2017, the country's president was impeached and forced from office following an investigation into corruption.

Korea's principal antitrust law is the Monopoly Regulation and Fair Trade Act (henceforth "MRFTA" or "Act") which was enacted in 1980. The need for such legislation was demonstrated in the 1960s as the producers of some important products, including sugar, cement, and wheat, engaged in price fixing cartels. Moreover, for some time, the Korean economy was dominated by the *chaebols*, a form of large business group or conglomerate. The Korean Government was formerly supportive of the *chaebols*, but, since the enactment of the MRFTA, the government has sought to encourage competition among them to avoid monopolies.

In addition to considering the text of the MRFTA, readers should be aware of the Presidential Enforcement Decree which accompanies the Act and provides additional rules and standards governing the law. The most recent version of the Enforcement Decree available in English is No. 25840 effective in 2015.

As Article 1 of the MRFTA proclaims, the statute's purpose is to promote fair and free competition and to protect consumers by preventing the abuse of market dominance and excessive concentration of economic power, as well as by regulating improper cartels and unfair business practices.

§17.02 KFTC ENFORCEMENT POWERS

The MRFTA is enforced by the Korea Fair Trade Commission ("KFTC") which is a ministerial level central administrative organization operating under the authority of the Prime Minister. It also functions as a quasi-judicial body. The Chairman and Vice-Chairman are appointed by the President. There are nine commissioners serving three-year terms of office. The secretariat includes several hundred employees, including the Competition Policy Bureau, the Consumer Policy Bureau, the Anti-Monopoly Bureau, the Cartel Investigation Bureau, and the Business Trade Policy Bureau. The KFTC enforces twelve laws including the MRFTA and is considered immune from political influence.

Among these laws are the "fair trade laws," which are distinct from the antitrust laws. In Korea, small retailers and manufacturers have been considered to be victims of aggressive and unfair practices on the part of large firms, prompting special legislation. Among the fair trade and consumer protection related statutes enforced by the KFTC are the Act on Fair Labeling and Advertising, the Fair Transactions in Subcontracting Act, the Act on Door-to-Door Sales, the Fair Trade in Authorized Dealer Act, the Act on the Consumer Protection in Electronic Commerce, the Act on Fair Transactions in Large Franchise and Retail Business, the Installment Transactions Act, the Fair Transactions in Franchise Business Act, the Act on the Fair Trade in Large-Scaled Distribution Businesses, and the Act on the Regulation on Terms and Conditions. We will, however, limit our study to the antitrust regulation embodied in the MRFTA.

The enforcement focus of the MRFTA's antitrust efforts is directed at the activities of "undertakings" (in the English translation) or enterprises, meaning a person or firm who conducts a manufacturing business, service business, or any other business, including any person who acts in the interests of the enterprise.

An investigation by the KFTC can be triggered by an outside complaint or at the Commission's discretion. The alleged violator may be ordered to submit reports and given an opportunity to state its case. Experts, witnesses and others may also be asked to provide their views and information. The KFTC may carry out a "dawn raid" on the premises of the alleged violator to discover the existence of documents, books and other data pertinent to the investigation. Any person who does not cooperate with the KFTC's investigation without sufficient reason may be fined. In 2011, a consent order procedure was introduced, allowing the termination of an antitrust case by settlement.

If an administrative case is brought, the KFTC will file a decision. If a criminal case is to be brought, the case will be filed in a district court after the Public Prosecutor General has filed an arraignment.

Pursuant to Article 54(1) of the MRFTA, a party desiring review of an action of the KFTC may file a lawsuit in court, a procedure which is under the exclusive jurisdiction of the Seoul High Court. A judgment of the Seoul High Court can be appealed to the Supreme Court.

Article 56 of the MRFTA enables a party who suffers damages due to another's violation of the Act to sue in a private claim for damages. But the defendant can avoid such liability if he can show that the acts were not intentionally or negligently committed.

§17.03 CARTEL ACTIVITY PROHIBITION

A primary concern of the MRFTA is horizontal collaborative activity in the form of cartels or through bid rigging. Among the unjust concerted acts prohibited by Article 19 are agreements as to prices and other conditions of sales or services, concerted restrictions as to production, delivery, transportation or trade regions, and bid rigging, i.e., traditional cartel activity. The KFTC has issued *Guidelines for Concerted Practice Review* (2009) and also *Guidelines on Examination on Unfair Joint Conduct in Bidding*.

The *Guidelines for Concerted Practice Review* advise that the prohibited concerted activity can be in the form of a mutual understanding, not merely an express agreement. It is noteworthy also that, in a 2004 addition, Article 2-2 of the MRFTA provides that the Act applies to any extraterritorial conduct when it affects the domestic market.

These *Guidelines* also advise that, if the concerted practice can cause both restrictive effects and enhancements (efficiencies), as in the case of joint production, marketing, research and development, or purchasing, then both the positive and the negative effects must be examined to determine the propriety of the concerted activity.

The KFTC has a leniency policy which gives persons exemption or partial exemption from surcharges and corrective measures, depending on when the person made a voluntary report on the unlawful activity to the KFTC, i.e., before or after the commencement of an investigation into the matter.

After the KFTC's Cartel Policy Bureau has investigated alleged cartel activity, the Commission may issue a corrective order and impose surcharges where it finds that the enterprise has committed an unlawful collaborative act. Pursuant to Article 66, enterprises or persons that have committed unlawful collaborative acts are also subject to criminal sanctions, including imprisonment for up to three years or a fine of up to KRW 200 million. If the KFTC determines that the offense is sufficiently serious to warrant a criminal prosecution, the Commission must refer the case for prosecution to the Public Prosecutor General for arraignment.

§17.04 ABUSE OF A DOMINANT POSITION

Article 3-2 of the MRFTA prohibits abuses by "market dominating undertakings," including unjustly: (1) determining, maintaining or changing the price of goods or services; (2) controlling the sales of goods or the supply of services; (3) hindering the business activity of another undertaking; (4) unjustly impeding new competitors' market entry; or (5) transacting with the purpose of unjustly excluding competitors or unjustly and substantially impairing consumers' interests. The types of infringements and the criteria relating to abusive conduct are also further specified by the Enforcement Decree.

Article 2(7) defines a market dominating undertaking as meaning any enterprise holding a market position whereby it can determine, maintain or change the prices, quantity or quality of commodities or services or other terms and conditions of business as a supplier or customer in a particular business area individually or jointly with other enterprises. Article 7 further provides that, in order to determine whether an undertaking holds a market dominant position, market shares, barriers to entry, the relative size of competitors and any other relevant factors may be considered. In making the determination of dominance, the KFTC also considers possibilities of collusion, substitutability of goods and services, and financial strength.

Article 4 provides market share presumptions for abuse of dominance determinations. If an enterprise (except an undertaking whose amount of annual sales turnover or the amount of annual purchases in a certain line of trade is less than KRW 4 billion) has a market share in a particular business area of 50% or more, or the combined market share of three or fewer undertakings is 75% or more, then the applicable enterprise(s) is presumed to be dominant. However, in calculating these totals, enterprises with market shares of 10% or less are excluded.

In theory, at least, this description permits application of the concept of collective, as well as sole dominance.

The KFTC has issued *Guidelines for the Abuse of Market Dominant Position*, last amended in 2013, which provide standards for the determination of whether the conduct of a market dominant undertaking constitutes an abuse of a market dominant position under Article 3-2 of the MRFTA and Article 5 of the Enforcement Decree. Whether there is dominance is addressed by considering, *inter alia*, relevant market shares, entry barriers, relative size of competitors, the possibility of concerted practices and financial resources.

The criteria for determining abuse include whether there is evidenced on the part of the dominant firm a significant increase or slight decrease of the price of goods or services without any justifiable reason, a significant decrease in the volume of supply of goods and services without any justifiable reason, unjust hindrance of the business activity of other undertakings, or unjust impediments to new competitors' market entry.

Accordingly, practices which may indicate abuse of a dominant position include price abuses, supply abuses, interference abuses, restriction of market entry, exclusive dealing, tied selling, refusal to deal, predatory pricing, margin squeezing, and other exploitative conduct.

It will be seen that, by reason of the language employed in the MRFTA and the Enforcement Decree as indicated above, some of the vertical restraints which are covered in Articles 23 and 29 (discussed below) prohibiting unfair trade practices (whether or not they are collusive and irrespective of market share), including refusal to deal, exclusive dealing and tie-in selling, are also incorporated in the prohibitions applicable to abuse of a dominant position. This may lead to what some consider as "double counting." Indeed, in the *Microsoft* case in 2006 the KFTC decided that the company had abused its dominant position in the Windows PC system market, in violation of Article 3-2 of the MRFTA and also infringed Article 23 through its tie-in selling practices. By contrast, it should be noted that, in the EU's 2004 case against Microsoft Corp., the company was found only to have violated Article 82 of the EC Treaty (now Article 102 TFEU) for abusing its dominant position through the use of tie-ins.

Under Article 5 the KFTC is authorized to order a market dominant undertaking that has violated Article 3-2 to decrease prices, to halt such conduct, to announce the fact that it has received a corrective order, and the KFTC may order any other necessary measure. Article 6 authorizes the KFTC also to impose on the market dominating undertaking that has abused its dominant position an administrative fine (surcharge).

§17.05 PROHIBITION OF UNFAIR TRADE PRACTICES

Article 23 of the MRFTA prohibits unfair trade practices. It provides that no enterpriser shall commit any act which falls under any of the following subparagraphs, and which is likely to impede fair trade (acts hereinafter referred to as "unfair trade practices") or make an affiliated company or other enterprisers perform such act: (1) unfairly refusing any transaction, or discriminating against a certain transaction partner; (2) unfairly excluding competitors; (3) unfairly coercing or inducing customers of competitors to deal with oneself; (4) trading with a certain transaction partner by unfairly taking advantage of his/her trade position; (5) trading under the terms and conditions which unfairly restrict business activities of a counterpart or obstructing business activities of other enterprises; and (6) unjustly assisting persons who have "special interests." The Enforcement Decree also specifies a number of unfair trade practices.

The KFTC has published *Guidelines for Review of Unfair Trade Practices,* last revised in August 2009. They state at the outset that the prohibitions also apply to foreign firms when they operate in the domestic Korean market. We address some of these practices below:

Price discrimination: The practice is usually illegal where it helps to maintain market dominance, is intended to exclude a competitor, is not based on a rational cost standard and/or is continuous. The practice is usually legal, even if it has a competition restraining effect, where based on cost justified factors, such as quantity of goods sold, or where other reasonable grounds for the price discrimination exists, such as countervailing efficiency or consumer welfare. There is a "safe harbor" so that, if the market share of the firm committing the discrimination is less than 10% there is no violation or, where the market share cannot be calculated, the business is exempt if its annual sales are less than KRW 2 billion.

Granting unjustifiable discounts below cost sales: Unjustifiable discounts are prohibited. This involves continuing to supply goods or services at a price which is considerably lower than the supply cost without justifiable reason or to supply such goods or services at an unduly low price, thereby threatening the existence of another company or its affiliates.

Exclusive dealing: Whether dealing with another enterprise on the condition that the enterprise will not deal with competitors or potential competitors is an unfair trade practice depends on such factors as the extent of the restriction on competition, the market share of the enterprise imposing the condition, and the purpose of the exclusionary condition.

Customer or market restrictions: Whether imposing customer or market restrictions on a transaction partner is an unfair trade practice depends on such factors as the degree of the restriction imposed on the trading partner, the extent of interbrand competition in the market, and whether there is any resulting efficiency or consumer welfare enhancement.

Tied selling: Tied selling refers to an enterprise wrongfully forcing another enterprise to whom it supplies commodities or services to purchase another commodity or service from the supplier or from another business designated by the supplier. Relevant to the determination of unfairness are such considerations as whether the different goods are normally traded together in the market, the functional characteristics of the products, product integration and consumer recognition.

RPM: Article 29(1) of the MRFTA provides that no enterprise shall engage in RPM. However, a proviso adds that this prohibition shall not apply in situations of maximum price maintenance where there exist justifiable reasons. Special exceptions as to certain commodities which permit RPM are also specified, including in the case of designated literary works. Where the second party is a consignee who only receives a commission and acts as an agent, the prohibition does not apply. The KFTC has issued *Guidelines for Review of Resale Price Maintenance* (2009).

Thus, minimum price maintenance is *per se* illegal without analysis of any efficiency enhancing effects. For a violation, there must be "force" involved in that the second party has no choice but to follow the first party's instructions.

In the event of illegal unfair trade practices, the KFTC may order the enterprise to discontinue the practice, to delete any pertinent provisions from the relevant agreement, to announce the receipt of the corrective order to the public, or take other necessary corrective measures. The KFTC can also impose on the enterprise concerned an administrative surcharge.

In the case of RPM, pursuant to Article 31-2, the KFTC may impose an administrative surcharge of not more than 2% of the turnover prescribed by the Presidential Decree. In the absence of such turnover, an administrative surcharge of not more than KRW 500 million may be imposed.

Theoretically, as with other unfair trade practices, an enterprise found to have committed RPM may receive a prison term of not more than two years, but such criminal punishment is very rare.

License of intellectual property rights: Article 59 of the MRFTA provides that the statute does not apply to the exercise of rights based on the intellectual property laws. *The Review Guidelines on Unfair Exercise of Intellectual Property Rights* (2014) ("*IP Guidelines*") echo this statement. They add, however, that (at 2A) "even when the exercise seems rightful in its formality, the exercise could be subject to this Act when the actual exercise goes against the original purpose of the intellectual property rights policies so it cannot be considered as the rightful exercise of IPRs."

One of the rights of an intellectual property owner is normally the right to refuse to license another party or to license only on terms acceptable to the licensor. However, as the *IP Guidelines* point out, IP rights cannot be used as a tool for purposes of operating a cartel or for a company with overwhelming market dominance to act abusively by engaging in refusals to trade, discrimination or imposition of an excessive royalty scheme. Then the practice is likely to fall under one of the various prohibitions of the MRFTA. Also, the acquisition of IP rights as an essential part of a company's business may be evaluated as a business combination under Article 7 which deals with economic concentrations of power.

Therefore, territorial, customer and field of use restrictions, along with tying, may constitute an abuse of dominance or an unfair trade practice. This may require determination of a relevant market for purposes of analysis, including whether a technology or innovation market exists which is relevant to competition. Specific practices to be scrutinized for purpose and competitive effect include acquisition of patent rights, excusive grantbacks, exercise of patent rights by filing suits, royalty rates, refusals to license, and tying.

Patent pools, whereby patentees agree to collectively pool and manage technologies, should not be used to impede fair trade in the relevant market. Similarly, cross-licensing should not be used to result in collaborative practices among enterprises and exclude other competitors.

Settlement agreements made in the context of patent disputes are normally appropriate but should not be structured so as to extend monopolies or block market entry by competitors.

§17.06 MERGERS AND ACQUISITIONS

Mergers and acquisitions are referred to in the MRFTA as "business combinations." Chapter 3 addresses the "restriction of the combination of enterprises and control of economic power concentration." Article 7(1) of the MRFTA prohibits anyone from, either directly or through a person with a special interest, substantially restricting competition in a particular business area through a merger, stock acquisition, interlocking directorate, transfer of a business, or participation in the establishment of a new company. Joint ventures are covered where they are formed by one of these business methods.

Article 7(2) stipulates that the provisions of Article 7(1) will not apply if the parties concerned can prove to the KFTC that the proposed combination meets any of the following requirements: (1) that the promotion of efficiency attainable though the combination of enterprises is greater than the negative effect produced by the restricted competition; (2) the combination is with a nonviable company meeting the requirements prescribed by the Presidential Decree, for instance, a company whose total capital in its balance sheet is less than its paid-in capital for a reasonable period of time.

The KFTC has issued several *Guidelines* relevant to this area of regulation: *Guidelines for Reporting Business Combinations* (2012), *Guidelines for Notification on Combination of Enterprises* (2009), *Guidelines for Combination of Enterprises Remedies* (2011), and *Guidelines for the Combination of Enterprises Review* (2011).

Article 12 of the MRFTA and Article 18 of the Enforcement Decree describe the types and sizes of transactions that create a duty on the part of the acquiring party to file a notification with the KFTC. Pursuant to Article 12(6) of the MRFTA, the merger report must be filed within thirty days from the date of the merger. Where either party involved in the merger is a large corporation in terms of assets or turnover, preclosing notification is required. Many of the transactions reviewed by the KFTC in this fashion have involved mergers between foreign companies or between a domestic company and a foreign company.

After receiving notification, the KFTC undertakes its review of the proposed transaction. Transactions that are immediately deemed to lack competition-restrictive characteristics receive a "simplified review," and the results are notified to the party within fifteen days of filing the due reporting documents after the examination of the reported contents.

The Commission's review begins with determining a product market and a geographical market for examination of the relevant competitive picture for the transaction. Then the degree of post-merger market concentration is determined as the starting point for assessing the merger's effect on competition. The *Guidelines for the Combination of Enterprises Review* (as of 2011) advise that the KFTC utilizes the Herfindahl-Hirschman Index ("HHI") to determine post-merger concentration for the transaction.

In the case of horizontal mergers, the transaction is subject to simplified review if: (1) the HHI is less than 1,200; or (2) the HHI is more than 1,200 and less than 2,500 but the increase in HHI is less than 250; or (3) the HHI is more than 2,500 but the increase in HHI is less than 150. In the case of vertical or conglomerate mergers, the transaction is subject to simplified review if: (1) the HHI is less than 2,500 and the market share of the parties to the transaction is less than 25%; or (2) the ranking of each of the parties to the transaction in each area of trade is less than fourth.

With respect to horizontal mergers, in addition to the issue of market concentration, the factors to be considered include international competition factors, possibility of entries in the market, the possibility of collusion between competing businesses and the existence of similar goods and adjacent markets as a counterweight. The likely unilateral, coordination and buying power effects of the merger are also taken into account.

In determining whether a vertical combination of enterprises substantially restricts competition, the following factors are considered:

(1) in particular, the possible market foreclosure effect whereby a corporation is in a position to substantially restrict competition by hindering the purchase or sales channels of its competitors; and
(2) the increased possibility of concerted practices among rival enterprises.

In determining whether a conglomerate combination of enterprises will substantially restrict competition by eliminating potential competition, the following conditions are taken into account: (1) whether a situation is created which hinders potential competitors from entering the market; (2) whether the transaction will so significantly enhance the overall business capabilities of the combined firm that competitors will be eliminated based on factors other than price and quality; and (3) whether the combination in question will increase barriers to entry, e.g., by raising the minimum capital required for entering the market.

In general, factors that can be considered to ease any anticompetitive effect resulting from the combination include the existence of significant imports and/or of a formidable international competitor, the importance of export sales, the likelihood of new market entries, the existence of similar goods and adjacent markets, and whether buyer power exists.

Moreover, under the MRFTA, the KFTC is required to consider whether any efficiencies resulting from the merger outweigh any harm to competition. Suffice it to say that such a showing is difficult to establish.

If the KFTC decides, after reviewing a merger transaction, that it is anticompetitive, the Commission may apply any of several remedies. It may recommend or issue a corrective order requiring disposal of all or part of the stock, a divestiture of assets, transfer of the business, resignation of officers, or move to nullify a merger that has not yet occurred. For example, in 2015, the KFTC ordered Bayer Korea to dispose of its assets and rights related to an oral contraceptive pill acquired from MSD Korea.

The KFTC may also file a criminal complaint in a merger case but this is a very unusual remedy. Any party dissatisfied with the decision of the KFTC may file an objection stating the reasons thereof with the KFTC within thirty days from the receipt of notice of the decision.

§17.07 SOME CASE LAW

Since the landmark decision of the Supreme Court of Korea in 2007 in the *Posco* case, the KFTC has shown a greater caution in enforcing the abuse of dominance provisions of the MRFTA. In 1999 Posco Corporation refused to sell hot rolled coils to Hyundai Hysco Co. Ltd. ("Hysco") which wanted to manufacture the coils into cold steel plates for its affiliates. However, Posco also manufactured cold steel plates for similar purposes. The KFTC determined that Posco had abused its market dominance by unreasonably refusing to deal with Hysco. The KTFC ruling was affirmed on appeal by the Seoul High Court. However, the Supreme Court vacated this ruling, holding that, although Posco was indeed dominant, the KFTC had not proven that Posco's refusal to deal was unreasonable. The Court also found that the KFTC had failed to prove either that Posco had an anticompetitive intent or that the action was likely to cause anticompetitive effects in the market for cold steel plates. This decision has been viewed as creating an effects-based test for the abuse of a dominant position prohibition.

In recent years much of the KFTC's enforcement attention has been directed at cartel and bid rigging cases. In 2015, for example, it sanctioned companies in eighty-eight cases involving cartel-type activity but only five involving abuse of market dominance. In the first instance of foreign enterprises being criminally punished though referral by the KFTC, the court imposed criminal fines on Japanese bearing manufacturers who fixed prices in Japan which were implemented through their Korean branch offices.

In 2017, it imposed surcharges of KRW 3.24 billion on six companies which decided the agreed-upon winners, bidding prices and awarded bid amounts in the power cable industry. The KFTC also imposed fines against four Japanese and German car bearing manufacturers for fixing prices to auto parts makers and agreeing not to compete. Also in 2017, the Commission required divestiture remedies with respect to the Dow-DuPont merger.

One of the past cases which concerned an international cartel involved the imposition of fines on six global automakers, including Hyundai Motor Co., for fixing of truck prices. A very large damage suit involving the military oil bid rigging case was finally settled in 2013 for USD 132 million to be paid to the Korean Government. In 2012, the Supreme Court awarded damages in the flour cartel case. In doing so, the Court did not recognize the passing on defense, but adjusted the amount of damages to avoid double compensation.

The KFTC has kept a close eye on practices in the tech industries, given their significance in the Korean economy, if one considers, for example, the critical importance played by Samsung Electronics. A number of cases brought have involved some of the familiar US names in the technology industry (as well as in what we might call the antitrust industry), Microsoft, Intel, and Qualcomm. As we mentioned earlier, in 2005 the KFTC ruled that Microsoft had abused its dominant position by refusing to unbundle its instant messaging tools and Media Player from the package which it sold as the Windows Operating System. The Commission determined that Microsoft was also guilty of an unfair trade practice and fined it KRW 33 billion.

In 2008, after a three-year investigation, the KFTC fined Intel Corporation KRW 26 billion after finding that the company abused its dominant position in the central processing unit ("CPU") market. The Commission found that Intel offered a total of USD 370 million to Samsung Electronics and Trigem Computer between 2001 and 2005 on the condition that neither purchase CPUs from Intel's rival, AMD, Inc. Intel has faced similar challenges in various other jurisdictions, including Japan and in the EU.

The KFTC fined Qualcomm Inc. KRW 273 billion in 2009 for abusing its dominant position in CDMA modem chips, which were then used in handsets made by Samsung and LG Electronics. The Commission began a new investigation in 2014 after receiving complaints that the company was restricting competition by refusing or limiting licensing to rival chipmakers of its standard essential patents related to modem chips. The KFTC ruled in December 2016 that Qualcomm had abused its dominant position by forcing handset makers to pay royalties for an unnecessarily broad set of patents as part of its sales of modem chips. The KFTC fined Qualcomm KRW 1.03 trillion (USD 854 million). The company has had similar problems elsewhere, including in the EU and in China where it paid a USD 975 million fine. The Korean case is on appeal to the courts.

Other noteworthy developments have included the following: In 2011, the KFTC imposed fines on the multinational GlaxoSmithKline and on Dong-A Pharmaceutical, a leading pharmaceutical supplier in Korea, for entering into a "pay-for-delay deal" wherein the two agreed to share the market for original and generic drugs. These sanctions were approved by the Supreme Court in 2014. In 2014, the KFTC imposed corrective orders and penalty surcharges against Johnson & Johnson Korea for fixing minimum resale prices for Acuvue contact lenses sales to consumers by optical stores. Both the Seoul High Court and the Supreme Court rejected the company's lawsuit contesting the decision. In 2015, the KFTC signed a memorandum of understanding on antirust cooperation with the US antitrust agencies, one of a number of cooperation agreements entered into with that body's counterpart agencies.

Appendices

APPENDIX I
Selected Bibliography

A. SELECTED BOOKS AND ONLINE RESOURCES

Access to European Union Law, www.eur-lex.europa.eu.

American Bar Association, Section of Antitrust Law (various Antitrust Law Section Publications) www.americanbar.org.

American Bar Association, Section of Antitrust Law, *Competition Laws Outside the United States*, Volumes I and II (2011).

American Bar Association, Section of Antitrust Law, *FTC Practice and Procedural Manual*.

American Law Institute, *Restatement of the Foreign Relations Law of the United States* (1986).

Antitrust Division, U.S. Department of Justice, *www.justice.gov/atr*.

Antitrust Modernization Commission, *Report and Recommendations*, April 2007.

Areeda, P. and Hovenkamp, H., *Antitrust Law* (Wolters Kluwer Law & Business, 4th ed. 2013 and 2016 Supp.).

Blanke, G. and Landolt, P., *EU and US Arbitration* (Wolters Kluwer Law & Business, 5th ed. 2011).

Breyer, S., *The Court and the World* (Alfred Knopf, 2015).

Bureau of National Affairs, Inc., *Antitrust & Trade Regulation Report*, www.bna.com.

Dabbah, M.M. and Hawk, B.E., *Anti-Cartel Enforcement Worldwide*, Volumes I, II and III (Cambridge University Press 2009).

Elhauge, E. and Geradin, D., *Global Competition and Economics* (Hart Publishing, 2d ed., 2011).

European Commission-Competition, *www.ec.europa.eu/competition*.

Ewing, K., *Competition Rules for the 21st Century: Principles from America's Experience* (Kluwer Law International, 5th ed. 2016).

Ezrachi, A., *EU Competition Law* (Hart Publishing, 5th ed., 2016).

Faull, J. & Nikpay, A., *The EU Law of Competition* (Oxford University Press, 3rd ed., 2014).

Federal Trade Commission, *www.ftc.gov*.
Federal Trade Commission, *The Federal Trade Commission's International Antitrust Program*, April 2016, www.ftc.gov.
Fox, E.M. and Trebilcock, M.J., *The Design of Competition Law Institutions* (Oxford University Press 2013).
Fugate, W.L. and Simowitz, L.H., *Foreign Commerce and the Antitrust Laws* (Wolters Kluwer Law & Business, 5th ed. 2014).
Global Competition Review (Law Business Research Ltd), globalcompetitionreview.com.
Goyder, J. & Albors-Llorens A., *Goyder's EC Competition Law* (Oxford University Press, 5th ed., 2009).
Hawk, B.E. ed., *International Antitrust Law and Policy* (Fordham Corporate Law 2014).
Hovenkamp, H., *Federal Antitrust Policy* (West Academic Publishing, 5th ed. 2015).
Hüschelrath, K. & Schweitzer, *Public and Private Enforcement of Competition Law in Europe* (Springer-Verlag Berlin Heidelberg 2014).
International Competition Network, *internationalcompetitionnetwork.org*.
Jones, A. & Sufrin, B., *EU Competition Law: Texts, Cases, and Materials* (Oxford University Press 6th Ed. 2016).
Kerse, C. & Khan, N., *EU Antitrust Procedure* (Sweet & Maxwell, 6th ed. 2012).
Lianos, I. & Korah, V., *Competition Law: Texts, Cases and Materials* (Hart Publishing, 4th ed. 2015).
Pitofsky, R., Goldschmid, H. & Wood, D. *et al.*, *Trade Regulation Cases and Materials* (Foundation Press, 6th ed. 2016 Supp.).
Ramappa, T., *Competition Law in India* (Oxford University Press, 3rd ed. 2014).
Singh, A., *Competition Laws in India* (Easy Law Mate 2016).
Sullivan, L.A. and Grimes, W.S., *The Law of Antitrust: An Integrated Handbook* (West Academic Publishing, 3rd ed. 2015).
U.S. Department of Justice and Federal Trade Commission, *Antitrust Guidelines for International Enforcement and Cooperation*, 2017, *www.justice.gov*.
Van Bael, I & Bellis, J., *Competition Law of the European Community* (Kluwer Law International, 5th ed. 2009).
Whish, R. & Bailey, D., *Competition Law* (Oxford University Press, 8th ed. 2015).
Wright, C. A. *et al.*, *Federal Practice and Procedure* (3rd ed. and 2015 Supp.).

B. UNITED STATES CASE LAW

Able Sales Co. v. *Compania De Azucar De Puerto Rico*, 406 F.3d 56 (1st Cir. 2005), p. 193.
Access Telecom, Inc. v. *MCI Telecommunications Corp. et al.*, 197 F.3d 694 (5th Cir. 1999), *reh. en banc denied*, 210 F.3d 365 (2000), *cert. denied*, 531 U.S. 917 (2000), p. 52.
Alfred Dunhill of London, Inc. v. *Republic of Cuba*, 425 U.S. 682 (1976), p. 61.
Allied Tube & Conduit Corp. v. *Indian Head, Inc.*, 486 U.S. 492 (1988), p. 121.
American Banana Co. v. *United Fruit Co.*, 213 U.S. 347 (1909), pp. 45–46.
American Express Co. v. *Italian Colors Restaurant*, 133 S. Ct. 2304 (2013), p. 105.

Appendix I

American Gas Central Eastern Texas Gas Co. v. *Union Pacific Resources Group, Inc.*, 93 Fed. App'x. (5th Cir. 2004), p. 104.
American Needle, Inc. v. *National Football League*, 560 U.S. 183 (2010), p. 129.
American Society of Mechanical Engineers, Inc. v. *Hydrolevel Corp.*, 456 U.S. 556 (1982), p. 120.
American Tobacco Co. v. *United States*, 328 U.S. 781 (1946), p. 44.
Animal Science Products, Inc. v. *China Minmetals Corporation et al.*, 654 F.3d 462 (3d Cir. 2011), p. 54.
AOL/Time Warner, FTC press release of 14 December 2000, pp. 210, 384–385.
Application of Chase Manhattan Bank, 192 F.Supp. 817 (S.D.N.Y. 1961), *aff'd*, 297 F.2d 611 (2d Cir. 1962), p. 94.
Asahi Metal Industry Co. Ltd. v. *Superior Court*, 480 U.S. 102 (1987), p. 70.
Aspen Skiing Co. v. *Aspen Highlands Skiing Corp.*, 472 U.S. 585 (1985), p. 136.
Associated Press v. *United States*, 326 U.S. 1 (1945), p. 118.
Automatic Radio Manufacturing Co. v. *Hazeltine Research, Inc.*, 339 U.S. 827 (1950), p. 173.
Baxter Int'l Inc. v. *Abbott Laboratories*, 315 F.3d 829 (7th Cir. 2003), *reh. en banc denied*, 325 F.3d 954 (7th Cir. 2003), *cert. denied*, 540 U.S. 963 (2003), p. 103.
Bell Atlantic Corp. v. *Twombly et al.*, 550 U.S. 544 (2007), p. 108.
Boeing Co., et al., FTC File No. 971-0051, 1 July 1997, reported in 5 Trade Reg. Rpt. (CCH) ¶ 24,295, p. 218.
Branch v. Federal Trade Commission, 141 F.2d 31 (7th Cir. 1944), p. 181.
Brantley v. *NBC Universal, Inc.*, 675 F.3d 1192 (9th Cir. 2012), *cert.denied*, 133 S. Ct. 573 (2012), p. 155.
Broadcast Music Inc. v. *Columbia Broadcasting System, Inc.*, 441 U.S. 1 (1979), pp. 16–17.
Broadcom Corp. v. *Qualcomm, Inc.*, 501 F. 3d 297 (3d Cir. 2007), p. 121.
Brooke Group Ltd. v. *Brown & Williamson Tobacco Co.*, 509 U.S. 209 (1993), pp. 134, 191.
Brulotte v. *Thys*, 379 U.S. 29 (1964), pp. 162, 173.
Brunswick Corp. v. *Pueblo Bowl-O-Mat, Inc.*, 429 U.S. 477 (1977), p. 38.
Burger King v. *Rudzewicz*, 471 U.S. 462 (1985), p. 70.
Burke v. *Ford & Kune*, 389 U.S. 320 (1967), p. 23.
Business Electronics Corp. v. *Sharp Electronics Corp.*, 485 U.S. 717 (1988), p. 156.
California v. *American Stores Co.*, 495 U.S. 271 (1990), p. 198.
California Dental Association v. *Federal Trade Commission*, 526 U.S. 756 (1999), p. 17.
California v. ARC America Corp., 490 U.S. 93 (1989), p. 40.
Carpet Group Int'l v. Oriental Rug Importers Assn., 227 F.3d 62 (3d Cir. 2000), p. 118.
Carrier Corp. v. *Outokumpu Oyj*, 673 F.3d 430 (6th Cir. 2012), pp. 54, 71.
Ciba-Geigy, Ltd., 123 F.T.C. 842 (1997), 5 Trade Reg. Rep. (CCH) ¶ 24,182 (1997), p. 215.
Clayco Petroleum Corp. v. *Occidental Petroleum Corp.*, 712 F.2d 404 (9th Cir. 1983), *cert. denied*, 464 U.S. 1040 (1984), p. 62.
Continental Ore Co. v. *Union Carbide & Carbon Corp.*, 370 U.S. 690 (1962), pp. 63, 142.
Continental Paper Bag. Co. v. *Eastern Paper Bag Co.*, 210 U.S. 405 (1908), p. 136.

Appendix I

Continental T.V., Inc. v. *GTE Sylvania Inc.*, 433 U.S. 36 (1977), p. 158.
Copperweld Corp. v. *Independence Tube Corp.*, 467 U.S. 752 (1984), p. 18.
Dagher et al. v. *Saudi Refining, Inc., et al.*, 369 F.3d 1108 (9th Cir. 2004), *reversed sub nom. Texaco Inc.* v. *Dagher et al.*, 547 U.S. 1 (2006), p. 128.
Daimler AG v. *Bauman et al.*, 134 S. Ct. 746 (2014), p. 71.
Dee-K Enterprises, Inc. v. *Heveafil* SDN BHD, 299 F.3d 281 (4th Cir. 2002), *cert. denied*, 537 U.S. 1102 (2003), p. 78.
Dehydrating Process Co. v. *A.O. Smith Corp.*, 292 F.2d 653 (1st Cir. 1961), p. 171.
Den Norske Stats Oljeskelskap AS v. *HeereMac VOF et al.*, 241 F.3d 420 (5th Cir. 2001), *cert. denied*, 534 US. 1127, *reh. denied*, 535 U.S. 1012 (2002), p. 52.
Dr. Miles Medical Co. v. *John D. Park & Sons Co.*, 220 U.S. 373 (1911), pp. 17, 156.
Eastern R.R. Presidents Conference v. *Noerr Motor Freight, Inc.*, 365 U.S. 127 (1961), pp. 184.
Eastern States Retail Lumber Dealers' Ass'n v. *United States*, 234 U.S. 600 (1914), pp. 18, 108, 117.
Eastman Kodak Co. v. *Image Technical Services, Inc.*, 504 U.S. 451 (1992), pp. 133, 137, 154, 178.
EEOC v. *Arabian Am. Oil Co.*, 499 U.S. 244 (1991), p. 181.
Ethyl Gasoline Corp. v. *United States*, 309 U.S. 436 (1940), p. 172.
Fashion Originators' Guild of America, Inc. v. *Federal Trade Commission*, 312 U.S. 457 (1941), pp. 117–118.
F. Hoffman-La Roche, Ltd. v. *Empagran S.A.*, 542 U.S. 155 (2004), *on remand*, 388 F.3d 337 (D.C. Cir. 2004), *dismissed*, 417 F.3d 1267 (D.C. Cir. 2005), *cert. denied*, 74 U.S.L.W. 3380 (2006), pp. 33, 45, 52–55, 59, 127.
Federal Trade Commission v. *Actavis, Inc.*, 570 U.S. 756 (2013), pp. 17, 165, 183–185.
Federal Trade Commission v. *Advocate Health Care Network, et al.*, 841 F.3d 460 (7th Cir. 2016), p. 212.
Federal Trade Commission v. Anthem, 28 April 2017 (D.C. Cir. 2017), p. 212.
Federal Trade Commission v. *Borden Co.*, 383 U.S. 637 (1966), p. 188.
Federal Trade Commission v. *Brown Shoe Co.*, 384 U.S. 316 (1966), pp. 149, 182–183.
Federal Trade Commission v. *Caravel Co.*, 6 F.T.C. 198 (1923), pp. 180–181.
Federal Trade Commission v. *Compagnie de Saint Gobain Pont-a-Mousson*, 636 F.2d 1300 (D.C. Cir. 1980), p. 98.
Federal Trade Commission v. *Cement Institute*, 333 U.S. 683, *reh. denied*, 334 U.S. 839 (1948), p. 18.
Federal Trade Commission v. *H.J. Heinz Co.*, 116 F.Supp. 2d 190 (D.D.C. 2000), *rev.*, 246 F.3d. 708 (D.C. Cir. 2001), p. 204.
Federal Trade Commission v. *Morton Salt Co.*, 334 U.S. 37 (1948), pp. 189–191.
Federal Trade Commission v. *Motion Picture Advertising Service Co.*, 344 U.S. 392 (1953), *reh. denied*, 345 U.S. 914 (1953), pp. 148–149, 182.
Federal Trade Commission v. *Mylan Laboratories, Inc. et al.*, 62 F.Supp. 2d 25 (D.D.C. 1999), *revised and reaffirmed in pertinent part*, 99 F.Supp. 2d 1 (D.D.C. 1999), p. 183.
Federal Trade Commission v. *Nestles Food Co.*, 2 F.T.C. 171 (1919), p. 180.

Federal Trade Commission v. *Perrigo Co. and Alpharma Inc.*, Trade Reg. Rep. (CCH) ¶ 15,641 (D.D.C. 2004), p. 183.
Federal Trade Commission v. Penn State Hershey Medical Center, 838 F. 3d 327 (3d Cir. 2016), p. 212.
Federal Trade Commission v. *Procter & Gamble Co.*, 386 U.S. 568 (1967), pp. 207, 210–211.
Federal Trade Commission v. Staples/Office Depot, 10 May 2016 (D.D.C.), p. 211.
Federal Trade Commission v. *Staples, Inc.*, 970 F.Supp. 1066 (D.D.C. 1997), p. 208.
Federal Trade Commission v. *University Health, Inc.*, 938 F.2d 1206 (11th Cir. 1991), p. 204.
Federal Trade Commission v. *Whole Foods Market, Inc.*, 548 F.3d 1028 (D.C. Cir. 2008), p. 211.
Freedom Watch, Inc. v. *OPEC*, 766 F.3d 74 (D.C.Cir. 2014), *on remand*, D.D.C., filed 12/03/15, pp. 79–80.
General Chemicals, Inc. v. *Exxon Chemical Co., USA*, 625 F.2d 1231 (5th Cir. 1980), pp. 193–194.
General Talking Pictures Corp. v. *Western Electric Co.*, 304 U.S. 175 (1938), *on reh.*, 305 U.S. 124 (1938), p. 170.
Goodyear Dunlop Tires Operations, S.A. v. *Brown*, 564 U.S. 915 (2011), p. 71.
Grand Jury Subpoena Duces Tecum Addressed to Canadian Intl. Paper Co., In re, 72 F.Supp. 1013 (S.D.N.Y. 1947), p. 94.
Great Atlantic & Pacific Tea Co. v. *FTC*, 440 U.S. 69 (1979), p. 193.
Green Tree Financial Corp. v. *Bazzle et al.*, 539 U.S. 444 (2003), p. 105.
GTE New Media Services, Inc. v. *Bellsouth Corp., et al.*, 199 F.3d 1343 (D.C. Cir. 2000), p. 73.
Gulf Oil Corp. v. *Copp Paving Co., Inc.*, 419 U.S. 186 (1974), p. 193.
Hanson v. *Denckla*, 357 U.S. 235 (1958), p. 70.
Hartford Fire Insurance Co. v. *California*, 509 U.S. 764 (1993), p. 49.
Hilton v. *Guyot*, 159 U.S. 113 (1895), pp. 48–49.
Hoffman Motors Corp. v. *Alfa Romeo, S.p.A.*, 244 F.Supp. 70 (S.D.N.Y. 1965), pp. 75–76.
Hunt v. *Mobil Oil Co.*, 550 F.2d 68 (2d Cir. 1976), *cert. denied*, 434 U.S. 984 (1977), pp. 61–62.
Impression Products, Inc. v. *Lexmark International, Inc.*, U.S., slip opinion 30 May 2017, p. 165.
Infusion Resources Inc. v. *Minimed Inc.*, 351 F.3d 688 (5th Cir. 2003), *cert. denied*, 124 S. Ct. 2881 (2004), p. 191.
Illinois Brick Co. v. *Illinois*, 431 U.S. 720 (1977), p. 40.
Illinois Tool Works, Inc. et al. v. *Independent Ink, Inc.*, 547 U.S. 28 (2006), pp. 152, 164, 171.
Impression Products, Inc. v. *Lexmark International, Inc.*, 581 U.S. _ (2017), pp. 165.
In Re: Automotive Refinishing Paint Antitrust Litigation, 358 F.3d 288 (3d Cir. 2004), p. 94.
PolyGram Holding, Inc. v. *FTC*, 416 F.3d 29 (D.C. Cir. 2005), pp. 126, 183–184.

Appendix I

Intel Corp. v. *Advanced Micro Devices, Inc.*, 292 F.3d 664 (9th Cir. 2003), *aff'd*, 542 U.S. 241 (2004), p. 88.

Intergraph Corp. v. *Intel Corp.*, 195 F.3d 1346 (Fed. Cir. 1999), p. 137.

International Ass'n of Machinists & Aerospace Workers v. *Organization of Petroleum Exporting Countries*, 477 F.Supp. 553 (CD. Cal. 1979), *aff'd on other grounds*, 649 F.2d 1354 (9th Cir. 1981), *cert. denied*, 454 U.S. 1163 (1982), p. 62.

International Salt Co. v. *United States*, 332 U.S. 392 (1947), p. 170.

International Shoe Co. v. *Washington*, 326 U.S. 310 (1945), p. 70.

Investigation of World Arrangements with Relation to the Production, Transportation, Refining and *Distribution of Petroleum*, 13 F.R.D. 280 (D.D.C. 1952), p. 95.

Jefferson Parish Hospital District No. 2 v. *Hyde*, 466 U.S. 2 (1984), p. 154.

J. Truett Payne Co. v. *Chrysler Motors Corp.*, 451 U.S. 557 (1981), p. 38.

JLM Industries, Inc. v. *Stolt-Nielsen SA*, 387 F.3d 163 (2d Cir. 2004), p. 104.

K-Mart v. *Cartier, Inc.*, 486 U.S. 281 (1988), p. 169.

King Drug Co. of Florence, Inc. v. *SmithKline Beecham Corp.*, 791 F.3d 388 (3d Cir. 2015), *cert. denied*, 2016 WL 696150 (Nov. 7, 2016), p. 185.

Klor's Inc. v. *Broadway Hale Stores Inc.*, 359 U.S. 207 (1959), p. 117.

KM Enterp. Inc. v. *Global Traffic Tech, Inc.*, 725 F.3d 718 (7th Cir. 2013), pp. 72–73.

Kruman v. *Christie's Int'l plc*, 284 F.3d 384 (2d Cir. 2002), *cert. dismissed*, 539 U.S. 978 (2003), p. 52.

Laker Airways, Ltd. v. *Sabena, Belgian World Airlines*, 731 F.2d 909 (D.C. Cir. 1984), p. 47.

Kimble v. *Marvel Ent't*, 135 S. Ct. 2401 (2015), pp. 162, 173.

LaPeyre v. *Federal Trade Commission*, 366 F.2d 117 (5th Cir. 1966), pp. 173–174.

LePages Inc. v. *3M (Minnesota Mining and Manufacturing Co.)*, 324 F.3d 141 (3d Cir. 2003), *cert. denied*, 542 U.S. 953 (2004), p. 140.

Leegin Creative Leather Products, Inc. v. *PSKS, Inc.*, 551 U.S. 877 (2007), pp. 156–157.

Lotes Co., Ltd. v. *Hon Hai Precision Industry Co.*, 753 F.3d 395 (2d Cir. 2014), p. 54.

Luria Brothers & Co. v. *Federal Trade Commission*, 389 F.2d 847 (3d Cir. 1968), *cert. denied*, 393 U.S. 829 (1969), p. 185.

McWane Inc. v. *Federal Trade Commission*, 783 F.3d 814 (11th Cir. 2015), p. 149.

Mannington Mills v. *Congoleum Corp.*, 595 F.2d 1287 (3d Cir. 1979), p. 47.

McWane, Inc. v. *Federal Trade Commission*, 783 F.3d 814 (11th Cir. 2015), *cert. denied*, 136 S. Ct. 1452 (2016), p. 149.

Metallgesellschaft AG v. *Sumitomo Corporation of America*, 325 F.3d 836 (7th Cir. 2003), p. 52.

Metro Industries, Inc. v. *Sammi Corp.*, 82 F.3d 839 (9th Cir. 1996), *cert. denied*, 117 S.Ct. 181 (1996), pp. 50–51.

Minn-Chem, Inc. v. *Agrium, Inc.*, 683 F.3d 845 (7th Cir. 2012) (*en banc*), p. 55.

Mitsubishi Motors Corp. v. *Soler Chrysler-Plymouth, Inc.*, 473 U.S. 614 (1985), p. 101.

Monsanto Co. v. *Spray-Rite Service Corp.*, 465 U.S. 752 (1984), p. 156.

Montreal Trading, Ltd. v. *Amax, Inc.*, 661 F.2d 864 (10th Cir. 1981, *cert. denied*, 455 U.S. 1001 (1982), p. 47.

Motorola Mobility LLC v. *AU Optronics, et al.*, 775 F.3d 816 (7th Cir. 2014), *cert. denied*, 576 U.S. _ (2015), p. 55.

Mozart Co. v. Mercedes-Benz of North America, Inc., 833 F.2d 1342 (9th Cir. 1987), *cert. denied*, 109 S.Ct. 179 (1988), p. 155.
National Bank of Canada v. Interbank Card Association, 666 F.2d 6 (2d Cir. 1981), p. 47–48.
Nieman v. Dryclean U.S.A. Franchise Co., Inc., 178 F.3d 1126 (11th Cir. 1999), p. 181.
North Carolina State Board of Dental Examiners v. FTC, 135 S. Ct. 1101 (2015), p. 129.
Northern Pacific Ry. Co. v. United States, 356 U.S. 1 (1958), pp. 153–154.
Northwest Wholesale Stationers, Inc. v. Pacific Stationery and Printing Co., 472 U.S. 284 (1985), p.130.
OBB Personenverkher AG v. Sachs, 136 S. Ct. 390 (2015), p. 130–131.
Occidental Petroleum Corp. v. Buttes Gas & Oil Co., 331 F.Supp. 92 (C.D. Cal. 1971), *aff'd*, 461 F.2d 1261 (9th Cir. 1972), *cert. denied*, 409 U.S. 950 (1972), pp. 61.
Omni Capital International, Ltd. v. Rudolph Wolff & Co., 484 U.S. 97 (1987), p. 76.
O.S.C. Corporation and O.S.C. Corporation of California v. Toshiba America, Inc. and Tokyo Shibaura Electric Co., Ltd., 491 F.2d 1064 (9th Cir. 1974), p. 75.
Parker v. Brown, 317 U.S. 341 (1943), pp. 28, 130.
Palmer v. BRG of Georgia, 498 U.S. 46 (1990), p. 109.
Pennoyer v. Neff, 95 U.S. 714 (1878), pp. 69–70.
Perkins v. Standard Oil Co. of California, 395 U.S. 642 (1969), p. 192.
Perma Life Mufflers, Inc. v. International Parts Corp., 392 U.S. 134 (1968), p. 39.
Pfizer, Inc. v. Government of India, 434 U.S. 308 (1978), p. 40.
Polygram Holding, Inc. v. Federal Trade Commission, 416 F.3d 29 (D.C. Cir. 2005), pp. 126, 183–184.
Polypore Int'l Inc. v. FTC, 686 F.3d 1208 (11th Cir. 1212), *cert. denied*, 133 S. Ct. 2853 (2013), p. 205.
Prewitt Enterprises, Inc. v. Organization of Petroleum Exporting Countries, 353 F.3d 916 (11th Cir. 2003), *cert. denied*, 125 S.Ct. 62 (2004), pp. 78.
ProMedica Health Sys., Inc. v. FTC, 749 F.3d 559 (6th Cir. 2014), p. 204.
Queen City Pizza, Inc. v. Domino's Pizza, Inc., 124 F.3d 430 (3rd Cir. 1997), *cert. denied*, 523 U.S. 1059 (1998), p. 178.
Radiant Burners, Inc. v. People's Gas Light & Coke Co., 364 U.S. 656 (1961), p. 119.
Rio Properties, Inc. v. Rio Int'l Interlink, 284 F.3d 1007 (9th Cir. 2002), p. 78.
Rotec Industries, Inc. v. Mitsubishi Corp., 348 F.3d 1116 (9th Cir. 2003), *cert. denied*, 541 U.S. 1063 (2004), p. 194.
Saint Alphonsus Medical Center-Nampa, Inc. v. St. Luke's Health Sys., Ltd., 778 F.3d 775 (9th Cir. 2015), p. 204.
Scherk v. Alberto-Culver Co., 417 U.S. 506 (1974), p. 101.
Sheridan v. Marathon Petroleum Co., 530 F.3d 590 (7th Cir. 2008), p. 153.
Siegel v. Chicken Delight, Inc., 311 F.Supp. 847 (N.D. Cal. 1970), *modified*, 448 F.2d 43 (9th Cir. 1971), *cert. denied*, 405 U.S. 955 (1972), pp. 177–178.
Société Internationale pour Participations Industrielles et Commerciales, S.A. v. Rogers, 357 U.S. 197 (1958), pp. 95–96.
Société Nationale Industrielle Aérospatiale v. U.S. Dist. Court for District of Iowa, 482 U.S. 522 (1987), p. 92.
S.S. Lotus, Case of the, 2 World Court Rep. 20 (1935), p. 60.

Appendix I

St. Alphonsus Medical Center-Nampa v. *St. Luke's Health Sys. Ltd.*, 778 F.3d 775 (9th Cir. 2015), pp. 204, 212.
Standard Oil Co. of New Jersey v. *United States*, 221 U.S. 1 (1911), pp. 16, 108–109.
State Oil Co. v. *Khan*, 522 U.S. 3 (1997), pp. 17, 156–157.
Stolt-Nielsen SA v. *United States*, 352 F.Supp. 2d 553 (E.D. Pa. 2005), *reversed*, 442 F. 3d 177 (3d Cir. 2006), p. 36.
Susser v. *Carvel Corp.*, 206 F.Supp. 636 (S.D.N.Y. 1962), *aff'd*, 332 F.2d 505 (2d Cir. 1964), *cert. granted*, 379 U.S. 885, *cert. dismissed as improvidently granted*, 381 U.S. 125 (1965), p. 177.
Swift & Co. v. *United States*, 196 U.S. 375 (1905), p. 23.
Tampa Electric Co. v. *Nashville Coal Co.*, 365 U.S. 320 (1961), p. 148.
Texaco Inc. v. *Hasbrouck*, 496 U.S. 543 (1990), pp. 192–193.
Theatre Enterprises, Inc. v. *Paramount Film Distributing Corp.*, 346 U.S. 537 (1954), p. 18.
Timberlane Lumber Co. v. *Bank of America*, 549 F.2d 597 (9th Cir. 1976), pp. 46, 47.
Timberlane Lumber Co. v. *Bank of America*, 749 F.2d 1378 (9th Cir. 1984), *cert. denied*, 472 U.S. 1032 (1985), pp. 46, 47, 48, 50.
Toys "R" Us, Inc. v. *Federal Trade Commission*, 221 F.3d 928 (7th Cir. 2000), p. 149.
Turicentro, S.A. v. *American Airlines*, 303 F.3d 293 (3d Cir. 2002), p. 52.
Underhill v. *Hernandez*, 434 U.S. 308 (1978), p. 61.
Union Oil Co.,___ F.T.C ___, 5 CCH Trade Reg. Rep. ¶ 15,618 (2004), p. 184.
United States Alkali Export Association, Inc. v. *United States*, 325 U.S. 196 (1945), p. 30.
United States v. *Addison-Wesley Publishing Co.*, Civ. No. 74-5176, 1970–1979 Transfer Binder Trade Reg. Rpt. (CCH) ¶ 45,074, Case No. 2419,1976-2 Trade Cas. (CCH) ¶ 61,225 (S.D.N.Y. 1976), p. 169.
United States v. *Addyston Pipe & Steel Co.*, 85 F. 271 (6th Cir. 1898), *modified & aff'd*, 175 U.S. 211 (1899), pp. 15–16.
United States v. *Aluminum Co. of America*, 148 F.2d 416 (2d Cir. 1945), p. 132.
United States v. *Aluminum Co. of America (Rome Cable)*, 377 U.S. 271 (1964), p. 206.
United States v. *American Society of Mechanical Engineers, Inc. and the National Board of Boiler and Pressure Vessel Inspectors*, 1972 Trade Cas. (CCH) ¶ 92,028 (S.D.N.Y. 1972), p. 120.
United States v. *American Tel. & Tel. Co.*, 552 F.Supp. 131 (D.D.C. 1982), *aff'd*, 460 U.S. 1001 (1983), pp. 135–136.
United States v. *AMR Corp.*, 335 F.3d 1109 (10th Cir. 2003), pp. 134–135.
United States v. *American Tobacco Co.*, 221 U.S. 106 (1911), pp. 45, 109, 141.
United States v. Anthem, Inc., 28 April 2017 (CADC 2017), p. 212.
United States v. *Apple, Inc.*, 952 F. Supp. 2d 638 (S.D.N.Y. 2013), *aff'd*, 791 F. 2d 290 (2d Cir. 2015), *cert. denied*, 136 S. Ct. 1376 (2016), p. 120.
United States v. *Arnold, Schwinn & Co.*, 388 U.S. 365 (1967), p. 158.
United States v. *Baker Hughes, Inc.*, 908 F.2d 981 (D.C. Cir. 1990), p. 208
United States v. *Bausch & Lomb Optical Co. et al.*, 34 F. Supp. 267 (S.D.N.Y. 1940), p. 118.
United States v. *Booker*, 543 U.S. 220 (2005), p. 35.

Appendix I

United States v. *CIBA Corp.*, 1970 Trade Cas. (CCH) ¶ 73,269 (S.D.N.Y. 1970), pp. 215–216.
United States v. *Colgate & Co.*, 250 U.S. 300 (1919), p. 156.
United States v. *Concentrated Phosphate Export Association*, 393 U.S. 199 (1968), p. 30.
United States v. *Container Corp. of America*, 393 U.S. 333 (1969), p. 108.
United States v. *De Beers Consol. Mines Ltd.*, 325 U.S. 212 (1945), p. 142.
United States v. *Dentsply Int'l, Inc.*, 399 F.3d 181 (3d Cir. 2005), *cert. denied*, 546 U.S. 1089 (2006), p. 140.
United States v. *E.I. duPont de Nemours & Co. (Cellophane)*, 351 U.S. 377 (1956), pp. 22, 133, 167.
United States v. *Falstaff Brewing Corp.*, 410 U.S. 526 (1973), p. 207.
United States v. *General Dynamics Corp.*, 415 U.S. 486 (1974), p. 207.
United States v. *General Electric Co.*, 869 F.Supp. 1285 (S.D. Ohio 1994), pp. 110–111.
United States v. *General Electric Co.*, 82 F.Supp. 753 (D.N.J. 1949), pp. 141–142.
United States v. *Gillette Co.*, 1990–1992 Trade Cas. (CCH) ¶ 69,142 (D.D.C. 1990), p. 216.
United States v. *Grinnell Corp.*, 384 U.S. 563 (1966), p. 132.
United States v. *Hercules, Inc.*, 1973 Trade Cas. (CCH) ¶ 74,530 (D. Del. 1973), p. 125.
United States v. *Imperial Chemical Industries, Ltd.*, 105 F.Supp. 215 (S.D.N.Y. 1952), p. 148.
United States v. *Hsiung*, 778 F.3d 738 (9th Cir. 2015), *cert. denied*, 135 S. Ct. 2837 (2015), pp. 54–55.
United States v. *International Nickel Co. of Can. Ltd.*, Civ. No. 36-31, Federal Antitrust Laws with Summary of Cases 1890–1951, Case No. 849 (1952) (S.D.N.Y. 1946), p. 142.
United States v. *Jerrold Electronics Corp.*, 187 F.Supp. 545 (E.D. Pa. 1960), *aff'd per curiam*, 365 U.S. 567 (1961), p. 155.
United States v. *Jos. Schlitz Brewing Co.*, 253 F.Supp. 129 (N.D. Cal. 1966), *aff'd per curiam*, 385 U.S. 37 (1966), *reh. denied*, 385 U.S. 1021 (1967), pp. 214–215.
United States v. *Loew's Inc.*, 371 U.S. 38 (1962), p. 171.
United States v. *Marine Bancorporation*, 418 U.S. 602 (1974), pp. 196, 207.
United States v. *MCI Communications Corp. et al.*, 1994-2 Tr. Cas. (CCH), ¶ 70,730, p. 217.
United States v. *Microsoft Corp.*, 253 F.3d 34 (D.C. Cir. 2001) (*en banc*, per *curiam*), *cert. denied.*, 534 U.S. 952 (2001), pp. 20, 139, 161.
United States v. *Microsoft Corp.*, 84 F. Supp. 2d 9 (D.D.C. 1999) (*Findings of Fact*), pp. 20, 139.
United States v. *Microsoft Corp.*, 87 F.Supp. 2d 30 (D.D.C. 2000), *aff'd* in part, *rev.* in part, *remanded*, 253 F.3d 34 (D.C. Cir. 2001), (*Conclusions of Law*), pp. 20, 139.
United States v. *Microsoft Corp.*, 97 F.Supp. 2d 59 (D.D.C. 2000), *rev'd*, 253 F.3d 34 (D.C. Cir. 2001) (*en banc*, per *curiam*) (*Remedy I*), p. 20.
United States v. *Microsoft Corp.*, 215 F.Supp. 2d 1 (D.D.C. 2002) (*Tunney Act Proceedings*), p. 139.
United States v. *Microsoft Corp.*, 231 F.Supp. 2d 144 (D.D.C. 2002) (*U.S. Consent Decree*), pp. 20, 139.

Appendix I

United States v. *Microsoft Corp.*, 2002 WL 31654530 (D.D.C. 2002) (*Final Consent Decree*), pp. 20, 139.
United States v. *Minnesota Mining & Manufacturing Co.*, 92 F.Supp. 947 (D.Mass. 1950), pp. 151–152.
United States v. *Monsanto Co.* ("*Mobay*"), Civil No. 64-342 (W.D. Pa. 1967), 1967 Trade Cas. (CCH), ¶ 72,001, p. 124.
United States v. *National Lead Co.*, 63 F.Supp. 513 (S.D.N.Y. 1945), *aff'd*, 332 U.S. 319 (1947), p. 110.
United States v. *Nippon Paper Industries Co. Ltd.*, 109 F.3d 1 (1st Cir. 1997), *cert. denied*, 118 S.Ct. 685 (1998), *reh. denied*, 118 S.Ct. 1116 (1998), p. 51.
United States v. *Oracle Corp.*, 331 F.Supp. 2d 1098 (N.D. Cal. 2004), p. 388.
United States v. *Penn-Olin Chemical Co.*, 378 U.S. 158 (1964), pp. 205–206.
United States v. *Philadelphia National Bank*, 374 U.S. 321 (1963), p. 206.
United States v. *Scophony Corp. of America*, 333 U.S. 795 (1948), p. 74.
United States v. *Singer Manufacturing Co.*, 374 U.S. 174 (1963), p. 175.
United States v. *Sisal Sales Corp.*, 274 U.S. 268 (1927), pp. 46–45.
United States v. *Standard Oil Co.*, 1970 Trade Cas. (CCH) para. 72,988 (N.D. Ohio 1969), p. 217.
United States v. *Stolt-Nielsen S.A.*, 442 F.3d 177 (3d Cir. 2006), p. 36.
United States v. *Timken Roller Bearing Co.*, 83 F.Supp. 284 (N.D. Ohio 1949), *modified & aff'd*, 341 U.S. 593 (1951), pp. 167–169.
United States v. *Topco Associates, Inc.*, 405 U.S. 596 (1972), pp. 13, 109.
United States v. *United Shoe Machinery Corp.*, 258 U.S. 451 (1922), p. 153.
United States v. *Univis Lens Co.*, 316 U.S. 241 (1942), p. 170.
United States v. *VISA USA, Inc.*, 344 F.3d 229 (2d Cir. 2003), pp. 118–119.
United States v. *Von's Grocery Co.*, 384 U.S. 270 (1966), p. 206.
United States v. *Watchmakers of Switzerland Information Center, Inc.*, 1963 Trade Cas. (CCH), ¶ 70,600 (S.D.N.Y. 1962), *order modified*, 1965 Trade Cas. ¶ 71,352 (1965), pp. 117–118.
United States v. *Westinghouse Elec. Corp.*, 471 F.Supp. 532 (N.D. Cal. 1978), *aff'd*, 648 F.2d 642 (9th Cir. 1981), *cert. denied*, 454 U.S. 1083 (1981), pp. 175–176.
United States Steel Corp. v. *Fortner Enterprises, Inc.*, 429 U.S. 610 (1977), pp. 153–154.
Utah Pie Co. v. *Continental Baking Co.*, 386 U.S. 685 (1967), p. 191.
Verizon Communications, Inc. v. *Law Offices of Curtis V. Trinko, LLP*, 540 U.S. 398 (2004), pp. 19, 132, 136.
Vitamin C Antitrust Litigation, 837 F.3d 175 (2d Cir. 2016), p. 64.
Virgin Atlantic Airways Ltd. v. *British Airways PLC*, 257 F.3d 256 (2d Cir. 2001), p. 150.
Volkswagenwerk A.G. v. *Schlunk*, 486 U.S. 694 (1988), pp. 81–82.
Volvo Trucks North America Inc. v. *Reeder-Simco GMC Inc.*, 546 U.S. 164 (2006), pp. 188–190.
W.S. Kirkpatrick & Co. v. *Environmental Tectonics Corp.*, 493 U.S. 400 (1990), pp. 61, 62.
Water Splash, Inc. v. *Menon*, 581 U.S. _ (2017), p. 82.
Weyerhaeuser Co. v. *Ross-Simmons Hardwood Lumber Co., Inc.*, 549 U.S. 312 (2007), p. 135.

White Motor Co. v. *United States*, 372 U.S. 253 (1963), p. 158.
World-Wide Volkswagen Corp. v. *Woodson*, 444 U.S. 286 (1980), p. 70.
Yamaha Motor Co., Ltd. v. *F.T.C*, (Brunswick), 657 F.2d 971 (8th Cir. 1981), *cert. denied*, 456 U.S. 915 (1982), p. 125.
Zenith Radio Co. v. *Hazeltine Research, Inc.*, 395 U.S. 100 (1969), pp. 173, 175.
2660 Woodley Road Joint Venture v. *ITT Sheraton Corp.*, 369 F.3d 732 (3d Cir. 2004), p. 193.

C. EUROPEAN UNION CASE LAW

(1) EUROPEAN COURT OF JUSTICE, COURT OF FIRST INSTANCE AND GENERAL COURT DECISIONS

Ahlström & Others ("Woodpulp I"), ECJ 27 September 1988, [1988] ECR 5193, p. 257.
Ahlström & Others ('Woodpulp II") ECJ 31 March 1993, [1993] ECR I-1575, p. 257.
Airtours, CFI 6 June 2002, [2002] ECR II-2585, pp. 376, 385.
Areva/Urenco/ETCJV, ECJ 6 October 2004, p. 378.
AKZO Chemie, ECJ 3 July 1991, [1991] ECR I-3359, p. 331.
AKZO Nobel Chemicals and Akcros Chemicals, CFI 30 October 2003, [2003] ECR II-4771, *annulled in part*, ECJ 27 September 2004, p. 244.
Akzo Nobel NV and Others, ECJ 27 April 2017, p. 253.
Almelo and Others, ECJ 27 April 1994, [1994] ECR 1-1477, p. 343.
AM & S Europe Ltd., ECJ 18 May 1982, [1982] ECR 1575, pp. 243–244.
ANIC Partecipazioni, ECJ 8 July 1999, [1999] ECR I-4125, p. 259.
ASNEF-EQUIFAX Servicios de Información sobre Solvencia y Credito SL, ECJ 23 November 2006, [2006] ECR I -11125, [2007] 4 CMLR 6, p. 255.
BaByliss- SEB/Moulinex, CFI 3 April 2003, [2003] ECR II- 1279, p. 387.
Bayer AG, CFI 26 October 2000, *aff'd*, ECJ 6 January 2004, [2004] 4 CMLR 653, p. 298.
Bertelsmann AG v. IMPALA, ECJ 10 July 2008, p. 378.
Boehringer Ingelheim, ECJ 23 April 2002, [2002] ECR I-3759, p. 315.
Boehringer Mannheim ("Quinine Cartel"), ECJ 15 July 197, [1970] ECR 769, pp. 269, 284.
British Airways plc, CFI 17 December 2003, [2003] ECR II-5917, p. 338.
British Leyland Public Ltd. Co., ECJ 11 November 1986, [1986] ECR 3263, p. 332.
British Sugar, ECJ 29 April 2004, [2004] 5 CMLR 8, pp. 256, 330, 332.
Bronner/Mediaprint ("Oscar Bronner"), ECJ 26 November 1998, [1998] ECR I-1779, pp. 332–333, 341.
BRT v. SABAM, ECJ 30 January 1974, [1974] ECR 51, p. 341.
Cableuropa SA, CFI 3 September 2003, [2003] ECR-II -4251, p. 363.
Centrafarm v. *Sterling*, ECJ 31 October 1974, [1974] ECR 1147, p. 313.
Centrafarm BV v. *Winthrop BV*, ECJ 31 October 1974, [1974] ECR 1183, p. 313.
CEPSA Estaciones de Servicio SA v. LV Tobar e Hijos SL, ECJ 11 September 2008, [2008] ECR I-6681, p. 296.
CEWAL ("Fighting Ships"), ECJ 16 March 2000, 2000 [ECR] I-1365, pp. 343–344.
Coditel SA v. Cine Vog Films (No. I), ECJ 18 March 1980, [1980] ECR 881, p. 313.

Appendix I

Coditel SA v. Cine Vog Films (No. II), ECJ 6 October 1982, [1982] ECR 3381, p. 313.
Consten and Grundig, ECJ 13 July 1966, [1966] ECR 429, pp. 256, 259, 312.
Courage v. Crehan, ECJ 20 September 2001, 2001 ECR I-6297, p. 247.
Dansk Rørindustri, ECJ 28 June 2005; [2005] 5 CMLR 17, pp. 271, 324.
Deutsche Bahn AG and Others v. Commission, ECJ 18 June 2015, pp. 242–243.
Deutsche Börse/NYSE Euronext, GC 9 March 2015, p. 372.
Deutsche Grammophon v. Metro, ECJ 8 June 1971, [1971] ECR 487, p. 313.
Deutsche Telekom AG (II), ECJ 14 October 2010, [2010] ECR I – 9555, p. 331.
EDP – Energias de Portugal, CFI 21 September 2005 [2005] 5 CMLR 23, p.362.
EMC Development AB, GC 12 May 2010, ECR II-29, *appeal dismissed*, ECJ 31 March 2011, p. 279.
Europemballage Corporation and Continental Can Co. Inc., ECJ 21 February 1973, [1973] ECR 215, pp. 325, 327, 356–357.
Expedia, Inc. v. Autorité de la Concurrence, ECJ 13 December 2012, 4 CMLR 14, p. 260.
Gas Natural/Endesa, CFI 14 July 2006, p. 362.
Gencor Ltd., CFI 25 March 1999, [1999] ECR II-753, p. 258.
General Electric Co. (Honeywell), CFI 14 December 2005, ECR II-5575, pp. 211, 218–219, 374–375, 381–382.
General Motors Nederland BV, ECJ 6 April 2006, [2006] ECR- I -3173, p. 294.
General Motors Continental NV, ECJ 13 November 1975, [1975] ECR 1367, p. 330.
GlaxoSmithKline Services Unlimited, ECJ 6 October 2009, [2009] ECR I-9291, p. 294.
Gottrup Klim v. DLG, ECJ 15 October 1994, [1994] ECR I-5641, p. 277.
Greenwich Film Productions v. SACEM, ECJ 25 October 1979, [1979] ECR 3275, p. 341.
Groupements des Fabricants de Papiers Peints de Belgique ("Belgian Wallpapers"), ECJ 26 November 1975, [1975] ECR 1491, pp. 273–274.
GVL, ECJ 2 March 1983, [1983] ECR 483, p. 341.
Hag (No. I) (Van Zuylen Frères), ECJ 3 July 1974, [1974] ECR 731, p. 316.
Hag (No. II), ECJ 17 October 1990, [1990] ECR I-3711, p. 316.
Hilti AG, ECJ 2 March 1994, [1994] ECR I-667, pp. 332, 336.
Hilti AG, CFI 12 December 1991, ECR II-1439, p. 305.
Hoffmann-La Roche v. Centrafarm, ECJ 23 May 1978, [1978] ECR 1139, p. 339.
Hoffmann-La Roche ("Vitamins"), ECJ 13 February 1979, [1979] ECR 461, pp. 325, 327, 337, 339, 342.
Höfner and Elser v. Macrotron, ECJ 23 April 1991, [1991] ECR I-1979, p. 333.
Hugin-Liptons, ECJ 31 May 1979, [1979] ECR 1869, pp. 328, 332.
Ideal Standard, ECJ 22 June 1994, [1994] ECR I-2789, p. 317.
Imperial Chemical Industries and Others ("Dyestuffs"), ECJ 14 July 1972, [1972] ECR 619, pp. 254–255, 257, 269.
IMS Health, ECJ 29 April 2004, [2004] ECR I-5039, pp. 341–342.
Instituto Chemioterapico Italiano and Commercial Solvents Corporation ("Commercial Solvents"), ECJ 6 March 1974, [1974] ECR 223, pp. 328, 331–332.
Intel Corp, GC 12 June 2014, 5 CMLR 9, *rev*. ECJ, 20 September 2017, pp. 348–349.
Irish Sugar, CFI 7 October 1999, [1999] ECR II-2969, *aff'd*, ECJ 10 July 2001, [2001] ECR I-5333, p. 335.

Italian Flat Glass, CFI 10 March 1992, [1992] ECR II-1403, pp. 232, 338, 342.
Kali & Salz (France and Others v. Commission), ECJ 31 March 1998, [1998] ECR I-1375, p. 376.
L'Oréal v. PBVA, ECJ 11 December 1980, [1980] ECR 3775, p. 303.
Magill TV Guide/ITP BBC, ECJ 6 April 1995, [1995] ECR I-743, pp. 340–342.
Maize Seed, ECJ 8 June 1982, [1982] ECR 2015, pp. 318–319.
Marlines SA, CFI 11 December 2003; [2005] 5 CMLR 28, p. 254.
MasterCard Inc., ECJ 11 September 2014, pp. 118–119.
Maxicar and Others v. Renault, ECJ 5 October 1988, [1988] ECR 6039, p. 340.
MCI Inc., CFI 28 September 2004; [2004] 5 CMLR 26, p. 384.
Merci Convenzionali Porto di Genova SpA, ECJ 10 December 1991, [1991] ECR I-5889, p. 326.
Merck/Paranova, ECJ 23 April 2002, [2002] ECR I-3703, p. 315.
Metro v. Saba (No. I), ECJ 25 October 1977, [1977] ECR 1875, p. 302.
Metro v. Saba (No. II), ECJ 22 October 1986, [1986] ECR 3021, p. 302.
Michelin (No. I), ECJ 9 November 1983, [1983] ECR 3461, p. 337.
Michelin (No. II), CFI 30 September 2003, [2003] ECR II-4071, pp. 328, 337.
Microsoft Corp., CFI 17 September 2007, [2007] ECR II-3601, p. 347.
Microsoft Corp., GC 27 June 2012, EU:T:2012:323. p. 347.
Montecatini SpA, ECJ 8 July 1999, [1999] ECR I-4575, p. 259.
Municipality of Almelo, ECJ 27 April 1994, [1994] ECR I-1477, p. 343.
Neste Markkinointi v. Yötuuli Ky, ECJ 7 December 2000, [2000] ECR I-11121, p. 297.
Pacific Fruit Group v. Commission, ECJ 27 April 2017, p. 273.
Paranova, ECJ 8 May 2003, [2003] ECR I-4246, p. 315–316.
Parke, Davis v. Probel, ECJ 29 February 1968, [1968] ECR 55, p. 312.
Petrolessence SA, CFI 3 April 2003, [2003] ECR II-1161, p. 368.
Pharmacia & Upjohn SA v. Paranova A/S, ECJ 12 October 1999, [1999] ECR I-6954, pp. 315–316.
Philip Morris/Rothmans, ECJ 17 November 1987, [1987] ECR 4487, pp. 357–358.
Piau, CFI 26 January 2005, [2005] ECR II - 209, p. 344.
Post Danmark, ECJ 6 October 2015, EU:C:2015, p. 339.
Procter & Gamble/Gillette, ECJ 15 July 2005, p. 375.
Pronuptia de Paris GmbH v. Pronuptia de Paris Irmgard Schillgallis, ECJ 28 January 1986, [1986] ECR 353, p. 304.
Royal Philips Electronics BV, CFI 3 April 2003, [2003] ECR II-1433, pp. 363, 387.
RTE and ITP ("Magill"), ECJ 6 April 1995, [1995] ECR I-743, pp. 340–342, 346.
Ryanair Holdings plc, GC 6 July 2010, [2010] ECR II- 3457, p. 372.
SACEM (No. II), ECJ 13 July 1989, [1989] ECR 2811, p. 331.
Saint-Gobain Glass France SA and Others, GC 27 March 2014, p. 273.
Sandoz Prodotti Farmaceutici, ECJ 11 January 1990, [1990] ECR I-45, p. 254.
Schneider Electric SA, ECJ 20 July 2009, p. 386.
Schneider Electric SA, CFI 22 October 2002, [2002] ECR II-4071, p. 386.
Schneider Electric SA, CFI 11 July 2007, p. 386.
Secil / Holderbank/Cimpor – Portuguese Republic, ECJ 22 June 2004, p. 364.
Siemens/Areva, Press Release IP/12618, 18 June 2012, p. 379.

Appendix I

SPCA/Kali und Salz – MdK/Treuhand, ECJ 31 March 1998, [1998] ECR I-1375, pp. 373, 376.
Suiker Unie ("Sugar Cartel"), ECJ 16 December 1975, [1975] ECR 1663], p. 286.
Sun Chemical Group, CFI 9 July 2007, [2007] ECR II- 2149, pp. 369, 371.
Telefónica SA/ Portugal Telecom, GC 28 June 2016, p. 379.
Télémarketing v. CLT and IPB, ECJ 3 October 1985, [1986] ECR 3261, p. 332.
TeliaSonera Sverige, ECJ 17 February 2011, [2011] ECR I – 527, p. 331.
Terrapin (Overseas) v. Terranova, ECJ 22 June 1976, [1976] ECR 1039, 2 CMLR 482, p. 317.
Tetra Laval / Sidel, CFI 25 October 2002, [2002] ECR II-4381, pp. 375, 386.
Tetra Pak International SA (No. I), CFI 10 July 1990, [1990] ECR II-309, p. 339.
Tetra Pak International SA (No. II), ECJ 14 November 1996, [1996] ECR I-5951, pp. 330, 335, 336.
Thyssen Stahl AG, ECJ 2 October 2003, ECR I-10885, pp. 270–271.
Tiercé Ladbroke, CFI 12 June 1997, [1997] ECR II-923, p. 341.
Tomra Systems ASA and Others, ECJ 19 April 2012, pp. 338–339.
Tournier, ECJ 13 July 1989, [1989] ECR 2521, p. 341.
UK Agricultural Tractor Registration Exchange, CFI 27 October 1994, *aff'd*, ECJ 28 May 1998, [1998] ECR I-3175, p. 270.
United Brands, ECJ 14 February 1978, [1978] ECR 207, pp. 325, 329–330, 438.
UPS/TNT Express, GC 7 March 2017, p. 389.
Van Den Bergh Foods (HB Ice Cream), CFI 23 October 2003, [2003] ECR II-4653, pp. 265, 338.
Vereeniging van Cementhandelaren, ECJ 17 October 1972, [1972] ECR 977, p. 259.
Vichy, CFI 27 February 1992, [1992] ECR II-415, p. 303.
Viho Europe BV, ECJ 24 October 1996, ECR I-5457, p. 307.
Volkswagen v. Commission, ECJ 6 July 2000, p. 296.
Volvo v. Veng (UK), 5 October 1988, [1988] ECR 6211, p. 340.
Windsurfing International Inc., ECJ 25 February 1986, [1986] ECR 611, pp. 305, 336.
Zino Davidoff SA, ECJ 20 November 2001, [2001] ECR I-8691, pp. 314–315.

(2) EUROPEAN COMMISSION DECISIONS

Accor/Hilton/Six Continents, 19 May 2003, IP/03/706, p. 387.
Aegean/Olympic II, 9 October 2013, p. 373.
Aer Lingus/British Midland Airways, 26 February 1992, 1992 OJ L 96/34, p. 333.
Aérospatiale /Alenia /De Havilland, 2 October 1991, 1991 OJ L 334/42, p. 380.
Air France/ KLM/ Alitalia and Delta, Commission press release of 12 May 2015, p. 288.
Air Liquide/Messer, 15 March 2004, IP/04/342, p. 377.
Alcan Aluminium /Alusuisse Lonza Group, 14 March 2000; [2002] 5 CMLR 724, p. 385.
Anglo American Corp./Lonrho, 23 April 1997, 1998 OJ L 149/21, p. 361.
AOL/ Time Warner, 11 October 2000, p. 210.
Apple Inc. and Others (e-books), press release of 13 December 2012, IP / 12// 1367, p. 115.
Areva/Urenco/ETCJV, 6 October 2004, p. 378.

Appendix I

Astra, 23 December 1992, OJ L 20/23, [1994] 5 CMLR 226, p. 287.
AT&T / Time Warner, 14 March 2017, p. 385.
BASF/Eurodiol/Pantochim, 11 July 2001, IP/01/984, p. 373.
Belgian Wallpapers, 23 July 1974, 1974 OJ L 237, pp. 273–274.
Boeing/McDonnell Douglas, 30 July 1997, 1997 OJ L 336/16, p. 380.
British Airways, American Airlines and Iberia, 14 July 2010, p. 288.
BSCH/Champalimaud, 20 July 1999, M. 1616, p. 364.
BT/AT&T, 30 March 1999, p. 378.
BT/SES/Astra, 23 December 1992, 1993 OJ L 20/23, p. 287.
Burroughs/Delplanque, 22 December 1971, 1972 OJ L 13, pp. 317–318.
Burroughs-Geha, 22 December 1971, 1972 OJ L 13, pp. 317–318.
Cartonboard, 13 July 1994, 1994 OJ L 243/1; [1994] 5 CMLR 547, p. 271.
Celanese/Degussa/JV, 11 June 2003, 2004 OJ L 38/47, p. 387.
Cement Cartel, 30 November 1994, 1994 OJ L 343, p. 271.
Cemex/Holcim assets, 9 September 2014, p. 371.
Clearstream, 2 June 2004, IP/04/705; [2005] 5 CMLR 1302, p. 334.
Coca- Cola I, 13 October 1988, IP (88) 615 COCA-COLA, pp. 337–338.
Coca-Cola II, 22 June 2005, IP/05/775, pp. 337–338.
Covisint, 31 July 2001, IP/01/1155 (comfort letter), p. 278.
Continental Can, 9 December 1971, 1972 OJ L 7, pp. 325, 356–357.
Davide Campari Milana, 23 December 1977, 1978 OJ L 70, p. 314.
DeLaval/Stork, 25 July 1977, 1977 OJ L 215, p. 286.
De Post / La Poste, 5 December 2001, 2002 OJ L 61/32, p. 336.
Deutsche Börse / LSE, 29 March 2017, p. 389.
Deutsche Post, 25 July 2001, 2001 OJ L 331/40, p. 331.
Deutsche Buchpreisbindung, 22 March 2002, p. 306.
Deutsche Telekom II, 21 May 2003, IP/03/717, p. 331.
Distillers, 20 December 1977, 1978 OJ L 50, p. 307.
Dutch Brick Producers, 3 May 1994, 1994 OJ L 131/15, p. 275.
E.ON Ruhrgas, 8 July 2009, p. 273.
ECS/Akzo, 14 December 1985, 1985 OJ L 374, pp. 253, 325, 331.
Eurofix-Bauco v. Hilti, 22 December 1987, 1988 OJ L65/19, [1989] 4 CMLR677, p. 332.
Euro LIBOR and Yen LIBOR, 4 December 2013, p. 273.
European Cement Association (Cembureau), press release of 30 November 1994, p. 271.
Ford/Volkswagen, 23 December 1992, 1993 OJ L 20/14, p. 287.
Gas Natural/ Endesa, 15 November 2005, p. 362.
GEMA I, 2 June 1971, 1971 OJ L 134, p. 341.
Gencor / Lonrho, 24 April 1996, 1997 OJ L 11/30, pp. 361, 368, 376.
General Electric/Honeywell, 3 July 2001, 2004 OJ L 48/1, pp. 211, 218, 219, 375, 381, 382, 386–387.
General Electric Aircraft Engines/Pratt & Whitney, 14 September 1999, 2000 OJ L 58/16, pp. 287–288.
Gillette/Wilkinson, 11 November 1992, 1993 OJ L 116/21, p. 358.
Google/Doubleclick, 11 March 2008, p. 374.

Appendix I

Groupement des Fabricants de Papier Peints de Belgique ("Belgian Wallpapers"), 23 July 1974, 1974 OJ L 237, p. 273.
Guinness/Grand Metropolitan, 15 October 1997, 1998 OJ L 288/24, p. 374.
Holcim/Cemex West, 5 June 2014, p. 371.
Intel Corp., 13 May 2009, OJ C 227/07, p. 450.
Intel/McAfee, 26 January 2011, p. 375.
IBM, press release of 20 September 2011 IP/11/1044, p. 336.
Italian Flat Glass, 7 December 1988, 1989 OJ 133, pp. 232, 338, 342.
JCI/VB/ FLAMM, 5 October 2007, p. 373.
Kali und Salz/MdK/Treuhand (No. 1), 14 December 1993, 1994 OJ L 186/30, *rev.* ECJ 31 March 1998, 1998 ECR I-1375, p. 373.
Kali und Salz/MdK/Treuhand (No. 2), 9 July 1998, M. 308, p. 373.
Kodak, 30 June 1970, 1970 OJ L 147, p. 307.
Maize Seed, 21 September 1978, 1978 OJ L 286/23, pp. 318–319.
MasterCard Inc., 19 December 2007, p. 285.
MCI WorldCom/Sprint, 28 June 2000, 2003 OJ L 300/1, pp. 383–384.
Michelin (No. I), 7 October 1981, 1981 OJ L 353/33, *aff'd*, ECJ 9 November 1983, 1983 ECR 3461, pp. 326, 327, 337.
Michelin (No. II), 20 June 2001, 2002 OJ L 143/1, aff'd, CFI 30 September 2003, T-203/01, p. 337.
Microsoft Corp., 17 July 1994, [1994] 5 CMLR 143, p. 345.
Microsoft Corp., 24 March 2004, OJ 2007 L 32/23, p. 346.
Microsoft Corp., 12 July 2006, p. 347.
Microsoft Corp., 27 February 2008, p. 347.
Microsoft Corp. (Tying), 6 March 2013, pp. 335–336, 422.
Moosehead/Whitbread, 23 March 1990, 1990 OJ L 100, p. 314.
Motorola, Enforcement of GPRS standard essential patents, 29 April 2014, p. 279.
Napier Brown v. *British Sugar*, 18 July 1988, 1988 OJ L 284/41, p. 326.
National Sulphuric Acid Association, 9 July 1980, 1980 OJ L 260, pp. 277–278.
Nestlé/Perrier, 22 July 1992, 1992 OJ L 356/1, p. 376.
News Corp/BSkyB, 21 December 2010, p. 364.
NYNAS/Shell/Harburg Refinery, 2 September 2013, p. 373.
NV IAZ International Belgium, 8 November 1983, ECR 3369, p. 274.
Optical Fibers, 14 July 1986, 1986 OJ L 236/30, p. 287.
Oracle/PeopleSoft, 26 October 2004, IP/04/1312, p. 388.
Pfizer/Pharmacia, 27 February 2003, IP/03/293, pp. 387–388.
Plasterboard, 27 November 2002, 2005 OJ L 166/8, p. 272.
Polypropylene, 23 April 1986, 1986 OJ L 230/1, p. 270.
Pre-Insulated Pipe Cartel Re, 21 October 1998, OJ [1999] L 24/48; [1999] 4 CMLR 402, p. 271.
Procter & Gamble /Gillette, 15 July 2005, IP/05/ 955, p. 375.
Prym/Beka, 8 October 1973, 1973 OJ L 296, p. 284.
PVC (polyvinylchloride), 27 July 1994, OJ [1994] L 239/14, pp. 274–275.
Quinine Cartel, 16 July 1969, 1969 OJ L 192, pp. 269, 284.
Raymond/Nagoya Rubber Co., 9 June 1972, 1972 OJ L 143, p. 318.

Rolled Zinc, 14 December 1982, 1982 OJ L 362, p. 284.
Saint Gobain Glass, 12 November 2008, p. 273.
Samsung - Enforcement of UMTS standard essential patents, 29 April 2014, pp. 279–280.
Sanofi – Synthélabo/Aventis, 26 April 2004, IP/04/545, p. 388.
Sea Containers/Stena Sealink, 21 December 1993, 1994 OJ L 15/8, p. 333.
Shell/Montecatini, 8 June 1994, 1994 OJ L 332/48, p. 287.
Siemens/Areva, 20 December 2012, p. 379.
Slovak Telekom, 15 October 2014, p. 334.
SOCEMAS, 17 July 1968, 1968 OJ L 201/4, pp. 277–278.
Sogecable/Canalsatellite, 14 August 2002, M. 2845, p. 373.
Sony/BMG, 03 October 2007, p. 378.
Synthetic Fibres, 4 July 1984, OJ [1984] L 207/17, [1985] 1 CMLR 787, p. 275.
Telefónica SA/Portugal Telecom SGPS SA, 23 January 2013, p. 379.
Tetra Pak I, 26 July 1988, OJ [1988] L 272/27, [1988] 4 CMLR 881, pp. 339–340.
Tetra Pak II, 24 July 1991, OJ [1992] L 72, [1992] 4 CMLR 551, p. 336.
Thomson/Reuters, 19 February 2008, p. 374.
Twenty-First Century Fox, Inc / Sky, Commission press release of 7 April 2017, pp. 364–365.
Vacuum Interrupters, 20 January 1977, OJ [1977], L 48, p. 286.
Vichy, Re, 11 January 1991, OJ [1991] L75/57, p. 303.
Visa International-Multilateral Interchange Fee, 24 July 2002, OJ [2002] L 318/17, [2003] 4 CMLR 283, p. 285.
Vitamins Cartel, 21 November 2001, OJ [2003] L 6/1, p. 272.
Volvo/Scania, 29 May 2001, OJ [2001] L 143, [2001] 5 CMLR 11, p. 385.
WorldCom/MCI, 8 July 1998, OJ [1999] 116/1, [1999] 5 CMLR 876, pp. 383–384.
Zinc Producer Group, 6 August 1984, OJ [1984] L 220/27, [1985] 2 CMLR 108, p. 270.
3G Patent Platform Partnership, 16 July 2003, IP/03/1026, p. 322.

APPENDIX II

Council Regulation (EC) No 1/2003 of 16 December 2002 on the Implementation of the Rules on Competition Laid Down in Articles 81 and 82 of the Treaty[*]

(Text with EEA relevance)

Official Journal L 001, 04/01/2003 P. 0001 - 0025
Council Regulation (EC) No 1/2003
of 16 December 2002
on the implementation of the rules on competition laid down in Articles 81 and 82 of the Treaty
(Text with EEA relevance)
THE COUNCIL OF THE EUROPEAN UNION,
Having regard to the Treaty establishing the European Community, and in particular Article 83 thereof,
Having regard to the proposal from the Commission[1],
Having regard to the opinion of the European Parliament[2],
Having regard to the opinion of the European Economic and Social Committee[3],
Whereas:

(1) In order to establish a system which ensures that competition in the common market is not distorted, Articles 81 and 82 of the Treaty must be applied effectively and uniformly in the Community. Council Regulation No 17 of 6 February 1962, First

---

[*] © European Union, http://eur-lex.europa.eu/, 1998-2017.
1. OJ C 365 E, 19.12.2000, p. 284.
2. OJ C 72 E, 21.3.2002, p. 305.
3. OJ C 155, 29.5.2001, p. 73.

Appendix II

Regulation implementing Articles 81 and 82[4] of the Treaty[5], has allowed a Community competition policy to develop that has helped to disseminate a competition culture within the Community. In the light of experience, however, that Regulation should now be replaced by legislation designed to meet the challenges of an integrated market and a future enlargement of the Community.

(2) In particular, there is a need to rethink the arrangements for applying the exception from the prohibition on agreements, which restrict competition, laid down in Article 81(3) of the Treaty. Under Article 83(2)(b) of the Treaty, account must be taken in this regard of the need to ensure effective supervision, on the one hand, and to simplify administration to the greatest possible extent, on the other.

(3) The centralised scheme set up by Regulation No 17 no longer secures a balance between those two objectives. It hampers application of the Community competition rules by the courts and competition authorities of the Member States, and the system of notification it involves prevents the Commission from concentrating its resources on curbing the most serious infringements. It also imposes considerable costs on undertakings.

(4) The present system should therefore be replaced by a directly applicable exception system in which the competition authorities and courts of the Member States have the power to apply not only Article 81(1) and Article 82 of the Treaty, which have direct applicability by virtue of the case-law of the Court of Justice of the European Communities, but also Article 81(3) of the Treaty.

(5) In order to ensure an effective enforcement of the Community competition rules and at the same time the respect of fundamental rights of defence, this Regulation should regulate the burden of proof under Articles 81 and 82 of the Treaty. It should be for the party or the authority alleging an infringement of Article 81(1) and Article 82 of the Treaty to prove the existence thereof to the required legal standard. It should be for the undertaking or association of undertakings invoking the benefit of a defence against a finding of an infringement to demonstrate to the required legal standard that the conditions for applying such defence are satisfied. This Regulation affects neither national rules on the standard of proof nor obligations of competition authorities and courts of the Member States to ascertain the relevant facts of a case, provided that such rules and obligations are compatible with general principles of Community law.

(6) In order to ensure that the Community competition rules are applied effectively, the competition authorities of the Member States should be associated more closely with their application. To this end, they should be empowered to apply Community law.

---

4. The title of Regulation No 17 has been adjusted to take account of the renumbering of the Articles of the EC Treaty, in accordance with Article 12 of the Treaty of Amsterdam; the original reference was to Articles 85 and 86 of the Treaty.
5. OJ 13, 21.2.1962, p. 204/62. Regulation as last amended by Regulation (EC) No 1216/1999 (OJ L 148, 15.6.1999, p. 5).

Appendix II

(7) National courts have an essential part to play in applying the Community competition rules. When deciding disputes between private individuals, they protect the subjective rights under Community law, for example by awarding damages to the victims of infringements. The role of the national courts here complements that of the competition authorities of the Member States. They should therefore be allowed to apply Articles 81 and 82 of the Treaty in full.

(8) In order to ensure the effective enforcement of the Community competition rules and the proper functioning of the cooperation mechanisms contained in this Regulation, it is necessary to oblige the competition authorities and courts of the Member States to also apply Articles 81 and 82 of the Treaty where they apply national competition law to agreements and practices which may affect trade between Member States. In order to create a level playing field for agreements, decisions by associations of undertakings and concerted practices within the internal market, it is also necessary to determine pursuant to Article 83(2)(e) of the Treaty the relationship between national laws and Community competition law. To that effect it is necessary to provide that the application of national competition laws to agreements, decisions or concerted practices within the meaning of Article 81(1) of the Treaty may not lead to the prohibition of such agreements, decisions and concerted practices if they are not also prohibited under Community competition law. The notions of agreements, decisions and concerted practices are autonomous concepts of Community competition law covering the coordination of behaviour of undertakings on the market as interpreted by the Community Courts. Member States should not under this Regulation be precluded from adopting and applying on their territory stricter national competition laws which prohibit or impose sanctions on unilateral conduct engaged in by undertakings. These stricter national laws may include provisions which prohibit or impose sanctions on abusive behaviour toward economically dependent undertakings. Furthermore, this Regulation does not apply to national laws which impose criminal sanctions on natural persons except to the extent that such sanctions are the means whereby competition rules applying to undertakings are enforced.

(9) Articles 81 and 82 of the Treaty have as their objective the protection of competition on the market. This Regulation, which is adopted for the implementation of these Treaty provisions, does not preclude Member States from implementing on their territory national legislation, which protects other legitimate interests provided that such legislation is compatible with general principles and other provisions of Community law. In so far as such national legislation pursues predominantly an objective different from that of protecting competition on the market, the competition authorities and courts of the Member States may apply such legislation on their territory. Accordingly, Member States may under this Regulation implement on their territory national legislation that prohibits or imposes sanctions on acts of unfair trading practice, be they unilateral or contractual. Such legislation pursues a specific objective, irrespective of the actual or presumed effects of such acts on competition on the market. This is particularly the case of legislation which prohibits undertakings from imposing on their trading partners, obtaining or attempting to obtain from them terms and conditions that are unjustified, disproportionate or without consideration.

Appendix II

(10) Regulations such as 19/65/EEC[6], (EEC) No 2821/71[7], (EEC) No 3976/87[8], (EEC) No 1534/91[9], or (EEC) No 479/92[10] empower the Commission to apply Article 81(3) of the Treaty by Regulation to certain categories of agreements, decisions by associations of undertakings and concerted practices. In the areas defined by such Regulations, the Commission has adopted and may continue to adopt so called "block" exemption Regulations by which it declares Article 81(1) of the Treaty inapplicable to categories of agreements, decisions and concerted practices. Where agreements, decisions and concerted practices to which such Regulations apply nonetheless have effects that are incompatible with Article 81(3) of the Treaty, the Commission and the competition authorities of the Member States should have the power to withdraw in a particular case the benefit of the block exemption Regulation.

(11) For it to ensure that the provisions of the Treaty are applied, the Commission should be able to address decisions to undertakings or associations of undertakings for the purpose of bringing to an end infringements of Articles 81 and 82 of the Treaty. Provided there is a legitimate interest in doing so, the Commission should also be able to adopt decisions which find that an infringement has been committed in the past even if it does not impose a fine. This Regulation should also make explicit provision for the Commission's power to adopt decisions ordering interim measures, which has been acknowledged by the Court of Justice.

---

6. Council Regulation No 19/65/EEC of 2 March 1965 on the application of Article 81(3) (The titles of the Regulations have been adjusted to take account of the renumbering of the Articles of the EC Treaty, in accordance with Article 12 of the Treaty of Amsterdam; the original reference was to Article 85(3) of the Treaty) of the Treaty to certain categories of agreements and concerted practices (OJ 36, 6.3.1965, p. 533). Regulation as last amended by Regulation (EC) No 1215/1999 (OJ L 148, 15.6.1999, p. 1).
7. Council Regulation (EEC) No 2821/71 of 20 December 1971 on the application of Article 81(3) (The titles of the Regulations have been adjusted to take account of the renumbering of the Articles of the EC Treaty, in accordance with Article 12 of the Treaty of Amsterdam; the original reference was to Article 85(3) of the Treaty) of the Treaty to categories of agreements, decisions and concerted practices (OJ L 285, 29.12.1971, p. 46). Regulation as last amended by the Act of Accession of 1994.
8. Council Regulation (EEC) No 3976/87 of 14 December 1987 on the application of Article 81(3) (The titles of the Regulations have been adjusted to take account of the renumbering of the Articles of the EC Treaty, in accordance with Article 12 of the Treaty of Amsterdam; the original reference was to Article I 85(3) of the Treaty) of the Treaty to certain categories of agreements and concerted practices in the air transport sector (OJ L 374, 31.12.1987, p. 9). Regulation as last amended by the Act of Accession of 1994.
9. Council Regulation (EEC) No 1534/91 of 31 May 1991 on the application of Article 81(3) (The titles of the Regulations have been adjusted to take account of the renumbering of the Articles of the EC Treaty, in accordance with Article 12 of the Treaty of Amsterdam; the original reference was to Article 85(3) of the Treaty) of the Treaty to certain categories of agreements, decisions and concerted practices in the insurance sector (OJ L 143, 7.6.1991, p. 1).
10. Council Regulation (EEC) No 479/92 of 25 February 1992 on the application of Article 81(3) (The titles of the Regulations have been adjusted to take account of the renumbering of the Articles of the EC Treaty, in accordance with Article 12 of the Treaty of Amsterdam; the original reference was to Article 85(3) of the Treaty) of the Treaty to certain categories of agreements, decisions and concerted practices between liner shipping companies (Consortia) (OJ L 55, 29.2.1992, p. 3). Regulation amended by the Act of Accession of 1994.

(12) This Regulation should make explicit provision for the Commission's power to impose any remedy, whether behavioural or structural, which is necessary to bring the infringement effectively to an end, having regard to the principle of proportionality. Structural remedies should only be imposed either where there is no equally effective behavioural remedy or where any equally effective behavioural remedy would be more burdensome for the undertaking concerned than the structural remedy. Changes to the structure of an undertaking as it existed before the infringement was committed would only be proportionate where there is a substantial risk of a lasting or repeated infringement that derives from the very structure of the undertaking.

(13) Where, in the course of proceedings which might lead to an agreement or practice being prohibited, undertakings offer the Commission commitments such as to meet its concerns, the Commission should be able to adopt decisions which make those commitments binding on the undertakings concerned. Commitment decisions should find that there are no longer grounds for action by the Commission without concluding whether or not there has been or still is an infringement. Commitment decisions are without prejudice to the powers of competition authorities and courts of the Member States to make such a finding and decide upon the case. Commitment decisions are not appropriate in cases where the Commission intends to impose a fine.

(14) In exceptional cases where the public interest of the Community so requires, it may also be expedient for the Commission to adopt a decision of a declaratory nature finding that the prohibition in Article 81 or Article 82 of the Treaty does not apply, with a view to clarifying the law and ensuring its consistent application throughout the Community, in particular with regard to new types of agreements or practices that have not been settled in the existing case-law and administrative practice.

(15) The Commission and the competition authorities of the Member States should form together a network of public authorities applying the Community competition rules in close cooperation. For that purpose it is necessary to set up arrangements for information and consultation. Further modalities for the cooperation within the network will be laid down and revised by the Commission, in close cooperation with the Member States.

(16) Notwithstanding any national provision to the contrary, the exchange of information and the use of such information in evidence should be allowed between the members of the network even where the information is confidential. This information may be used for the application of Articles 81 and 82 of the Treaty as well as for the parallel application of national competition law, provided that the latter application relates to the same case and does not lead to a different outcome. When the information exchanged is used by the receiving authority to impose sanctions on undertakings, there should be no other limit to the use of the information than the obligation to use it for the purpose for which it was collected given the fact that the sanctions imposed on undertakings are of the same type in all systems. The rights of defence enjoyed by undertakings in the various systems can be considered as sufficiently equivalent. However, as regards natural persons, they may be subject to substantially different types of sanctions across the various systems. Where that is the case, it is necessary to

ensure that information can only be used if it has been collected in a way which respects the same level of protection of the rights of defence of natural persons as provided for under the national rules of the receiving authority.

(17) If the competition rules are to be applied consistently and, at the same time, the network is to be managed in the best possible way, it is essential to retain the rule that the competition authorities of the Member States are automatically relieved of their competence if the Commission initiates its own proceedings. Where a competition authority of a Member State is already acting on a case and the Commission intends to initiate proceedings, it should endeavour to do so as soon as possible. Before initiating proceedings, the Commission should consult the national authority concerned.

(18) To ensure that cases are dealt with by the most appropriate authorities within the network, a general provision should be laid down allowing a competition authority to suspend or close a case on the ground that another authority is dealing with it or has already dealt with it, the objective being that each case should be handled by a single authority. This provision should not prevent the Commission from rejecting a complaint for lack of Community interest, as the case-law of the Court of Justice has acknowledged it may do, even if no other competition authority has indicated its intention of dealing with the case.

(19) The Advisory Committee on Restrictive Practices and Dominant Positions set up by Regulation No 17 has functioned in a very satisfactory manner. It will fit well into the new system of decentralised application. It is necessary, therefore, to build upon the rules laid down by Regulation No 17, while improving the effectiveness of the organisational arrangements. To this end, it would be expedient to allow opinions to be delivered by written procedure. The Advisory Committee should also be able to act as a forum for discussing cases that are being handled by the competition authorities of the Member States, so as to help safeguard the consistent application of the Community competition rules.

(20) The Advisory Committee should be composed of representatives of the competition authorities of the Member States. For meetings in which general issues are being discussed, Member States should be able to appoint an additional representative. This is without prejudice to members of the Committee being assisted by other experts from the Member States.

(21) Consistency in the application of the competition rules also requires that arrangements be established for cooperation between the courts of the Member States and the Commission. This is relevant for all courts of the Member States that apply Articles 81 and 82 of the Treaty, whether applying these rules in lawsuits between private parties, acting as public enforcers or as review courts. In particular, national courts should be able to ask the Commission for information or for its opinion on points concerning the application of Community competition law. The Commission and the competition authorities of the Member States should also be able to submit written or oral observations to courts called upon to apply Article 81 or Article 82 of the Treaty. These observations should be submitted within the framework of national procedural

rules and practices including those safeguarding the rights of the parties. Steps should therefore be taken to ensure that the Commission and the competition authorities of the Member States are kept sufficiently well informed of proceedings before national courts.

(22) In order to ensure compliance with the principles of legal certainty and the uniform application of the Community competition rules in a system of parallel powers, conflicting decisions must be avoided. It is therefore necessary to clarify, in accordance with the case-law of the Court of Justice, the effects of Commission decisions and proceedings on courts and competition authorities of the Member States. Commitment decisions adopted by the Commission do not affect the power of the courts and the competition authorities of the Member States to apply Articles 81 and 82 of the Treaty.

(23) The Commission should be empowered throughout the Community to require such information to be supplied as is necessary to detect any agreement, decision or concerted practice prohibited by Article 81 of the Treaty or any abuse of a dominant position prohibited by Article 82 of the Treaty. When complying with a decision of the Commission, undertakings cannot be forced to admit that they have committed an infringement, but they are in any event obliged to answer factual questions and to provide documents, even if this information may be used to establish against them or against another undertaking the existence of an infringement.

(24) The Commission should also be empowered to undertake such inspections as are necessary to detect any agreement, decision or concerted practice prohibited by Article 81 of the Treaty or any abuse of a dominant position prohibited by Article 82 of the Treaty. The competition authorities of the Member States should cooperate actively in the exercise of these powers.

(25) The detection of infringements of the competition rules is growing ever more difficult, and, in order to protect competition effectively, the Commission's powers of investigation need to be supplemented. The Commission should in particular be empowered to interview any persons who may be in possession of useful information and to record the statements made. In the course of an inspection, officials authorised by the Commission should be empowered to affix seals for the period of time necessary for the inspection. Seals should normally not be affixed for more than 72 hours. Officials authorised by the Commission should also be empowered to ask for any information relevant to the subject matter and purpose of the inspection.

(26) Experience has shown that there are cases where business records are kept in the homes of directors or other people working for an undertaking. In order to safeguard the effectiveness of inspections, therefore, officials and other persons authorised by the Commission should be empowered to enter any premises where business records may be kept, including private homes. However, the exercise of this latter power should be subject to the authorisation of the judicial authority.

(27) Without prejudice to the case-law of the Court of Justice, it is useful to set out the scope of the control that the national judicial authority may carry out when it

Appendix II

authorises, as foreseen by national law including as a precautionary measure, assistance from law enforcement authorities in order to overcome possible opposition on the part of the undertaking or the execution of the decision to carry out inspections in non-business premises. It results from the case-law that the national judicial authority may in particular ask the Commission for further information which it needs to carry out its control and in the absence of which it could refuse the authorisation. The case-law also confirms the competence of the national courts to control the application of national rules governing the implementation of coercive measures.

(28) In order to help the competition authorities of the Member States to apply Articles 81 and 82 of the Treaty effectively, it is expedient to enable them to assist one another by carrying out inspections and other fact-finding measures.

(29) Compliance with Articles 81 and 82 of the Treaty and the fulfilment of the obligations imposed on undertakings and associations of undertakings under this Regulation should be enforceable by means of fines and periodic penalty payments. To that end, appropriate levels of fine should also be laid down for infringements of the procedural rules.

(30) In order to ensure effective recovery of fines imposed on associations of undertakings for infringements that they have committed, it is necessary to lay down the conditions on which the Commission may require payment of the fine from the members of the association where the association is not solvent. In doing so, the Commission should have regard to the relative size of the undertakings belonging to the association and in particular to the situation of small and medium-sized enterprises. Payment of the fine by one or several members of an association is without prejudice to rules of national law that provide for recovery of the amount paid from other members of the association.

(31) The rules on periods of limitation for the imposition of fines and periodic penalty payments were laid down in Council Regulation (EEC) No 2988/74[11], which also concerns penalties in the field of transport. In a system of parallel powers, the acts, which may interrupt a limitation period, should include procedural steps taken independently by the competition authority of a Member State. To clarify the legal framework, Regulation (EEC) No 2988/74 should therefore be amended to prevent it applying to matters covered by this Regulation, and this Regulation should include provisions on periods of limitation.

(32) The undertakings concerned should be accorded the right to be heard by the Commission, third parties whose interests may be affected by a decision should be given the opportunity of submitting their observations beforehand, and the decisions taken should be widely publicised. While ensuring the rights of defence of the undertakings concerned, in particular, the right of access to the file, it is essential that

---

11. Council Regulation (EEC) No 2988/74 of 26 November 1974 concerning limitation periods in proceedings and the enforcement of sanctions under the rules of the European Economic Community relating to transport and competition (OJ L 319, 29.11.1974, p. 1).

business secrets be protected. The confidentiality of information exchanged in the network should likewise be safeguarded.

(33) Since all decisions taken by the Commission under this Regulation are subject to review by the Court of Justice in accordance with the Treaty, the Court of Justice should, in accordance with Article 229 thereof be given unlimited jurisdiction in respect of decisions by which the Commission imposes fines or periodic penalty payments.

(34) The principles laid down in Articles 81 and 82 of the Treaty, as they have been applied by Regulation No 17, have given a central role to the Community bodies. This central role should be retained, whilst associating the Member States more closely with the application of the Community competition rules. In accordance with the principles of subsidiarity and proportionality as set out in Article 5 of the Treaty, this Regulation does not go beyond what is necessary in order to achieve its objective, which is to allow the Community competition rules to be applied effectively.

(35) In order to attain a proper enforcement of Community competition law, Member States should designate and empower authorities to apply Articles 81 and 82 of the Treaty as public enforcers. They should be able to designate administrative as well as judicial authorities to carry out the various functions conferred upon competition authorities in this Regulation. This Regulation recognises the wide variation which exists in the public enforcement systems of Member States. The effects of Article 11(6) of this Regulation should apply to all competition authorities. As an exception to this general rule, where a prosecuting authority brings a case before a separate judicial authority, Article 11(6) should apply to the prosecuting authority subject to the conditions in Article 35(4) of this Regulation. Where these conditions are not fulfilled, the general rule should apply. In any case, Article 11(6) should not apply to courts insofar as they are acting as review courts.

(36) As the case-law has made it clear that the competition rules apply to transport, that sector should be made subject to the procedural provisions of this Regulation. Council Regulation No 141 of 26 November 1962 exempting transport from the application of Regulation No 17[12] should therefore be repealed and Regulations (EEC) No 1017/68[13], (EEC) No 4056/86[14] and (EEC) No 3975/87[15] should be amended in order to delete the specific procedural provisions they contain.

---

12. OJ 124, 28.11.1962, p. 2751/62; Regulation as last amended by Regulation No 1002/67/EEC (OJ 306, 16.12.1967, p. 1).
13. Council Regulation (EEC) No 1017/68 of 19 July 1968 applying rules of competition to transport by rail, road and inland waterway (OJ L 175, 23.7.1968, p. 1). Regulation as last amended by the Act of Accession of 1994.
14. Council Regulation (EEC) No 4056/86 of 22 December 1986 laying down detailed rules for the application of Articles 81 and 82 (The title of the Regulation has been adjusted to take account of the renumbering of the Articles of the EC Treaty, in accordance with Article 12 of the Treaty of Amsterdam; the original reference was to Articles 85 and 86 of the Treaty) of the Treaty to maritime transport (OJ L 378, 31.12.1986, p. 4). Regulation as last amended by the Act of Accession of 1994.

Appendix II

(37) This Regulation respects the fundamental rights and observes the principles recognised in particular by the Charter of Fundamental Rights of the European Union. Accordingly, this Regulation should be interpreted and applied with respect to those rights and principles.

(38) Legal certainty for undertakings operating under the Community competition rules contributes to the promotion of innovation and investment. Where cases give rise to genuine uncertainty because they present novel or unresolved questions for the application of these rules, individual undertakings may wish to seek informal guidance from the Commission. This Regulation is without prejudice to the ability of the Commission to issue such informal guidance,

HAS ADOPTED THIS REGULATION:

CHAPTER I

PRINCIPLES

Article 1

Application of Articles 81 and 82 of the Treaty

1. Agreements, decisions and concerted practices caught by Article 81(1) of the Treaty which do not satisfy the conditions of Article 81(3) of the Treaty shall be prohibited, no prior decision to that effect being required.

2. Agreements, decisions and concerted practices caught by Article 81(1) of the Treaty which satisfy the conditions of Article 81(3) of the Treaty shall not be prohibited, no prior decision to that effect being required.

3. The abuse of a dominant position referred to in Article 82 of the Treaty shall be prohibited, no prior decision to that effect being required.

Article 2

Burden of proof

In any national or Community proceedings for the application of Articles 81 and 82 of the Treaty, the burden of proving an infringement of Article 81(1) or of Article 82 of the Treaty shall rest on the party or the authority alleging the infringement. The undertaking or association of undertakings claiming the benefit of Article 81(3) of the Treaty shall bear the burden of proving that the conditions of that paragraph are fulfilled.

---

15. Council Regulation (EEC) No 3975/87 of 14 December 1987 laying down the procedure for the application of the rules on competition to undertakings in the air transport sector (OJ L 374, 31.12.1987, p. 1). Regulation as last amended by Regulation (EEC) No 2410/92 (OJ L 240, 24.8.1992, p. 18).

Article 3

Relationship between Articles 81 and 82 of the Treaty and national competition laws

1. Where the competition authorities of the Member States or national courts apply national competition law to agreements, decisions by associations of undertakings or concerted practices within the meaning of Article 81(1) of the Treaty which may affect trade between Member States within the meaning of that provision, they shall also apply Article 81 of the Treaty to such agreements, decisions or concerted practices. Where the competition authorities of the Member States or national courts apply national competition law to any abuse prohibited by Article 82 of the Treaty, they shall also apply Article 82 of the Treaty.

2. The application of national competition law may not lead to the prohibition of agreements, decisions by associations of undertakings or concerted practices which may affect trade between Member States but which do not restrict competition within the meaning of Article 81(1) of the Treaty, or which fulfil the conditions of Article 81(3) of the Treaty or which are covered by a Regulation for the application of Article 81(3) of the Treaty. Member States shall not under this Regulation be precluded from adopting and applying on their territory stricter national laws which prohibit or sanction unilateral conduct engaged in by undertakings.

3. Without prejudice to general principles and other provisions of Community law, paragraphs 1 and 2 do not apply when the competition authorities and the courts of the Member States apply national merger control laws nor do they preclude the application of provisions of national law that predominantly pursue an objective different from that pursued by Articles 81 and 82 of the Treaty.

CHAPTER II

POWERS

Article 4

Powers of the Commission

For the purpose of applying Articles 81 and 82 of the Treaty, the Commission shall have the powers provided for by this Regulation.

Article 5

Powers of the competition authorities of the Member States
The competition authorities of the Member States shall have the power to apply Articles 81 and 82 of the Treaty in individual cases. For this purpose, acting on their own initiative or on a complaint, they may take the following decisions:

- requiring that an infringement be brought to an end,
- ordering interim measures,

Appendix II

- accepting commitments,
- imposing fines, periodic penalty payments or any other penalty provided for in their national law.

Where on the basis of the information in their possession the conditions for prohibition are not met they may likewise decide that there are no grounds for action on their part.

Article 6

Powers of the national courts

National courts shall have the power to apply Articles 81 and 82 of the Treaty.

CHAPTER III

COMMISSION DECISIONS

Article 7

Finding and termination of infringement

1. Where the Commission, acting on a complaint or on its own initiative, finds that there is an infringement of Article 81 or of Article 82 of the Treaty, it may by decision require the undertakings and associations of undertakings concerned to bring such infringement to an end. For this purpose, it may impose on them any behavioural or structural remedies which are proportionate to the infringement committed and necessary to bring the infringement effectively to an end. Structural remedies can only be imposed either where there is no equally effective behavioural remedy or where any equally effective behavioural remedy would be more burdensome for the undertaking concerned than the structural remedy. If the Commission has a legitimate interest in doing so, it may also find that an infringement has been committed in the past.

2. Those entitled to lodge a complaint for the purposes of paragraph 1 are natural or legal persons who can show a legitimate interest and Member States.

Article 8

Interim measures

1. In cases of urgency due to the risk of serious and irreparable damage to competition, the Commission, acting on its own initiative may by decision, on the basis of a prima facie finding of infringement, order interim measures.

2. A decision under paragraph 1 shall apply for a specified period of time and may be renewed in so far this is necessary and appropriate.

Appendix II

Article 9

Commitments

1. Where the Commission intends to adopt a decision requiring that an infringement be brought to an end and the undertakings concerned offer commitments to meet the concerns expressed to them by the Commission in its preliminary assessment, the Commission may by decision make those commitments binding on the undertakings. Such a decision may be adopted for a specified period and shall conclude that there are no longer grounds for action by the Commission.

2. The Commission may, upon request or on its own initiative, reopen the proceedings:

- (a) where there has been a material change in any of the facts on which the decision was based;
- (b) where the undertakings concerned act contrary to their commitments; or
- (c) where the decision was based on incomplete, incorrect or misleading information provided by the parties.

Article 10

Finding of inapplicability

Where the Community public interest relating to the application of Articles 81 and 82 of the Treaty so requires, the Commission, acting on its own initiative, may by decision find that Article 81 of the Treaty is not applicable to an agreement, a decision by an association of undertakings or a concerted practice, either because the conditions of Article 81(1) of the Treaty are not fulfilled, or because the conditions of Article 81(3) of the Treaty are satisfied.
The Commission may likewise make such a finding with reference to Article 82 of the Treaty.

CHAPTER IV

COOPERATION

Article 11

Cooperation between the Commission and the competition authorities of the Member States

1. The Commission and the competition authorities of the Member States shall apply the Community competition rules in close cooperation.

2. The Commission shall transmit to the competition authorities of the Member States copies of the most important documents it has collected with a view to applying Articles 7, 8, 9, 10 and Article 29(1). At the request of the competition authority of a

Member State, the Commission shall provide it with a copy of other existing documents necessary for the assessment of the case.

3. The competition authorities of the Member States shall, when acting under Article 81 or Article 82 of the Treaty, inform the Commission in writing before or without delay after commencing the first formal investigative measure. This information may also be made available to the competition authorities of the other Member States.

4. No later than 30 days before the adoption of a decision requiring that an infringement be brought to an end, accepting commitments or withdrawing the benefit of a block exemption Regulation, the competition authorities of the Member States shall inform the Commission. To that effect, they shall provide the Commission with a summary of the case, the envisaged decision or, in the absence thereof, any other document indicating the proposed course of action. This information may also be made available to the competition authorities of the other Member States. At the request of the Commission, the acting competition authority shall make available to the Commission other documents it holds which are necessary for the assessment of the case. The information supplied to the Commission may be made available to the competition authorities of the other Member States. National competition authorities may also exchange between themselves information necessary for the assessment of a case that they are dealing with under Article 81 or Article 82 of the Treaty.

5. The competition authorities of the Member States may consult the Commission on any case involving the application of Community law.

6. The initiation by the Commission of proceedings for the adoption of a decision under Chapter III shall relieve the competition authorities of the Member States of their competence to apply Articles 81 and 82 of the Treaty. If a competition authority of a Member State is already acting on a case, the Commission shall only initiate proceedings after consulting with that national competition authority.

Article 12

Exchange of information

1. For the purpose of applying Articles 81 and 82 of the Treaty the Commission and the competition authorities of the Member States shall have the power to provide one another with and use in evidence any matter of fact or of law, including confidential information.

2. Information exchanged shall only be used in evidence for the purpose of applying Article 81 or Article 82 of the Treaty and in respect of the subject-matter for which it was collected by the transmitting authority. However, where national competition law is applied in the same case and in parallel to Community competition law and does not lead to a different outcome, information exchanged under this Article may also be used for the application of national competition law.

3. Information exchanged pursuant to paragraph 1 can only be used in evidence to impose sanctions on natural persons where:

- the law of the transmitting authority foresees sanctions of a similar kind in relation to an infringement of Article 81 or Article 82 of the Treaty or, in the absence thereof,
- the information has been collected in a way which respects the same level of protection of the rights of defence of natural persons as provided for under the national rules of the receiving authority. However, in this case, the information exchanged cannot be used by the receiving authority to impose custodial sanctions.

Article 13

Suspension or termination of proceedings

1. Where competition authorities of two or more Member States have received a complaint or are acting on their own initiative under Article 81 or Article 82 of the Treaty against the same agreement, decision of an association or practice, the fact that one authority is dealing with the case shall be sufficient grounds for the others to suspend the proceedings before them or to reject the complaint. The Commission may likewise reject a complaint on the ground that a competition authority of a Member State is dealing with the case.

2. Where a competition authority of a Member State or the Commission has received a complaint against an agreement, decision of an association or practice which has already been dealt with by another competition authority, it may reject it.

Article 14

Advisory Committee

1. The Commission shall consult an Advisory Committee on Restrictive Practices and Dominant Positions prior to the taking of any decision under Articles 7, 8, 9, 10, 23, Article 24(2) and Article 29(1).

2. For the discussion of individual cases, the Advisory Committee shall be composed of representatives of the competition authorities of the Member States. For meetings in which issues other than individual cases are being discussed, an additional Member State representative competent in competition matters may be appointed. Representatives may, if unable to attend, be replaced by other representatives.

3. The consultation may take place at a meeting convened and chaired by the Commission, held not earlier than 14 days after dispatch of the notice convening it, together with a summary of the case, an indication of the most important documents and a preliminary draft decision. In respect of decisions pursuant to Article 8, the meeting may be held seven days after the dispatch of the operative part of a draft

Appendix II

decision. Where the Commission dispatches a notice convening the meeting which gives a shorter period of notice than those specified above, the meeting may take place on the proposed date in the absence of an objection by any Member State. The Advisory Committee shall deliver a written opinion on the Commission's preliminary draft decision. It may deliver an opinion even if some members are absent and are not represented. At the request of one or several members, the positions stated in the opinion shall be reasoned.

4. Consultation may also take place by written procedure. However, if any Member State so requests, the Commission shall convene a meeting. In case of written procedure, the Commission shall determine a time-limit of not less than 14 days within which the Member States are to put forward their observations for circulation to all other Member States. In case of decisions to be taken pursuant to Article 8, the time-limit of 14 days is replaced by seven days. Where the Commission determines a time-limit for the written procedure which is shorter than those specified above, the proposed time-limit shall be applicable in the absence of an objection by any Member State.

5. The Commission shall take the utmost account of the opinion delivered by the Advisory Committee. It shall inform the Committee of the manner in which its opinion has been taken into account.

6. Where the Advisory Committee delivers a written opinion, this opinion shall be appended to the draft decision. If the Advisory Committee recommends publication of the opinion, the Commission shall carry out such publication taking into account the legitimate interest of undertakings in the protection of their business secrets.

7. At the request of a competition authority of a Member State, the Commission shall include on the agenda of the Advisory Committee cases that are being dealt with by a competition authority of a Member State under Article 81 or Article 82 of the Treaty. The Commission may also do so on its own initiative. In either case, the Commission shall inform the competition authority concerned.

A request may in particular be made by a competition authority of a Member State in respect of a case where the Commission intends to initiate proceedings with the effect of Article 11(6).

The Advisory Committee shall not issue opinions on cases dealt with by competition authorities of the Member States. The Advisory Committee may also discuss general issues of Community competition law.

Article 15

Cooperation with national courts

1. In proceedings for the application of Article 81 or Article 82 of the Treaty, courts of the Member States may ask the Commission to transmit to them information in its possession or its opinion on questions concerning the application of the Community competition rules.

2. Member States shall forward to the Commission a copy of any written judgment of national courts deciding on the application of Article 81 or Article 82 of the Treaty. Such copy shall be forwarded without delay after the full written judgment is notified to the parties.

3. Competition authorities of the Member States, acting on their own initiative, may submit written observations to the national courts of their Member State on issues relating to the application of Article 81 or Article 82 of the Treaty. With the permission of the court in question, they may also submit oral observations to the national courts of their Member State. Where the coherent application of Article 81 or Article 82 of the Treaty so requires, the Commission, acting on its own initiative, may submit written observations to courts of the Member States. With the permission of the court in question, it may also make oral observations.

For the purpose of the preparation of their observations only, the competition authorities of the Member States and the Commission may request the relevant court of the Member State to transmit or ensure the transmission to them of any documents necessary for the assessment of the case.

4. This Article is without prejudice to wider powers to make observations before courts conferred on competition authorities of the Member States under the law of their Member State.

Article 16

Uniform application of Community competition law

1. When national courts rule on agreements, decisions or practices under Article 81 or Article 82 of the Treaty which are already the subject of a Commission decision, they cannot take decisions running counter to the decision adopted by the Commission. They must also avoid giving decisions which would conflict with a decision contemplated by the Commission in proceedings it has initiated. To that effect, the national court may assess whether it is necessary to stay its proceedings. This obligation is without prejudice to the rights and obligations under Article 234 of the Treaty.

2. When competition authorities of the Member States rule on agreements, decisions or practices under Article 81 or Article 82 of the Treaty which are already the subject of a Commission decision, they cannot take decisions which would run counter to the decision adopted by the Commission.

CHAPTER V

POWERS OF INVESTIGATION

Article 17

Investigations into sectors of the economy and into types of agreements

Appendix II

1. Where the trend of trade between Member States, the rigidity of prices or other circumstances suggest that competition may be restricted or distorted within the common market, the Commission may conduct its inquiry into a particular sector of the economy or into a particular type of agreements across various sectors. In the course of that inquiry, the Commission may request the undertakings or associations of undertakings concerned to supply the information necessary for giving effect to Articles 81 and 82 of the Treaty and may carry out any inspections necessary for that purpose.

The Commission may in particular request the undertakings or associations of undertakings concerned to communicate to it all agreements, decisions and concerted practices.

The Commission may publish a report on the results of its inquiry into particular sectors of the economy or particular types of agreements across various sectors and invite comments from interested parties.

2. Articles 14, 18, 19, 20, 22, 23 and 24 shall apply mutatis mutandis.

Article 18

Requests for information

1. In order to carry out the duties assigned to it by this Regulation, the Commission may, by simple request or by decision, require undertakings and associations of undertakings to provide all necessary information.

2. When sending a simple request for information to an undertaking or association of undertakings, the Commission shall state the legal basis and the purpose of the request, specify what information is required and fix the time-limit within which the information is to be provided, and the penalties provided for in Article 23 for supplying incorrect or misleading information.

3. Where the Commission requires undertakings and associations of undertakings to supply information by decision, it shall state the legal basis and the purpose of the request, specify what information is required and fix the time-limit within which it is to be provided. It shall also indicate the penalties provided for in Article 23 and indicate or impose the penalties provided for in Article 24. It shall further indicate the right to have the decision reviewed by the Court of Justice.

4. The owners of the undertakings or their representatives and, in the case of legal persons, companies or firms, or associations having no legal personality, the persons authorised to represent them by law or by their constitution shall supply the information requested on behalf of the undertaking or the association of undertakings concerned. Lawyers duly authorised to act may supply the information on behalf of their clients. The latter shall remain fully responsible if the information supplied is incomplete, incorrect or misleading.

5. The Commission shall without delay forward a copy of the simple request or of the decision to the competition authority of the Member State in whose territory the seat of

Appendix II

the undertaking or association of undertakings is situated and the competition authority of the Member State whose territory is affected.

6. At the request of the Commission the governments and competition authorities of the Member States shall provide the Commission with all necessary information to carry out the duties assigned to it by this Regulation.

Article 19

Power to take statements

1. In order to carry out the duties assigned to it by this Regulation, the Commission may interview any natural or legal person who consents to be interviewed for the purpose of collecting information relating to the subject-matter of an investigation.

2. Where an interview pursuant to paragraph 1 is conducted in the premises of an undertaking, the Commission shall inform the competition authority of the Member State in whose territory the interview takes place. If so requested by the competition authority of that Member State, its officials may assist the officials and other accompanying persons authorised by the Commission to conduct the interview.

Article 20

The Commission's powers of inspection

1. In order to carry out the duties assigned to it by this Regulation, the Commission may conduct all necessary inspections of undertakings and associations of undertakings.

2. The officials and other accompanying persons authorised by the Commission to conduct an inspection are empowered:

(a) to enter any premises, land and means of transport of undertakings and associations of undertakings;
(b) to examine the books and other records related to the business, irrespective of the medium on which they are stored;
(c) to take or obtain in any form copies of or extracts from such books or records;
(d) to seal any business premises and books or records for the period and to the extent necessary for the inspection;
(e) to ask any representative or member of staff of the undertaking or association of undertakings for explanations on facts or documents relating to the subject-matter and purpose of the inspection and to record the answers.

3. The officials and other accompanying persons authorised by the Commission to conduct an inspection shall exercise their powers upon production of a written authorisation specifying the subject matter and purpose of the inspection and the penalties provided for in Article 23 in case the production of the required books or other

Appendix II

records related to the business is incomplete or where the answers to questions asked under paragraph 2 of the present Article are incorrect or misleading. In good time before the inspection, the Commission shall give notice of the inspection to the competition authority of the Member State in whose territory it is to be conducted.

4. Undertakings and associations of undertakings are required to submit to inspections ordered by decision of the Commission. The decision shall specify the subject matter and purpose of the inspection, appoint the date on which it is to begin and indicate the penalties provided for in Articles 23 and 24 and the right to have the decision reviewed by the Court of Justice. The Commission shall take such decisions after consulting the competition authority of the Member State in whose territory the inspection is to be conducted.

5. Officials of as well as those authorised or appointed by the competition authority of the Member State in whose territory the inspection is to be conducted shall, at the request of that authority or of the Commission, actively assist the officials and other accompanying persons authorised by the Commission. To this end, they shall enjoy the powers specified in paragraph 2.

6. Where the officials and other accompanying persons authorised by the Commission find that an undertaking opposes an inspection ordered pursuant to this Article, the Member State concerned shall afford them the necessary assistance, requesting where appropriate the assistance of the police or of an equivalent enforcement authority, so as to enable them to conduct their inspection.

7. If the assistance provided for in paragraph 6 requires authorisation from a judicial authority according to national rules, such authorisation shall be applied for. Such authorisation may also be applied for as a precautionary measure.

8. Where authorisation as referred to in paragraph 7 is applied for, the national judicial authority shall control that the Commission decision is authentic and that the coercive measures envisaged are neither arbitrary nor excessive having regard to the subject matter of the inspection. In its control of the proportionality of the coercive measures, the national judicial authority may ask the Commission, directly or through the Member State competition authority, for detailed explanations in particular on the grounds the Commission has for suspecting infringement of Articles 81 and 82 of the Treaty, as well as on the seriousness of the suspected infringement and on the nature of the involvement of the undertaking concerned. However, the national judicial authority may not call into question the necessity for the inspection nor demand that it be provided with the information in the Commission's file. The lawfulness of the Commission decision shall be subject to review only by the Court of Justice.

Article 21

Inspection of other premises

1. If a reasonable suspicion exists that books or other records related to the business and to the subject-matter of the inspection, which may be relevant to prove a serious

violation of Article 81 or Article 82 of the Treaty, are being kept in any other premises, land and means of transport, including the homes of directors, managers and other members of staff of the undertakings and associations of undertakings concerned, the Commission can by decision order an inspection to be conducted in such other premises, land and means of transport.

2. The decision shall specify the subject matter and purpose of the inspection, appoint the date on which it is to begin and indicate the right to have the decision reviewed by the Court of Justice. It shall in particular state the reasons that have led the Commission to conclude that a suspicion in the sense of paragraph 1 exists. The Commission shall take such decisions after consulting the competition authority of the Member State in whose territory the inspection is to be conducted.

3. A decision adopted pursuant to paragraph 1 cannot be executed without prior authorisation from the national judicial authority of the Member State concerned. The national judicial authority shall control that the Commission decision is authentic and that the coercive measures envisaged are neither arbitrary nor excessive having regard in particular to the seriousness of the suspected infringement, to the importance of the evidence sought, to the involvement of the undertaking concerned and to the reasonable likelihood that business books and records relating to the subject matter of the inspection are kept in the premises for which the authorisation is requested. The national judicial authority may ask the Commission, directly or through the Member State competition authority, for detailed explanations on those elements which are necessary to allow its control of the proportionality of the coercive measures envisaged. However, the national judicial authority may not call into question the necessity for the inspection nor demand that it be provided with information in the Commission's file. The lawfulness of the Commission decision shall be subject to review only by the Court of Justice.

4. The officials and other accompanying persons authorised by the Commission to conduct an inspection ordered in accordance with paragraph 1 of this Article shall have the powers set out in Article 20(2)(a), (b) and (c). Article 20(5) and (6) shall apply mutatis mutandis.

Article 22

Investigations by competition authorities of Member States

1. The competition authority of a Member State may in its own territory carry out any inspection or other fact-finding measure under its national law on behalf and for the account of the competition authority of another Member State in order to establish whether there has been an infringement of Article 81 or Article 82 of the Treaty. Any exchange and use of the information collected shall be carried out in accordance with Article 12.

2. At the request of the Commission, the competition authorities of the Member States shall undertake the inspections which the Commission considers to be necessary

Appendix II

under Article 20(1) or which it has ordered by decision pursuant to Article 20(4). The officials of the competition authorities of the Member States who are responsible for conducting these inspections as well as those authorised or appointed by them shall exercise their powers in accordance with their national law.

If so requested by the Commission or by the competition authority of the Member State in whose territory the inspection is to be conducted, officials and other accompanying persons authorised by the Commission may assist the officials of the authority concerned.

CHAPTER VI

PENALTIES

Article 23

Fines

1. The Commission may by decision impose on undertakings and associations of undertakings fines not exceeding 1 % of the total turnover in the preceding business year where, intentionally or negligently:

   (a) they supply incorrect or misleading information in response to a request made pursuant to Article 17 or Article 18(2);
   (b) in response to a request made by decision adopted pursuant to Article 17 or Article 18(3), they supply incorrect, incomplete or misleading information or do not supply information within the required time-limit;
   (c) they produce the required books or other records related to the business in incomplete form during inspections under Article 20 or refuse to submit to inspections ordered by a decision adopted pursuant to Article 20(4);
   (d) in response to a question asked in accordance with Article 20(2)(e),
       - they give an incorrect or misleading answer,
       - they fail to rectify within a time-limit set by the Commission an incorrect, incomplete or misleading answer given by a member of staff, or
       - they fail or refuse to provide a complete answer on facts relating to the subject-matter and purpose of an inspection ordered by a decision adopted pursuant to Article 20(4);
   (e) seals affixed in accordance with Article 20(2)(d) by officials or other accompanying persons authorised by the Commission have been broken.

2. The Commission may by decision impose fines on undertakings and associations of undertakings where, either intentionally or negligently:

   (a) they infringe Article 81 or Article 82 of the Treaty; or
   (b) they contravene a decision ordering interim measures under Article 8; or
   (c) they fail to comply with a commitment made binding by a decision pursuant to Article 9.

Appendix II

For each undertaking and association of undertakings participating in the infringement, the fine shall not exceed 10 % of its total turnover in the preceding business year. Where the infringement of an association relates to the activities of its members, the fine shall not exceed 10 % of the sum of the total turnover of each member active on the market affected by the infringement of the association.

3. In fixing the amount of the fine, regard shall be had both to the gravity and to the duration of the infringement.

4. When a fine is imposed on an association of undertakings taking account of the turnover of its members and the association is not solvent, the association is obliged to call for contributions from its members to cover the amount of the fine.

Where such contributions have not been made to the association within a time-limit fixed by the Commission, the Commission may require payment of the fine directly by any of the undertakings whose representatives were members of the decision-making bodies concerned of the association.

After the Commission has required payment under the second subparagraph, where necessary to ensure full payment of the fine, the Commission may require payment of the balance by any of the members of the association which were active on the market on which the infringement occurred.

However, the Commission shall not require payment under the second or the third subparagraph from undertakings which show that they have not implemented the infringing decision of the association and either were not aware of its existence or have actively distanced themselves from it before the Commission started investigating the case.

The financial liability of each undertaking in respect of the payment of the fine shall not exceed 10 % of its total turnover in the preceding business year.

5. Decisions taken pursuant to paragraphs 1 and 2 shall not be of a criminal law nature.

Article 24

Periodic penalty payments

1. The Commission may, by decision, impose on undertakings or associations of undertakings periodic penalty payments not exceeding 5 % of the average daily turnover in the preceding business year per day and calculated from the date appointed by the decision, in order to compel them:

(a) to put an end to an infringement of Article 81 or Article 82 of the Treaty, in accordance with a decision taken pursuant to Article 7;
(b) to comply with a decision ordering interim measures taken pursuant to Article 8;
(c) to comply with a commitment made binding by a decision pursuant to Article 9;

(d) to supply complete and correct information which it has requested by decision taken pursuant to Article 17 or Article 18(3);
(e) to submit to an inspection which it has ordered by decision taken pursuant to Article 20(4).

2. Where the undertakings or associations of undertakings have satisfied the obligation which the periodic penalty payment was intended to enforce, the Commission may fix the definitive amount of the periodic penalty payment at a figure lower than that which would arise under the original decision. Article 23(4) shall apply correspondingly.

CHAPTER VII

LIMITATION PERIODS

Article 25

Limitation periods for the imposition of penalties

1. The powers conferred on the Commission by Articles 23 and 24 shall be subject to the following limitation periods:

(a) three years in the case of infringements of provisions concerning requests for information or the conduct of inspections;
(b) five years in the case of all other infringements.

2. Time shall begin to run on the day on which the infringement is committed. However, in the case of continuing or repeated infringements, time shall begin to run on the day on which the infringement ceases.

3. Any action taken by the Commission or by the competition authority of a Member State for the purpose of the investigation or proceedings in respect of an infringement shall interrupt the limitation period for the imposition of fines or periodic penalty payments. The limitation period shall be interrupted with effect from the date on which the action is notified to at least one undertaking or association of undertakings which has participated in the infringement. Actions which interrupt the running of the period shall include in particular the following:

(a) written requests for information by the Commission or by the competition authority of a Member State;
(b) written authorisations to conduct inspections issued to its officials by the Commission or by the competition authority of a Member State;
(c) the initiation of proceedings by the Commission or by the competition authority of a Member State;
(d) notification of the statement of objections of the Commission or of the competition authority of a Member State.

Appendix II

4. The interruption of the limitation period shall apply for all the undertakings or associations of undertakings which have participated in the infringement.

5. Each interruption shall start time running afresh. However, the limitation period shall expire at the latest on the day on which a period equal to twice the limitation period has elapsed without the Commission having imposed a fine or a periodic penalty payment. That period shall be extended by the time during which limitation is suspended pursuant to paragraph 6.

6. The limitation period for the imposition of fines or periodic penalty payments shall be suspended for as long as the decision of the Commission is the subject of proceedings pending before the Court of Justice.

Article 26

Limitation period for the enforcement of penalties

1. The power of the Commission to enforce decisions taken pursuant to Articles 23 and 24 shall be subject to a limitation period of five years.

2. Time shall begin to run on the day on which the decision becomes final.

3. The limitation period for the enforcement of penalties shall be interrupted:

   (a) by notification of a decision varying the original amount of the fine or periodic penalty payment or refusing an application for variation;
   (b) by any action of the Commission or of a Member State, acting at the request of the Commission, designed to enforce payment of the fine or periodic penalty payment.

4. Each interruption shall start time running afresh.

5. The limitation period for the enforcement of penalties shall be suspended for so long as:

   (a) time to pay is allowed;
   (b) enforcement of payment is suspended pursuant to a decision of the Court of Justice.

CHAPTER VIII

HEARINGS AND PROFESSIONAL SECRECY

Article 27

Hearing of the parties, complainants and others

Appendix II

1. Before taking decisions as provided for in Articles 7, 8, 23 and Article 24(2), the Commission shall give the undertakings or associations of undertakings which are the subject of the proceedings conducted by the Commission the opportunity of being heard on the matters to which the Commission has taken objection. The Commission shall base its decisions only on objections on which the parties concerned have been able to comment. Complainants shall be associated closely with the proceedings.

2. The rights of defence of the parties concerned shall be fully respected in the proceedings. They shall be entitled to have access to the Commission's file, subject to the legitimate interest of undertakings in the protection of their business secrets. The right of access to the file shall not extend to confidential information and internal documents of the Commission or the competition authorities of the Member States. In particular, the right of access shall not extend to correspondence between the Commission and the competition authorities of the Member States, or between the latter, including documents drawn up pursuant to Articles 11 and 14. Nothing in this paragraph shall prevent the Commission from disclosing and using information necessary to prove an infringement.

3. If the Commission considers it necessary, it may also hear other natural or legal persons. Applications to be heard on the part of such persons shall, where they show a sufficient interest, be granted. The competition authorities of the Member States may also ask the Commission to hear other natural or legal persons.

4. Where the Commission intends to adopt a decision pursuant to Article 9 or Article 10, it shall publish a concise summary of the case and the main content of the commitments or of the proposed course of action. Interested third parties may submit their observations within a time limit which is fixed by the Commission in its publication and which may not be less than one month. Publication shall have regard to the legitimate interest of undertakings in the protection of their business secrets.

Article 28

Professional secrecy

1. Without prejudice to Articles 12 and 15, information collected pursuant to Articles 17 to 22 shall be used only for the purpose for which it was acquired.

2. Without prejudice to the exchange and to the use of information foreseen in Articles 11, 12, 14, 15 and 27, the Commission and the competition authorities of the Member States, their officials, servants and other persons working under the supervision of these authorities as well as officials and civil servants of other authorities of the Member States shall not disclose information acquired or exchanged by them pursuant to this Regulation and of the kind covered by the obligation of professional secrecy. This obligation also applies to all representatives and experts of Member States attending meetings of the Advisory Committee pursuant to Article 14.

Appendix II

CHAPTER IX

EXEMPTION REGULATIONS

Article 29

Withdrawal in individual cases

1. Where the Commission, empowered by a Council Regulation, such as Regulations 19/65/EEC, (EEC) No 2821/71, (EEC) No 3976/87, (EEC) No 1534/91 or (EEC) No 479/92, to apply Article 81(3) of the Treaty by regulation, has declared Article 81(1) of the Treaty inapplicable to certain categories of agreements, decisions by associations of undertakings or concerted practices, it may, acting on its own initiative or on a complaint, withdraw the benefit of such an exemption Regulation when it finds that in any particular case an agreement, decision or concerted practice to which the exemption Regulation applies has certain effects which are incompatible with Article 81(3) of the Treaty.

2. Where, in any particular case, agreements, decisions by associations of undertakings or concerted practices to which a Commission Regulation referred to in paragraph 1 applies have effects which are incompatible with Article 81(3) of the Treaty in the territory of a Member State, or in a part thereof, which has all the characteristics of a distinct geographic market, the competition authority of that Member State may withdraw the benefit of the Regulation in question in respect of that territory.

CHAPTER X

GENERAL PROVISIONS

Article 30

Publication of decisions

1. The Commission shall publish the decisions, which it takes pursuant to Articles 7 to 10, 23 and 24.

2. The publication shall state the names of the parties and the main content of the decision, including any penalties imposed. It shall have regard to the legitimate interest of undertakings in the protection of their business secrets.

Article 31

Review by the Court of Justice

The Court of Justice shall have unlimited jurisdiction to review decisions whereby the Commission has fixed a fine or periodic penalty payment. It may cancel, reduce or increase the fine or periodic penalty payment imposed.

Appendix II

Article 32

Exclusions

This Regulation shall not apply to:

(a) international tramp vessel services as defined in Article 1(3)(a) of Regulation (EEC) No 4056/86;
(b) a maritime transport service that takes place exclusively between ports in one and the same Member State as foreseen in Article 1(2) of Regulation (EEC) No 4056/86;
(c) air transport between Community airports and third countries.

Article 33

Implementing provisions

1. The Commission shall be authorised to take such measures as may be appropriate in order to apply this Regulation. The measures may concern, inter alia:

(a) the form, content and other details of complaints lodged pursuant to Article 7 and the procedure for rejecting complaints;
(b) the practical arrangements for the exchange of information and consultations provided for in Article 11;
(c) the practical arrangements for the hearings provided for in Article 27.

2. Before the adoption of any measures pursuant to paragraph 1, the Commission shall publish a draft thereof and invite all interested parties to submit their comments within the time-limit it lays down, which may not be less than one month. Before publishing a draft measure and before adopting it, the Commission shall consult the Advisory Committee on Restrictive Practices and Dominant Positions.

CHAPTER XI

TRANSITIONAL, AMENDING AND FINAL PROVISIONS

Article 34

Transitional provisions

1. Applications made to the Commission under Article 2 of Regulation No 17, notifications made under Articles 4 and 5 of that Regulation and the corresponding applications and notifications made under Regulations (EEC) No 1017/68, (EEC) No 4056/86 and (EEC) No 3975/87 shall lapse as from the date of application of this Regulation.

Appendix II

2. Procedural steps taken under Regulation No 17 and Regulations (EEC) No 1017/68, (EEC) No 4056/86 and (EEC) No 3975/87 shall continue to have effect for the purposes of applying this Regulation.

Article 35

Designation of competition authorities of Member States

1. The Member States shall designate the competition authority or authorities responsible for the application of Articles 81 and 82 of the Treaty in such a way that the provisions of this regulation are effectively complied with. The measures necessary to empower those authorities to apply those Articles shall be taken before 1 May 2004. The authorities designated may include courts.

2. When enforcement of Community competition law is entrusted to national administrative and judicial authorities, the Member States may allocate different powers and functions to those different national authorities, whether administrative or judicial.

3. The effects of Article 11(6) apply to the authorities designated by the Member States including courts that exercise functions regarding the preparation and the adoption of the types of decisions foreseen in Article 5. The effects of Article 11(6) do not extend to courts insofar as they act as review courts in respect of the types of decisions foreseen in Article 5.

4. Notwithstanding paragraph 3, in the Member States where, for the adoption of certain types of decisions foreseen in Article 5, an authority brings an action before a judicial authority that is separate and different from the prosecuting authority and provided that the terms of this paragraph are complied with, the effects of Article 11(6) shall be limited to the authority prosecuting the case which shall withdraw its claim before the judicial authority when the Commission opens proceedings and this withdrawal shall bring the national proceedings effectively to an end.

Article 36

Amendment of Regulation (EEC) No 1017/68

Regulation (EEC) No 1017/68 is amended as follows:

1. Article 2 is repealed;

2. in Article 3(1), the words "The prohibition laid down in Article 2" are replaced by the words "The prohibition in Article 81(1) of the Treaty";

3. Article 4 is amended as follows:

   (a) In paragraph 1, the words "The agreements, decisions and concerted practices referred to in Article 2" are replaced by the words "Agreements, decisions and concerted practices pursuant to Article 81(1) of the Treaty";
   (b) Paragraph 2 is replaced by the following:

Appendix II

"2. If the implementation of any agreement, decision or concerted practice covered by paragraph 1 has, in a given case, effects which are incompatible with the requirements of Article 81(3) of the Treaty, undertakings or associations of undertakings may be required to make such effects cease."

4. Articles 5 to 29 are repealed with the exception of Article 13(3) which continues to apply to decisions adopted pursuant to Article 5 of Regulation (EEC) No 1017/68 prior to the date of application of this Regulation until the date of expiration of those decisions;

5. in Article 30, paragraphs 2, 3 and 4 are deleted.

Article 37

Amendment of Regulation (EEC) No 2988/74
In Regulation (EEC) No 2988/74, the following Article is inserted:

"Article 7a

Exclusion

This Regulation shall not apply to measures taken under Council Regulation (EC) No 1/2003 of 16 December 2002 on the implementation of the rules on competition laid down in Articles 81 and 82 of the Treaty[16]."

Article 38

Amendment of Regulation (EEC) No 4056/86
Regulation (EEC) No 4056/86 is amended as follows:

1. Article 7 is amended as follows:

   (a) Paragraph 1 is replaced by the following:

   "1. Breach of an obligation

   Where the persons concerned are in breach of an obligation which, pursuant to Article 5, attaches to the exemption provided for in Article 3, the Commission may, in order to put an end to such breach and under the conditions laid down in Council Regulation (EC) No 1/2003 of 16 December 2002 on the implementation of the rules on competition laid down in Articles 81 and 82 of the Treaty[17] adopt a decision that either prohibits them from carrying out or requires them to perform certain specific acts, or withdraws the benefit of the block exemption which they enjoyed."

---

16. OJ L 1, 4.1.2003, p. 1.
17. OJ L 1, 4.1.2003, p. 1.

(b) Paragraph 2 is amended as follows:
   (i) In point (a), the words "under the conditions laid down in Section II" are replaced by the words "under the conditions laid down in Regulation (EC) No 1/2003";
   (ii) The second sentence of the second subparagraph of point (c)(i) is replaced by the following:

"At the same time it shall decide, in accordance with Article 9 of Regulation (EC) No 1/2003, whether to accept commitments offered by the undertakings concerned with a view, inter alia, to obtaining access to the market for non-conference lines."

2. Article 8 is amended as follows:

   (a) Paragraph 1 is deleted.
   (b) In paragraph 2 the words "pursuant to Article 10" are replaced by the words "pursuant to Regulation (EC) No 1/2003".
   (c) Paragraph 3 is deleted;

3. Article 9 is amended as follows:

   (a) In paragraph 1, the words "Advisory Committee referred to in Article 15" are replaced by the words "Advisory Committee referred to in Article 14 of Regulation (EC) No 1/2003";
   (b) In paragraph 2, the words "Advisory Committee as referred to in Article 15" are replaced by the words "Advisory Committee referred to in Article 14 of Regulation (EC) No 1/2003";

4. Articles 10 to 25 are repealed with the exception of Article 13(3) which continues to apply to decisions adopted pursuant to Article 81(3) of the Treaty prior to the date of application of this Regulation until the date of expiration of those decisions;

5. in Article 26, the words "the form, content and other details of complaints pursuant to Article 10, applications pursuant to Article 12 and the hearings provided for in Article 23(1) and (2)" are deleted.

Article 39

Amendment of Regulation (EEC) No 3975/87

Articles 3 to 19 of Regulation (EEC) No 3975/87 are repealed with the exception of Article 6(3) which continues to apply to decisions adopted pursuant to Article 81(3) of the Treaty prior to the date of application of this Regulation until the date of expiration of those decisions.

Appendix II

Article 40

Amendment of Regulations No 19/65/EEC, (EEC) No 2821/71 and (EEC) No 1534/91

Article 7 of Regulation No 19/65/EEC, Article 7 of Regulation (EEC) No 2821/71 and Article 7 of Regulation (EEC) No 1534/91 are repealed.

Article 41

Amendment of Regulation (EEC) No 3976/87
Regulation (EEC) No 3976/87 is amended as follows:

1. Article 6 is replaced by the following:

 "Article 6

 The Commission shall consult the Advisory Committee referred to in Article 14 of Council Regulation (EC) No 1/2003 of 16 December 2002 on the implementation of the rules on competition laid down in Articles 81 and 82 of the Treaty[18] before publishing a draft Regulation and before adopting a Regulation."

2. Article 7 is repealed.

Article 42

Amendment of Regulation (EEC) No 479/92
Regulation (EEC) No 479/92 is amended as follows:

1. Article 5 is replaced by the following:

 "Article 5

 Before publishing the draft Regulation and before adopting the Regulation, the Commission shall consult the Advisory Committee referred to in Article 14 of Council Regulation (EC) No 1/2003 of 16 December 2002 on the implementation of the rules on competition laid down in Articles 81 and 82 of the Treaty[19].'

2. Article 6 is repealed.

Article 43

Repeal of Regulations No 17 and No 141

1. Regulation No 17 is repealed with the exception of Article 8(3) which continues to apply to decisions adopted pursuant to Article 81(3) of the Treaty prior to the date of application of this Regulation until the date of expiration of those decisions.

2. Regulation No 141 is repealed.

---

18. OJ L 1, 4.1.2003, p. 1.
19. OJ L 1, 4.1.2003, p. 1.

3. References to the repealed Regulations shall be construed as references to this Regulation.

Article 44

Report on the application of the present Regulation

Five years from the date of application of this Regulation, the Commission shall report to the European Parliament and the Council on the functioning of this Regulation, in particular on the application of Article 11(6) and Article 17.
On the basis of this report, the Commission shall assess whether it is appropriate to propose to the Council a revision of this Regulation.

Article 45

Entry into force

This Regulation shall enter into force on the 20th day following that of its publication in the Official Journal of the European Communities.
It shall apply from 1 May 2004.
This Regulation shall be binding in its entirety and directly applicable in all Member States.
Done at Brussels, 16 December 2002.
For the Council
The President
M. Fischer Boel

APPENDIX III
Antitrust Guidelines for International Enforcement and Cooperation

Issued by the:

U.S. DEPARTMENT OF JUSTICE

and

FEDERAL TRADE COMMISSION

January 13, 2017

TABLE OF CONTENTS

1. Introduction
2. Relevant Antitrust and Related Statutes
   - 2.1 Sherman Antitrust Act
   - 2.2 Federal Trade Commission Act
   - 2.3 Clayton Antitrust Act
   - 2.4 Hart-Scott-Rodino Antitrust Improvements Act of 1976
   - 2.5 Antitrust Criminal Penalty Enhancement and Reform Act of 2004
   - 2.6 International Antitrust Enforcement Assistance Act
   - 2.7 National Cooperative Research and Production Act
   - 2.8 Webb-Pomerene Act
   - 2.9 Export Trading Company Act of 1982
   - 2.10 Wilson Tariff Act
   - 2.11 Trade Act of 1974, Section 301
   - 2.12 Tariff Act of 1930
3. Agencies' Application of U.S. Antitrust Law to Conduct Involving Foreign

Appendix III

        Commerce
        3.1   Conduct Involving Import Commerce
        3.2   Conduct Involving Non-Import Foreign Commerce
        3.3   Conduct Involving U.S. Government Financing or Purchasing
4.   Agencies' Consideration of Foreign Jurisdictions
        4.1   Comity
        4.2   Consideration of Foreign Government Involvement
              4.2.1 Foreign Sovereign Immunity
              4.2.2 Foreign Sovereign Compulsion
              4.2.3 Act of State Doctrine
              4.2.4 Petitioning of Sovereigns
5.   International Cooperation
        5.1   Investigations and Cooperation
              5.1.1 Investigative Tools
              5.1.2 Confidentiality
              5.1.3 Legal Bases for Cooperation
              5.1.4 Types of Information Exchanged and Waivers of Confidentiality
              5.1.5 Remedies
        5.2   Special Considerations in Criminal Investigations

ANNEX Defined Terms

1.   INTRODUCTION

"The heart of our national economic policy long has been faith in the value of competition,"[1] and the U.S. antitrust laws have stood as the ultimate protector of competition in our free market economy. That policy and these laws rest "on the premise that the unrestrained interaction of competitive forces will yield the best allocation of our economic resources, the lowest prices, the highest quality and the greatest material progress."[2] To protect U.S. consumers and businesses from anticompetitive conduct in foreign commerce, the federal antitrust laws have applied to "commerce with foreign nations" since their inception.[3]

Since the 1995 release of the Antitrust Enforcement Guidelines for International Operations, trade between the United States and other countries has expanded at a tremendous rate. With this expansion, the federal antitrust laws have played an increasingly important role in protecting consumers and businesses purchasing in U.S. import commerce and exporters selling in U.S. export commerce from anticompetitive conduct. In addition, anticompetitive conduct—from price-fixing cartels to competition-reducing mergers and monopolization—increasingly is subject to investigation and, in some cases, remedial action by foreign authorities.

---

1. *Standard Oil Co. v. Fed. Trade Comm'n*, 340 U.S. 231, 248 (1951).
2. *N. Pac. Ry. Co. v. United States*, 356 U.S. 1, 4 (1958).
3. *See infra* Sections 3.1 and 3.2 for a discussion of the meaning of "commerce with foreign nations."

Appendix III

The Department of Justice (the "Department") and the Federal Trade Commission (the "Commission" or "FTC") (collectively the "Agencies") are charged with enforcement of the federal antitrust laws, an essential component of which is the application of these laws to foreign commerce. Moreover, the Agencies cooperate on their antitrust enforcement with foreign authorities wherever appropriate.

In furtherance of that enforcement and in recognition of the role of international cooperation, the Agencies issue these Antitrust Guidelines for International Enforcement and Cooperation ("International Guidelines"), which replace the 1995 Antitrust Enforcement Guidelines for International Operations. The International Guidelines provide updated guidance to businesses engaged in international activities on questions that concern the Agencies' international enforcement policy as well as the Agencies' related investigative tools and cooperation with foreign authorities.

Many nations share our faith in the value of competition, and as of 2017, over 130 jurisdictions have enacted antitrust laws as a means to ensure open and free markets, promote consumer welfare, and prevent conduct that impedes competition. Accordingly, the Agencies have expanded their efforts and committed greater resources to building and maintaining strong relationships with foreign authorities to promote greater policy engagement. This engagement with foreign authorities has multiple goals, notably: increasing global understanding of different jurisdictions' respective antitrust laws, policies, and procedures; contributing to procedural and substantive convergence toward best practices; and facilitating enforcement cooperation internationally. The Agencies have championed and continue to promote this engagement, focusing on substantive enforcement standards that seek to advance consumer welfare based on sound economics, procedural fairness, transparency, and non-discriminatory treatment of parties.

In furtherance of these goals, the Agencies raise important policy and practical antitrust issues with foreign authorities bilaterally and through multilateral organizations such as the Competition Committee of the Organisation for Economic Co-operation and Development ("OECD"), the International Competition Network ("ICN"), the United Nations Conference on Trade and Development ("UNCTAD"), and the Asia-Pacific Economic Cooperation ("APEC") forum. These efforts have resulted in the development and implementation of standards of international best practice and consensus guidance on substantive antitrust and procedural fairness.[4] Consistent approaches to competition law, policy, and procedures across jurisdictions facilitate cooperation among competition agencies, and increase the effectiveness and predictability of enforcement, which benefits the Agencies, consumers, and the business community.

---

4. *See, e.g.*, Int'l Competition Network, *Guidance on Investigative Process*, http://www.internationalcompetitionnetwork.org/uploads/library/doc1028.pdf; Org. for Econ. Co-Operation & Dev., *Recommendation Concerning International Co- operation on Competition Investigations and Proceedings* (2014), http://www.oecd.org/daf/competition/2014-rec-internat-coop-competition.pdf; Int'l Competition Network, *Recommended Practices on the Assessment of Dominance/Substantial Market Power*; http://www.internationalcompetitionnetwork.org/uploads/library/doc317.pdf; Int'l Competition Network, *Recommended Practices for Merger Notification and Review Procedures*, http://www.internationalcompetitionnetwork.org/uploads/library/doc588.pdf; Org. for Econ. Co-Operation & Dev., *Recommendation Concerning Effective Action Against Hard Core Cartels* (1998), https://www.oecd.org/daf/competition/2350130.pdf.

Appendix III

In the United States, the Agencies are responsible for international antitrust policy engagement and cooperation. The Agencies also work within the U.S. government to ensure that broader U.S. policy and engagement appropriately reflects an understanding of complex international antitrust issues and accepted principles of competition law, economics, and policy. Consumers and businesses are welcome to contact the Agencies concerning the application and enforcement of antitrust law and policy internationally.

In addition to this introductory chapter, the International Guidelines are divided into four other chapters. Chapter 2 provides a brief summary of the antitrust and related laws that are likely to have the greatest significance for businesses engaged in international activities. Chapter 3 describes what connections to the United States are sufficient for the Agencies to investigate or bring enforcement actions challenging conduct occurring abroad or involving or affecting foreign commerce.

Chapter 4 describes the Agencies' consideration of international comity concerns and the role of foreign government involvement in determining whether to open an investigation or bring an enforcement action. Chapter 5 provides guidance on the Agencies' pertinent investigatory tools and their enforcement cooperation with foreign authorities. These International Guidelines also include a number of examples that are intended to illustrate how the principles and policies discussed may operate in certain contexts.[5]

As is the case with all guidelines issued by the Agencies, users should rely on qualified counsel to assist them in evaluating the antitrust risk associated with any contemplated transaction or activity.[6] No set of guidelines could possibly indicate how the Agencies will assess the particular facts of every case. Persons seeking more specific advance statements of enforcement intentions with respect to the issues discussed in the International Guidelines should use other procedures, which may include the Department's Business Review procedure[7] and the Commission's Advisory Opinion procedure.[8] Other existing Department and Commission guidelines and statements are not qualified, modified, or otherwise amended by the issuance of these International Guidelines. The International Guidelines are not intended to, do not, and may not be relied upon to create any rights, substantive or procedural, enforceable at law by any party in any matter, civil or criminal. Nor are any limitations hereby placed on otherwise lawful litigative prerogatives of the Department or Commission.

---

5. The ultimate outcome of the analysis in a particular case, *i.e.*, in determining whether or not a violation of the federal antitrust laws has occurred, or the manner in which the Agencies may cooperate with foreign authorities, depends on the specific facts and circumstances of the case.
6. Users also should evaluate separately the risk of private litigation by competitors, consumers, and suppliers, as well as the risk of enforcement by state prosecutors under state and federal antitrust laws.
7. 28 C.F.R. § 50.6.
8. 16 C.F.R. §§ 1.1-1.4.

2. RELEVANT ANTITRUST AND RELATED STATUTES

Cases involving foreign commerce or foreign conduct can involve almost any provision of the federal antitrust laws. The Agencies do not discriminate in the enforcement of the antitrust laws based on the nationality of the parties. Nor do the Agencies employ their statutory authority to further non-antitrust goals. When the Agencies determine that a sufficient nexus to the United States exists to apply the antitrust laws[9] and that neither international comity nor the involvement of a foreign jurisdiction precludes investigation or enforcement,[10] the Agencies apply the same substantive rules to all cases. The following is a brief summary of the antitrust and related statutes that are likely to have the greatest significance for businesses engaged in international activities.

2.1 Sherman Antitrust Act

The Sherman Antitrust Act ("Sherman Act") sets forth general antitrust prohibitions.[11] Section 1 of the Sherman Act outlaws contracts, combinations, and conspiracies that unreasonably restrain "trade or commerce among the several States, or with foreign nations."1[12] Section 2 outlaws monopolization, attempts to monopolize, and conspiracies to monopolize "any part of the trade or commerce among the several States, or with foreign nations."[13] Section 6a, added by the Foreign Trade Antitrust Improvements Act of 1982 ("FTAIA"), clarifies the Sherman Act's application to conduct involving only non-import foreign commerce.[14]

Violations of the Sherman Act may be prosecuted as civil or criminal offenses. The Department has sole responsibility for the criminal enforcement of the Sherman Act and criminally prosecutes traditional per se offenses of the law, which typically involve price fixing, customer allocation, bid rigging, or other cartel activities that would also be violations of the law in many countries. Criminal violations of the Act are punishable by fines and imprisonment. The Sherman Act provides that corporate defendants may be fined up to $100 million and individual defendants may be fined up to $1 million and sentenced to up to 10 years imprisonment.[15]

---

9. *See infra* Sections 3.1-3.3.
10. *See infra* Sections 4.1-4.2.
11. 15 U.S.C. §§ 1-7.
12. *Id.* § 1.
13. *Id.* § 2.
14. *Id.* § 6a; *see infra* Sections 2.9, 3.1, and 3.2.
15. 15 U.S.C. §§ 1-3. Defendants may be fined up to twice the gross pecuniary gain or loss caused by their offense in lieu of the Sherman Act fines, pursuant to 18 U.S.C. § 3571(d). Defendants may also be placed on probation for up to five years. The U.S. Sentencing Commission Guidelines provide advisory sentences or sentencing ranges for antitrust offenses. *See* U.S.S.G. § 2R1.1 & ch. 8. In determining the appropriate sentence, the court must consider the Guidelines' advisory sentence or sentencing range, as well as the other factors in 18 U.S.C. § 3553(a) and also, for fines, the factors in 18 U.S.C. § 3572(a). The Department generally seeks sentences consistent with the Guidelines.

Appendix III

In a civil proceeding, the Department may obtain equitable relief to prevent and restrain violations of the Sherman Act.[16] It may also obtain treble damages if the U.S. government is injured in its business or property by a violation, for example as a purchaser of affected goods or services.[17] Private plaintiffs may also obtain injunctive and treble damage relief for violations of the Sherman Act.[18]

2.2 Federal Trade Commission Act

Section 5 of the Federal Trade Commission Act ("FTC Act") declares unlawful "unfair methods of competition in or affecting commerce, and unfair or deceptive acts or practices in or affecting commerce."[19] Pursuant to its authority to prevent unfair methods of competition, the Commission may take administrative action against conduct that violates the Sherman Act or the Clayton Antitrust Act ("Clayton Act"), as well as anticompetitive practices that do not fall within the scope of the Sherman or Clayton Acts.[20] The Commission may also seek injunctive relief in federal court under Section 13(b) of the FTC Act.[21] These International Guidelines pertain only to the Commission's antitrust enforcement authority under Section 5's prohibition of unfair methods of competition. Section 5(a)(3) of the FTC Act, added by the Foreign Trade Antitrust Improvements Act of 1982, clarifies the FTC Act's application to conduct involving only non-import foreign commerce.[22]

2.3 Clayton Antitrust Act

The Clayton Act expands on the general prohibitions of the Sherman Act and addresses anticompetitive problems in their incipiency.[23] Section 7 of the Clayton Act prohibits any merger or acquisition of stock or assets "where in any line of commerce or in any activity affecting commerce in any section of the country, the effect of such acquisition may be substantially to lessen competition, or to tend to create a monopoly."[24] The Agency reviewing a transaction that would violate Section 7 can seek a federal court order enjoining its consummation.[25] In addition, the Commission may seek a cease and

---

16. 15 U.S.C. § 4.
17. *Id.* § 15a.
18. *See id.* §§ 15, 26.
19. *Id.* § 45.
20. *Id.* § 45(b). *See* Fed. Trade Comm'n, *Statement of Enforcement Principles Regarding "Unfair methods of Competition" Under Section 5 of the FTC Act*, https://www.ftc.gov/public-statements/2015/08/statement-enforcement-principles-regarding-unfair-methods-competition.
21. 15 U.S.C. § 53(b).
22. *Id.* § 45(a)(3).
23. *Id.* §§ 12-27. Under the Clayton Act, "commerce" includes "trade or commerce among the several States and with foreign nations," and "person" includes corporations or associations existing under or authorized either by the laws of the United States or any of its states or territories, or by the laws of any foreign country. *Id.* § 12.
24. *Id.* § 18. The asset acquisition clause applies to "person[s] subject to the jurisdiction of the Federal Trade Commission" under the Clayton Act.
25. *Id.* § 25 (Clayton Act); *id.* § 53(b) (FTC Act). On August 19, 2010, the Agencies issued revised Horizontal Merger Guidelines, which outline their principal analytical techniques, practices, and

desist order in an administrative proceeding against a merger under Section 11 of the Clayton Act, Section 5 of the FTC Act, or both.[26] Private parties and state Attorneys General may also seek injunctive relief under the Clayton Act.[27]

Section 3 of the Clayton Act prohibits any person engaged in commerce from conditioning the lease or sale of goods or commodities upon the purchaser's agreement not to use the products of a competitor, if the effect may be "to substantially lessen competition or tend to create a monopoly in any line of commerce."[28] In evaluating transactions, courts use the same analysis employed in the evaluation of tying under Section 1 of the Sherman Act to assess a defendant's liability under Section 3 of the Clayton Act.[29]

Section 2 of the Clayton Act, as amended by the Robinson-Patman Act,[30] prohibits price discrimination in certain circumstances. In practice, the Commission has exercised principal responsibility for enforcing this provision.

2.4 Hart-Scott-Rodino Antitrust Improvements Act of 1976

Title II of the Hart-Scott-Rodino Antitrust Improvements Act of 1976 ("HSR Act") facilitates the Agencies' enforcement of the antitrust laws with respect to anticompetitive mergers and acquisitions. It requires that persons provide notice to the Agencies of certain proposed mergers or acquisitions and imposes a waiting period on these mergers or acquisitions.[31] Transactions are subject to these requirements only if they meet certain conditions, including minimum size thresholds.[32] Some transactions are

---

enforcement policy with respect to mergers and acquisitions involving actual or potential competitors under the federal antitrust laws. U.S. Dep't of Justice & Fed. Trade Comm'n, *Horizontal Merger Guidelines* (2010), https://www.justice.gov/sites/default/files/atr/legacy/2010/08/19/hmg-2010.pdf.

26. 15 U.S.C. § 21 (Clayton Act); *id.* § 45 (FTC Act).
27. *Id.* §§ 15c, 26.
28. *Id.* § 14.
29. *See, e.g., Sheridan v. Marathon Petroleum Co.*, 530 F.3d 590, 592 (7th Cir. 2008) ("Though some old cases say otherwise, the standards for adjudicating tying under the two statutes are now recognized to be the same.").
30. 15 U.S.C. §§ 13-13b, 21a. The Robinson-Patman Act applies only to purchases involving commodities "for use, consumption, or resale within the United States." *Id.* § 13(a). It has been construed not to apply to sales for export. *See, e.g., Gen. Chem., Inc. v. Exxon Chem. Co.*, 625 F.2d 1231, 1234 (5th Cir. 1980). Intervening domestic sales, however, would be subject to the Act. *See Raul Int'l Corp. v. Sealed Power Corp.*, 586 F. Supp. 349, 351-55 (D.N.J. 1984).
31. 15 U.S.C. § 18a. The scope of the Agencies' jurisdiction under Section 7 of the Clayton Act, *id.* § 18, exceeds the scope of those transactions subject to the premerger notification requirements of the HSR Act. Enforcement responsibility in particular cases is allocated to either the Department or the Commission typically based on prior agency expertise in the relevant product market at issue.
32. *Id.* § 18a(a). As a result of a 2000 amendment to the HSR Act, all minimum thresholds in the Act are adjusted annually based on changes in the gross national product. *Id.* § 18a(a)(2). The adjusted annual thresholds are announced in January of each year in the Federal Register, and are effective 30 days after publication. The current adjusted annual thresholds are available on the Commission's website at https://www.ftc.gov/enforcement/premerger-notification-program/current-thresholds.

Appendix III

explicitly exempted from these requirements by the statute's text.[33] The HSR Act and the Hart-Scott-Rodino Premerger Notification Rules ("HSR Rules")[34] exempt from the notification requirements certain international transactions (typically those having little nexus to U.S. commerce) that otherwise meet the statutory thresholds.[35] Transactions not subject to the HSR Act's notification and waiting period requirements may still be subject to the Sherman Act, the FTC Act, or the Clayton Act, and the Agencies may seek to block or undo an anticompetitive merger or acquisition or seek other equitable relief when any of those statutes applies.

If a transaction is subject to the HSR Act's requirements, the parties must typically wait 30 days after providing notice to the Agencies before they may consummate it; the parties to cash tender offers must wait only 15 days.[36] The Agency reviewing the transaction may request additional documents or information concerning a transaction, known as a "Second Request," during this waiting period. Issuing a Second Request extends the waiting period until a certain number of days after the Agency has received the requested material and the party certifies substantial compliance; typically 30 days, but only 10 days for cash tender offers.[37]

Failure to comply with the HSR Act is punishable by court-imposed and potentially substantial civil monetary penalties.[38] A court also may order injunctive relief to remedy a substantial failure to comply with the HSR Act.[39]

The HSR Act and the HSR Rules are necessarily technical and should be consulted directly. Businesses may seek an interpretation of their obligations under the HSR Act and the HSR Rules from the Commission's Premerger Notification Office.[40]

2.5 Antitrust Criminal Penalty Enhancement and Reform Act of 2004

The Antitrust Criminal Penalty Enhancement and Reform Act of 2004 ("ACPERA") limits the liability for civil damages claims in private state or federal antitrust actions of a qualifying person cooperating with a criminal antitrust investigation by the Department.[41] Specifically, for claims against a corporation that enters into an antitrust leniency agreement with the Department pursuant to its Corporate Leniency Policy[42] or

---

33. 15 U.S.C.§ 18a(c).
34. 16 C.F.R. pt. 801-03.
35. 16 C.F.R. §§ 801.1(e), (k) & 802.50-53.
36. 15 U.S.C. § 18a(b); 16 C.F.R. § 803.1; see also 11 U.S.C. § 363 (b)(2) (regarding certain transactions involving parties in bankruptcy).
37. 15 U.S.C. § 18a(e).
38. Id. § 18a(g)(1). In August 2016, the limit on these penalties was adjusted upward to $40,000 for each day a violation continues. That limit adjusts periodically based on inflation. 28 U.S.C. § 2461 note; 16 C.F.R. § 1.98(a).
39. 15 U.S.C. § 18a(g)(2).
40. See 16 C.F.R. § 803.30.
41. Pub. L. 108-237, 118 Stat. 661 (codified as 15 U.S.C. § 1 note). Originally set to expire in 2009, the provision has been twice extended. Pub. L. 111-190, 124 Stat. 1275 (2010); Pub. L. 111-30, 123 Stat. 1775 (2009). It is currently set to expire, absent further extension by Congress, on June 22, 2020.
42. For information on the Department's Antitrust Corporate Leniency Policy, see https://www.justice.gov/atr/leniency-program.

a cooperating individual covered by such an agreement, a claimant cannot recover damages exceeding the "portion of the actual damages sustained by such claimant which is attributable to the commerce done by the applicant in the goods or services affected by the violation."[43] To qualify for this limitation, the corporation or cooperating individuals must meet the conditions of the Corporate Leniency Policy, including cooperating fully with the Department's investigation, and must meet certain requirements in connection with the claimant's civil action. These requirements include providing the claimant with a full account of all facts known to the corporation or cooperating individual that are potentially relevant to the civil action, furnishing the claimant with potentially relevant documents and other items wherever located, and, in the case of cooperating individuals, making himself or herself available for interviews, depositions, or testimony in connection with the civil action as the claimant may reasonably require.

2.6 International Antitrust Enforcement Assistance Act

The International Antitrust Enforcement Assistance Act ("IAEAA")[44] authorizes the Agencies to enter into antitrust-specific mutual assistance agreements with foreign authorities.[45] Under such agreements, U.S. and foreign authorities may share evidence relating to antitrust violations already in their possession and provide each other with investigatory assistance in obtaining evidence, including statutorily protected confidential information.[46] The IAEAA does not apply to materials submitted pursuant to the HSR Act.[47] The Agencies entered into an IAEAA agreement with Australia in 1999.[48]

2.7 National Cooperative Research and Production Act

The National Cooperative Research and Production Act ("NCRPA"), as amended by the Standards Development Organization Advancement Act of 2004,[49] clarifies the substantive application of the state and federal antitrust laws to joint ventures and standards development organizations ("SDOs") while engaged in standards development activity. It requires U.S. courts to judge the competitive effects of a challenged

---

43. 15 U.S.C. § 1 note.
44. 15 U.S.C. § 6201 et seq.
45. Information relevant to antitrust enforcement may also be provided under generalized legal assistance treaties in force between the United States and a wide range of foreign partners. See infra Sections 5.1.3 and 5.2.
46. 15 U.S.C. § 6201. Agreements entered into under the IAEAA's authority must include, among other requirements, assurances that the foreign authority will protect the confidentiality of the information exchanged, id. § 6211(2)(A)-(C), and provisions addressing the permitted use of the evidence exchanged, id. § 6211(2)(E)(i), (ii).
47. Id. § 6204(1).
48. Agreement Between the Government of the United States of America and The Government of Australia on Mutual Antitrust Enforcement Assistance, U.S.-Aus. (1999), reprinted in 4 Trade Rep. Reg. (CCH) ¶ 13,502A, available at https://www.ftc.gov/policy/cooperation-agreements/usaaustralia-mutual-antitrust-enforcement-assistance-agreement.
49. 15 U.S.C. §§ 4301-06.

joint venture or SDO covered by the Act under a rule-of-reason standard.[50] This approach is consistent with the Agencies' general analysis of joint ventures.[51] The Act further provides for the possible recovery of attorney's fees by joint ventures and SDOs that are prevailing parties in damage actions brought against them under the antitrust laws.

The NCRPA also establishes a voluntary procedure pursuant to which parties to a joint venture or an SDO that meet certain criteria may notify the Agencies of their intention to engage in standards development activity. Under the statute, if participants provide notice to the Agencies, the amount of monetary relief obtainable in a private civil suit challenging the standards-development activity is limited to actual, rather than treble, damages so long as the challenged conduct is within the scope of the notification. This benefit is not available to joint production ventures, unless "(1) the principal facilities for such production are located in the United States or its territories, and (2) each person who controls any party to such venture (including such party itself) is a United States person, or a foreign person from a country whose law accords antitrust treatment no less favorable to United States persons than to such country's domestic persons with respect to participation in joint ventures for production."[52]

2.8 Webb-Pomerene Act

The Webb-Pomerene Act provides a limited antitrust exemption for the formation and operation of associations of otherwise competing businesses to engage collectively in export sales.[53] The exemption applies only to the export of "goods, wares, or merchandise."[54] It does not apply to conduct that has an anticompetitive effect in the United States or that injures domestic competitors of the members of an export association. Nor does it provide any immunity from prosecution under foreign antitrust laws.[55] Associations seeking an exemption under the Webb- Pomerene Act must file their

---

50. *Id.* § 4302.
51. *See, e.g.*, U.S. Dep't of Justice & Fed. Trade Comm'n, *Antitrust Guidelines for the Licensing of Intellectual Property* 5 (2017), https://www.justice.gov/atr/IPguidelines/download; Fed. Trade Comm'n & U.S. Dep't of Justice, *Antitrust Guidelines for Collaborations Among Competitors*, (2000), *available at* https://www.ftc.gov/sites/default/files/documents/public_events/joint-venture-hearings-antitrust-guidelines-collaboration-among-competitors/ ftcdojguidelines-2.pdf; Fed. Trade Comm'n & U.S. Dep't of Justice, *Statements of Antitrust Enforcement Policy in Health Care*, Stmt. 2 (1996), *available at* https://www.ftc.gov/sites/default/files/attachments/competition-policy-guidance/statements_of_antitrust_enforcement_policy_in_health_care_august_1996.pdf (outlining a four-step approach for joint venture analysis). *See generally Am. Needle, Inc. v. Nat'l Football League*, 560 U.S. 183 (2010); *Texaco, Inc. v. Dagher*, 547 U.S. 1 (2006); *Fed. Trade Comm'n v. Ind. Fed'n of Dentists*, 476 U.S. 447 (1986); *Nat'l Collegiate Athletic Ass'n v. Bd. of Regents of Univ. of Okla.*, 468 U.S. 85 (1984). *See generally also In re Mass. Board of Registration in Optometry*, 110 F.T.C. 549 (1988).
52. 15 U.S.C. § 4306(2).
53. *Id.* §§ 61-65.
54. *Id.* § 61.
55. *See, e.g.*, Case C-89/85, *Ahlström v. Comm'n*, 1988 E.C.R. 5193 (finding Webb- Pomerene association was not exempt from violations of European antitrust law); Commission Decision of 19 December 1990 Relating to a Proceeding Under Article 85 of the EEC Treaty, 1991 O.J. (L 152) 16-20 (denying antitrust exemption to soda ash Webb-Pomerene association); *Competition*

Appendix III

articles of agreement and annual reports with the Commission, but pre-formation approval from the Commission is not required. Few associations file reports with the FTC; those reports are available on the Commission's website.[56]

2.9 Export Trading Company Act of 1982

The Export Trading Company Act of 1982 ("ETC Act")[57] is designed to increase U.S. exports of goods and services in several ways.[58] In Title II, it encourages more efficient provision of export trade services to U.S. producers and suppliers by reducing restrictions on trade financing provided by financial institutions.[59] In Title III, it reduces uncertainty concerning the application of the U.S. antitrust laws to export trade through the creation of a procedure by which persons engaging in U.S. export trade may obtain an export trade certificate of review ("ETCR").[60] In Title IV, also known as the Foreign Trade Antitrust Improvement Act of 1982 or FTAIA, it clarifies the application of the Sherman Act and the FTC Act to conduct involving only non-import foreign commerce.[61] The Title III certificates are discussed briefly here; the application of the Sherman Act and FTC Act is treated below in Chapter 3.

Export trade certificates of review are issued by the Secretary of Commerce with the concurrence of the Department. Persons named in the ETCR obtain limited immunity from suit under both federal and state antitrust laws for activities that are specified in the certificate and that comply with the terms of the certificate.[62] To obtain an ETCR, an applicant must show that proposed export conduct will:

1. result in neither a substantial lessening of competition or restraint of trade within the United States nor a substantial restraint of the export trade of any competitor of the applicant;
2. not unreasonably enhance, stabilize, or depress prices in the United States of the class of goods or services covered by the application;
3. not constitute unfair methods of competition against competitors engaged in the export of the class of goods or services exported by the applicant; and
4. not include any act that may reasonably be expected to result in the sale for consumption or resale in the United States of such goods or services.[63]

Comm'n v. Am. Nat. Soda Ash Corp., 2008 ZACT 92 (South Africa) (settlement by Webb-Pomerene association with Competition Tribunal South Africa for violations of antitrust laws).
56. Webb-Pomerene Act filings are available at https://www.ftc.gov/policy/reports/webb-pomerene-act-filings. Two associations filed reports with the FTC for 2015.
57. Pub L. No. 97-290, 96 Stat. 1233 (codified in scattered sections of 15 U.S.C.).
58. 15 U.S.C. § 4001(b).
59. *See* 12 U.S.C. §§ 372, 635 a-4, 1841, 1843. Because Title II does not implicate the antitrust laws, it is not discussed further in these Guidelines.
60. 15 U.S.C. §§ 4011-21.
61. *Id.* § 6a (Sherman Act); *id.* § 45(a)(3) (FTC Act); *see infra* Sections 3.1-3.3.
62. H.R. REP. NO. 97-924, at 26 (1982); *see* 15 U.S.C. § 4021(6).
63. 15 U.S.C. § 4013(a).

Congress intended that these standards "encompass the full range of the antitrust laws," as defined in the ETC Act.[64]

The protections provided by an ETCR from the federal and state antitrust laws are not unlimited. First, conduct that falls outside the scope of a certificate remains fully subject to private and governmental enforcement actions. Second, an ETCR that is obtained by fraud is void from the outset and thus offers no protection under the antitrust laws. Third, any person that has been injured by certified conduct may recover actual (though not treble) damages if that conduct is found to violate any of the statutory criteria described above.[65] In any such action, certified conduct enjoys a presumption of legality, and the prevailing party is entitled to recover costs and attorneys' fees.[66] Fourth, an ETCR does not constitute, explicitly or implicitly, an endorsement or opinion by the Secretary of Commerce or by the Department concerning the legality of such business plans under the laws of any foreign country. Finally, an ETCR does not insulate conduct from investigation or enforcement by a foreign antitrust authority.

The Secretary of Commerce may revoke or modify an ETCR if the Secretary or the Department determines that the applicant's export activities have ceased to comply with the statutory criteria for obtaining a certificate.[67] The Department may also bring suit under Section 15 of the Clayton Act to enjoin conduct that threatens a "clear and irreparable harm to the national interest,"[68] even if the conduct has been pre-approved as part of an ETCR.

The Commerce Department, in consultation with the Department, has issued guidelines setting forth the standards used in reviewing ETCR applications.[69]

2.10 Wilson Tariff Act

The Wilson Tariff Act[70] prohibits "every combination, conspiracy, trust, agreement, or contract" made by or between two or more persons or corporations, either of whom is engaged in importing any article from a foreign country into the United States, where the agreement is intended to restrain trade or increase the market price in any part of the United States of the imported articles, or of "any manufacture into which such imported article enters or is intended to enter." Violation of the Wilson Tariff Act is a

---

64. H.R. REP. NO. 97-924, at 26(1982); see 15 U.S.C. § 4021(6).
65. 15 U.S.C. § 4016(b)(1).
66. See id. § 4016(b)(3), (b)(4).
67. Id. § 4014(b).
68. Id. § 4016(b)(5); see also id. § 25.
69. See Int'l Trade Admin. (U.S. Dep't of Commerce), *The Export Trade Certificate of Review Program - The Competitive Edge for U.S. Exporters: Guidelines* (2015), http://trade.gov/mas/ian/etca/tg_ian_002140.asp. The Commerce Department's Export Trading Company Guidebook provides information on establishing and using an export trading company, including factors to consider when applying for an ETCR. Int'l Trade Admin. (U.S. Dep't of Commerce), *The Export Trading Company Guidebook* (1987). As of the date of these Guidelines, there are approximately 80 active certificates.
70. 15 U.S.C. §§ 8-11.

misdemeanor, punishable by a maximum fine of $5,000 or one year in prison. This Act also provides for seizure of the imported articles.[71]

2.11 Trade Act of 1974, Section 301

Section 301 of the Trade Act of 1974 provides that the U.S. Trade Representative ("USTR"), subject to the specific direction, if any, of the President, may take action, including restricting imports, to enforce rights of the United States under any trade agreement, to address acts inconsistent with the international legal rights of the United States, or to respond to unjustifiable, unreasonable or discriminatory practices of foreign governments that burden or restrict U.S. commerce.[72] Interested parties may initiate such actions through petitions to the USTR, or the USTR may itself initiate proceedings. Section 301(d)(3)(B)(i)(IV) includes the "toleration by a foreign government of systematic anticompetitive activities by enterprises or among enterprises in the foreign country that have the effect of restricting . . . access of United States goods or services to a foreign market" as one of the "unreasonable" practices that might justify such a proceeding.[73] The Department participates in the interagency committee that makes recommendations to the President on what actions, if any, should be taken.

2.12 Tariff Act of 1930

The Tariff Act of 1930[74] provides remedies for certain violations of the trade laws with antitrust implications, including violations of the laws regarding countervailing and anti-dumping duties.[75] Significant for purposes of the Agencies' enforcement of the federal antitrust laws, certain settlements of trade disputes entered under specific procedures set forth in the U.S. trade laws are granted implied immunity under this Act, even if the settlement involves price and quantity agreements or otherwise implicates the antitrust laws.[76] Agreements among competitors that do not comply with specific procedures in the U.S. trade laws or go beyond the measures authorized by such laws, however, are subject to the antitrust laws to the same extent as conduct unrelated to the settlement of a trade dispute.

---

71. *Id.* § 11.
72. 19 U.S.C. § 2411.
73. *Id.*
74. *Id.* §§ 1202 *et seq.*
75. *Id.* §§ 1671, 1673.
76. *See, e.g.*, Letter from Charles F. Rule, Acting Assistant Attorney General, Antitrust Division, Department of Justice, to Mr. Makoto Kuroda, Vice-Minister for International Affairs, Japanese Ministry of International Trade and Industry, July 30, 1986 (concluding that a suspension agreement did not violate the antitrust laws on the basis of factual representations that the agreement applied only to products under investigation, that it did not require pricing above levels needed to eliminate sales below foreign market value, and that assigning weighted-average foreign market values to exporters who were not respondents in the investigation was necessary to achieve the purpose of the anti-dumping law).

Appendix III

In the absence of legal authority, the fact, without more, that U.S. or foreign government officials were involved in or encouraged measures that would otherwise violate the antitrust laws does not immunize such arrangements.[77]

3. AGENCIES' APPLICATION OF U.S. ANTITRUST LAW TO CONDUCT INVOLVING FOREIGN COMMERCE

In making investigative and enforcement decisions, the Agencies focus on whether there is a sufficient connection between the anticompetitive conduct and the United States such that the federal antitrust laws apply and the Agencies' enforcement would redress harm or threatened harm to U.S. commerce and consumers. This Chapter describes circumstances under which a sufficient connection exists. If the Agencies determine that a sufficient connection exists, the Agencies generally will proceed in the normal course, subject to the considerations described in Chapter 4 and principles of prosecutorial discretion.

It is well established that the federal antitrust laws apply to foreign conduct that has a substantial and intended effect in the United States.[78] In 1982, Congress reaffirmed the applicability of the antitrust laws to conduct involving foreign commerce when it passed the FTAIA, which added Section 6a to the Sherman Act and Section 5(a)(3) to the FTC Act.[79] These provisions clarify whether the antitrust laws reach conduct—regardless of where it takes place—that involves trade or commerce with foreign nations.[80] Specifically, Section 6a provides:

> Sections 1 to 7 of [the Sherman Act] shall not apply to conduct involving trade or commerce (other than import trade or import commerce) with foreign nations unless—
> (1) such conduct has a direct, substantial, and reasonably foreseeable effect—

---

77. Cf. *United States v. Socony-Vacuum Oil Co.*, 310 U.S. 150, 226 (1940) ("Though employees of the government may have known of those programs and winked at them or tacitly approved them, no immunity would have thereby been obtained. For Congress had specified the precise manner and method of securing immunity [in the National Industrial Recovery Act]. None other would suffice. . . ."); see also *Otter Tail Power Co. v. United States*, 410 U.S. 366, 378-79 (1973).
78. *Hartford Fire Ins. Co. v. California*, 509 U.S. 764, 796 (1993); *United States v. Nippon Paper Indus. Co.*, 109 F.3d 1, 9 (1st Cir. 1997); *United States v. Aluminum Co. of Am.*, 148 F.2d 416, 444 (2d Cir. 1945).
79. 15 U.S.C. § 6a (Sherman Act); id. § 45(a)(3) (FTC Act).
80. The Supreme Court and other courts have declined to consider whether Section 6a amended existing law or merely codified it. *Hartford Fire*, 509 U.S. at 796 n.23; *Nippon Paper*, 109 F.3d at 4. Other courts have held that Section 6a supplanted the prior standard for the extraterritorial reach of the Sherman Act. *McGlinchy v. Shell Chem. Co.*, 845 F.2d 802, 813 n.8 (9th Cir. 1988); *The In Porters, S.A. v. Hanes Printables, Inc.*, 663 F. Supp. 494, 497 (M.D.N.C. 1987). If both the prior precedent and Section 6a apply in a single case, their requirements likely yield the same results. Conduct that either involves U.S. import commerce, see infra Section 3.1, or has a direct, substantial, and reasonably foreseeable effect on U.S. commerce, see infra Section 3.2, likely has a substantial and intended effect in the United States. In the Agencies' view, however, a separate showing of substantial and intended effects is unnecessary when some of the challenged conduct takes place in the United States because such a case would involve application, at least in part, of the U.S. antitrust law to territorial conduct.

(A) on trade or commerce which is not trade or commerce with foreign nations, or on import trade or import commerce with foreign nations; or

(B) on export trade or export commerce with foreign nations, of a person engaged in such trade or commerce in the United States; and

(2) such effect gives rise to a claim under the provisions of sections 1 to 7 of this title, other than this section.

If sections 1 to 7 of this title apply to such conduct only because of the operation of paragraph (1)(B), then sections 1 to 7 of this title shall apply to such conduct only for injury to export business in the United States.[81]

Section 5(a)(3) of the FTC Act closely parallels this provision.[82] Although the FTAIA clarified the reach of the Sherman Act and the FTC Act, it did not address the reach of the Clayton Act. Nevertheless, the Agencies would apply the principles outlined below when making enforcement decisions regarding mergers and acquisitions involving trade or commerce with foreign nations.

3.1 Conduct Involving Import Commerce

In general, the proscriptions in the Sherman Act and the FTC Act apply to conduct subject to Congress' constitutional power "to regulate commerce with foreign nations," among other things.[83] The FTAIA places "conduct involving trade or commerce (other than import trade or import commerce) with foreign nations" beyond the reach of these statutes, unless the conduct satisfies the FTAIA's effects exception described below.[84] The parenthetical language, however, excludes from the FTAIA's operation conduct involving import trade and import commerce. This provision is commonly referred to

---

81. 15 U.S.C. § 6a.
82. See 15 U.S.C § 45(a)(3). The federal courts of appeals have expressed differing views as to whether the FTAIA goes to a claim's merits or a court's subject-matter jurisdiction. Compare In re Monosodium Glutamate Antitrust Litig., 477 F.3d 535, 537 (8th Cir. 2007) (treating FTAIA as a question of subject-matter jurisdiction), Empagran S.A. v. F. Hoffmann-LaRoche, Ltd., 417 F.3d 1267, 1269 (D.C. Cir. 2005) (same), United States v. Anderson, 326 F.3d 1319, 1329-30 (11th Cir. 2003) (same), and Den Norske Stats Oljeselskap As v. HeereMac Vof, 241 F.3d 420, 424-25 (5th Cir. 2001) (same), with Minn-Chem, Inc. v. Agrium, Inc., 683 F.3d 845, 852 (7th Cir. 2012) (en banc) (FTAIA relates to merits of a claim), overruling United Phosphorus, Ltd. v. Angus Chem. Co., 322 F.3d 942, 951-52 (7th Cir. 2003) (en banc) (FTAIA relates to court's subject-matter jurisdiction), United States v. Hsiung, 778 F.3d 738 (9th Cir. 2015) (merits), overruling United States v. LSL Biotechs., 379 F.3d 672, 677 (9th Cir. 2004) (subject-matter jurisdiction), Lotes Co., Ltd. v. Hon Hai Precision Indus. Co., 753 F.3d 395, 405 (2d Cir. 2014) (merits), overruling Filetech S.A. v. France Telecom S.A., 157 F.3d 922, 929-32 (2d Cir. 1998) (subject-matter jurisdiction), and Animal Sci. Prods., Inc. v. China Minmetals Corp., 654 F.3d 462, 467-68 (3d Cir. 2011) (merits), overruling Carpet Grp. Int'l v. Oriental Rug Importers Ass'n, Inc., 227 F.3d 62, 69-70 (3d Cir. 2000) (subject-matter jurisdiction). This difference will not affect the Agencies' decisions about whether to proceed with an investigation or an enforcement action because the Agencies will not proceed when the FTAIA precludes the claim on the merits or strips the court of jurisdiction.
83. U.S. Const. art. I, § 8, cl. 3; see, e.g., 15 U.S.C. § 1 (outlawing conspiracies in unreasonably restraint of "trade or commerce ... with foreign nations"); id. §§ 44, 45(a)(1) (outlawing "unfair methods of competition in or affecting" "commerce ... with foreign nations"); see generally United States v. Se. Underwriters Ass'n, 322 U.S. 533, 588 (1944); Fed. Trade Comm'n v. Klesner, 274 U.S. 145, 151 (1927).
84. See infra Section 3.2.

Appendix III

as the "import commerce exclusion."[85] As a result of this exclusion, conduct involving U.S. import commerce, like conduct involving commerce within the United States, is "subject to the Sherman Act's [or FTC Act's] general requirements for effects on commerce, not to the special requirements spelled out in the FTAIA."[86]

The import commerce exclusion does not apply to conduct merely because those participating in the conduct are also engaged in import commerce. Rather the conduct being challenged must itself involve import commerce.[87] Conversely, the import commerce exclusion may apply to conduct even if the participants themselves do not act as importers. For example, a firm cannot escape liability for unreasonably restraining or monopolizing import commerce by outsourcing the delivery of its product to the United States.

Conduct may "involve" import commerce even if it is not directed specifically or exclusively at import commerce and even if the import commerce involved constitutes a relatively small portion of the worldwide commerce involved in the anticompetitive conduct.

Illustrative Example A

Situation: Corporation 1 and Corporation 2 have factories in Country Alpha where they manufacture Widget X. Corporation 1 and Corporation 2 agree to charge higher prices for Widget X. They sell Widget X to customers around the world, including in the United States.

Discussion: Corporation 1 and Corporation 2 manufacture Widget X outside the United States and sell Widget X in or for delivery to the United States. Thus their conspiracy to fix the price of Widget X is conduct involving U.S. import commerce. Accordingly, the conduct is prohibited by Section 1 of the Sherman Act as a conspiracy in restraint of "trade . . . with foreign nations," and Section 6a would not exempt this conspiracy from the antitrust laws. The circumstance that the price-fixing agreement concerned worldwide sales and did not specifically identify sales into the United States would not change the analysis. Likewise, even if the sales of Widget X in import commerce were a relatively small proportion or dollar amount of the price-fixed goods sold worldwide, the analysis would remain unchanged.[88]

Illustrative Example B

Situation: Shipping Corporation 1 and Shipping Corporation 2 are located in Country Alpha and provide international shipping services on various routes to the United States. Shipping Corporation 1 and Shipping Corporation 2 agree to charge higher prices for shipping services on select routes, including some routes to the United States.

Discussion: Shipping Corporation 1 and Shipping Corporation 2's conspiracy to fix the price of shipping services, which are closely connected to the importation of

---

85. See, e.g., Minn-Chem, 683 F.3d at 855.
86. Id. at 854; see Hsiung, 778 F.3d at 754; cf. H.R. REP. NO. 97-686, at 9 (1982) (explaining that "import restraints, which can be damaging to American consumers, remain covered by the law").
87. Carpet Grp., 227 F.3d at 71.
88. See generally Hsiung, 778 F.3d at 754-56 (affirming Sherman Act convictions on ground that evidence that conspirators sold price-fixed components in or for delivery to the United States satisfied Section 6a's import commerce exclusion).

goods into the United States, is conduct involving import commerce. Moreover, the conduct would also involve import commerce if Shipping Corporation 1 and Shipping Corporation 2 sold shipping services to customers in the United States for the transport of goods to the United States. In either case, the conduct is prohibited by Section 1 of the Sherman Act as a conspiracy in restraint of "trade ... with foreign nations," and Section 6a would not exempt this conspiracy from the antitrust laws. The conduct also likely has a direct, substantial, and reasonably foreseeable effect on import commerce by raising the price of importing goods into the United States or of the imported goods themselves, in which case it would also satisfy the FTAIA's effects exception, described below.[89]

3.2 Conduct Involving Non-Import Foreign Commerce

The FTAIA initially places conduct involving non-import foreign commerce, which means U.S. export commerce and wholly foreign commerce, outside the reach of the Sherman Act and FTC Act.[90] What is commonly referred to as the FTAIA's "effects exception"[91] brings such conduct back within the reach of the Acts if the conduct has a direct, substantial, and reasonably foreseeable effect on commerce within the United States, U.S. import commerce, or the export commerce of a U.S. exporter, and that effect gives rise to a claim.[92]

Whether an alleged effect on such commerce is direct, substantial, and reasonably foreseeable is a question of fact. An effect on commerce is "direct" if there is a reasonably proximate causal nexus, that is, if the effect is proximately caused by the alleged anticompetitive conduct.[93] In other words, an effect is direct if, in the natural or ordinary course of events, the alleged anticompetitive conduct would produce an effect on commerce. The substantiality requirement does not provide a minimum pecuniary threshold, nor does it require that the effects be quantified.[94] Finally, the "reasonable foreseeability" requirement is an objective test, requiring that the effect be foreseeable to "a reasonable person making practical business judgments."[95]

---

89. *See infra* Section 3.2.
90. *F. Hoffmann-La Roche Ltd. v. Empagran S.A.*, 542 U.S. 155, 162-63 (2004).
91. *See, e.g., Animal Sci. Prods., Inc. v. China Minmetals Corp.*, 654 F.3d 462, 471 (3d Cir. 2011).
92. *Empagran*, 542 U.S. at 162.
93. *See Minn-Chem*, 683 F.3d at 857; *Lotes Co. v. Hon Hai Precision Indus. Co.*, 753 F.3d 395, 409-13 (2d Cir. 2014). Although one court of appeals has held that an effect on U.S. commerce is "direct" for purposes of Section 6a only if it follows "as an immediate consequence" of the defendant's activity, *United States v. LSL Biotechs.*, 379 F.3d 672, 680 (9th Cir. 2004), the proximate cause standard is more consistent with the language of the statute. As the Seventh Circuit explained "[s]uperimposing the idea of 'immediate consequence' on top of the full [integrated] phrase ['direct, substantial, and reasonably foreseeable'] results in a stricter test than the complete text of the statute can bear" and "comes close to ignoring the fact that straightforward import commerce has already been excluded from the FTAIA's coverage." *Minn-Chem*, 683 F.3d at 857. Nevertheless, any difference between these two tests is unlikely to yield different results in the vast majority of cases.
94. *Cf. McLain v. Real Estate Bd. of New Orleans, Inc.*, 444 U.S. 232, 243 (1980) ("Nor is jurisdiction defeated in a case relying on anticompetitive effects by plaintiff's failure to quantify the adverse impact of defendant's conduct."); *Goldfarb v. Va. State Bar*, 421 U.S. 773, 785 (1975) ("[O]nce an effect is shown, no specific magnitude need be proved").
95. *Animal Sci.*, 654 F.3d at 471.

Appendix III

Illustrative Example C

Situation: Corporation 1 and Corporation 2 have factories in Country Alpha where they manufacture Component X, a piece of high-tech hardware used in electronic products. Corporation 1 and Corporation 2 agree to raise prices for Component X sold to finished product integrators. These integrators have factories in Country Beta where they incorporate Component X into finished electronic products sold in the United States.

Discussion: Assuming Corporation 1 and Corporation 2 do not sell Component X in or for delivery to the United States, their conspiracy to fix the prices of Component X is conduct involving wholly foreign commerce, that is, commerce between Countries Alpha and Beta, and thus would not fall within the FTAIA's import commerce exclusion.

The conduct would still fall within the reach of the Sherman Act if it has a (1) direct, (2) substantial, and (3) reasonably foreseeable effect on U.S. import commerce in finished electronic products that incorporate Component X.

Assessing the conduct's effects can be a fact-intensive inquiry. Here the Agencies would collect and analyze evidence to determine whether the price fixing of the component had an effect on U.S. import commerce. If it does, the Agencies would further analyze the evidence and collect additional evidence, as necessary, to determine: (1) whether the price fixing was the proximate cause of that effect, (2) whether the effect was substantial, and (3) whether that effect was a result of the price fixing that was foreseeable to a reasonable person making practical business judgments.

The fact that the price-fixed component was first sold to integrators in Country Beta, where it was incorporated into finished electronic products which were then sold in, or for delivery to, the United States would not render indirect an effect on import commerce in those products. Nor would the fact that the finished products were sold around the world or that Corporation 1 and Corporation 2 were unaware or indifferent to whether the finished products were sold in the United States render insubstantial or not reasonably foreseeable the effect on import commerce. In this context, substantiality is not a question of proportion. So long as the effect on import commerce is substantial, it does not matter if that effect is smaller than the conduct's effect outside the United States. Reasonable foreseeability is an objective standard, which asks not whether the conspirators actually foresaw the effect, but rather whether a reasonable person would foresee the effect on import commerce.

The relative size of Component X as a cost component of the finished electronic products may be relevant to determining whether the price- fixing conduct has the requisite effect, but it is not dispositive. For example, Component X may account for a large portion of the cost of the finished product, but competition from substitutes for the finished electronic products that do not incorporate Component X makes it unlikely that a price increase on Component X will affect import commerce in the finished products. Conversely, Component X may account for a small fraction of the cost of the finished product but the finished electronic product pricing is closely tied to input costs due to market conditions or contractual arrangements, or for other reasons. Thus, any price increase on Component X could, as a practical matter, have the requisite effect on import commerce in the finished electronic product.

Evidence that the conspirators actually expected their conduct to cause an effect on import commerce in the finished products would help to show that a direct, substantial, and reasonably foreseeable effect existed. Such evidence might include Corporation 1 and Corporation 2's contacts with purchasers in the United States, including negotiations regarding Component X pricing, as well as Corporation 1 and Corporation 2's discussing market conditions and tracking sales of the finished products in the United States. But the presence or absence of such evidence would not fundamentally alter the Agencies' analysis.[96]

Illustrative Example D

Situation: Company 1 and Company 2 are located in Country Alpha, where they extract Mineral X. Company 3 is located in the United States, where it extracts Mineral X. Company 3 is able to meet the entire U.S. demand for Mineral X and does so. Company 1 and Company 2 supply the rest of the world with Mineral X, but not the United States. By mutual agreement, Company 1 and Company 2 reduce their sales of Mineral X, significantly driving up the price of Mineral X outside the United States. Because of the increased price for Mineral X outside the United States, Company 3 begins to export much of the U.S. supply of Mineral X. No other firms replace Company 3's diverted sales, and the price of Mineral X rises inside the United States.

Discussion: Company 1 and Company 2's conspiracy to reduce their sales of Mineral X outside the United States is conduct involving wholly foreign commerce. Such conduct would fall within the reach of the Sherman Act if it has a direct, substantial, and reasonably foreseeable effect on U.S. interstate commerce in Mineral X. Here, the conspiracy had the effect of raising prices on interstate sales of Mineral X. That effect appears to be direct, substantial, and reasonably foreseeable.[97]

The FTAIA's effects exception also requires that the effect on commerce within the United States, U.S. import commerce, or the export commerce of a U.S. exporter "gives rise to" a claim under the antitrust laws. In a damages action brought under the antitrust laws, this provision requires that the effect on U.S. commerce be an adverse one and that the effect proximately cause the plaintiff's antitrust injury.[98] It is therefore appropriate for courts to distinguish among damages claims based upon the underlying transaction that forms the basis of the injury to ensure that each claim redresses injury

---

96. *See generally Hsiung*, 778 F.3d at 756-60 (affirming Sherman Act convictions on alternate ground that evidence that price fixing of components sold abroad had a direct effect on U.S. import commerce in finished products containing price-fixed components satisfied Section 6a's effects exception).
97. *Cf.* H.R. REP. NO. 97-686, at 13 (1982) ("For example, if a domestic export cartel were so strong as to have a 'spillover' effect on commerce within this country—by creating a world-wide shortage or artificially inflated world-wide price that had the effect of raising domestic prices—the cartel's conduct would fall within the reach of our antitrust laws. Such an impact would, at least over time, meet the test of a direct, substantial and reasonably foreseeable effect on domestic commerce.").
98. *F. Hoffmann-La Roche Ltd. v. Empagran S.A.*, 542 U.S. 155, 173 (2004); *Lotes Co., Ltd. v. Hon Hai Precision Industry Co.*, 753 F.3d 395, 414 (2d Cir. 2014); *In re Dynamic Random Access Memory*

Appendix III

consistent with the requirements of the antitrust laws, including the FTAIA. For example, when anticompetitive conduct affects commerce around the world, a plaintiff whose antitrust injury arises from that conduct's effect on U.S. import commerce may recover damages for that injury, but a plaintiff that suffers a foreign injury that is independent of, and not proximately caused by, the conduct's effect on U.S. commerce cannot recover damages under the U.S. antitrust laws.[99]

Similarly, when the United States is a plaintiff seeking damages under Section 4A of the Clayton Act for injury to its business or property, the United States must establish that the alleged conduct's effect on U.S. commerce proximately caused the injury to the United States' business or property.

Civil actions for equitable relief brought by the Agencies or criminal enforcement actions brought by the Department, on behalf of the United States, do not seek to redress a pecuniary injury to the government. Instead, such actions are brought by the sovereign to enjoin or prosecute a violation of its laws. In such cases, a direct, substantial, and reasonably foreseeable effect on U.S. commerce would give rise to the sovereign's claim.[100]

Thus, as a result of the effects exception's "gives rise to" provision, the Sherman Act can apply and not apply to the same conduct, depending upon the circumstances, including the plaintiff bringing the claim, the nature of the claim, and the injury underlying the claim.[101]

3.3 Conduct Involving U.S. Government Financing or Purchasing

The Agencies may, in appropriate cases, take enforcement action when the U.S. government is a purchaser, or substantially funds the purchase, of goods or services for consumption or use abroad. Cases in which the effect of anticompetitive conduct with respect to the sale of these goods or services falls primarily on U.S. taxpayers may

---

Antitrust Litig., 546 F.3d 981, 987 (9th Cir. 2008); *In re Monosodium Glutamate Antitrust Litig.*, 477 F.3d 535, 538 (8th Cir. 2007); *Empagran S.A. v. F. Hoffmann-La Roche Ltd.*, 417 F.3d 1267, 1271 (D.C. Cir. 2005).

99. *Empagran*, 542 U.S. at 165, 169-73 (the federal antitrust laws "reflect a legislative effort to redress *domestic* antitrust injury that foreign anticompetitive conduct has caused") (emphasis added)); *see also Lotes*, 753 F.3d at 413-15.

100. The Department's Antitrust Corporate Leniency Policy requires applicants to make restitution to the victims of their offense. *See supra* n.42. Consistent with the Supreme Court's and courts of appeals' interpretation of the "gives rise to" provision that damages for violations of the Sherman Act are not available for foreign injuries independent of and not proximately caused by any adverse effect on U.S. commerce, *supra* n.98, the Department construes the leniency policy to not require restitution to victims whose antitrust injuries are independent of and not proximately caused by an adverse effect on (i) trade or commerce within the United States, (ii) import trade or commerce, or (iii) the export trade or commerce of a person engaged in such trade or commerce in the United States, which effect was proximately caused by the anticompetitive activity being reported.

101. *Empagran*, 542 U.S. at 174; *see also Motorola Mobility LLC v. AU Optronics Corp.*, 775 F.3d 816, 820, 825 (7th Cir. 2014) (noting that the FTAIA "would not block the Department of Justice from seeking criminal or injunctive remedies" for price fixing that had the requisite effect on U.S. commerce, while holding private plaintiff could not recover damages because the injury did not arise from that effect).

qualify for redress under the federal antitrust laws.[102] The requisite U.S. government involvement could include an actual purchase of goods by the U.S. government for shipment abroad, a U.S. government grant to a foreign government that is specifically earmarked for the transaction, or a U.S. government loan specifically earmarked for the transaction that is made on such generous terms that it amounts to a grant. The Agencies consider U.S. government interests to be sufficiently affected when, as a result of its payment or financing, the U.S. government bears a substantial portion of the cost of the transaction. U.S. government interests would not be considered to be sufficiently implicated with respect to a transaction that is merely funded by an international agency, or a transaction in which the foreign government received non-earmarked funds from the United States as part of a general government-to-government aid program.

4. AGENCIES' CONSIDERATION OF FOREIGN JURISDICTIONS

4.1 Comity

In enforcing the federal antitrust laws, the Agencies consider international comity. Comity itself reflects the broad concept of respect among co-equal sovereign nations and plays a role in determining "the recognition which one nation allows within its territory to the legislative, executive or judicial acts of another nation."[103] In determining whether to investigate or bring an action, or to seek particular remedies in a given case, the Agencies take into account whether significant interests of any foreign sovereign would be affected.[104] A decision to take an investigative step or to prosecute an antitrust action under the federal antitrust laws represents a determination that the importance of antitrust enforcement outweighs any relevant foreign policy concerns.

---

102. See *United States v. Anderson*, 326 F.3d 1319 (11th Cir. 2003) (applying Sherman Act to bid rigging on USAID-funded construction projects in Egypt). *Cf. United States v. Concentrated Phosphate Exp. Ass'n*, 393 U.S. 199, 208 (1968). ("[A]lthough the fertilizer shipments were consigned to Korea and although in most cases Korea formally let the contracts, American participation was the overwhelmingly dominant feature. The burden of noncompetitive pricing fell, not on any foreign purchaser, but on the American taxpayer. The United States was, in essence, furnishing fertilizer to Korea. . . . The foreign elements in the transaction were, by comparison, insignificant."); *United States v. Standard Tallow Corp.*, No. 85-cv-2062, 1988 WL 72620 (S.D.N.Y. Jan. 28, 1988) (consent decree) (barring suppliers from fixing prices or rigging bids for the sale of tallow financed in whole or in part through grants or loans by the U.S. Government to the Government of Egypt); *United States v. Anthracite Exp. Ass'n*, No. 70-cv-9171, 1970 WL 540 (M.D. Pa. Nov. 12, 1970) (consent decree) (barring price-fixing, bid-rigging, and market allocation in Army foreign aid program).
103. *Hilton v. Guyot*, 159 U.S. 113, 164 (1895).
104. The Agencies, like other competition authorities around the world, consider the legitimate interests of foreign sovereigns in accordance with the recommendations of the OECD and various bilateral agreements, and may, as appropriate, discuss these issues with foreign counterparts. See *infra* Chapter 5.

That determination is entitled to deference.[105] Some courts have undertaken a comity analysis in disputes between private parties.[106]

In performing this comity analysis, the Agencies consider a number of relevant factors. The relative weight given to each factor depends on the facts and circumstances of each case. Among other things, the Agencies weigh: the existence of a purpose to affect or an actual effect on U.S. commerce; the significance and foreseeability of the effects of the anticompetitive conduct on the United States; the degree of conflict with a foreign jurisdiction's law or articulated policy; the extent to which the enforcement activities of another jurisdiction, including remedies resulting from those enforcement activities, may be affected; and the effectiveness of foreign enforcement as compared to U.S. enforcement.

An investigation or enforcement action by a foreign authority will not preclude an investigation or enforcement action by either the Department or the Commission. Rather, the Agency will determine whether, in light of actions by the foreign authority, investigation or enforcement is warranted to address harm or threatened harm to U.S. commerce and consumers from anticompetitive conduct. In cases in which an Agency opens an investigation or brings an enforcement action concerning conduct under investigation by a foreign authority, it may coordinate with that authority.[107]

Several of the comity factors considered by the Agencies warrant further discussion.

First, when considering the degree of conflict with foreign laws, the Agencies review the relevant laws of the interested foreign sovereigns. In the context of the Agencies' enforcement, conflicts of law are rare. As more jurisdictions have adopted and enforce antitrust laws that are compatible with those of the United States, it has become increasingly common that no conflict exists between U.S. antitrust enforcement interests and the laws or policies of a foreign sovereign. Further, no conflict of law exists if a person subject to the laws of two sovereigns can comply with both.[108] Moreover, no conflict exists in cases where foreign law is neutral as to particular conduct, because it remains possible for the parties in question to comply with the U.S. antitrust laws without violating foreign law. In situations where a conflict of law exists, however, comity may counsel in favor of declining enforcement.

Second, the Agencies will assess the articulated interests and policies of a foreign sovereign beyond whether there is a conflict with foreign law. In determining whether to investigate or bring an enforcement action regarding an alleged antitrust violation, the Agencies consider the extent to which a foreign sovereign encourages or discourages certain courses of conduct or leaves parties free to choose among different courses of conduct.

Third, the Agencies consider whether the objectives sought to be obtained by U.S. enforcement could be achieved by foreign enforcement. The Agencies may consult with interested foreign authorities with the purpose of working to understand and

---

105. *See, e.g.*, *United States v. Baker Hughes, Inc.*, 731 F. Supp. 3, 6 n.5 (D.D.C.), *aff'd*, 908 F.2d 981 (D.C. Cir. 1990).
106. *See, e.g.*, *Timberlane Lumber Co. v. Bank of Am.*, 549 F.2d 597, 614-16 (9th Cir. 1976).
107. *See infra* Chapter 5.
108. *Hartford Fire Ins. Co. v. California*, 509 U.S. 764, 798-99 (1993).

address harm or threatened harm to U.S. commerce and consumers from anticompetitive conduct.

4.2 Consideration of Foreign Government Involvement

In some instances, a foreign government may be involved in anticompetitive conduct that involves or affects U.S. commerce. In determining whether to conduct an investigation or to file an enforcement action in cases in which foreign government involvement is known or suspected, the Agencies consider four legal doctrines that lie at the intersection of government action and the antitrust laws: (1) foreign sovereign immunity; (2) foreign sovereign compulsion; (3) act of state; and (4) petitioning of sovereigns.[109]

4.2.1 Foreign Sovereign Immunity

In civil cases, the Foreign Sovereign Immunities Act of 1976 ("FSIA")[110] provides the "sole basis for obtaining jurisdiction over a foreign state in the courts of this country."[111] The FSIA shields foreign states[112] from the civil jurisdiction of the courts of the United States, subject to certain enumerated exceptions and to treaties in place at the time of the FSIA's enactment.[113] Under the FSIA, federal courts have jurisdiction over foreign states in certain cases in which the foreign state has:

a. waived immunity explicitly or by implication;
b. engaged in commercial activity;
c. expropriated property in violation of international law;
d. acquired rights to property in the United States;
e. committed certain torts within the United States; or
f. agreed to arbitration of the dispute.[114]

---

109. In some cases, investigation may be necessary to assess the nature of foreign government involvement and the applicability of the principles discussed below, even where an Agency ultimately refrains from enforcement.
110. 28 U.S.C. § 1330 *et seq.*
111. *Argentine Republic v. Amerada Hess Shipping Corp.*, 488 U.S. 428, 443 (1989).
112. The FSIA defines "foreign state" to include a "political subdivision of a foreign state or an agency or instrumentality of a foreign state." 28 U.S.C. § 1603(a). It further defines an "agency or instrumentality of a foreign state" to mean any entity "(1) which is a separate legal person, corporate or otherwise; and (2) which is an organ of a foreign state or political subdivision thereof, or a majority of whose shares or other ownership interest is owned by a foreign state or political subdivision thereof; and (3) which is neither a citizen of a State of the United States [as defined elsewhere in Title 28 of the U.S. Code], nor created under the laws of any third country." *Id.* § 1603(b). The majority-ownership prong of this definition encompasses state-owned corporations, so long as the "foreign state itself owns a majority of the corporation's shares." *Dole Food Co. v. Patrickson*, 538 U.S. 468, 477 (2003). The Act does not, however, apply to cases brought against individual foreign officials, whose immunity is governed instead by the common law. *Samantar v. Yousuf*, 560 U.S. 305, 319 (2010).
113. 28 U.S.C. § 1604.
114. *See generally id.* § 1605.

Appendix III

The "commercial activity" exception is the most relevant exception for antitrust purposes.[115] The FSIA provides that a foreign state is not immune from jurisdiction of U.S. courts when:

> the action is based upon a commercial activity carried on in the United States by the foreign state; or upon an act performed in the United States in connection with a commercial activity of the foreign state elsewhere; or upon an act outside the territory of the United States in connection with a commercial activity of the foreign state elsewhere and that act causes a direct effect in the United States.[116]

"Commercial activity" is defined to include "either a regular course of commercial conduct or a particular commercial transaction or act," and the FSIA provides that "the commercial character of an activity shall be determined by reference to the nature of the course of conduct or particular transaction or act, rather than by reference to its purpose."[117] Commercial activity is distinct from sovereign activity inasmuch as the former is understood to include "those powers that can also be exercised by private citizens," while the latter is understood to include "powers peculiar to sovereigns."[118] In other words, the principal question is whether the government is acting "not as a regulator of a market, but in the manner of a private player within it."[119]

To determine whether an action is "based upon" a commercial activity, a court must focus on "the particular conduct on which the plaintiff's action is based," *i.e.*, "those elements that, if proven, would entitle a plaintiff to relief and the gravamen of the complaint."[120]

As a practical matter, most activities of foreign state-owned enterprises operating in the commercial marketplace are "commercial" and, therefore, such enterprises are not immune from the jurisdiction of the U.S. courts in actions to enforce the antitrust laws by virtue of the FSIA. The commercial activities of these enterprises are subject to the U.S. antitrust laws to the same extent as the activities of privately owned foreign firms.

---

115. *Id.* § 1605(a)(2); *see also id.* § 1603(e) (defining "commercial activity carried on in the United States by a foreign state" as "commercial activity carried on by such state and having substantial contact with the United States").
116. *Id.* § 1605(a)(2).
117. *Id.* § 1603(d).
118. *Alfred Dunhill of London, Inc. v. Republic of Cuba*, 425 U.S. 682, 704 (1976).
119. *Republic of Arg. v. Weltover, Inc.*, 504 U.S. 607, 614 (1992); *see also Saudi Arabia v. Nelson*, 507 U.S. 349, 360 (1993); *Universal Trading & Inv. Co. v. Bureau for Representing Ukrainian Interests in Int'l & Foreign Courts*, 727 F.3d 10, 19-20 (1st Cir. 2013); *Cmty. Fin. Grp., Inc. v. Republic of Kenya*, 663 F.3d 977, 980 (8th Cir. 2011); *Jurisdiction of U.S. Courts in Suits Against Foreign States: Hearings on H.R. 11315 Before Subcomm. on Admin. Law & Governmental Relations of the House Comm. on the Judiciary*, 94th Cong. 53 (1976) (statement of Monroe Leigh, Legal Advisor, U.S. Dep't of State) (courts should "inquire whether the activity in question is one which private parties ordinarily perform or whether it is peculiarly within the realm of governments").
120. *OBB Personenverkher AG v. Sachs*, 136 S. Ct. 390, 395 (2015) (citing *Saudi Arabia v. Nelson*, 507 U.S. 349, 356-57 (1993)) (internal quotation marks and alterations omitted).

4.2.2 Foreign Sovereign Compulsion

Because U.S. antitrust laws can extend to foreign persons and conduct with a sufficient connection to the United States, some persons may find themselves subject to foreign legal requirements that conflict with the laws of the United States. In these circumstances, courts have recognized a limited defense against application of the U.S. antitrust laws when a foreign sovereign compels the very conduct that the U.S. antitrust law would prohibit.[121] If it is possible, however, for a party to comply with both the foreign law and the U.S. antitrust laws, the existence of the foreign law does not provide any legal excuse for actions that do not comply with U.S. law.[122] Similarly, that conduct may be lawful, approved, or encouraged in a foreign jurisdiction does not, in and of itself, bar application of the U.S. antitrust laws—even when the foreign jurisdiction has a strong policy in favor of the conduct in question.[123]

Two rationales underlie the limited defense of foreign sovereign compulsion. First, Congress enacted the U.S. antitrust laws against the background of well-recognized principles of international law and comity, pursuant to which U.S. authorities give due deference to the official acts of foreign governments. A defense for actions compelled by foreign sovereigns under certain circumstances serves to accommodate equal sovereigns. Second, fairness considerations require a mechanism to provide a predictable rule of decision for those seeking to conform their behavior to all applicable laws. The Agencies recognize and consider this foreign sovereign compulsion defense when determining whether to bring an enforcement action. Because of the limited scope of the defense, however, the Agencies will refrain from bringing an enforcement action based on considerations of foreign sovereign compulsion only when certain criteria are satisfied.

First, the foreign government must have compelled the anticompetitive conduct under circumstances in which a refusal to comply with the foreign government's command would give rise to the imposition of penal or other severe sanctions. As a general matter, the Agencies regard the foreign government's formal representation that refusal to comply with its command would have such a result as being sufficient to establish that the conduct in question has been compelled. To be sufficient, however, the representation must contain enough detail to enable the Agencies to see precisely how the compulsion would be accomplished under foreign law.[124] Foreign government

---

121. *See, e.g., Mannington Mills, Inc. v. Congoleum Corp.*, 595 F.2d 1287, 1293-94 (3d Cir. 1979); *Trugman-Nash, Inc. v. N.Z. Dairy Bd.*, 954 F. Supp. 733, 736 (S.D.N.Y. 1997); *Interamerican Refining Corp. v. Texaco Maracaibo, Inc.*, 307 F. Supp. 1291, 1304 (D. Del. 1970).

  The defense of foreign sovereign compulsion is distinct from the state action doctrine articulated in *Parker v. Brown*, 317 U.S. 341 (1943). The state action doctrine applies to the actions of U.S. states and their subdivisions, and also to private anticompetitive conduct that is both: (1) undertaken pursuant to clearly articulated state policies and (2) actively supervised by the state. *See N.C. State Bd. of Dental Exam'rs v. Fed. Trade Comm'n*, 135 S. Ct. 1101 (2015).

122. *Hartford Fire Ins. Co. v. California*, 509 U.S. 764, 798-99 (1993).

123. *Id.* Discretionary conduct is also outside the protections afforded by this defense. *See Continental Ore Co. v. Union Carbide & Carbon Corp.*, 370 U.S. 690, 706-07 (1962).

124. For example, the Agencies may not regard as dispositive a statement that is unsupported or ambiguous, or that, on its face, appears to be internally inconsistent. The Agencies may inquire

measures short of compulsion do not suffice for this defense, although they may be a relevant comity consideration if, for example, the measures reflect an articulated policy of the foreign government.

Second, the defense generally applies only when the compelled conduct can be accomplished entirely within the foreign sovereign's own territory. If the compelled conduct occurs in the United States, the Agencies will not recognize the defense.[125] For example, the defense would not apply if a foreign government required the U.S. subsidiaries of several firms to organize a cartel in the United States to fix the price at which products would be sold in the United States.

Third, the order must come from the foreign government acting in its governmental capacity.[126] The defense does not arise from conduct that would fall within the FSIA commercial activity exception.

Illustrative Example E

Situation: Increased quantities of Commodity X have flooded the world market over the last several years, including substantial amounts coming into the United States. The officials of Countries Alpha, Beta, and Gamma meet with their respective domestic firms and urge them to "rationalize" production of Commodity X by cooperatively cutting back. Going one step further, the government of Country Gamma orders cutbacks from its domestic firms, subject to substantial penalties for non-compliance. Producers from Countries Alpha and Beta agree among themselves to institute comparable cutbacks, but their governments do not require them to do so. The overseas production cutbacks have sufficient effects on U.S. commerce for the antitrust laws to apply.

Discussion: The Agencies would not find that foreign sovereign compulsion precludes prosecution of the agreement in restraint of trade entered into by the participants from Countries Alpha and Beta.[127] The Agencies would acknowledge a defense of sovereign compulsion, however, for the participants from Country Gamma.

4.2.3 Act of State Doctrine

The act of state doctrine prevents courts from "declar[ing] invalid the official act of a foreign sovereign performed within its own territory."[128] Applying this doctrine, courts decline to adjudicate claims or issues that would require the court to judge the validity

---

  into the circumstances underlying the statement and may request further information if the source of the power to compel is unclear.
125. See *Linseman v. World Hockey Ass'n*, 439 F. Supp. 1315, 1324-25 (D. Conn. 1977).
126. See *supra* Section 4.2.1.
127. As in all such cases, the Agencies would also consider whether comity factors counsel against bringing an enforcement action for the conduct. See *supra* Section 4.1.
128. *W.S. Kirkpatrick & Co. v. Envt'l Tectonics Corp., Int'l*, 493 U.S. 400, 405 (1990); *Banco Nacional de Cuba v. Sabbatino*, 376 U.S. 398, 401 (1964); *Underhill v. Hernandez*, 168 U.S. 250, 252 (1897) ("Every sovereign state is bound to respect the independence of every other sovereign state, and the courts of one country will not sit in judgment on the acts of the government of

of the sovereign act of a foreign state in its own territory.[129] This doctrine is rooted in considerations of international comity and the separation of powers.[130]

The doctrine does not apply to every act taken by an individual or entity affiliated with a sovereign state. For instance, it does not apply to the acts of individual government officials acting outside their official capacity.[131] Nor does it apply to private actors, even when those acts are approved or condoned by the foreign government in question.[132] Accordingly, when a restraint on competition arises directly from the act of a foreign sovereign, such as the grant of a license, award of a contract, or expropriation of property, the Agencies may refrain from bringing an enforcement action based on the principles animating the act of state doctrine. More specifically, the Agencies may exercise enforcement discretion and decline to challenge foreign acts of state if the facts and circumstances indicate that: (1) the specific conduct complained of is a public act of the sovereign, (2) the act was taken within the territorial jurisdiction of the sovereign, and (3) the conduct relates to a matter that is governmental, rather than commercial.[133]

4.2.4 *Petitioning of Sovereigns*

Under the *Noerr-Pennington* doctrine, a genuine effort to obtain or influence action by governmental entities in the United States falls outside the scope of the Sherman Act, even if the intent or effect of that effort is to restrain or monopolize trade.[134] It is the view of the Agencies that the principles undergirding this doctrine apply to the petitioning of foreign governments. The Agencies, therefore, will not challenge under the antitrust laws genuine efforts to obtain or influence action by foreign government entities.[135] But as with *Noerr-Pennington*, the Agencies will not exercise this discretion when faced with "sham" activities, in which petitioning "ostensibly directed toward influencing governmental action, is a mere sham to cover . . . an attempt to interfere

---

another, done within its own territory. Redress of grievances by reason of such acts must be obtained through the means open to be availed of by sovereign powers as between themselves.").

129. *See W.S. Kirkpatrick*, 493 U.S. at 406 ("Act of state issues only arise when a court *must decide*—that is, when the outcome of the case turns upon—the effect of official action by a foreign sovereign. When that question is not in the case, neither is the act of state doctrine.").

130. *Id.* at 404; *Sabbatino*, 376 U.S. at 423 (the doctrine "express[es] the strong sense of the Judicial Branch that its engagement in the task of passing on the validity of foreign acts of state may hinder rather than further this country's pursuit of goals . . . in the international sphere").

131. *Republic of Iraq v. ABB AG*, 768 F.3d 145, 165 (2d Cir. 2014).

132. *See, e.g., In re Potash Antitrust Litig.*, 686 F. Supp. 2d 816, 825 (N.D. Ill. 2010).

133. *See Alfred Dunhill of London, Inc. v. Republic of Cuba*, 425 U.S. 682, 704 (1976) (plurality op. of White, J.). *Cf. supra* Section 4.2.1.

134. *See United Mine Workers of Am. v. Pennington*, 381 U.S. 657 (1965); *E.R.R. Presidents Conference v. Noerr Motor Freight, Inc.*, 365 U.S. 127 (1961); *see also Cal. Motor Transp. Co. v. Trucking Unlimited*, 404 U.S. 508 (1972) (extending protection to petitioning before "all departments of Government," including the courts).

135. *Cf. Amarel v. Connell*, 102 F.3d 1494, 1520 (9th Cir. 1996).

Appendix III

directly with the business relationships of a competitor,"[136] or when *Noerr-Pennington* would otherwise not apply.[137]

Illustrative Example F

Situation: Corporation 1 and Corporation 2 have mines in Country Alpha where they extract Mineral X. Corporation 1 and Corporation 2 use different techniques to extract Mineral X. Corporation 1 launches a campaign designed to foster the adoption and retention of regulations that would effectively outlaw Corporation 2's mining technique. As part of this broader campaign, Corporation 1 files a complaint with Country Alpha's Ministry of Mines alleging severe health and safety concerns stemming from Corporation 2's mining technique and demanding the permanent closure of Corporation 2's mine. If successful, Corporation 1 would have an effective monopoly on the U.S. market for Mineral X. The Country Alpha Ministry of Mines decides to investigate the complaint, leading to the temporary shutdown of Corporation 2's operations.

Discussion: Had Corporation 1's activities been directed at a U.S. government entity and the *Noerr-Pennington* doctrine applied, the Agencies would not take action against Corporation 1. Applying like principles here, the Agencies would not institute enforcement action against Corporation 1 for lodging a complaint with the Country Alpha Ministry of Mines.

5. INTERNATIONAL COOPERATION

Effective enforcement of the U.S. antitrust laws in a global economy benefits from cooperation with foreign authorities. The Agencies are committed to cooperating with foreign authorities on both policy and investigative matters. This cooperation contributes to convergence on substantive enforcement standards that seek to advance consumer welfare, based on sound economics, procedural fairness, transparency, and non-discriminatory treatment of parties. The Agencies' international policy work and case cooperation are closely connected. As noted above, consistent approaches to competition law, policy, and procedures across jurisdictions facilitate case cooperation among competition authorities. Moreover, through case cooperation, the Agencies and cooperating authorities often raise important substantive and procedural issues as they arise in practice, which can lead to greater convergence in substantive analysis and procedures. In keeping with these Guidelines' focus on international enforcement and practice, this Chapter focuses on investigations and case cooperation.

International case cooperation helps agencies investigating a particular matter to identify issues of common interest, gain a better understanding of relevant facts, and achieve consistent outcomes. Cooperation can yield better results for competition and promote efficiency for both cooperating agencies and subjects of an investigation. It

---

136. *Prof'l Real Estate Investors, Inc. v. Columbia Pictures Indus.*, 508 U.S. 49, 56 (1993) (internal quotations omitted).
137. *See, e.g., Allied Tube & Conduit Corp. v. Indian Head, Inc.*, 486 U.S. 492 (1988); *Walker Process Equip., Inc. v. Food Mach. & Chem. Corp.*, 382 U.S. 172 (1965).

can improve substantive analyses and procedures, and ensure that investigations and remedies are as consistent and predictable as possible, which improves outcomes, and reduces uncertainty and expense to firms doing business across borders. When either Agency reviews a case that raises possible competitive concerns in jurisdictions outside of the United States, it may consult with the relevant foreign authorities about the matter and coordinate and cooperate with those authorities conducting parallel investigations.[138] As described in greater detail throughout this chapter, cooperation can include a broad range of practices, from initiating informal discussions and informing cooperating authorities of the different stages of their investigations, to engaging in detailed discussions of substantive issues, exchanging information, conducting interviews at which two or more agencies may be present, and coordinating remedy design and implementation, as relevant and appropriate.[139]

5.1 Investigations and Cooperation

Increasingly, the Agencies' investigations involve conduct, entities, individuals, and information located outside the United States. The Agencies employ a combination of their own investigative tools and cooperation with foreign authorities in investigating and seeking appropriate remedies in certain international matters.

5.1.1 *Investigative Tools*

When practical and consistent with enforcement objectives, the Agencies may request that parties and third parties voluntarily: provide documents; submit to interviews; or provide other information related to an investigation. These requests may seek documents or information located outside the United States.

The Agencies also may use compulsory measures to obtain documents and information. Specifically, the Agencies may compel production of documents or information via civil investigative demand ("CID") or subpoena.[140] U.S. law provides authority for such compulsory measures directed to persons over whom the courts have personal

---

138. An Agency may continue that cooperation when either it or the foreign authority has closed its investigation. The Agencies may also engage in general discussions with foreign authorities on matters in which only one authority has an open investigation.
139. The Agencies do not conduct "joint investigations" with foreign authorities; neither Agency exercises control over foreign authorities regarding their investigations, nor accepts direction from foreign authorities regarding its own investigations. The Agencies, however, do cooperate with foreign authorities conducting parallel investigations. "[R]obust information-sharing and cooperation across parallel investigations" do not transform multiple parallel investigations into a joint investigation. *United States v. Getto*, 729 F.3d 221, 231 (2d Cir. 2013).
140. The Department may issue CIDs pursuant to the Antitrust Civil Process Act, 15 U.S.C.§ 1312, and the FTC may issue CIDs and subpoenas pursuant to the FTC Act. *Id.* §§ 49, 57b-1(c). In merger investigations, the Agencies utilize the mechanisms of the HSR Act to gather information from parties. *Id.* § 18(a). *See also* U.S. Dep't of Justice, *Crim. Resource Manual* § 279 (discussing availability of subpoenas reaching individuals and evidence located abroad), https://www.justice.gov/usam/criminal-resource-manual-279-subpoenas.

Appendix III

jurisdiction.[141] The Agencies may compel the production of documents or information, including documents or information located outside the United States, when the documents or information sought are within the "possession, custody, or control" of an individual or entity subject to the jurisdiction of the United States and are not protected by the attorney-client privilege or the work-product doctrine.[142]

When one of the Agencies investigates a transaction notified under the HSR Act, it may issue a request for additional documents or information, typically called a "Second Request."[143] Compliance with a Second Request requires production of all responsive documents and information, no matter where located.

Conflicts can arise where foreign statutes purport to prevent individuals or entities from disclosing documents or information for use in U.S. proceedings. The mere existence of such statutes, however, does not excuse noncompliance with a request for documents or information from one of the Agencies.[144]

Because unilaterally collecting documents or information from individuals or entities located abroad can adversely affect law enforcement relationships with foreign countries, the Agencies use compulsory measures after carefully considering the importance of the documents or information to the investigation or prosecution and the availability of other means to obtain them.[145] When such compulsory measures are warranted, the Agencies may seek to work with the foreign authority involved as appropriate.

5.1.2 Confidentiality

The Agencies' enforcement activities benefit greatly from access to sensitive, nonpublic information from businesses and consumers. The Agencies recognize the importance of protecting the confidentiality of sensitive, nonpublic information received from parties and foreign authorities. The Agencies protect the confidentiality of all such information received, be it from businesses or consumers located domestically or abroad, or from foreign authorities, under applicable provisions of U.S. law.

Several statutes require the Agencies to treat as confidential certain information obtained in the course of an investigation. The HSR Act prohibits the Agencies from disclosing information obtained pursuant to the act, including the fact that the parties filed notice of a proposed transaction and confidential business information provided

---

141. *In re Grand Jury Proceedings (Bank of Nova Scotia)*, 740 F.2d 817, 828-29 (11th Cir. 1984); *United States v. First Nat'l City Bank*, 396 F.2d 897, 900-901 (2d Cir. 1968); *see also, e.g.*, 28 U.S.C. § 1783(a) (authorizing a U.S. court to order the issuance of a subpoena "requiring the appearance as a witness before it, or before a person or body designated by it, of a national or resident of the United States who is in a foreign country, or requiring the production of a specified document or other thing by him," under circumstances identified in the statute).
142. 15 U.S.C. § 57b-1(c)(1) (FTC Act); *id.* § 1312(a) (Antitrust Civil Process Act).
143. See Section 2.2.4, *supra*, regarding the HSR Act.
144. The Agencies do not view the mere existence of blocking statutes as creating a conflict of law for purposes of the comity analysis. *Cf. Société Nationale Industrielle Aérospatiale v. U.S. Dist. Court*, 482 U.S. 522, 542-44 & n. 29 (1987). Comity is addressed in Section 4.1.
145. U.S. Dep't of Justice, *Crim. Resource Manual* § 279, https://www.justice.gov/usam/criminal-resource-manual-279-subpoenas.

Appendix III

in a filing or in response to a document or information request.[146] The FTC Act restricts disclosure of information that the Commission receives pursuant to compulsory process, or produced voluntarily in lieu of process, in a law enforcement investigation.[147] The FTC Act also prohibits the Commission from making public any trade secret or any commercial or financial information it obtains that is privileged or confidential, except in limited circumstances.[148] The Antitrust Civil Process Act prohibits the Department from disclosing documents or testimony obtained pursuant to a CID without the consent of the person that produced the materials, except in limited circumstances.[149] Other federal laws also require the Agencies to treat specific types of information as confidential, without regard to the manner in which the information is obtained. For example, laws governing privacy, national security information, and trade secrets require that the Agencies treat certain information as confidential.[150]

There are certain, discrete circumstances in which the Agencies may disclose a person's confidential information for a specific use. The HSR Act, the FTC Act, and the Antitrust Civil Process Act do not bar the Agencies' use of a person's confidential information in judicial and administrative proceedings.[151] However, the Federal Rules of Civil Procedure and FTC Rules of Practice include procedures to protect confidential information used in judicial proceedings or FTC administrative proceedings.[152]

The Agencies also are subject to the Freedom of Information Act ("FOIA"), which provides the public with a right of access to certain agency records.[153] This statute, however, contains several exemptions that protect information provided to the Agencies. It permits the Agencies to withhold certain categories of documents from requesters, including information protected by statute (such as the HSR Act or FTC Act), "commercial or financial information obtained from a person [that is] privileged or confidential," inter- or intra-agency memoranda or letters that would be routinely privileged in civil discovery, and "files the disclosure of which would constitute a

---

146. See 15 U.S.C. § 18a(h).
147. 15 U.S.C. §§ 57b-2(b), 57b-2(f). Section 21(f) of the FTC Act also explicitly protects from disclosure any materials received from a non-U.S. competition authority when "the foreign law enforcement agency or other foreign government agency has requested confidential treatment, or has precluded such disclosure under other use limitations, as a condition of providing the material." Id. § 57b-2(f).
148. Id. § 46(f).
149. See 15 U.S.C. § 1313(c)(2), (d).
150. For example, U.S. law imposes confidentiality obligations regarding certain classes of information, including personally identifiable information. See, e.g. 5 U.S.C. § 552a (Privacy Act of 1974).
151. In addition, the FTC Act, with regard to the Commission, and HSR Act do not prevent the Agencies from complying with information requests from Congress. In the event of such a request, however, the Agency receiving the request must notify the submitter of the information, and the Agency can request confidential treatment of any information that may be shared.
152. For instance, the person providing information may seek a protective order to prevent confidential information from being made public or from being used outside the court proceeding. See Fed. R. Civ. P. 26(c); 16 C.F.R. § 3.31(d) (requiring Administrative Law Judge in FTC proceeding to issue a specific protective order).
153. 5 U.S.C. § 552.

Appendix III

clearly unwarranted invasion of personal privacy."[154] In addition, an exemption from FOIA's disclosure regime applies to certain information compiled for law enforcement purposes, including when disclosure could interfere with enforcement proceedings or disclose the identity of a confidential source.[155]

5.1.3 Legal Bases for Cooperation

The Agencies' authority to cooperate with foreign authorities is inherent in their ability to act in furtherance of their mandates. The Department and FTC, therefore, each has the discretion to cooperate, including when it furthers its enforcement interests. Cooperation can be facilitated by bilateral and multilateral arrangements.[156] The Agencies have also developed best practices and guidance documents on cooperation for specific types of investigations.[157] These arrangements and guidance documents can serve as a catalyst for cooperation and provide useful guidance to coordinate and facilitate enforcement activities. They are not necessary for cooperation to take place,

---

154. *Id.* § 552(b)(3)-(6).
155. *Id.* § 552(b)(7).
156. For example, the United States or the Agencies have bilateral cooperation agreements with eleven jurisdictions or competition agencies: Germany (1976); Australia (1982); the European Union (1991); Canada (1995); Brazil, Israel, and Japan (1999); Mexico (2000); Chile (2011); Colombia (2014); and Peru (2016). The Agencies also have entered into memoranda of understanding with the Russian Federal Antimonopoly Service (2009), the three Chinese antimonopoly enforcement agencies (2011), the Indian competition authorities (2012), and the Korea Fair Trade Commission (2015). These arrangements are available at https://www.justice.gov/atr/antitrust-cooperation-agreements and https://www.ftc.gov/policy/international/international-cooperation-agreements. Multilateral arrangements include the Recommendation of the OECD Council Concerning Co-Operation on Competition Investigations and Proceedings, and the ICN Framework for Merger Cooperation. Org. for Econ. Co-Operation & Dev., Recommendation of the OECD Council Concerning Co-Operation on Competition Investigations and Proceedings (2014), http://www.oecd.org/competition/international-coop-competition-2014-recommendation.htm; Int'l Competition Network, Framework for Merger Cooperation (2012), http://www.internationalcompetitionnetwork.org/uploads/library/doc803.pdf.
157. *See, e.g.,* US-EU Merger Working Grp., *Best Practices on Cooperation in Merger Investigations* (2011), https://www.justice.gov/atr/best-practices-cooperation-merger-investigations; China Ministry of Comm., Fed. Trade Comm'n, U.S. Dep't of Justice, *Guidance for Case Cooperation between the Ministry of Commerce and the Department of Justice and Federal Trade Commission on Concentration of Undertakings (Merger) Cases* (2011), https://www.ftc.gov/system/files/attachments/press-releases/federal-trade-commission-department-justice-meet-chinese-ministry-commerce-merger-enforcement/111129mofcom.pdf; U.S.- Can. Working Grp., *Best Practices on Cooperation in Merger Investigations* (2014), https://www.justice.gov/sites/default/files/atr/legacy/2014/03/25/304654.pdf; Int'l Competition Network, *Anti-Cartel Enforcement Manual,* http://www.internationalcompetitionnetwork.org/working-groups/current/cartel/manual.aspx; Int'l Competition Network, *Recommended Practices for Merger Notification and Review Procedures,* http://www.internationalcompetitionnetwork.org/uploads/library/doc588.pdf; Int'l Competition Network, *Recommended Practices for Merger Analysis,* http://www.internationalcompetitionnetwork.org/uploads/library/doc316.pdf; Int'l Competition Network, *Practical Guide to Enforcement Cooperation in Mergers,* http://www.internationalcompetitionnetwork.org/uploads/library/doc1031.pdf; Org. for Econ. Co-Operation & Development, *Best Practices for Formal Exchange of Information Between Competition Authorities in Hard Core Cartel Investigations* (2005), http://www.oecd.org/competition/cartels/35590548.pdf.

and the Agencies may cooperate with relevant foreign authorities in the absence of any formal arrangement. These bilateral and multilateral arrangements do not change the signatories' laws, including laws concerning the treatment of confidential information. The IAEAA authorizes the Agencies to enter into antitrust-specific mutual assistance agreements with foreign authorities that allow the Agencies to share evidence relating to antitrust violations already in their possession and provide each other with investigatory assistance in obtaining evidence, subject to certain limitations.[158] As noted in Section 2.6, the IAEAA does not apply to materials submitted pursuant to the HSR Act.[159]

5.1.4 Types of Information Exchanged and Waivers of Confidentiality

If a transaction or conduct under antitrust investigation in the United States is also being investigated by a foreign authority, the Department or the Commission may contact the authority. The Agencies may share with these foreign authorities relevant publicly available information.[160] Similarly, it remains in the Agencies' discretion whether to share with cooperating foreign authorities agency non-public information, which is information that the Agencies are not statutorily prohibited from disclosing, but that the Agencies normally treat as non-public and withhold from public disclosure.[161] Examples of agency non-public information include the existence of an open investigation and the Agencies' staff views as to the merits of a case, market definition, competitive effects, substantive theories of harm, and remedies. Before exchanging agency non-public information, the Agencies will have reached an understanding that the foreign authority will maintain the information in confidence and in accordance with that authority's laws and rules. This may be through bilateral or multilateral cooperation agreements or arrangements, or other means.

While confidentiality obligations generally prohibit the Agencies from disclosing to foreign authorities confidential information submitted by a person,[162] that person can enable the Agencies to engage in more meaningful cooperation with foreign authorities by granting the Agencies a waiver of confidentiality as to information that may be otherwise protected from disclosure. The Agencies issued a joint model waiver of confidentiality for use in civil matters, which serves to streamline the waiver process[163]

---

158. 15 U.S.C. § 6201 et seq., discussed supra Section 2.6. Mutual Legal Assistance Treaties may be used in the criminal context, discussed infra Section 5.2.
159. Id. § 6204(1).
160. The types of relevant publicly available information that the Agencies may share with foreign authorities include background information regarding a particular industry or company and public records, such as court or securities filings.
161. See, e.g., 5 U.S.C. § 552(b)(5).
162. See supra Section 5.1.2.
163. Fed. Trade Comm'n & Dep't of Justice, Model Waiver of Confidentiality (2013), https://www.ftc.gov/sites/default/files/attachments/international-waivers-confidentiality-ftc-antitrust-investigations/model_waiver.pdf.

Appendix III

and published explanatory materials that provide further details on waivers of confidentiality, applicable confidentiality rules, and the process for providing a waiver of confidentiality.[164].

A waiver identifies the terms under which a person agrees to waive statutory confidentiality protections vis-à-vis the agency that originally received the person's confidential information. A waiver also describes an agency's policy regarding how it will treat the information it receives from another agency pursuant to a waiver, although it is not an agreement signed by the agency. Waivers are limited in scope to a specific, named matter and designate the agencies that may share the waiving person's confidential information. Waivers generally allow the cooperating authorities to share documents, statements, data, and other information.

Waivers enable deeper communication, cooperation, and coordination among competition authorities concurrently reviewing a matter. They can lead to more effective, efficient investigations and better-informed, more consistent enforcement decisions based on the Agencies' increased ability to share information.

The Agencies will protect information received from a foreign authority pursuant to a waiver under applicable provisions of U.S. law. The Agencies will not seek information that is privileged under U.S. law from foreign authorities through waivers or other cooperative activities.[165]

Similarly, the Agencies will provide information to foreign authorities pursuant to a waiver when they have reached an understanding with the recipient agency that it will maintain the confidentiality of such information consistent with its laws and rules. Generally, a person that has waived the confidentiality of its information as to one of the Agencies also will provide a separate waiver of confidentiality to the relevant foreign authority, based on the waiving person's understanding of the foreign authority's confidentiality protections.

The Agencies may request a waiver of confidentiality, but the decision whether to provide one rests solely with the producing person. Refusal to provide a waiver will not prejudice the outcome of an investigation, though, in some cases, the absence of a waiver may have practical effects such as increasing the risk of inconsistent outcomes between jurisdictions. Further, declining to grant a waiver will not preclude the Agencies from sharing publicly available or agency non-public information with foreign authorities.

Illustrative Example G

Situation: Corporation 1 and Corporation 2 each manufacture Product X and Product Y. Corporation 1 and Corporation 2 enter into an agreement to merge. The proposed merger meets the threshold for premerger notification in the United States under the HSR Act and the thresholds for premerger notification in several other jurisdictions.

---

164. U.S. Dep't of Justice & Fed. Trade Comm'n, *Model Waiver of Confidentiality for Use in Civil Matters Involving Non-U.S. Competition Auths. Frequently Asked Questions* (2015), www.justice.gov/sites/default/files/atr/legacy/2015/05/11/300916.pdf

165. *Id.*

Corporation 1 and Corporation 2 inform the U.S. Agency reviewing the merger as well as reviewing foreign authorities that the merger will be notified or reviewed in multiple jurisdictions. Pre-notification consultations and pre-merger filings are timed to facilitate communication and cooperation among reviewing authorities at key decision-making stages of their respective investigations.

Discussion: After learning that the merger will be notified or reviewed in more than one jurisdiction, the U.S. Agency contacts the foreign reviewing authorities to discuss review timetables and assess the potential for cooperation. The extent of cooperation with each foreign authority reviewing the matter will vary depending on factors including the depth of that authority's investigation, the competitive conditions in that authority's jurisdiction, and the scope of potential remedies likely to be considered. The U.S. Agency requests a waiver of confidentiality from Corporation 1 and Corporation 2 to allow for the exchange of confidential information with the reviewing authorities in Countries Alpha, Beta, and Gamma, given the nature of the competitive concerns raised by the merger in these jurisdictions.

Corporation 1 and Corporation 2 voluntarily grant these waivers, as well as the waivers of confidentiality requested by each of these reviewing authorities. The U.S. Agency cooperates with the reviewing authorities in Countries Delta and Epsilon on the basis of publicly available and agency non-public information, without exchanging confidential business information.

As reviews of the merger proceed, the U.S. Agency and the other reviewing authorities arrange communications between and among themselves as appropriate to their investigations. The U.S. Agency and authorities of Alpha, Beta, and Gamma each arrange regular, bilateral calls and, in some instances, certain of these agencies conduct interviews together, facilitated by waivers. These reviewing agencies, as well as the reviewing authorities of Delta and Epsilon, also conduct status calls, based on publicly available and agency non-public information to update each other on the timing of reviews and theories of harm. The reviewing authorities of Delta and Epsilon identify that the merger's effects in their jurisdictions are likely to be insignificant, and that they will close their investigations accordingly.

5.1.5 Remedies

The Agencies seek remedies that effectively address harm or threatened harm to U.S. commerce and consumers, while attempting to avoid conflicts with remedies contemplated by their foreign counterparts.[166] An Agency will seek a remedy that includes conduct or assets outside the United States only to the extent that including them is needed to effectively redress harm or threatened harm to U.S. commerce and consumers[167] and is consistent with the Agency's international comity analysis.[168]

---

166. *United States v. General Elec. Co. et al.*, No. 15-cv-1460 (D.D.C. 2015); *In re Panasonic Corp. et al*, Dkt. No. C-4274 (FTC Jan. 8, 2010) (allowed for extension of divestiture deadline if necessary to obtain approval for divestiture from the European Commission).
167. *Polypore Int'l, Inc. v. Fed. Trade Comm'n*, 686 F.3d 1208, 1219 (11th Cir. 2012) (affirming Commission decision in a merger matter with remedy including assets located outside the

Appendix III

When multiple authorities are investigating the same transaction or same conduct, the Agencies may cooperate with other authorities, to the extent permitted under U.S. law, to facilitate obtaining effective and non-conflicting remedies.[169] Cooperation also may facilitate the development of a proposed remedies package that comprehensively addresses the concerns of multiple authorities.[170] In some circumstances, cooperation may result in one authority closing an investigation without remedies after taking another authority's remedies into account.[171]

Illustrative Example H

Situation: After investigating the merger as outlined in Illustrative Example G, the U.S. Agency finds that the merger is likely to substantially lessen competition in the U.S. market for Product X, and therefore that the merger would violate Section 7 of the Clayton Act.

The U.S. Agency determines that these competitive concerns likely can be addressed through a divestiture of Corporation 1's assets related to Product X. Countries Alpha, Beta, and Gamma also find that the merger will harm competition in their markets for Product X, and Country Gamma has additional concerns about a reduction of competition in Gamma's market for Product Y.

Discussion: The U.S. Agency and the authorities in Alpha, Beta, and Gamma discuss, among themselves and with Corporation 1 and Corporation 2, a proposed remedy for the competitive concerns regarding Product X, in an effort to identify a package of assets for divesture that addresses the reviewing agencies' competitive concerns.

In this instance, the U.S. Agency and the foreign reviewing authorities agree that the same divestiture remedy for Product X will effectively address the competitive concerns in their respective jurisdictions.

Corporation 1 and Corporation 2 enter into a consent decree in the United States that includes divestiture of specified assets of Corporation 1's related to Product X, and the

---

United States); *United States. v. Cont'l AG & Veyance Technologies*, No. 14-cv-2087 (D.D.C. 2014) (facilities in Mexico divested); *U.S. v. Anheuser-Busch InBev SA/NV & Grupo Modelo S.A.B. DE C.V.*, No. 13-cv-127 (D.D.C 2013) (brewery in Mexico divested); *In re Victrex, plc*, Dkt. No. C-4586 (FTC July 14, 2016) (remedy prohibiting contract provisions that could result in exclusivity, including when products are manufactured or sold abroad for use in products sold or cleared for use in the United States); *In re Intel Corp.*, Dkt. No. 9341 (FTC Nov. 2, 2010) (remedy including requirements regarding licensing with foreign CPU maker that potentially competed with Intel in order to restore competition in United States). These remedies are often entered into voluntarily pursuant to consent decrees.

168. *See supra* Section 4.1.
169. As with other aspects of cooperation, a person's grant of waivers can enhance the efficacy of such discussions between the Agencies and foreign authorities.
170. *See* U.S.- Can. Working Grp., *Best Practices on Cooperation in Merger Investigations* (2014), https://www.ftc.gov/system/files/attachments/international-competition-consumer-protecti on-cooperation-agreements/canada-us_merger_cooperation_best_practices.pdf; US-EU Merger Working Grp., *Best Practices on Cooperation in Merger Investigations* (2011), https://www.justice.gov/sites/default/files/atr/legacy/2011/10/27/276276.pdf.
171. *See* United States Submission to OECD Competition Committee regarding Remedies in Cross-Border Merger Cases, DAF/COMP/WP3/WD(2013) (discussing cooperation and remedies in: *In the Matter of Agilent Technologies*; *In the Matter of Panasonic Corporation/Sanyo Electric Co., Ltd.*; *UTC/Goodrich*; *Cisco/Tandberg*; and other matters).

Appendix III

authority in Alpha seeks the same divestiture remedy to ensure enforceability of the remedy in its jurisdiction. Country Beta concludes that the remedies secured in the United States and in Country Alpha are sufficient to address its competitive concerns and closes its investigation. Country Gamma seeks a remedy identical to that entered into in the United States and Country Alpha regarding Product X, coupled with an additional remedy to address the competitive harm in its jurisdiction regarding Product Y.

5.2 Special Considerations in Criminal Investigations

Among the Department's top priorities is the criminal investigation and prosecution of international price-fixing cartels. Because these cartels often involve foreign- located defendants, witnesses, and evidence, antitrust enforcement in this context can present not only an investigatory challenge but also a special need for international cooperation and coordination. Mutual Legal Assistance Treaties ("MLATs") are an important basis for international cooperation in the Department's criminal antitrust enforcement. MLATs are used often in criminal investigations to gather evidence located outside the United States. Parties to these agreements have agreed to assist one another in criminal law enforcement matters.[172] The specific provisions of MLATs vary, but they generally provide for assistance in obtaining evidence and in serving documents in one jurisdiction at the request of the other.

The Department also coordinates with foreign authorities when they are conducting cartel investigations parallel with the Department's own. The Department sometimes shares information to coordinate investigative steps. For example, to minimize the risk of document destruction, the Department and foreign authorities can time dawn raids and searches to coincide in multiple jurisdictions. And the Department and foreign authorities may also coordinate on logistical aspects of their parallel investigations to help minimize overlapping and inconsistent demands placed on cooperating individuals and firms. The Department recognizes that such coordination has the benefit of decreasing the costs to cooperators and increasing the pace of the investigations and is committed to engaging in such coordination where practicable.

The Department's ability to share information with foreign authorities is not unlimited, however. An essential component in the investigation and enforcement of the criminal antitrust laws is the grand jury, which is subject to the grand jury secrecy rule. Through its subpoenas, a grand jury can "compel the production of evidence or the testimony of witnesses as it considers appropriate, and its operation generally is unrestrained by the technical procedural and evidentiary rules governing the conduct of criminal trials."[173]

---

172. The United States' MLAT with Germany is unique in that it also provides for U.S. assistance to Germany in administrative cartel matters. *See* Mutual Legal Assistance Treaty, U.S.-Ger., S. Treaty Doc. 108-27 (2003), *available at* https://www.congress.gov/108/cdoc/tdoc27/CDOC-108tdoc27.pdf.

173. *United States v. Calandra*, 414 U.S. 338, 343 (1974); *see also Branzburg v. Hayes*, 408 U.S. 665, 688 (1972). The "powers of the grand jury are not unlimited," *id.*; for example, a grand jury subpoena does not override a valid privilege and may be quashed or modified by a court if compliance would be "unreasonable or oppressive." Fed. R. Crim. P. 17(c)(2).

Appendix III

The Department is prohibited, however, from disclosing matters occurring before the grand jury absent an applicable exception.[174] This prohibition cannot be waived by a subject of the investigation, a grand jury witness, or a recipient of a grand jury subpoena. The prohibition, however, does not apply to these persons and therefore does not generally prohibit disclosures by them.

In addition, a criminal investigation can gather information through the assistance of an applicant under the Department's Corporate and Individual Leniency Policies for antitrust crimes.[175] To qualify for leniency under those policies, the applicant is required, among other things, to report the wrongdoing with candor and completeness and provide full, continuing, and complete cooperation. That required cooperation includes the production of all documents, information, or other materials in the applicant's possession, custody, or control, wherever located, that are requested by the Department in connection with the criminal antitrust investigation and are not protected by the attorney-client privilege or the work- product doctrine.

The Department holds the identity of leniency applicants and the information they provide in strict confidence. The Department does not publicly disclose the identity of an applicant or information provided by the applicant, absent prior disclosure by the applicant, unless required to do so by a court order in connection with litigation. A leniency applicant can agree to waive this confidentiality assurance and allow the Department to share the applicant's identity and information with a foreign authority. Such waivers of confidentiality for information sharing with a foreign authority are common when the applicant has also applied for leniency under the foreign authority's leniency policy.

Lastly, the Department sometimes seeks the cooperation of foreign jurisdictions to obtain indicted fugitives. It can seek the issuance of an INTERPOL "Red Notice," which operates as an international "wanted" notice that, in some INTERPOL member countries, serves as a request, should the fugitive enter their jurisdiction, to arrest the subject, with a view toward extradition. And the Department can request that a foreign jurisdiction extradite a fugitive defendant located in that jurisdiction to the United States.[176]

ANNEX 1. DEFINED TERMS

ACPERA	Antitrust Criminal Penalty Enhancement and Reform Act of 2004
Agencies	The Department of Justice and Federal Trade
Commission APEC	Asia-Pacific Economic Cooperation
CID	Civil Investigative Demand Clayton

---

174. Fed. R. Crim. P. 6(e).
175. For information on these policies, see https://www.justice.gov/atr/leniency-program.
176. Extradition ordinarily depends on the presence and terms of an extradition treaty with the foreign jurisdiction.

Appendix III

Act	Clayton Antitrust Act Commission Federal Trade
Commission Department	The Department of Justice
ETC Act	Export Trading Company Act of 1982
ETCR	Export Trade Certificate of Review
FTC	Federal Trade Commission
FTC Act	Federal Trade Commission Act
FSIA	Foreign Sovereign Immunities Act of 1976
FTAIA	Foreign Trade Antitrust Improvements Act of 1982
FOIA	Freedom of Information Act
HSR Act	Hart-Scott-Rodino Antitrust Improvements Act of 1976
HSR Rules	Hart-Scott-Rodino Premerger Notification Rules
IAEAA	International Antitrust Enforcement Assistance Act
ICN	International Competition Network
International Guidelines	Antitrust Guidelines for International Enforcement and Cooperation
MLATs	Mutual Legal Assistance Treaties
NCRPA	National Cooperative Research and Production Act
OECD	Organisation for Economic Co-operation and Development
Sherman Act	Sherman Antitrust Act
SDOs	Standards Development Organizations
UNCTAD	United Nations Conference on Trade and Development
USTR	U.S. Trade Representative

Index

A

Abuse, 323-353, 434, 443-445
Access to essential facilities, 368
Acquisitions, 195-220, 424-429, 447-449
Act of state doctrine, 61-63, 65, 532-533
Administrative
  guidance, 405, 406, 418
  surcharges, 410, 446
Advertising, 17, 27, 126, 148, 181, 182, 186, 190, 210, 302, 350, 442
Affecting, 4, 25, 27-28, 37, 39, 43, 44, 51, 52, 54, 56, 68, 69, 82, 97, 148, 149, 159, 176, 180, 185, 188, 196, 197, 216, 229, 241, 256, 257, 284, 285, 293, 318, 327, 328, 333, 381, 418, 419, 510, 512
Agreement on Trade-Related Aspects of Intellectual Property Rights, 159
Agreements
  or contracts, 24, 518
Airlines, 52, 65, 114, 134, 206, 211, 212, 218, 288, 338, 376, 380, 389, 408, 428
AMA See Antimonopoly Act (AMA)
Analysis, 201-205, 369-375, 426-427
Ancillary restraints, 15, 124, 126-129, 167, 206, 378-379
Antidumping Act, 27
Antimonopoly Act (AMA), 405, 407, 409, 417, 418, 421, 423, 426

Antitrust Civil Process Act, 85, 98, 537
Antitrust Criminal Penalty Enhancement and Reform Act of 2004, 35, 111, 514-515, 544
Antitrust Enforcement Guidelines for International Operations, 41, 508, 509
Antitrust Guidelines
  for Collaborations Among Competitors, 123, 206
  for the Licensing of Intellectual Property, 41, 163, 207
Antitrust Modernization Commission (AMC), 42, 187
Antitrust Procedures and Penalties Act, 34
APEC, 5, 9, 509, 544
Arbitration, 89, 100-106, 176, 280, 369, 529
Asia-Pacific Economic Cooperation, 5, 509, 544
Associations, 18, 27, 30, 31, 38, 44, 77, 117, 121, 180, 231, 234, 236-240, 242, 251, 253, 257, 271, 293, 344, 351, 394, 395, 397, 405, 417, 475, 476, 480, 483, 484, 490-499, 502, 516, 517
Attempted, 19, 36, 79, 90, 94, 100, 120, 122, 131, 132, 137, 139, 141, 161, 211, 214, 216, 288, 316, 317, 341, 343, 383, 414
Attorney-client privilege, 83, 243, 409, 536, 544

Index

B

BE Regulation, 290-297, 299-301, 303-306, 308, 337
Best practices, 6, 9, 211, 219, 239, 245, 360, 368, 381, 509, 538
Bid-rigging, 57
Block exemptions, 281-285, 317-322
Blocking statutes, 59, 84, 92-94, 96
Boycotts, 7, 17, 18, 28, 38, 107, 116-119, 121, 130, 149, 164, 182, 248, 259, 273-274, 276, 300, 411, 417, 422
Brussels, 99, 225-227, 298, 350, 355

C

Canada, 3, 9, 47, 94, 107, 113, 120, 175, 187, 214, 272, 365, 374, 385
Car distribution, 307-308
Cartels, 2, 4, 7, 29, 31, 38, 60, 62, 107, 109-115, 122, 141, 167, 196, 240, 249, 253, 258, 268, 272, 273, 274, 277, 306, 396, 398, 405-407, 410, 411, 417-419, 433, 436, 441-443, 508, 543
Cases involving, 92, 105, 109, 127, 142, 171, 173, 214, 217, 218, 279, 286, 315, 331, 333, 364, 470, 450, 511
CIDs See Civil Investigative Demands (CIDs)
Civil
  cases, 35, 38, 72, 76, 77, 85, 411, 529
  suits, 14, 25, 29, 34, 36, 38, 82, 85, 87, 95, 107, 516
Civil Investigative Demands (CIDs), 83, 98, 535, 537, 544
Class actions, 8, 14, 33, 38, 39, 78, 105, 106, 112, 115, 136, 248, 412
Clayton Act, 24-27, 30, 33, 34, 36, 38, 40, 68, 72-77, 79, 82, 117, 124, 125, 137, 146-149, 151-153, 161, 170, 179, 182, 183, 193, 196-199, 205, 210, 212, 214, 216, 383, 512-514, 518, 521, 526, 542
Collaborations Among, 123, 206
Collective
  boycotts, 116-119, 274, 417
  dominance, 141, 327, 342, 344, 370, 375-377, 384, 385
  or joint, 375
Combination or conspiracy, 15, 18, 34, 108, 117
Combinations, 17-18, 107-109
Combines Investigation Act, 3
Comfort letters, 262, 263
Comity
  analysis, 49, 51, 59, 93, 528, 541
Commerce, 22-24, 43-57, 107-143, 145-178, 193-194
Commercialization agreements, 280
Commission, 26-27, 36-38, 97-98, 179-194, 226-227, 239-246, 408-410, 433
Common law, 1, 2, 15, 40, 91, 100, 161, 228
Common Market, 4, 223, 230, 256, 257, 258, 260, 269, 275, 284, 286, 289, 297, 306, 311, 324, 326-328, 333, 334, 338, 339, 355, 357, 359, 366, 370, 373, 376, 378, 381-384, 387, 473, 490
Competition Act, 3, 53, 394-399, 432-439
Competition Appeal Tribunal, 249, 395
Competition Commission, 211, 362, 367, 379, 381, 394, 395, 400, 401, 432, 433, 435

Competitive injury, 134, 135, 188-193
Competitors, 251-288
Concentrations, 360-362, 370-371
Concerted
 practices, 251-322
Conglomerate
 mergers, 197, 204, 207, 218, 220, 370, 373-375, 381, 427, 448
Conspiracy, 14, 15, 17, 18, 21, 23, 24, 28, 34, 36, 40, 44, 49, 52-55, 63, 78, 83, 104, 108-112, 114-120, 124, 128, 129, 141, 142, 148, 155-157, 174, 175, 186, 352, 419, 518, 522-525
Contingency fees, 8, 248
Contracts, 17-18, 107-109
Conventions, 80-82, 90-94
Convergence, 6-8, 362, 509, 534
Cooperation agreements, 9, 211, 227, 260, 275, 276, 278-282, 284-288, 365, 383, 403, 451, 539
Copyright, 28, 137, 145, 159, 160, 162, 163, 166, 167, 169-172, 299, 308, 310-311, 313, 314, 319, 327, 340, 341, 344, 413, 416, 423
Countervailing duty law, 28, 133
Country of origin, 186
Court of First Instance (CFI), 223, 228, 229, 232, 243, 244, 246, 247, 253, 254, 258, 265, 266, 270, 272, 273, 279, 285, 298, 303, 305, 328, 331, 335-344, 347-349, 353, 361-363, 367-369, 371, 372, 375-379, 381, 382, 384-387, 389
Courts, 41-42, 68, 85-90, 228-229
Criminal
 Proceedings, 38, 84, 90, 419
 prosecutions, 14, 34, 35, 83-85, 395, 419, 443

Crisis, 274, 441
Cross-licensing, 167, 175, 176, 447

D

De minimis doctrine, 260, 292, 305
Decentralization, 262, 263-267, 399
Decisions, 244-246, 251-322
Defenses, 16, 58, 62-64, 67-69, 86, 95, 97, 130, 170, 188, 190, 192, 193, 203, 204, 209, 225, 238, 243, 245, 246, 248, 249, 295, 307, 350, 373, 380, 386, 389, 396, 418, 450, 531, 532
Definition, 7, 21, 23, 44, 65, 133, 138, 180, 191, 202, 219, 261, 282, 325, 326, 359, 377, 388, 397, 413, 421, 426, 432, 539
Depositions, 87-90, 97, 515
Directives, 93, 96, 115, 226, 229, 230, 232, 233, 249, 309-311, 315, 316, 320, 344, 345, 396
Director General of Fair Trading, 393
Directorate-General for Competition, 89, 113, 226, 227, 245, 246, 355, 366
Disclosure of information, 96, 537
Discovery, 82-98
Discrimination, 2, 3, 25, 42, 120, 121, 154, 173, 174, 187-193, 202, 210, 217, 230, 231, 261, 300, 306-307, 335, 341, 394, 420, 423, 431, 445, 447, 513
Distribution, 300-303, 307-308
Distribution Systems and Business, 407, 421
Divestiture, 26, 34, 183, 198, 199, 205, 208-210, 212, 215, 216, 360, 367, 368, 374, 375, 377, 378, 380, 383, 388, 389, 401, 415, 416, 427, 437, 449, 450, 542, 543

Division of territories, 169
Documents, 60, 67, 77, 79-92, 94, 95, 97, 98, 111, 115, 200, 201, 236, 238, 241-243, 245, 246, 273, 290, 409, 426, 435, 442, 448, 479, 485-487, 489, 491, 498, 514, 515, 535-538, 540, 543, 544
Dominance, 2, 19, 21, 69, 75, 131, 133, 136, 141, 177, 209, 218, 325, 327, 336, 338, 342-345, 349, 350, 356, 368, 370, 373, 375-377, 381-385, 414, 434, 438, 442, 444, 445, 447, 449, 450
Dominant position, 323-353, 443-445
Due process of law, 69-74
Duopoly, 209, 376, 377, 385, 401

E

EC Treaty, 89, 224, 229, 230, 233, 234, 255, 270, 312, 316, 317, 356, 358, 386, 394, 395, 445
ECMR, 358, 363, 387
Effects test, 46, 48, 50, 51, 60, 257
Efficiency
 defense, 204, 209, 295, 380
Enforcement
 of competition laws, 8
 of judgments, 99-100
 procedures, 67-106
Enterprise Act 2002, 249, 395
Environmental agreements, 280, 284
Equity joint ventures, 122, 196
Essential facilities, 128, 136, 175, 206, 326, 332, 333, 368
European Coal and Steel Community (ECSC), 223, 224, 275, 325, 358

European Commission, 5, 8, 31, 89, 112, 116, 139, 196, 213, 216, 218, 219, 225, 226, 239, 242-243, 247, 253, 259, 268, 271, 272, 279, 287, 342, 345, 348, 349, 351, 352, 355, 362, 364, 370, 374, 375, 377, 379, 381, 383, 385, 388-390, 396, 398, 401, 403, 419, 428, 429
European Community (EC)
 law, 248, 396, 397
 merger
 control, 360
 regulation, 368, 399
European Court of Justice (ECJ), 137, 223, 228, 229, 233, 243, 244, 246, 247, 252-256, 258, 259, 261, 265, 270, 273, 274, 279, 284, 285, 296-299, 304, 305, 307, 312-318, 324-326, 328, 329, 331, 333-337, 339-343, 346, 356, 364, 369, 375, 376, 378, 386, 396, 397, 403, 438
European Economic Area (EEA), 231, 243, 314, 315, 320, 338, 349, 378, 380, 381, 402
European Economic Community (EEC), 4, 223, 224, 344, 356
European Parliament, 223, 224, 226-228, 232, 249, 285, 312, 505
European Union, 223-249, 272, 294, 297, 310, 342, 355-390, 402
Exclusionary conduct, 6, 105, 137-140, 329, 414
Exclusive
 dealing, 7, 25, 139, 140, 146-153, 164, 179, 182, 268, 273, 296, 336-340, 394, 414, 422, 431, 432, 444, 446

Index

supply, 185, 218, 303, 433
Exemptions, 28-33, 281-285, 317-322, 413
Export
  associations, 30, 151
  trade, 29-31, 48, 151, 176, 180, 181, 193, 414, 517, 521
Export Trading Company Act (ETCA), 29, 31-32, 517-518
Exports, 5, 28, 30, 31, 54, 127, 142, 151, 180, 216, 225, 254, 257, 271, 285-286, 293, 302, 307, 312, 517
Extraterritoriality, 60, 397

F

Failing company
  defense, 203, 373
Fair Trading Act, 393, 394, 399, 400
Federal Competition Commission, 211
Federal Rules
  of Civil Procedure, 39, 76, 77, 85, 92, 93, 97, 98, 537
  of Criminal Procedure, 76, 90
Federal Trade Commission (FTC), 36-38, 97-98
Federal Trade Commission (FTC) Act, 26-27, 32, 33, 36, 37, 48, 85, 97, 98, 125, 126, 146, 147, 151, 153, 156, 157, 165, 170, 174, 179-183, 205, 216, 512, 513, 514, 517, 520-523, 537
Fines, 239-240
Fixing, 109-115, 268-273
Flow of
  commerce doctrine, 23
Foreign
  commerce, 21-24, 32, 34, 43-57
  corporations, 24, 45, 71, 73, 77, 99, 194, 197
  governments, 28, 29, 34, 38, 40, 43, 45, 50, 56-66, 79, 88, 95, 96, 109, 142, 510, 519, 520, 527, 529-534

law, 47, 50, 51, 63, 77, 80, 94-96, 151, 166, 528, 531
markets, 29, 127, 133, 155, 159, 167, 186, 519
parties, 43-67, 84, 92, 127, 163, 168, 187, 407
sovereign, compulsion, 60, 63-64, 529-532
immunity, 40, 60, 64-66, 529-530
Foreign Proceedings, 59, 89
Foreign Sovereign Immunities Act (FSIA), 64, 529
Foreign Trade Antitrust Improvements Act (FTAIA), 29, 49, 511, 512,
Franchise rule, 177, 181
Franchising, 176-178, 303-304
FTC See Federal Trade Commission (FTC)
FTC Act See Federal Trade Commission (FTC) Act
Full-line forcing, 399

G

General Court (GC) See Court of First Instance (CFI)
General jurisdiction, 71, 72, 77
General Agreement on Tariffs and Trade, 27
Globalization, 5, 195, 217, 288, 309
Gray market, 168, 169
Guidelines, 40-41, 55-57, 276-281, 292-294

H

Hague Conference on Private International Law, 80, 81, 91, 100
Hague Evidence Convention, 82, 88, 90-94
Hague Service Convention, 79-82, 91
Hart-Scott-Rodino Antitrust Improvements Act, 198, 513-514

Index

Herfindahl-Hirschman Index (HHI), 203, 204, 212, 370, 371, 373, 427, 448
Horizontal
  agreements, 17, 148, 149, 157, 273, 274, 433, 437
  effects, 369
  mergers, 41, 197, 199, 202, 204, 208, 359, 371, 373, 427, 448
  restraints, 31
Horizontal Cooperation, 260, 275-282, 284-286
Horizontal Merger Guidelines, 41, 202, 204

I

Imports, 27-28
Index, 203
Individual, 1, 2, 8, 13, 14, 18, 23, 26, 33-36, 39, 40, 44, 57, 59, 63, 67, 69, 73, 76-79, 83, 84, 86-88, 99, 104, 105, 110, 111, 113-115, 117, 128, 129, 145, 149, 160, 172, 174, 203, 211, 226, 229-231, 234, 236, 239, 240, 241, 246, 247, 252, 262, 264, 266, 269, 271, 277, 282, 284, 291, 292, 295-297, 300, 302, 305, 306, 308, 309, 317, 318, 321, 337, 338, 341, 344, 347, 351, 369, 378, 390, 393-395, 397, 398, 403, 410, 413, 419, 436, 444, 475, 482
Information exchange, 32, 255, 270, 271, 276, 281, 286, 477, 481, 486, 487, 539-541
Innovation markets, 124, 216, 447
Institutions, 39, 100, 224, 225-230, 246, 253, 360, 361, 386, 402, 410, 517
Integration, 2, 4, 164, 176, 200, 205, 218, 223, 231, 255, 291, 297, 299, 309, 327, 329, 381, 427, 434, 437, 446

Intellectual property rights (IPR), 28, 164, 174, 292, 303, 309, 320, 348, 439, 446-447
International
  cooperation, 8-9, 92, 211, 352, 509, 534-543
  law, 43, 46, 47, 50, 53, 57-60, 69, 80, 8, 91, 98, 100, 258, 259, 361, 529, 531
  transactions, 43-66, 200, 202, 401, 514
International Antitrust Enforcement Assistance Act (IAEAA), 34, 515, 539
International Competition Network (ICN), 6-9, 113, 187, 365, 509
International Guidelines, 41, 51, 54-57, 61, 63, 64, 83, 96, 123, 200, 509, 510, 512
International Trade Commission (ITC), 27, 28, 162, 163, 167
Internet, 20, 59, 65, 73, 161, 177, 182, 210, 211, 289, 298, 302, 306, 311, 347, 349, 350, 383, 384, 387, 416, 441
Interstate commerce, 3, 23, 24, 107, 109, 154, 187, 197, 214, 525
Investigation and discovery, 67, 82-98

J

Japan, 405-429
Japan Fair Trade Commission (JFTC), 113, 272, 405, 408-429
Japanese law, 103, 418
Joint
  action, 1, 16, 117, 291
  purchasing, 130, 131, 276-278, 288
  ventures, 122-130, 205-206, 286-288, 377-378
Judicial, 246-247, 369
Jurisdiction, 68, 69-82, 180-182

K

Keiretsu, 406, 421

Know-how, 159, 160, 163, 176, 205, 215, 282, 299, 303, 304, 308, 309, 314, 318, 319-321

L

Leniency policy, 35, 36, 111, 411, 443, 514, 515, 544
Licensing, 159-176, 423-424
Limitation of, 281, 284, 318, 332, 398

M

Maastricht Treaty, 224, 225, 227
Market share, 370-371
McCarran Ferguson Act, 28, 50
Merger control, 5, 7, 196, 197, 206, 213, 232, 239, 286, 355-390, 394, 400, 431, 483
Merger Enforcement, 196
Merger Regulation, 233, 258, 286-288, 324, 342, 355-359, 361, 363-366, 368-370, 375-378, 380, 383, 384, 389, 399, 400, 425
Mergers and acquisitions, 7, 25, 185, 195-220, 232, 357, 361, 407, 408, 424-429, 436, 437, 447-449, 513, 521
Mexico, 6, 7, 9, 53, 180, 187
Minimum contacts, 69-75, 77
Monopolies and Mergers Commission (MMC), 393, 394
Monopolization, 19-22, 107-143, 413-417

N

National
  treatment, 163, 308
National Cooperative Research and Production Act (NCRPA), 29, 32, 122, 123, 515-516
Nationality, 46, 47, 56, 59, 93, 213, 217, 244, 351, 511
Negative clearance, 233, 277, 287, 317, 318

Noerr-Pennington doctrine, 29, 121, 184, 533-534
Noncompete obligation, 296, 299-300, 303, 304, 322, 379
Noncompliance, 7, 59, 90, 243, 368, 400, 532, 536
Non-Horizontal Merger Guidelines, 41, 202, 204, 207
Notification, 7, 122, 198-201, 208, 213, 217, 233, 248, 262-267, 278, 356, 358, 359, 362, 365-367, 383, 384, 388, 394, 402, 418, 425, 426, 448, 474, 496, 497, 500, 514, 516, 540, 541

O

Objective territorial principle, 46, 60
Office of Fair Trading (OFT), 114, 393, 395, 398-402
Oligopoly, 7, 295, 344, 375-377
Organization for Economic Co-operation and Development (OECD), 9, 218, 258, 381, 509
Organization of Petroleum Exporting Countries (OPEC), 62, 63, 65, 78-80, 109
Other countries, 59, 91, 99, 113, 159, 169, 196, 215, 330, 341, 350, 508

P

Package
  licensing, 172, 309
Parallel
  conduct, 18, 108, 255, 417
  imports, 274, 294, 299, 308, 311-316, 318, 332
Patent
  infringement, 163, 165-167, 170, 175, 184
  misuse doctrine, 162, 170, 172
Per se rule, 138, 139, 154, 156-158, 163, 175

Permanent Court of International
  Justice, 60
Personal
  jurisdiction, 44, 53, 60, 67-84, 92-94,
    99, 193, 214, 215
Power, 442-443
Practices, 134-143, 182-185, 251-322,
    329-344, 420-423, 445-447
Predatory
  practices, 2, 4, 150, 414
  pricing, 3, 7, 20, 134-136, 150, 191,
    272, 394, 431, 438, 444
Pre-merger notification, 7
Price
  fixing, 1, 14, 17, 23, 33-36, 40, 53, 55,
    57, 62, 63, 65, 78, 107, 109-
    116, 118, 128, 147, 152, 156,
    157, 159, 164, 175, 182, 196,
    231, 253, 259, 269, 268-273,
    276, 280, 306, 395, 398,
    410-412, 417-420, 441, 508,
    511, 522, 524, 543
Pricing, 134-136, 306-307
Private parties, 29, 40, 41, 60, 63, 68,
    104, 198, 229, 407, 478, 513,
    528
Privilege, 2, 19, 68, 70, 71, 73, 80, 83,
    86, 87, 173, 243, 244, 409, 536,
    537, 540, 544
Production
  limitation, 109-115, 231, 417
Prohibited agreements, 253-255,
    435
Protection of Trading Interests Act, 59
Public interest, 13, 34, 103, 139, 198,
    237, 364, 394, 400, 401, 413,
    417, 477, 485
Purchasing agreements, 130, 277, 278,
    297

R

R&D, 276, 278, 282, 283, 286, 293, 320
Reciprocity, 99

Refusal to deal, 21, 117, 118, 248, 327,
    331, 341, 421, 422, 444, 449
Regulation, 233-238, 291-292, 317-322,
    356-369
Relevant
  geographic, 21, 133, 202, 212, 215,
    261, 300, 326, 346, 428
  market, 19, 21, 116, 124, 129, 131,
    132, 137, 138, 142, 148, 150,
    164, 178, 203, 204, 205, 208,
    211, 256, 260, 261, 265, 270,
    281-283, 292, 309, 320, 325-
    327, 339, 342, 367, 370, 371,
    387, 436-438, 444, 447
  product, 21, 22, 124, 133, 202, 208,
    261, 272, 326, 346, 357, 388,
    428, 434, 436
Remedies, 27-28, 133-134, 328, 367-369,
    410-411
Requirements contracts, 148, 152, 415
Resale price maintenance, 3, 156-157,
    295-296, 431
Research and development agreements,
    266, 282-283
Restraints, 146-159, 289-295, 378-379,
    417-420
Restriction, 166-170, 297-299, 305-306
Robinson-Patman Act, 3, 25, 36, 42, 117,
    140, 179-194, 306, 327, 513
Royalties, 116, 153, 162, 172-174, 184,
    313, 318, 321, 331, 341, 345,
    447, 450
Rule of reason, 7, 15-17, 29, 32, 46-48,
    51, 60, 103, 108, 116, 118, 120,
    122-124, 126-131, 139, 146-
    148, 150, 151, 154, 155, 157,
    158, 164, 165, 183, 185, 260,
    265, 267, 290, 432, 433, 516

S

Sanctions, 8, 64, 80, 84, 87, 89, 90, 95,
    96, 194, 234, 235, 246, 247,
    368, 421, 443, 450, 451, 475,
    477, 483, 487, 531

Selective, 102, 167, 291, 293, 298, 300-303, 321, 352, 399
Sentencing, 35
Sentencing Guidelines, 35
Service of process, 76-82
Services, 76-82
Sherman Act, 13-24, 43-57, 107-143
Shipping, 29, 104, 175, 230, 266, 343, 344, 420, 522-523
Single branding, 296-297
Single European Act, 223, 228
Sovereign, 63-64
   compulsion, 60, 63-64, 531-532
   immunity, 40, 60-62, 64-66, 529-530
Specialization agreements, 266, 276, 283-284, 286, 293, 320
Specific jurisdiction, 71
Standardization, 108, 119-122, 276, 278-280, 284, 286, 424
Stream of, 70, 71, 73
Subject matter, 91, 101, 102, 227, 236, 333, 370, 479, 486, 491, 493, 494
   jurisdiction, 33, 43, 44, 47, 49, 54, 59, 67, 68, 83, 107, 521
Submarkets, 21, 22, 208, 209, 211, 348, 413
Subpoenas, 37, 83-85, 88, 90, 95, 97, 98, 113, 543
Subsidiaries, 18, 54, 55, 71, 74, 75, 81, 99, 111, 113, 114, 125, 141, 142, 168, 214-216, 227, 240, 243, 244, 252-254, 257, 258, 291, 294, 298, 332, 337, 338, 355, 357, 359, 361, 378, 384, 389, 416, 422, 428, 429, 481, 532

T

Tariff Act of 1930, 28, 162, 168, 169, 519-520
Technology, 317-322, 344-353
licensing, 31, 290, 322
Territorial, 30, 45, 46, 59, 60, 62, 67, 69, 70, 74, 98, 103, 146, 157-159, 164, 166-169, 180, 181, 190, 231, 258, 259, 289, 291, 298, 299, 306, 314, 318, 420, 422, 431, 447, 533
Trade
   and development, 9
   associations, 27, 117, 121, 169, 180, 271, 397, 405, 410-412, 417, 421
   secrets, 87, 145, 159-163, 167, 173, 537
Trademarks, 28, 145, 156, 159-162, 167-169, 171, 176-178, 215, 289, 298, 299, 303, 308-310, 312-317, 321, 327, 339, 368, 415
   and service marks, 145, 160, 176, 177
Transfer, 160-162, 164, 165, 168, 198, 211, 266, 282, 284, 285, 293, 299, 309, 312, 317-322, 356, 379, 387, 394, 395, 407, 410, 425, 428, 447, 449
Treaty
   of Amsterdam, 227, 474, 476, 481
   of Nice, 224, 228
   of Paris, 223, 224
   on European Union, 224, 225, 402
Treaty Establishing the European Community, 473
TRIPS, 159, 308, 309
Tunney Act, 34, 37, 139
Turnover, 237, 238, 239, 256, 271, 272, 338, 349, 357, 358, 360-362, 365, 377, 380, 400, 407, 425, 435, 436, 439, 444, 446, 448, 494, 495
Tying
   arrangements, 7, 25, 105, 137-140, 146, 152-155, 164, 170, 171, 178, 335

Index

U

UK, 114, 167, 169, 217, 224, 258, 270, 277, 287, 313-315, 317, 333, 338, 364, 365, 374, 385, 389, 393-403
Undertakings, 240-241, 252-253
Unfair
  competition, 162, 180, 185, 298
  trade practices, 407, 408, 410-412, 414, 417, 420-425, 431, 444-447, 450
United Kingdom, 45, 50, 51, 113, 114, 187, 224, 249, 313, 314, 332, 376, 377, 384, 393-403
United Nations Conference on Trade and Development (UNCTAD), 9, 509
U.S.
  state courts, 99
  Supreme Court, 13, 15-19, 21-24, 27, 28, 30, 33, 35, 38, 39-42, 45, 46, 48-50, 52-55, 58, 61-72, 74, 76, 81, 82, 88-90, 92-96, 101, 103-105, 108-110, 116-121, 126-130, 132-138, 140-142, 147-149, 153, 154, 156-158, 160, 162, 164-166, 168-173, 175, 178, 181-185, 188-193, 196, 198, 202, 204-208

V

Venue, 6, 67, 68, 72, 73, 75
Vertical
  agreements, 145-146, 149, 157, 266, 284, 289-294, 297, 300, 302, 308, 337, 398, 399, 433, 437
  mergers, 41, 197, 205, 209-210, 213, 374
  restraints, 6, 17, 41, 146-159, 255, 260, 268, 280, 289-294, 300, 301, 303, 305, 437, 444
Vertical Restraint Guidelines, 147

W

Webb-Pomerene Act, 3, 29-32, 151, 180, 181, 258, 516-517
Wilson Tariff Act, 24, 46, 518-519
World Trade Organization, 27, 28, 159, 163, 227, 308